Price and Value

A Guide to Equity Market Valuation Metrics

George Calhoun

Price and Value: A Guide to Equity Market Valuation Metrics

George Calhoun
Jersey City, NJ, USA

ISBN-13 (pbk): 978-1-4842-5551-3   ISBN-13 (electronic): 978-1-4842-5552-0
https://doi.org/10.1007/978-1-4842-5552-0

Copyright © 2020 by George Calhoun

This work is subject to copyright. All rights are reserved by the Publisher, whether the whole or part of the material is concerned, specifically the rights of translation, reprinting, reuse of illustrations, recitation, broadcasting, reproduction on microfilms or in any other physical way, and transmission or information storage and retrieval, electronic adaptation, computer software, or by similar or dissimilar methodology now known or hereafter developed.

Trademarked names, logos, and images may appear in this book. Rather than use a trademark symbol with every occurrence of a trademarked name, logo, or image we use the names, logos, and images only in an editorial fashion and to the benefit of the trademark owner, with no intention of infringement of the trademark.

The use in this publication of trade names, trademarks, service marks, and similar terms, even if they are not identified as such, is not to be taken as an expression of opinion as to whether or not they are subject to proprietary rights.

While the advice and information in this book are believed to be true and accurate at the date of publication, neither the authors nor the editors nor the publisher can accept any legal responsibility for any errors or omissions that may be made. The publisher makes no warranty, express or implied, with respect to the material contained herein.

    Managing Director, Apress Media LLC: Welmoed Spahr
    Acquisitions Editor: Susan McDermott
    Development Editor: Laura Berendson
    Coordinating Editor: Rita Fernando

Cover image by Stevens Institute of Technology

Distributed to the book trade worldwide by Springer Science+Business Media New York, 233 Spring Street, 6th Floor, New York, NY 10013. Phone 1-800-SPRINGER, fax (201) 348-4505, e-mail orders-ny@springer-sbm.com, or visit www.springeronline.com. Apress Media, LLC is a California LLC and the sole member (owner) is Springer Science + Business Media Finance Inc (SSBM Finance Inc). SSBM Finance Inc is a **Delaware** corporation.

For information on translations, please e-mail rights@apress.com, or visit http://www.apress.com/rights-permissions.

Apress titles may be purchased in bulk for academic, corporate, or promotional use. eBook versions and licenses are also available for most titles. For more information, reference our Print and eBook Bulk Sales web page at http://www.apress.com/bulk-sales.

Any source code or other supplementary material referenced by the author in this book is available to readers on GitHub via the book's product page, located at www.apress.com/9781484255513. For more detailed information, please visit http://www.apress.com/source-code.

Printed on acid-free paper

"Measuring the price of something and measuring its value ... are two different tasks."
—*The Economist magazine (2019)*

"Price and value... Find the disconnect."
—*Forbes magazine (2018)*

"Price is what you pay. Value is what you get."
—*Warren Buffett (2008)*

"Nowadays people know the price of everything and the value of nothing."
—*Oscar Wilde (1890)*

Table of Contents

About the Author xi

About the Technical Reviewer xiii

Acknowledgments xv

Preface xvii

Introduction xxiii

Chapter 1: The Ford Dollar: The Mysterious Multiple 1
   1.1 P/E As a Measure of How "Expensive" a Company Is 4
   1.2 P/E As a Predictor of Future Share Price 6
   1.3 P/E As a Predictor of Future Returns 9
   1.4 The Mysterious Multiple 16

Chapter 2: The Value Triangle 19
   2.1 Accounting Valuations: The Limitations of "Book Value" 20
   2.2 The Shortcomings of Financial Models 25
   2.3 The Pros and Cons of Market-Based Valuation Metrics 30
      2.3.1 Disney vs. Netflix 31
      2.3.2 Ford vs. Tesla 33
   2.4 Triangulating Intrinsic Value: The Use of Valuation Ratios 36
      2.4.1 Price-to-Book 37
      2.4.2 Return-on-Assets 38
      2.4.3 Price-to-Earnings 39
   2.5 Summary 40

Chapter 3: Valuation Ratios 41

   3.1 Trailing P/E, or P/E$_{ttm}$ 42

   3.2 Forward P/E 44

       3.2.1 PER (Relative P/E) 49

       3.2.2 Normalized P/E 49

       3.2.3 Improving on P/E? 50

   3.3 Price-to-Operating Earnings 50

       3.3.1 Pro Forma Earnings 54

       3.3.2 Core Earnings 57

   3.4 Dividends 59

       3.4.1 Dividend Ratios: Significance and Trends 60

   3.5 Price-to-Sales 65

   3.6 Metrics Based on Cash Flow 74

       3.6.1 EBITDA and EV/EBITDA 75

       3.6.2 Free Cash Flow 76

       3.6.3 Do Cash Flow Metrics Improve Upon Earnings-Based Multiples? 78

   3.7 Price-to-Book 83

   3.8 Tobin's Q 86

   3.9 Return-on-Assets 88

   3.10 Adjustments to the Denominator: Cyclically Adjusted P/E (CAPE$_1$) 90

       3.10.1 Critics and Critiques 94

       3.10.2 CAPE Performance 96

       3.10.3 CAPE: An Assessment 107

   3.11 Adjustments to the Numerator: Cash-Adjusted P/E (CAPE$_2$) 113

   3.12 *What* About *the PEG Ratio?* 120

   3.13 Composite P/E Ratios 123

   3.14 Summary 126

TABLE OF CONTENTS

Chapter 4: Interpretations: P/E As a Dependent Variable 131
4.1 What Does the P/E Really Measure? 132
4.2 Firm-Level Drivers 135
4.2.1 Growth 135
4.2.2 Profitability, and "Quality" 146
4.2.3 Size 156
4.2.4 "Risk" and Cost of Capital 159
4.2.5 Shareholder Return 162
4.2.6 Strategy and Business Model Issues 168
4.2.7 Earnings Volatility 185
4.2.8 Share Price Volatility (Beta) 188
4.2.9 Leverage 194
4.2.10 Accounting Issues 201
4.2.11 Governance 202
4.3 Sector-Level and Market-Level Drivers 207
4.3.1 Sentiment ("Animal Spirits") 207
4.3.2 Sector Discounts and Premiums 212
4.3.3 Regulation 219
4.3.4 Monetary Policy 222
4.3.5 Fiscal Policy 226
4.3.6 Inflation 228
4.3.7 Interest Rates and Bond Yields 233
4.3.8 International Differences 240
4.4 Summary 245

Chapter 5: Applications: P/E As an Independent Variable 249
5.1 Using Multiples to Forecast Stock Prices 250
5.1.1 The General Case: P/E As a Contrarian Indicator 250
5.2 Screening for "Value" 256
5.2.1 Evidence for the Value Anomaly 257
5.2.2 Explanations of the Value Anomaly 261
5.2.3 Comparing Multiples As Value Screens 273

5.3 Index Construction 286
5.4 Factor Models and "Smart Beta" 288
    5.4.1 The Proliferation of Factors 290
    5.4.2 The "Value" Cornerstone 292
5.5 Valuing Corporate Transactions 293
    5.5.1 Deal Pricing 293
    5.5.2 Sum-of-the-Parts Analyses (the Conglomerate Discount) 296
5.6 Diagnosing Market Regimes 299
    5.6.1 Monetary Policy Impact 300
    5.6.2 Bubble Detection 304
    5.6.3 Illuminating the "Fine Structure" of Market Regimes 308
5.7 Summary 314

Chapter 6: Assessments and Qualifications 317

6.1 The Best Metric Today (2019): The P/E 317
    6.1.1 P/E Tends to Prevail (but Not Always), and It Only Explains So Much 319
    6.1.2 Substituting Earnings Measures Other Than GAAP-Compliant Net Earnings Does Not Reliably Improve Performance (Yet) 320
    6.1.3 The Performance of All Multiples Is Highly Dependent on the Market Regime 320
    6.1.4 The Performance of Some Multiples Has Diminished Significantly over Time 321
    6.1.5 Sensitivity Varies, but Favors P/E 321
    6.1.6 A Future Orientation Tends to Improve Short-Term Performance, but Only So Much 322
    6.1.7 Prediction Tends to Improve Significantly as the Holding Period Increases 323
    6.1.8 Cash Flow Multiples Are Less Reliable 323
    6.1.9 Averaging (Trend-Smoothing) Multiples: An Under-explored Concept 324
    6.1.10 P/E Wins the Industry Popularity Contest 324
6.2 Shifting Definitions 326
    6.2.1 GAAP, Non-GAAP, Core, and So On: The Validity Problem for "Earnings" 327
    6.2.2 Street Earnings 328
    6.2.3 IFRS vs. GAAP 331
    6.2.4 Changing Accounting Standards 332
    6.2.5 Earnings Management 1: Gaming the Numbers 334

6.2.6 Earnings Management 2: Buybacks and EPS Enhancement 336

6.2.7 Cash Dilution ("Nonoperating Financial Assets") 340

6.2.8 Taxes 341

6.2.9 The Effect of Asset-Light Business Models 343

6.2.10 The Effect of Alternate Growth Strategies: Acquisition vs. Internal Development 347

6.3 Problems with Price-to-Book 349

6.4 ROA: An Incomplete Picture 352

6.5 Concluding Comments: The Uncertainty Principle(s) in Finance 355

    6.5.1 The Academic Confusion Factor 355

    6.5.2 Reflexivity and the "Human Uncertainty Principle" 357

    6.5.3 Fischer Black's Proposition 360

    6.5.4 Price-Insensitive Markets 363

Appendix A: A Critical Examination of Discounted Cash Flow Valuation Methods 365

The End of Book Value 365

Discounted Cash Flow Modeling: A Critical Assessment 369

    The DCF Best Case 370

    What Is DCF, Really? 371

    Uncertainties, Compounded 372

    DCF Manipulation 376

    Is DCF Actually Used by Market Practitioners? 377

    DCF: Assessments 378

Afterword: Fair Price, True Value 381

Index 385

About the Author

George Calhoun

- Professor and Founding Director of the Quantitative Finance Program – *Stevens Institute of Technology*

- Executive Director of the Hanlon Financial Systems Center, at *Stevens*

- Area Coordinator for graduate and undergraduate finance programs, at *Stevens*

- Series Editor for the Stevens Series in Quantitative Finance and Data Sciences, a book series launched in 2014 with *Springer/Apress*

- PhD from the *Wharton School*

- 30 years of experience in the technology industry, in executive and board-level positions at several public companies, including as Chief Executive Officer (CEO), Chairman of the Board (two companies), and Audit Committee Chairman (four companies)

- Extensive experience in capital acquisition through public offerings (five), convertible and straight debt offerings, private placements, joint ventures, and venture capital transactions

- Author of three books on advanced signal processing technology and applications to the telecommunications field

About the Technical Reviewer

Dr. Jonathan Kaufman has more than 25 years of experience investing in various securities and other markets. Prior to graduate school, Dr. Kaufman was an account executive at Johnston, Lemon and Co., stockbrokers in Washington, D.C. From 1990 to 1994, Dr. Kaufman was a corporate tax attorney with the New York law office of Cravath, Swaine and Moore. Dr. Kaufman reentered the financial services industry in 1994 with Salomon Brothers/Citigroup, where he subsequently became Head of North American Capital Structuring for Salomon Brothers/Citigroup in New York and Managing Director, and a member of the Global Senior Management Committee of Global Capital Structuring. In April 2003, Dr. Kaufman left Salomon Brothers/Citigroup to pursue private investment management service opportunities in the financial services industry. Since that time, he has been Chairman and Chief Executive Officer of Kaufman Global Capital Advisors and a partner in Olympus Capital Management, both hedge fund and capital advisory firms.

Dr. Kaufman was awarded a PhD in Economics from the Department of Economics at the University of Chicago, as well as a Juris Doctorate from the University of Chicago Law School. Dr. Kaufman was awarded Bachelor of Arts in Biology and History from Brown University.

Acknowledgments

This work is the product of years of collective conversation, for which in many respects I am only the scribe. I am grateful to the friends and colleagues at *Stevens Institute of Technology* who have contributed in many ways to my thinking, including Khaldoun Khashanah, Germán Creamer, Jon Kaufman, Stefano Bonini, Hamed Ghoddusi, Tom Lonon, Suman Banerjee, Pape Ndiaye, Dragos Bozdog, Zhenyu Cui, Majeed Simaan, Ann Murphy, Michael zur Muehlen, Richard Anderson, Paul Rohmeyer, Ted Stohr, Giuseppe Ateniese, Ted Lappas, Gaurav Sabnis, Feng Mai, Chihoon Lee, Elaine Henry, Rupak Chatterjee, Steve Yang, Jeff Nickerson, Manos Hatzakis, Eleni Gousgounis, Dami Kazeem, Elizabeth Awosogba, Nicole Malantchouk, Michelle Crilly, Lisa Cavanaugh, Susan Pavelchek, Zheng Xing, and Brandon Griffin.

Of course I also owe a great deal to my students. Teaching is the active mode of Knowing. The effort of distilling Fact and Theory into a form suitable for the classroom is what finally brings a higher degree of coherence to one's ideas.

I would like to give special thanks to Sean Hanlon, a generous friend who has helped propel *Stevens* to the forefront of this field; to Gregory Prastacos, a visionary dean who has steered the School in the right direction and has kindly tolerated my idiosyncrasies; and to Ionut Florescu, who can always be counted on for the creative provocation that helps move us forward.

There is also the patient, rather lonely undertaking, the writing of the thing, a strange process which produces, eventually, out of scraps of knowledge and experience, a Book. It is something of a pleasure, and something of an ordeal – and for her help in getting me through it, and for all the rest, I give thanks daily (!) for the support of my partner, Virginia.

Preface

Every Fall, in my introductory course on Quantitative Finance, I begin with the basic metrics that are a starting point for thinking about whether a stock is valued correctly: the Price-to-Earnings (P/E) ratio and its variants. The topic is pedagogically fruitful, combining a seeming simplicity in construction – just ratios, no complex math – with intriguing difficulties in interpretation and an abundance of counterintuitive and thought-provoking applications.

The students soon realize that these metrics do not always give clear answers. But they do raise interesting questions. Korean stocks typically carry a lower P/E – that is, they are less expensive, or more undervalued – than American stocks. Why? *Morgan Stanley* trades at a premium to *Goldman Sachs*. Why? Why does a dollar of earnings at *Costco* create 50% more stock market value than a dollar of *Walmart's* earnings? Why are *Pepsi's* earnings usually priced more cheaply than *Coke's*? What should we make of the exorbitant P/E ratio (ten times the market average) that *Amazon* carries?[1] Questions like these are the seeds of the broader curriculum, highlighting the complexities of the financial markets.

A few years later, as the students are completing their degrees, ready to enter the working world of Finance, armed with extensive math and computer science skills, and having taken a wide range of courses related to Quantitative Finance in all its dimensions, somehow we seem to have circled back to that same starting point: the question of *valuation* and the market's perspective on it. The students' vocabulary has expanded; they now speak of "factor models" and "smart beta"; they converse easily about "momentum" and "mean reversion"; they use portfolio optimization techniques to balance "risk and return"; they know how to scrutinize the "market microstructure" to analyze "liquidity" and "volatility"; they have learned how to hedge different types of market risk with complex derivatives. But underlying these advanced concepts and techniques, there is

---

[1] All factual references phrased in the present tense in this book refer to the period from mid-2018 to mid-2019.

still the basic mystery: *How does the market determine the correct price for the assets that it trades? How does it ascribe value to a complex and dynamic business enterprise?* And this always brings us back, at some point, to the basic valuation metrics.

Ratios like the P/E are by far the most common type of valuation tool used by practitioners. For investors, the ratios link fundamental corporate performance (e.g., sales, profit) with share prices, to quickly diagnose potentially undervalued or overvalued companies. Financial analysts use them to calibrate, and validate, more "sophisticated" models based on calculating future discounted cash flows (DCFs) or to help price mergers and acquisitions or to characterize different market regimes (e.g., for detecting "bubbles"). But many market professionals view the use of these ratios as mere shortcuts – even somehow a kind of "cheating," not quite the "real thing" in terms of enterprise valuation. Business education reinforces this perspective. DCF models are taught and rehearsed in every finance course in the universe, elaborated in weighty textbooks; valuation ratios are relegated to a quick chapter or two, if presented at all. Sometimes the P/E can seem almost too self-evident to require formal instruction.

The subject deserves a systematic treatment. The mystery, and the potency, of a simple ratio like the P/E stems from its incongruous nature. It is a direct and explicit *apples-to-oranges comparison*. The two halves of the ratio are derived from different sources, based on different conceptual frameworks. The numerator comes from the market, reflecting its emotions, its peculiar "weather," and its purported wisdom of the crowd; the denominator is an objective measure of residual cash flows, groomed and adjusted according to standardized rules of accounting, and has nothing to do with the market. This hybrid signal is both ambiguous and unstable (or "nonstationary" as the statisticians say). That is, the significance of the P/E – its momentarily "correct" interpretation – changes from time to time and from company to company. This does not impair its usefulness, but it does challenge the user to approach the matter carefully, alert to its complexities, and to handle the results with caution.

This book is intended to shed light on the use of market ratios for enterprise valuation, to assess the quantity and quality of the information they contain, and to highlight the questions they raise. I have tried to adopt a consistent critical perspective – which is often missing from other presentations. Many investment advisers present their chosen formula as *The One Best Way*, without any sort of comparative assessment. For example, in the past few years, there has been a surge of interest in what are called "cyclically adjusted" metrics that incorporate long-term averages of certain variables. These come with a plausible rationale: it is suggested that valuation accuracy can be improved by averaging over the business cycle, or by smoothing out short-term earnings volatility. But does this rationale hold true? It is an open question. Little work has been done to critically evaluate the performance of cyclically adjusted metrics compared with traditional versions they are proposed to replace, and when comparisons have been made, the results have often failed to support the claims of superior accuracy for the cyclical versions.[2] (We will examine this particular question in detail in later chapters.)

The Power of Triangulation

The phrase "mixing apples and oranges" connotes an improper comparison of supposedly incommensurable entities. But the usefulness of evaluating a difficult question with results from very different measurement methodologies has come to be recognized in several of the hard sciences as "an essential protection against flawed ideas."

> Triangulation... is the strategic use of multiple approaches to address a single question. Each approach has its own unrelated assumptions, strengths, and weaknesses.[3]

Note how this idea draws on the logic of *diversification* – which is central to Finance – by seeking to explicitly de-correlate the methodological portfolio. A prominent economist has made this point in a broad critique of econometrics research:

> Diversification is good in research strategy as in most other things... Successful pieces of pragmatic empirical work [are not bound by a methodological] straitjacket. Many different types of data are examined... A persuasive pattern emerges from the totality.[4]

Triangulation approaches have been applied in fields such as environmental science, cellular biology, medicine, and climatology, which pose multidimensional research questions involving unruly data sets with complex and sometimes elusive statistical

---

[2]For example, Jim Masturzo, "CAPE Fatigue," *Research Affiliates White Paper*, June 2017.

[3]Marcus Munafò and George Davey Smith, "Repeating Experiments is Not Enough," *Nature*, Vol. 553 (January 25, 2018), pp. 399–401.

[4]Lawrence Summers, "The Scientific Illusion in Empirical Macroeconomics," *Scandinavian Journal of Economics*, Vol. 93, No. 2 (1991), pp. 129–148.

characteristics. For example, this assessment comes from a critical survey of research methods in the field of epidemiology:

> Etiological epidemiology – understanding what causes differing levels of disease in populations – is central to the science of epidemiology. However, there is considerable debate about the circumstances under which causality can be tested or assumed.... [Triangulation is] the practice of strengthening causal inferences by integrating results from several different approaches, where each approach has different (and assumed to be largely unrelated) key sources of potential bias.[5]

The financial markets also generate huge, noisy, and heterogeneous data sets (prices, orders, transactions, etc.), and extracting useful signals can be tricky. The underlying causal variables are often confounded and difficult to separate. An apples-and-oranges approach based on the market ratios offers one of the best ways to cope with this complexity and to unlock the mysteries of Price and Value.

The field of Finance presents an odd mixture of advanced mathematics and ultra-pragmatic "cash value" thinking, incorporating advice from professors, pit traders, and everyone in between. Operating between the opposite poles of abstract certainty and messy market outcomes, academicians and practitioners alike may find themselves feeling at times overwhelmed and in doubt. Of course, Mr. Market is always right there, in your face, to affirm or deny your pet theories, which either way may seem like progress. But the next day or the next quarter or the next millisecond, the rules will change, and incoherence will prevail again – until revised models are trundled forth (for the next slaughter). It is one of the things that makes it an interesting business.

I tell students that the market mutates, frequently, perhaps more frequently than it used to. I tell them this means that unlike physics, where a textbook written decades ago is still valid, for the most part – the "laws" of physics are unchanging – a textbook purporting

---

[5] Debbie Lawlor, Kate Tilling, and George Davey Smith, "Triangulation in Aetiological Epidemiology," *International Journal of Epidemiology*, Vol. 45, No. 6 (December 2016), pp. 1866–1886.

to explain the behavior of the financial markets will be substantially obsolete almost before the ink has dried. Worse than obsolete, it will likely be wrong, misleading, and even dangerous. The "laws" of Finance are rewritten all the time, and without warning.

Nevertheless, students' understandable need for structure in the educational process has forced me to think about how to teach this material in a way that can survive the next market downturn or the latest policy pronouncement by the money commissariat (the central banks). That thought process, evolved over the last ten years, has led to this book.

George Calhoun
Rome, 2019

Introduction

Enterprise Valuation: Goals, Challenges, Methods

Enterprise valuation is hardcore Finance. It takes on tough questions:

- How to set a fair and accurate price for an active, ongoing business
- How to benchmark that price against the valuations for similar firms or the market as a whole
- How to account not just for the value of the company's current earnings and assets, but also its future prospects (for growth or decline)
- How to reflect the dynamism of the company's operating environment in a competitive economy, with all its possibilities for surprise, opportunity, and disruption
- How to do all this quickly, before things change too much, before the data goes stale...

It can be a hazardous undertaking. Valuation errors have killed deals, wrecked court cases, ruined careers, crashed markets, and overturned governments. The financial crisis of 2008 was precipitated by the sudden catastrophic *re*valuation of vast portfolios of incorrectly marked assets, which brought down giant institutions – *Bear Stearns, Fannie Mae, Freddie Mac, Wachovia, Merrill Lynch, AIG, Lehman Bros., etc.* Across the global economy, the "discrepancies" were measured in trillions.

Valuation is also central to the calmer day-to-day side of Finance – analyzing investments, buying and selling real estate, underwriting insurance, pricing corporate acquisitions, and preparing financial statements. Accurate valuation is at the heart of the banking business. It animates the capital markets. It is essential for auditing, credit rating, hedging, and risk management. Financial innovations, from index construction and the design of ETFs to the securitization of mortgages, credit card debt, and student loans, depend upon it.

INTRODUCTION

There is no important decision in Finance that does not require a sound valuation methodology.

And yet, the traditional and widely taught valuation methods – financial accounting for computing "book value" and discounted cash flow modeling to estimate "net present value"– are deeply flawed, as we shall see.

This book focuses on a different approach, which uses data drawn from the financial markets to construct value metrics that can be applied to individual companies, industry sectors, or the entire market. These metrics share a common structure: they are based on ratios that link the *market price* of the company's shares to some measure of *fundamental performance* (sales, earnings, cash flow, etc.). The classic example is the Price/Earnings ratio – the P/E "Multiple" – and there are many variations on this basic idea, involving substitutions or adjustments to both the numerator and the denominator.

"Multiples" are pervasive in Finance today. Among professional equity analysts, they are the overwhelming choice as a valuation tool.[1] (See Figure 1.)

There are good reasons for this popularity. Market ratios are *more accurate, easier to use*, and *more versatile* than other valuation methods. Even when other techniques are used, market ratios are often employed as a comparative checkpoint. They shed light on a wide range of questions related to investment decisions, corporate transactions, and the assessment of business models and corporate strategies and even broad economic questions relating to business cycles, the health of the financial system, the impact of government regulation, monetary policies, the effects of technological innovation, and the comparison of different international economic regimes – almost any question relating to the creation (or destruction) of economic value.

They are also the most *actionable* value metrics. Because they incorporate the *current market price*, the valuations they yield are directly linked to the price points where a real transaction can be executed.

---

[1]Paul Asquith, Michael B. Mikhail, and Andrea S. Au, "Information Content of Equity Analyst Reports," *Journal of Financial Economics*, Vol. 75, No. 2 (February 2005), pp. 245-282. See also Andreas Schreiner, "Equity Valuation Using Multiples: An Empirical Investigation," *Doctoral Dissertation,* University of St. Gallen Graduate School of Business Administration, 2007.

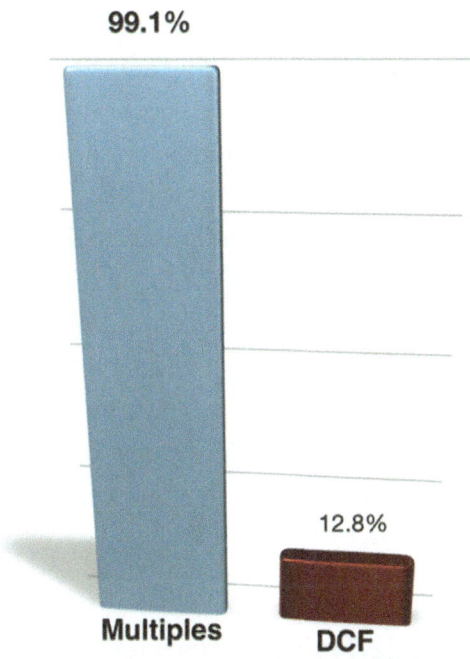

Figure 1. *Analysts Prefer the Multiple As a Valuation Metric*

But these ratios are often applied *ad hoc,* as rules of thumb, treated as suggestive, but not definitive, or dismissed as a "tool for the unsophisticated"[2] or even as a "violation" of sound reasoning.[3] Or they may be used uncritically; of the different ratios to choose from, practitioners often have their favorites, and it is rare to find a comparative analysis to justify the choice of a particular alternative.[4] The academic literature is (as usual) full

---

[2] A. Damodaran, *On Valuation*, Wiley (2006), p. 235.
[3] Stephen Penman, *Accounting for Value,* Columbia (2011), p. 23.
[4] An exception: Savita Subramanian et al., at *Bank of America/Merrill Lynch* – e.g., see their report "What do oil and high beta stocks have in common?" *Equity and Quant Strategy Report*, April 15, 2015.

of contradictory findings. To be fair, no one is quite sure exactly what the P/E means. Is a high P/E good news or not so good? (Are we buying or selling today?) Its significance depends very much on the application.

There is also a kind of "Black Box" quality to these metrics. They respond quickly to new information. But we are not always sure how the market calculates. The P/E is an exquisite "dependent variable" – a sensitive signal that adjusts rapidly and with seeming precision to changes in a company's situation – but it is not always clear *what* it is signaling, which "independent variable" is driving it. These ratios can seem at once transparent and opaque.

Penetrating this opaqueness is the motivation for this book. Given the pervasive use of these ratios, especially in the investment end of the financial industry, the subject calls out for a systematic assessment. Which metrics work best? What drives them? What do they mean? Shedding light on these questions is the goal here. I have not undertaken (very much) original study; I intend to survey the highlights of the published research and practical experience involving these metrics. Hopefully we can at least establish some useful guidelines and clarify what we know, what we don't know, and what we half-know (and there's a lot of that!).

The Challenges of Enterprise Valuation

Valuing an individual asset – a truck, a plot of land, a case of vintage Bordeaux – is straightforward. We look to recent transactions involving similar assets. Houses, used cars, antiques, works of art, and the like are appraised, priced, and put up for sale by referring to "comparables."[5]

Valuing a live business is different matter. It is much more than a static collection of assets. It is a dynamic socio-technical system, a "going concern," continuously generating new quanta of value that accountants call "sales" and "earnings" and creating or acquiring new assets. The valuation process must consider the value in hand today and the value that will come to hand in a month or a year or ten years – which is of course shrouded in uncertainty. Enterprise valuation has to somehow account for all the chickens, both the hatched and the unhatched.

---

[5]The other alternative is to simply use the original purchase price – "historical cost" – perhaps discounted. But if much time has passed, this will not serve the purpose.

INTRODUCTION

For large companies, there are few transactions of a similar nature, close enough in time, to allow for meaningful price-benchmarking. In fact, the nature of the modern economic system is such that most companies specialize. They seek competitive advantage through *differentiation*. They develop differentiated products, brands, technologies, business models, and competitive strategies. The "comparables" approach is hard to apply.

Consider, for example, *Coke* and *Pepsi* – that is, *The Coca-Cola Company* and *Pepsico*. We think of them as a pair, as archrivals, twins almost, competing head-to-head. Actually their businesses are rather dissimilar. Virtually all of *Coke's* revenue is derived from selling beverages (juice, soft drinks, tea, coffee, water, sports drinks). On the other hand, over half of *Pepsi's* revenue comes from food products, especially snacks (*Frito-Lay* is *Pepsi's* biggest and most profitable business unit) – a different business model.[6] *Coke* derives just 20% of its sales from North America. Almost 60% of *Pepsi's* revenue comes from the US market. The two companies actually do not match up very well. Any attempt to value *Coke's* business by comparing it to *Pepsi* would require a lot of tricky adjustments.

Many important business decisions require enterprise valuations. Three urgent applications stand out:

- **Investment decisions**, whether to acquire shares of stock representing partial claims on the underlying value of the business – *Is Coke or Pepsi the better investment right now?*

- **Pricing decisions for acquisitions, mergers, and other strategic corporate transactions**, involving the transfer of ownership of an entire operating business – *If Pepsi were to divest its snacks division (as it has been under pressure to do), what would be the proper price?*

- **Credit decisions**. For a bank considering a loan or an investor considering the purchase of a company's bonds or a credit rating agency asked to rate those bonds, it is necessary to value the company's operating business – *Is Coke a better credit risk? Can it carry higher levels of debt than Pepsi in the current economic environment?*

---

[6]In fact, *Pepsico* is often grouped with food companies such as *Kraft Heinz*, *Nestlé*, and *Kellogg* – see John Tell, "Big Food is Going to Get Even Bigger," *Fortune*, March 15, 2017.

INTRODUCTION

Three Approaches to Enterprise Valuation[7]

There are three professionally recognized methodologies to address these questions:

- **Financial accounting**, which generates a measure called ***Book Value***
- **Financial modeling** techniques that rely on the concept of ***Discounted Cash Flows* (DCFs)**, borrowed from the world of bond pricing, which calculates the ***Net Present Value*** of the company's current and projected future cash flows
- **Market Multiples**, which use the price signals generated by the financial markets, to produce ***Valuation Ratios***

We will examine these three approaches in the following chapters, but to be clear up front, **market ratios are superior** to the other methods, broadly on grounds of the timeliness, observability, and concreteness of the market prices that compose them.[8]

---

[7]These three methods are recognized by the **American Institute of Certified Public Accountants (AICPA)**, as the methods to derive "fair value" for accounting purposes. AICPA Task Force, *Valuation of Portfolio Company Investments of Venture Capital and Private Equity Funds and Other Investment Companies*, Draft (May 15, 2018), Chapter 5. The publication refers to the methods as "the market, income, and assets approaches." Paragraph 5.03.

[8]The AICPA recognizes this, giving preference to market data in defining "fair value": *"[a] quoted price in an active market provides the most reliable evidence of fair value and shall be used without adjustment to measure fair value whenever available... An active market is defined as '[a] market in which transactions for the asset or liability take place with sufficient frequency and volume to provide pricing information on an ongoing basis'"* (AICPA Task Force, *Valuation of Portfolio Company Investments of Venture Capital and Private Equity Funds and Other Investment Companies*, Draft (May 15, 2018), Chapter 2, paragraph 2.20).

Also: *"The fair value hierarchy gives the highest priority to quoted prices (unadjusted) in active markets for identical assets or liabilities, and the lowest priority to unobservable inputs. [It] requires that valuation techniques maximize the use of relevant observable inputs and minimize the use of unobservable inputs. As such, even in situations in which the market for a particular asset is deemed not to be active, relevant prices or inputs from this market would still need to be considered in the determination of fair value. It would not be appropriate to default solely to a model's value based on unobservable inputs."* (paragraph 2.21).

See also Chapter 5 of the AICPA document for the discussion of the use of specific market ratios (multiples).

And there are five additional reasons:

First – **Raw Data Quality.**[9] Market metrics draw upon high-quality data generated and updated continuously by the financial markets. *Market price* is the simplest of all the data types, the easiest to obtain, the most objective, the least subject to uncertainty, and the most difficult to manipulate. (The only other data type of similar quality is the Dividend.) *All* the other data types used in the other valuation methods are subject to some uncertainty.[10] They may incorporate large and disputable assumptions, unstable definitions, and methodological bias or manipulation.

Second – **Much Broader Applicability.** Enterprise valuation often calls for the analysis of broad segments of the market. We may want to compare the value of our investment to the market benchmark. Or we may want to compare the valuations in the US market with those in the Chinese market or to detect whether the stock market is entering into "bubble" territory. Market metrics enable this sort of analysis. Other methods have trouble. For example, consider the simple question of how well a company is doing competitively within its sector. Is it a leader? Or a weak player? Is its star rising or falling? These are reflections of its true value certainly. This question is quickly illuminated by market metrics. It would be difficult to perform the same quick comparison with DCF modeling for a sector that might include dozens of companies and harder still to keep it updated for the impact of fresh news or shifts in the competitive landscape (whereas the market metrics update continuously). To use DCF modeling to study the valuation trends in the broader market – say the S&P 500 – is infeasible. DCF is typically used for point-in-time valuations; it is unsuited to track valuation changes over time in an efficient manner even

---

[9]The word "quality" here does not mean the quality of the *information* that the data can provide. Market signals can be ambiguous and difficult to interpret, as we shall discuss. "Raw data quality" refers to the reliability of the data as *a measure of what it purports to measure.* Two bathroom scales, based on differing technologies (say, a mechanical spring scale and an electronic strain-gauge scale), may differ considerably in raw data quality, one giving much more variable readings than the other. A price quote from the stock exchange is a measure of the quoted price, plain and simple. There are no hidden assumptions or adjustments. In contrast, the "Earnings" figure from an income statement incorporates many assumptions, some of them not necessarily explicit, and bears a much more complicated relationship to the company's actual profit level, even before we enter into any question of how to interpret the information it contains. This qualification applies even more forcefully to *forecasts* of cash flows and the future values of other variables used in DCF modeling.

[10]This applies even to accounting categories like "earnings." See Chapter 6.

for a single company. It is too arduous and fraught with multiple sources of uncertainty. Book Value also suffers from systematic shortcomings that limit its application in cross-industry or market-wide comparisons.[11]

Third – **Detection of Mispricings.** Market metrics can often identify possible mispricings – of obvious interest to investors – through a variety of simple tests (see Chapter 5). By itself, a DCF model cannot detect overvaluation or undervaluation. DCF does not supply a benchmark; it gives us a data point – "the Net Present Value of the company is approximately X" – and it is only by cross-checking against the corresponding Market Value that one can gain a perspective on possible mispricings. The same is true for Book Value.

Fourth – **Accuracy.** Applied critically, market metrics have a strong claim to produce more accurate estimates of enterprise value (EV) than GAAP accounting[12] or DCF modeling. GAAP numbers are incomplete, and stale, by design. DCF models are full of uncertainties and far too sensitive to small changes in input values (most of which are based on assumptions rather than hard data).[13] We cannot perhaps observe a company's "true value" directly. But we can use Market Value to construct metrics, ratios, that triangulate that Value, bound it, and give us a reasonable estimate of this hidden variable.

Fifth – T**he Market Price Is Actionable**. The market price will always be close to the price where the transaction *can actually be executed at that moment.*[14] (Accounting-based "Book Value" and DCF-derived "Net Present Value" figures don't necessarily meet this test.) The market price possesses this inherent realism; it defines what is possible. It is a valuation that investors must be willing to accept in order to buy or sell shares today. In corporate transactions involving public companies, the changes in the market price

---

[11]These issues are examined more closely in the Appendix.

[12]GAAP = "Generally Accepted Accounting Principles" – i.e., officially sanctioning financial reporting.

[13]See Chapter 2 on these shortcomings of the GAAP and DCF approaches.

[14]What the AICPA calls the "measurement date. *"The objective of a fair value measurement is 'to estimate the price at which an orderly transaction to sell the asset or to transfer the liability would take place between market participants at the measurement date under current market conditions.' Therefore, a fair value measurement considers market conditions as they exist at the measurement date (not at some point in the future), information which is known or knowable at the measurement date, and is intended to represent the current value of the asset or liability, not the potential value of the asset or liability at some future date"* (AICPA Task Force, *Valuation of Portfolio Company Investments of Venture Capital and Private Equity Funds and Other Investment Companies*, Draft (May 15, 2018), Chapter 2, paragraph 2.14).

will quickly signal the likely value point that will allow the deal to go through. ("Book Value" and "Net Present Value" may serve as inputs to a decision; the market price – when available[15] – *is* the decision, to take or leave.)

The Challenge of Using Market Metrics

Market ratios are easy to calculate and use. This sometimes leads to carelessness in how they are handled. There has been surprisingly little systematic analysis of the various alternatives and parameters affecting these ratios. Even obvious questions – such as whether and under what conditions a P/E based on *historical* earnings is better or worse at predicting various outcomes than a P/E based on *forecast* earnings – have not been thoroughly studied. As a result, market ratios are often difficult to interpret and therefore sometimes hard to apply. There is no standards-setting body for "Multiples," no public methodology for comparing different versions applied to different problems.[16] The "same" ratio may be constructed differently by different users, without necessarily making it clear. Are the earnings adjusted for inflation or seasonality? Does the denominator of the P/E ratio include all shares issued or only some of them? Where do the forecasts of future earnings come from? The lack of methodological control is a weakness today of the Market Value-based approach. The interpretation of even a simple P/E ratio – as we shall see in the next chapter – can be elusive.

The goal of this book, then, is to give some order to an important set of questions and research findings related to the application of market ratios to a range of valuation objectives, especially those related to investment decisions. Regarding specific questions (such as whether Trailing or Forward P/E is more accurate), the answers are often still unclear. But progress can still be made by putting a framework in place that can hopefully ensure that the proper questions are raised and future research efforts brought into sharper focus.

---

[15] Obviously, a market price is not available directly for private transactions. But the transaction is still referenced in most cases to comparable public market valuations.

[16] GAAP accounting and DCF modeling have this advantage. The process of calculating "Book Value" is regulated by the standards bodies of the accounting profession – i.e., the Financial Accounting Standards Board, which promulgates Generally Accepted Accounting Principles in the United States, and the International Accounting Standards Board, which develops the International Financial Reporting Standards used in most of the rest of the world. DCF models – for all their shortcomings – are also methodologically transparent. Their assumptions and techniques – however strained – are clearly stated.

CHAPTER 1

The Ford Dollar: The Mysterious Multiple

Suppose you want to enter into a financial contract with a reliable counterparty to receive a cash payment of $1.00 every year on December 31, for some number of years into the future. Let us assume the counterparty is a large corporation – say, *Ford Motor Company* – operating a successful ongoing business which generates a reliable cash flow.

What would you expect to pay up front for this annuity?

Setting a fair price for this sort of financial instrument is straightforward. Simply project the stream of annual $1.00 payments into the future as far as your contract specifies, and discount each future payment back to its "present value" using a discount factor to reflect the lower value of a future dollar relative to a dollar in hand today. The farther out into the future, the larger the discount. Then add up the stream of discounted payments. Thus, we obtain the Net Present Value, which should equal the Price you have to pay to acquire this contract.

© George Calhoun 2020
G. Calhoun, *Price and Value*, https://doi.org/10.1007/978-1-4842-5552-0_1

CHAPTER 1   THE FORD DOLLAR: THE MYSTERIOUS MULTIPLE

The only tricky part is deciding on the discount rate, which in principle should reflect *Ford's* riskiness as a counterparty or *Ford's* cost of capital and perhaps other considerations (the expected inflation rate?). For purposes of this example, we can set the discount rate equal to the "risk-free interest rate" (the rate of interest paid on the highest-quality government debt, such as Treasury bonds) – plus perhaps some premium to reflect *Ford's* status as a private sector corporation exposed to diverse sources of business risk. If we assume, say, a discount rate of 8%, then the present value of next year's $1.00 payment is about 92 cents. The discount effect compounds as the time horizon extends. The present value of an *infinite* stream of $1.00 payments, discounted at 8%, eventually converges asymptotically to a very finite $12.50. For a shorter period, the present value – and the fair price – would be less. A ten-year annuity stream would be worth about $6.70.

But let's make the question a little messier. Assume now that the contract entitles you to some sort of *claim* on $1.00 of *Ford's* earnings. However, under this new arrangement, *Ford* is not required to pay out the full amount each year. The company may decide in good faith to retain some portion of "your" dollar, to reinvest in the business (with your interests in mind of course), to grow the company, so that down the road they may be able to pay you even more than $1.00 a year. As the payout rate grows, perhaps in time you might be receiving $2.00 a year, or more.[1]

Now also assume that the contract is *transferable* – you can sell this annuity to anyone you choose, at any time, for whatever price you may negotiate. This adds a so-called *terminal value (TV)* to your calculation, on top of the annual cash payments.

How much would you have to pay for such a contract?

This is a more difficult question. There are many uncertainties – how much of your $1.00 claim will *Ford* actually pay out in cash this year? How much will they retain? How much next year and the year(s) after? What exactly will they do with the retained portion? If they reinvest it in the business, how successful will those reinvestments be? How much will the company grow? When and by how much will your quasi-annuity

---

[1] Interestingly, Finance theory makes an argument that the value of the claim is not dependent upon whether the cash is paid out. This is the famous (and perhaps spurious) "dividend irrelevance theorem" proposed by Miller and Modigliani some 50 years ago. *"Value does not depend on payout. Value is indeed based on expected cash flows over the life of an investment, but the timing of the payout is not important; the value is independent of whether the firm pays out dividends in the short term or only pays out dividends on liquidation of the firm"* (Stephen Penman, *Accounting for Value,* Columbia Press (2011), p. 38).

CHAPTER 1 THE FORD DOLLAR: THE MYSTERIOUS MULTIPLE

increase in value? What is the risk of a recession next year or five years from now? (This is an important question, since we know that the automotive business is rather sensitive to the business cycle.) Perhaps there will be tariffs and trade wars, labor troubles, new foreign competition, or new and disruptive technologies (e.g., electric cars). What would be the impact of these factors on *Ford's* performance?

In short, *your* future cash flows are hard to predict. You can no longer count on receiving a certain dollar every year. You can't be sure whether, or by how much, the future cash payments might increase (or decrease). And then there is the question of the terminal value you might expect at some future date if you were to sell the contract to someone else. That is also uncertain. Finally, there is still the discount factor, one more uncertainty to apply to all these uncertain future payments.

There's much to consider and calculate. It would be daunting to model, if you were inclined to do so. We might expect that any answer we obtain would be very approximate and uncertain. But in fact, there is already a precise quantitative answer to this question. There is an exact, executable price that you can pay, right now, to acquire this contract. On May 4, 2018, the cost of this contract was exactly $5.89. For a bit more than the cost of a cafe latte, you could have purchased a claim on a perpetual earnings stream of $1.00 per year.[2]

As you have probably realized by now, the contract in question is of course one share of *Ford's* common stock. On May 4, 2018, you would have paid $11.20 for that share. *Ford's* earnings the previous year amounted to $1.90 for each share. So – doing the math – each dollar of *Ford's* earnings is apparently valued at $5.89 (in terms of share price). And remember ownership of the share gives you a claim not just on this year's dollar of earnings, but on an ongoing stream of earnings, for as long as you hold it.

What you have just calculated is the fundamental valuation metric known as the Price-to-Earnings ratio, or P/E.

---

[2] *Ford* is currently paying out 60 cents of that claim in cash, as its common stock dividend. The rest is reinvested in the presumed hope of growing the business and increasing the payout in future years. Five years previously, *Ford* was paying out only 40 cents per share; so the dividend payout has grown by 50%. Other companies have been more successful in growing the payouts. *Johnson & Johnson* (JNJ), a so-called dividend aristocrat, has increased its dividend by a factor of ten in the last 20 years. These examples help illustrate the rationale of viewing a "claim" on a dollar of earnings as a valid and valuable proposition, even if the entire dollar is not paid out in the current period.

CHAPTER 1   THE FORD DOLLAR: THE MYSTERIOUS MULTIPLE

$$\frac{Price\ per\ share}{Earnings\ per\ share} = \frac{\$11.20}{\$1.90} = 5.89\ (the\ P/E)$$

The P/E tells you the price of a *Ford* Dollar, your quasi-annuity, a claim on $1.00 of *Ford's* earnings stream. The price, on May 4, 2018, was $5.89. That number bundled all the uncertainties mentioned earlier into a single price point. It was not abstract. It was not uncertain. It was a firm offer that was available to anyone, right then, on the spot. Consider for a moment how extraordinary this is. The stock market is capable of processing all these uncertainties, all of *Ford's* possible futures, into a single hard number, instantaneously.

1.1 P/E As a Measure of How "Expensive" a Company Is

So, on May 4, 2018, a *Ford* Dollar would have cost you $5.89. Was that a good deal?

Well, a *GM* Dollar would have cost $6.71 (i.e., *GM* had a P/E of 6.71). A *Toyota* Dollar would have cost $8.66. A *Chrysler* Dollar was priced at $8.54. In the automotive sector at least, *Ford* looked like the best offer.

How about other industries? An *Apple* Dollar cost $18.60. A *Starbucks* Dollar cost $18.91. A Cornflakes Dollar (i.e., *Kellogg's*) was on sale for $15.23.

A *Goldman Sachs* Dollar was priced at $25.97. (But *Morgan Stanley's* Dollar was only $16.55 – a better bargain if you want the cachet of a premier investment bank as your counterparty.)

Then there was *Facebook*, a darling of the market lately. If you wanted one of Mark Zuckerberg's Dollars, it would have cost you $32.40 – five-and-a-half times the price of a *Ford* Dollar. (See Figure 1-1.)

CHAPTER 1   THE FORD DOLLAR: THE MYSTERIOUS MULTIPLE

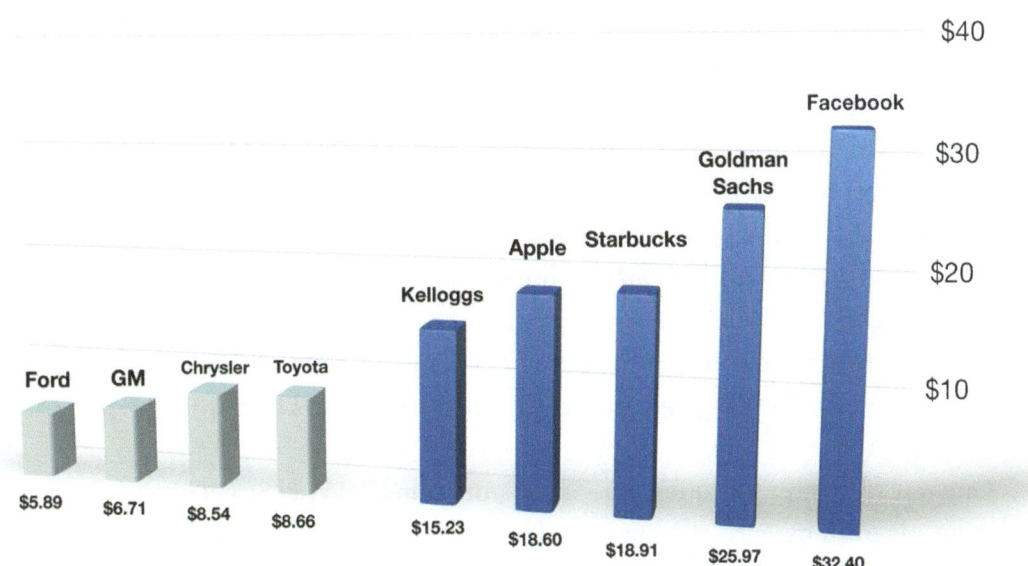

Figure 1-1. Price of $1 Claim for Various Companies

And what can we say about *Amazon*? On May 4, 2018, a Bezos Dollar would have cost you exactly *$254 (and 76 cents)*. It was so expensive it has been left off the chart here because it would distort the graphic perspective.

So, *Ford* looks like a bargain. But why? After all, the dollars in the annuity stream, and the dollars that all these companies are earning, are units of the same currency – US dollars, fully interchangeable. Presumably a dollar in cash you might receive from *Ford* has exactly the same purchasing power as a dollar in cash from Facebook. Of course, the companies don't have to pay out in cash. So is the value of a *claim* on *Ford's* earnings less certain than a claim on *Facebook's* earnings? *Ford* pays out between two-thirds and three-quarters of its actual earnings to its shareholders, in cash, year after year. *Facebook* has never paid out a dime of its earnings. Therefore, the *quality* of the claim on *Ford's* earnings would seem to be stronger. So why would you pay five-and-a-half times more to obtain the *Facebook* Dollar? In market parlance, *Ford* is cheap, and *Facebook* is expensive. If you want that annuity, at the best price, buy *Ford*.

CHAPTER 1   THE FORD DOLLAR: THE MYSTERIOUS MULTIPLE

1.2 P/E As a Predictor of Future Share Price

Or maybe not. There is also the "terminal value" of the *Ford* Dollar – that is, the price you'll get for it if you decide to sell it at some point in the future, instead of holding onto the earnings claim. Let us now assume you plan to retain the *Ford* share for one year and then sell it. The price today (May 4, 2018 – your "cost basis") is $11.20. If that price were to increase by, say, 15% in the coming year, to around $13, and you sold it then, you would at least double the profit on your investment (compared to the annuity or dividend payout).[3] In buying a share of *Ford's* common stock, you not only purchased a claim on *Ford's* earnings but a sort of option on its future share price as well. It may well be that the terminal value turns out to be the larger part of your gains. So, to decide whether the $5.89 price of the *Ford* Dollar is a good deal or not, you also want to know what the price of that share is likely to be in a year.

One way to answer this question – in fact, the standard Wall Street way to answer this question – is to study *Ford's* business in detail, review its financial statements, interview its management if possible, listen to the forecasts for its future sales, assess its profit margins, check what the competition is doing… and come up with an estimate for next year's earnings per share (EPS – the denominator in the P/E ratio). Let's say, having done this hard work, you conclude that *Ford* will have an excellent year and will earn $2.90 per share next year (vs. $1.90 per share last year). Clearly, the company will have increased in value, and this should be reflected in the share price, which should also increase. But by how much?

Here's a rough answer: take the extra $1.00 in EPS, and *multiply* it by the P/E ratio – to forecast the expected gain in share price. Applied in this way, the P/E ratio is commonly referred to as the *Multiple*.[4] All things being equal, if you are right about *Ford's* earnings next year, the price of *Ford's* common stock should increase by approximately $5.89 ($1.00 increase in EPS times the Multiple of 5.89) to reach about $17 a share – a 50% return. Sounds like good news.

---

[3] That is, you would receive $1.90 in cash payments – all of its earnings – from *Ford* (in this imaginary example) plus a capital gain of about $1.80 from the sale of your share in the market.

[4] Of course, the multiple (the P/E ratio) itself may change. The analyst may wish to adjust the multiple to take into account other expected changes in the situation – say, new regulations that may constrain the growth prospects of the business in some way. But the general principle holds: the P/E ratio is seen as a metric that can allow us to relate future fundamental performance – changes in sales, earnings, and so on – to the future share price. It is first and foremost a forecasting tool.

CHAPTER 1   THE FORD DOLLAR: THE MYSTERIOUS MULTIPLE

But what if *Ford* had *Facebook's* multiple? With $2.90 in earnings/share, *Ford's* stock would be worth almost $95 a share. (See Figure 1-2.)

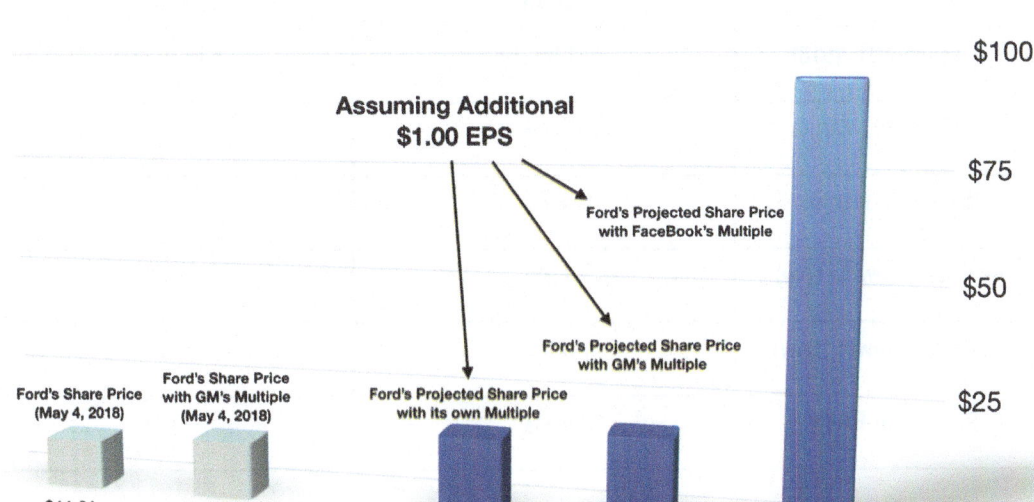

Figure 1-2. *The Effect of the Multiple on the Share Price Forecast*

Of course, *Ford* is no *Facebook*. But even if *Ford* only had *GM's* multiple, its shares next year would be worth 15% more (even with *no* increase in earnings). If it had *Toyota's* multiple, it would be worth $16.71 a share today – almost as much as the payoff from what would be an impressive and challenging 50% gain in earnings next year.

The key question now seems to be: *Why* does *Ford* get a lower value for its earnings dollar than *GM* or *Toyota*? These are similar companies, with similar products, similar customers, and similar broad business prospects. One of the standard interpretations of the P/E ratio holds that a higher P/E is associated with faster growth and generally with superior performance.[5] Yet a comparison of *Ford* and *GM* for the most recent prior quarter (Q1 2018) shows *Ford* was doing rather better than *GM*. (See Table 1-1.)

---

[5]See Chapter 4, Section 4.2.1.

CHAPTER 1   THE FORD DOLLAR: THE MYSTERIOUS MULTIPLE

Table 1-1. *Ford vs. GM*

	Ford	GM
Revenue (Q1 2018)	$41.95 Bn	$36.10 Bn
Gross Profit Margin	9.2%	8.0%
Net Profit Margin	4.1%	2.8%
Revenue Growth (yoy)	7.2%	-3.1%
Earnings Growth (yoy)	9.0%	-60.0%
Return on Equity	4.7%	3.0%

Ford had higher revenue, was more profitable, and was growing faster. Its business appeared healthier in every way. *Ford* paid out more of its earnings in cash dividends (65%) than *GM* (52%). The cash value of the dollars that *Ford* earns and pays out is the same as that of the dollars that *GM* earns and pays out. So why was *Ford's* earnings stream selling at a discount? The answer is not clear.

Consider also how the Multiple relates to the company's strategic outlook. Shareholder value is driven by a very simple equation:

$$EPS\,(Earnings) * P/E\,(The\ Multiple) = Share\ Price$$

So if *Ford* wants to increase its share price by 15% this year – a decent return for its shareholders – it has two options. On the one hand, it can grow earnings. It can invest and execute well, to design better vehicles and sell more of them, more profitably, and it may be able to increase the earnings per share by 15%. The share price should rise, all things being equal.

Or the company can take steps to somehow increase the Multiple. If *Ford* can figure out how to change the market's perception of its earnings stream, to persuade the market to view its earnings in the same way that the market views *GM's* earnings, the share price will rise even without an increase in earnings. But it is not clear just how that can be done.

Analysts know how to model the company's fundamental business, forecast sales and earnings, and how to use the (fixed) Multiple to predict the future share price. It is harder to understand what it might take to *change* the Multiple, to change the value that the market places on each *Ford* Dollar, or how to raise it to parity with the *GM* Dollar.

It seems unfair. *Ford* receives less credit – measured in terms of shareholder value – for its hard work to earn each dollar of net profit than *GM* or any of its peers in the industry. The future value of *Ford's* shares will be handicapped by this, unless the Multiple changes for the better.

1.3 P/E As a Predictor of Future Returns

Let us now pose a different question, not *What will the future share price be?* but *What is the return on the investment can we expect, if we purchase a share of Ford's stock today?*

Here we enter into one of the mysteries of the market: the inverse relationship between P/E and returns.

To observe this phenomenon, we dial the clock back to some suitably distant starting point (say, 20 years ago), and we divide the universe of stocks (say, the S&P 500) into ten buckets ranked by the value of the P/E on the start date of the analysis. That is, the lowest 10% of stocks ranked by their P/E ratios are placed in the first bucket, the next higher 10% in the second bucket, and so forth. Then we run the clock forward for, say, 10 years. (See Figure 1-3.)

CHAPTER 1   THE FORD DOLLAR: THE MYSTERIOUS MULTIPLE

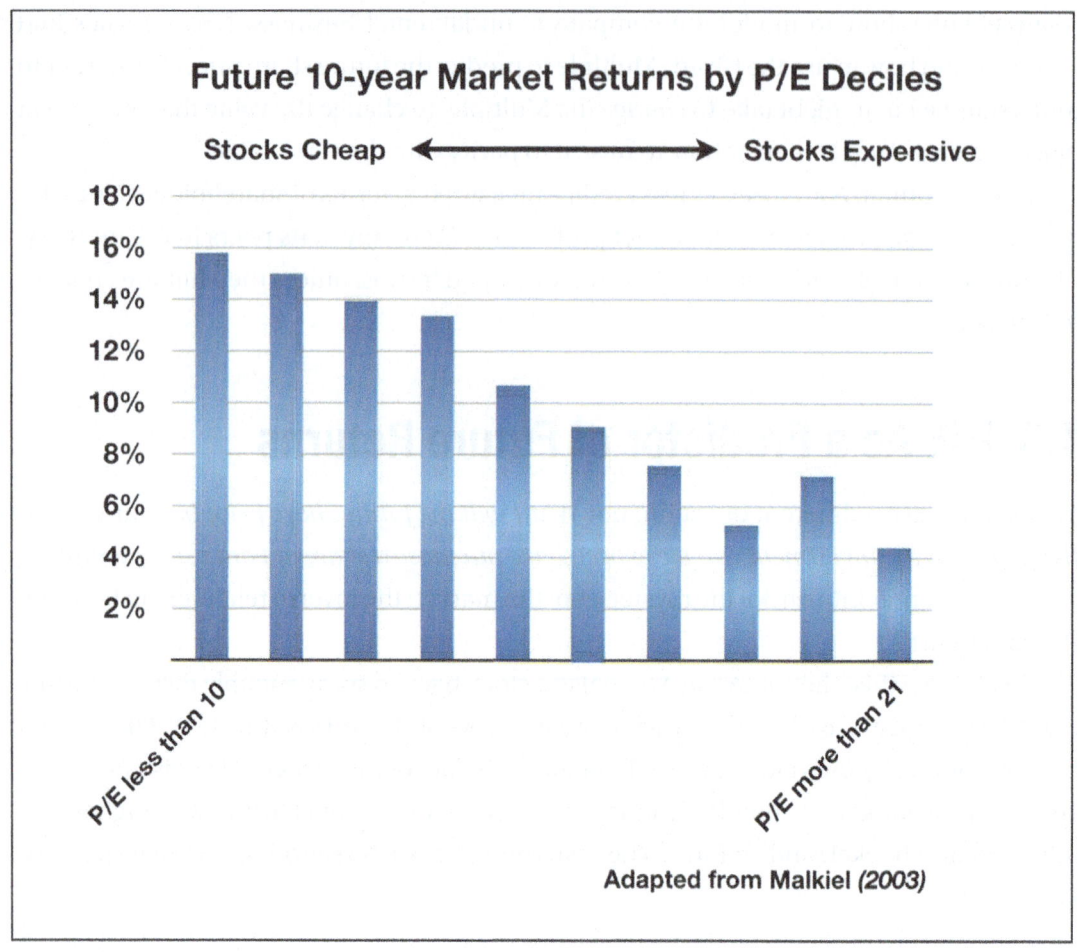

Figure 1-3. P/E Multiples by Decile[6]

The results are surprising, and should be.[7] The stocks with the "worst" Multiples significantly outperform. By "worst" we mean well below the market average P/E. And why "worst"? Because generally a low P/E is a sign that the company is out of favor, that it has problems, and that the business has underperformed. Stocks are usually discounted for a reason. It may be a flawed business model, aggressive competition, an accounting scandal,

---

[6]Adapted from Burton G. Malkiel, "The Efficient Market Hypothesis and its Critics," *Journal of Economic Perspectives*, Vol. 17, No. 1, Winter 2003, pp. 59–82.

[7]Burton G. Malkiel, "The Efficient Market Hypothesis and its Critics," *Journal of Economic Perspectives*, Vol. 17, No. 1, Winter 2003, pp. 59–82.

or simply a string of bad quarters. Companies that are doing well – with strong management, successful products, high profit margins, and expanding markets – have a bright future and usually carry high multiples. One would expect that investing in these successful companies would pay off much more than investing in the "dogs" of the market.

It doesn't work out that way. It is one of the profound "anomalies" of the market that the companies that have underperformed, the companies with problems, inferior products, legal troubles, bad management teams, and regulatory headaches; the companies that are struggling in the competitive market, are the companies whose shares will on average outperform the more successful companies going forward.

This pattern has been confirmed time and again, in hundreds of studies, over many decades. The chart in Figure 1-4, prepared by the Federal Reserve Bank of San Francisco, relates the P/E (averaged over a 10-year period) to the returns of those stocks over the following 10 years.[8] The downward slope is inexorable. If the pattern holds, a stock with a *Facebook*-ish P/E of 30 can be expected to return, on average, approximately 0% gain over the next 20 years, while a *Ford*-type stock with a P/E of 5 or 6 could be expected to gain 5, 10, or 12% *per year* for the next 20 years, on average.

---

[8]This data is apparently derived in part from Robert J. Shiller, *Irrational Exuberance*, 2nd Edition, 2006.

CHAPTER 1   THE FORD DOLLAR: THE MYSTERIOUS MULTIPLE

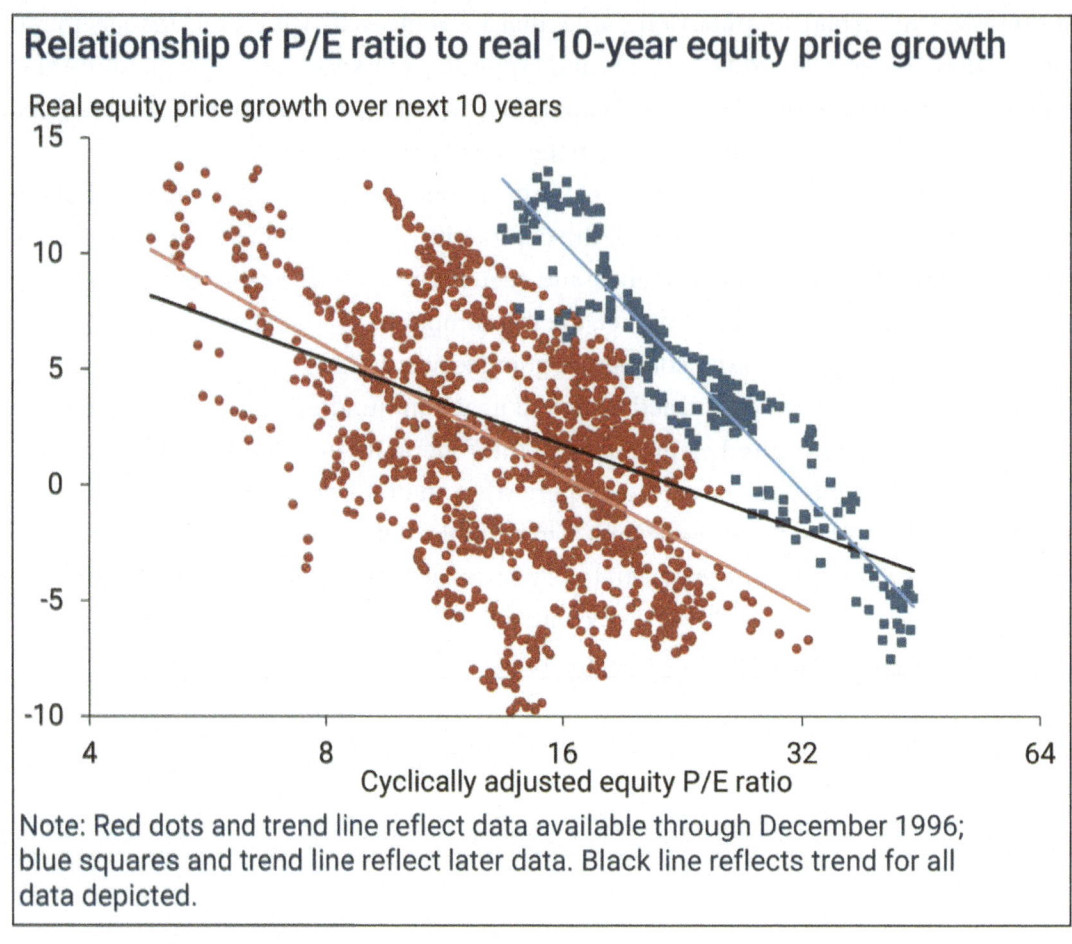

Figure 1-4. P/E 10-Year Rates of Return[9]

---

[9]Reprinted with permission from the **Federal Reserve Bank of San Francisco**, "Valuation Ratios for Households and Businesses," *FRBSF Economic Letter 2018-01,* January 8, 2018, www.frbsf.org/economic-research/publications/economic-letter/2018/january/valuation-ratios-for-households-and-businesses/. The opinions expressed in this article do not necessarily reflect the views of the management of the Federal Reserve Bank of San Francisco or of the Board of Governors of the Federal Reserve System.

CHAPTER 1   THE FORD DOLLAR: THE MYSTERIOUS MULTIPLE

In 1982, Tom Peters and Robert Waterman published *In Search of Excellence*, a bestseller in its day, which provided a list of 36 of "America's Best-Run Companies" – selected on the basis of solid financial metrics such as asset growth, return on capital, and so forth. A few years later, an analyst checking up on the actual stock market performance of these "excellent" companies also decided, "out of curiosity," to screen for the very opposite sort of company – she called it going "in search of disaster" – and used the same fundamental metrics to select the very worst companies in the S&P 500.[10] A comparison of the "excellents" against the "unexcellents" on the basis of the prior fundamentals presents a stark contrast of superior vs. inferior business performance. (See Figure 1-5.)

---

[10]Michelle Clayman, "In Search of Excellence: The Investor's Viewpoint," *Financial Analysts Journal,* May-June 1987, pp. 54–63.

CHAPTER 1   THE FORD DOLLAR: THE MYSTERIOUS MULTIPLE

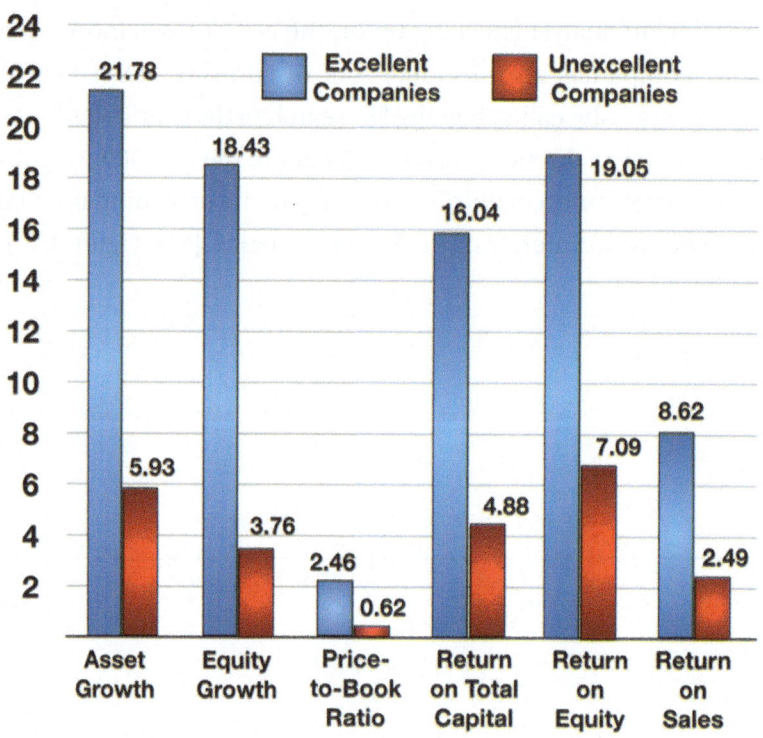

Figure 1-5. Excellent and "Unexcellent" Companies Compared on Fundamental Performance[11]

But the performance of the companies' shares showed the opposite pattern: the "disasters" nearly tripled in value, far surpassing Peters and Waterman's selection of "best-run companies."[12] (See Figure 1-6.)

---

[11]Adapted from Michelle Clayman, "In Search of Excellence: The Investor's Viewpoint," *Financial Analysts Journal*, May–June 1987, pp. 54–63.

[12]The "disasters" beat the S&P 500 average by an astounding 12.4% per year. And they had virtually the same "beta" (a measure of market "risk" or volatility) as the "excellent" companies.

CHAPTER 1   THE FORD DOLLAR: THE MYSTERIOUS MULTIPLE

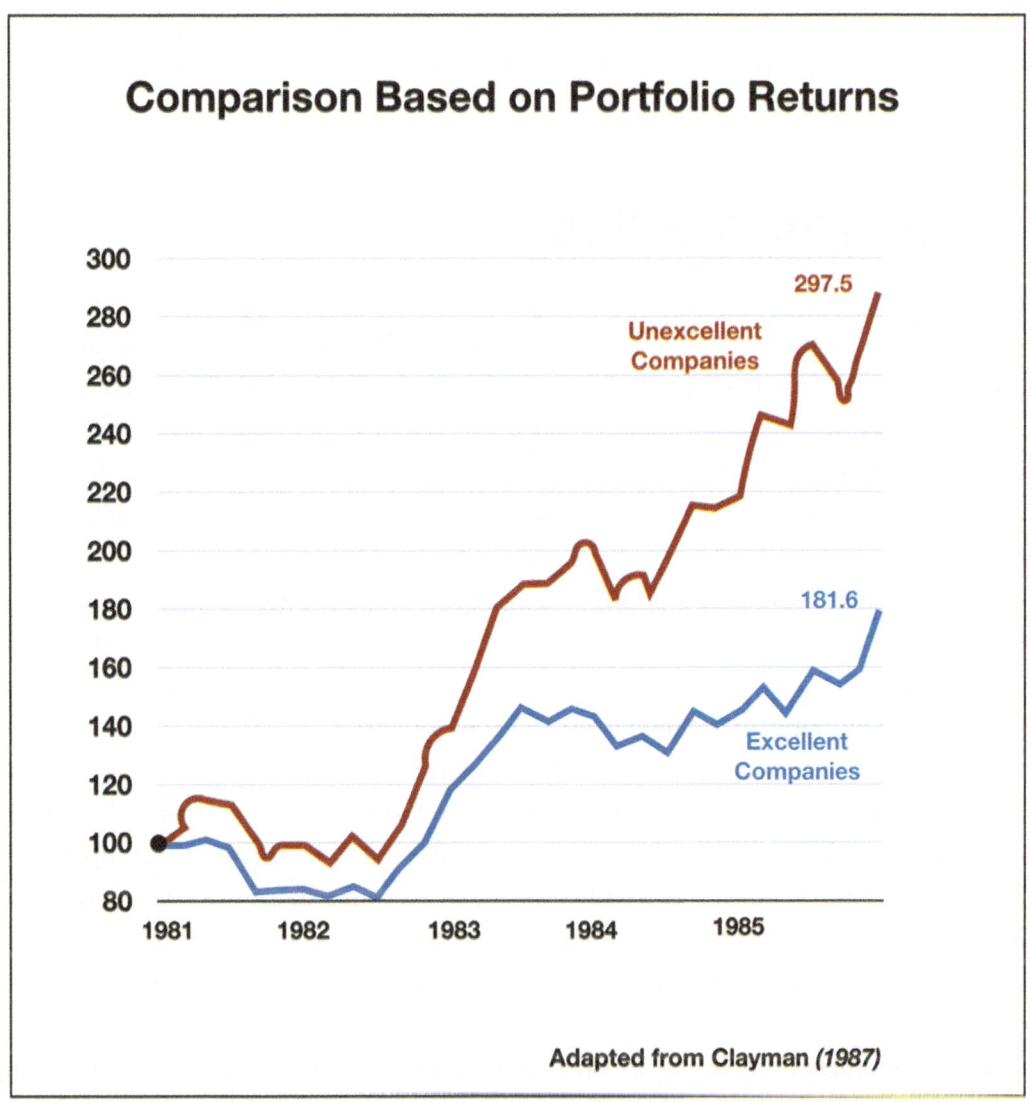

Figure 1-6. Excellent and "Unexcellent" Companies Compared on Market Returns[13]

---

[13]Adapted from Michelle Clayman, "In Search of Excellence: The Investor's Viewpoint," *Financial Analysts Journal*, May–June 1987, pp. 54–63.

CHAPTER 1   THE FORD DOLLAR: THE MYSTERIOUS MULTIPLE

This is not a freak outcome. As we will see later on in this book (Chapter 5), the contrarian pattern of stock market returns as a function of P/E and other multiples is a pervasive feature of the financial markets.

1.4 The Mysterious Multiple

The P/E ratio commingles a diverse set of signals, with very different practical implications. It seems to point in several directions at the same time, because it possesses an inherently incoherent constitution that mixes sober accounting calculations with the animal spirits of the stock market.[14]

This makes interpretation difficult. Is a high P/E better than a low P/E or vice versa? The low cost of a *Ford* Dollar (the claim on *Ford's* earnings) looks like a bargain for the simple annuity seeker (low beats high), until we use the Multiple to forecast *Ford's* future price (the "terminal value" of the investment), which exposes the chronic discount that the capital gains seeker will suffer; *Ford* lags inexplicably behind its peers (high beats low). But then again, we see that other companies with *Ford*-like Multiples in the past have tended to outperform the high flyers (low beats high).

It is paradoxical. Managers work hard to create shareholder value and to build the sort of company that will support a high P/E, but when the company carries a high P/E, it means shareholders are likely to suffer. Successful companies tend to have higher multiples than less successful ones – but the price of "excellence" is often share price stagnation and investor disappointment. Struggling companies often carry very low Multiples on what earnings they do manage to generate; a low P/E might therefore seem like an obvious danger signal. Yet for years, so-called "value investors" have used a low P/E screen to find these seemingly unattractive prospects that often go on to generate market-beating returns – despite the fact that classical finance theory says they should not be able to do so.

Yet as challenged, and challenging, and self-contradictory as it may be, the Multiple is central to security analysis methodologies in use today. Why is such an unstable, ambiguous, difficult-to-interpret metric so popular?

---

[14]It is as though a statistician were to perform a careful regression analysis on his data – and then add a factor to reflect his mood at that particular moment. No one would think of doing something like that, but that is in a sense what the P/E embodies: a combination of hard fact and raw sentiment.

The answer lies in the concept of triangulation, described briefly in the Preface. Looking at something by means of different and dissimilar methodologies – in effect, triangulating the phenomenon from two or more philosophically well-separated standpoints – has gained acceptance in a number of fields where the subject matter is complex and noisy (as the financial markets are).

In the case of enterprise valuation, the P/E ratio is best understood as an example of triangulation – using two different and supposedly incompatible valuation techniques to triangulate the "true value" of the enterprise. The next chapter develops this idea further.

CHAPTER 2

The Value Triangle

As of 2018, *the Ford Motor Company* operated in dozens of countries, with around 75 production facilities on five continents and tens of thousands of dealers. It employed over 166,000 people to design, produce, and sell hundreds of different products and services, to millions of customers, generating a continuous stream of cash flows, profits, and dividends and providing the fuel for innovation and reinvestment to allow for future cash flows to continue and hopefully to grow. The company buys, sells, invests, divests, and distributes

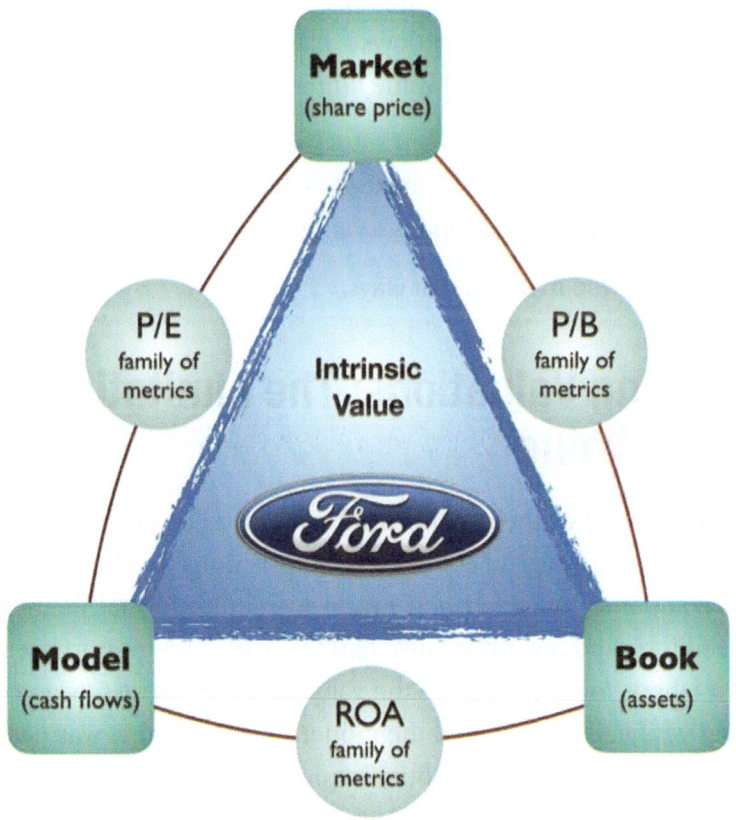

© George Calhoun 2020
G. Calhoun, *Price and Value*, https://doi.org/10.1007/978-1-4842-5552-0_2

CHAPTER 2   THE VALUE TRIANGLE

various assets continuously, transacting in many currencies and under many systems of commercial and financial regulation around the world. Its fortunes are constantly in flux, depending on its strategic choices (and those of its competitors) and on the changes in its economic environment (trends in regulation, business cycles, credit conditions). *Ford's* value is not just a function of the present moment; it incorporates a broad horizon of expectations regarding the future performance of the company and future states of its environment.

How then should we calculate the value of *Ford's* business?

We begin with three "snapshots" which capture different aspects of *Ford's* enterprise value – often referred to as Book, Model, and Market:

- **Book**: Drawn from the balance sheet, the list of the assets (and offsetting liabilities) that *Ford* currently owns, from which we derive the company's "book value."

- **Model**: Starting with the income statement as a simplified model of the *Ford's* ongoing operations, linking the various streams of revenues, expenses, earnings, and cash flows – elaborate financial models can be developed to forecast and value *future* earnings performance.

- **Market**: The market price of *Ford's* stock, as set and reset constantly by investors, traders, and market makers – which represents the market's current appraisal of the company's value.

Each approach is flawed in important ways.

2.1 Accounting Valuations: The Limitations of "Book Value"

Accounting was developed in the preindustrial era, *not* as a valuation technique *per se*, but as a method for keeping track of commercial transactions (the bookkeeping function). As large public companies emerged and began to require formal financial reports for shareholders, creditors, and tax authorities, and for management purposes, accountants extended their methods to try to capture the value of corporate assets and liabilities in a standardized and verifiable format, and the modern balance sheet was developed. Thus, today, as we all know, "assets minus liabilities" equals Book Value (also called Net Assets or Equity). For a long time, this simple formula was sufficient to value a business.

No longer. Public accounting today is a field in crisis. It fails to recognize the key assets that actually generate most of a modern company's earnings and drive the appreciation of its share price. This becomes clear by comparing Book Value with Market Value (market capitalization, that is, the value of the company's outstanding shares of stock, its equity value). In principle, both aim to measure the same thing – the residual value of the business net of its liabilities. Both often carry the same label – "Equity" – although they are derived from very different sources. And indeed, until about 1985, Book and Market *were* in general agreement: the average Market-to-Book ratio (called "Price-to-Book," or P/B)[1] across the economy was approximately 1 to 1. (Market Value trended slightly higher, but this was usually explained as a symptom of investors' "animal spirits" or overoptimism – accountants relied on their disciplined methods to keep these emotions in check.)

Then, beginning in the mid-1980s, these two measures began to diverge. The P/B ratio climbed from near parity to as high as 7:1 and has ranged between 2.5 and 5 over most of the last 30 years.[2] (See Figure 2-1.) Individual companies often have much higher Price-to-Book ratios. *Apple's* P/B is 7.3 to 1.[3] *Facebook* is 6.8 to 1. Chipmaker *Nvidia* is 19.5 to 1. *Amazon* is 27.5 to 1. The phenomenon is not limited to technology companies. *Coca-Cola* has a Price-to-Book ratio of 10.5 to 1. *Pepsi* is higher – 12.7 to 1. *Kellogg's* is 9.4 to 1. *Starbucks* is 14.0 to 1. *Marriott Hotels* is 13.3 to 1.

---

[1] For some reason, many academics prefer to use the inverted form: a Book/Price ratio, B/P. Keeping in mind that, in the nature of any ratio, a high P/B will correspond to a low B/P, the metrics are otherwise the same. Whether this confusion serves any other purpose...

[2] Baruch Lev, *Intangibles: Management, Measurement, and Reporting* (Washington, D.C.: Brookings, 2001).

[3] All figures as of mid-2018.

CHAPTER 2   THE VALUE TRIANGLE

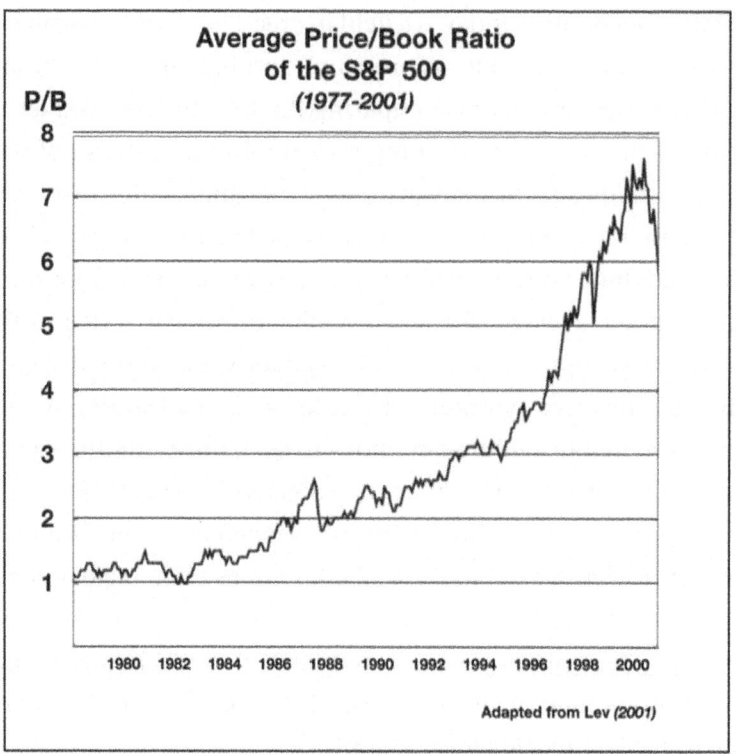

Figure 2-1. *Price-to-Book Ratio for the S&P 500*[4]

The explanation is simple: the key value-creating assets of these companies are missing from the balance sheet. *Coke's* most important asset is its *brand,* which is often listed by brand valuation specialists as among the most valuable intellectual property assets in the world – and goes unrecognized by accountants. *Nvidia's* business is based on its proprietary *technology* – the result of years of heavy investment in R&D, all of which has been "expensed," written off as a "cost," as though it were similar to paying the electric bill – and is therefore not recorded on the balance sheet as a long-lived, valuable, and value-creating asset. *Facebook's* principal asset is the *data* it collects from its subscribers, which it monetizes by selling to advertisers for targeted product messaging. None of these value drivers appear in the companies' financial statements.

---

[4]Adapted from Baruch Lev, Intangibles: Management, Measurement, and Reporting (Washington, D.C.: Brookings, 2001).

Accountants sometimes sidestep the question by referring to these as "intangible" assets, suggesting they are not significant.[5] At one time, intangibles were a small part of the picture. An analysis by *Ocean Tomo* (a specialist in intellectual property valuation) reports that in 1975 only 17% of the value of all the companies in the S&P 500 index was derived from *intangible* assets. (See Figure 2-2.) But by 2015, intangibles accounted for 84% of market value.[6] This means that the financial market places a value on the American economy that is *five times greater* than the value given to traditional hard assets on the balance sheet by accountants.

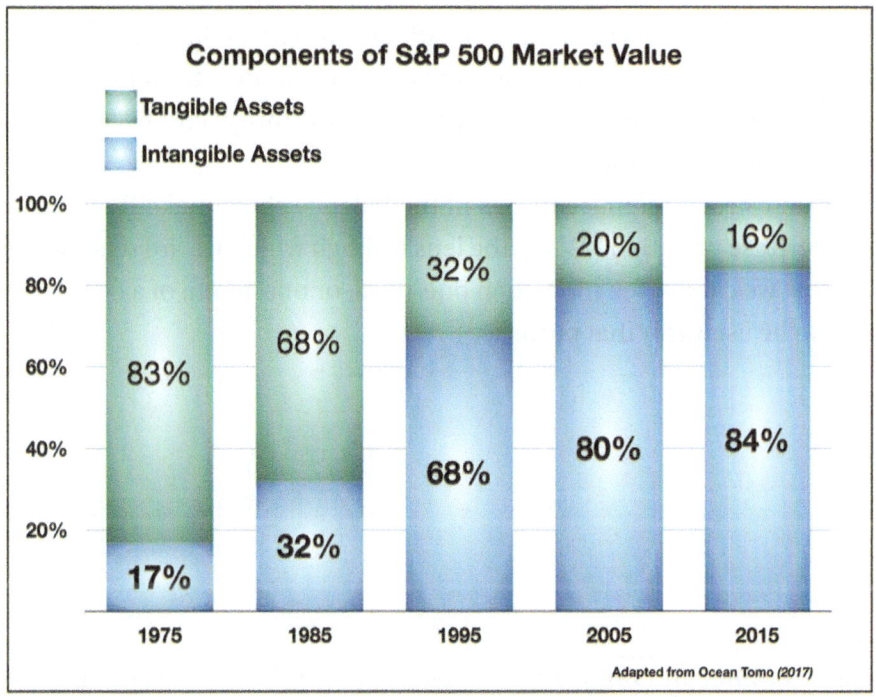

Figure 2-2. Tangible vs. Intangible Assets: The Evolution of "Book Value"[7]

---

[5]The category "intangible assets" does sometimes appear on the balance sheet, typically when a company has purchased them, and the cost of acquisition can be specified. But the vast bulk of the "intangibles" are simply *invisible* and show up nowhere in the financial statements. For example, in 2018, Coca-Cola listed several categories of intangible assets on its balance sheet: Trademarks ($6.7 Bn), Goodwill ($9.4 Bn), and "Other Intangibles" ($368 Mn) – a total of about $16 Bn of identified intangibles. But Coke's Market Capitalization was about $180 Bn, compared to just $17 Bn in Book Value. Something over $150 Bn in valuation is unaccounted for.

[6]*Intangible Asset Market Value Study*, Ocean Tomo, 2017. *"IAMV is determined by subtracting a company's net tangible asset value from its market cap to determine its net intangible asset value."*

[7]Adapted from *Intangible Asset Market Value Study*, Ocean Tomo, 2017.

CHAPTER 2   THE VALUE TRIANGLE

This shift in the asset mix from mostly tangible assets to mostly intangible assets reflects a broad trend in the American economy, with modern business models increasingly based on assets like monetizable data, brand equity, customer equity, and intellectual property – which require less capital to generate each dollar of revenue and earnings.

There are other problems with Book Value. Balance sheet figures are nearly always out of date. This is by design. Generally Accepted Accounting Principles (GAAP) require that assets be valued based on their historical cost – that is, the verifiable price paid to acquire them. This has two implications. First, assets that are *developed* through internal investments rather than acquired – such as *Coke's* brand equity or *Nvidia's* technology – cannot be valued "at cost" (according to GAAP) because no auditable price was paid for them and therefore go unrecognized as assets by accountants. Second, asset values do change over time. Balance sheet figures that are tied to historical cost become stale as true values of those assets rise or fall.[8]

The gaps and structural inaccuracies of the balance sheet make Book Value a poor choice for enterprise valuation.[9] When the lens through which we are searching for value is so cloudy that we cannot see more than one-third, or one-tenth, of a company's assets, it has ceased to be useful for that purpose.[10]

---

[8]The **American Institute of Certified Public Accountants** has acknowledged this problem in their Draft guidelines for assessing the fair value of an enterprise: *"A historical reporting basis, such as cost, does not provide meaningful comparability across investments"* (AICPA Task Force, *Valuation of Portfolio Company Investments of Venture Capital and Private Equity Funds and Other Investment Companies*, Draft (May 15, 2018), paragraph 2.07.

[9]There are other problems with respect to the use of Book Value as a measure of enterprise value. Many of the standard balance sheet asset categories are arguably not assets in the true sense, but more like liabilities. Inventory is a good example; excess inventory is widely seen as a danger signal. Even cash can become more of a liability than an asset under some circumstances. See Chapter 3 for a discussion on Cash-Adjusted Price-to-Earnings.

[10]An argument can be made that Book Value is still useful in evaluating firms in the financial sector, since the majority of their assets are *financial* assets (e.g., cash, tradable securities, loans with good credit standing), which have values that are easy to convert into current dollars. The financial sector has the lowest P/B ratio of all the sectors in the S&P 500, about 1.68 as of this writing [May 2018].

2.2 The Shortcomings of Financial Models

Financial modeling is often seen as a central pillar of modern Finance. Spreadsheet software has facilitated the construction of models that were once very time-consuming to build and use. Borrowing valuation concepts from bond pricing methods and working with data derived from standard income statements, along with many assumptions and estimates of future values for key variables, it has become the standard approach to valuation for many purposes.

Essentially, all financial models are based on the concept of valuing a stream of estimated *future* cash flows. The first application of this approach was the Dividend Discount Model (DDM), which asserts that the value of a company is "simply" the discounted sum of its expected future dividends. The DDM dates back several decades to the work of John Burr Williams, and later Myron Gordon, who offered it as an alternative to the more speculative and "psychological" interpretations of market pricing that were then popular among practitioners.[11] The dividend stream is viewed as an infinite series of cash payments, similar to the interest payments on a debt instrument, which invites the use of standard bond pricing concepts (with an added factor to account for dividend growth).[12]

---

[11] John Burr Williams, *The Theory of Investment Value*. Harvard University Press, 1938. The opposing view was perhaps best characterized by John Maynard Keynes, a sort of Behavioral Economist *avant la lettre*, who held that "animal spirits" played a large and perhaps decisive role, instead of formal calculation of returns, as Williams argued (J. M. Keynes, *The General Theory of Employment*, London, 1938).

[12] The only important nuance was whether dividends alone were sufficient or should net earnings forecasts also come into the valuation picture. Gordon (writing in 1959) put it this way: *"The three possible hypotheses with respect to what an investor pays for when he acquires a share of common stock are that he is buying (1) both the dividends and the earnings, (2) the dividends and (3) the earnings. It may be argued that most commonly he is buying the price at some future date, but if the future price will be related to the expected dividends and/or earnings on that date, we need not go beyond the three hypotheses stated"* (M. J. Gordon, "Dividends, Earnings, and Stock Prices," *The Review of Economics and Statistics*, Vol. 41, No. 2 (May 1959), pp. 99–105). Of course the orthodox view – embodied in the Miller-Modigliani "dividend irrelevance" proposition – would imply that the first of Gordon's hypotheses is the correct one. See Chapter 1, Footnote 1.

CHAPTER 2   THE VALUE TRIANGLE

Later, the DDM framework was expanded to take into account the "terminal value" of the company or its shares (which may represent the sale price of the shares at the end of some time period or the sum total of all the future dividend payments beyond some forecast period or perhaps the liquidation proceeds). So-called "multi-period" models were developed to allow for a more dynamic representation of future growth trajectories. For example, early fast-growth periods may be followed by slow-growth or steady-state no-growth periods. Over time, the models have become more elaborate. Discount factors have been picked apart into their various components, the "cost of capital" estimated, and various "risk premiums" hypothesized.

Today the financial modeling approach most used in enterprise valuation is based on the **Discounted Cash Flow (DCF) method**. Instead of projecting future dividends, DCF forecasts earnings and positive and negative cash flows. DCF is used for capital budgeting, advising on corporate acquisitions, and valuing potential equity investments. It appeals to some because it seems to portray value in a logical manner (rather than just accepting the opaque verdict of "animal spirits"). The complex arithmetic lends an impression of accuracy.

It is often a false impression. I will summarize here some of the inherent difficulties and shortcomings of financial modeling of the DCF type, as applied to enterprise valuation, and refer the reader to the Appendix for more detailed treatment.

A DCF modeling process goes through two stages – forecasting and discounting – to assign value to unrealized future earnings. It is important to remember that both stages involve construction of hypothetical quantities rather than measurement of real ones. Here is the standard form of the DCF equation, at its simplest:

$$Company\ Value = \sum_{t=0}^{n} \frac{FCF_t}{(1+r)^t} + Terminal\ Value.$$

FCF stands for "Free Cash Flow" – which is not a standard GAAP figure and may be subject to varying definitions. ***t*** is the year-counter for the future forecasts of FCF, repeated and summed between now and ***n*** years from now. (***n*** is typically 5–15.) ***r*** stands for the so-called discount rate applied to adjust the value of each future cash flow estimate back to its "present value" (based on the general principle that a dollar paid one year from today is worth less than a dollar paid today). **Terminal Value** is the residual sum of all the projected cash flows that would take place *after **n*** years, carried "to infinity."

CHAPTER 2   THE VALUE TRIANGLE

These are not hard numbers. They are not data. They are forecasts and constructions, based on multiple assumptions, and are structurally complex. Building a DCF model is an arduous undertaking; each component (e.g., the Free Cash Flow projection) requires its own sub-model. There are many definitional subtleties (e.g., the calculation of the discount factor may involve estimating future bond yields, inflation rates, the firm's cost of capital, and other complex variables).

Thus, the quality of the inputs used by DCF-type financial models is rather tenuous. "Book Value" may be problematic, as noted, but at least accountants attempt to deal in verifiable (auditable) hard numbers. They segregate the "known unknowns" and refrain from making too many or too sweeping assumptions. By contrast, the DCF method incorporates ambitious assumptions about almost all the key elements of the calculation. The individual variables can be complex and opaque. (What is the true inflation rate deflator, for example? Or the "equity risk premium"?) The DCF construction process embeds quite a few "unknown unknowns."

DCF models are also rather delicate. The calculations are very sensitive to tiny changes in the underlying assumptions. Uncertainty is compounded by complexity, subject to judgments which can differ honestly from one analyst to another, and which may produce very different answers. The DCF method suffers from what one careful and not unsympathetic analyst has called a "massive assumption bias."[13]

Consider an example (see Table 2-1, drawn from Steiger). It shows the estimated future cash flows of *BASF*, the German chemical company, along with their discounted values. The estimates were developed by the investment bank *Credit Suisse*. The model covers a five-year forecast (2008–2013) plus a terminal value based on an assumed "perpetual growth rate" of 1.5% beyond five years.

Table 2-1. BASF DCF Estimates

Period	2008E	2009E	2010E	2011E	2012E	2013E	TV
FCFF	4,284	4,405	4,866	5,409	6,148	6,212	-
NPV	3,930	3,708	3,758	3,832	3,996	3,704	44,923
EV	67,850						

---

[13]Florian Steiger, "The Validity of Company Valuation Using Discounted Cash Flow Methods," European Business School, 2008.

CHAPTER 2   THE VALUE TRIANGLE

A key variable is the discount rate, defined in this case as the "weighted average cost of capital" (WACC), which involves a complex calculation. A sensitivity analysis focused on this input gives the results shown in the following chart (see Figure 2-3).

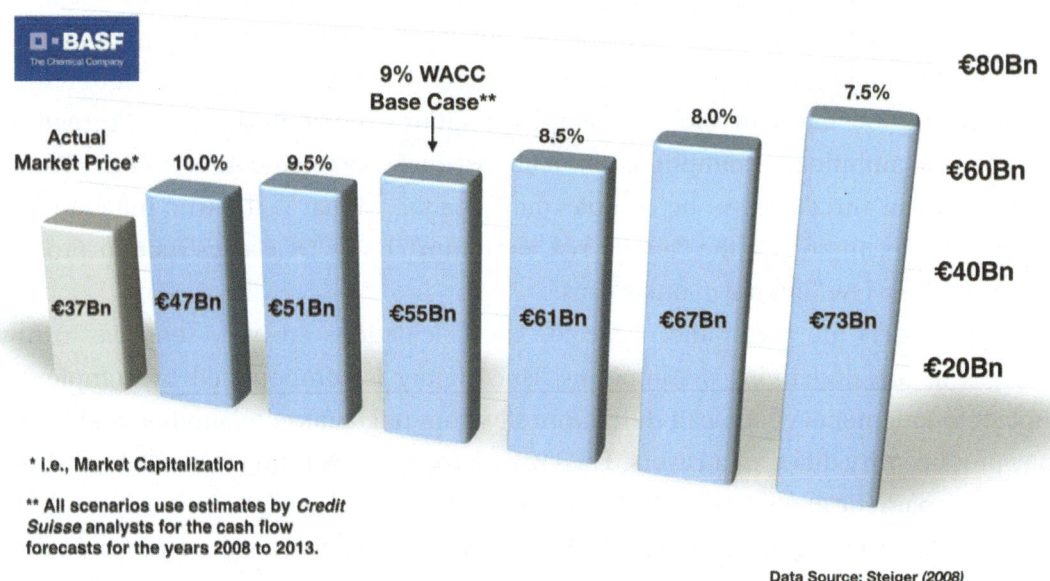

Figure 2-3. DCF – "Massive Assumption Bias"[14]

Note that the base case DCF valuation (at 9% WACC, calculated by *Credit Suisse*) was almost 50% higher than *BASF's* then-current market capitalization. Note also the extreme sensitivity of the results to the input assumptions. Each shift of 50 basis points in the discount factor produces *an 800–1000 basis point change in the company's valuation* – a 1:20 ratio of input variability to output variability, which in this case amounts to a €5–10 Bn difference in enterprise value for each half-percentage point step in the WACC. To put

---

[14]Data drawn from Florian Steiger, "The Validity of Company Valuation Using Discounted Cash Flow Methods," European Business School, 2008.

the possibility of such a small shift in WACC in context, we cite another study[15] which found that professional equity analysts (like those who prepared the *Credit Suisse* forecasts of *BASF's* earnings) show a consistent bias in estimating the cost of equity capital. The average magnitude of the error in the WACC was found to be 280 basis points. If that level of bias applies here, the potential error in the final valuation is close to 100%.

There is also an important practical problem: DCF modeling is a lengthy process, even with modern software. It requires substantial effort to perform a thorough DCF analysis for even a single company. It is not feasible to use DCF for screening broad segments of the market or for applications requiring very frequent updating. For internal capital projects or small-scale asset pricing, where market prices are not available, financial models may be the only option. Valuing an entire ongoing enterprise as complex as *the Ford Motor Company* is a different matter. When applied to enterprise valuation, financial models require aggressive simplifying assumptions about future events and states of the world.

(Aside from the methodological issues, DCF often does not perform well as a valuation tool, as the BASF case illustrates, with its large discrepancy between the results of the model and the market price. DCF does not produce actionable valuations in many cases – that is, the "deal" often gets done at a very different price point. However, critiquing the DCF model in detail is not our main purpose here. The reader is referred to the Appendix for a more extended technical discussion of the inadequacies of DCF for valuing a business enterprise. It is enough to observe that a methodology that is based on uncertain and biased forecasts of future cash flows that will occur 5, 10, or more years into the future, compounded with a discount rate so sensitive that small changes can produce wildly different outcomes, cannot be viewed as a sound basis in and of itself for the accurate valuation of an operating business, when better methods are available.[16])

---

[15]Stephanie Larocque, "Analysts' earnings forecast errors and cost of equity capital estimates," *Review of Accounting Studies,* Vol. 18 (2013), pp. 135–166.

[16]Of course, for some purposes, the DCF method may be the "least worst" answer. Valuing a private asset, which has no public market, may invite DCF modeling, if there are no good market-based comparables or similar transactions to consult. Some types of assets – e.g., a rental property with fixed rental agreements for long-term tenants in a stable neighborhood – may be somewhat more suitable for DCF. But for a dynamic public company, in a competitive market, in a typically changeable economic and regulatory environment, the DCF approach will not do. The market price is a superior starting point for valuation analysis. It is noteworthy that the **Financial Accounting Standards Board** – the guardian of accounting orthodoxy –has recognized this principle: *"A quoted price in an active market provides the most reliable evidence of fair value and shall be used without adjustment to measure fair value whenever available"* (*FASB 820, Fair Value Measurement* (May 2011), paragraph 820-10-35-41).

CHAPTER 2   THE VALUE TRIANGLE

2.3 The Pros and Cons of Market-Based Valuation Metrics

To know values is to comprehend the market.
—Charles Dow (1920)[17]

There is no accepted theory by which to understand the worth of stocks.
—Robert Shiller (1984)[18]

What about the most obvious and accessible measure of value: the company's share price? If an asset is worth what someone will pay for it, doesn't *Ford's* share price then tell us what *Ford* is really worth?

It depends. Whether we accept the market price (i.e., market capitalization, or the market value of the company's equity) as a valid measure of enterprise value depends on which theoretical view of the financial market we adopt.

Mainstream opinion among academic financial economists is still dominated by the so-called **Efficient Market Hypothesis** (EMH). According to this controversial idea, the current market price of the company's stock is all we need – it faithfully reflects all the available information about the company's current and future prospects, and it values the company accurately, or as accurately as possible. It may not turn out to be a perfect predictor of *future* value, as events unfold, but it cannot be improved upon because, by definition, if better information about the future becomes available, the market will absorb and disseminate it very rapidly and prices will adjust accordingly. Believers assure us that no one can "beat the market."

The EMH has been highly influential. It is the theoretical basis for so-called "passive investing" strategies, using index funds that seek simply to track the market without attempting to pick winners (which would require an information advantage that the EMH tells us is impossible to achieve). The underlying notion is that the financial

---

[17]Charles Henry Dow, *Scientific Stock Speculation*, The Magazine of Wall Street (1920), p. 37.
[18]Robert Shiller, "Stock Prices and Social Dynamics," *Brooking Papers on Economic Activity*, Vol. 1984, No. 2 (1984), pp. 457–510.

market is equilibrium-seeking, and the share price is the mechanism for establishing the equilibrium point. In sum, according to EMH, Price reflects the company's full and fair Value, or the best available approximation of it (on a per share basis). There is no such thing as a (significantly, persistently) mispriced stock. Any mispricing will be minor, unexploitable, meaningless – just "noise" – and fleeting.[19]

It has become clear that markets don't work like this. There are many forms of persistent mispricing that can affect broad categories of stocks – academics initially labeled them "anomalies" (later rebranded as "factors") – and there are indeed demonstrable ways to "beat the market" by exploiting these anomalies (although it is not always easy and the techniques do not work all the time). Very few practitioners accept the EMH today. There is also a growing challenge to the EMH from within the walls of academia, under the heading of "Behavioral Economics" or "Behavioral Finance." Instead of a rational, equilibrium-seeking, and unbeatable market, the Behavioral branch sees the financial markets as dominated by agents (investors) with realistic human cognitive and psychological characteristics and limitations, who display persistent "irrational" biases and whose decisions are therefore prone to systematic error. The result (in this view) is a market that is full of mispriced assets, where opportunities for market-beating strategies abound.

This would mean that the Price set by the market is not necessarily an accurate indication of true value. The cloudiness of the market signal can be illustrated with a couple of current examples.

2.3.1 Disney vs. Netflix

In the Spring of 2018, one of the leading stories in the financial press focused on the suddenly surging market value of *Netflix*, which had nearly overtaken the market capitalization of the mighty *Walt Disney Company*. (See Figure 2-4.)

---

[19]The Efficient Market Hypothesis accepts, in its revised versions, that there is some degree of "noise" in the market, which causes the constant small fluctuations in the price viewed over small timescales. Some revisionists also accept that the EMH can allow for small lags in adjusting to new information, so that small and temporary mispricings can occur while preserving the overall context of an equilibrium-seeking efficiency.

CHAPTER 2   THE VALUE TRIANGLE

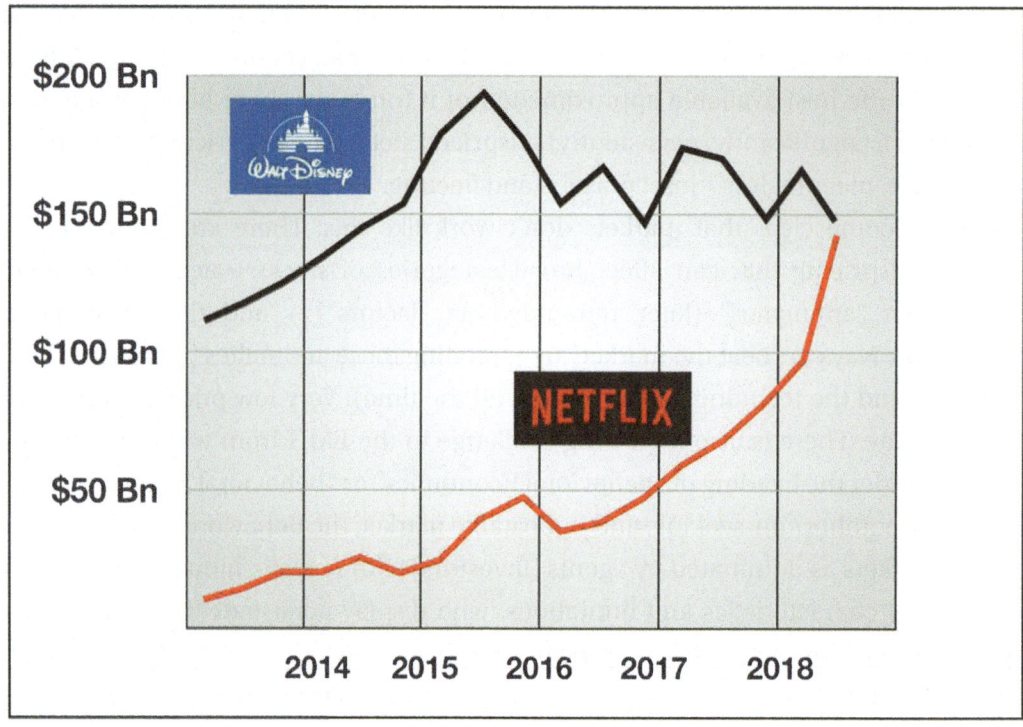

Figure 2-4. *Disney vs. Netflix (2018)*

Disney was a much larger and much more profitable company, with a long track record of success, a much more diversified business model, and extremely strong financial metrics (see Table 2-2). Disney's *net* profit margin was twice the market average and comparable to *Apple* and *Google*. It had a much stronger revenue stream per customer than *Netflix* (for its subscription services, the most directly comparable business segment). Its credit rating was five steps above "junk" level – while *Netflix* was four steps below. *Disney* was expected to generate $10 Bn in cash flow in 2018, compared to a $3.1 Bn cash *burn* for *Netflix*. As Q1 2018 ended, *Disney* was coming off of two huge blockbuster successes in this period in its movie business: *Black Panthe*r (worldwide box office of $1.3 Bn) and *Avengers: The Infinity War* ($1.8 Bn). Each of these movies earned more net profit than *Netflix* earned in all of 2017. *Disney's* track record is terrific: they have had the top-grossing films worldwide in six of the last seven years.[20] *Netflix* is an exciting new business model in some respects, but is it really worth almost as much as a full-fledged media powerhouse like *Disney*? The

---

[20]Aaron Black, "Walt Disney Has Good Reasons to Remain in Fox Chase," *The Wall Street Journal*, June 21, 2018.

market is saying yes, but we have a right to be skeptical. Or is it that *Disney* is deeply flawed in some way? Some analysts see it that way: "The stock valuation suggests that investors view *Disney* as having fallen hopelessly behind *Netflix*."[21] Who knows? The point is the Price alone cannot answer these questions. In all likelihood, the price of either *Disney* or *Netflix* is "wrong" (mispriced, not in line with true enterprise value), but we can't be sure which one.

Table 2-2. Disney vs. Netflix

Q1 2018	The Walt Disney Company	Netflix
Market Capitalization	$153.1 Bn	$144.8 Bn
Revenue	$55.7 Bn	$12.7 Bn
Free Cash Flow (2018 est)	$10.0 Bn	– $3.1 Bn
Gross Profit Margin	44.6%	31.3%
Net Profit Margin	19.6%	5.3%
Quarterly Earnings Growth (yoy)	78.4%	62.8%
Revenue/Subscriber	$28/month	$11/month

2.3.2 Ford vs. Tesla

In another major business story in 2017, electric vehicle startup *Tesla* surpassed the "venerable" *Ford Motor Company* in market value. This is an even more striking comparison (see Table 2-3).

---

[21]Jack Hough, "This Picture Could Still Have a Happy Ending," *Barron's*, April 30, 2018.

CHAPTER 2   THE VALUE TRIANGLE

Table 2-3. Ford vs. Tesla

2018	Ford	Tesla
Market Capitalization	$45.4 Bn	$46.9 Bn
Revenue	$159.6 Bn	$12.4 Bn
Free Cash Flow (2017)	$11.1 Bn	– $4.4 Bn
Net Profit Margin	4.9%	-18.8%
Vehicles Sold	6,600,000	103,000
Market Cap./Vehicle Sold	~ $7,000	~ $460,000

Are there mispricings here? If so, is it *Ford* that is undervalued? Or is it *Tesla* that is overvalued? From the Price alone, we cannot be sure. Valuation "experts" disagree; some say that "it could be a decade before it is possible to properly value *Tesla*."[22]

Market signals can behave in peculiar ways.[23] The only tentative conclusion we can draw from Price alone is that the market seems to be evaluating these two companies using two different yardsticks – which means that one way or another the Efficient Market Hypothesis in the classical sense cannot be correct here. The market price, taken in isolation, is not consistently reliable as a measure of enterprise value. There may well be

---

[22]Matthew DeBord, "It's Become Almost Impossible to Figure Out What Tesla is Actually Worth," *Business Insider,* August 19, 2017.

[23]For example, on Sunday, May 20, 2018, *Tesla* CEO Elon Musk announced (on *Twitter*) that the forthcoming flagship Model 3 – the company's key mass market offering – would be delayed and perhaps even canceled. He said that actually trying to produce the low-priced Model 3 *Tesla* could cause the company to "lose money and die" – an unusually dire assessment from a CEO, prompting *The Wall Street Journal* to ask "Is Tesla Abandoning the Mass Market?" [May 21, 2018.] Still, the price of *Tesla's* shares jumped 5% on the following Monday morning. Did Musk's pessimism suddenly create several billion dollars of shareholder value?

explanations for the premium valuations carried by innovative newcomers like *Netflix* and *Tesla* or for discounts endured by old-line companies like *Ford* and *Disney*. But to discover them, we will need more than just the simple share price metric.

Book, Model, and Market – each perspective provides a snapshot of enterprise value, but none of them gives a complete and accurate picture. A summary of the arguments in this chapter is shown in Table 2-4.

Table 2-4. Summary of Book, Model, and Market

Valuation Method	Inadequacies for Purposes of Enterprise Valuation
"Book Value"	• Incomplete accounting of assets • Many key value-creating assets unrecognized • Stale data: Asset values carried as historical cost • Some assets tainted with liability-like characteristics • Increased use of leverage affects book value inconsistently
Discounted Cash Flow	• Requires forecasts of earnings far into the future • Inherent optimistic bias in forecasts • Complex assumptions required to create discount factor • Uses discredited CAPM model in WACC calculations • Often dominated by terminal value • Outcomes sensitive to small changes in assumptions • Time-consuming to construct, unsuited for many uses • Easy to manipulate the outcome
Market Value	• Unclear interpretation of extreme valuations • Price Volatility can obscure the value signal • Different companies respond to different value drivers • Price signals are often ambiguous

Intrinsic value – "True" Enterprise Value – is *unobservable*. Our knowledge of it is always indirect and uncertain. No single perspective can resolve the matter reliably. What we *can* do is to use these snapshots – book value, cash flow, market price – *comparatively*, to *triangulate* the unknown true value of *Ford's* ongoing business and set some bounds on the inherent uncertainty.

2.4 Triangulating Intrinsic Value: The Use of Valuation Ratios

The diagram at the beginning of this chapter depicts what we are calling the Value Triangle. The vertices of the Triangle represent the three single-focus perspectives on enterprise value – none of which, taken in isolation, provides a complete and accurate picture.

To deal with these shortcomings, the financial industry often adopts a *comparative* approach, based on simple ratios, such as P/E, P/B, and ROA, represented by the sides of the Triangle. By comparing, say, the market view of value (Price) to fundamental operating performance (Earnings), we hope to gain insight that neither Price nor Earnings alone can provide.

The theoretical justification for these comparisons is not always clear. Take the P/E. The financial market is a complex system, the functioning of which is the subject of much controversy. How Mr. Market arrives at a price (P) for *Ford's* shares remains something of a mystery, if we are honest about it. It is a blend of sentiment, hard information, rumor, expectation, market weather, fear, and greed, all swirling through a complex supercomputer (actually, a network of dozens of trading platforms) that in the end produces a unitary price point.[24] On the other hand, the number that is the arguably best earnings figure (E) – the estimate of the company's one-year forward earnings – is also a blend of a large number of known and partially known factors that affect or could affect the company's performance in the coming year. Using one mystery to illuminate another is tricky. Exactly how a dollar of next year's *earnings* relates to *a dollar of market value* turns out to be quite a deep question (as the puzzles in Chapter 1 have suggested). Nevertheless, there is reason to argue that the use of ratios is superior to any of the single-focus methods.

---

[24]Lately this price point has even acquired a name – the NBBO (National Best Bid and Offer) – and a formidable legal significance. Actually, the complexity of the exchange network today allows for the existence of multiple price points (within a small range) simultaneously on different platforms – which complicates market regulation considerably. As well, the exchange network produces other signals, such as trading volume, bid and ask spreads, order types (e.g., limit vs. market orders), and order book depth, which have some applications but generally do not bear on enterprise value *per se*.

There are three "families" of ratios, represented by the three sides of the Value Triangle: ratios that compare Market Value to Book Value (Price-to-Book), ratios that compare Operating Performance to Book Value (such as Return-on-Assets, ROA), and ratios that compare Market Value to Operating Performance (Price-to-Earnings and its siblings). The P/E ratio is undoubtedly the most popular. But each has certain advantages.

2.4.1 Price-to-Book

P/B is the conservative choice, stylistically at least. The academic literature tends to favor it, particularly for analyses of so-called "value investing" – the search for deeply undervalued companies.[25] In its "normal" state, P/B is assumed to be properly equal to 1 (or nearly so).[26] However, the difficulty of working with Book Value is clear from the previous discussion. As the denominator in the P/B ratio, its inherent flaws inevitably compromise the accuracy of the ratio. P/B today often deviates very significantly from 1, as we have seen. It is a very poor predictor of profitability (either Operating Margin or Net Margin) or return on equity (ROE).

---

[25] Algy Hall, "Taking Price-to-Book Ratio to Book," *Investors Chronicle (Financial Times)*, May 25, 2018: *"The price-to-book ratio (P/BV) has a very special place in the hearts of many 'value' investors. Indeed, the ratio was made a value classic by no less than 'the father of value investing' Benjamin Graham. In his 1949 value-investing bible,* The Intelligent Investor, *he suggested the ratio be used to identify not only potentially superior returns, but also to measure the 'margin of safety' of an investment. Adding to P/BV's status as a key ratio for identifying value was the evidence of the relationship between low P/BV and improved long-term investment return presented in the hugely influential three-factor model developed by academics Eugene Fama and Kenneth French."*

[26] Alexander Nezlobin, Madhav V. Rajan, and Stefan Reichelstein, "Structural properties of the price-to-earnings and price-to-book ratios," *Review of Accounting Studies*, Vol. 21 (2016), pp. 438–472: *"Textbooks frequently view a P/B ratio equal to one as 'normal,' though it is commonly understood that both anticipated future profitability and conservative valuation of incumbent assets tend to push this ratio above one."*

Still, the Price-to-Book ratio can serve some limited purposes. It can be used negatively, so to speak, to identify companies that have large and important intangible assets. The fact that *Coke* trades at a P/B ratio of 10 alerts us to look for the missing "dark matter" – the intangibles that don't show up on the balance sheet (in *Coke's* case, it is mainly brand equity). P/B can also be useful for comparisons between companies in the same sector, which have similar business models and accounting policies. Differences in Sector P/B can highlight differences between business models. A related measure, adopted by many academics – Tobin's Q – is based not on the historical cost of the company's assets, but on their replacement value, which tends to mitigate, conceptually, the problem of stale "at-cost" balance sheet values (although it is much more difficult to construct than conventional Book Value). We will look at both of these ratios in more detail in the following chapter.

2.4.2 Return-on-Assets

Return-on-Assets (Earnings-to-Net Assets, ROA) ought to be an outstanding choice for business valuation. It is similar to concepts like Return on Investment (ROI) and Return on Equity (ROE) which are the cornerstone of investment analysis and capital budgeting.[27] Conceptually, the efficiency with which a company can generate sales and earnings as a function of each dollar of assets it owns ought to be a key measure of strategic fitness. And as noted earlier, the focus on asset efficiency has lately acquired a larger significance. The entire economy is shifting from asset-heavy business models based on large fixed investments (like factories, equipment, real estate) to leaner models based on mostly intangible franchise assets like brand, design, customer loyalty, and technology. The overall ROA in the US economy is probably rising. A company like *Ford*, still committed to heavy capital expenditures on fixed assets, has an ROA of about 1–2%. *Facebook's* ROA is 17%. Importantly, ROA appears to be better correlated with profitability than either P/B or P/E.[28]

---

[27] The difference – and I believe the advantage – is that ROA is unconcerned with how the productive assets were financed, whether through external investment or retained earnings, debt, or equity. It measures the operational value of the business, rather than the value returned to the shareholder as a function of her invested capital.

[28] See examples in Chapter 4.

Unfortunately, ROA, like P/B, is tainted by the problems introduced by the use of Book Value in the denominator, especially the exclusion of key franchise assets. There are also questions as to the proper choice of the numerator – whether net earnings or Operating Earnings (before the effect of leverage) would be more appropriate. The impact of increasing leverage also affects the accuracy of ROA and makes comparisons over time and across industries more difficult. Finally, ROA lacks the immediacy of the Price term, relying entirely on accounting data that is updated only once a quarter. Still, for whatever reason, ROA gets less attention than it probably should.

2.4.3 Price-to-Earnings

The P/E is the "mainstay of valuation practice."[29] There are several reasons for this.

Both the numerator and the denominator are highly reliable measures of their target quantities. "Price" equals the market's valuation (per share), by definition. "Earnings" means actual net earnings,[30] within the limits of GAAP procedures (which are much less flawed with respect to the income statement, compared to the balance sheet). There is no time lag (or not much of one – none for the numerator and no more than 90 days for the denominator). Both P and E are auditable and reasonably reliable.[31] The P/E, and its many variants, will be the primary focus throughout the remainder of this book.

---

[29]Efthimios G. Demirakos, Norman C. Strong, and Martin Walker, "What Valuation Models Do Analysts Use?" *Accounting Horizons*, Vol. 18, No. 4 (2004) pp. 221–240.

[30]This is for Trailing P/E. The Forward P/E uses a forecast of next year's earnings. See Chapter 3.

[31]Although, even if we rule out "fraud" in the E denominator – a very rare issue in the American markets – we are still left with a set of definitional uncertainties, some of which can be significant. We will consider these in Chapter 6.

2.5 Summary

Valuation is difficult and uncertain. Yet it is essential to almost any decision involving the acquisition or divestiture of business assets, any decision to invest in public or private companies, and most decisions to extend or validate credit. The traditional valuation methods that rely upon a single perspective – Book, Model, or Market alone – are inadequate. GAAP accounting has lost track of many of the key value-creating assets that are central to modern business models. Financial modeling techniques like Discounted Cash Flow analysis cannot cope with the large uncertainties created by the forecasts and the assumptions they require or the extreme sensitivity of the model outputs to small and economically insignificant differences in the inputs. And while the Stock Market publishes its opinions on public company valuations instantaneously throughout the trading day, its judgments can be inconsistent and heterogeneous – there are too many different valuation yardsticks implicit in the single-point prices of traded shares to use them in their raw form.

The strategy embraced by professionals whose livelihood depends on an accurate understanding of enterprise value is based on using multiple valuation methods comparatively. The use of valuation ratios has become the standard practice in the financial industry and has been taken up by much of the academic literature as well. The following chapter provides an overview of these comparative metrics.

CHAPTER 3

Valuation Ratios

The market ratios commonly used for enterprise valuation include the following (Table 3-1).

Table 3-1. Valuation Ratio Characteristics

Valuation Ratios	Chief Characteristics
Trailing P/E	• Uses prior year earnings – audited, realized numbers • Backward-looking
Forward P/E	• Uses Analysts' 1-Year Forecast Earnings – estimated numbers • Forward-looking
Price/Operating Earnings	• Uses Operating Earnings in calculating EPS • Avoids distortions due to leverage and "extraordinary charges" • Better for comparison's across different time periods • Avoids distortions due to tax effects
Price/Dividend (Dividend Yield)	• Dividends traditionally considered most concrete metric of shareholder value
Price/Sales	• Useful for companies in "sales-volume driven" businesses (e.g., retail) • Useful for companies without earnings • Useful for within-sector comparisons
Price/Cash Flow	• Aligns with "Cash is King" arguments • Many options for defining Cash Flow – Earnings Before Interest, Taxes, Depreciation, and Amortization (EBITDA), Free Cash Flow most popular • Avoids distortions due to non-cash charges in the current period
Price/Book	• Useful for identifying "gaps" in the balance sheet (unaccounted-for assets) • Often applied to companies in the Financial sector
Tobin's Q	• Based on "replacement value" of assets; hard to construct • Occasionally used by academics
Return-on-Assets	• Non-market based – used to assess efficiency of asset exploitation • Strongly aligned with profitability
Cyclically Adjusted P/E	• Averages the Earnings denominator over a multi-year period • Smooths out earnings to mitigate short-term volatility • Purports to counteract effects of the business cycle
Cash-Adjusted P/E	• Removes dilutive effect of "unproductive" cash holdings
PEG Ratio	• Includes Earnings Growth into the metric

CHAPTER 3   VALUATION RATIOS

3.1 Trailing P/E, or P/E$_{ttm}$

The Trailing Price/Earnings ratio is the original market valuation metric:[1]

$$\frac{price\,/\,share}{earnings\,/\,share_{ttm}}$$

Price (P) refers to the *current market price of the company's shares*.[2]

Earnings-per-share$_{ttm}$ (E) is a ratio of the "Earnings" reported by the company in the prior year to the total number of "Shares" issued by the company ("*ttm*" stands for "Trailing Twelve Months").

The default definition of **Earnings** is *Net Earnings,* the bottom line of the income statement, reported quarterly. It may also be referred to as *GAAP earnings*[3] or As *reported earnings*.[4]

The default definition of **per-share** is based on the number of Shares of Common Stock Outstanding – that is, shares that have been issued by the company and are currently in the hands of investors. It may involve the calculation of a weighted average number of shares, if new shares were issued or existing shares were bought back by the company over the prior year.[5] EPS excludes Treasury Shares (shares held in the company's own account for possible future issuance).

---

[1] The P/E was actually not always the go-to option. In the 19th and into the 20th centuries, **dividend yield** (Section 3.4) was the preferred metric. *"In the US, bond issues during the 1800s and early 1900s outweighed stock issues 3 to 1. The stock market consisted largely of railway stocks, with utilities and then industrials only becoming more important by 1900. In these circumstances it is hardly surprising that dividend yield was the favored method of deciding whether a stock was cheap or expensive because dividend yield could be directly compared to the yield on a bond."* The P/E came into fashion with the stock market boom of the 1920s, as growth and capital gains it began to supplement and then displace dividends as the predominant component of shareholder returns. See Nilesh Soman, "Retracing the History of the Price to Earnings Ratio," January 7, 2014. Online at www.moneycontrol.com/news/business/personal-finance/retracinghistoryprice-to-earnings-ratio--1185979.html

[2] This is true for almost all of the forms of the Multiple discussed in this chapter. Price is always the current price, not a forecast. Deviations from this principle are rare. An exception is the Cash-Adjusted P/E (Section 3.11).

[3] GAAP of course refers to Generally Accepted Accounting Principles, which is the American accounting standard for the preparation of financial statements.

[4] David Blitzer, Robert Friedman, and Howard Silverblatt, "Measures of Corporate Earnings," *Standard & Poor's*, May 14, 2002.

[5] There are many nuances attached to the figure for the number of shares to be used in calculating EPS. We will review some of these in Chapter 6.

[*Nuances*: Calculations of EPS may adjust the Earnings figure for "Dividends on Preferred Shares," to report "Earnings Available to Common Shareholders." Few companies issue preferred shares, and the overall market is small – less than 1% of the value of the equities market generally.[6]

Calculations of the number of Shares may also be adjusted to reflect "Fully Diluted Shares" – which accounts for shares that would be issued in connection with the future exercise of stock options, or convertible debt instruments. This difference does not appear to be significant, in most cases.[7]]

The Trailing P/E is the most "objective" of all the Multiples (except for Dividend Yield). "Price" is based on the most recent market transactions. "Earnings" is based on realized and reported results. P/E_{ttm} is reasonably uncompromised by forecasts, assumptions, or estimates other than those which are GAAP-approved, and likely conservative.[8]

This emphasis on hard numbers is considered to be the strength of the Trailing P/E by its advocates. The weakness of Trailing P/E is that it is backward-looking. Most valuation applications adopt a forward-looking perspective. Investors buy the future, not the past. We invest in *Ford* because of the future returns we hope it will generate, not because of how well it did last year. The usefulness of last year's performance is principally as a predictor of next year's performance. So Trailing P/E provides only an indirect indication.

---

[6] As of February 27, 2009, the S&P US Preferred Stock Index had 72 constituents (or about 14% of the S&P 500). The total market value of the Preferred was approx. $100 billion – about 1% of the value of the total equities market (Standard & Poor's, Preferred Stock Primer, March 25, 2009). Following the financial crisis, Preferred Shares fell further out of favor. By 2018, this has declined to less than 1% (*Janney Investment Group, Investable Themes: Preferred Securities*, September 2018) – not quite negligible, but nearly so.

[7] Tech companies that grant a lot of employee options might be expected to show a significant effect related to dilution calculations that would reflect unexercised options. But perhaps not. For example, the difference between *Facebook*'s "basic earnings per share" and "diluted earnings per share" is less than 1% (2018), despite the liberal use of employee options. *Netflix* also shows a less than 1% difference (2018).

[8] There may be minor assumptions or estimates incorporated in the calculation of net earnings, such as reserves to account for bad debt (customers' failure to pay), possible warranty expenses, or product returns.

CHAPTER 3   VALUATION RATIOS

It is also true that share prices themselves "lean forward" – that is, even though we are using the current Price in the P/E multiple, it is generally assumed that that Price incorporates an implicit forecast of corporate performance and economic conditions several quarters ahead. If the ratio combines this inherently forward-oriented "Price" with the inherently backward-oriented "Earnings," it may be seen as somehow out of alignment.

3.2 Forward P/E

The other common form of the Earnings Multiple is Forward P/E:

$$\frac{price\,/\,share}{forward\,earnings\,/\,share_{ttm}}$$

Here **P** (the numerator) is again *the current price* (and specifically *not* a prediction of a future price). But **E** in the denominator refers to a *forecast* of the coming year's earnings per share, which is derived from earnings estimates prepared by a "select group" of analysts, typically financial industry professionals who follow the company, model its performance, and publish their estimates of its next year's EPS.[9]

Introducing any forecast adds uncertainty. We have seen how the accumulating uncertainties of multi-year forecasts undermine the Discounted Cash Flow approach. To control this, the Forward P/E ratio usually focuses on a one-year earnings projection. It is true that the accuracy of analysts' 3-year forecasts is consistently found to be biased – too optimistic, most of the time. But as the chart here shows, analysts' estimates tend to start high and then pare back to align with reality. One year out from the actuals, the forecasts are quite accurate, as the flat right-hand tails in most of these trend lines indicate.[10] (See Figure 3-1.)

---

[9] *"For valuation purposes, analyst consensus is the preferred method of determining future EPS. Analyst consensus represents the average (or 'consensus') of all the equity research analysts that cover a stock and submit their estimates to IBES on Bloomberg or another data set."* (a typical definition, from the **Corporate Finance Institute**, available at https://corporatefinanceinstitute.com/about-cfi/).

[10] James Mackintosh, "Hope Springs but Profit Pitfalls Lurk," *The Wall Street Journal*, January 6, 2017.

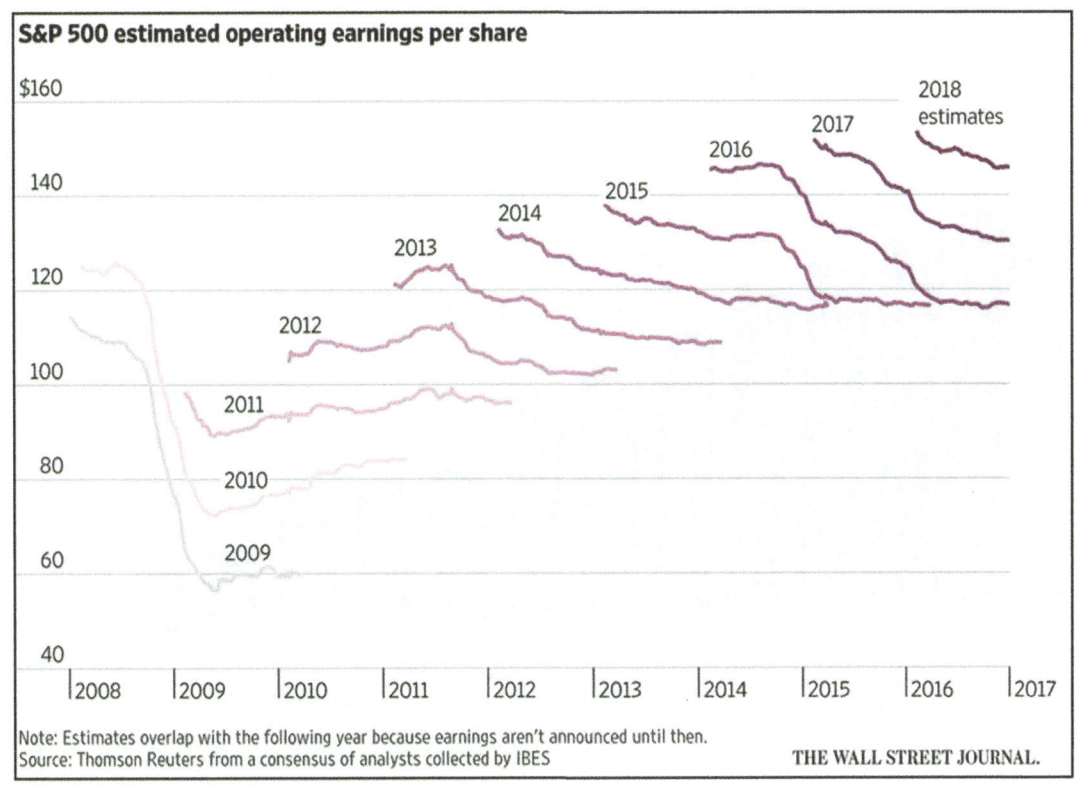

Figure 3-1. *Adjustment of Forward Earnings Estimates Over Time*[11]

A 2012 academic study confirmed that analysts' forecasts are more accurate than simple projections generated by random-walk time-series models (a proxy for an un-informed extrapolation of the past trend – the implicit perspective of the Trailing P/E). But this is true only for 12-month forecasts. Analysts' performance advantage declined steadily as the time frame lengthened. Longer-range forecasts showed no sustainable advantage over the un-informed projection.[12] (See Figure 3-2.)

---

[11]James Mackintosh, "Hope Springs but Profit Pitfalls Lurk," *The Wall Street Journal*, January 6, 2017. Reproduced by permission from *The Wall Street Journal*.

[12]Mark T. Bradshaw, Michael S. Drake, James N. Myers, and Linda A. Myers, "A re-examination of analysts' superiority over time-series forecasts of annual earnings," *Review of Accounting Studies*, Vol. 17 (2012), pp. 944–968. However, as with so many "findings" in the academic literature on the financial markets, other studies point in the opposite direction. Liu et al., in 2002, found that *"forward earnings perform the best, and performance improves if the forecast horizon lengthens (1-year to 2-year to 3-year out EPS forecasts)."* (Jing Liu, Doron Nissim, and Jacob Thomas, "Equity Valuation Using Multiples," *Journal of Accounting Research*, Vol. 40, No. 1 (March 2002), pp. 135–172).

CHAPTER 3   VALUATION RATIOS

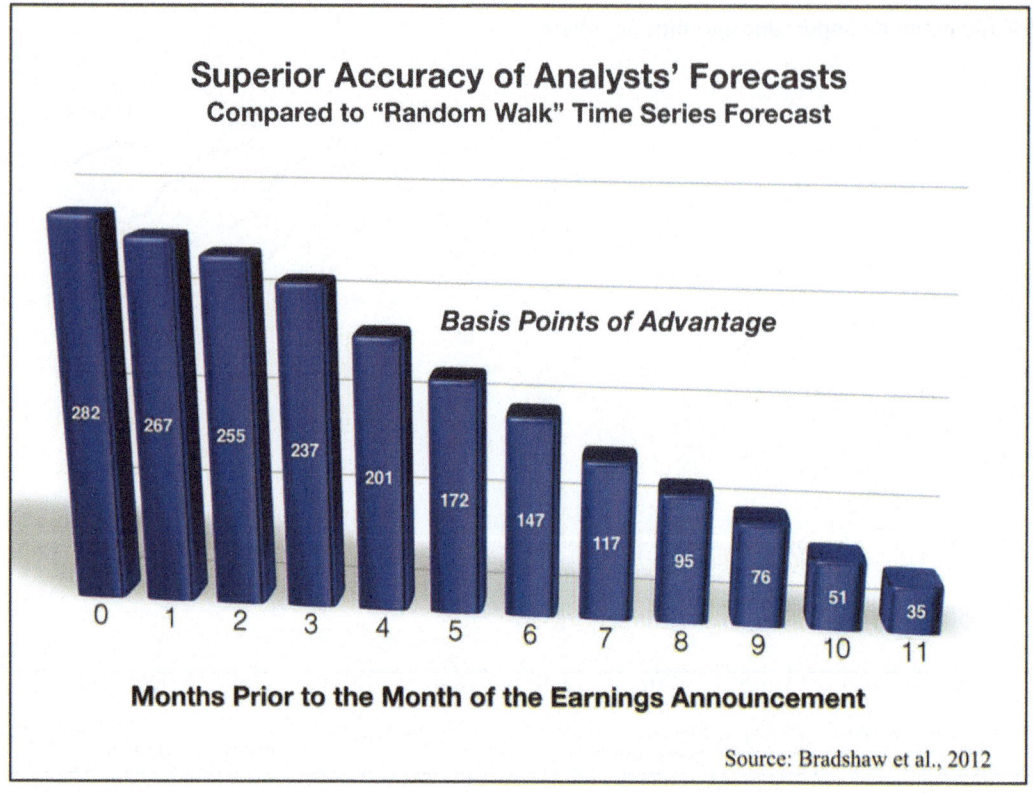

Figure 3-2. Superior Accuracy of Analysts' Forecasts Compared to "Random-Walk" Time-Series Forecast[13]

Forward vs. Trailing P/E: A Comparison

Which is better? To a considerable extent, the choice is a matter of style. Optimistic or "bullish" investors may prefer the Forward multiple, because of its future orientation. More risk-averse investors like the objectivity and auditability of the Trailing EPS and accept its limitations and perhaps an extra degree of conservatism, in favor of avoiding too much uncertainty about as-yet unrealized performance.

---

[13]Based on Mark T. Bradshaw, Michael S. Drake, James N. Myers, and Linda A. Myers, "A re-examination of analysts' superiority over time-series forecasts of annual earnings," *Review of Accounting Studies*, Vol. 17 (2012), pp. 944–968.

It should be noted that in general, for companies whose earnings are expected to grow, the Forward P/E will be lower than the Trailing P/E. The numerator is the same for both: the current Price. If the next year's earnings are projected to increase, raising the denominator will therefore lower the value of the ratio. Also, because forecasts are generally less volatile than actual earnings, the trend for the Forward P/E will also tend to be somewhat smoother. Forecast earnings also generally focus on the fundamental operations of the company, rather than on trying to predict one-time events, and may be less volatile for this reason.

The case for trailing P/E is often based on a concern about analysts' bias. A recent study of earnings estimates developed by Wall Street equity analysts concludes

> Forecasts are pervasively and significantly upward biased...
>
> Bias may be avoided by estimating value based on *realized* earnings rather than biased earnings *forecasts*.[14] *[Emphasis in the original]*

But there may be a bias in a too strict policy of bias avoidance. It is true that forecasts have been shown to be biased to some degree; nevertheless, **there is evidence that the Forward P/E is superior to the Trailing P/E as a predictor of future performance**.[15] (See Chapter 5.) It would appear that analysts do add value to the forecast over the coming 1-year period and perhaps longer, compared to a simple extrapolation of the prior year's trend. For this reason, as well as the fact that a forward focus aligns better with the actual

---

[14] Peter Easton and Gregory Sommers, "Effect of Analysts' Optimism on Estimates of the Expected Rate of Return Implied by Earnings Forecasts," *Journal of Accounting Research*, Vol. 45, No. 5, December 2017, p. 1013.

[15] Jing Liu, Doron Nissim, and Jacob Thomas, "Equity Valuation Using Multiples," *Journal of Accounting Research*, Vol. 40, No. 1 (March 2002), pp. 135–172. See also John Authers, "Number Crunchers Are Socially Desirable," *Financial Times*, July 11, 2017. The FT piece cites also Jing Liu, Doron Nissim, and Jacob Thomas, "Is Cash Flow King in Valuations?" *Financial Analysts Journal*, Vol. 63, No. 2 (March/April 2007) pp. 56–68; but with respect to the comment on the superiority of Forward P/E to Trailing P/E, this piece appears to be based largely on the earlier 2002 article by Liu et al., cited first.

investment perspective, the Forward P/E is gaining the advantage in popular usage.[16] The *American Institute of Certified Public Accountants,* in its Draft Handbook for enterprise valuation, observes that "valuations are forward-looking":

> Multiples...are essentially a proxy for market participant expectations regarding future cash flow, growth and risk... If available, forward multiples are likely to provide more relevant information, especially for high growth businesses.[17]

An assessment by analysts at the *Federal Reserve Bank of Cleveland* concludes

> Since the forward P/E ratio uses projections of future earnings, it has the advantage of looking at expected earnings, rather than current earnings, which may be high or low because of one-time factors that don't reflect the prospects of the firm. On the other hand, a company's forward P/E can be artificially *deflated* by a rosy earnings estimate, particularly in a boom period.[18]

This "deflation" effect has been noted elsewhere and is often read as an indicator of forthcoming positive market trends (allowing that even "rosy" earnings estimates have some validity in the 1-year forecast, as indicated by the studies cited previously).[19]

---

[16] According to a *Bank of America/Merrill Lynch* study, the Forward PE is preferred by a more than 2 to 1 margin over the Trailing P/E among individual investors. Another recent study gives a 6 to 1 advantage to Forward P/E vs. Trailing P/E in use by professionals (Jerald Pinto, Thomas Robinson, and John Stowe, "Equity Valuation: A Survey of Professional Practice," *CFA Institute*, September 7, 2015).

[17] AICPA Task Force, *Valuation of Portfolio Company Investments of Venture Capital and Private Equity Funds and Other Investment Companies, Draft* (May 15, 2018), paragraphs 5.22 and 5.38.

[18] Joseph G. Haubrich, Sara Millington, and Brendan Costello, "Comparing Price-to-Earnings Ratios: The S&P 500 Forward P/E and the CAPE," *Economic Trends: The Federal Reserve Bank of Cleveland,* August 10, 2014.

[19] "*Forward p/e ratios...are above their abysmal levels from the worst of the post-Lehman crisis, but beyond that they are as cheap as they have been in decades... Forecast profits...look rosy... Optimistic forecasts might make forward multiples artificially low.*" (John Authers, "Optimists Say This is the Time to Buy Equities," *Financial Times,* July 10, 2011). We may note that the aftermath of the post-Lehman crisis (late 2008 or early 2009) would have been the very best time to enter the market in decades, and even investors entering in July 2011 would have enjoyed a more-the-100% gain since that time. So the "abnormally low" Forward P/E does seem to have predicted well the boom in future returns.

3.2.1 PER (Relative P/E)

An early paper on the low P/E anomaly (discussed in Chapter 5) proposed a modification to eliminate "sector bias" – that is, to compensate for the fact that some sectors carry higher or lower average P/E multiples than others.[20] For example, from 2013 to 2018, the healthcare sector had an average P/E more than 70% higher than the average of the financial sector.[21] To offset this "industry effect," the researchers calculated each individual firm's P/E relative to the average P/E of all the firms in its sector. This so-called PER seems like a reasonable adjustment, for certain applications. It has not been widely adopted.

3.2.2 Normalized P/E

The phrase "Normalized P/E" has also become popular. It has been used in two very different senses, however.

The more correct usage defines it as Price divided by "Normalized EPS" – where normalization means the elimination of "the effects of seasonality, revenue and expenses that are unusual or one-time influences... non-recurring charges or gains." This is the approach sanctioned by the American Institute of Certified Public Accountants for valuing private investments.[22] In this sense, Normalized P/E is similar to Price/Operating Earnings (see Section 3.3), with the additional feature of smoothing out seasonal effects.[23]

"Normalized P/E" has also sometimes been used (inaptly) to refer to a P/E ratio where the Earnings denominator is averaged over the prior 10 years. This is simply a version of the Cyclically Adjusted P/E ($CAPE_1$ – see Section 3.10) – except that it does not adjust earnings for inflation.

---

[20] David Goodman and John Peavy, "Industry Relative Price-Earnings Ratios as Indicators of Investment Returns," *Financial Analysts Journal* (July/August 1983) pp. 60–66.

[21] See Chapter 4, Section 4.3.2.

[22] AICPA Task Force, *Valuation of Portfolio Company Investments of Venture Capital and Private Equity Funds and Other Investment Companies, Draft* (May 15, 2018), paragraph 5.34.

[23] This is the common usage. See, e.g., Savita Subramanian, "US Equity Strategy Year Ahead: 2017," *Bank of America/Merrill Lynch*, 2017.

3.2.3 Improving on P/E?

The classic Price-to-Earnings ratio, in both forms, is by far the most popular valuation metric in use today.[24] But the fact that it "explains" only part of the movements in share prices (probably less than half), the fact that it seems sometimes to respond to contrary influences and in general to move in mysterious ways, and the fact that it is *so* simple and old-school have inspired analysts to search for ways to make it better.

The following alternatives are attempts to improve the P/E – either by modifying the denominator or, less often, the numerator. As a summary statement, it seems at this point that none of these innovations have been able to displace the simple P/E Multiple as the preferred alternative. Still, some of these supplementary perspectives on enterprise value may add to the accuracy or persuasiveness of the valuation analysis.

3.3 Price-to-Operating Earnings

Some analysts suggest substituting *Operating Earnings* (in place of Net Earnings) as the denominator of the P/E Multiple:

$$\frac{price\,/\,share}{operating\,earnings\,/\,share}$$

Others regard this move with apprehension:

> *International Business Machines* is joining tech peers in a race to the accounting bottom. It released figures showing how its last 10 quarters would have changed using non-GAAP "operating" earnings.[25]

---

[24] It is used in 90% or more of professional analysts' reports. See Footnote 1 in the Introduction. It is also reported that 80% of individual investors make use of the P/E multiple (Maggie Fitzgerald, "Everyone Still Relies on Stock's P/E Ratio..." *CNBC,* June 2019, citing a *BofA Merrill Lynch* study).

[25] *The Wall Street Journal,* September 1, 2010.

But is this really a "race to the bottom"? Should we really suspect the buttoned-down management of *IBM* of trying to debase their financial reports? Is it accurate to label it "non-GAAP"?[26]

Operating Earnings is based on a reasonable idea. Here is *Standard & Poor's* definition:

> This measure focuses on the *earnings from a company's principal operations, with the goal of making the numbers comparable across different time periods*. Operating earnings are usually considered to be 'as reported' earnings with some charges reversed to exclude corporate or one-time expenses.[27] *[Emphasis added]*

This point is often lost: the use of Operating Income facilitates comparisons of company performance from one time period to the next, by eliminating charges (or gains) arising from events that do not regularly recur. In principle, this should improve the quality of the Earnings metric for valuation purposes.

The definition of Operating Earnings also proposes "to exclude *corporate*…expenses" – expenses created by the corporate superstructure within which the business operates, such as the choice of the capital structure (debt vs. equity) used to finance the business or the tax status of the corporation.

Typically, therefore, Operating Income excludes

- **Interest on debt financing**: This expense is related to the capital structure, the manner in which the company has financed itself, and not to the profitability of the operating business per se (following the same logic that excludes dividends, another "expense" determined by the capital structure, from Net Earnings).

---

[26]"Operating Income" appears as a line in a GAAP-approved income statement. Some analysts use other definitions of "earnings" which are non-GAAP (although still permitted with the appropriate caveats and reconciliations). There is confusion over closely related terms, such as Earnings Before Interest and Taxes (EBIT), a standard though non-GAAP figure. Some have argued that Operating Income (GAAP) should be differentiated from Operating Earnings (non-GAAP), but this seems to me to be a misnomer. I believe that Operating Income, Operating Profit, and Operating Earnings are used synonymously for the GAAP category describing the residual after all operating expenses are subtracted from revenues and before interest, taxes, investment income, gains or losses from disposal of assets, and various "extraordinary," "unusual," or "irregular" items.

[27]David Blitzer, Robert Friedman, and Howard Silverblatt, "Measures of Corporate Earnings," *Standard & Poor's,* May 14, 2002.

- **Taxes**: This expense varies from country to country and with changes in the tax laws, as well as special credits, "holidays," abatements, and subsidies, and is less connected to the operating model of the firm.[28]
- **"Extraordinary" Items**: Also referred to as "one-time" or "non-recurring" items, either expenses or gains that arguably lie outside the framework of the normal ongoing business.[29]

This last category creates much of the concern over the use of Operating Earnings, especially the so-called "one-time charges" or "write-offs" that often result from strategic restructurings or from unusual events.[30] The principle of handling non-recurring

---

[28]For example, a "tax holiday" to encourage repatriation of foreign earnings, which may create a spike in tax expenses, depressing earnings, raising the trailing P/E, would have little to do with a company's success in making and selling its products; In 2004, a tax holiday for US multinational companies allowed them to repatriate foreign profits to the United States at a 5.25% tax rate, rather than the existing 35% corporate tax rate. Under this law, corporations brought $362 billion into the American economy ["Repatriation tax holiday," *Wikipedia*].

[29]The terminology has been changing. **The Financial Accounting Standards Board** (FASB) has recently eliminated the term "extraordinary items" from the accounting vocabulary [FASB *Accounting Standards Update No. 2015-01*, "Income Statement – Extraordinary and Unusual Items (Subtopic 225-20) – Simplifying Income Statement Presentation by Eliminating the Concept of Extraordinary Items," January 2015].

[30]For example, in 2017, *Valero* – the largest American oil refining company – suffered a shutdown and loss of business due to the impact of Hurricane Harvey on its Gulf Coast refining operations. In its financial statements, it chose to separate some of those costs from Operating Income, as "other expenses." These one-time charges were nevertheless subtracted to arrive at Net Earnings. This would have temporarily depressed Net Earnings and raised the Trailing P/E. The Price-to-Operating Earnings metric might have avoided this "spurious" volatility. Such charges include facility shutdowns – when *Ford* closes a factory permanently because it is ceasing production of a particular model, it has to write off the remaining value of that factory which it had been carrying on its balance sheet. If it exits a major line of business entirely, selling it at a book value loss or ceasing operations altogether, it may incur such a charge. Other examples might include damage suffered from unexpected natural or manmade disasters – floods, fires, strikes, wars – and perhaps large adverse financial judgments or settlements associated with lawsuits brought against the company. The general idea is that these events are "irregular" or "unusual" or "non-recurring" – and therefore should be set aside when evaluating the current ongoing business. (The rules governing the determination of which expenses can be considered, or must be considered, as either non-recurring or extraordinary are elaborate. It is not within our scope here to parse the changing terminology of "extraordinary," "unusual," "irregular," "non-recurring," etc. applied to expenses (and gains) or to track which ones allow or require particular accounting treatments that may rule them either in or out of "Operating Income" calculations.)

expenses in this way is not illogical. By removing them from the Earnings calculation, the proponents of Operating Earnings argue that it presents a truer picture of a company's actual performance. (They are of course still included in Net Earnings.)

Operating Earnings are generally *higher* than Net Earnings. Therefore, the P/E based on Operating Earnings is generally *lower* than the standard Trailing P/E.[31] As shown here, the "gap" between the two has tended to grow – becoming especially significant at certain stages of the business cycle.[32] It has been quite large in recent recessions, reaching nearly 24% in the 2009 downturn (see Figure 3-3).

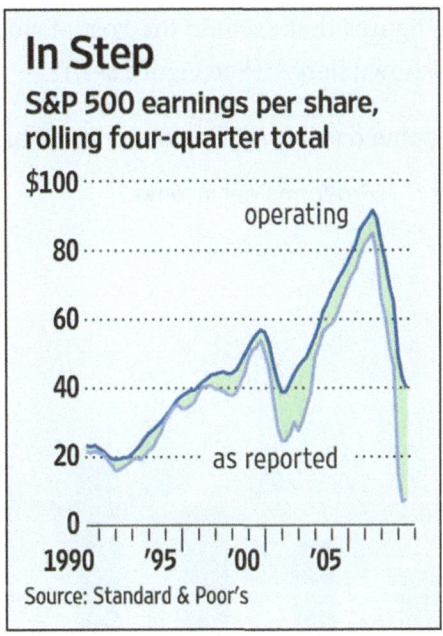

Figure 3-3. *GAAP Earnings vs. Operating Earnings*[33]

There is a tendency for companies with larger discrepancies to underperform. Because of the variability and the judgment involved in deciding which expenses to classify as "extraordinary," the definition of Operating Earnings in practice has become blurred.

---

[31]Though not always – sometimes there is an extraordinary gain, as when an asset is sold for a much higher price than its book value.

[32]Gretchen Morgenson, "What? They Never Heard of WorldCom?" *The New York Times*, March 21, 2005; and Mark Gongloff, "Investors, It Pays to Mind the GAAP Gaps," *The Wall Street Journal*, September 18, 2009.

[33]Mark Gongloff, "Investors, It Pays to Mind the GAAP Gaps," *The Wall Street Journal*, September 18, 2009. Reproduced by permission from *The Wall Street Journal*.

CHAPTER 3   VALUATION RATIOS

3.3.1 Pro Forma Earnings

The concept of Operating Earnings shades into a broader spectrum of non-GAAP earnings formulas, in which companies attempt (in good faith, in many cases; in others, perhaps not) to better portray their performance by presenting an alternative view of their "true" earnings. Pro forma earnings are constructed in different ways by different companies. These measures are non-GAAP, but are permitted (within limits) as long as the companies provide a clear reconciliation with GAAP earnings.

The justifications for using a pro forma measure vary considerably. Many tech companies present income figures that exclude the cost of stock-based compensation.[34] *Facebook* is a case in point, shown here.[35] (See Figure 3-4.)

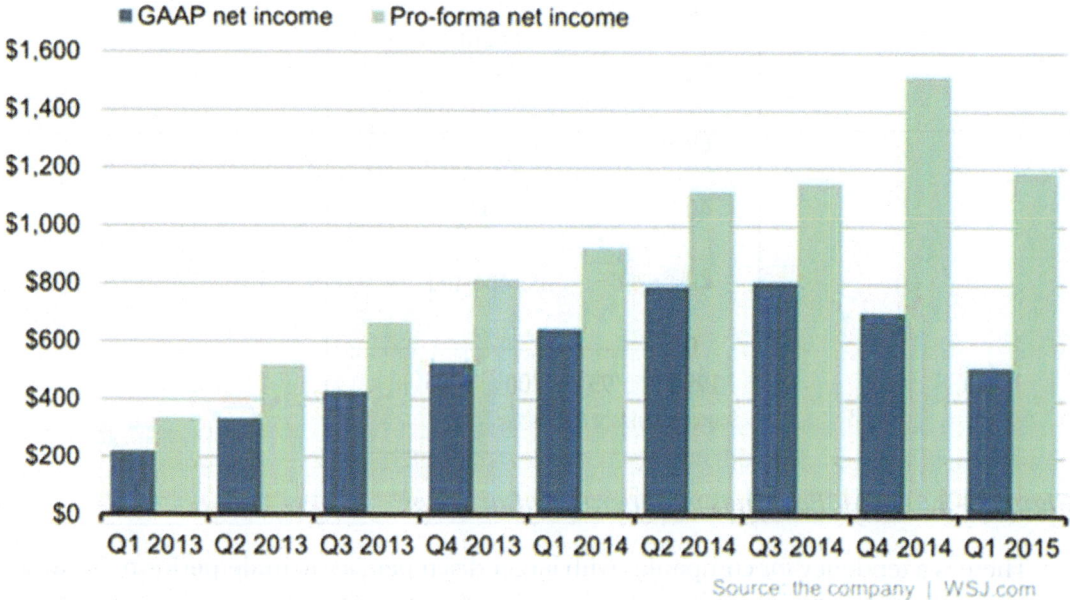

Figure 3-4. *Pro Forma Earnings for Facebook (Q1 2013–Q1 2015)*[36]

---

[34] A personal comment here: From my own experience in the tech industry, I am in general agreement that accounting for incentive stock options granted by tech companies (and others) to their employees as though it were the same as cash compensation is seriously misleading as to the nature of the "expense."

[35] Miriam Gottfried, "Blowing the Froth off of Big Tech Earnings," *The Wall Street Journal*, May 20, 2015.

[36] Miriam Gottfried, "Blowing the Froth off of Big Tech Earnings," *The Wall Street Journal*, May 20, 2015. Reproduced by permission from *The Wall Street Journal*.

There are many reasons for which a company may offer pro forma earnings to supplement standard GAAP reporting. Some energy companies have argued that big swings in oil prices (driven by events in the global energy markets rather than by company operations) affect their asset values and drive charges to GAAP earnings, which should be eliminated to provide a better picture of their actual performance. *Berkshire Hathaway* has argued that accounting treatments of some of its acquisitions have created "non-real" charges to earnings, which obscure the true picture for investors. It is worth quoting Warren Buffett's 2015 Letter to Shareholders here:

> Amortization charges of $1.1 billion have been deducted as expenses. We would call about 20% of these 'real,' the rest not. The 'non-real' charges, once non-existent at *Berkshire*, have become significant because of the many acquisitions we have made. Non-real amortization charges are likely to climb further as we acquire more companies.[37]

In Buffett's case, we can grant that his reasoning is probably correct, even if he does not fully explain it. In some cases, the use of non-GAAP pro forma figures may be more suspect.

> Most companies with negative GAAP earnings have positive non-GAAP earnings, suggesting that companies with low earnings are more likely to adjust upward.[38]

---

[37]Luke Kawa, "Warren Buffett's [2015] Shareholder Letter, Annotated," *Bloomberg Online*, February 27, 2016.

[38]Mark Fahey, "Mind the GAAP: Buffett warns of deceptive earnings," *CNBC Online*, March 1, 2016.

CHAPTER 3   VALUATION RATIOS

In any case, across the market, the "GAAP Gap" has grown in recent years.[39] (See Figure 3-5.) In 2015, S&P pro forma earnings were 25% above GAAP earnings. Moreover, there is evidence that investors increasingly prefer pro forma earnings to GAAP earnings and find them more informative.[40] There is also evidence that some non-GAAP metrics are better predictors of future performance, and value, than GAAP numbers.[41]

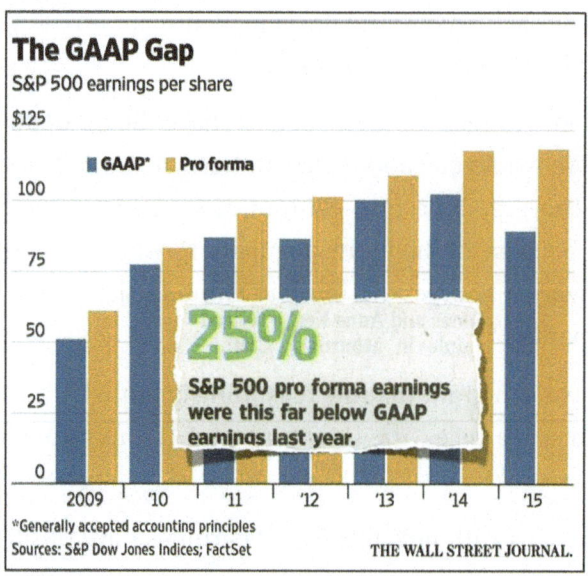

Figure 3-5. S&P 500 Earnings per Share Under Generally Accepted Accounting Principles vs. Pro Forma (2009–2015)[42]

---

[39]Justin Lahart, "S&P 500 Earnings: Far Worse Than Advertised," *The Wall Street Journal*, February 24, 2016.

[40]Dirk Black, Ervin Black, Theodore Christensen, and William Heninger, "Has the Regulation of Pro Forma Reporting in the US Changed Investors' Perceptions of Pro Forma Earnings Disclosures?" *Journal of Business Finance & Accounting*, Vol. 39, No. 7 (September/October 2012), pp. 876–904. Also Susan Albring, Maria Cabán-Garcia, and Jacqueline Reck, "The Value Relevance of a non-GAAP Performance Metric to the Capital Markets," *Review of Accounting and Finance*, Vol. 9, No. 3 (2010) pp. 264–284.

[41]Elmar Venter, David Emanuel, and Steven Cahan, "The Value Relevance of Mandatory Non-GAAP Earnings," *ABACUS*, Vol. 50, No. 1 (2014) pp. 1–24. The conclusion of Albring et al., op cit: "The non-GAAP measure is significantly associated with equity market values and returns and is significantly more value-relevant than the GAAP measure."

[42]Justin Lahart, "S&P 500 Earnings: Far Worse Than Advertised," *The Wall Street Journal*, February 24, 2016. Reproduced by permission from *The Wall Street Journal*.

To the extent that pro forma earnings figures are accepted as an adequate or even a superior measure, they may appear in the denominator of Earnings Multiples. However, the lack of standardization and general definitional confusion related to non-GAAP metrics will restrain this process. Pro forma earnings have been misused in some cases, leading to broad investor skepticism. *Standard & Poor's* offers a typically dismissive assessment:

> Originally, the use of the term *pro forma* meant a special analysis of a major change, such as a merger, where adjustments were made for an "as if" review. In such cases, pro forma measures are very useful. However, the specific items being considered in an "as if" review must be clear. In some recent cases, "as if" has come to mean "as if the company didn't have to cover proper expenses." In the most extreme cases, pro forma is nicknamed EBBS, or "earnings before bad stuff."[43]

3.3.2 Core Earnings

Standard & Poor's has made an effort to clarify this situation by introducing its own proprietary measure – Core Earnings.[44] It is described as follows:

> Core Earnings begins with as reported earnings and then makes a series of adjustments. 'As Reported' is earnings as defined by GAAP, with three exclusions – extraordinary items, cumulative effect of accounting changes, and discontinued operations, all as defined by GAAP.

---

[43]David Blitzer, Robert Friedman, and Howard Silverblatt, "Measures of Corporate Earnings," *Standard & Poor's*, May 14, 2002.

[44]Henny Sender, "S&P to Change its Methodology for Calculating Operating Profit," *The Wall Street Journal*, May 13, 2002. Other financial information providers have made similar proposals.

> Core Earnings focus on a company's ongoing operations. They should include all the revenues and costs associated with those operations and exclude revenues or costs that arise in other parts of the business, such as unrealized gains or losses from hedging activities. Items that reflect ongoing operations include compensation of employees, expenditures for materials and supplies, and depreciation of capital equipment used in production.
>
> Items that are not related to operations include litigation settlements, expenses related to mergers or acquisitions, and costs related to financing. These revenues or expenses are important and may be significant, but they are not representative of the company's core operations.[45]

The idea of a more rigorous and standardized definition of Operating Earnings was widely welcomed by many in the academic and business community. *The New York Times* called it one of the "Best Ideas of the Year" for 2002.[46] To the limited extent that Core Earnings has been studied as a predictor of performance and value, it appears to be superior to GAAP earnings in certain respects. A 2014 article in the *Management Accounting Quarterly* concluded that "Core Earnings is consistently more informative and value relevant than GAAP earnings."[47]

Still, two decades on, it is rare to find Core Earnings in use in the financial industry. The concept has not met with market success. But it points to a recognized need for a better and more uniform definition of Operating Earnings (and, implicitly, to the shortcomings of GAAP earnings).

---

[45]David Blitzer, Robert Friedman, and Howard Silverblatt, "Measures of Corporate Earnings," *Standard & Poor's*, May 14, 2002.

[46]Dahlia Robinson, Mark Dawkins, Babajide Wintoki, and Michael Dugan, "Has S&P's Core Earnings Lived Up to its Expectations? Assessing the Usefulness of Core Earnings Relative to GAAP Earnings," *University of Georgia Working Paper*, September 5, 2008: http://media.terry.uga.edu/documents/accounting/dawkinspaper.pdf

[47]Matthew M. Wieland, Mark C. Dawkins, and Michael T. Dugan, "The Value Relevance of S&P's Core Earnings vs. GAAP Earnings," *Management Accounting Quarterly*, Vol. 15, No. 4 (Summer 2014), pp. 18–26. See also Matthew M. Wieland, Mark C. Dawkins, and Michael T. Dugan, "The Differential Value Relevance of S&P's Core Earnings Versus GAAP Earnings: The Role of Stock Option Expense," *Journal of Business Finance & Accounting*, Vol. 40, No. 1/2 (January/February 2013), pp. 55–81.

In summary, Operating Earnings, pro forma earnings, and similar measures suffer from a lack of consistent definitions, which can lead even experienced analysts to confuse and mingle data from different categories.[48] The general observation that Operating Earnings are consistently higher, and pro forma earnings higher still, appears to hold, but the definitional problems make it difficult to use this metric to compare different companies and sectors and across different periods.

3.4 Dividends

Dividends are "the ultimate cash flow"[49] – unmixed with forecasts, assumptions, interpretations, or accounting contrivances:

$$\frac{price/share}{dividend/share} \quad \text{or} \quad \frac{dividend/share}{price/share}$$

In an earlier era, investors looked to dividends as the true foundation of value. This is still often true today.

> The power of this ratio comes from the fact that unlike earnings, dividends cannot be "massaged" by creative accounting. They are either declared and paid in cash or they aren't.[50]

The classic Dividend Discount Model (DDM) equates the market price of a stock with the sum of all its future dividends discounted back to their present value. Some version of this formula is still to be found in many textbooks.

---

[48]For example, Jeremy Siegel would have us accept that "the terms non-GAAP earnings, pro forma earnings, and earnings from continuing operations all refer to operating earnings" – a careless use of language. From "The Shiller CAPE Ratio: A New Look," *Financial Analysts Journal*, Vol. 72, No. 3 (2016) pp. 41–50.

[49]Peter Suozzo, Stephen Cooper, Gillian Sutherland, and Zhen Deng, "Valuation Multiples: A Primer," *UBS Warburg Global Equity Research*, November 2001.

[50]"Why the Price Dividend Ratio is Better than the PE Ratio," *Seeking Alpha*, October 13, 2008.

CHAPTER 3   VALUATION RATIOS

Dividends are undoubtedly a major driver of value. Dividend-payers outperform the rest of the market.[51] From 1972 to 2012, dividends accounted for the largest proportion of total stock market returns in most countries, much more than P/E expansion.[52] In the United States, from 1940 to 2006, 64% of the annualized return on the S&P 500 came from reinvested dividends.[53] Investing strategies based on screening for dividend yield have substantially beaten the market.[54] Index funds that use dividends as a weighting factor have beaten their market capitalization-weighted peers over certain periods.[55] The case for using a market valuation ratio based on dividends would appear to be a strong one.

3.4.1 Dividend Ratios: Significance and Trends

Dividend ratios are presented in two logically equivalent forms: Price-to-Dividend (P/D) and Dividend-to-Price ("Dividend Yield").

Unlike P/E which only measures a "claim" on earnings (without the certainty that the shareholder will directly benefit), Price-to-Dividend and its inverse, Dividend Yield, measure precisely the cost of acquiring $1.00 in cash paid out by the company.

Low P/D (which equates to high D/P or high dividend yield) means that the company's dividend dollar is "cheap," just as a low P/E tells us that the "claim" on an earnings dollar is cheap. Since dividends constitute the bulk of the returns from stock ownership, on average, dwarfing capital gains, one would expect that cheap P/D stocks will outperform – and they generally do, on average. Low P/D (high yield) is regarded as a strong "value"

---

[51]Spencer Jakab, "Idea of a Dividend Bubble Has Some Pop," *The Wall Street Journal*, June 8, 2012; also "Veni Divi Vici," *Financial Times*, March 30, 2010.

[52]Andrew Lapthorne, "Global Quality Income Index," *Société Générale Cross Asset Research*, May 24, 2012.

[53]Shirley A. Lazo, "Dividend Savant?" *Barron's*, August 21, 2006.

[54]Scott Cendrowski, "Dividends for the Long Run," *Fortune*, November 23, 2009: *"Since 1972, companies that increase or begin paying dividends have returned 9.5% a year, soundly beating the 6.8% return of the S&P 500."*

[55]For example, the family of fundamentally weighted index funds offered by the firm *Wisdom Tree* (which emphasize dividends) outperformed the cap-weighted market average during an earlier phase of the recent bull market (although in other periods they have underperformed) ("Get Your Coupon," *Financial Times*, January 14, 2012).

signal. Many value-investing screens and strategies incorporate dividend-based ratios.[56] (See Figure 3-6.) Dividend Yield tends to mirror the P/E ratio,[57] with Low P/E and high Dividend Yield both pointing to undervalued companies and associated with strong future returns.[58] (See Figure 3-7.)

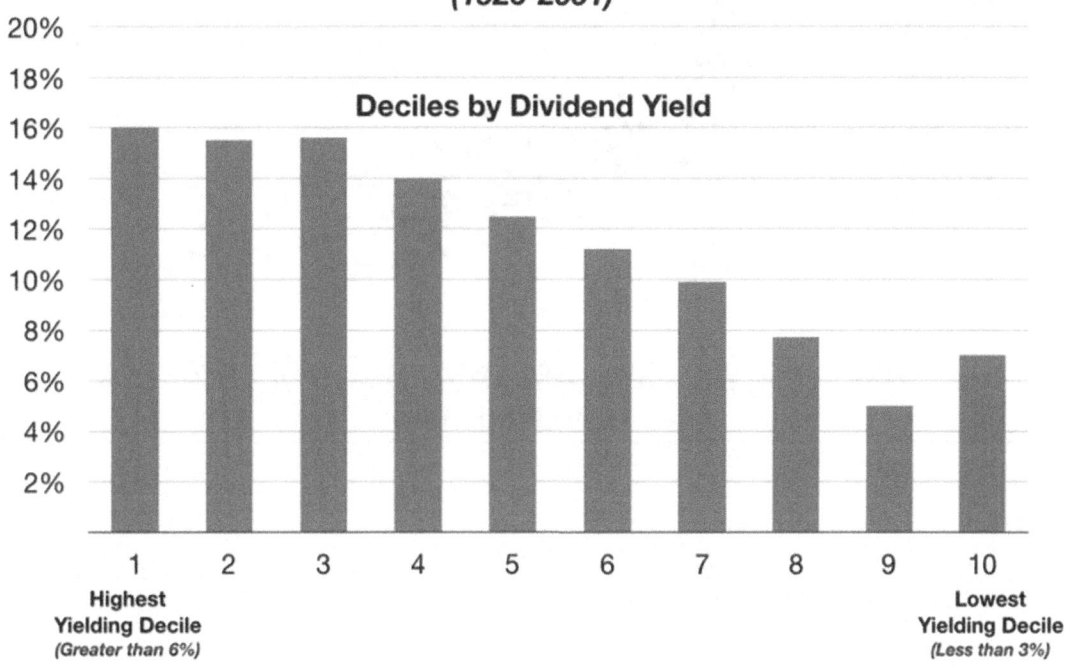

Figure 3-6. Future 10-Year Rates of Return for Stocks Purchased at Alternative Initial Dividend Yields (1926–2001)[59]

---

[56]For example, the well-known "Dogs of the Dow" formula is based on Dividend Yield. The strategy involves buying the ten *Dow Jones Industrial Average* component companies with the highest dividend yields, using a high Dividend Yield to screen for an underpriced stock. Elizabeth O'Brien, "History Says These Dogs are Usually Barking Up the Right Tree," *The Wall Street Journal*, August 13, 2012.

[57]Chart source: Crestmont Research.

[58]Burton G. Malkiel, "The Efficient Market Hypothesis and its Critics," *Journal of Economic Perspectives*, Vol. 17, No. 1, Winter 2003, pp. 59–82.

[59]Adapted from Burton G. Malkiel, "The Efficient Market Hypothesis and its Critics," *Journal of Economic Perspectives*, Vol. 17, No. 1, Winter 2003, pp. 59–82.

CHAPTER 3   VALUATION RATIOS

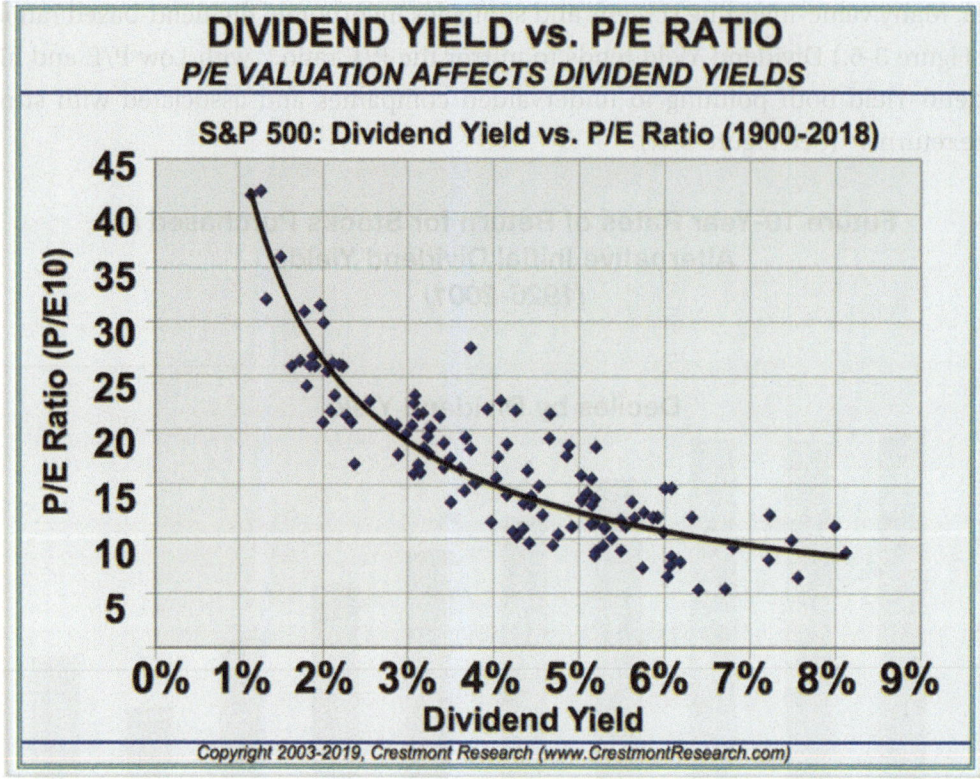

Figure 3-7. *Dividend Yield and P/E*[60]

International comparisons suggest that inadequate dividend *payouts* in some markets may be associated with much lower P/E ratios and lower market valuations generally. Korean companies pay out much less than companies in other parts of the world. *The Economist* magazine concludes "Low dividends are thought to be part of the reason for the 'Korea Discount': the relatively low valuations of Korean firms."[61] (See Figure 3-8.)

---

[60]Reproduced by permission of *Crestmont Research*.
[61]"A Tempting Target," *The Economist*, September 27, 2014.

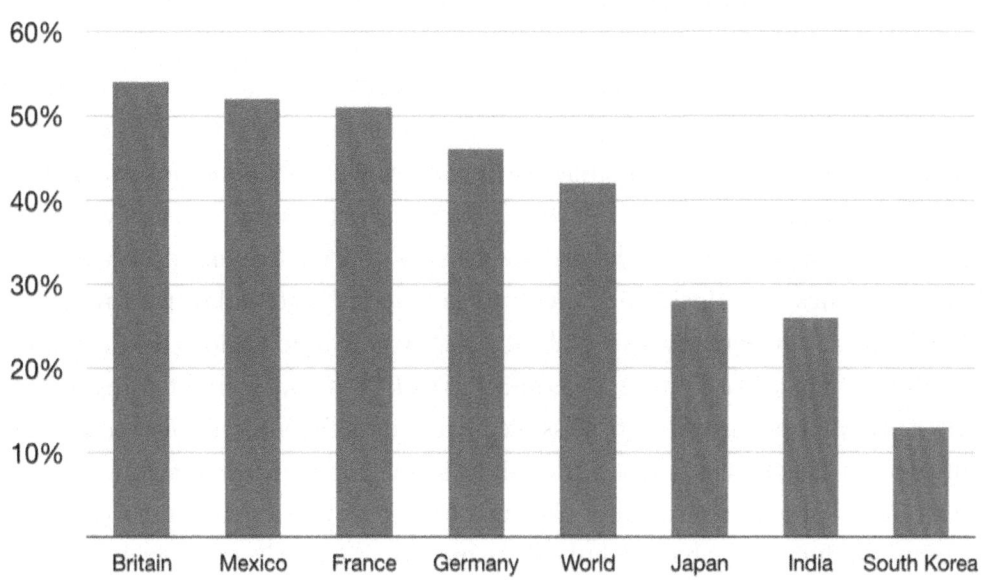

Figure 3-8. *Dividends Paid as a Percentage of Net Profit*[62]

Payout trends in the United States have also been declining.[63] The dividend yield has fallen over the long term, from an average of 4% in the 1980s to less than 2% today.[64] The decline is partly due to the growing popularity of share buybacks, a topic we will return to in later chapters.

---

[62]Adapted from "A Tempting Target," *The Economist*, September 27, 2014.
[63]John Authers, "Hordes of Hoarders," *Financial Times*, January 30, 2012.
[64]Morgan Housel, "How To Boost Income in an Era of Low Stock Dividends," *The Wall Street Journal*, October 4, 2014.

It is also unclear how dividend signals should be interpreted. Differences in the Price/Earnings ratio from one company to another can be seen in terms of different expectations about future earnings. The Dividend Discount Model holds that the share price values the entire dividend stream, so greater uncertainty about *future* dividends could result in lower market prices per dividend dollar (and therefore higher yields). But dividends are much less volatile than earnings.[65] As well, dividend dollars might be expected to have roughly equal value. Cash is cash. Yet it costs around $16 today to buy $1 of *AT&T* dividend payments, while *Johnson & Johnson* sells its dividend dollar for about $36. Both companies are considered "dividend aristocrats" with solid track records of increasing dividend payments over several decades, so there is no obvious justification for differentiating them based on future uncertainty. *AT&T* does have a credit rating of BBB+ from S&P (a proxy for potential future possible dividend risk); *Johnson & Johnson* is rated AAA. But *AT&T's* rating reflects strategic decisions by the company's management to take on more leverage, supported by a utility-like business model and a steadier cash flow than the consumer products and pharmaceutical business of *J&J*, and is arguably unrelated to risk of impairment to the dividend.[66]

This underscores the cloudiness of dividend-based ratios as a valuation metric. Dividends – cash in hand – are one thing. Dividend yield – the price (market value) of that cash in hand – is something else. The absolute value of dividends is a very important driver of returns: in one classic study by Robert Shiller, dividend payments had a correlation of 90% with market price changes over the long run.[67]

---

[65] In a seminal 1981 study by Robert J. Shiller, price volatility was found to be five to thirteen times greater than dividend volatility ("Do Stock Prices Move Too Much to be Justified by Subsequent Changes in Dividends?" *The American Economic Review*, Vol. 71, No. 3 (June 1981), pp. 421–436).

[66] The lower credit rating does reflect "default risk" officials, according to S&P. But given *AT&T's* history and business model, it is hard to credit this assessment. *AT&T* could easily restructure its balance sheet, which might reduce returns to shareholders, but it seems unlikely that it is at any true risk of default which it could not take measures to mitigate.

[67] Robert Shiller, "Stock Prices and Social Dynamics," *Brookings Papers on Economic Activity*, Vol. 1984, No. 2 (1984), pp. 457–510.

Aggregate real stock prices are fairly highly correlated over time with aggregate real dividends. The simple correlation coefficient between the Standard and Poor's composite stock price index and the corresponding annual real dividend series between 1926 and 1983 is 0.91... Much of the movements of the stock market that we often regard as inexplicable can be traced to movements in dividends.

But this same study found that the *ratio* of dividend to market price "explained" just 6% of stock returns over that period across the market. A high Dividend Yield may signal a good investment prospect, but paradoxically it does not seem to track value creation very well in the broader market, especially over shorter (but more realistic) investment horizons. *The Wall Street Journal* has noted that

The five-year rolling correlation between the S&P 500 dividend yield and the [S&P 500] index's performance [has] an average of minus -0.1 dating back to 1941.[68]

Another study by *Vanguard*, covering the period of 1926–2011, found that the Trailing P/E had over *twice* the predictive power of Dividend Yield with respect to 10-year-ahead stock returns.[69]

3.5 Price-to-Sales

Price-to-Sales (P/S) – where the denominator is based on the revenue figure from the top line of the income statement – would appear to be an attractive valuation metric:

$$\frac{price/share}{sales/share}$$

---

[68] Ben Eisen, "Dividends Are What Matter Now," *The Wall Street Journal*, August 25, 2016.

[69] Joseph Davis, Roger Aliaga-Díaz, and Charles Thomas, "Forecasting Stock Returns: What Signals Matter, and What Do They Say Now?" *Vanguard Research*, October 2012. The R2 of trailing dividends is about 10% for one year and 18% for 10 years. The explanatory power is thus quite weak.

CHAPTER 3 VALUATION RATIOS

Revenue is often assumed to be less subject to the complexities and controversies that affect Earnings calculations.[70] Sales are seen as less volatile than Earnings. A dollar of Sales received by the company "across the counter" has a certain concreteness to it. It recalls the original transactional character of the business, before the accountants in the back office have had their way with the numbers. There are no adjustments for depreciation, tax holidays, or write-offs.

But this seemingly superior integrity of "revenue" is illusory. A "dollar of sales" is not a simple concept and does not always mean the same thing from one industry to the next or for different companies in the same industry or from one period to the next.[71] There are discounts, rebates, warranty reserves, bad debts, product returns, gift cards that are not redeemed, sales commissions, and certain kinds of taxes. All these offsets and adjustments contribute to the difference between Gross Sales and Net Sales (the Net number is the denominator in the P/S ratio.) There are questions related to booking revenue for multi-year contracts. There are complex rules governing the recognition of *software* revenue that can distort the economic reality of the transaction (in the view of some). For example, *Apple* reported in 2009 that its actual dollar revenue received was 17% higher than what they were allowed to report, because of the requirement to spread a portion of the sales price of the iPhone over eight fiscal quarters. (This issue later led to an accounting rule change.[72])

---

[70]A. J. Senchack and Hojn D. Martin, "The Relative Performance of the PSR and PER Investment Strategies," *Financial Analysts Journal* (March/April 1987), pp. 46–56.

[71]In some industries, there is the question of whether to book revenue when products are sold to an intermediary wholesaler or distributor or to wait until the product is "sold through" to the end user. (GAAP allows either approach.) For example, in 2006 it was reported that the semiconductor manufacturer *Texas Instruments* used "sell-in" revenue recognition, where sales were recorded when product was shipped to the distributor (not the end customer). *Intel*, a direct competitor, used "sell-through" revenue recognition where sales were not recorded until the intermediary distributors sold the *Intel* product to the final customers. A number of the examples of companies switching from one form of revenue recognition to the other are cited, which obviously means that P/S (and perhaps other multiples) is not readily comparable from before and after the switch (Herb Greenberg, "A Shift to 'Sell-In' Accounting Could Be a Clue to Brewing Trouble," *The Wall Street Journal*, June 18, 2006).

[72]Martin Peers, "Investors Should Focus on Apple's Core," *The Wall Street Journal*, September 24, 2009. Also Michael Rapoport, Yukare Iwatani Kane, and Ben Worthen, "U.S. Accounting to Aid Tech Firms," *The Wall Street Journal*, September 24, 2009.

Revenue recognition is a tricky field. A full discussion of the complications, loopholes, and improprieties associated with revenue accounting might fill an entire volume. Just one recent change in revenue recognition policy (2018) forced a majority of S&P 500 companies to redefine their accounting procedures.[73] This sort of adjustment clearly impacts the P/S metric, and the effects may not be consistent across the market.

Beyond definitional changes, the possibility of manipulation also creates a problem for the P/S metric. In a 2005 *Wall Street Journal* article, it was reported that over half of the class action lawsuits brought against public companies the previous year had to do with alleged irregularities in revenue recognition.[74] As well, "revenue recognition continues to remain one of the highest causes of restatements" of financial reports.[75]

So when *is* P/S appropriate?

Sometimes P/S has been used in direct comparisons of archrivals, where some external factor may skew the picture. For example, in a 2014 comparison, *Apple* was valued at 2.5 times the annual sales, while *Samsung* was valued at just 50% of its annual sales.[76] That 5 to 1 P/S advantage for *Apple* is well above the difference in their P/E ratios, (which has fluctuated in recent years between 1.2 and 2 times in favor of *Apple)*. The fact that *Samsung's* sales are even more undervalued than its earnings raises an interesting question for the valuation exercise. It is likely that this discrepancy is related to difference between valuations in the two home country markets – Korean companies trade at much lower multiples than their American counterparts, in part due to less reliable financial

---

[73] *"Some companies expect the new rules to accelerate revenue, while others say the timing of when they can record revenue as earned will be delayed, even though their underlying business remains unchanged."* (Tatyana Shumsky, "Updated Accounting Rules Reverberate," *The Wall Street Journal*, June 13, 2018).

[74] Gene Colter, "Bull Market for Securities Lawsuits," *The Wall Street Journal*, March 30, 2005.

[75] Herb Greenberg, "A Shift to 'Sell-In' Accounting Could Be a Clue to Brewing Trouble," *The Wall Street Journal*, June 18, 2006.

[76] Andrew Bary, "Samsung Rising," *Barron's*, October 13, 2014.

reporting (resulting in lower investor confidence in reported revenue and earnings figures).[77] It could also indicate that *Samsung's* "quality of revenue" is fundamentally lower (e.g., less repeatable, showing lower customer loyalty) than *Apple's*.

P/S can also be useful when the company's business model is tied to maximizing *sales volume*, throughput, and "turnover" and selling identical or nearly identical products, with low profit margins – as is often the case for classic retailers. An onion, or a jar of mayonnaise, is essentially the same product whether it sits on the shelf at *Kroger* or at *Walmart* or at *Whole Foods*. Differences in the value of each dollar of "mayonnaise revenue" point to differences in the underlying business model, which enable more successful companies to generate higher enterprise value. *Walmart* gets more than twice the market value that *Kroger* gets per dollar of sales, by leveraging groceries with general consumer merchandise (while Kroger sells only groceries). In turn, *Whole Foods* routinely received more than twice the market value for each dollar of its sales compared to *Walmart* (and five-and-a-half times *Kroger's* value per sales dollar). The *Whole Foods* model leveraged brand equity and product quality, and probably higher customer loyalty, to drive higher margins. The P/S ratio seems to discriminate these differences.[78] (See Figure 3-9.)

---

[77]Korea is rated in comparative studies near the bottom of the international scale in terms of Financial Reporting Quality – see Jennifer Martínez-Ferrero, "Consequences of financial reporting quality on corporate performance. Evidence at the international level," *Estudios de Economia*, Vol. 41, No. 1 (June 2014), pp. 49–88. See also T. H. Choi and Jinhan Pae, "Business Ethics and Financial Reporting Quality: Evidence from Korea," *Journal of Business Ethics*, Vol. 103 (2011), pp. 403–427. Acknowledging the deficits in Financial Reporting Quality in Korea and commenting on the adoption of IFRS, the international accounting standard, which in general allows even more flexibility than GAAP for the interpretation of "revenue recognition" principles, the authors state: *"IFRS, which is a principles-based accounting system requiring the sound judgment and interpretation of accounting standards by managers, Financial Reporting Quality will depend on how Korean companies apply and interpret IFRS even more than before."*

[78]Spencer Jakab, "Cleaning Up in Aisle Five with Kroger," *The Wall Street Journal*, September 12, 2013. Of course, *Whole Foods* is now a subsidiary of *Amazon*.

CHAPTER 3   VALUATION RATIOS

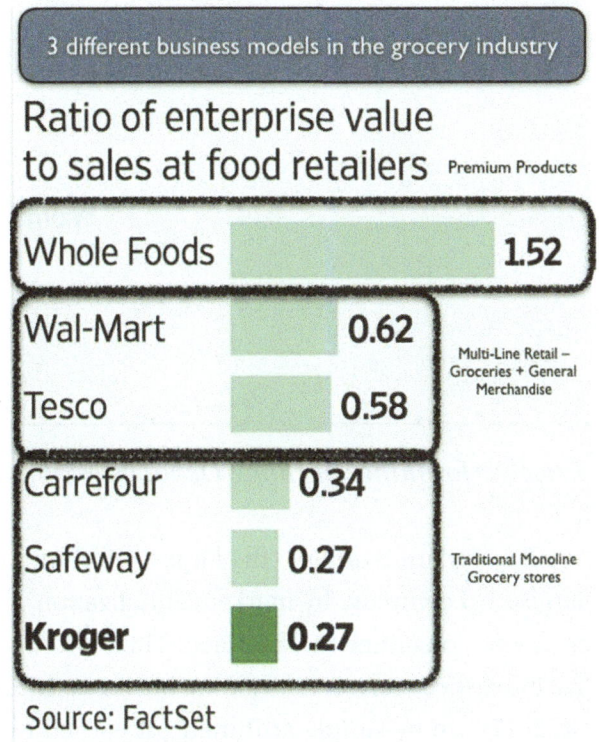

Figure 3-9. *EV/S for Food Retailers*[79]

Sometimes the P/S will point to important strategic or structural distinctions. For example, in May 2018, *Home Depot* and *Walmart* enjoyed identical Price-to-Earnings multiples (25.66 and 25.65, respectively). But *Home Depot's* Price-to-Sales ratio was four times higher (2.14 vs. 0.50), reflecting stronger customer loyalty and stronger pricing power. The P/S metric aligns much better with the market performance. (See Figure 3-10.)

---

[79]Spencer Jakab, "Cleaning Up in Aisle Five with Kroger," *The Wall Street Journal,* September 12, 2013. Reproduced by permission from *The Wall Street Journal.*

CHAPTER 3   VALUATION RATIOS

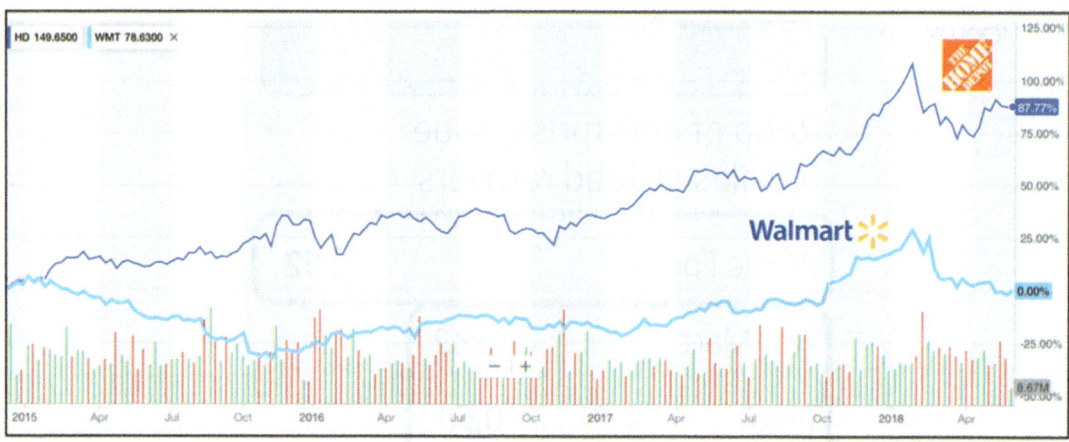

Figure 3-10. *Share Price Performance of Home Depot vs. Walmart (2015–2018)*

The two giants of retail today are *Walmart* (the largest US company by revenue) and *Amazon* (the second largest US company by market capitalization), locked in a historic contest for dominance of the consumer marketplace. Their profit margins are almost identical – 1.97% and 2.04%, respectively. It is a volume business. *Walmart* sold two-and-a-half times as much in 2017 – so by simple arithmetic, it earned two-and-a-half times what *Amazon* earned. But *Amazon* has a stratospheric P/E (over 260) – too high to tell us much. On the other hand, the P/S comparison is informative. (See Figure 3-11.)

CHAPTER 3   VALUATION RATIOS

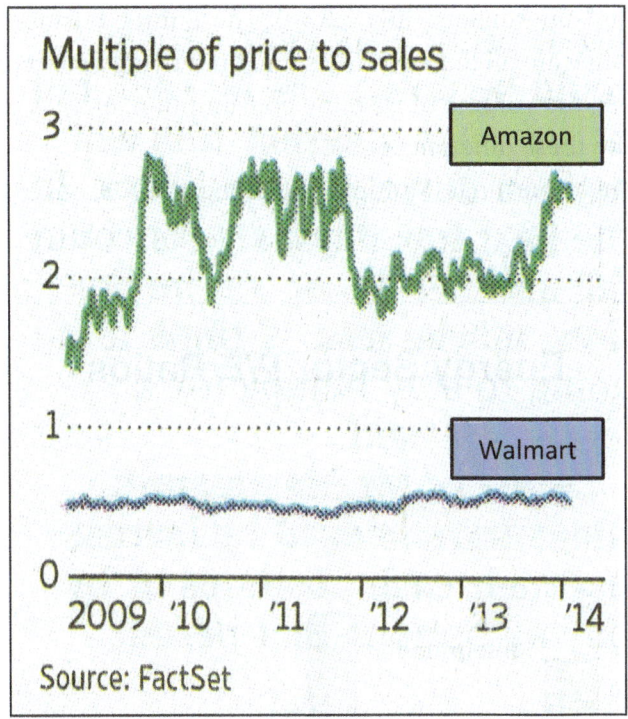

Figure 3-11. *Amazon vs. Walmart P/S*[80]

Amazon generates four to seven times more value per dollar of sales. *Amazon's* P/S has also fluctuated more than 100% over this period, while *Walmart* logged a steady 50 cents per sales dollar, quarter after quarter. The market evidently has a good fix on *Walmart's* business model, but it is still uncertain about how to value *Amazon's* sales.[81]

P/S can sometimes be more useful than P/E for comparisons within a sector, especially when some companies are losing money and/or taking unusual write-offs that depress Net Earnings. An example is the energy sector, as it looked in 2018. This sector is divided into three segments: Upstream (oil and gas exploration and production), Downstream (oil and gas refining and marketing), and Integrated Oil and Gas (companies which do

---

[80]Spencer Jakab, "Amazon's Growth Story Continues to Sell," *The Wall Street Journal*, January 30, 2014. Reproduced by permission from *The Wall Street Journal*.

[81]*Amazon's* business model has evolved in very diverse fields, from retail to cloud computing to entertainment. This is a confounding factor in interpreting the P/S signal vs. a much more focused competitor such as *Walmart*.

CHAPTER 3   VALUATION RATIOS

both – including the "supermajors" like *Exxon*). These three business models are quite different, although they are all linked to the same underlying economic drivers (such as the price of crude oil, the volume of gasoline consumption, etc.). A useful Value Metric ought to shed light on these differences.

The comparison of Earnings Multiples (Trailing P/E) is not very revealing. (See Figure 3-12.)

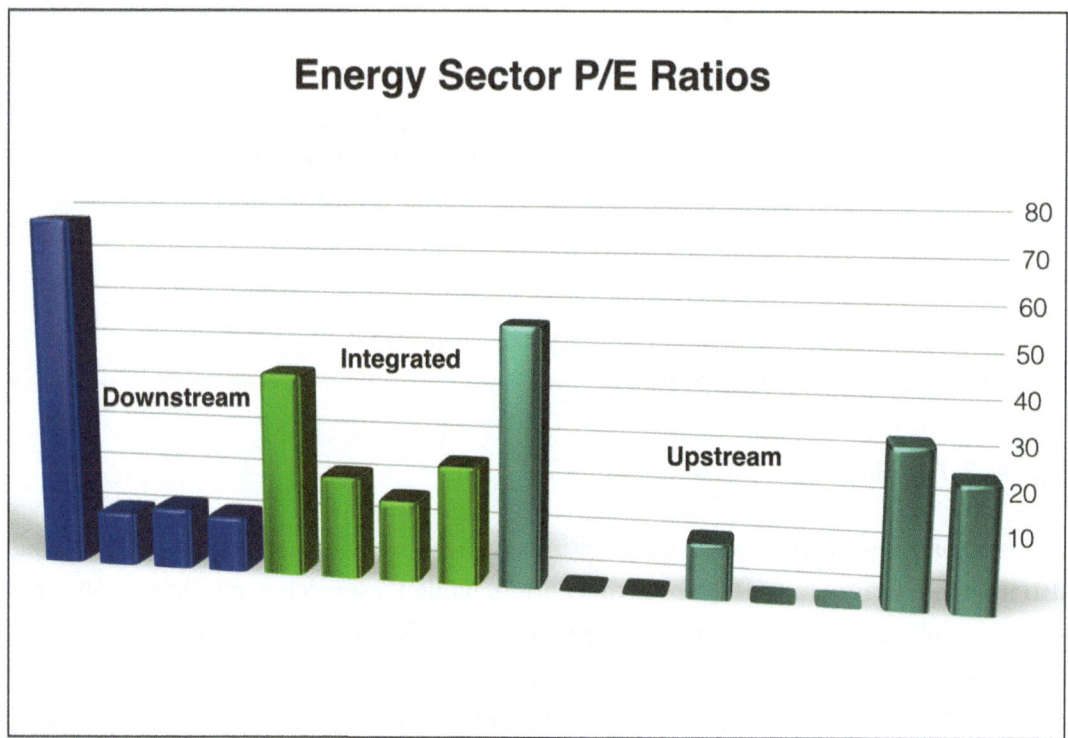

Figure 3-12. *Energy Sector P/E Ratios*

There is no meaningful pattern here. The highest P/E belongs to a Downstream company and the second and fourth highest to Upstream companies; but half the Upstream players reported losses (i.e., P/E=N/A). The P/E Multiples do not provide a particularly useful perspective on valuation of these companies.

The P/S ratio is more coherent. It reveals an important difference in value-driving relationships across the three sectors. (See Figure 3-13.)

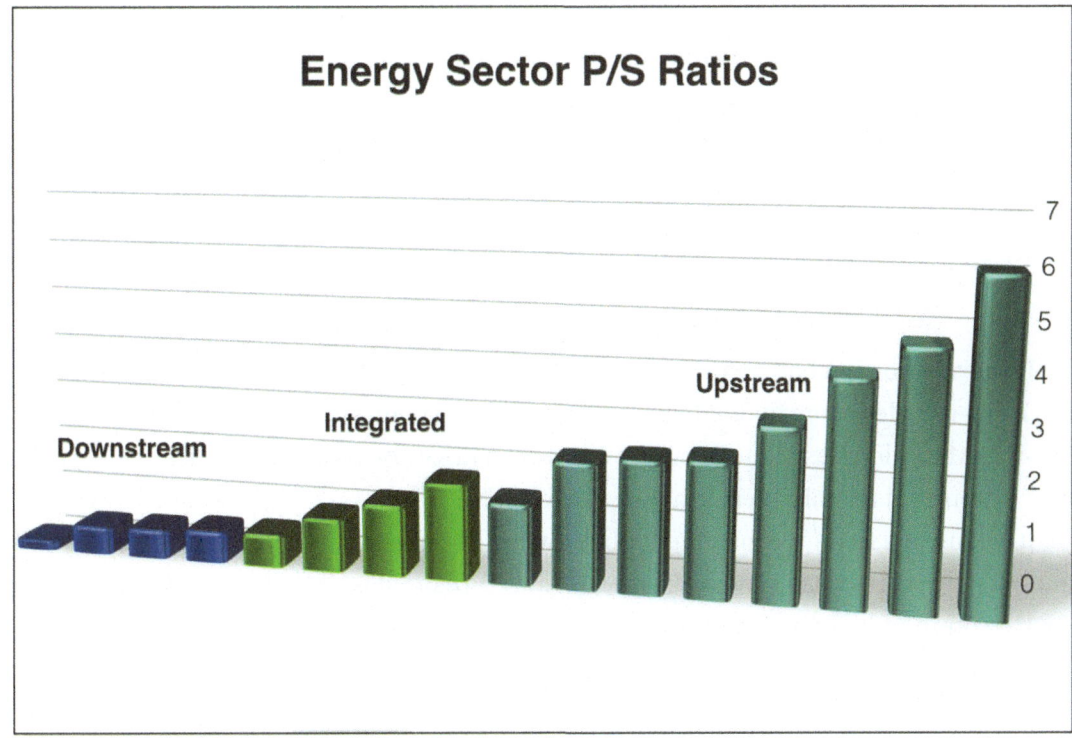

Figure 3-13. *Energy Sector P/S Ratios*

Still, P/S is little used and not much studied. Why not? The results of the rather small number of studies of this metric are mixed. One group found that it performed as well as the P/E, at least for the Taiwan stock market.[82] A study of Finnish stocks found that P/E multiples adjusted to market mispricings rapidly, compared to P/S ratios which were much more sluggish to respond.[83] An older study (1987) of the American market concluded that P/S was inferior as an investment screen for value stocks:

---

[82]Peter Chou and Tung Liao, "The relative performance of the PER and PSR filters with stochastic dominance: evidence from the Taiwan Stock Exchange," *Applied Financial Economics*, Vol. 6 (1996), pp. 119–27.

[83]Eero Patari and Timo Leivo, "Persistence in Relative Valuation Difference between Value and Glamour Stocks: The Finnish Experience," *Banking and Finance Letters*, Vol. 2, No. 3, pp. 319–324.

Low price-earnings ratio (PER) stocks dominate low price-to-sales ratio (PSR) stocks on both an absolute and risk-adjusted basis. The PER strategy also appears to offer better discrimination between potential winners and losers. Moreover, the relative performance of low PER stocks seems to be more consistent over different time periods than that of low PSR stocks; the low PER portfolios produced a higher return than the low PSR portfolios in 68 per cent of the quarters studied.[84]

Finally, a more recent, comprehensive study of the full range of market metrics found that Price-to-Sales came in dead last in accuracy, well behind both Forward and Trailing Earnings Multiples, Cash Flow Multiples, and even Price-to-Book. "Among drivers derived from historical data, sales performance the worst."[85]

It seems this news has been absorbed by the profession. In one study of 103 equity analysts' reports covering major US companies, Price/Sales was cited as the basis of a stock recommendation in just a single case. (Price/Earnings was cited in 76 cases.)[86]

In short, P/S is not popular, and perhaps deservedly so.

3.6 Metrics Based on Cash Flow

If "Sales" is less solid than it seems, what about "Cash"?

There is a growing interest among analysts, managers, and investors in the use of Cash Flow metrics. "Cash" seems as though it ought to count for something more certain than mere "Earnings." Many investors have never quite trusted accrual accounting. "Cash is a fact, Profit is an opinion."[87] Perhaps it is possible to construct a more useful valuation metric with Cash Flow in the denominator. However, there are many different definitions of Cash Flow. Most deviate from GAAP.

---

[84] A. J. Senchack and Hojn D. Martin, "The Relative Performance of the PSR and PER Investment Strategies," *Financial Analysts Journal* (March/April 1987), pp. 46–56.

[85] Jing Liu, Doron Nissim, and Jacob Thomas, "Equity Valuation Using Multiples," *Journal of Accounting Research*, Vol. 40, No. 1 (March 2002), pp. 135–172.

[86] Mark Bradshaw, "The Use of Target Prices to Justify Sell-Side Analysts' Stock Recommendations," *Accounting Horizons*, Vol. 16, No. 1 (March 2002), pp. 27–41.

[87] Alfred Rappaport, *Creating Shareholder Value: A Guide for Managers and Investors, Revised and Updated* (New York: Free Press, 1997), p. 15.

3.6.1 EBITDA and EV/EBITDA

One popular measure of Cash Flow for valuation purposes is EBITDA (Earnings Before Interest, Taxes, Depreciation, and Amortization) – which begins with the Net Earnings (the GAAP bottom line) and adds back the four accounts mentioned in its title: Interest and Taxes, considered as unrelated to the *operational* aspect of the business (as previously mentioned in the discussion of Price-to-Operating Income ratio), and Depreciation and Amortization as two important categories of expenses that are carried over from previous years' investments or acquisitions and do not correspond to cash outflows in the current period.

EBITDA is used frequently as the denominator in a ratio called EV/EBITDA. It has become the second most popular valuation multiple, after the P/E:[88]

$$\frac{enterprise\ value\ /\ share}{EBITDA\ /\ share}$$

The numerator – Enterprise Value – is itself a compound construction. It is the sum of the market value of the company's equity (the market capitalization) and the company's debt, minus cash on hand (considered an offset to the debt). It often includes further adjustments.[89] The underlying principle is that EV represents the cost for an acquirer to obtain a full claim on 100% of the cash flows generated by the company, including earnings, dividends, and payouts to creditors (bank loans, bondholders).[90] Or to state it more simply, it is the price to acquire the company in a debt-free state:

---

[88] EBITDA is a relatively recent and somewhat controversial innovation: *"EBITDA came into vogue during the dot-com era of the 1990s. It was a period when many startup technology companies, telecoms, and other fragile startup companies could not generate a profit and needed an alternative metric besides GAAP earnings to convey a positive picture to investors."* (Stanley Block, "Methods of Valuation: Myths vs. Reality," *The Journal of Investing* (Winter 2010), pp. 7–14).

[89] There may be additional adjustments for preferred stock, pension liabilities, etc. EV is not a standardized metric (it is non-GAAP); it is not always constructed in the same way.

[90] By analogy with a simple real estate transaction, EV would be equivalent conceptually to the purchase price on a leveraged property – buying a house and paying the seller his equity claim plus paying off the seller's mortgage. (It has always puzzled me somewhat why if the numerator includes the value of the company's debt, the denominator (EBITDA) excludes the payments to service that debt. The use of EV/EBITDA has become fairly common, but it seems in this and in other respects to be rather unexamined, another of the "received ideas" that have proliferated in the field of Finance.)

$$\frac{(market\ capitalization + total\ debt - cash)/share}{EBITDA/share}$$

This definition entails certain quirks. First, a company with a large cash balance, and without much debt, has an EV *lower* than its market cap. On June 1, 2018, *Google (Alphabet)* had a market cap of $774 Bn, but with $100 Bn in cash and just $3 Bn in debt, its EV (with other adjustments) was much lower – about $650 Bn. This is relevant for valuations supporting merger and acquisition analyses, because the company's cash can effectively be used to partially fund its acquisition, reducing the cost to a potential buyer. Used as a valuation metric in EV/EBITDA, the cash balance is considered in a sense separate from the main business and deducted from its value. (This adjustment for cash holdings is similar in spirit to the Cash-Adjusted P/E described in a later section of this chapter.)

It also follows, of course, that a heavily indebted company will have a much higher EV than its market price would indicate. *Ford* had a market cap of $46 Bn but an EV of $175 Bn.

EV is useful, even necessary, in situations like these. If a company has an unusually large cash balance (and little debt) or a large debt load (and a normal cash balance), EV probably gives a better picture of the value of the business than market capitalization (Price) alone. In such cases, the EV/EBITDA metric may have an edge over P/E, although the question has not been systematically studied.

3.6.2 Free Cash Flow

A valuation metric gaining popularity is Price-to-Free-Cash-Flow (P/FCF – also EV/FCF):

$$\frac{price/share}{(operating\ cash\ flow - CAPEX)/share}$$

The concept of "Free Cash Flow" is based on the idea that not all of the company's positive cash flow is available for discretionary use. Some portion of it has to be reinvested in the company to ensure that future cash flows continue as expected.[91] The residual – after

---

[91] The cash cow gives her milk, but some of the proceeds from the sale of that milk today have to be spent on her feed and care, so that she will give more milk tomorrow.

required reinvestment – is Free Cash Flow. It is the cash which the company's management has at its disposal for dividends, share buybacks, investing in growth, or acquisitions and new adventures.

The idea of Free Cash Flow as a central measure of performance has caught on with corporate managers. It is increasingly common for companies to calculate some form of this metric.[92] The simplest formula – depending on the business model – is often to subtract capital expenditures from operating cash flow.[93]

FCF is also becoming popular with analysts and investors. "Break from the herd – Consider Free Cash Flow," urges one investment firm.[94] There are now indexes based on FCF for the S&P 500. There are Exchange Traded Funds (ETFs) that allow retail investors to bet on FCF metrics. It seems to be the coming thing.

On the other hand, some accounting studies of the relation between earnings (which include non-cash accruals) and market value, compared to the relation of cash flow (which excludes accruals) to market value, argue that accrual accounting is superior:

> Accrual accounting rules prescribe that earnings add to shareholder value, but cash flow is irrelevant to the valuation of equity. The stock market prices equity shares according to this prescription. Earnings are priced positively but, given earnings, a dollar more of free cash flow from a business – cash flow from operations minus cash investment – is, on average, associated with approximately a dollar less in the market value of the business and has no association with changes in the market value of the equity claim on the business.[95]

---

[92]There are various labels used, and differing definitions, for this sort of metric, e.g., "Free Cash Flow Excluding Certain Items" (*Pepsico*, 2017), "Net cash provided by operating activities reduced by capital expenditures" (*Kellogg*, 2017), "Management Operating Cash Flow" (many companies).

[93]There is no standard formula. Companies often develop idiosyncratic metrics that they believe in good faith will better represent certain aspects of their performance. For example, *United Rentals* – in the business of renting heavy machinery to its customers – uses "Adjusted EBITDA," which they define as follows: *"Adjusted EBITDA represents EBITDA plus the sum of the merger related costs, restructuring charge, stock compensation expense, net, and the impact of the fair value mark-up of acquired fleet."*

[94]Pacer ETFs – www.paceretfs.com

[95]Stephen H. Penman and Nir Yehuda, "The pricing of earnings and cash flows and an affirmation of accrual accounting," *Review of Accounting Studies*, Vol. 14 (2009), pp. 453–479.

This study found that a dollar invested (Capex) returned $1.30 in enterprise value, while a dollar of "Free Cash Flow" caused a *drop* in enterprise value of "slightly more than $1.00."

The relationship of Free Cash Flow to enterprise value *is* conceptually ambiguous. High FCF may be a sign of a healthy business with resources available for strategic initiatives and/or distribution of cash to shareholders. The widespread reporting of FCF metrics by companies (88% of US public companies in 2017 reported some form of Free Cash Flow in their financial statements[96]) would indicate that it is generally seen as a positive, informational, and value-creating factor.

On the other hand, high FCF could also be the result of underinvestment, which may reflect either a lack of growth opportunities and a stagnant outlook or a diversion of resources away from sustaining the business (e.g., through excessive and expensive share buybacks).[97] Either of these explanations would entail negative implications for enterprise value. If Free Cash Flow is equated with "idle cash" that is allowed to languish (like an undistributed dividend), the evidence for the negative value of accumulated cash would support this view (see Section 3.11).

3.6.3 Do Cash Flow Metrics Improve Upon Earnings-Based Multiples?

Regarding EV/EBITDA, does the use of the Enterprise Value (which includes the firm's debt) instead of market capitalization (based solely on share price, sometimes called the Equity Value in comparisons) improve performance of the metric? Does EBITDA outperform Earnings? These are empirical questions.

Early assessments were not favorable. In a comprehensive 2002 study, EV was found to be inferior:

> Using Enterprise Value, rather than Equity Value... reduces [investment] performance...[98]

---

[96]Alexandra Scaggs, "Financial Reporting Relativism is Running Deep as Lines Become Blurred," *Financial Times*, May 5, 2018.

[97]The *Sears* scenario - Gretchen Morgenson, Michael Barbaro, and Geraldine Fabrikant, "Saving Sears Doesn't Look Easy Anymore," *The New York Times*, January 27, 2008.

[98]Jing Liu, Doron Nissim, and Jacob Thomas, "Equity Valuation Using Multiples," *Journal of Accounting Research*, Vol. 40, No. 1 (March 2002), pp. 135-172.

The same study concluded

> Cash flow measures, defined in various forms, perform poorly.

Cash flow multiples took a while to catch on. A 2004 study of 104 analysts' reports from major investment banks for large UK companies found that *none* of them used price-to-cash-flow for their valuations.[99] A similar study of 103 reports on US firms found that only 15% mentioned using a Cash Flow metric.[100]

With respect to Free Cash Flow, the 2009 study cited previously found that FCF did not "explain" changes in enterprise value (whereas GAAP accounting did):

> Price-deflated free cash flows and operating income are not highly correlated, indicating their information content (if any) is quite different. While earnings and operating income are positively correlated with contemporaneous stock price changes... free cash flows have near-zero or negative correlation with these price changes.[101]

But it may be too early to draw conclusions. FCF is an evolving, fluid concept. Experience in different market regimes is still being gathered. Recent surveys (2015) show a large swing toward EBITDA-based metrics – at least to supplement traditional P/E Multiples.[102] Whether this trend reflects improved accuracy of cash flow metrics is unclear.[103]

---

[99] Efthimios G. Demirakos, Norman C. Strong, and Martin Walker, "What Valuation Models Do Analysts Use?" *Accounting Horizons*, Vol. 18, No. 4 (2004), pp 221–240.

[100] Mark T. Bradshaw, "The Use of Target Prices to Justify Sell-Side Analysts' Stock Recommendations," *Accounting Horizons*, Vol. 16, No. 1 (March 2002), pp. 27–41.

[101] Stephen H. Penman and Nir Yehuda, "The pricing of earnings and cash flows and an affirmation of accrual accounting," *Review of Accounting Studies*, Vol. 14 (2009), pp. 453–479.

[102] Jerald Pinto, Thomas Robinson, and John Stowe, "Equity Valuation: A Survey of Professional Practice," *CFA Institute*, September 7, 2015.

[103] Note that the study also indicates high frequency of use for Price/Book and Price/Sales, both of which have been shown to be rather ineffective in recent years. This may be a sign of "box checking" by the survey participants, rather than an indication of actual pragmatic value.

CHAPTER 3 VALUATION RATIOS

In 2017, it was reported that FCF-based multiples may perform better than traditional metrics:

> Back in 2000 US listed companies spent $2 on capex for every $1 they gave to shareholders. That has fallen to $1.... Markets currently value a dollar paid out more highly than a dollar reinvested. *[Note: This contradicts the Penman and Yehuda study a decade earlier.]*
>
> Using FCF yield *[i.e., P/FCF in some form]* to pick stocks has been much more successful than other more traditional valuation metrics such as price/earnings or dividend yield.[104]

A UBS study from 2001 argues for the superiority of Free Cash Flow metrics over EBITDA, taking the telecom industry as an example. (See Figure 3-14.)

> UBS favors using EV to operating free cash flow over EV/EBITDA when looking at multiples versus growth because they feel that the relationship over time has been more significant and is more useful in predicting future performance.[105]

---

[104]Robert Buckland, "Trend for Payout Over Capex Shows No Signs of Reversing," *Financial Times*, August 30, 2017.

[105]Peter Suozzo et al., *Valuation Multiples: A Primer*, UBS Warburg Global Equity Research, November 2001, p. 22.

CHAPTER 3   VALUATION RATIOS

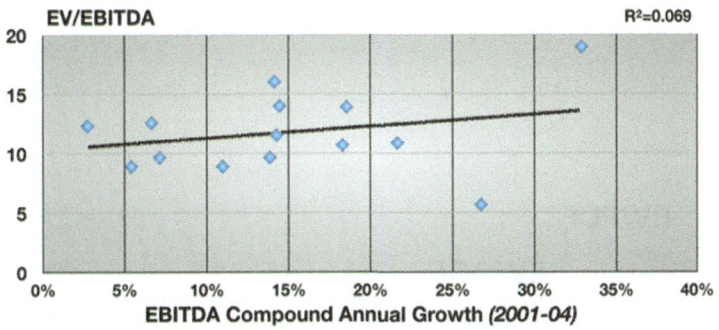

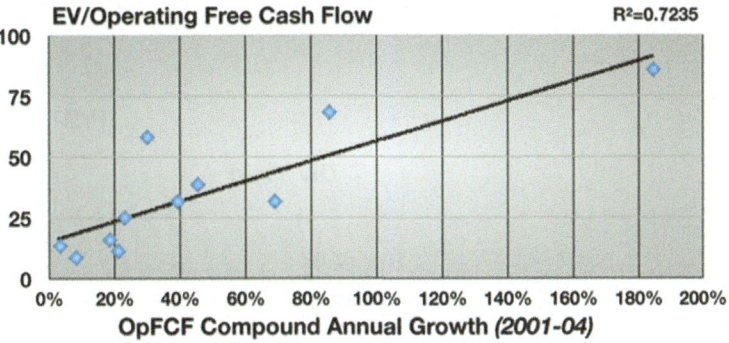

Figure 3-14. *EBITDA vs. Operating Free Cash Flow*[106]

The growth rate in cash flow "explains" 72% of the EV/FCF multiple vs. just 7% of the EV/EBITDA.

In another recent analysis, summarized in the following chart (Figure 3-15), FCF-based measures show the highest annualized returns (over a 28-year period, shown on the Y-axis) and the lowest percentage of "bad calls" (negative 12-month returns, shown on the X-axis).[107]

---

[106]Adapted from Peter Suozzo et al., *Valuation Multiples: A Primer*, UBS Warburg Global Equity Research, November 2001, p. 22.

[107]Pacer ETFs – www.paceretfs.com – *The Pacer Perspective*, January 2017.

CHAPTER 3   VALUATION RATIOS

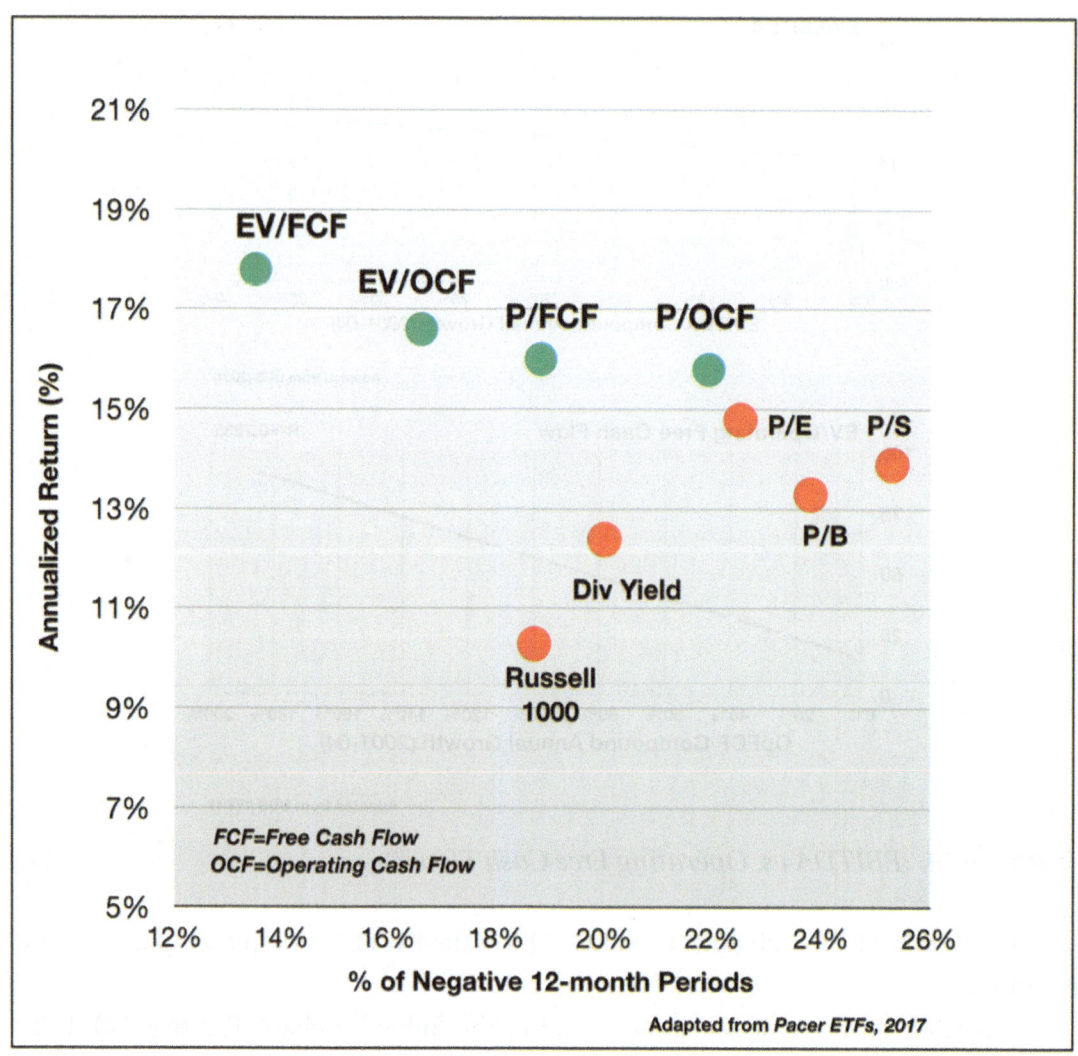

Figure 3-15. *Comparison of Various Multiples with respect to Return and Frequency of 12-Month Negative Outcomes*[108]

In sum, the Free Cash Flow approach to valuation, combining some version of FCF with Price or Enterprise Value in a new Multiple, seems promising. Standardized definitions will help clarify this prospect.

---

[108] Adapted from Pacer ETFs – www.paceretfs.com – *The Pacer Perspective*, January 2017.

3.7 Price-to-Book

Price/Book is frequently used as a "value" screen – that is, as a way to identify undervalued stocks. It is the basis of the original definition in the academic literature of the so-called "Value Factor" – one of the first significant adjustments to the strict Efficient Market Hypothesis:[109]

$$\frac{price\,/\,share}{book\,value\,/\,share}$$

However, the reliance on Book Value to construct this metric is problematic. Its proponents see it as a conservative choice, but it is "conservative" mainly because accounting rules tie balance sheet values to historical cost – which is usually out of date, by design.[110] More serious is the fact that Book Value ignores major classes of business assets that are becoming more important as the economy evolves – assets like technology, brand, and monetizable data. It is not surprising therefore that P/B today is typically found to be among the least successful metrics in tracking market returns, the least "value-relevant." One study concludes "it would appear to be a myth that price/book carries a special meaning."[111]

This was not always the case. Joseph Mezrich of *Nomura Securities* has analyzed the evolution of the P/B signal over the past several decades. In the mid-1980s, Price-to-Book was in fact the number one "driver" of market returns out of 21 value metrics studied (including P/E Trailing and Forward, EV/EBITDA, the PEG ratio, Dividend Yield, etc.). But by 2010, Price-to-Book was dead last.[112] In other words, P/B shifted from being a strong BUY signal to become, if anything, a strong SELL signal. (See Figure 3-16.) A 2015 article, citing Mezrich, quantified the significance of this effect:

---

[109]Eugene Fama and Kenneth French, "The Cross-Section of Expected Stock Returns," *The Journal of Finance*, Vol. 47, No. 2 (June 1992), pp. 427–465.

[110]Asset values only change when a major event requires a "write-down" (never a "write-up") – which is almost always late in coming.

[111]Stanley Block, "Methods of Valuation: Myths vs Reality," *The Journal of Investing* (Winter 2010), pp. 7–14.

[112]Joseph Mezrich, "Quantitative Strategy: Wisdom of crowds/Madness of crowds," *Nomura Research*, April 30, 2012.

CHAPTER 3   VALUATION RATIOS

Stocks that were cheap based on book value [i.e those with a low P/B] began to track a company's chance of default, while cheap stocks based on earnings [low P/E] became closely linked with profitability... So far this year [2015] while the cheapest stocks based on book value have lagged behind the most expensive ones by 15 percentage points, the cheapest on earnings have outperformed the most expensive by 13.6 points.[113]

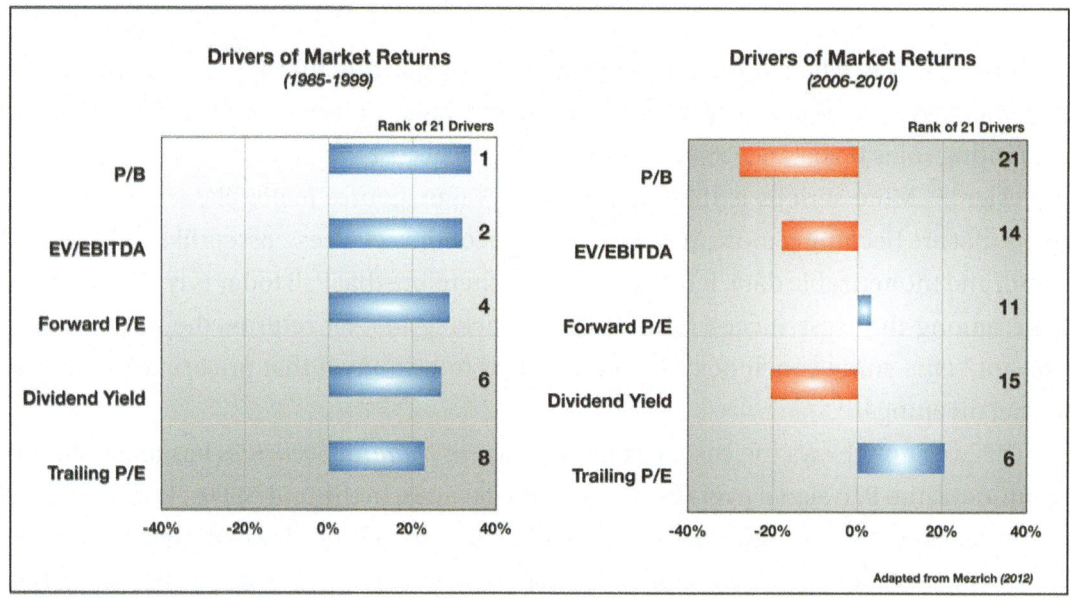

Figure 3-16. Comparison of Various Metrics as Drivers of Returns[114]

This loss of value relevance corresponds with the divergence of Book Value and Market Value. In the 1980s, the two metrics were in sync – P/B readings were approximately 1:1 for the market as a whole. But by the turn of the century, Market Value had jumped to three and four times the level of Book Value.

---

[113]Ben Levisohn, "Have We Misplaced Value? *Barron's*," December 7, 2015.
[114]Adapted from Joseph Mezrich, "Quantitative Strategy: Wisdom of crowds/Madness of crowds," *Nomura Research*, April 30, 2012.

Another recent study argues that the main driver of Book Value is "retained earnings" – that is, the "accumulated total earnings the firm generated over its history, less accumulated dividend distributions."[115] But even this modified interpretation of P/B, construed as Price/Retained Earnings, has declined as a proportion of the total Book Value in recent decades. This may account for the diminished effectiveness of Price/Book metric as a value screen.[116]

Some academics still argue that "price/book is still the best measure of value."[117] Such views may reflect a degree of intellectual inertia. The evidence is clear that P/B has lost much of its value relevance. As early as 1980, Fischer Black observed

> The variability of book value to price ratios exceeds the variability of earnings to price ratios, both across the universe of stocks and over time, suggesting that the earning figure is a better measure of value than the book value figure.[118]

In his 2018 letter to his *Berkshire Hathaway* shareholders, even Warren Buffett – a long-time advocate of conservative accounting – reached the conclusion that "book-value has become increasingly out of touch with economic reality."[119]

---

[115] Ray Ball, Joseph Gerakos, Juhanio Linnainmaa, and Valeri Nikolaev, "Earnings, retained earnings, and book-to-market in the cross section of expected returns," Working Paper, September 5, 2018 [Forthcoming in the *Journal of Financial Economics*].

[116] Mark Hulbert, "'Value' Stocks Aren't What They Used to Be," *The Wall Street Journal*, September 10, 2018. Over the last decade, Value stocks derived by screening for low P/B have underperformed in the market, reversing a long-term pattern of outperformance.

[117] Reshma Kapadia, "Are Value Stocks About to Grow?" *Barron's*, April 30, 2018.

[118] Fischer Black, "The Magic in Earnings: Economic Earnings versus Accounting Earnings," *Financial Analysts Journal* (November/December 1980), pp. 19–24.

[119] Warren Buffett's 2018 Annual *Berkshire Hathaway* Shareholder Letter.

CHAPTER 3 VALUATION RATIOS

3.8 Tobin's Q

This metric is favored by some academic economists. In spirit, it proposes to correct the problem of stale asset values associated with the accounting entries that comprise Book Value, by inserting in the denominator the "replacement or reproduction cost: the price *in the market [emphasis added]* for newly produced commodities."[120] In other words, it is a "Mark-to-Market" approach: it aims to use current market prices, rather than historical cost, to value assets on the balance sheet. It is named after its chief popularizer, the economist James Tobin:

$$\frac{price\ /\ share}{replacement\ cost\ /\ share}$$

If it were practical to calculate accurate replacement values for all of the company's productive assets (and it is not), Tobin's Q might at least mitigate one of the problems with Price/Book (the stale balance sheet figures). But it does not address the problem of incompleteness – that is, the failure to recognize key franchise assets such as brand or technology – and indeed the trend for this metric shows the same pattern as that of Book Value: a growing divergence from Market Value, due to the shift in the economy to "intangible" assets.[121] (See Figure 3-17.)

---

[120]James Tobin and William C. Brainard, 1976. "Asset Markets and the Cost of Capital," *Cowles Foundation Discussion Papers 427*, Cowles Foundation for Research in Economics, Yale University.

[121]Data from FRED (Federal Reserve Economic Data), the *Federal Reserve Bank of St. Louis*, 2019. There are a number of ways in which this metric is calculated, resulting in quite different values. However, the general trend highlighted here is evident in all the versions I have seen.

CHAPTER 3 VALUATION RATIOS

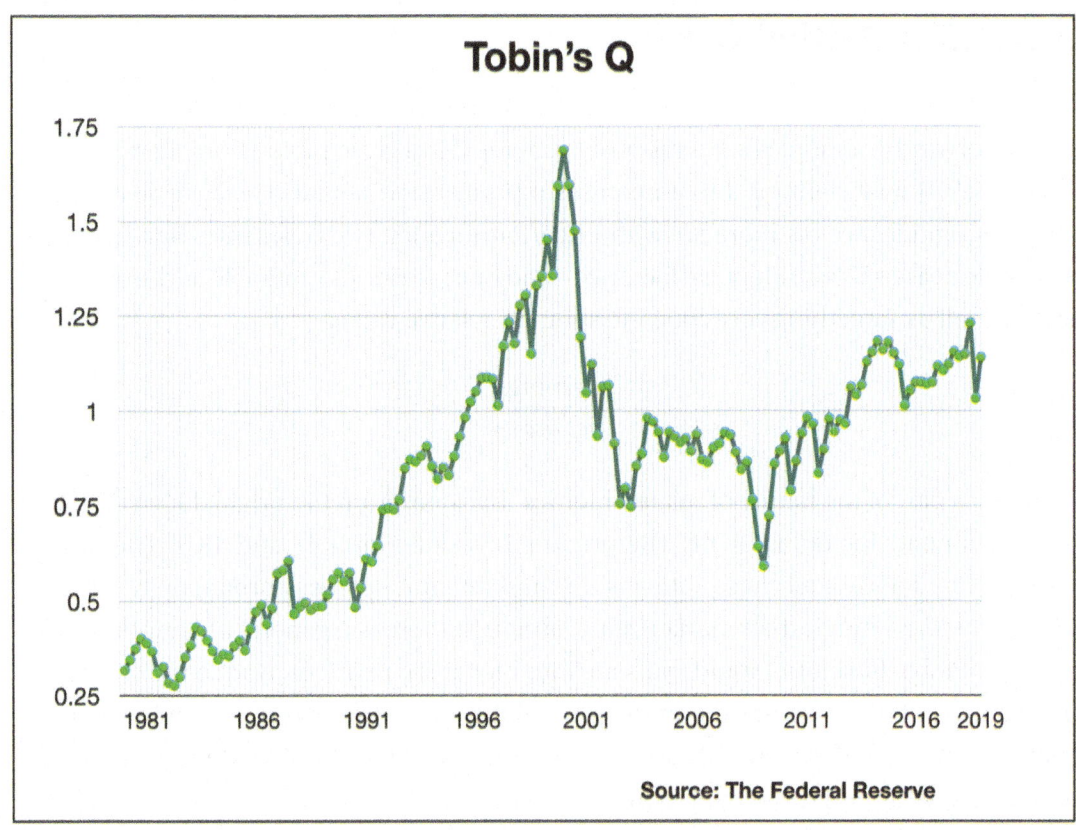

Figure 3-17. *Tobin's Q – the Trend*[122]

Tobin's *Q* is rarely used by practitioners. It does not appear among the 22 value-relevant metrics cited earlier by Mezrich. It is not clear that it can be put to practical use. It does not appear even to succeed in performing its main theoretical function, to predict capital investment trends. One recent and thorough study of corporate investment trends points to "the empirical failure of *q* in explaining aggregate investment."[123]

---

[122]Data from the *Federal Reserve*.
[123]Gustavo Grullon, John Hund, and James P. Weston, "Concentrating on q and Cash Flow," *Journal of Financial Intermediation*, Vol. 33 (2018), pp. 1–15.

CHAPTER 3   VALUATION RATIOS

3.9 Return-on-Assets

ROA is not a market metric; hence, there is no per-share calculation. It illuminates a straightforward question: What is the profit generated in a given period from the company's asset base? How efficiently is the company using its invested capital? There are no mysteries about its significance (as there are with Price/Earnings). If two businesses have the same ensemble of assets – say, identical factories – and one is twice as profitable as the other, this ought to tell us something very concrete about its relative value:

$$\frac{earnings}{net\ assets}$$

ROA is part of the family of related metrics that stem from the original idea of Return on Investment, including ROIC (Return on Invested Capital) and ROE (Return on Equity). The focus of all these ratios is on fundamental business productivity – that is, its *profitability* – rather than market value, although there is a general assumption that a more profitable business should translate into higher share prices. And to the extent that the value of a business is based on the profitability of its operations, as a going concern (rather than the static value of its assets), measures like ROA should in theory be a useful tool for assessing enterprise valuation.

Indeed, in Mezrich's analysis, Return on Equity (ROE, a close cousin of ROA) moved up to the number one position among his selection of 22 value metrics after the year 2000.

I have charted the interrelationships of several market valuation metrics for a small and rather diverse sample of prominent US public companies.[124] Interestingly, P/E is essentially unrelated to profitability metrics such as Gross Margin, Operating Margin, and Net Margin. (See Figure 3-18.) P/B and P/S fare no better.

---

[124]Stock symbols: consumer sector – PEP, K, CFB, GIS; automotive sector – F, GM, TM; semiconductors – INTC, NVDA, QCOM; and tech giants – MSFT, AAPL, GOOG, FB, AMZN. Admittedly a nonscientific sample, but perhaps enough diversity to expose the relationships of interest.

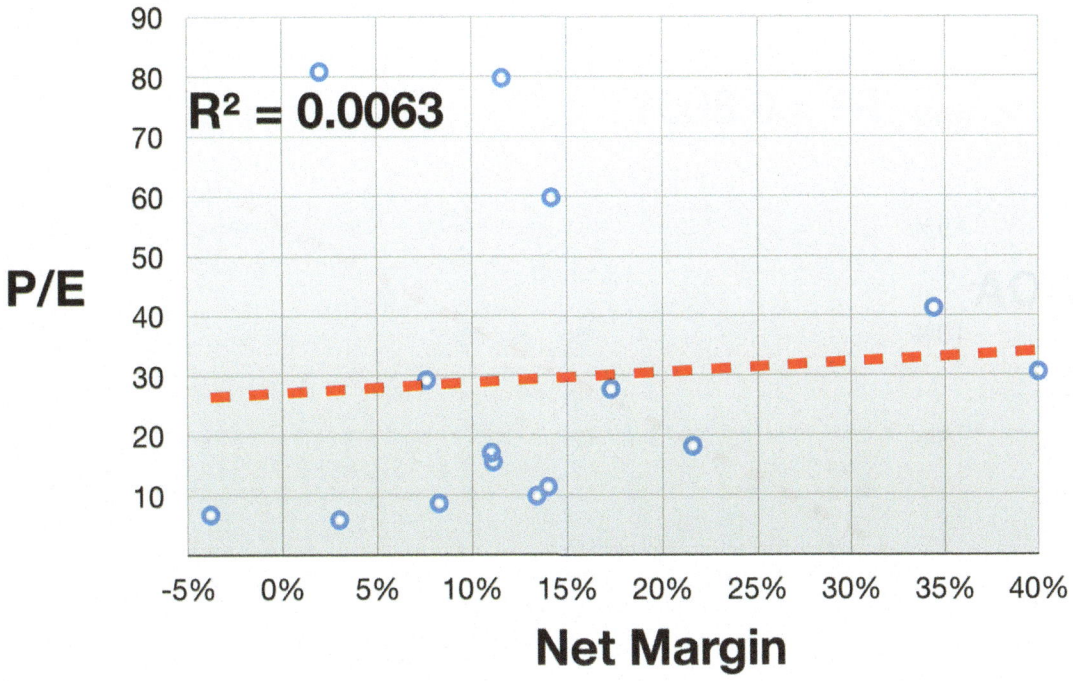

Figure 3-18. Price-to-Earnings Ratio and Profitability

On the other hand, ROA is strongly predictive for profitability. (See Figure 3-19.)

CHAPTER 3   VALUATION RATIOS

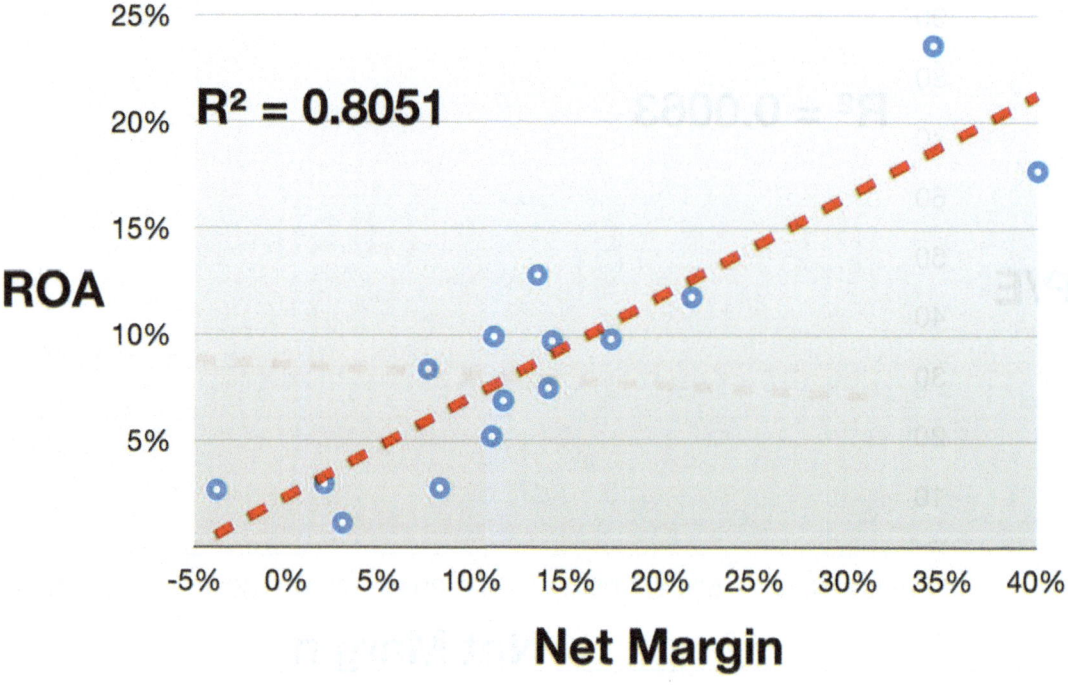

Figure 3-19. Return-on-Assets Ratio and Profitability

It is odd that such an accurate indicator of fundamental business success would not correlate with P/E, but it points to something quite interesting: if success in business is about profitability, then it would seem that *the P/E is not really a signal of (current) business success.*

So, what *is* P/E signaling? (This question is the starting point for the next chapter.)

Before trying to answer that question, however, there are two more "adjusted" forms of the Multiple which have been advanced in recent years as improvements upon the basic P/E: $CAPE_1$ and $CAPE_2$.

3.10 Adjustments to the Denominator: Cyclically Adjusted P/E ($CAPE_1$)

Stock prices are volatile. Earnings are volatile. The P/E Multiple is doubly afflicted, with volatility in both the numerator and the denominator. Yet we presume that the underlying intrinsic value of the firm is not so unstable, that it changes more slowly and with fewer discontinuities. So how can we compensate for the jumpiness in the metric?

An obvious answer is to average the signal over a longer time period. Volatility is a time-domain phenomenon which affects data sets in many branches of science. Longer observation windows can help smooth out the noise and sometimes clarify the underlying signal. Early investment theorists recognized this and argued pragmatically for metrics calculated over a multi-year period.[125]

Academics eventually caught up to the problem. In the 1980s, economist Robert Shiller studied the problem of "excess" volatility in stock prices and found that indeed "measures of stock price volatility over the past century appear to be too high – five to thirteen times too high – to be attributed to new information about dividends." This was a blow to the Dividend Discount theory of share prices and an early crack in the facade of the Efficient Market Hypothesis.[126] (We will we have more to say about this paper in the Appendix on problems with the DCF model.) In a subsequent article, the idea of "a long moving average" of earnings was tentatively introduced.[127] Later Shiller applied the averaging concept to the P/E Multiple, settling on a 10-year time-averaging window, with an inflation adjustment – and the Cyclically Adjusted P/E, or CAPE, was born. The branding nomenclature – "cyclically adjusted" – referred to the claim that the 10-year window was designed to even out the effects of the normal business cycle (expansion/ recession/recovery).

CAPE has caught the fancy of the media in recent years. It has tended to run "hot" in the last decade – generating what can look like alarming signals that the market is overpriced. (CAPE is often applied to the entire market.) It serves as a prompt for cautionary analyses of market trends.

CAPE has also seemed particularly appealing as a way to adjust for the extreme fluctuations in the market surrounding the 2008 financial crisis:

---

[125]In their 1934 classic security analysis, Benjamin Graham and David Dodd argued for adopting long-term horizons, both forward and backward, generally in analyzing a company's earning power. They suggested that seven to ten years of earnings (historical or projected) should be the assumed timescale for valuation purposes.

[126]Robert J. Shiller, "Do Stock Prices Move Too Much to be Justified by Subsequent Changes in Dividends?" *The American Economic Review*, Vol. 71, No. 3 (June 1981), pp. 421–436.

[127]John Y. Campbell and Robert J. Shiller, "Stock Prices, Earnings, and Expected Dividends," *The Journal of Finance*, Vol. 43, No. 3 (July 1988), pp. 661–676.

Its advantage is that it corrects for extreme good times and bad times by valuing share prices based on 10 years of earnings, rather than one year. That smooths out periods just like prior to the housing bust, when unusually strong earnings made stocks look reasonably priced, and post-recession recoveries, when weak earnings make stocks look expensive.[128]

What Is CAPE, and What Is It Not?

CAPE is defined as the ratio between the current market price and the 10-year moving average of earnings:

$$\frac{price \: / \: share}{10 \: year \: moving \: average \: of \: real \: earnings \: / \: share}$$

The denominator is inflation-adjusted (that is what the term "real earnings" signifies). The principle of averaging is used to smooth out (1) short-term volatility in a company's earnings (if applied at the firm level) or (2) the ups and downs of the business cycle (if applied to the entire market).

We should be clear about what is on offer here: CAPE is *not* a product of theory; it is a pragmatic adjustment of the classic (and still mysterious) market metric, the P/E Multiple. Like the PE1 – as the standard P/E is labeled in many comparisons with CAPE, called the PE10 – the CAPE is understood as a rule-of-thumb solution to the problem of valuation. PE10 may (or may not) perform better than PE1. But it is based on a series of still largely under-researched questions, including the following:

- Why is 10 years selected as the averaging window? Why not 5 years or 15 years? What is the effect on the performance of CAPE as a function of the length of the window? How much better is PE10 than PE5, or PE1 for that matter?

---

[128] Justin Lahart, "This Key Metric Rings a False Alarm," *The Wall Street Journal*, October 6, 2016.

- The answer sometimes offered is that 10 years captures the full "business cycle"[129] – do we know that this is the case? Is 10 years the best window on the business cycle?[130]

- Does the 10-year window sometimes capture too many business cycles, as some critics contend?

- If applied to individual firms or sectors, which vary considerably in their sensitivity to the business cycle, how does the metric adjust for this?

- Does the "business cycle" have different meanings for different companies or sectors? (Think of the effect of crude oil prices on the energy sector, the yield curve on the banking sector or the seasonality characteristic of retail.)

An underlying question here is whether the so-called business cycle manifests sufficient regularity to clearly define the length of the appropriate averaging period. And why *should* we be trying to average out the business cycle in the first place? (We'll come back to that question in the following.)

More questions:

- Does the "normal level" of CAPE shift over time? [There is evidence that it has – see in the following.] If so, what sort of calibration is required?

- Does the significance of CAPE (i.e., the direction and strength of its predictive force) undergo change over time, similar to what happened with Price-to-Book over the last three decades (as described earlier)?

---

[129] Oliver Bunn, Arne Staal, Ji Zhuang, Anthony Lazanas, Cenk Ural, and Robert Shiller, "Escaping from Overvalued Sectors: Sector Selection Based on the Cyclically Adjusted Price-Earnings (CAPE) Ratio," *The Journal of Portfolio Management* (Fall 2014), pp. 16–32.

[130] Lately, the regularity of the "business cycle" has come into question. *"There are real indications that the economy is less beholden to traditional cycles than it used to be... Business cycles are themselves contained within longer ones, which economists call 'financial cycles.' .... Economists have long struggled to separate the two types of cycles."* (Jon Sindreu, "Recession Worry is Overblown for Now," *The Wall Street Journal*, June 8, 2019).

- Unlike P/E which is based on two variables (Price and Earnings), CAPE is based on three – it includes Inflation. Is it appropriate to treat inflation correction as simply an adjustment, or is there a more fundamental interaction effect between inflation and valuation?

- How sensitive is CAPE to various changes in the *definitions* of its complex components, such as Earnings or Inflation?

- How sensitive is CAPE to changing market regimes, for example, the long decline in bond interest rates, amplified by central bank monetary policies (e.g., quantitative easing)? What effect would this have on the levels and predictive power of CAPE?

- And, fundamentally, does CAPE actually add value to the analysis? Does it increase predictive power compared to PE1?

3.10.1 Critics and Critiques
3.10.1.1 Accounting Changes

A major problem with CAPE is similar to the problem with PE1: the changing accounting rules that affect the definition of Earnings. We will consider this question more broadly in Chapter 6, but with respect to CAPE, several examples stand out in the published commentaries:

- FASB 142: A 2001 change in the treatment of so-called goodwill and other intangible assets

- FASB 123R: A 2004 revision of the rules for expensing of stock options issued to employees as compensation

- Mark-to-Market accounting generally, applied extensively following the 2008 financial crisis

The official statement for FASB 142 warned explicitly that "there may be more volatility in reported income than under previous standards."[131] The magnitude of this change has been estimated at over $300 Bn. The question of expensing employee options (FASB 123) generated even more controversy and continues to do so.[132] And Mark-to-Market accounting can force write-downs of impaired assets held on companies' books when their market value has demonstrably declined, but does not permit "write-ups" unless the assets are sold.[133]

In terms of the accuracy of the metric, all of these accounting changes will affect CAPE when they fall inside the 10-year averaging window. CAPE values on either side of such an accounting change will be inconsistent with each other.[134]

3.10.1.2 Dominance of Large Losses by a Few Firms

The CAPE captures and magnifies disaster, by its nature. In 2008, several financial firms experienced huge paper losses – Mark-to-Market write-downs of impaired assets – which swamped the overall S&P index. Jeremy Siegel has called this the "aggregation bias" of the S&P 500 earnings:

> Before 2008, there was never a loss in *any* quarter in the historical reported earnings data that Shiller used, including the Great Depression of the 1930s. But GAAP earnings in the fourth quarter of 2008 experienced a loss of $23.25 Bn, caused primarily by the huge write-downs of two financial firms – *AIG* and *Citigroup* – and *Bank of America*, which together lost in excess of $80 Bn. None of these losses would have been recorded in GAAP earnings before FAS Nos. 115, 142, and 144 were issued....

---

[131] *Statement of Financial Accounting Standards No. 142: Goodwill and Other Intangible Assets*, Financial Accounting Standards Board, June 2001, p. 5.

[132] Mary E. Barth, Ian D. Gow, and Daniel J. Taylor, "Why do pro forma and Street earnings not reflect changes in GAAP? Evidence from SFAS 123R," *Review of Accounting Studies*, Vol. 17 (2012), pp. 526–562.

[133] Jeremy Siegel, "Don't Put Faith in Cape Crusaders," *Financial Times*, August 19, 2013.

[134] Laurence Siegel, "CAPE Crusaders: The Shiller-Siegel Shootout at the Q Group Corral," *Advisor Perspectives*, February 18, 2014. Available at www.advisorperspectives.com/articles/2014/02/18/cape-crusaders-the-shiller-siegel-shootout-at-the-q-group-corral

> *AIG* alone had a weight of only under 0.2% in the S&P 500 at the time, yet its $63 billion loss more than wiped out the aggregate profits of the 30 most profitable companies in the S&P 500 in Q4 2008 – companies whose market values composed almost half the index. This dramatic decline in reported earnings of the S&P 500 is a major reason why the CAPE ratio has remained so far above its mean since the financial crisis.

All in all, mandated write-downs by S&P 500 companies in 2008 reached over $300 Bn – enough by one estimate "to bump up the CAPE by a full point."[135] And once captured, these losses are baked into CAPE for the following 10 years, depressing average earnings and pushing the CAPE value higher.

> Any stock return forecast issued before 2018 will include the extraordinarily low earnings of 2008–2009 and may be biased downward.[136]

2008 was a bad year for investors, certainly. But is it still relevant to valuation assessments five or ten years later?

3.10.2 CAPE Performance

CAPE has gained public attention in recent years as a sort of flashing red light, warning of a severely overvalued stock market.[137] (See Figure 3-20.)

---

[135] Laurence Siegel, "CAPE Crusaders: The Shiller-Siegel Shootout at the Q Group Corral," *Advisor Perspectives*, February 18, 2014. Available at www.advisorperspectives.com/articles/2014/02/18/cape-crusaders-the-shiller-siegel-shootout-at-the-q-group-corral

[136] Jeremy Siegel, "The Shiller CAPE Ratio: A New Look," *Financial Analysts Journal*, Vol. 72, No. 3 (2016), pp. 41–50.

[137] Alexandra Scaggs, "Nobelist's Valuation Measure Draws Questions," *The Wall Street Journal*, November 22, 2013.

CHAPTER 3   VALUATION RATIOS

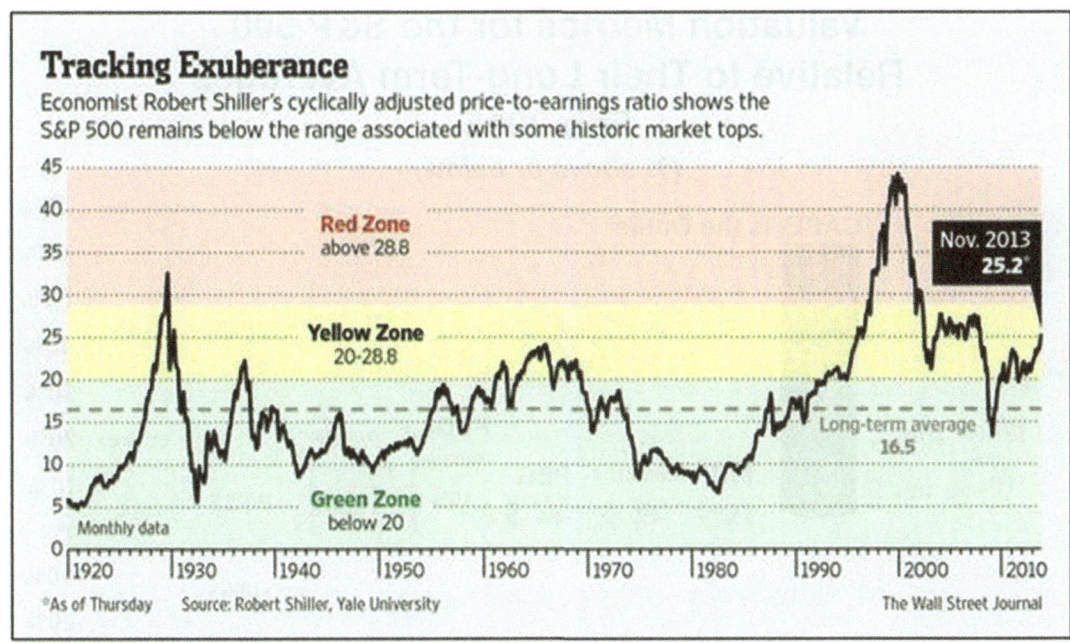

Figure 3-20. *CAPE (Cyclically Adjusted Price/Earnings) Ratio*[138]

The problem has been that the light is always flashing, at least since the CAPE averaging process swallowed the 2001 dot-com crash and later the 2008 financial crisis. Averaged in, these disasters dragged down the 10-year moving average of earnings in the denominator and elevated the CAPE ratio. CAPE has consistently forecast a bearish future – but the market has gone the other way, tripling and more in the ten years following the start of the recovery in 2009. In a 2013 study by *Merrill Lynch*, CAPE was the only one of 15 market valuation metrics running above its long-term average. Updated in 2015, CAPE was still the outlier.[139] (See Figure 3-21.)

---

[138]Alexandra Scaggs, "Nobelist's Valuation Measure Draws Questions," *The Wall Street Journal*, November 22, 2013. Reproduced by permission from *The Wall Street Journal*.

[139]Savita Subramanian et al, "What do oil and high beta stocks have in common?" *Equity and Quant Strategy Report, Bank of America/Merrill Lynch*, April 15, 2015.

CHAPTER 3   VALUATION RATIOS

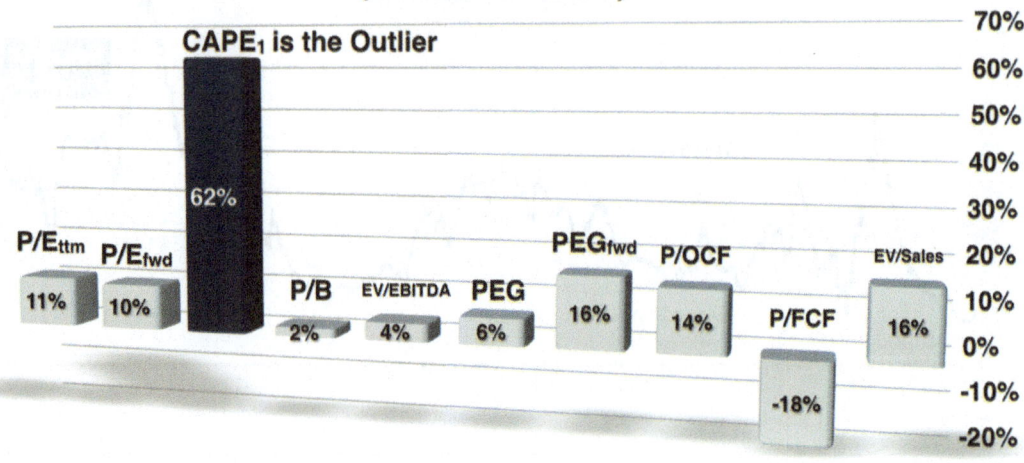

Source: Subramanian et al, 2015

Figure 3-21. Valuation Metrics for the S&P 500 Relative to Their Long-Term Averages, February 2015 (% Above or Below)

The market was up 40% in the following three years; there was no overvaluation. CAPE was flashing the wrong signal.

Indeed, it has become clear that CAPE is – in the words of even one of its ardent defenders – "notoriously unreliable in picking market peaks and troughs."[140] More specifically, it does not meet the criterion that interests most market professionals: reasonably accurate, monetizable predictions for the performance of the market over the reasonably near term. "[CAPE] completely failed to predict the bull market of 2009-2014 *[which has continued on through the date of this writing, 2019]*."[141]

---

[140] Rob Arnott, Vitaki Klesnik, and Jim Masturzo, "CAPE Fear: Why CAPE Naysayers Are Wrong," *Research Affiliates*, January 2018.

[141] Laurence Siegel, "CAPE Crusaders: The Shiller-Siegel Shootout at the Q Group Corral," *Advisor Perspectives*, February 18, 2014. Available at www.advisorperspectives.com/articles/2014/02/18/cape-crusaders-the-shiller-siegel-shootout-at-the-q-group-corral

CHAPTER 3   VALUATION RATIOS

In terms of shedding light on *past* performance of the stock market, statistical analyses inform us that "CAPE has explained about one-third of the variation in actual subsequent 10-year stock returns."[142] This is considered impressive in academic circles, because stock returns are devilishly difficult to "explain" (statistically speaking). Indeed, to give due credit, in *Vanguard's* analysis, PE10 comes out on top, "explaining" 43% of the variation in stock prices from 1926 to 2011, edging out the standard PE1, which explains 38%.

Yet as the authors comment:

> We do not find a clear 'winner' or 'optimal' smoothing mechanism for earnings.... The difference in R^2 statistics ranges from 0.38 to 0.43. Our interpretation is that the difference of 0.05 is not a wide enough margin to conclusively reject one model [PE1] in favor of the other [PE10].[143]

To state the question clearly: Does CAPE actually improve very much upon the traditional P/E Multiple?

The answer seems to be: not really (Figure 3-22).

---

[142]Ibid.

[143]Joseph Davis, Roger Aliaga-Díaz, and Charles Thomas, "Forecasting Stock Returns: What Signals Matter, and What Do They Say Now?" *Vanguard Research*, October 2012. Interestingly (given how infrequently these studies confirm one another), Ang and Zhang found exactly the same R2 of 38% for Earnings Growth as an explanatory variable for PEttm for the period from 1953 to 2009 (Andrew Ang and Xiaoyan Zhang, "Price-Earnings Ratios: Growth and Discount Rates," *The Research Foundation of the CFA Institute* (2011), pp. 130–142).

CHAPTER 3   VALUATION RATIOS

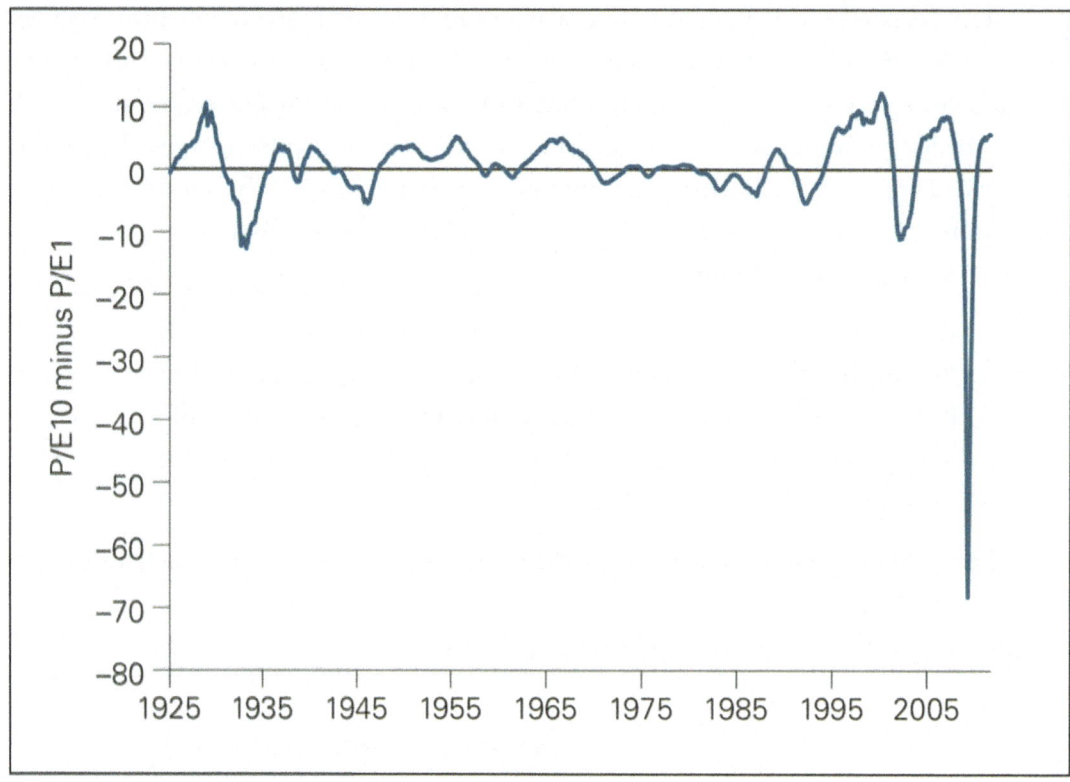

Figure 3-22. *The Traditional P/E vs. CAPE*[144]

Except briefly during the 2008 crisis (which probably accounts for most of the R^2 discrepancy), since 1925 there has been very little in the way of a persistent, tradeable difference in the *Vanguard* results between the traditional 1-year Trailing P/E and a 10-year smoothed P/E.

And further, if the 1-year and 10-year P/E's are so similar, what is the real impact of the length of the averaging window? That doesn't seem to matter much either (Figure 3-23).

---

[144]Joseph Davis, Roger Aliaga-Díaz, and Charles Thomas, "Forecasting Stock Returns: What Signals Matter, and What Do They Say Now?" *Vanguard Research*, October 2012. Reproduced by permission from *Vanguard Research*.

CHAPTER 3   VALUATION RATIOS

Figure 3-23. *The Effect of the Averaging Window on CAPE Forecasting Accuracy*[145]

There is a slight bump here around the 10-year mark, but is it significant?

It is worth repeating that the narrative embedded in the P/E metrics (and indeed in *all* market metrics) – including both the Trailing 1-year and the CAPE – is *contrarian*: companies with low Multiples, which signal generally negative market sentiment and often serious business challenges (the "Dogs"), outperform the more successful and popular high P/E companies (the "Stars"). Here then is the down-sloping regression analysis performed by the *Vanguard* study (Figure 3-24).

---

[145] Joseph Davis, Roger Aliaga-Díaz, and Charles Thomas, "Forecasting Stock Returns: What Signals Matter, and What Do They Say Now?" *Vanguard Research*, October 2012. Reproduced by permission from *Vanguard Research*.

CHAPTER 3 VALUATION RATIOS

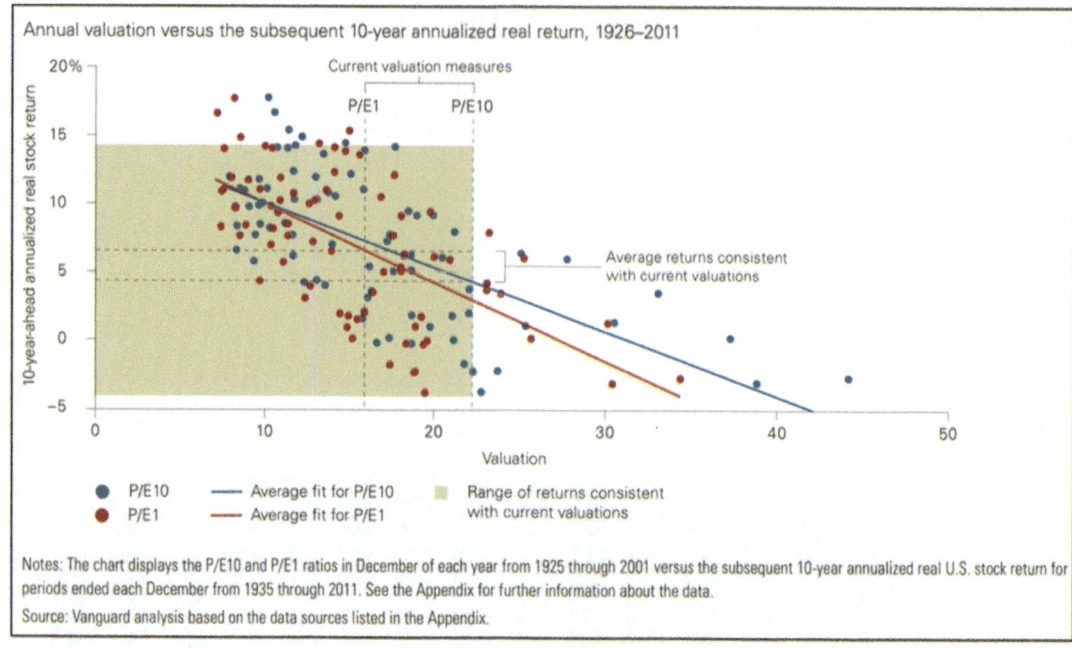

Figure 3-24. Annual Valuation vs. the Subsequent 10-Year Annualized Return, P/E vs. CAPE[146]

Note the rather slight difference between the 1-year and the 10-year versions. It does not appear that smoothing has much effect on the nature of the relationship.

In another recent study, CAPE was compared to a more classical model based on dividend yield and earnings growth. CAPE showed significant errors in forecasting actual returns, and it underperformed over most of the last 40 years (Figure 3-25):

> The difference between actual and predicted returns in each decade, beginning in 1920, shows that CAPE has routinely missed the market return by more than 3% annually over a 10-year horizon. For example, the 1970s value of −3.1% indicates that for predictions of return using CAPE made in the 1970s, the actual market return over the next 10 years was 3.1% lower than predicted by CAPE alone,

---

[146]Joseph Davis, Roger Aliaga-Díaz, and Charles Thomas, "Forecasting Stock Returns: What Signals Matter, and What Do They Say Now?" *Vanguard Research*, October 2012. Reproduced by permission from *Vanguard Research*.

In Yield-plus-Growth, Yield is defined as the dividend yield in each period, and Growth is the long-term growth rate, which is trend earnings per share growth up to the start of the period. When we add the Yield-plus-Growth model to our decade-by-decade CAPE results, we find that CAPE initially had a great run, winning the five consecutive decades beginning in the 1920s, but lost three of the last four decades: 1970s, 1990s, and 2000s.[147]

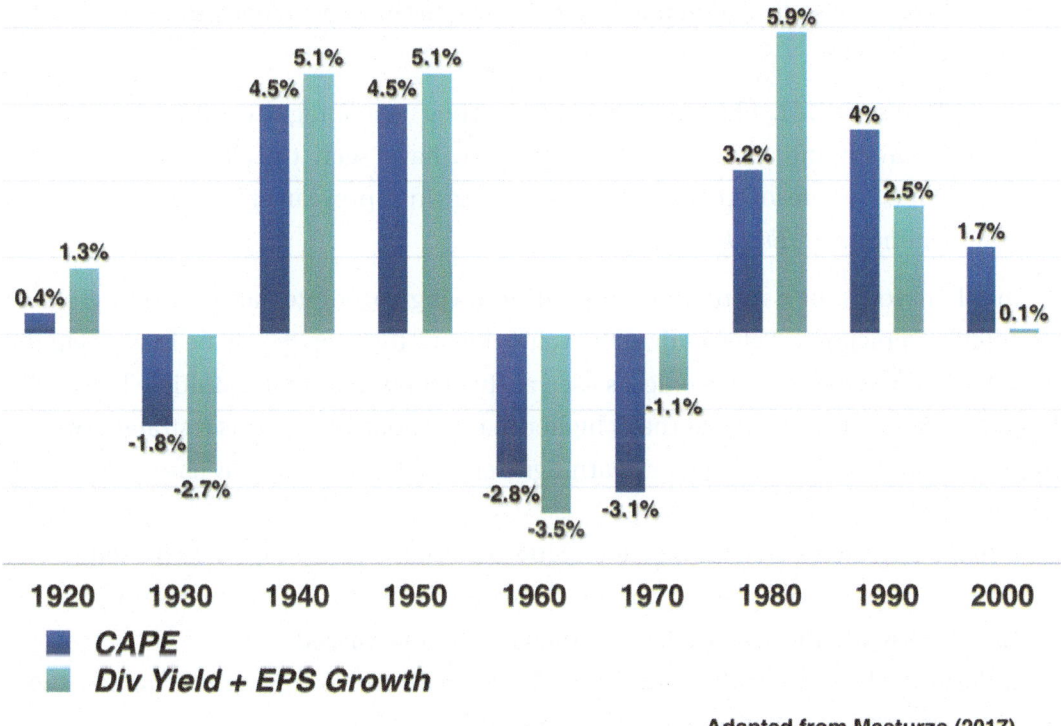

Figure 3-25. *CAPE Forecasting Error*[148]

---

[147]Jim Masturzo, "CAPE Fatigue," *Research Affiliates White Paper*, June 2017.
[148]Jim Masturzo, "CAPE Fatigue," *Research Affiliates White Paper*, June 2017.

Is the CAPE actually biased? Some would say it is and perhaps even embrace the bias:

> The CAPE provides a high estimate of the "true" or underlying PE that it is trying to measure. This is because real earnings tend to grow over time, so that the true PE is probably somewhere between the CAPE, which reflects five-year-old earnings numbers on average, and the current year's PE.
>
> So the expected return as measured by the CAPE... *is a low estimate of the true expected return.* The amount by which this estimate is low depends on how fast earnings have been growing; if fast, then very low; if not so fast, then not so low; if earnings have been declining, then high.
>
> That's OK. I like low estimates. They encourage cautious behavior and modest expectations. We have seen the damage done, to pension plans and individual savings programs, by high estimates.[149] *[Emphasis added]*

In other words, in a rising trend (as with growing corporate earnings or a growing economy), averaging will always drag the value down – the average will be lower than the last value in the series. If that average is used as the denominator for a Multiple like CAPE, that ratio will be pushed up – perhaps higher than it should be. This is a straightforward property of averages applied to rising earnings trends. It has been largely ignored by CAPE proponents.

Is the CAPE stable? That is, does it tend toward a "normal" average over the long term, so that we can say with reasonable confidence when it is "high" and when it is not? Can we use CAPE to say whether the market is "expensive" or overpriced?

Unfortunately, even aside from the problems with the averaging mechanics, there appears to be a structural instability in this metric:

---

[149] Laurence Siegel, "CAPMing the CAPE" available at https://larrysiegeldotorg.files.wordpress.com/2016/09/siegel_capming-the-cape_2016_09_08.pdf

From 1926 to 1990, the average CAPE reading was 14.7X. However, from 1990 to the present [2015] the average reading has been 25.6X, 74% higher. This would suggest that stocks have been overvalued for 25+ years. However this isn't borne out by performance data. From 1926 though 1990, then S&P 500 posted an annualized return of 10%. From the beginning of 1991 through November 2015, the Index posted an identical return of 10% despite trading at elevated CAPE levels throughout the period.[150]

Since 1997, the average for the CAPE is 27.[151] (See Figure 3-26.) There are several possible explanations. Certainly there has been a long-term trend to tighten the definition of GAAP earnings, reducing the denominator and boosting the CAPE. This is a structural change, and we shouldn't expect a reversion to "normal" levels seen in decades long past.

---

[150]"Beware the CAPE Crusaders," *Renaissance Investment Management*, December 2015. Available at www.reninv.com/large-cap-growth/

[151]Liam Pleven, "Stocks: Are They Too High?" *The Wall Street Journal*, May 16, 2015.

CHAPTER 3   VALUATION RATIOS

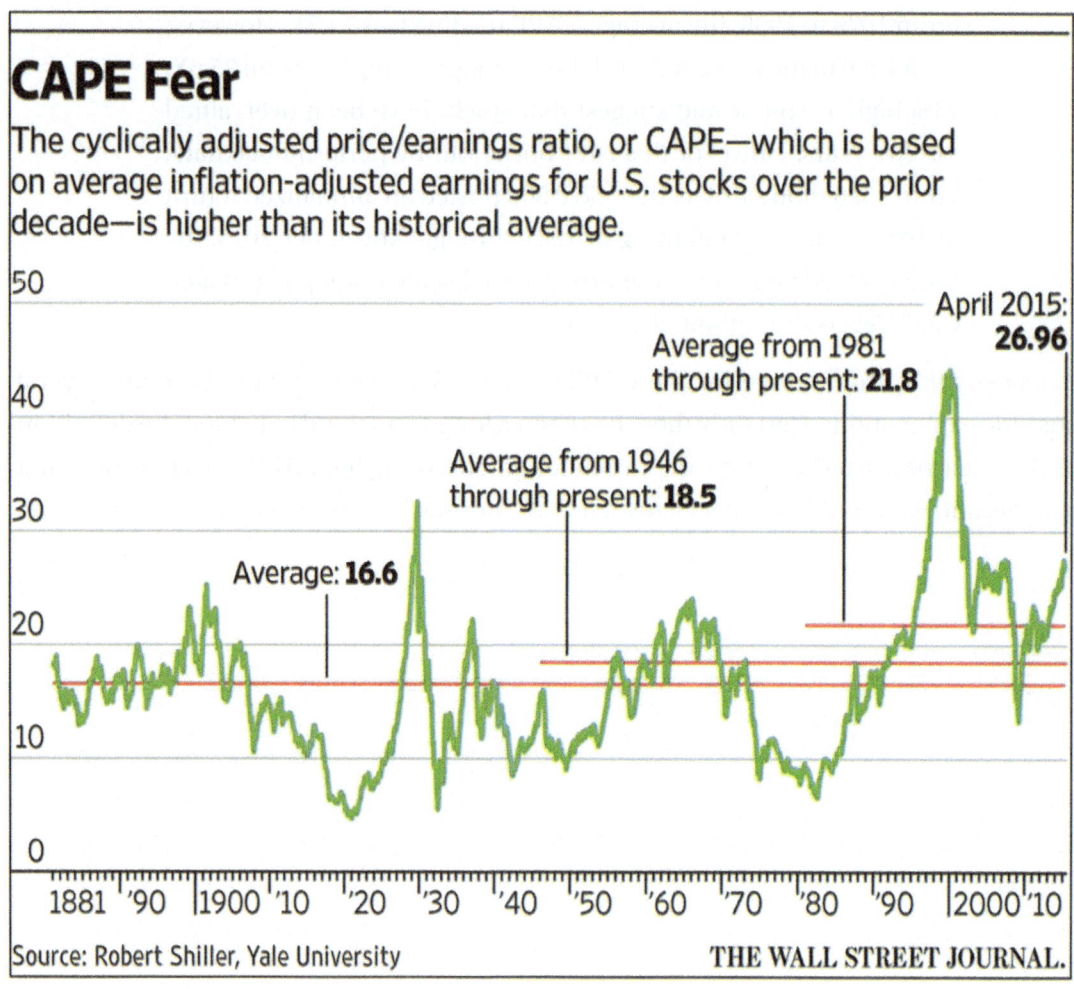

Figure 3-26. *CAPE Rising Trend* [152]

This is of more than just historical interest. If the signal is not reliable, it undermines to the value of CAPE as a guide to investing forward. The same study analyzed three CAPE-triggered portfolio strategies, based on using the CAPE at various thresholds as a signal to exit a presumably overheated market. The results speak for themselves. (See Figure 3-27.)

---

[152] Liam Pleven, "Stocks: Are They Too High?" *The Wall Street Journal*, May 16, 2015. Reproduced by permission from *The Wall Street Journal*.

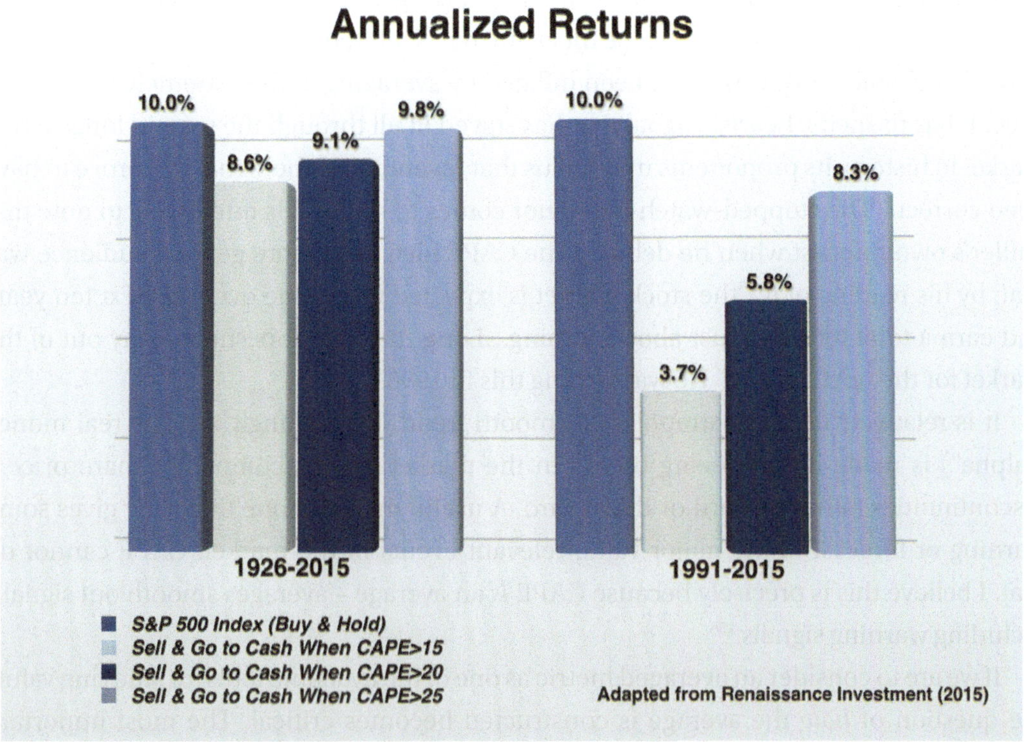

Annualized Returns

Figure 3-27. *CAPE Ineffective as a Sell Signal*[153]

Bars (1926–2015): S&P 500 Index (Buy & Hold) 10.0%; Sell & Go to Cash When CAPE>15 8.6%; Sell & Go to Cash When CAPE>20 9.1%; Sell & Go to Cash When CAPE>25 9.8%.

Bars (1991–2015): S&P 500 Index (Buy & Hold) 10.0%; Sell & Go to Cash When CAPE>15 3.7%; Sell & Go to Cash When CAPE>20 5.8%; Sell & Go to Cash When CAPE>25 8.3%.

Adapted from Renaissance Investment (2015)

3.10.3 CAPE: An Assessment

In the end, a new market metric is judged first and foremost by how well it measures or predicts or explains the behavior of the stock market. The results here are mixed.

The deeper question is: *Does averaging really clarify the signal we are looking for or conceal it? Does it produce information or destroy it?*

This is an old question in Statistics.[154] There is always the story of the man who drowned crossing a stream with an average depth of six inches. The long business cycle

---

[153] "Beware the CAPE Crusaders," *Renaissance Investment Management*, December 2015. Available at www.reninv.com/large-cap-growth/

[154] As long ago as 1947, T. J. Koopmans argued against the practice of averaging in the analysis of economic data: *"Smoothing is found to be wasteful of information and to complicate mathematical treatment, because it mixes up the effects of successive disturbances as well as blurs the time-shape of exogenous variables."* [from "Measurement without Theory," *The Review of Economic Statistics*, Vol. 29, No. 3 (August 1947), pp. 161–172].

certainly has an impact on intrinsic enterprise valuation, which should be reflected in stock market prices. But the market is forward-looking, and for most purposes we need a *current* price. The CAPE offers a value measure that is diluted with nine years' worth of old news. For a while now, CAPE has been inflated by averaging in the extremely bad year in 2008. It has flashed a bearish signal that has stayed lit all through the second longest bull market in history. Its proponents may tell us that "eventually" the signal will prove to have been correct. (The stopped-watch metaphor comes to mind. It is interesting to note that Shiller's own forecast when he debuted the CAPE idea for a more general audience was that, by his reading of it, "the stock market is expected to decline over the next ten years and earn a total return of just about nothing...Long run investors should stay out of the market for the next decade." He was writing this in 1996.)[155]

It is relatively easy to extrapolate a smooth trend. Misleadingly so. The real money ("alpha") is made by foreseeing breaks in the market or in a company's share price – discontinuities either upward or downward. A useful metric is one that truly gives some warning or forecast of the major value-relevant events in the market. CAPE cannot do that. I believe this is precisely because CAPE *is* an average – averages smooth out signals, including warning signals.[156]

If we are to consider an averaged metric as one of the available tools for studying value, the question of *how* the average is constructed becomes critical. The most important aspect of this question is the length of the time window over which the average is taken. Ten years is a very long window. Certainly it is a long time in the history of any individual corporation. In ten years, most companies today will have changed leadership teams at

---

[155] Robert Shiller, "Price-Earnings Ratios as Forecasters of Returns: The Stock Market Outlook in 1996," Yale, *The Cowles Foundation,* July 1996. In fact, ten years later, the market had roughly doubled, and the S&P 500 index has never dropped below the level it was at when Shiller offered this advice. Much later, in 2013, with CAPE still signaling an overpriced market, Prof. Shiller again suggested that investors should reduce their holdings. The market was up over 50% in the following five years – reported in Alexandra Scaggs, "Nobelist's Valuation Measure Draws Questions," *The Wall Street Journal,* November 22, 2013.

[156] Koopmans extends this critique by arguing that the economic system itself (and subsystems such as individual business enterprises) is in effect averaging functions, smoothing out the impact of "shocks" and spreading the effects over longer time periods: *"One of the reasons why business cycle analysis is a difficult undertaking is that the economic system itself is such an effective smoothing agent of the random shocks to which it is exposed. The analytical problem is one of de-smoothing rather than smoothing"* [from "Measurement without Theory," *The Review of Economic Statistics,* Vol. 29, No. 3 (August 1947), pp. 161–172].

least once. They will have developed new products and strategies. They will have likely faced great changes in their competitive situation. In terms of the market as a whole, the ongoing evolution of accounting standards and the resulting modifications to the definition of "Earnings" are a systematic constraint on the comparison of averaged measures over long periods. The idea that CAPE or any market metric has validity in comparing business and market performance over many decades, even a century or more, is unsupportable.

Is CAPE "the most oversold, overhyped metric I've ever seen" (in the words of one academic specialist)?[157] That is likely premature. The time constant in today's market metrics is typically one year, which is taken from the accounting framework. There is nothing "organic" about a 1-year horizon for valuation.[158] Different businesses track different earnings cycles. The idea of adjusting the time window for the definition of Earnings is certainly worth exploring. But it should be done systematically, dare we say "scientifically" – not *ad hoc*.[159] In the process, we should pay close attention to the real variations in earnings patterns for different industries and different market regimes and as a function of other aspects of economic weather (such as monetary policy, demographic trends, or even political election cycles). Is it too much to hope that some sort of a "smart CAPE" will eventually emerge?

It may be in the works. There are a number of recent adaptations of the CAPE concept that point the way forward. *The Wall Street Journal* developed a version of CAPE using alternative data sets sourced from the US Commerce Department (for Earnings) and the Federal Reserve (for Prices). The resulting metric shows a more plausible (lower) number for the CAPE. Interestingly, it appears that the difference lies largely in the accounting for the write-offs, which affects the denominator of CAPE:

---

[157] Aswath Damodaran, quoted in Justin Lahart, "This Key Metric Rings a False Alarm," *The Wall Street Journal*, October 6, 2016.

[158] Keith Anderson and Chris Brooks, "The Long-Term Price-Earnings Ratio," *Journal of Business Finance & Accounting*, 33(7) and (8), (September/October 2006), pp. 1063–1086.

[159] Anderson and Brooks, *op. cit.*, writing in 2006, comment on the shallowness of research in this area: *"We have been unable to find any previous academic research into whether knowledge of earnings of previous years will improve the ability of the P/E ratio to predict future returns on individual shares. Graham and Dodd recommended the use of average earnings over a period of at least five years and preferably over seven to ten years, to give the analyst a more reliable view of the true value of a company. Yet their conjecture does not seem to have been tested by any academic research."*

CHAPTER 3   VALUATION RATIOS

The two measures tracked each other almost perfectly for decades until 2008, when banks and other businesses, required to follow the latest GAAP rules, suffered huge write-downs that cut earnings. The Commerce Department's measure treats bad-debt expenses, asset write-downs and loan-loss provisions as capital losses that reduce the value of corporate assets, rather than cutting earnings. Since both of these measures rely on 10 years of earnings, the disparity stemming from the financial crisis has persisted.[160]

The black line here shows the Commerce Department's figures for corporate earnings – a non-GAAP but well-constructed and standardized Earnings metric that may help rescue CAPE (Figure 3-28).

Figure 3-28. *CAPE Alternative (1)*[161]

---

[160]Justin Lahart, "This Key Metric Rings a False Alarm," *The Wall Street Journal*, October 6, 2016; also Justin Lahart, "Taking Stock Market at Face Value," *The Wall Street Journal*, February 18, 2012.

[161]Justin Lahart, "Taking Stock Market at Face Value," *The Wall Street Journal*, February 18, 2012. Reproduced by permission from *The Wall Street Journal*.

A different version of CAPE, which uses Operating Earnings instead of GAAP (to avoid the problem of incorporating the extraordinary write-downs) and takes the series only back to 1960, is shown here (Figure 3-29).[162]

Figure 3-29. CAPE Alternative (2)[163]

Roger Ibbotson and Philip Straehl have proposed another "cyclically adjusted" metric, CATY, modeled on CAPE, but instead of using Earnings in the denominator, they use "Total Yield"[164] – the "distributable cash flows (i.e., dividends and buybacks)." Just as the volatility of annual earnings is the motivation for averaging them over a longer period for CAPE, Ibbotson and Straehl point to the volatility of buybacks as a motivation for averaging these cash flows. They claim a modest improvement in performance.[165]

---

[162] E. S. Browning, "Is the Market Overvalued?" *The Wall Street Journal*, April 9, 2011.

[163] E. S. Browning, "Is the Market Overvalued?" *The Wall Street Journal*, April 9, 2011. Reproduced by permission from *The Wall Street Journal*.

[164] Philip U. Straehl and Roger G. Ibbotson, "The Long-Run Drivers of Stock Returns: Total Payouts and the Real Economy," *Financial Analysts Journal* (Q3 2017), pp. 32–52.

[165] They show an R2 of 11% for the 5-year CAPE and an R2 of 25% for the 5-year CATY.

CHAPTER 3   VALUATION RATIOS

Still another version of CAPE is based on the observation that monetary policy and moves by the Federal Reserve and its Open Market Committee (the FOMC) in particular have become a major factor in moving markets (see Section 4.3.4). Market responses on FOMC meeting days are said to account for 25% or more of market gains from 1985 to 2016, driving the P/E multiple significantly higher. Since this short-term factor is not held to be related to the underlying fundamentals, it can be subtracted from the nominal P/E by taking out those few days from the time series of market prices. The result has been called the MAPE, or the Monetary Policy–Adjusted P/E.[166]

These are interesting initiatives. The challenges of incorporating what would seem to be obvious adjustments – averaging, inflation adjustment – should not be underestimated, however. The basic P/E Multiple contains two variables – "Price" and "Earnings" – both of which, and especially "Earnings," are more complex than they first appear. The CAPE adds two more variables, each a new can of worms: the "Inflation" variable used to convert "nominal values" into "real values" (which is much more problematic than is generally realized)[167] and the entire framework by which the Average is constructed.[168] There is some hard work to be done here.

---

[166]http://thewallstreetchallenger.com/Index/valuation.html; see also www.advisorperspectives.com/commentaries/2016/03/23/the-stock-market-as-monetary-policy-junkie-quantifying-the-fed-s-impact-on-the-s-p-500

[167]Laurence Siegel struggles with this issue: *"in order to be useful, the CAPE needs to be reconciled with the Capital Asset Pricing Model (CAPM). Specifically, CAPE-based estimates of the expected equity return need to be adjusted for fluctuations in interest rates, that is, for changes in the expected return on bonds...."* – this is a line of reasoning which leads far afield, and on unsteady ground, as CAPM is by now rather thoroughly discredited (see Appendix A). From Laurence Siegel, "CAPMing the CAPE" available at https://larrysiegeldotorg.files.wordpress.com/2016/09/siegel_capming-the-cape_2016_09_08.pdf

[168]Bunn et al. summarize the questions relating to the design of the average used in CAPE as follows: *"The original definition of the cyclically adjusted price-earnings ratio in Campbell and Shiller [1988] divides the most recent price information by the arithmetic average of the logarithm of (inflation-adjusted) one-year earnings observations, thereby calculating a geometric ten-year earnings average. Campbell and Shiller later use a simplified definition and arithmetically average (inflation-adjusted) 1-year earnings observations, which is the conceptual version that we rely on here. Shiller [later] calculates the 10-year earnings average from monthly (inflation-adjusted) earnings observations, where each number captures income information for the past twelve months. This calculation, however, down-weights the most recent (as well as, less importantly, the most distant) earnings information, which we would not like to incorporate."* In short, even defining the Average is not a simple matter. From Oliver Bunn, Arne Staal, Ji Zhuang, Anthony Lazanas, Cenk Ural, and Robert Shiller, Escaping from Overvalued Sectors: Sector Selection Based on the Cyclically Adjusted Price-Earnings (CAPE) Ratio," *The Journal of Portfolio Management* (Fall 2014), pp. 16–32.

3.11 Adjustments to the Numerator: Cash-Adjusted P/E (CAPE$_2$)

The numerator of the P/E multiple has also been the subject of proposed improvements. One of the most interesting is the suggestion to strip out Cash from the market price, for companies sitting on very large cash balances:

$$\frac{(price/share)-(cash/share)}{earnings-interest\ income\ from\ cash/share}$$

The idea is simple and plausible, although counterintuitive (it turns "cash is king" thinking on its head).

Starting in the 1990s, US corporations (excluding financial firms) began accumulating record amounts of cash on their balance sheets. Cash holdings grew by six times from 1990 to 2012 in absolute value.[169] As a percentage of total assets, cash grew to about 6% of total assets[170] and the equivalent of 10% of total market value.[171] (For large companies, the figure for cash plus repurchased shares had already reached 20% of market value in 2006.[172]) The issue pushed into the headlines and began to draw attention from market analysts.[173]

---

[169] Ben Casselman, "Cautious Companies Stockpile Cash," *The Wall Street Journal*, December 7, 2012; Jonathan Cheng, "Firms Weigh Options for those Piles of Cash," *The Wall Street Journal*, August 23, 2010.

[170] Justin Lahart, "U.S. Firms Build Up Record Cash Piles," *The Wall Street Journal*, June 11, 2010.

[171] David Reilly, "Companies Should Keep Their Cash Stashes," *The Wall Street Journal*, May 10, 2010.

[172] Ian McDonald, "Capital Pains: Big Cash Hoards," *The Wall Street Journal*, July 21, 2006.

[173] A discussion of the reasons for this cash accumulation lie outside the scope of this work. But it is likely that they have to do with the business model shift previously alluded to – namely, the shift to reliance on intangible assets with inherently higher ROA and higher levels of profitability, with a reduction in the need for Capex, the traditional consumer of excess corporate cash.

CHAPTER 3   VALUATION RATIOS

Good news? Not really. In 2012 it was called "the $1.7 Tn problem" by the *Financial Times* in an article subtitled *"Companies' Growing Cash Piles are Irking Shareholders and Stunting Growth."*[174] In the ultralow interest rate environment prevailing at that time, *The Wall Street Journal* observed that "there is little use in so much cash lying fallow on corporate balance sheets."[175] Meanwhile, the share prices of many cash-rich companies showed signs of being depressed. One analyst calculated that across the entire equity market, the cash hoard had reduced the P/E Multiple by 1.4 points and asked

> Why pay a stock market multiple for a company that is essentially acting like a bank – and a bad one at that?[176]

A bad bank? *Apple* has been the worst "offender" with a cash pile that reached $66 Bn by 2011 – the financial return on all that cash was 0.75%.[177]

To put this in perspective, consider that in 2018 *Apple* and *ExxonMobil* had identical revenues ($247 Bn and $248 Bn, respectively). But *Exxon* – a very profitable enterprise with large capital expenditures and real liquidity needs – carried just $4 Bn in cash on its balance sheet. *Apple* – much more of an asset-light business model based on intangible assets – carried 22 times as much. The disparity in revenue generated per dollar of cash is striking; by this measure, *Exxon* is far more efficient. (See Figure 3-30.)

---

[174]John Authers, "Hordes of Hoarders," *Financial Times*, January 30, 2012.
[175]Kelly Evans, "Companies Like Bed Bath Need Capital Ideas," *The Wall Street Journal*, September 22, 2010.
[176]Roben Farzad, "When Cash Takes a Vacation," *Bloomberg/BusinessWeek*, July 12, 2010.
[177]Martin Peers, "Cash Returns: Where Apple Lags Rivals," *The Wall Street Journal*, May 23, 2011. *Apple's* cash later reached $200 Bn. Despite instituting a generous dividend and large cash buybacks, *Apple* still has $88 Bn in cash on hand as of this writing.

CHAPTER 3 VALUATION RATIOS

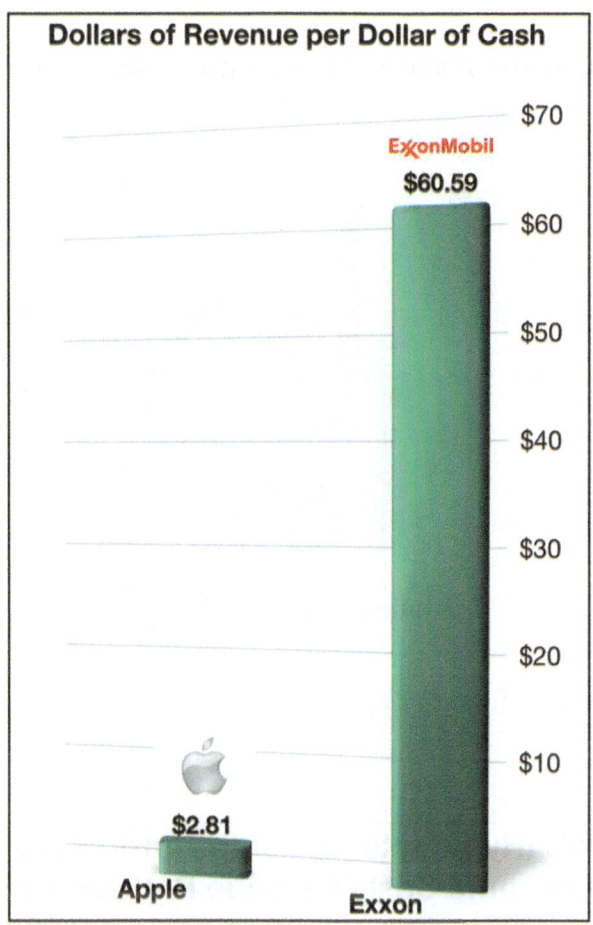

Figure 3-30. *Apple vs. Exxon*

The impact on the company's operating performance is significant (Figure 3-31). At the end of 2017, *Apple* and *ExxonMobil* have similar sized balance sheet accounts for Total Assets ($375 Bn and $348 Bn). Cash and Cash-like accounts made up almost 20% of *Apple's* total assets, but less than 1% of *ExxonMobil's* total assets. If *Apple* were able to manage its business with a level of cash similar to *ExxonMobil's*, its Return-on-Assets would have improved from ~11% to ~14% (Figure 3-32). Applying the correlation shown earlier in the chapter between ROA and Profitability, we might expect to see the company's net profit margin increase by 200 basis points or more.

CHAPTER 3 VALUATION RATIOS

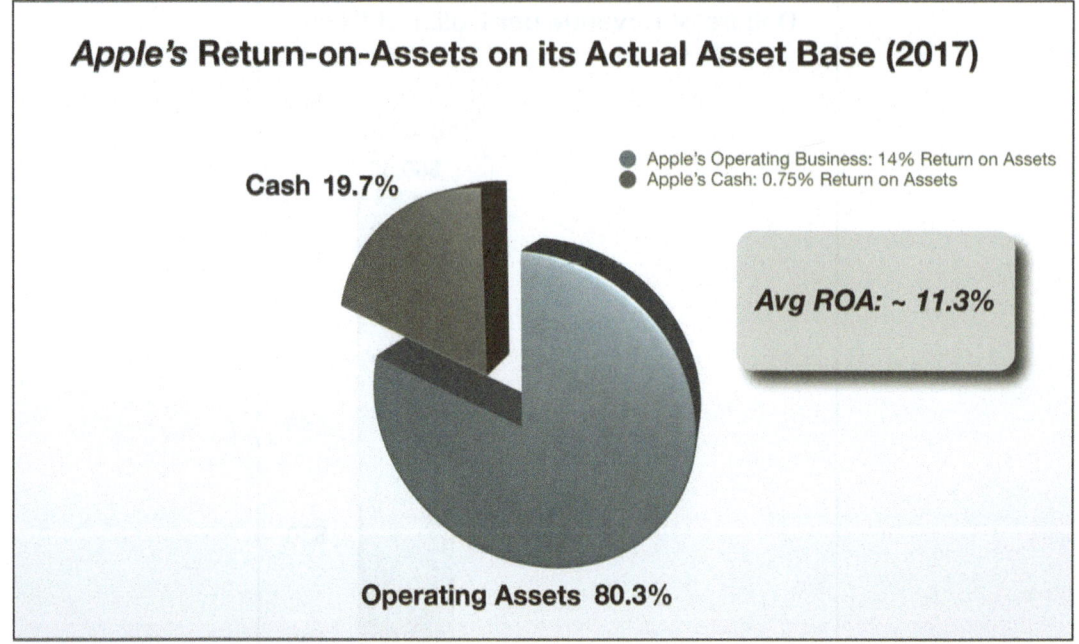

Figure 3-31. Apple as It Actually Is (2017)

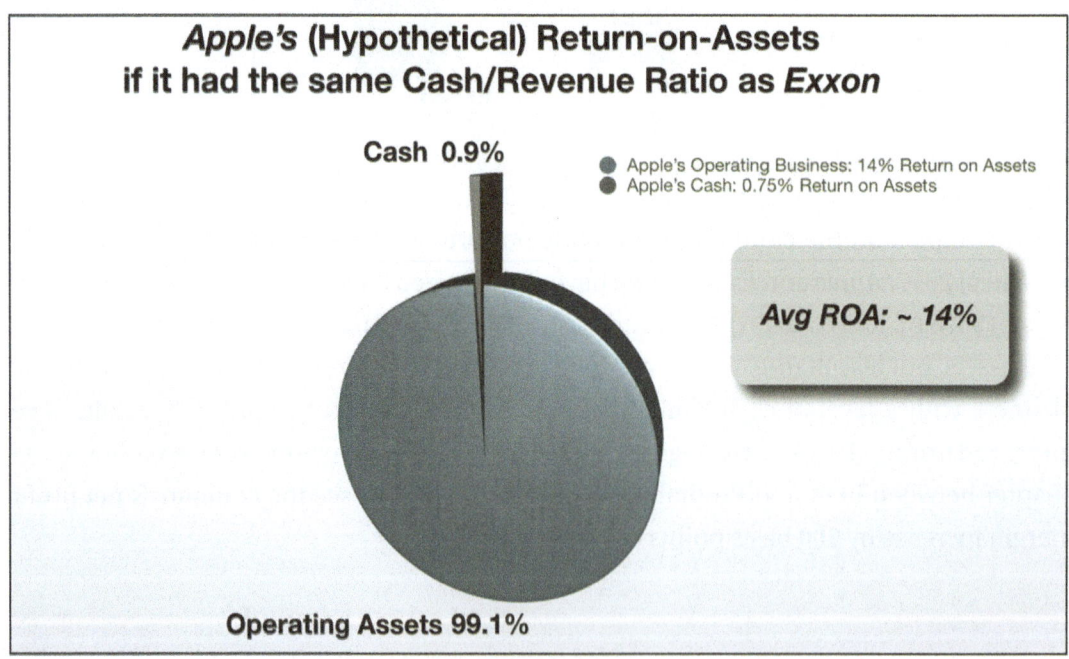

Figure 3-32. Apple, Shown as if It Had the Same Asset Profile as Exxon (2017)

CHAPTER 3 VALUATION RATIOS

CAPE$_2$ is a version of the P/E Multiple which adjusts for the problem of excess cash holdings. *Apple* is composed of a very profitable and successful business, which generates essentially all of its earnings, and a huge pile of cash that generates a market return of less than 1%.

Apple's Total Market Cap = Value of Apple's Business + Value of Apple's Cash

Taking the reasonable position that the market would value each $1.00 of cash held in *Apple's* account at $1.00 of market cap, CAPE$_2$ strips out the value of the cash pile from the company's market capitalization, to more properly value the operating business itself.

In 2011, *Barron's* magazine performed this type of analysis, using the then-current financials of *Apple*.[178] (See Figure 3-33.)

| Company | Recent price | 2011E | | | | Net Cash | | |
		EPS	P/E		P/E ex Net Cash	Total ($bil)	Per Share	% of Price
AAPL	$334.64	$22.98	14.6		11.8	$59.70	$63.98	19%

Figure 3-33. Apple's Cash-Adjusted Price-to-Earnings Ratio[179]

Apple had $64 per share in Cash. Valued dollar for dollar, this is taken to imply that $64 of *Apple's* then-current share price of $334 can be attributed to the cash holding. The remaining $270 of the share price corresponds to the value of the company's actual business – which generates virtually all of the $23/share in earnings.

---

[178] Andrew Bary, "Silicon Skinflints Still Skimp on Payouts," *Barron's*, March 21, 2011.
[179] Adapted from Andrew Bary, "Silicon Skinflints Still Skimp on Payouts," *Barron's*, March 21, 2011.

CHAPTER 3   VALUATION RATIOS

$$\textit{Apple's Market Cap per Share}\,(\$334) = \textit{Apple's Cash, per Share}\,(\$64) \\ + \textit{the Value of Apple's Business,} \\ \textit{per Share}\,(\$270)$$

So the company's P/E of 14.6 ($334/$22.98) becomes the $CAPE_2$ of 11.8 ($270/$22.98). This seems entirely reasonable, at least as an alternative view of *Apple's* value. It corresponds to the logic underlying the EV metric ("Enterprise Value") discussed in the section on EV/EBITDA, which would tell us that the cost to acquire *Apple* would need to be discounted by the value of the net cash on hand. Stripping the cash out of the Price in the numerator is another way to get at this same concept.

The problem of excessive cash accumulation is associated in recent years with the tech industry in the United States. But it may be even more of a problem overseas. (See Figure 3-34.) Germany has seen cash accumulations growing in its core industrial sectors, described there as "overcapitalization" with cash hoards sitting on the balance sheets "earning very little return at all."[180] And if US levels of corporate cash were high (11% of GDP in 2014), they were stratospheric in East Asia – reaching 34% of GDP in South Korea and 44% in Japan! (Yes, that is worth an exclamation point.)[181]

---

[180] Chris Bryant, "Pressure Rises on German Groups as Cash Piles Grow," *Financial Times*, July 26, 2011.

[181] "Corporate Saving in Asia: A $2.5 Trillion Problem," *The Economist*, September 27, 2014.

CHAPTER 3   VALUATION RATIOS

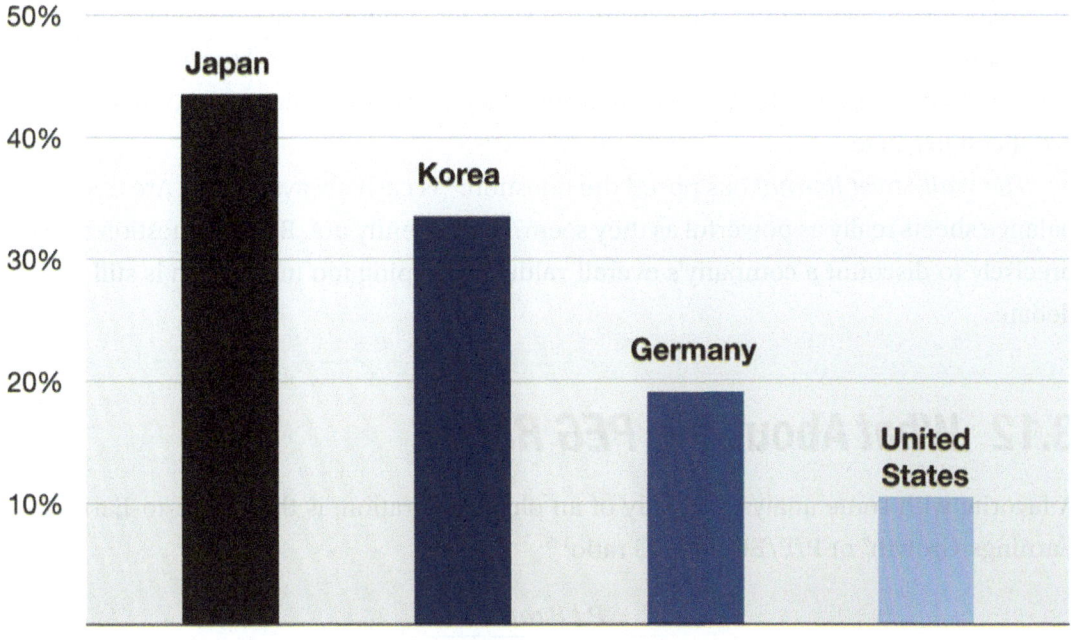

Figure 3-34. Corporate Cash[182]

Why is $CAPE_2$ not more popular? (It has hardly been studied at all by academia.) One reason may be that its useful application would seem to be limited in the United States to a small number of very large companies, mostly in the tech sector. But the numbers shown here would suggest that any serious analysis of corporate valuations in Korea or Japan ought to take full account of this matter.

EV/EBITDA performs a very similar adjustment to the numerator of the Multiple. Large net cash positions (net of debt) will result in a reduced EV compared to the market cap. This may mitigate the need for a new metric like $CAPE_2$. As well, the accumulation of cash by US companies was due in part to American tax law that encouraged the accumulation

---

[182]Adapted from "Corporate Saving in Asia: A $2.5 Trillion Problem," *The Economist*, September 27, 2014.

of cash overseas, where often there were not sufficient opportunities for reinvestment.[183] Credit raters like *Moody's* have applied explicit discounts (up to 30%) to cash balances at companies like *Pfizer* and *Johnson & Johnson*. The effect of tax policies on company value is difficult to gauge.

The Wall Street Journal has posed the question: "Is cash always liquid? Are cash-rich balance sheets really as powerful as they seem?"[184] Evidently not. But the question of how precisely to discount a company's overall value for keeping too much cash is still up for debate.

3.12 *What* About *the PEG Ratio?*

A favorite with some analysts, mostly of an older generation, is the "Price-to-Earnings/Earnings-Growth" or P/E/EG, or PEG ratio[185]:

$$\frac{P/E \text{ ratio}}{\text{annual EPS growth}}$$

It incorporates into the valuation metric the standard interpretive "theory" of the meaning of the P/E multiple itself – namely, that the P/E reflects, or is driven by, the earnings *growth* rate (see Chapter 4). According to the conventional view, companies whose earnings are growing rapidly will carry high P/E Multiples. This has been called

---

[183] The cash could not be brought back to the United States for dividends or buybacks or domestic investment without paying a large penalty of up to 35%. This law has recently changed. But while it was in effect, it may have reduced the market's perceived value of the cash so sequestered. At the very least, this sort of cash needs to be discounted for the likely eventual tax payment.

[184] John Jannarone and Sara Silver, "Cash (Kept at Home) is King," *The Wall Street Journal*, January 14, 2009.

[185] Peter Easton, "PE Ratios, PEG Ratios, and Estimating the Implied Expected Rate of Return on Equity Capital," *The Accounting Review*, Vol. 79, No. 1 (January 2004), pp. 73–95 – offers a sincere attempt to make sense of the PEG ratio in a more "theoretical" framework. It is not entirely clear to me what this paper "proves." The conclusion: "I develop and demonstrate a procedure for simultaneously estimating the implied market expectation of the rate of return and the implied market expectation of the long-run change in abnormal growth in earnings." I am not sure what the value of showing a correlation between these "expectations" is, beyond confirming that the typical psychology of investors links earnings growth and stock market gains.

a "long-standing and well-known truism."[186] Or maybe it's the other way around, and "low growth firms should have higher PEG ratios than high growth firms."[187] Or perhaps it is both (Figure 3-35).[188] It is easy to explain things when your metric can point in either direction.[189]

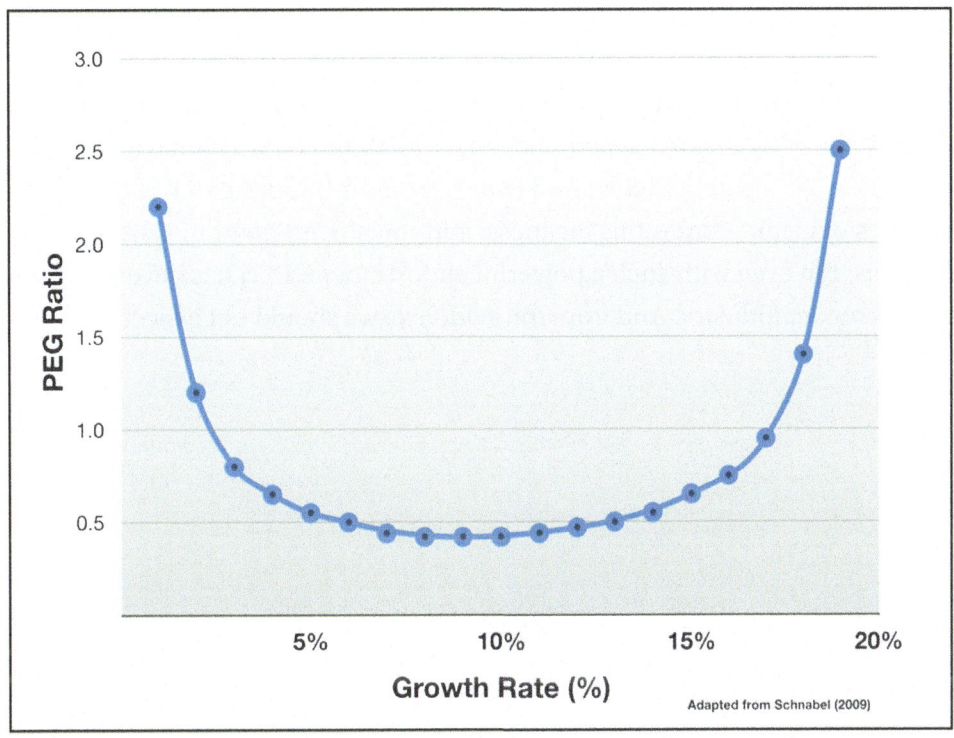

Figure 3-35. *The PEG Is a Convex Function of the Earnings Growth Rate*[190]

---

[186]Jacques Schnabel, "Benchmarking the PEG Ratio," *The Journal of Wealth Management*, Winter 2009, pp. 89–94.

[187]Mark Trombley, "Understanding the PEG Ratio," *The Journal of Investing*, Spring 2008, pp. 22–25.

[188]Jacques Schnabel, "Benchmarking the PEG Ratio," *The Journal of Wealth Management*, Winter 2009, pp. 89–94.

[189]It would appear that the academic community has reached the conclusion that PEG is a nonstarter. There is very little published research on the PEG; what is available is mostly in the form of short journalistic "investment advice" pieces in the popular press.

[190]Adapted from Jacques Schnabel, "Benchmarking the PEG Ratio," *The Journal of Wealth Management*, Winter 2009, pp. 89–94.

CHAPTER 3   VALUATION RATIOS

The PEG ratio tries to bring "Earnings Growth" directly into the calculation of the value metric. Unfortunately, it doesn't seem to work. According to the *Vanguard* study cited previously, the 3-year and the 10-year earnings growth rates are completely uncorrelated with future returns. Earnings growth rates have zero predictive power.[191] Another comparison of the PEG with the simple P/E Multiple found no benefit: "the PEG ratio is not an effective tool over P/E."[192]

Why then do we still hear about the PEG ratio from time to time? Probably because Peter Lynch – a legendary stock picker – touted it as his particular formula for success. He claimed that "the P/E ratio of any company that's fairly priced will equal its growth rate." That is, a PEG of 1 is a potential Buy. And Lynch certainly has done well with it. There are many sources of inspiration in this business, and there is no point in gainsaying a track record like his. But even with such a powerful endorsement, PEG has never really caught on with the broader industry. And from the evidence, we should not expect it to.[193]

---

[191] Joseph Davis, Roger Aliaga-Díaz, and Charles Thomas, "Forecasting Stock Returns: What Signals Matter, and What Do They Say Now?" *Vanguard Research*, October 2012. In fact, the earnings growth rates have less "explanatory" power with respect to future real stock returns than the meaningless dummy variable (annual rainfall) introduced by the *Vanguard* authors to benchmark the threshold of obvious non-causality.

[192] Bharat Meher and Saurabh Sharma, "Is PEG Ratio a Better Tool for Valuing the Companies as Compared to P/E Ratio? (A Case Study on Selected Automobile Companies)," *International Journal of Banking and Risk*, Vol. 3, No. 2 (September 2015), pp. 48–52.

[193] Block analyzes the PEG ratios of the 30 Dow component companies (December 2009) and concludes *"As a guideline on Wall Street, stocks that trade at a P/E greater than their five-year growth rate (a PEG greater than 1) should be subject to special observation to make sure they are not overvalued. This would have to qualify as a myth; 27 of the DJIA stocks traded over 1 [in fact all of the Dow components with positive earnings, for which a PEG could be calculated], and few of the firms would have been considered to be overvalued based on other metrics."* (Stanley Block, "Methods of Valuation: Myths vs Reality," *The Journal of Investing* (Winter 2010), pp. 7–14).

3.13 Composite P/E Ratios

Finally, when P/E is calculated for portfolios based on sectors or entire markets, it can be affected by the composition of the indices that define those portfolios. For example, the P/E for emerging market equities has been critiqued on the basis that its recent apparent "cheap" valuation relative to P/E's for developed markets may be an artifact resulting from a difference in the composition of the indices for these two markets. (See Figure 3-36.) Emerging market indices tend to be weighted toward out-of-favor sectors, with lower multiples:

> Emerging markets have far more banks and commodity producers, which trade at lower valuations than more fashionable areas. Adjust the sector weights too match those of developed markets, and emerging-market indexes trade at the same price-to-forward-earnings ratio as the FTSE World index.[194]

---

[194] James Mackintosh, "Emerging Markets Are No Bargains," *The Wall Street Journal*, September 4, 2018.

CHAPTER 3   VALUATION RATIOS

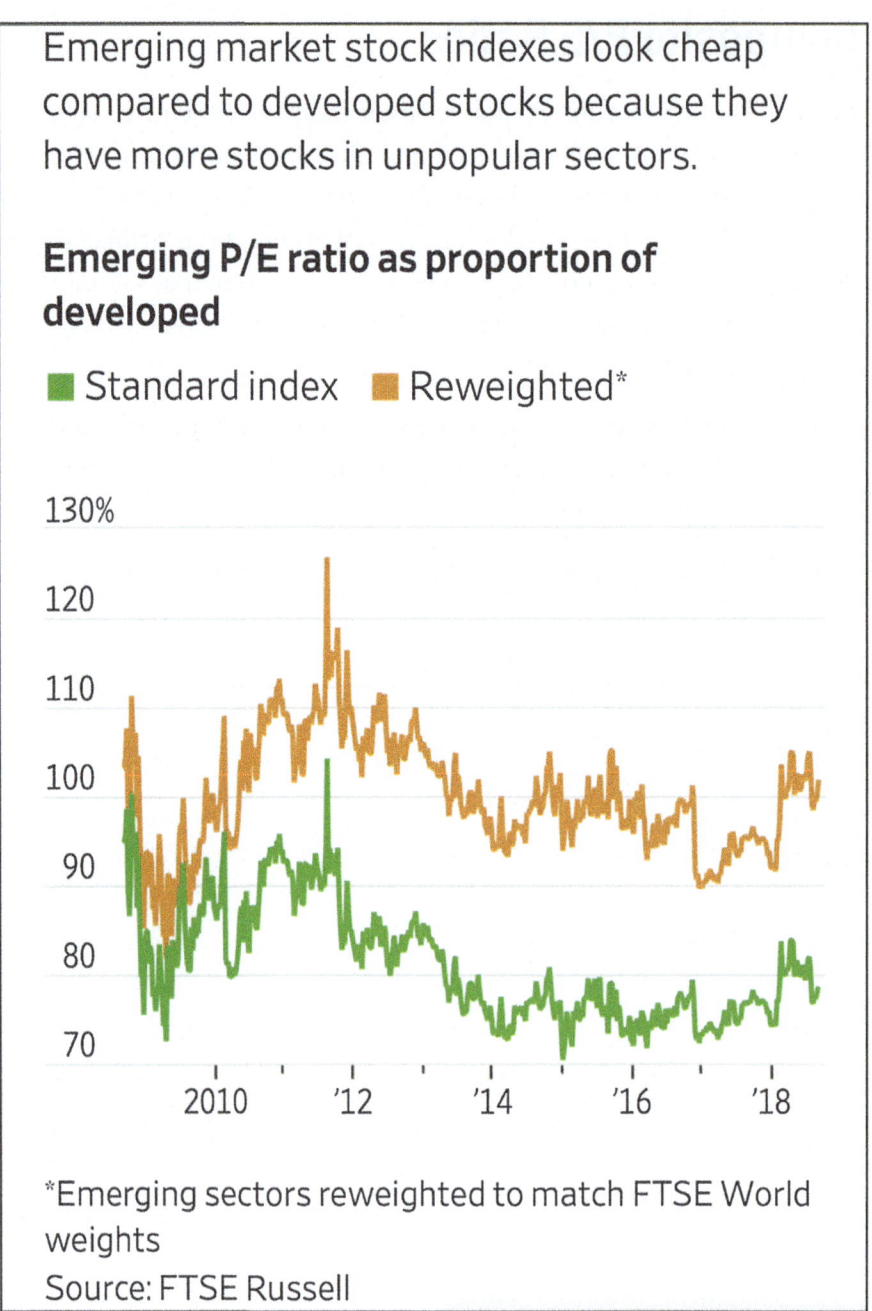

Figure 3-36. Adjusting for Sector Weighting in Broad Market Indices[195]

---

[195]James Mackintosh, "Emerging Markets Are No Bargains," *The Wall Street Journal*, September 4, 2018. Reproduced by permission from *The Wall Street Journal*.

This example reveals the existence of a "hidden variable" in our seemingly simple P/E calculation. The P/E for any aggregate set is affected by the composition of that set. If the composition changes, the P/E will change. This affects the P/E multiples for sectors when the definition of sector membership changes. In 2018, two of the leading sector index providers – S&P and MSCI – announced plans to change their sector compositions. These are sweeping changes. More than 10% of the S&P 500 companies are being reclassified.[196] In total, some 225 companies in the United States are being reclassified. Globally, more than 1,100 companies are affected, in China (170), Japan (140), Canada (57), the United Kingdom (51), and so on. The impact on the revised "tech sector" of the S&P 500 will have the effect of lowering the sector P/E by a full point, to 17.7.[197]

This effect is also present in a financial time series like the S&P 500 P/E – as a function of changes in the composition of the index and also as the listed companies evolve their business models and capital structures. Since the 1970s, several broad trends in the American economy have emerged: for example, the significant increase in corporate leverage (reflected in the virtual disappearance of AAA-rated companies) and the shift to asset-light business models (reflected in the growing disparity between market value and book value). Corporate profit margins have generally increased, and capital Expenditures have declined, in relative terms. Sectors like tech and finance have boomed. The overall weighting of the tech sector in the S&P 500 reached 26% in 2018 – several times its relative weight in the mid-1990s. This qualitative evolution of the economy skews the P/E multiple of the overall market, as high-growth and generally high-P/E companies outweigh or displace lower-growth, lower-P/E companies.[198]

In short, the S&P 500 index of today measures a rather different economy than the S&P 500 index of the 1970s or the 1980s. As well, many accounting rules have changed (as we will discuss in later chapters), affecting the calculation of the earnings denominator of the Multiple. The point is obvious, but we should always keep in mind that the P/E is not a stable, invariant metric, but also reflects the *qualitative* characteristics of the current economic context.

---

[196] Matthew Bartolini and Anqi Dong, "GICS Sector Structure Changes: What Do They Mean for Investors?" *State Street Global Advisors*, 2018.

[197] Daren Fonda, "Reshaping the Market's Sectors," *Barron's*, September 3, 2018.

[198] "S&P 500 Sector Weightings: Tech Nears 26%," *Seeking Alpha*, May 10, 2018; available online at https://seekingalpha.com/article/4172093-s-and-p-500-sector-weightings-tech-nears-26-percent

CHAPTER 3   VALUATION RATIOS

One more factor obtrudes. Index compositions change from time to time, as companies merge or drop out of the rankings. Arnott has looked at the valuations of companies being dropped vs. those being added:

> Stocks added to capitalization-weighted indices are routinely priced at a substantial premium to market valuation multiples (i.e., buying high), while discretionary deletions (excepting removals related to mergers, acquisitions, and other corporate actions) are routinely of deep-discount value stocks (i.e., selling low). In fact, additions tend to be priced at valuation multiples – using a blend of price-to-earnings (P/E), price-to-cash-flow (P/CF), price-to-book (P/B), price-to-sales (P/S), and (if available) price-to-dividends (P/D) ratios – that average over *three times as expensive as those of deletions*.[199] [Emphasis added]

This would indicate that an index like the S&P 500 (and possibly any capitalization-weighted index[200]) is structurally biased and "overvalued" in some sense relative to the market as a whole. In other words, the S&P 500 index members are "high multiple," and the non-S&P 500 stocks are a "low-multiple" set.

3.14 Summary

This chapter has been mainly focused on general definitions of the different multiples and their relationships to enterprise value, their "accuracy" in a somewhat static sense. The results are somewhat incoherent or "multidimensional" (and not all the dimensions are fully connected to one another). Some metrics appear to work well for some purposes, others for others. Some work in certain periods, with certain kinds of markets, and break down unexpectedly as the market conditions change. "Rigorous" studies often contradict each other on even the most basic questions – which reflects the *ad hoc* nature of much of the available research. The practitioner literature is often crafted in the spirit of revealing the "one true answer," while the peer-reviewed literature often amounts to little more than a numbers game and may not go very deep (regress the data set against some interesting variable and write it up).

---

[199]Rob Arnott, Vitali Kalesnik, PhD, and Lillian Wu, "Buy High and Sell Low with Index Funds!" *Research Affiliates*, June 2018.
[200]A "cap-weighted" index is one that assigns weighting to the individual stocks in the index based on their relative market capitalizations. Most indexes today are cap-weighted.

There is also the inevitable partisanship. Analysts have their favorite metrics. Academics have theirs. The impulse to simplify is very strong in this field, and I feel it is almost always wrong to do so. In confronting obvious complexity in the markets, it would make more sense if our responses were more complex, more admitting of multiple perspectives. Perhaps at some point, in this age of machine learning and artificial intelligence, someone will undertake a thorough and comprehensive evaluation of all the available metrics, in all their variations in construction and nuances of interpretation, to help us decide which measures shed the most light on which questions. But we are not there yet.

In the next two chapters, we will look more closely at how Multiples are *used*.

The primary application of the Multiples is for the interpretation of stock market behavior, which has two aspects: the power to *predict* – that is, to use the Multiples as signals to guide forward-looking decisions, such as investments – and the power to *explain*, to help find and interpret a coherent historical pattern. Prediction presumes to tell us *what* will (or may) happen; explanation tries to tell us *why*.

But aren't explanation (of the past) and predictions (of the future) really the same thing, or at least hand-in-glove? If we can explain the past pattern, doesn't that give us the ability to predict the future? It would – if we could assume *invariance, t*hat is, if we could assume that the system in question (the financial market or the business firm or the economy as a whole) behaved in a deterministic manner, that its patterns of behavior would not change, and that the laws governing those patterns, once discovered, could be applied with confidence to future decisions. This assumption is often implicit in studies of financial markets.[201]

---

[201]For example, extrapolating the CAPE from the starting year of 1871 (as its proponents routinely do) and constructing "normal" benchmarks or historical averages drawn over that entire period clearly presupposes that the market and the economy are essentially invariant over that very long period.

CHAPTER 3 VALUATION RATIOS

But the market mutates. We know this before we run a single regression. Its behavior changes, abruptly and unpredictably. Metrics that "meant" one thing two or three decades ago – or two or three quarters ago – may now come to mean something very different. Even the definitions that we take to be fundamental – like "earnings" – prove not to be so. Therefore, I believe we *do* face two separate questions: Can we explain what happened? Can we predict what will happen next? Can the Multiples help answer these questions? (That sets us up for Chapters 4 and 5.)

The Multiples have other virtues – they may shed light on aspects of value that are not otherwise obvious. Price-to-Sales neatly parses the energy industry into upstream and downstream business models. Of course we didn't need P/S to perform that analysis; but it is interesting that it does discriminate this difference where P/E and other metrics fail to do so. Many nuances of business strategy may be amenable to systematic study in this way; a strong and innovative strategy should have a higher value than a weak or imitative one; this may be the message behind the huge discrepancies between the multiples for *Amazon* and *Walmart* (two gigantic retail powerhouses, otherwise so similar in their current financial fundamentals). Indeed, it is not just strategy, but questions like "quality of revenue" and "quality of earnings" or "pricing power" that come to mind, or perhaps something like the "moats" that Warren Buffett looks for in the companies he invests in. If we remember that the larger question here is the value of the business enterprise and consider how many factors bear upon that, it must be likely that there are other uses for these metrics beyond predicting and explaining stock prices.

To conclude then, here is a brief overview of the metrics covered in this chapter. (See Table 3-2.)

CHAPTER 3 VALUATION RATIOS

Table 3-2. Concluding Overview and Summary

Valuation Ratios	Assessment
Trailing P/E	• The traditional Standard • Not as accurate as forward P/E in predicting future performance
Forward P/E	• Best predictor of future performance in some studies • Forward forecasts are accurate 1 year out in some studies, longer in others
Price/Operating Earnings	• Inconsistent definitions of "Operating Earnings" in use (Non-GAAP) • Generally weaker predictive/explanatory power compared to standard P/E
Price/Dividend (Dividend Yield)	• Weak and declining predictive/explanatory value • Growing use of share buybacks has diluted dividend signals
Price/Sales	• Useful for certain sectors (e.g., Retail) • Very weak predictor of Value • Can shed light on business model differences
Price/Cash Flow	• Mixed results, but generally weaker than standard P/E • Inconsistent definitions of "cash flow" in use (Non-GAAP)
Price/Book	• Suffers a significant and growing misalignment with market valuations • Major flaws in the calculation of "Book Value" for the denominator
Tobin's Q	• Proposes to use market values to adjust balance sheet values • However it is generally infeasible to calculate Replacement Value of assets • Not widely used outside of academic circles
Return-on-Assets	• Strong predictor of profitability • Not a strong predictor of market returns • Inherent flaws in "Book Value" as the denominator
Cyclically Adjusted P/E	• Moderate explanatory power for long-term historical returns (similar to std P/E) • Unsuccessful as a predictor of Market returns going forward • Inherent biases and structural problems
Cash-Adjusted P/E	• Not widely used • Limited applicability in the U.S; potentially more relevant in foreign markets
PEG Ratio	• Very weak indicator; contradictory signals

CHAPTER 4

Interpretations: P/E As a Dependent Variable

What information does the P/E contain? What does it *signify*?

There are two ways to construe this question:

1. What causes the P/E signal to take on a particular value? What sets its level? What fundamental aspect of a company's performance, or its environment, is associated with a high Multiple or a low one? What might cause it to change?

2. What is the P/E signal telling us to do? How can we use it to make decisions?

The first perspective is historical. The second is forward-looking. In general, the first question is of interest to academics; the second is what investors want to know.

The first perspective positions the P/E as a *dependent variable*, the value of which is determined by something else. In other words, it "measures" something:

$$P/E = f(X)$$

The second perspective sees the P/E as the *independent variable* that "explains" something else. It "predicts" something:

$$X = f(P/E)$$

Any discussion of the full meaning of the P/E (and other multiples) inevitably blends both aspects – retrospective and prospective, analytical and pragmatic. In this chapter, we will concentrate on the first perspective: how does the P/E come to have the value that it does? What factors create a high (or low) P/E value? We will turn to the second question in the next chapter.

CHAPTER 4   INTERPRETATIONS: P/E AS A DEPENDENT VARIABLE

4.1 What Does the P/E Really Measure?

The apparent simplicity of the Earnings Multiple – composed of two numbers, simple, objective, readily available – inspires a lot of seemingly decisive "quick answers." Unfortunately, the discussion often then drifts into incoherence. Here is a sample, drawn from some of the leading textbooks[1]:

> The single most important variable determining the P/E ratio of an individual stock is the expectation of future earnings growth... However P/E ratios are influenced by other factors such as interest rates, risk attitudes of investors, taxes, and liquidity, among others. [Authority #1]

> Intuitively, firms with higher growth rates, less risk, and greater cash-flow-generating potential should trade at higher multiples... The key determinants of the P/E ratio are the expected growth rate in earnings per share, the cost of equity, and the payout ratio... A firm's multiples are likely to increase more as risk decreases than as growth increases... But not all growth is created equal, and companies that generate growth more efficiently should trade at higher values... return on equity and net profit margins are additional variables... [Authority #2]

> It is a mathematical identity that high P/E ratios reflect some combination of low discount rates and/or high expected earnings growth rates....Historical analysis suggests that P/E has been more closely related to inflation than to nominal or real bond yields or any growth metrics.... What P/E drivers are there besides inflation? Other useful explanatory variables include output volatility (e.g., rolling GDP volatility), profit/GDP ratio, and demographic patterns... Even though P/E ratios are conceptually a forecast of future growth, they have had a limited correlation with actual growth. [Authority #3]

---

[1]The quotes are anonymized here.

> The normal forward P/E ratio is equal to the reciprocal of the firm's cost of capital... [or] the reciprocal of the difference between the firm's cost of capital and the anticipated growth rate in earnings.... The firm with newer assets will have a higher P/E ratio.... The P/E ratio is increasing with the firm's pricing power....Higher growth in future periods will unambiguously increase the P/E ratio, unless the firm operates in a competitive industry... [Authority #4][2]

Quite a muddle – this "array of competing descriptions"[3] – but the fact is that there is no simple answer. The Price-to-Earnings ratio is responsive to many influences. The market price in the numerator is the complex product of various "factors" – the company's past performance, its future prospects, broad market sentiment, the general economic conditions, and the inflation rate, among other things. The "earnings" denominator can also be quite complex (as discussed in the previous chapter). It is challenging to pick apart this "simple ratio," statistically and conceptually.

That said, we can list some of the main factors considered by practitioners, and to some extent studied in the academic literature, as drivers of the P/E and other multiples. These factors can be divided into those that seem to act at the level of the individual firm vs. those that affect entire sectors, or the market as a whole.

Firm-level drivers include

- Earnings Growth
- Profitability, or "Quality" (e.g., Profit Margin, Return on Equity)
- Size
- "Risk" and cost of capital
- Dividend and Share Repurchase Policies
- Various aspects of the company's strategy or business model

---

[2]Alexander Nezlobin, Madhav V. Rajan, and Stefan Reichelstein, "Structural properties of the price-to-earnings and price-to-book ratios," *Review of Accounting Studies*, Vol. 21 (2016), pp. 438–472.

[3]Stephen H. Penman, "The Articulation of Price-Earnings Ratios and Market-to-Book Ratios and the Evaluation of Growth," *Journal of Accounting Research*, Vol. 34, No. 2 (Autumn, 1996), pp. 235–259.

CHAPTER 4 INTERPRETATIONS: P/E AS A DEPENDENT VARIABLE

- Earnings volatility
- Share price volatility (beta)
- Leverage
- Accounting issues (e.g., quality of earnings, accruals)
- Corporate governance

The drivers which seem to act at the level of a sector or the market as a whole include

- Market sentiment (market regimes)
- Sector-related discounts and premiums
- Regulation effects
- Government monetary policy
- Government fiscal policy
- Inflation
- Interest rates
- International differences

Caveat: These categories overlap. The definition and assumptions are often ambiguous. For example, the common assertion that P/E is linked to Earnings Growth requires further specification. Does the P/E reflect *past* Earnings Growth? Does it forecast future growth? What time periods are involved? What *is* the exact definition of Earnings? Too often, even such basic points are not clear in the published literature. The following survey should be seen as a "best efforts" attempt to sort out these factors and summarize the relevant research findings.

CHAPTER 4   INTERPRETATIONS: P/E AS A DEPENDENT VARIABLE

4.2 Firm-Level Drivers
4.2.1 Growth

Many explanations of the P/E and other multiples invoke a common theme: the Multiple is driven by the growth of the business, specifically earnings or sales growth.

> The core principle [is] that growth in earnings explains to price-to-earnings ratio.[4]

> A central organizing principle [is] that firms with a relatively large P/E ratio ought to have a relatively large growth in expected earnings... Such a relation would seem to be beyond dispute.[5]

The default assumption is that fast-growing companies will carry higher multiples. Why does *Amazon* have a Price/Sales ratio so much higher than *Walmart's*? Because its sales are growing much faster.[6] (See Figure 4-1.)

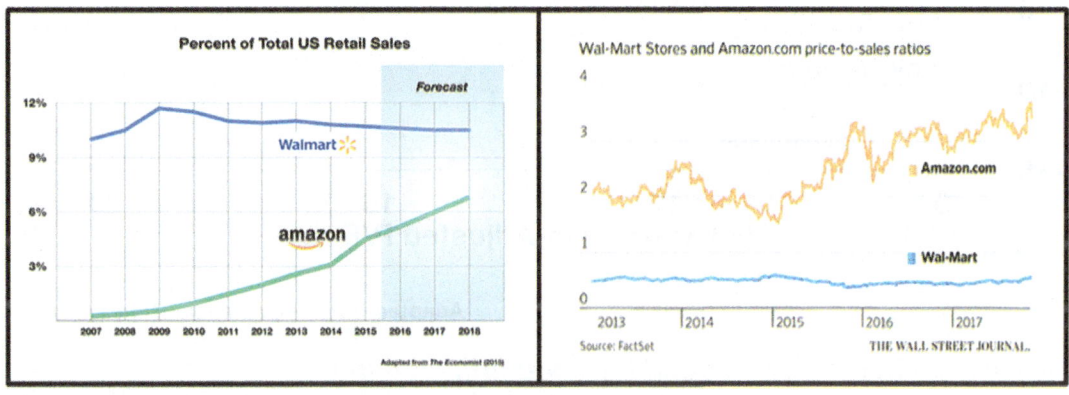

Figure 4-1. *Walmart vs. Amazon – the Effect of Growth*[7]

---

[4]James Ohlson and Zhan Gao, "Earnings, Earnings Growth and Value," *Foundations and Trends in Accounting*, Vol. 1, No. 1 (2006), pp. 1–70.

[5]James Ohlson and Beate Juettner-Nauroth, "Expected EPS and EPS Growth as Determinants of Value," *Review of Accounting Studies*, Vol 10 (2005), pp. 349–365.

[6]"Walmart: Thinking Outside the Box," *The Economist*, June 4, 2016; Justin Lahart, "Wal-Mart Should Worry Amazon," *The Wall Street Journal*, November 17, 2017.

[7]Left: Adapted from "Walmart: Thinking Outside the Box," *The Economist*, June 4, 2016. Right: Justin Lahart, "Wal-Mart Should Worry Amazon," *The Wall Street Journal*, November 17, 2017. Reproduced by permission from *The Wall Street Journal*.

CHAPTER 4   INTERPRETATIONS: P/E AS A DEPENDENT VARIABLE

There is some support for this interpretation. Here, from *the Financial Times* in 2014, is a plot of Revenue Growth vs. P/E for some of the leading companies in the tech sector, showing at least a rough correlation.[8] (See Figure 4-2.)

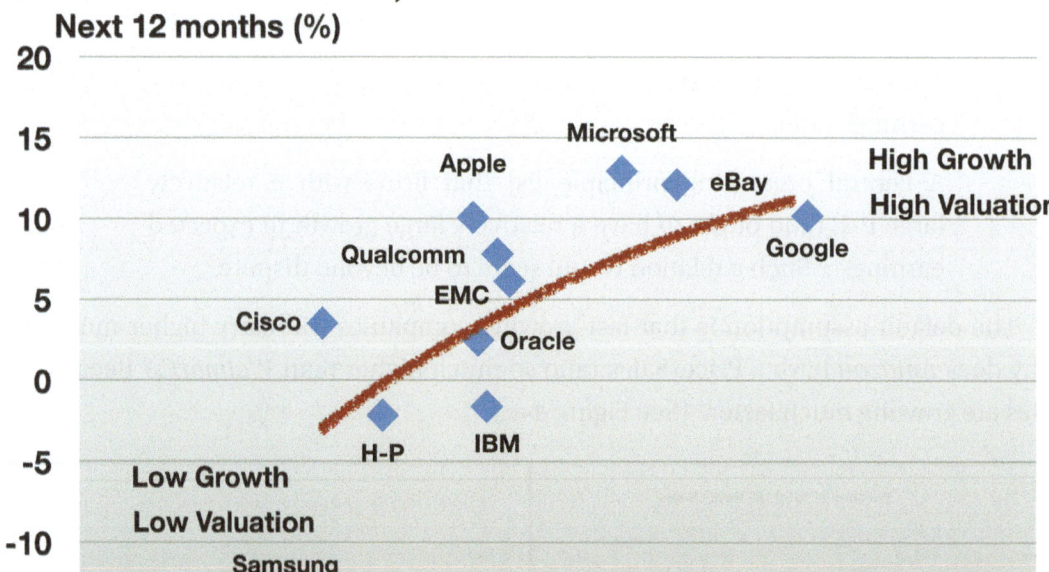

Adapted from *The Financial Times* (2014)

Figure 4-2. *Revenue Growth and Price-to-Earnings Ratio*[9]

Another example, with a different multiple – the Forward version of the EV/EBITDA – shows the projected 1-year growth in cash flow for companies in the European telecom sector.[10] (See Figure 4-3.)

---

[8]"Close to the Tree," *Financial Times*, October 11, 2014.
[9]Source: 2014, "Close to the Tree," *Financial Times*, October 11. Used under license from the *Financial Times*. All Rights Reserved.
[10]"Dot to Dot," *Financial Times*, January 27, 2015.

CHAPTER 4   INTERPRETATIONS: P/E AS A DEPENDENT VARIABLE

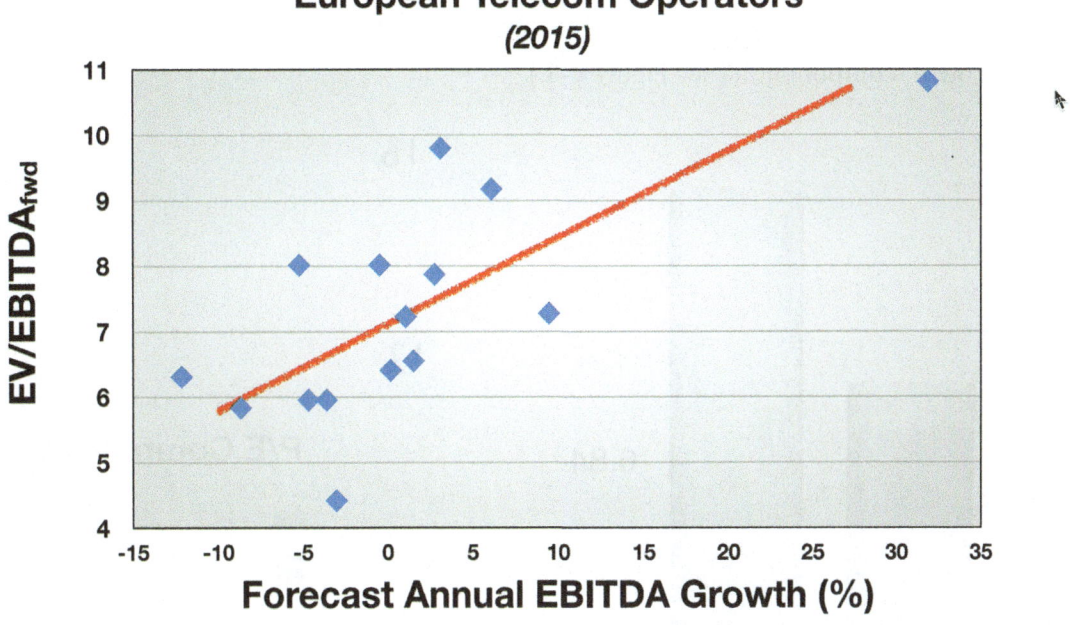

Adapted from *The Financial Times (2015)*

Figure 4-3. Cash Flow Growth and EV/EBITDA Ratio[11]

A nuanced version of this argument recognizes that even if no growth is predicted, a company's "steady-state" earnings still have value. A report by *Citigroup's* Financial Strategy Group splits the Earnings multiple into a "base" component – reflecting the profits from the existing business – and a "growth" component, which captures the expected increase in future earnings.[12] In April 2009 – near the bottom of the stock market crash – the Forward P/E of the S&P 500 was 11.5, of which 92% was attributed to the "base" component and only a small residual to the forecast of future earnings. This pessimistic view reflected the dire conditions of the economy at that time, still in the trough of the deepest recession in decades; growth was not in the picture. But nine months later, in

---

[11]Source: 2015, "Dot to Dot," *Financial Times*, January 27. Used under license from the *Financial Times*. All Rights Reserved.

[12]Liam Denning, "New American Cash Conundrum: Too Much," *The Wall Street Journal*, January 21, 2010.

CHAPTER 4   INTERPRETATIONS: P/E AS A DEPENDENT VARIABLE

January 2010, the market was beginning to forecast an economic recovery. Revived animal spirits now set a market P/E some 30% higher at 15.2 – of which almost half was attributed to the "growth" component.[13] (See Figure 4-4.)

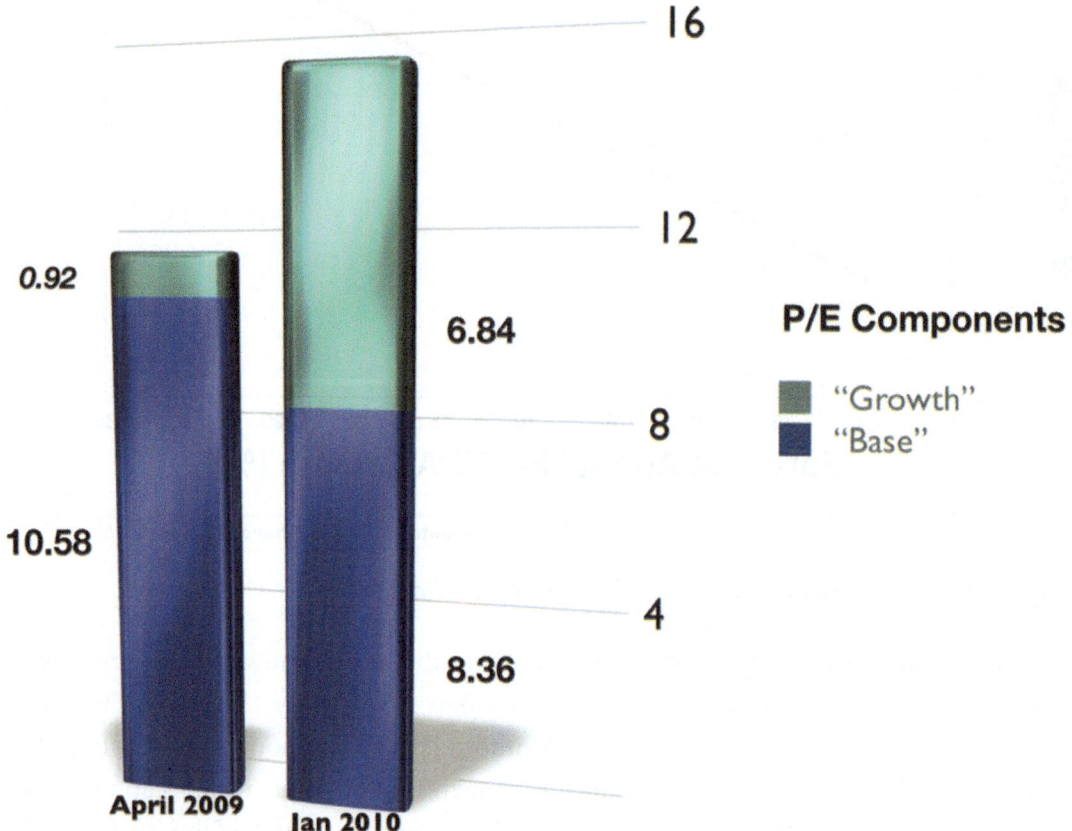

Figure 4-4. *P/E Decomposed into Base and Growth Components*[14]

We see a similar pattern in the following chart of the P/E multiples of selected companies in the pharmaceutical industry in 2014.[15] (See Figure 4-5.)

---

[13]These distinctions are unobservable – like many aspects of Value – and the calculations are speculative. The thesis is unprovable, but plausible.

[14]Data from Liam Denning, "New American Cash Conundrum: Too Much," *The Wall Street Journal*, January 21, 2010.

[15]"Are you on Drugs?" *Financial Times*, April 2, 2014.

CHAPTER 4   INTERPRETATIONS: P/E AS A DEPENDENT VARIABLE

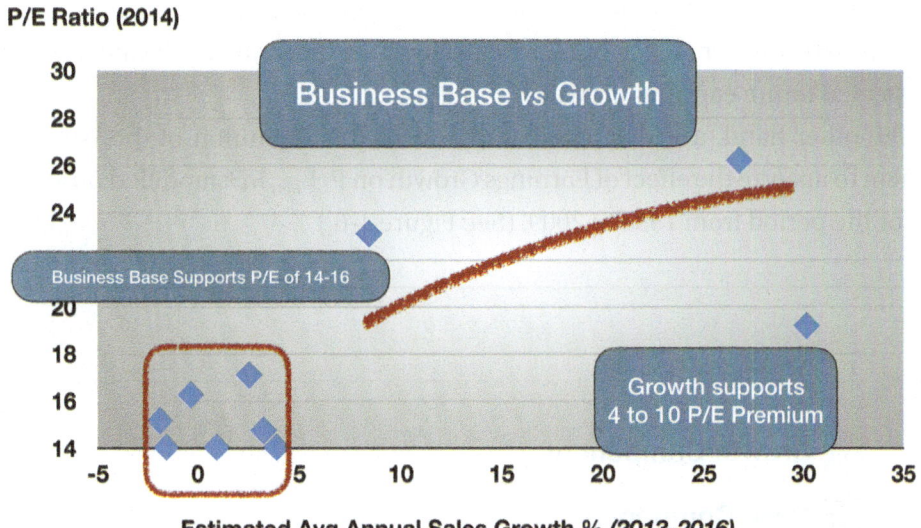

Figure 4-5. *Base and Growth P/E Components in the Pharmaceutical Industry*[16]

The idea of a *Base + Growth* decomposition of the multiple – where the *Total value of the firm = Steady-state value + "Future value creation"* – is now quite common. There are of course different ideas about how to separate out the two components. The steady-state component is said to be that part of the business which is "sustainable indefinitely" from its own proceeds (presumably), but will not grow or generate returns at a rate in excess of the cost of capital. For this portion of the business, one approach is to set the steady-state P/E equal to the reciprocal of the cost of capital, or the discount rate.[17]

$$\text{Steady-state price-earnings multiple} = \frac{1}{\text{Cost of equity}}$$

---

[16]Source: 2014, "Are you on Drugs?" *Financial Times*, April 2. Used under license from the *Financial Times*. All Rights Reserved.

[17]Michael J. Mauboussin and Dan Callahan, "What Does a Price-Earnings Multiple Mean?" *Global Financial Strategies, Credit Suisse,* January 29, 2014. The terminology should not confuse. For this purpose, the company's cost of capital is assumed to be equal to (i.e., used as) the discount rate.

139

CHAPTER 4   INTERPRETATIONS: P/E AS A DEPENDENT VARIABLE

If we accept this formula, then, given a figure for the "cost of equity" – not a simple calculation – we can determine the steady-state P/E. In the study cited here, the cost of equity is taken to be 8% – which allows us to define the steady-state P/E as 12.5. If a particular firm has an actual P/E of 25, we can conclude that half of that valuation is based on its expected future earnings growth.[18]

On the other hand, a widely cited study[19] uses this definition of the "steady-state" component to analyze the effect of Earnings Growth on P/E_{ttm}, in a modified *Base + Growth* model, for the period from 1953 to 2009. (See Figure 4-6.)

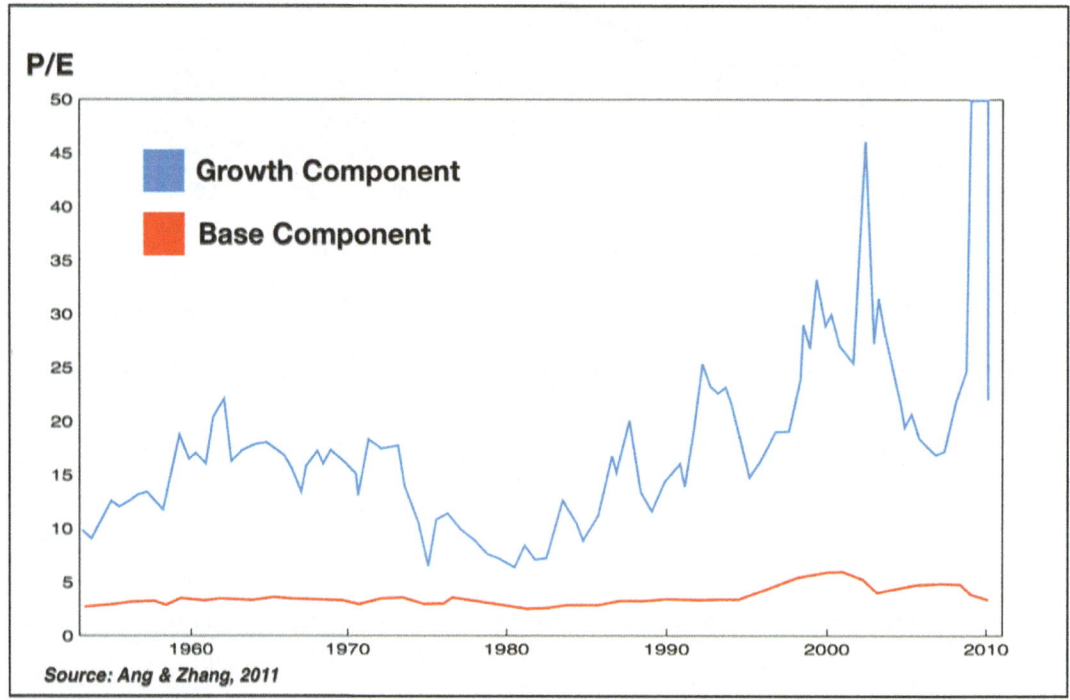

Figure 4-6. *Base and Growth P/E Components*[20]

---

[18]If you find this reasoning opaque, you are not alone. The "cost of equity" is composed of the "risk-free rate" – which of course is variable – and the "equity risk premium," a cloudy quantity at best, which often serves as the plug variable to explain deviations in other valuation metrics. See the Appendix for a more in-depth critique.

[19]Andrew Ang and Xiaoyan Zhang, "Price-Earnings Ratios: Growth and Discount Rates," *The Research Foundation of the CFA Institute* (2011), pp. 130–142.

[20]Adapted from Andrew Ang and Xiaoyan Zhang, "Price-Earnings Ratios: Growth and Discount Rates," *The Research Foundation of the CFA Institute* (2011), pp. 130–142.

Among their findings:

- The average P/E for the period is 18.5.

- The no-growth or steady-state P/E is only 3.8; the growth component is 14.7.

- The variability of the P/E is driven almost entirely by the growth component.

These results should be viewed with caution. If the steady-state component of the Earnings Multiple is the reciprocal of the cost of capital, then a steady-state value of 3.8 implies a long-term cost of equity in the United States of over 26% – which is clearly not correct. What these models label the "growth component" is simply the part of the Multiple that is *not explained* (statistically) by steady-state earnings. It is a *residual*, and a large one. The steady-state component is shown as quite static, decade after decade, which seems unlikely in light of other trends in the economy, the business cycle, and rising corporate profitability and leverage.[21] The growth component probably rolls up many other factors (discussed later in this chapter) in addition to expected EPS growth. The *Citibank* model conveys more realism, I believe, about the size and variability of the two components.

4.2.1.1 The Case for Growth

So how well does the total P/E "measure" or correlate with *actual* earnings growth?

It is not clear. Some early studies found *no* relationship between growth and P/E at the firm level.[22] However, when later researchers aggregated "portfolios" to "diversify out the noise at the individual stock level," they observed a fairly strong correlation.

---

[21]The concept of a P/E component based on "steady-state" earnings, while it sounds plausible, is probably more difficult to define than it seems. For example, a company with steady-state earnings based on typical retail sales (e.g., a department store) might carry a lower P/E on those earnings than a company with a subscription-based business model (e.g., a telecommunications company). More generally, the quality of revenue and earnings matters. This effect may operate at the level of the economy as a whole; as American firms have shifted to asset-light strategies and subscription-based business models, the value of earnings may be changing.

[22]Joseph Murphy and Harold Stevenson, "Price/Earnings Ratios and Future Growth of Earnings and Dividends," *Financial Analysts Journal* (November/December 1967), pp. 111–114.

CHAPTER 4   INTERPRETATIONS: P/E AS A DEPENDENT VARIABLE

EPS growth "explained" 58% of the variance in the P/E 1 year forward, dropping to 25% for EPS growth 2 years out and essentially to zero thereafter.

> In general the pattern behaves as if market participants, in determining prices, cannot forecast growth beyond two years.[23]

(This is in line with the assessments of analysts' forecasting accuracy cited in Chapter 3.)

R^2 values of around 34% (from 1881 to 2013, for 3-year forward growth) to 38% (from 1953 to 2009, for 1-year forward growth) have been reported – implying that earnings growth may retrospectively "explain" a bit more than one-third of the P/E.[24] (This of course means that two-thirds of the phenomenon is left unexplained.) Moreover, in some studies the effect of earnings per share growth appears to be much stronger in the aggregate – that is, at the level of the market, say – than at the firm level. Penman (1996) found that for "portfolios" of approximately 130 firms each, EPS growth 3 years out explains 43% of the P/E variance.[25] But for individual companies, the EPS growth has almost no explanatory value (5%). Worse, updated studies seem to show that – strangely – in the last few years the relationship has disappeared.[26] (See Figure 4-7 – another side effect of loose monetary policy?[27])

---

[23] William Beaver and Dale Morse, "What Determines Price-Earnings Ratios?" *Financial Analysts Journal* (July/August 1978), pp. 65–76. A follow-up study focusing on a very short-term and rather specialized data set (1964–1968) found an even stronger correlation – an R^2 of 70% – between "long-term growth expectations" (obtained from reading analysts' reports) and P/E. This may be viewed as a sentiment metric, however. Paul Zarowin, "What Determines Earnings-Price Ratios: Revisited," *Journal of Accounting, Auditing, and Finance*, Vol. 5, No. 3 (1990), pp. 439–457.

[24] Rick Ferri, "P/E Doesn't Predict Future Earnings," *Forbes*, October 29, 2013.

[25] I hope I am reading this right. The study covers 2574 firms from 1968 to 1985 and constructs ten portfolios ranked by P/E (Stephen H. Penman, "The Articulation of Price-Earnings Ratios and Market-to-Book Ratios and the Evaluation of Growth," *Journal of Accounting Research*, Vol. 34, No. 2 (Autumn, 1996), pp. 235–259).

[26] David Trainer, "EPS growth rate has almost no correlation with P/E," *ValueWalk*, January 15, 2017. Available at www.valuewalk.com/2017/01/real-earnings-season-doesnt-start-february/. See also David Trainer, "Here's Why P/E Ratios Are A Poor Way To Measure Value," *Forbes*, December 16, 2015. Also Andrew Ang and Xiaoyan Zhang, "Price-Earnings Ratios: Growth and Discount Rates," *The Research Foundation of the CFA Institute* (2011), pp. 130–142.

[27] On the assumption that quantitative easing has changed the thinking and the motivation of investors, stimulating the equity markets to go "beyond the fundamentals" – thus attenuating the linkage between earnings and market prices (and valuation metrics).

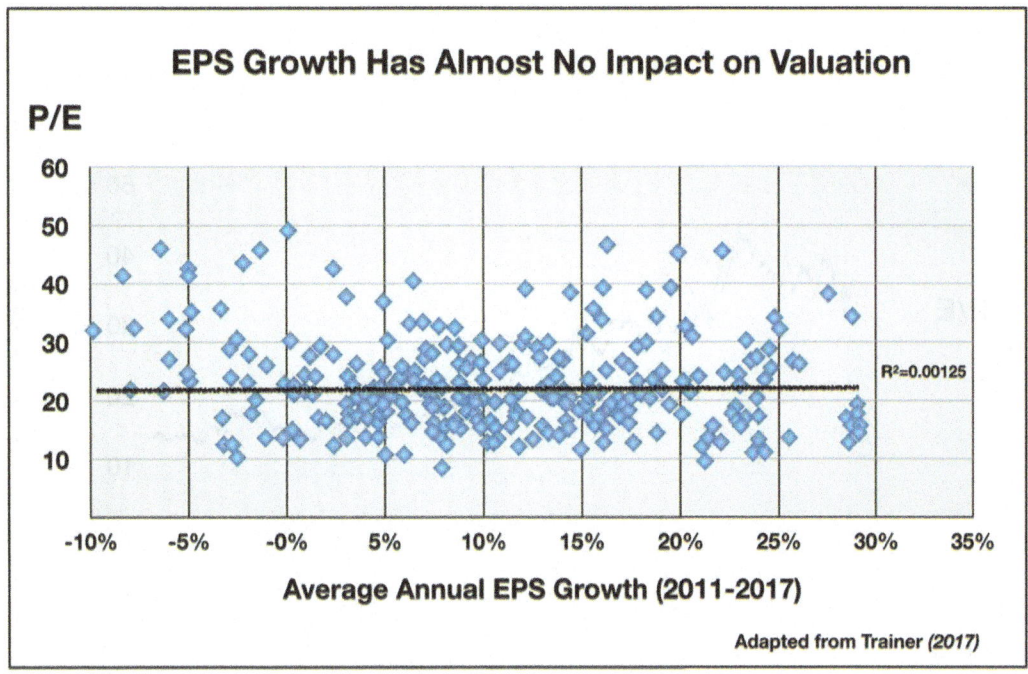

Figure 4-7. *EPS Growth vs. P/E Ratio for the S&P 500*[28]

A contrary theme also emerges from the data: at a certain point in a company's evolution, growth seems to lose its relevance as a driver of valuation. The P/E sags even though the firm is still experiencing robust growth in sales and earnings.

For example, between 2000 and 2010, Walmart *tripled* its earnings per share. But its P/E contracted from around 45 to about 14.[29] As a result, the share price stagnated. (See Figure 4-8.)

---

[28]Adapted from David Trainer, "EPS growth rate has almost no correlation with P/E," *ValueWalk*, January 15, 2017.

[29]Lawrence C. Strauss, "Home on the Range," *Barron's*, September 21, 2009; Sandra Ward, "Load Up the Shopping Cart," *Barron's*, July 12, 2010; John Jannarone, "Walmart Shifts Into Slow Lane of Growth," *The Wall Street Journal*, May 19, 2010; John Jannarone, "Wal-Mart's Tough Work Experience," *The Wall Street Journal*, February 23, 2011.

CHAPTER 4   INTERPRETATIONS: P/E AS A DEPENDENT VARIABLE

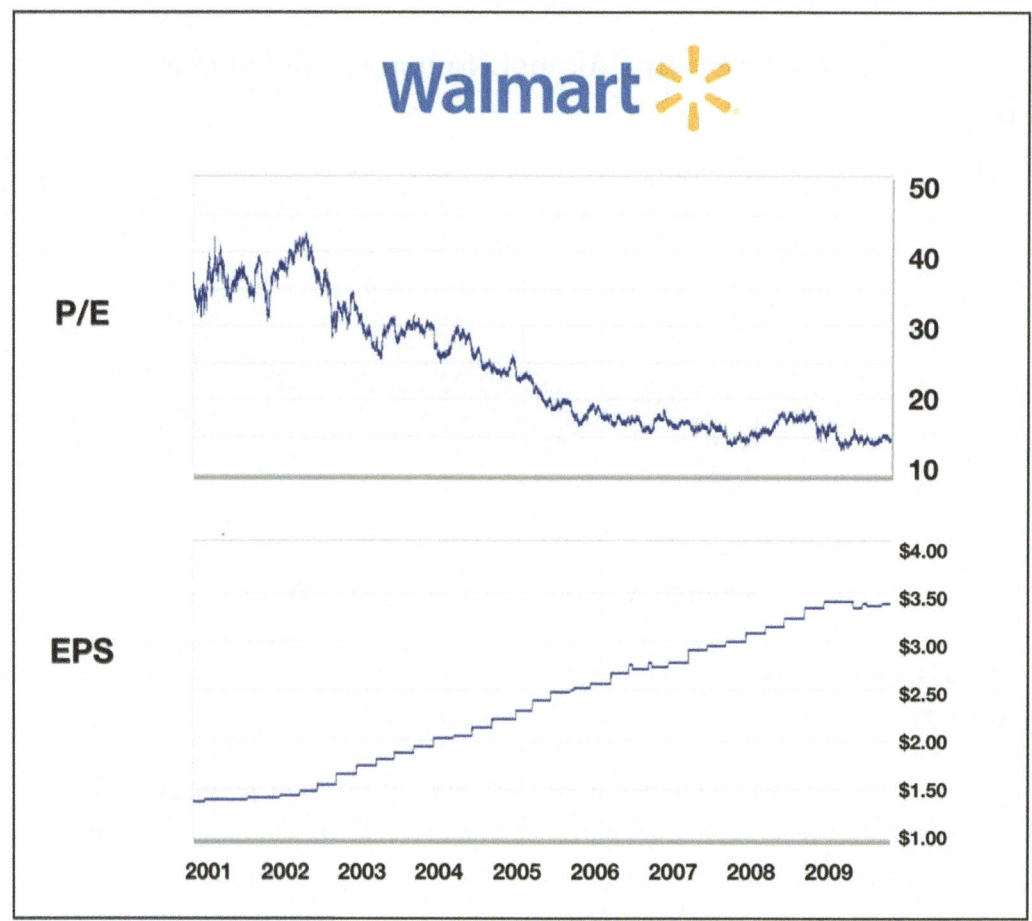

Figure 4-8. *P/E Compression*

Microsoft is a similar case.[30] From 2000 to 2010, its revenue tripled and its earnings more than doubled. It repurchased its shares on a massive scale. But the company's P/E fell by a factor of 4, and the share price was flat. (See Figure 4-9.)

---

[30]Liam Denning, "Exxon and Microsoft: Riding Into the Sunset," *The Wall Street Journal*, May 18, 2011; Tiernan Ray, "Memo to Microsoft: Show Us the Money," *Barron's*, July 18, 2011; Spencer Jakab, "Windows Opportunity Opens at Microsoft," *The Wall Street Journal*, April 19, 2012; Randall Stross, "Even with all its Profits, Microsoft Has a Popularity Problem," *The New York Times*, July 25, 2010.

CHAPTER 4   INTERPRETATIONS: P/E AS A DEPENDENT VARIABLE

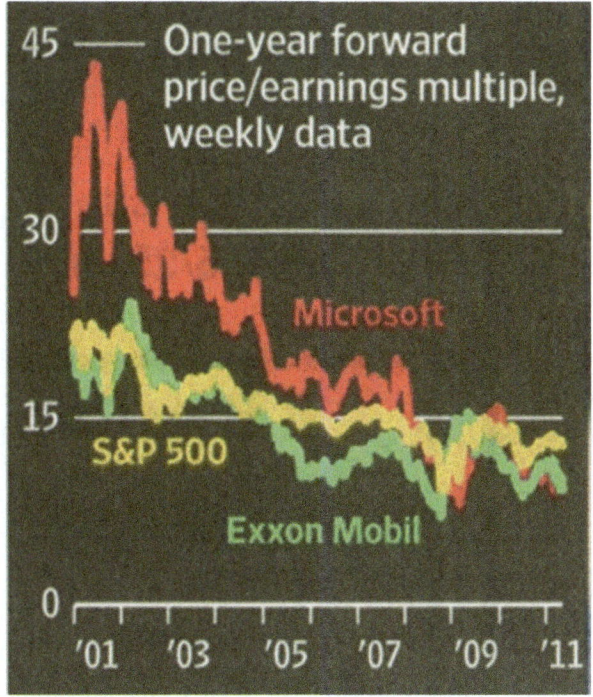

Figure 4-9. *P/E Compression*[31]

Between 2005 and 2015, *Cisco's* sales doubled, and its EPS grew even faster.[32] The share price was flat as its multiple declined.

These examples illustrate what might be termed a Maturity Reset, in which the P/E multiple shifts from a focus on growth to a focus on the mature, steady-state business – even though the company is still growing vigorously. It points to the complex, inconsistent relationship between growth and P/E multiples.

There are of course many pitfalls associated with the P/E, especially with the variability of the denominator, which undercut (potentially) the Earnings-Growth-as-Driver argument. As noted in the previous chapter, GAAP-approved Net Earnings can bounce around because of one-time charges or gains. A large one-time loss can bump up the P/E and compromise its value as a measure of earnings growth potential. Share buybacks – addressed later in this chapter – also disrupt the case for viewing the

---

[31]Liam Denning, "Exxon and Microsoft: Riding Into the Sunset," *The Wall Street Journal*, May 18, 2011. Reproduced by permission from *The Wall Street Journal*.
[32]Quentin Hardy, "Tech's Transition Reaches Cisco," *The New York Times*, May 5, 2015.

CHAPTER 4   INTERPRETATIONS: P/E AS A DEPENDENT VARIABLE

P/E as a measure of earnings growth, by introducing a "non-fundamental" source of EPS augmentation.

A more profound question about the relationship between growth and the multiple, a conundrum that anticipates the discussion in following chapter – involves the use of the P/E as an independent variable, to forecast stock market returns. If high P/E signals high future growth, shouldn't that predict strong future stock market returns – since presumably a company that is growing its earnings should see its share price increase, as a rule (keeping the Maturity Reset phenomenon in mind)?

But this is *not* what we see. As an *independent* variable, as a predictor of market performance, the P/E signal is contrarian: a high P/E generally signals *poor* stock market returns going forward. How is it that a projected high future growth could drive poor returns?[33]

4.2.2 Profitability, and "Quality"

Companies are in business to make a profit. Oddly, though, profitability as such has not been studied much in relation to valuation – there may be a bias in academia which sees "profit" as too superficial or "mechanical"[34] to be interesting. Researchers are therefore sometimes surprised to discover what should be obvious: profitability *is* an important driver of enterprise value.[35]

---

[33]Some academics talk around this problem by arguing that "theory" somehow supports this dichotomous set of facts. *"Both intuitive and formal analyses of the factors that determine price-earnings (P/E) ratios predict a positive relation with anticipated growth and a negative relation with expected rates of return"* (Jacob Thomas and Huai Zhang, "Another Look at P/E Ratios," Working Paper, Yale School of Management, 2006 – which is otherwise a very useful resource). I cannot agree that it is "intuitive" – the commonsense view is that a fast-growing company is one whose share price will appreciate.

[34]Robert Novy-Marx, "The Other Side of Value: The Gross Profitability Premium," *Journal of Financial Economics,* Vol. 108 (2013), pp. 1–28.

[35]Recently, a widely cited article in a prestigious academic journal could announce an amazing discovery… (wait for it): *"Profitable firms generate significantly higher returns than unprofitable firms"* (Robert Novy-Marx, "The Other Side of Value: The Gross Profitability Premium," *Journal of Financial Economics,* Vol. 108 (2013), pp. 1–28). This study uses *Gross Profit* as its central metric. There is also this, based on a *Net Profit* metric: *"Higher positive profitability tends to be associated with higher returns"* (E. Fama and K. French, "Dissecting Anomalies," *Journal of Finance,* Vol. 63, No. 4 (August 2008), pp. 1653–1678). This perspective – that profit potential is important in determining value – is of course what keeps the Discounted Cash Flow modelers in business.

The basic intuition *is* obvious; moreover, the assumption connecting earnings *growth* to valuation multiples (Section 4.2.1) suggests that earnings (profit) should receive greater attention, not just as a trend (growth) but also as a structural variable (profitability). Yet "Profit" – a standard accounting measure – is different from "Profitability," which encompasses a broader set of considerations, including the nature of the underlying cost structure of the company's business model, the customer profiles, accounting policies (the use, or avoidance, of accruals), and the reliability or repeatability of the revenue streams.

In any case, the idea of Profitability has two different interpretations.

From the standpoint of the business, Profitability is a neutral accounting measure, based on some version of Revenue-Minus-Expenses. Depending on which categories of expenses are subtracted from top-line Revenue, there are several profitability metrics to choose from, such as Gross Margin, Operating Margin, Net Margin, Cash Flow Margin.

From the standpoint of the investor, profitability is viewed as the return to the invested capital.[36] Common metrics are Return on Equity (ROE) and Return on Total Capital (also referred to as Return on Invested Capital [ROIC] or Return on Capital Employed [ROCE]). The denominator of ROE is the equity capital (only), invested by shareholders. ROIC is based on both equity and debt capital invested in the company.

Finally, in a related development, the study of valuation anomalies has recently led to the identification of a "Quality Factor" which may drive abnormal positive stock returns (similar to the more familiar "Value" and "Size or Small Cap" factors). "Quality" is typically seen as multidimensional, including some measure of "Profitability" along with various other considerations.

---

[36]This does **not** refer to stock market returns, or an investor's "profit" on share sold.

4.2.2.1 Gross Profit Metrics

Among the various accounting categories, Gross Profit – *Net Revenue minus Variable Product Costs* – is said to provide the best measure of "true economic profitability."[37] It is used to construct scale-normalized metrics such as

- Gross Margin: Gross Profit/Net Revenues
- Gross Profit/Total Assets (which some prefer to the more traditional Return-on-Assets measure, which uses Net Profits in the numerator)

Novy-Marx, in an important recent study of the relationship between Gross Profit and Market Value, finds that profitable firms have significantly higher valuation ratios (the Price-to-Book ratio, in this study – although presented in the inverse form, Market-to-Book). The author concludes that "the ratio of a firm's gross profits to its assets has roughly the same power as [the P/B, or B/P] for predicting average [stock market] returns." The relationship is strongest for companies with the highest gross profit metrics, which is in line with macroeconomic trends that favor companies that leverage "intangible" assets like brand and technology (which lowers the value of the P/B denominator while typically increasing the gross margin).[38] (See Figure 4-10.)

---

[37] *"Gross profits is the cleanest accounting measure of true economic profitability. The farther down he income statement one goes, the more polluted profitability measures become."* (Robert Novy-Marx, "The Other Side of Value: The Gross Profitability Premium," *Journal of Financial Economics,* Vol. 108 (2013), pp. 1–28).

[38] The correlation between Book/Market (the inverse of Price-to-Book) and gross profit is negative 0.18 – judged "highly significant" by the author (Robert Novy-Marx, "The Other Side of Value: The Gross Profitability Premium," *Journal of Financial Economics,* Vol. 108 (2013), pp. 1–28). Earlier studies found that Gross Profit does contain more information than Net Earnings (Robert C. Lipe, "The Information Contained in the Components of Earnings," *Journal of Accounting Research: Studies on Alternative Measures of Accounting Income,* Vol. 24 (1986), pp. 37–64). This is confirmed in the study by James Ohlson and Stephen Penman, "Disaggregated Accounting Data as Explanatory Variables for Returns," *Journal of Accounting, Auditing, & Finance,* Vol. 7, No. 4 (Fall 1992), pp. 553–573.

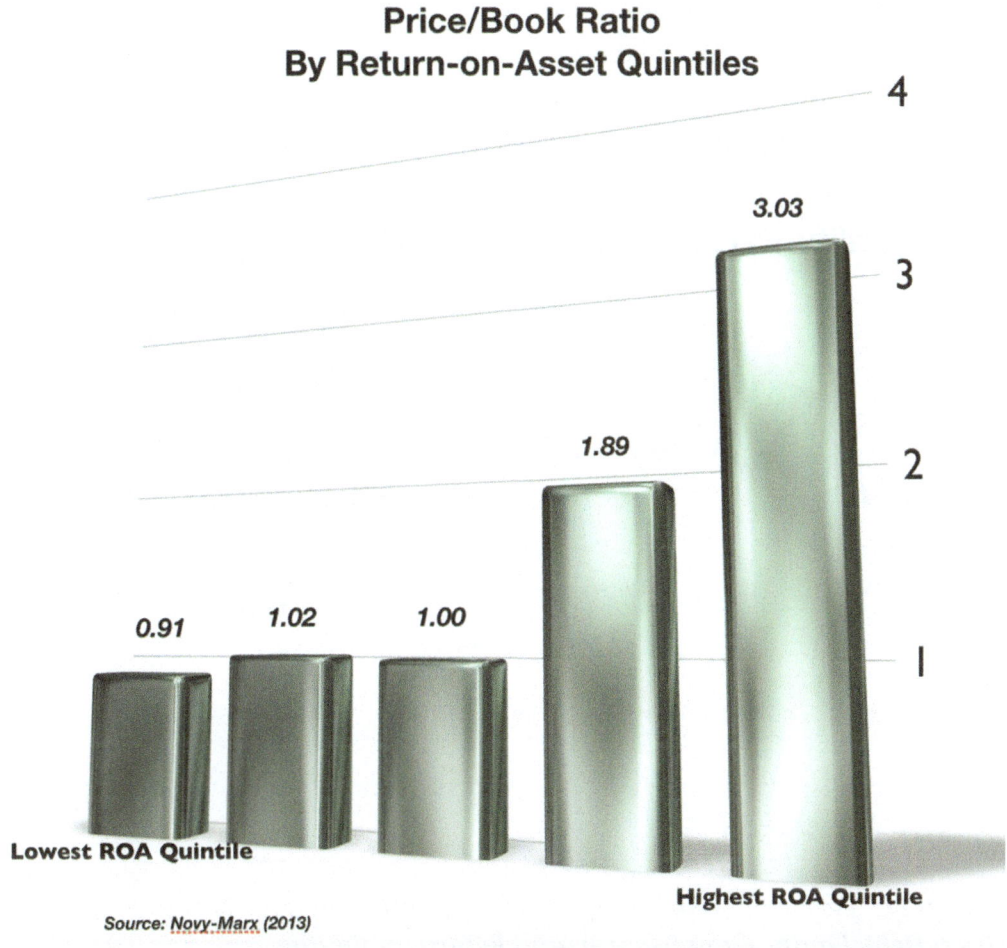

Figure 4-10. Return-on-Assets and Price-to-Book

4.2.2.2 Return on Equity

The most studied metric of profitability from an investment perspective is *Return on Equity*. The standard assumption is that, of two similar firms, the one with the higher Return on Equity should show stronger market returns, a higher valuation, and presumably a higher market multiple.

>It is easy to verify that the P/E ratio increases with ROE.[39]

>Firms with high P/E ratios tend to have lower ROE.[40]

---

[39]Zvi Bodie, Alex Kane, and Alan Marcus, *Investments* (McGraw-Hill, 2002), p. 577.

[40]Wan-Ting Wu, "The P/E Ratio and Profitability," *Journal of Business and Economic Research,* Vol. 12, No. 1 (Q1 2014) pp. 67–76.

CHAPTER 4   INTERPRETATIONS: P/E AS A DEPENDENT VARIABLE

The findings are mixed. *MSCI* reports that ROE is the strongest predictor of market returns out of several "quality" metrics (including debt/equity ratio, earnings volatility).[41] *S&P* reports the same result.[42] *FactorResearch*,[43] provides a revealing decomposition of its "Quality" metric, which shows the dominance of the ROE component. (See Figure 4-11.)

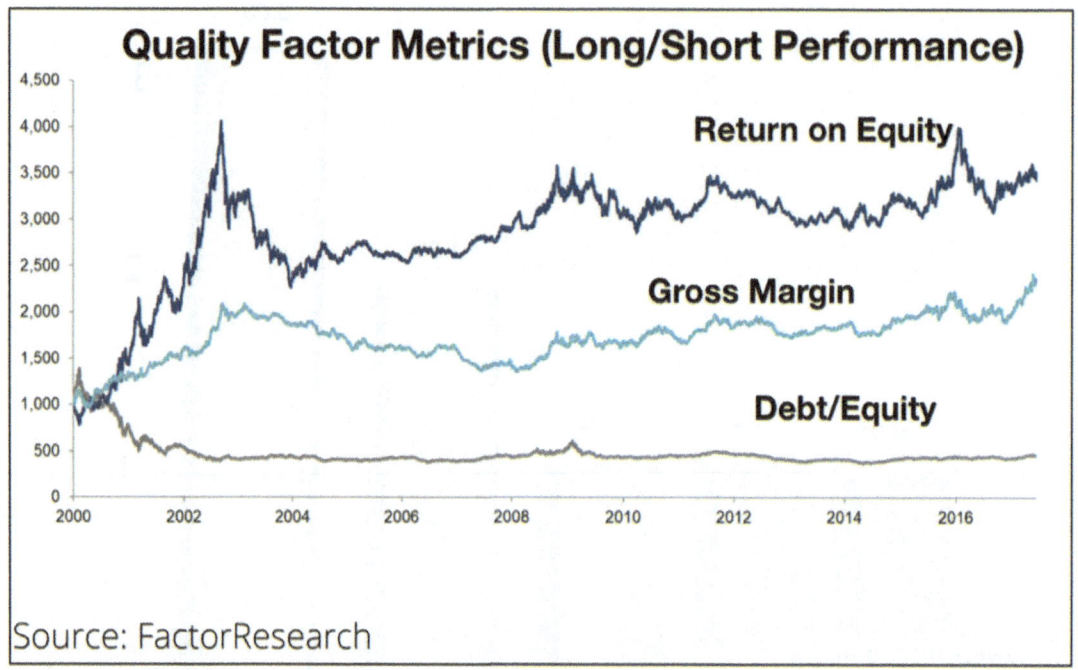

Figure 4-11. *Performance of Long/Short Portfolios Based on Three Quality Factor Metrics: Debt/Equity, Gross Margin, and Return on Equity*[44]

---

[41]MSCI, "Playing Defense: Using the MSCI Quality Factor," www.msci.com/quality-factor

[42]S&P Dow Jones Indices, "S&P Quality Indices - Methodology," January 2019, https://us.spindices.com/documents/methodologies/methodology-sp-quality-indices.pdf

[43]Nicolas Rabener, "Quality Factor: How to Define It?" *FactorResearch*, July 2017.

[44]Nicolas Rabener, "Quality Factor: How to Define It?" *FactorResearch*, July 2017.

These sources do not directly analyze the relationship of ROE to P/E. However, FactorResearch concludes that "companies that are more profitable [higher ROE] than others should be trading at higher valuations" – implying that they will carry higher P/E's. The study does sort companies by Price-to-Book and shows a strong positive relationship with profitability (ROE).[45] (See Figure 4-12.)

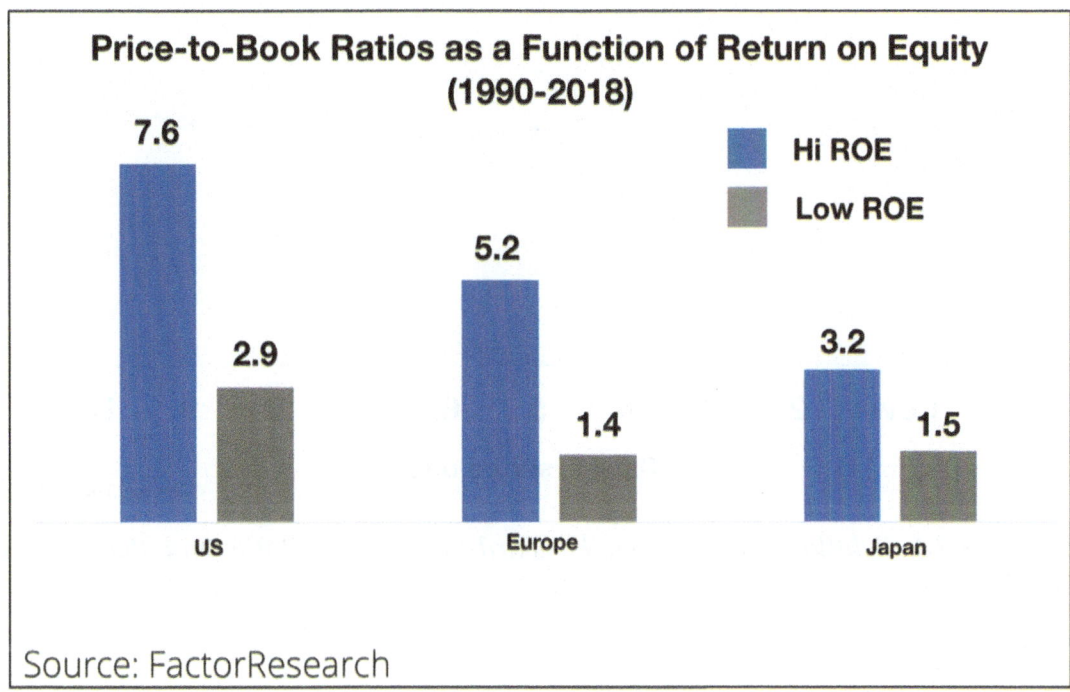

Figure 4-12. *Performance of Long/Short Portfolios Based on Price-to-Book*[46]

On the other hand… an academic study from 2014 found a more ambiguous relationship with the *earnings* multiple. The forward P/E was *highest* for firms with the *lowest* ROEs – that is, a *high* P/E was associated with *low* profitability – and the relationship followed a U-shape over the spectrum of firms sorted by ROE. (See Figure 4-13.)

---

[45]Nicolas Rabener, "The Odd Factors" Profitability and Investment," *FactorResearch*, November 2018.

[46]Nicolas Rabener, "The Odd Factors" Profitability and Investment," *FactorResearch*, November 2018.

CHAPTER 4   INTERPRETATIONS: P/E AS A DEPENDENT VARIABLE

Forward P/E Ratio

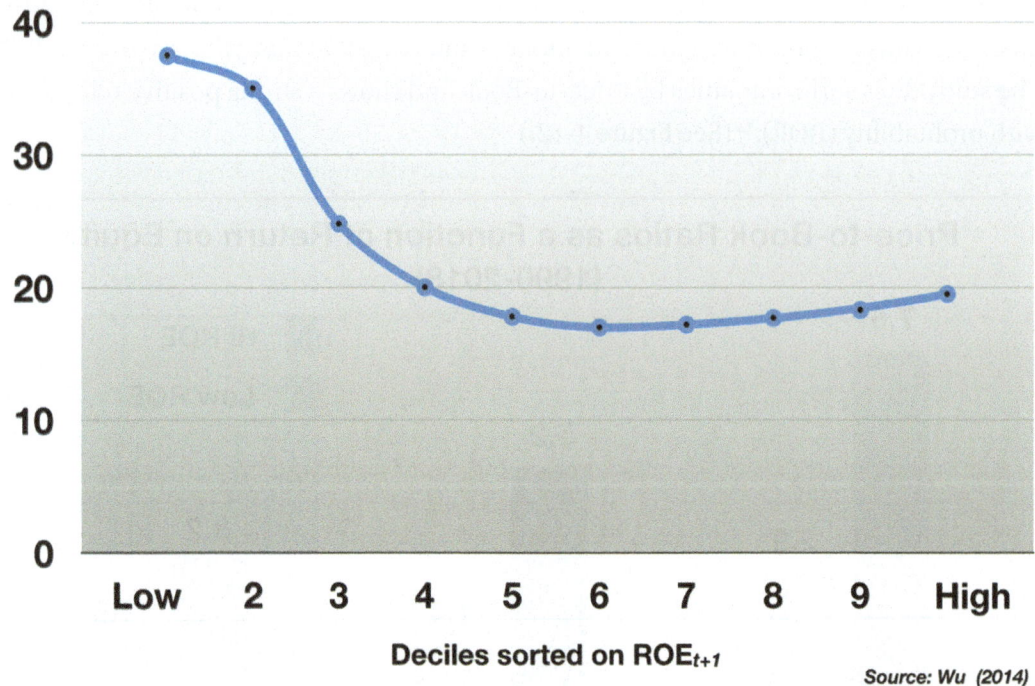

Figure 4-13. Relationship Between Forward-to-Earnings Ratio and Return on Equity[47]

Moreover:

> Firms with higher forward P/E ratios achieve *lower* ROE in the subsequent years and the distribution of their realized ROE is more volatile and widespread than firms with lower forward P/E ratios.[48]

I have personally analyzed the relationship between ROE and P/E_{fwd} for firms in several sectors (pharmaceutical, energy, consumer products), and I have found virtually zero correlation in the data for the recent period (2018).

---

[47]Adapted from Wan-Ting Wu, "The P/E Ratio And Profitability," *Journal of Business and Economics Research* – Vol 12, No. 1 (2014), pp. 67–76.

[48]Wan-Ting Wu, "The P/E Ratio And Profitability," *Journal of Business and Economics Research* – Vol. 12, No. 1 (2014), pp. 67–76.

4.2.2.3 The "Quality" Factor

The discovery that higher "quality" businesses demonstrably outperform the rest of the field is a late revelation of the academic literature. Practitioners are working to develop appropriate metrics. The definition of "Quality" varies and typically combines a number of dimensions related to fairly conventional views of what comprises a "good business." Some examples are the following:

- **MSCI:** "A company's quality can be evaluated along five key dimensions: profitability, earnings quality, financial leverage, asset growth and corporate governance. Various descriptors can be used to define each of these dimensions, but we have constructed the MSCI Quality Index using these three: Return on Equity, Debt to Equity, Earnings Variability."[49]

- **S&P:** "The S&P 500 Quality Index…is a composite measure of ROE, accruals, and leverage."[50]

- **FactorResearch:** Noting that Quality is "the factor where opinions are the most diverse regarding the definition," *FactorResearch* chooses to focus on debt equity, ROE, and gross margin (without specifying the mix precisely).[51]

None of these sources directly link the "Quality" factor to the P/E multiple. However, the P/E_{ttm} of several Exchange Traded Funds that track major Quality indices (e.g., S&P, MSCI) traded a discount of 12–22% compared to the P/E_{ttm} of the broad market, as of December 31, 2018 – suggesting that the "Quality" factor is associated with a *lower* P/E multiple, at least some of the time.[52] (See Figure 4-14.)

---

[49] MSCI, "Playing Defense: Using the MSCI Quality Factor," www.msci.com/quality-factor

[50] S&P Dow Jones Indices, "S&P Quality Indices – Methodology," January 2019, https://us.spindices.com/documents/methodologies/methodology-sp-quality-indices.pdf

[51] Nicolas Rabener, "Quality Factor: How to Define It?" *FactorResearch*, July 2017.

[52] Over a ten-year period, the *S&P Quality Index* underperformed the broad *S&P 500* index by more than 5%.

CHAPTER 4   INTERPRETATIONS: P/E AS A DEPENDENT VARIABLE

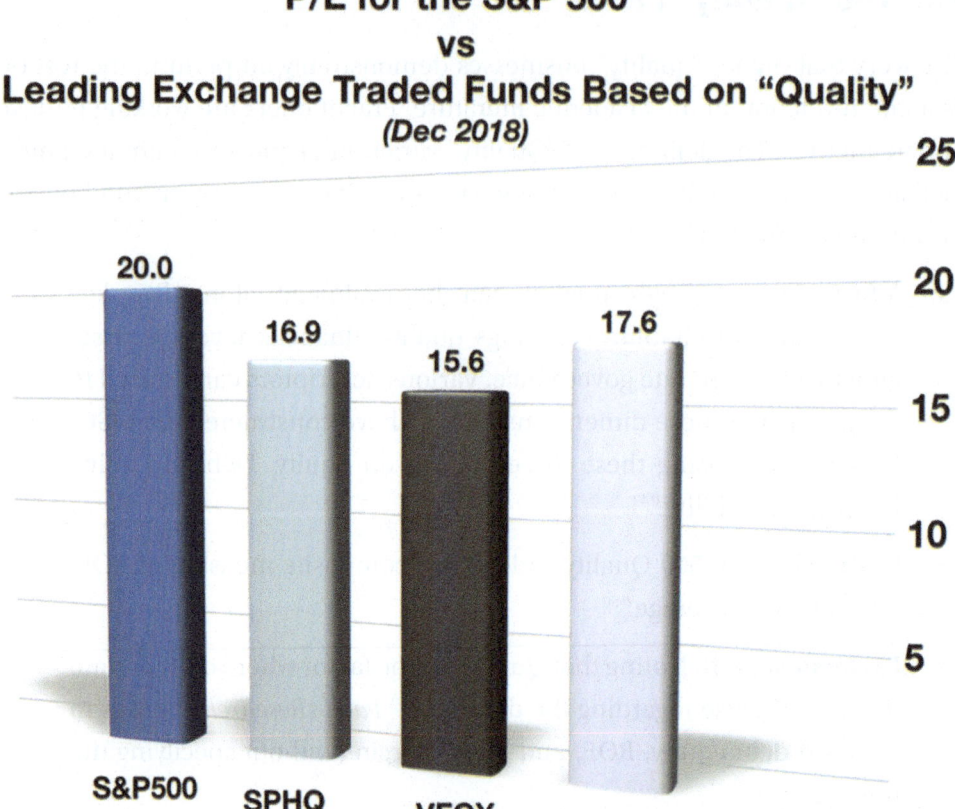

Figure 4-14. *P/E for the S&P 500 vs. Leading Exchange Traded Funds Based on "Quality" (Dec 2018)*

The relationship between the Market Multiples and Profitability or Quality is an under-researched topic. The results so far are as follows:

- Gross Profit metrics correlate rather modestly (18%) with P/B ratios; the relationship is strongest at the high end of the P/B scale – asset-light companies and companies with significant intangible assets.

- Return on Equity – as a measure of Profitability – shows a complex relationship with the market multiples; it appears to correlate well with P/B – that is, high P/B and high ROE go together; but the relationship with the earnings multiple is less clear; indeed, the least profitable firms (in terms of ROE) show the highest P/E multiples

- "Quality" metrics are not yet standardized, but several ETFs tracking "Quality" trade at significant discounts to the overall market (at year-end 2018).

It is a puzzle. Surely, in principle, successful companies, more "profitable" companies, and companies with "higher-quality" business models (smoother earnings, higher gross margins, etc.) *should* be worth more and should carry higher valuations. The problem, in part, is that defining "Quality" or even "Profitability" is complex and conceptually challenging. The simple components of the metrics – "Gross margin," "return" (i.e., net profit), "equity" as a balance sheet category, "total assets" – are all accounting conventions, and we have seen in the previous chapter how accounting has lost its connection to enterprise valuation. Accounting measures of profit may not correspond closely to "true economic profit" – which may be as hard to pin down as "true intrinsic value." Adding in conventional notions of sound business practice – like maintaining modest debt levels or avoiding accruals – may not in fact improve the accuracy of the quality metric. As for including "governance" criteria... do we really understand yet how these factors are related to business success or value creation? (See Section 4.2.12.)

One possibility is that the "Quality" metrics being developed – as well as the basic traditional metrics like ROE – are *biased toward conservatism*. That is, they concede some of the available market value (return) for the sake of "prudence" or to avoid excessive risk. This may be only natural, psychologically speaking. The market brings together risk-takers and risk-avoiders, and the latter may be more inclined to "safe and sound" business practices, which trade off some of the upside, some of the value, to the more adventurous. Yet it is strange that "Quality" is cheaper (by the ETF evidence) than the rest of the market; by definition, for most things, "Quality" costs more.

"Profitability" (as opposed to "Profit" or "Earnings") transcends accounting. It incorporates concepts of risk, sustainability, repeatability, and growth – all of which point forward to future prospects that accounting categories are not intended to capture. Simple accounting metrics like gross margin, or Return on Equity, are at best crude proxies, for purposes of valuation – which is perhaps why the correlation with the market's valuation is ambiguous.

CHAPTER 4   INTERPRETATIONS: P/E AS A DEPENDENT VARIABLE

4.2.3 Size

Large companies usually command a higher P/E than do smaller companies.[53]

On average global small caps have traded on a 61% premium P/E to large caps since 2007.[54]

Size is another factor that affects P/E, and, like most things in Finance, the relationship is complex (or unstable). Empirical studies have yielded contradictory results. One study found that from 1975 to 2003, Large Cap companies carried a premium.[55] (See Figure 4-15.)

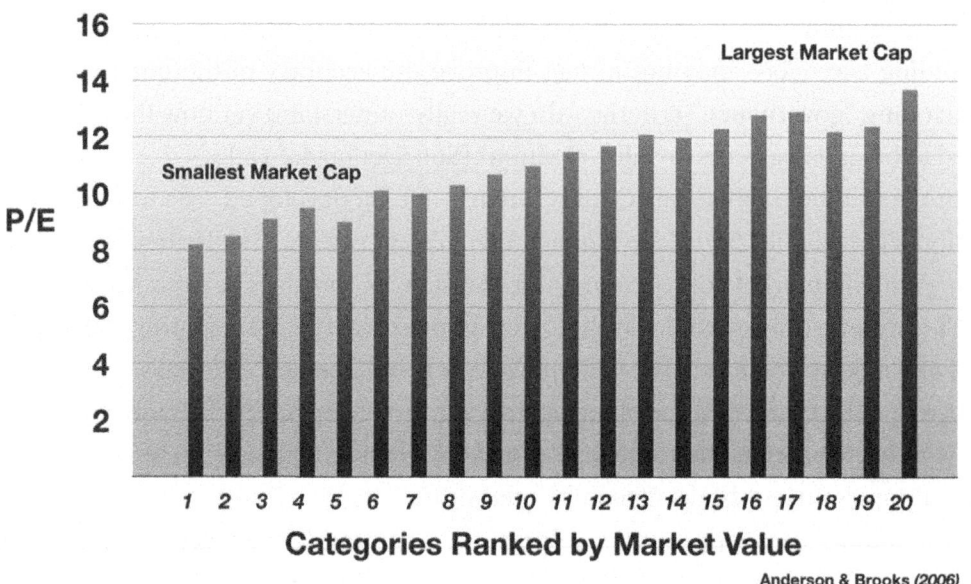

Figure 4-15. Price-to-Earnings Ratio and Size (Market Capitalization)[56]

---

[53]Keith Anderson and Chris Brooks, "Decomposing the Price-earnings Ratio," *Journal of Asset Management*, Vol. 6, No. 6 (March 2006) pp. 456–469.

[54]David Brett, "Small Cap vs. Large Cap: How Valuations Compare," *Schroders Fund Newsletter*, March 27, 2017.

[55]Keith Anderson and Chris Brooks, "Decomposing the Price-earnings Ratio," *Journal of Asset Management*, Vol. 6, No. 6 (March 2006) pp. 456–469.

[56]Adapted from Keith Anderson and Chris Brooks, "Decomposing the Price-earnings Ratio," *Journal of Asset Management*, Vol. 6, No. 6 (March 2006), pp. 456–469.

In general, the opposite pattern prevails. Over the last 15 years, small companies have carried a premium of 15-20% over large companies[57] – and perhaps as high as 40-60% (depending on the time period and how the categories are measured).[58] However, during the late stages of the previous bull market (1998-2000), Large Cap P/E's soared as much as 30% above Small Cap P/E's. In 2018, Large Cap P/E's again moved slightly ahead of Small Cap P/E's, perhaps signaling once again the top of the market run.

"Theory" offers uncertain guidance on this point. Commenting on the data from the earlier period (through 2003), the argument for a Large Cap premium is summarized as follows:

> Large companies usually command a high P/E... Liquidity constraints suffered by large fund managers may account for a significant proportion of this premium, since only the largest companies can offer the necessary liquidity in their shares if the fund manager is not to move the market price adversely. Managers of large funds therefore naturally gravitate towards investing in larger companies.[59]

This is a valid argument and might be extended. Large investment funds are also biased to larger cap companies because of the need to keep the number of positions they manage within reasonable limits and to avoid taking too large a position in any one company. As well, it has been observed that small positions in Small Cap companies – even when successful – do not "move the needle" as much for large funds, which also pushes those managers toward the Large Cap end of the market.[60]

On the other hand, a Small Cap P/E premium is predicted by the classic Risk/Return framework of modern finance theory. Small Caps are in several senses "riskier" than Large Caps. They are more volatile (higher "financial risk") and more vulnerable to adverse business conditions (higher "economic risk"), and so should carry a higher "risk premium" and a higher P/E.

---

[57] Edward Yardeni, "Investment Style Guide," *Yardeni Research*, October 22, 2018.

[58] David Brett, "Small Cap vs, Large Cap: How Valuations Compare," *Schroders Fund Newsletter*, March 27, 2017.

[59] Keith Anderson and Chris Brooks, "Decomposing the Price-earnings Ratio," *Journal of Asset Management*, Vol. 6, No. 6 (March 2006), pp. 456-469.

[60] David Reilly and Shefali Anand, "Small-Cap Funds: The Big Case for Thinking Small," *The Wall Street Journal*, January 19, 2007.

CHAPTER 4   INTERPRETATIONS: P/E AS A DEPENDENT VARIABLE

It may also be that the overall environment for equities was different in the first period (1975–2003) than in the second (post-2003). During the 1970s, the economic scene was dominated by large diversified companies. The era of the "startup" did not really get underway until the 1980s. The 1990s saw the top of the bull market with another period of dominance by large caps (including some of the tech startups now grown up, like *Intel, Cisco,* and *Microsoft*). After the dot-com bubble, the market cooled, and the Large Cap premium disappeared, as shown here.[61] (See Figure 4-16.)

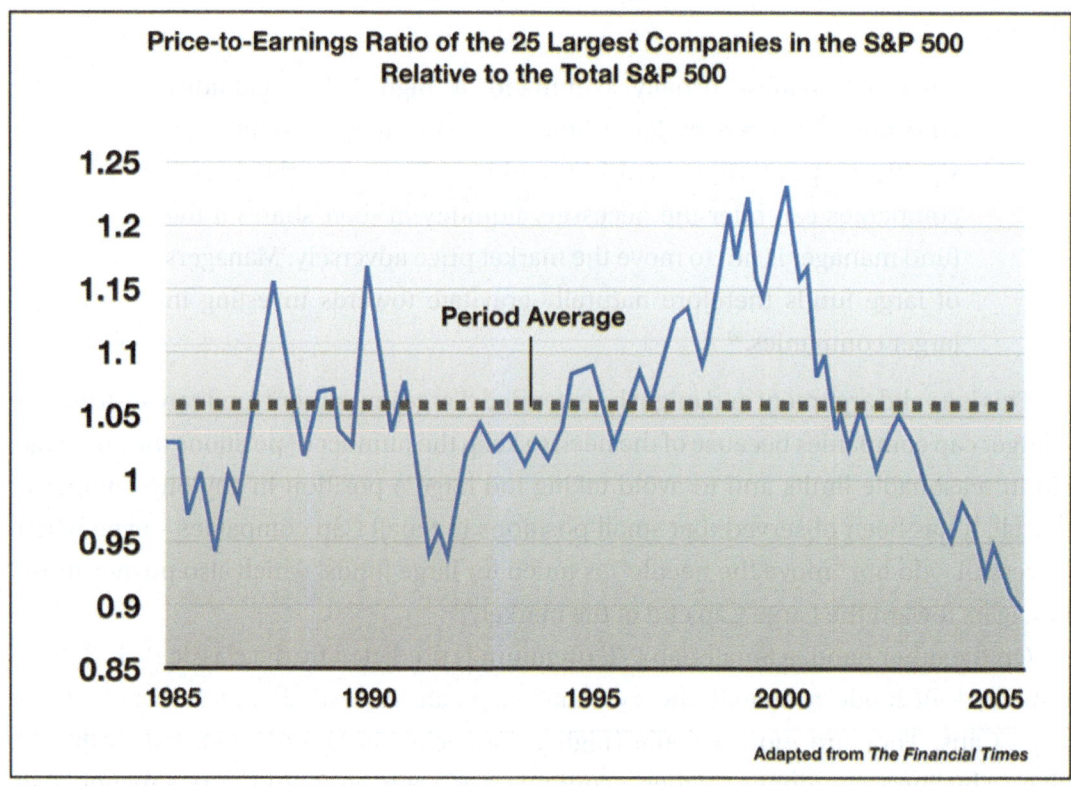

Figure 4-16. Price-to-Earnings Ratios: Large Caps Relative to the Entire Market[62]

---

[61]Dan Roberts and John Authers, "The Harder They Fall: Conglomerates are Stricken by a Shift in Investor Preference," *Financial Times,* October 28, 2005.

[62]Adapted from Dan Roberts and John Authers, "The Harder They Fall: Conglomerates are Stricken by a Shift in Investor Preference," *Financial Times,* October 28, 2005.

4.2.4 "Risk" and Cost of Capital

The PE ratio is a function of the perceived risk of a firm, and the effect shows up in the cost of equity. A firm with a higher cost of equity will trade at a lower multiple of earnings than a similar firm with a lower cost of equity.[63]

This is a theory-driven pronouncement, repeated constantly in the literature, which is enough to raise suspicion. Do companies with a low P/E always have a higher cost of capital? Does *Goldman Sachs* (P/E of 7.7) really have a higher cost of capital than, say, *Netflix* (P/E 135)? Does low-P/E *General Motors* pay a higher rate than a small biotech firm? Do we actually know how to measure cost of capital? And how does the causation run? Does a company somehow suffer a high cost of capital, a strategic handicap which weighs on its share price and lowers its P/E? Or does the low valuation assigned by the market to the company's earnings somehow raise its cost to borrow (or sell shares)?

In any case, there is considerable evidence against the assertion. For example, we see that small cap stocks have consistently higher cost of equity *and* higher P/E multiples, at least in the recent period.

> Global small caps' 10-year median P/E is 25.8, compared with large caps' P/E of 16. So on average global small caps have traded on a 61% premium to large caps since 2007.
>
> The premium is currently 46%. Small cap P/E's have risen to 30.8 from 27.5 in 2007, while large cap P/E's have climbed to 21 from 16.3.[64]

With respect to the cost of equity capital, a 2018 *EY* study finds that European small companies have a significant additional "size premium" – equal to more than half of the basic market risk premium – included in the calculation of the cost of capital. (See Figure 4-17.)

---

[63] A. Damodaran, *Investment Valuation*, p. 475.
[64] David Brett, "Small Cap vs. Large Cap: How Valuations Compare," *Schroders Fund Newsletter*, March 27, 2017.

CHAPTER 4 INTERPRETATIONS: P/E AS A DEPENDENT VARIABLE

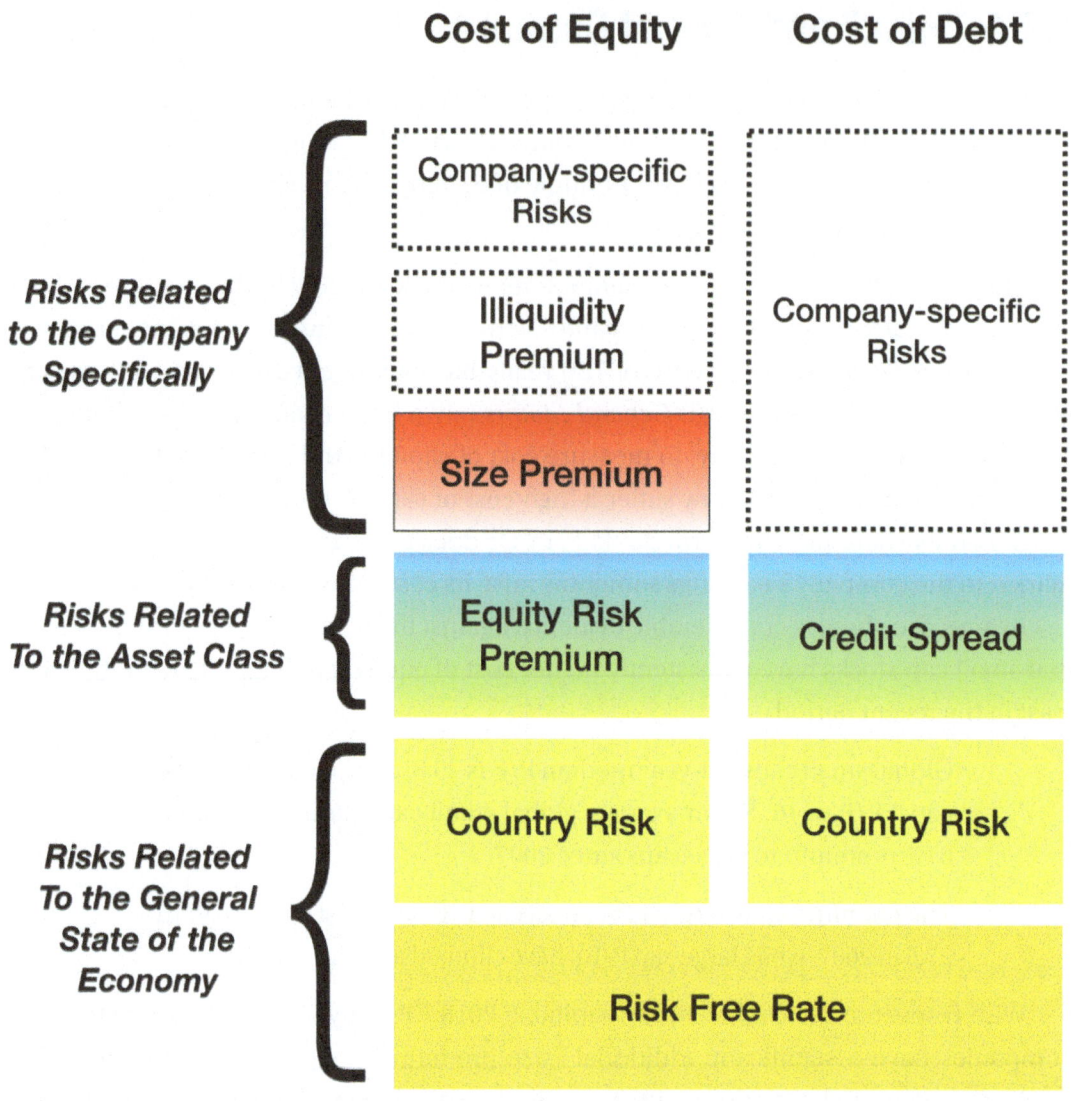

Figure 4-17. *Breakdown of Risk Premia for Equity and Debt*[65]

The authors conclude "The smaller a company's market capitalization, the higher the size premium."[66] (See Figure 4-18.)

---

[65] Adapted from Hannes Schobinger and Marc Filleux, *Practitioner's Guide to Cost of Capital and WACC Calculation*, EY (February 2018).

[66] Hannes Schobinger and Marc Filleux, *Practitioner's Guide to Cost of Capital and WACC Calculation*, EY (February 2018).

CHAPTER 4   INTERPRETATIONS: P/E AS A DEPENDENT VARIABLE

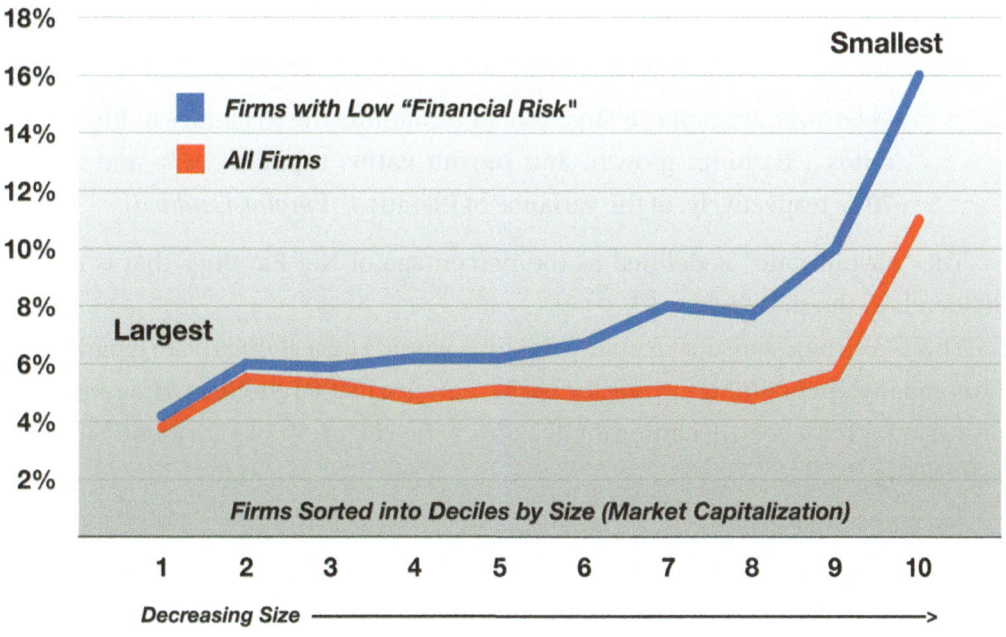

Figure 4-18. Breakdown of Risk Premia for Equity and Debt[67]

The same "cost of capital handbook" (updated 2017) cites a size premium for the cost of capital for the smallest market cap decile of companies of 3.6–5.6%.[68]

There is thus frequently an association of *higher* cost of capital with *higher* P/E multiples. Indeed, if there is any relationship, it seems that higher "risk" (in the classic, if misleading, finance-theoretic sense of "volatility" of returns) is associated with higher P/E multiples over the long run (but not the short run – see Section 4.2.7), at least when comparing Small Cap with Large Cap.[69]

---

[67] Adapted from Hannes Schobinger and Marc Filleux, *Practitioner's Guide to Cost of Capital and WACC Calculation*, EY (February 2018).

[68] Roger Grabowski et al., *2017 Valuation Handbook: U.S. Guide to Cost of Capital*, Wiley (2017).

[69] David Templeton, "Continuing To Favor U.S. Large Cap Stocks Over U.S. Small Cap Stocks," *Seeking Alpha*, February 18, 2018.

CHAPTER 4   INTERPRETATIONS: P/E AS A DEPENDENT VARIABLE

4.2.5 Shareholder Return

4.2.5.1 Dividends

The CFA Institute study[70] cited earlier also looked at the "drivers of the PE Ratio" – the variables that explain (statistically speaking) its variations over time.

> Macro variables play a large role in explaining the dynamics of PE ratios... Earnings growth, and **payout ratios** explain... 38% and **70%**, respectively, of the variance of PE ratios. *[Emphasis added]*

The "payout ratio" is defined as the percentage of Net Earnings that is paid out in Dividends to the shareholders.[71]

This is a strong statistical result. This study would suggest that the P/E mainly reflects the company's policy for returning the cash it earns to its shareholders. However, dividend payout ratios have been declining for decades.[72] (See Figure 4-19.) Dividend Yield has also been falling.[73]

---

[70]Andrew Ang and Xiaoyan Zhang, "Price-Earnings Ratios: Growth and Discount Rates," *The Research Foundation of the CFA Institute* (2011), pp. 130–142.

[71]These are Trailing 12-month dividends, dividends that have actually been received by shareholders.

[72]John Authers, "Hordes of Hoarders," *Financial Times*, January 30, 2012.

[73]Morgan Housel, "How To Boost Income in an Era of Low Stock Dividends," *The Wall Street Journal*, October 4, 2014.

CHAPTER 4   INTERPRETATIONS: P/E AS A DEPENDENT VARIABLE

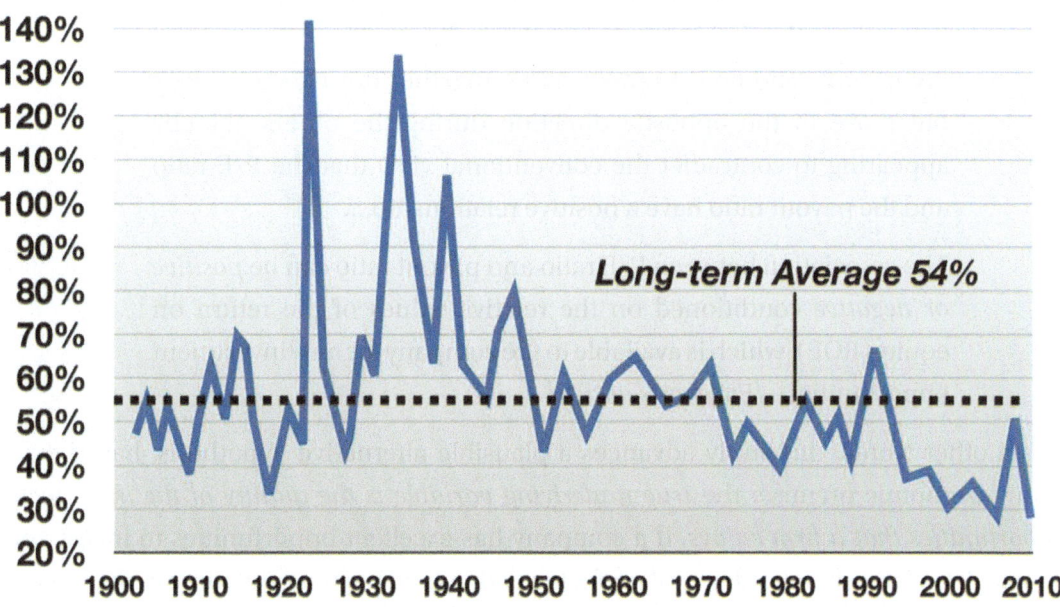

Figure 4-19. Dividend Payout Ratios[74]

And yet, the P/E has been generally rising. The traditional dividend-driven model of valuation is changing.

A recent study focusing on the last 20 years highlights the "nonlinear" relationship between *dividend* payout ratios and P/E multiples.[75] (See Figure 4-20.)

> It is customary for a vast body of prior research to employ a linear regression model and unanimously conclude that the P/E ratio is positively associated with the dividend payout ratio...

---

[74]Adapted from John Authers, "Hordes of Hoarders," *Financial Times*, January 30, 2012.

[75]Boonlert Jitmaneeroj, "The impact of dividend policy on price-earnings ratios: The role of conditional and nonlinear relationship," *Review of Accounting and Finance,* Vol. 16 No. 1 (2017) pp. 125–140.

> Nevertheless, these studies provide a narrow understanding because they overlook [the fact] that the relationship between P/E ratio and payout ratio is not always linear. The P/E ratio and the payout ratio tend to move along together during some years but move in the opposite direction during the others, thereby appearing to contradict the conventional view that the P/E ratio and the payout ratio have a positive relationship....
>
> The association between P/E ratio and payout ratio can be *positive or negative* conditioned on the relative values of the return on equity (ROE) [which is available to the company for new investment opportunities]. *[Emphasis added]*

In other words, this study advances a plausible alternative hypothesis, based on a strong economic premise: the *true underlying variable is the quality of the investment opportunities that a firm enjoys.* If a company has excellent opportunities to invest and earn high returns, shareholders will prefer lower dividend payouts and more cash directed to growth. In this scenario, a low payout ratio will drive a higher P/E multiple. On the other hand, if the company lacks promising opportunities to invest (or simply has more cash than it can use), shareholders will prefer to receive their dividends. In this case, a high payout ratio will drive a higher P/E. (Such is the argument.)

CHAPTER 4 INTERPRETATIONS: P/E AS A DEPENDENT VARIABLE

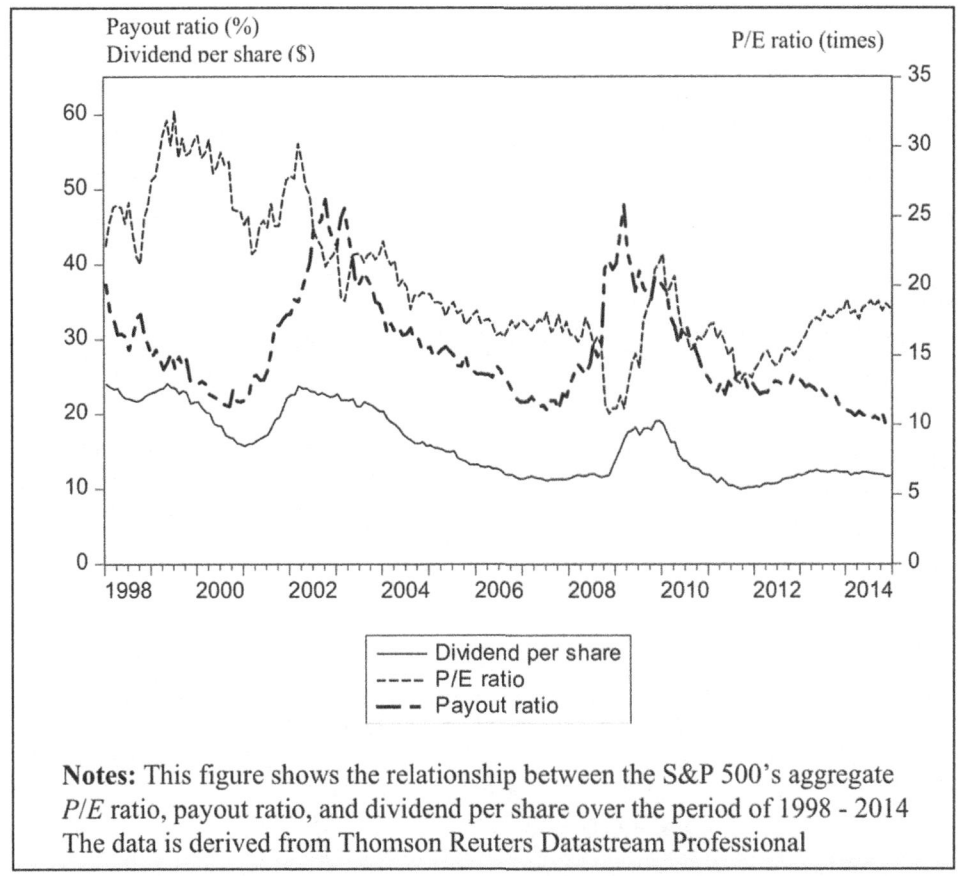

Notes: This figure shows the relationship between the S&P 500's aggregate P/E ratio, payout ratio, and dividend per share over the period of 1998 - 2014 The data is derived from Thomson Reuters Datastream Professional

Figure 4-20. *Payout Ratio vs. Price-to-Earnings Ratio*[76]

The payout ratio is understood as merely a proxy for what is the truly significant factor: the profit potential of economic landscape in which the company operates. But this is a profoundly complex matter: "investment opportunities" reflect many factors – the company's management and its strategic "vision," the state of technology and innovation in the sector, moves by the competition (who may be pursuing the same opportunities), government programs and policies that incentivize or dis-incentivize certain investments, and on and on.

---

[76] Boonlert Jitmaneeroj, "The impact of dividend policy on price-earnings ratios: The role of conditional and nonlinear relationship," *Review of Accounting and Finance*, Vol. 16 No. 1 (2017) pp. 125–140. Reproduced by permission of *Review of Accounting and Finance*.

CHAPTER 4   INTERPRETATIONS: P/E AS A DEPENDENT VARIABLE

4.2.5.2 Buybacks

The rise of share buybacks as an alternative to dividends complicates the picture. Buybacks have often outpaced dividends in recent years and are far more variable. Lately, the cash returned through buybacks has been double the amount returned through dividend payments. In 2019, buybacks are expected to reach nearly $1 Tn.[77] (See Figure 4-21.)

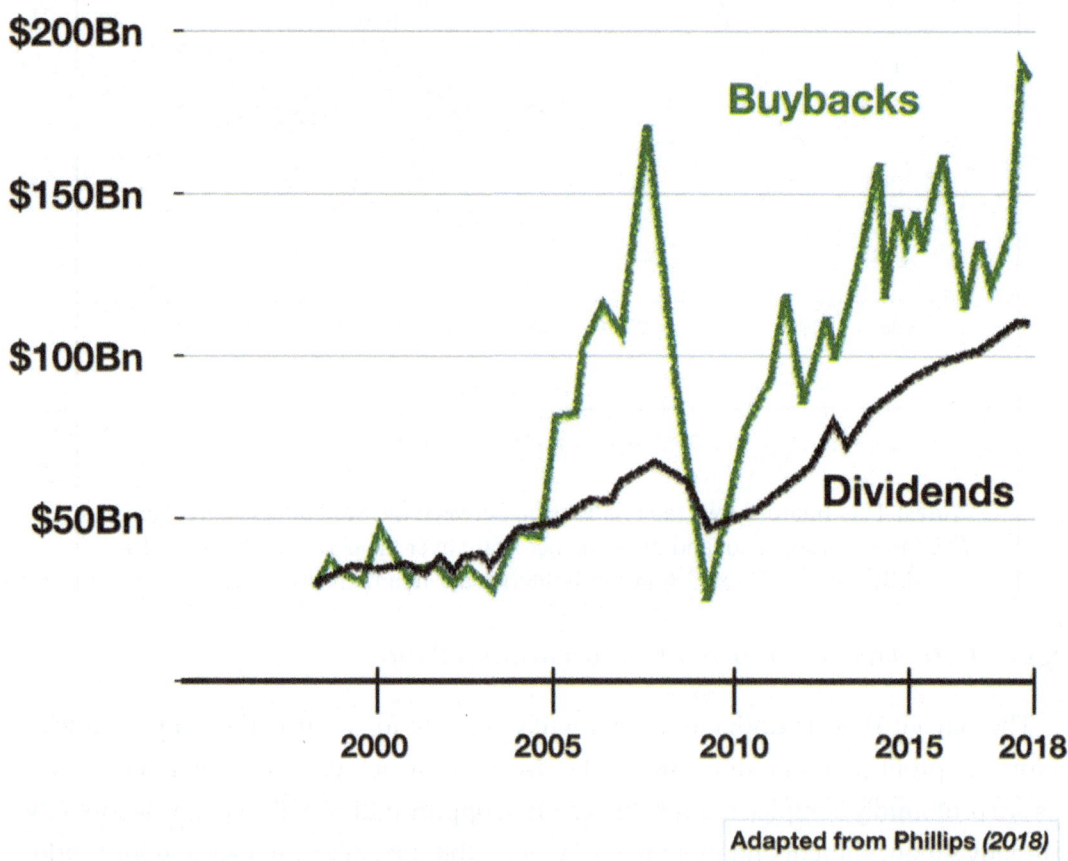

Figure 4-21. Dividends vs. Buybacks (Quarterly)[78]

Buybacks have also outpaced *reinvestment* as a use of cash flow. A *Citibank* report calculates the ratio of *corporate investment* (defined as capital expenditures plus R&D) to *total payout* (defined as dividends plus share buybacks). This metric sheds considerable light on

---

[77]Matt Phillips, "Buybacks Dip Could Factor into a Sell-off," *The New York Times*, October 12, 2018.
[78]Adapted from Matt Phillips, "Buybacks Dip Could Factor into a Sell-off," *The New York Times*, October 12, 2018.

the connection between shareholder returns and P/E multiples, across regions and sectors: "We find a clear relationship between the corporate investment/payout ratio and valuations. The higher the ratio the lower the PE."[79] In other words, traditional Capex "investment" may be value-destroying – a counterintuitive result perhaps. (See Figure 4-22.)

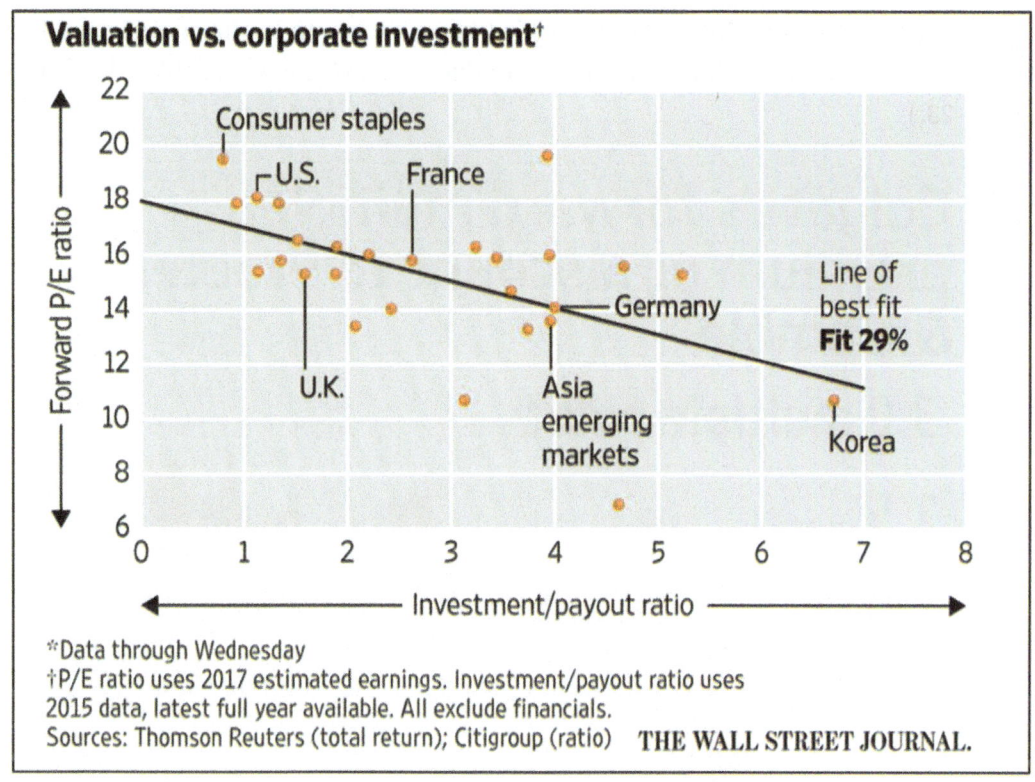

Figure 4-22. Investment/Payout Ratio and the Forward P/E[80]

New metrics (like the Investment/Payout ratio) are needed to capture "shareholder returns" accurately; but it appears that high payouts do indeed drive high P/E multiples. Returning cash to shareholders, through dividends and buyouts, makes the claim on earnings – which the P/E represents – perhaps more concrete and therefore more valuable. As the authors of the *Citi* report observe, "CEO's who want a higher PE (and to avoid the attention of activist investors) should take note."

---

[79]Robert Buckland et al., "Market Wants Cash Cows," *Citi Research*, March 19, 2015; James Mackintosh, "Who's Right: Warren Buffett or Larry Fink?" *The Wall Street Journal,* March 2, 2017.
[80]James Mackintosh, "Who's Right: Warren Buffett or Larry Fink?" *The Wall Street Journal*, March 2, 2017.

4.2.6 Strategy and Business Model Issues

The P/E is a signal of enterprise value, and it reflects events and policies that affect that value. It is sensitive to changes in business strategy in the short term and will reflect the quality of a firm's business model over the somewhat longer term.

The sensitivity of the Multiple to strategic fitness shows up in the comparison here between two direct competitors, *Colgate-Palmolive* and *Proctor & Gamble (P&G)*. (See Figure 4-23.)

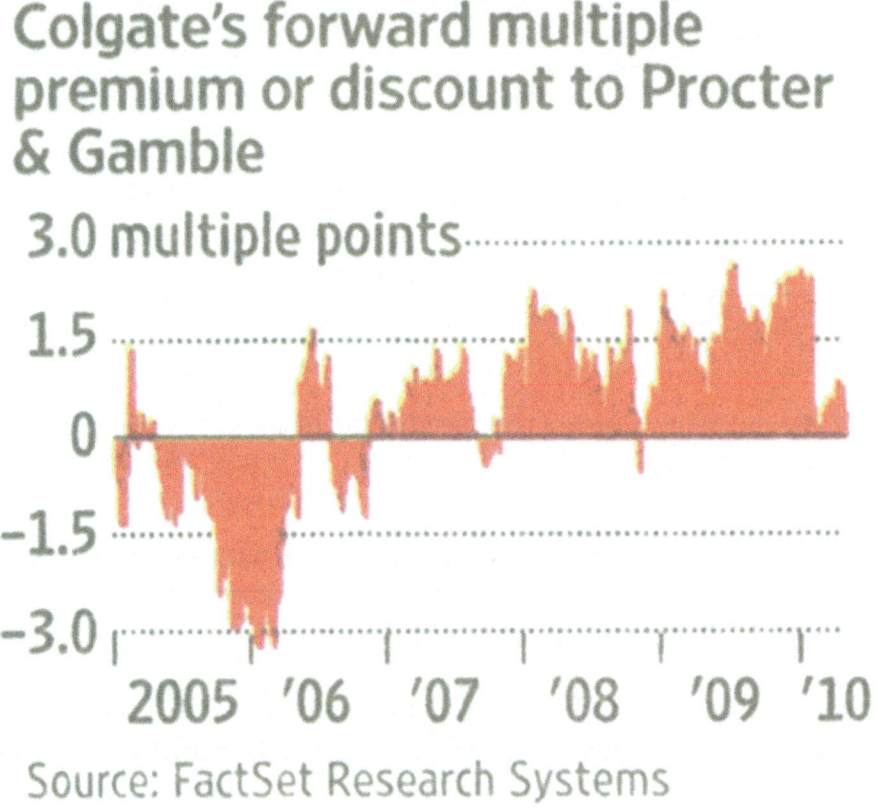

Figure 4-23. Colgate vs. Proctor & Gamble – the P/E as Indicator of Strategic Fitness[81]

---

[81]John Jannarone, "Gambling on Procter and Gamble's Return," *The Wall Street Journal*, April 28, 2010. Reproduced by permission from *The Wall Street Journal*.

CHAPTER 4 INTERPRETATIONS: P/E AS A DEPENDENT VARIABLE

In the first part of this period, *P&G* (arguably the category leader) trades at a significant premium to *Colgate*. This relationship flips around with the looming financial crisis and the recession. *Colgate* now sports a premium. This is attributed by the *Wall Street Journal* to its business model being more recession-proof:

> *Colgate* relies less on high-end products that consumers have foregone and has a stronger emerging-markets position [i.e., markets where the effects of the recession were viewed as less severe].[82]

Events of strategic significance are often registered early and decisively by shifts in the P/E, before the full impact on actual sales or earnings. In 2014, *American Express (Amex)'s* forward Multiple drifted downward by 10–12% in just a few months, which was attributed to the loss of its long-time partnership with retail giant *Costco*.[83] On April 10, 2015, *General Electric* announced it would be exiting the financial services industry.[84] GE's multiple jumped by 10% in the next few days. The market had effectively priced it as a blend of industrial and financial businesses, with a multiple positioned between the two categories. Jettisoning the financial component caused the multiple to rise toward the industrial peer group average.[85] (See Figure 4-24.)

---

[82] John Jannarone, "Gambling on Procter & Gamble's Return," *The Wall Street Journal*, April 28, 2010; Emily Glazer et al., "P&G's Stumbles Put CEO on Hot Seat for Turnaround," *The Wall Street Journal*, September 27, 2012.

[83] John Carney, "American Express Faces Struggle to Keep Up," *The Wall Street Journal*, April 7, 2015.

[84] Charley Grant, "Why GE's Diet Should Carry More Weight," *The Wall Street Journal*, September 28, 2015.

[85] Spencer Jakab, "Scrutinizing GE's Bright Idea," *The Wall Street Journal*, April 17, 2015.

CHAPTER 4   INTERPRETATIONS: P/E AS A DEPENDENT VARIABLE

Figure 4-24. *GE Valuation Shift Based on Divestiture of Finance*[86]

Thus, the P/E multiple is often useful as a "strategy barometer," illuminating aspects of strategic fitness, including factors such as

- Quality of Revenue – for example, recurring vs. non-recurring
- The Conglomerate Discount
- Capex Intensity
- Excess Cash Accumulation
- Exposure to the Business Cycle

4.2.6.1 Quality of Revenue

Morgan Stanley and *Goldman Sachs* have followed different strategies in recent years. *Goldman* focused on trading and *Morgan Stanley* on wealth management.[87] (See Figure 4-25.)

---

[86] Adapted from Spencer Jakab, "Scrutinizing GE's Bright Idea," *The Wall Street Journal*, April 17, 2015.
[87] Justin Baer and Peter Rudegeair, "Banks' Recipes for Profit Differ," *The Wall Street Journal*, April 21, 2015.

CHAPTER 4   INTERPRETATIONS: P/E AS A DEPENDENT VARIABLE

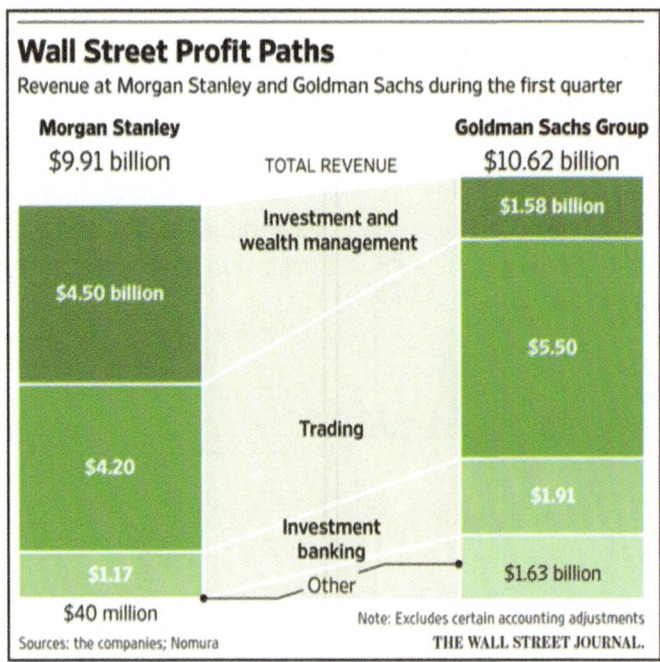

Figure 4-25. Morgan Stanley and Goldman Sachs – Different Revenue Models (Q1 2015)[88]

In time, the market began to register a difference in the quality of revenue derived from these two different business models, and the difference was captured in the valuation ratios of the two companies:

> In 2013, *Morgan Stanley* and *Goldman Sachs* were both at similar multiples to forward earnings. Now [2015] *Morgan Stanley* trades above 12 times, while Goldman is close to 10 times...
>
> Trading revenue has fallen out of favor with investors. It is seen as volatile, opaque and costly in terms of regulatory capital.
>
> [Meanwhile] *Morgan Stanley* trimmed its trading operations and bought *Smith Barney*...to boost its more predictable and steady unit that manages money for wealthy individuals.[89]

---

[88]Adapted from Justin Baer and Peter Rudegeair, "Banks' Recipes for Profit Differ," *The Wall Street Journal*, April 21, 2015.

[89]John Carney, "Morgan Stanley Hits Wrong Chord," *The Wall Street Journal*, April 21, 2015; also Justin Bare and Peter Rudegeair, "Banks' Recipes for Profit Differ," *The Wall Street Journal*, April 21, 2015.

CHAPTER 4   INTERPRETATIONS: P/E AS A DEPENDENT VARIABLE

The impact on the Price/Book ratio – always important for financial firms – was even more dramatic. In this period, *Morgan Stanley's* multiple went from a 30% discount to *Goldman Sachs* to a 9% premium.[90] (See Figure 4-26.)

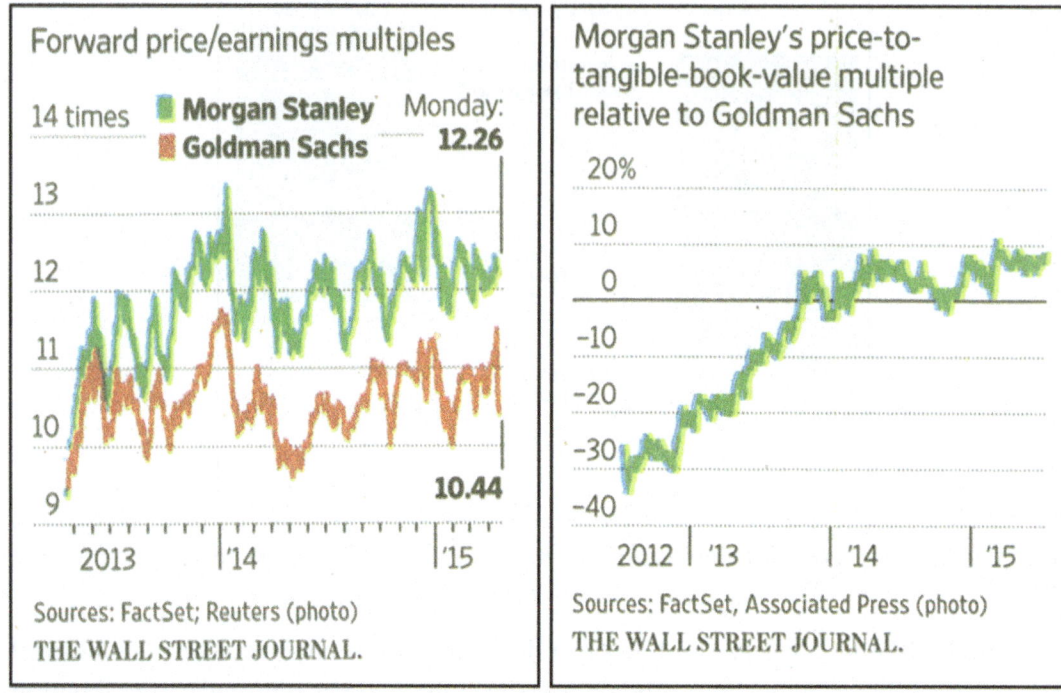

Figure 4-26. *Morgan Stanley and Goldman Sachs – P/E and P/B Comparisons (2015)*[91]

Following the financial crisis of 2008, *Walmart* and *Target* traded consistently at much lower multiples than *Costco*.[92] (See Figure 4-27.) This was despite (or because of?) *Costco's* nearly 50% higher hourly labor costs and despite significantly lower operating profit margins. In fact, the *Costco* multiple rose even in the face of decelerating sales trends.[93]

---

[90]David Reilly, "Fickle Trading Wind Hits Goldman," *The Wall Street Journal*, July 17, 2015.

[91]John Carney, "Morgan Stanley Hits Wrong Chord," *The Wall Street Journal*, April 21, 2015. Reproduced by permission from *The Wall Street Journal*. David Reilly, "Fickle Trading Wind Hits Goldman," *The Wall Street Journal*, July 17, 2015. Reproduced by permission from *The Wall Street Journal*.

[92]Spencer Jakab, "Bulking Up on Costco is Getting Pricey," *The Wall Street Journal*, October 10, 2012; Spencer Jakab, "End of Fee Fillip Will Slow Costco's Growth," *The Wall Street Journal*, December 11, 2013.

[93]Spencer Jakab, "Frostbitten Costco is on Thin Ice," *The Wall Street Journal*, March 5, 2015.

CHAPTER 4   INTERPRETATIONS: P/E AS A DEPENDENT VARIABLE

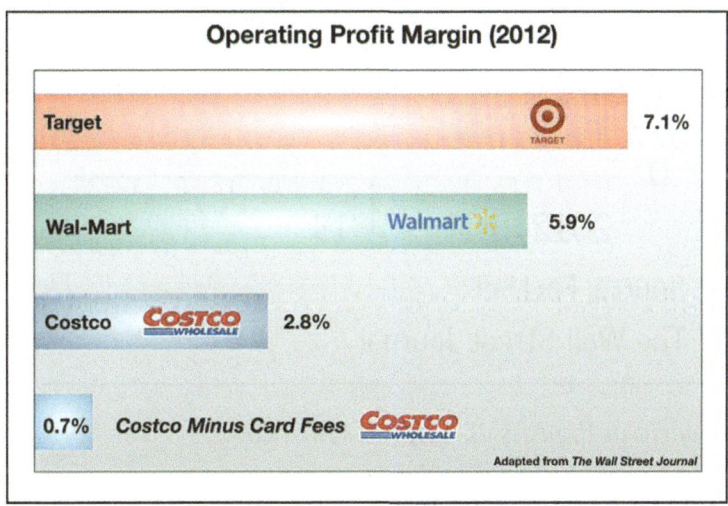

Figure 4-27. Costco vs. Walmart and Target – and Profitability (2012, 2013)[94]

---

[94](Top) Spencer Jakab, "End of Fee Fillip Will Slow Costco's Growth," *The Wall Street Journal*, December 11, 2013. Reproduced by permission from *The Wall Street Journal*. (Bottom) Adapted from Spencer Jakab, "End of Fee Fillip Will Slow Costco's Growth," *The Wall Street Journal*, December 11, 2013.

CHAPTER 4 INTERPRETATIONS: P/E AS A DEPENDENT VARIABLE

The likely explanation is *Costco's* business model. Seventy percent of the company's profits come from membership fees, which are renewed annually by 90% or so of its customers, even with price increases.[95] *Costco's* recurring revenue is highly valued by investors, compared with *Walmart* and *Target* which depend on traditional and less predictable retail product sales.

American Express carries a significant premium multiple compared to *Capital One*.[96] There are two quality of revenue–related reasons for this: (1) Amex has higher membership fees (recurring) and (2) it attracts higher-quality customers, who spend more and default less frequently. (See Figure 4-28.)

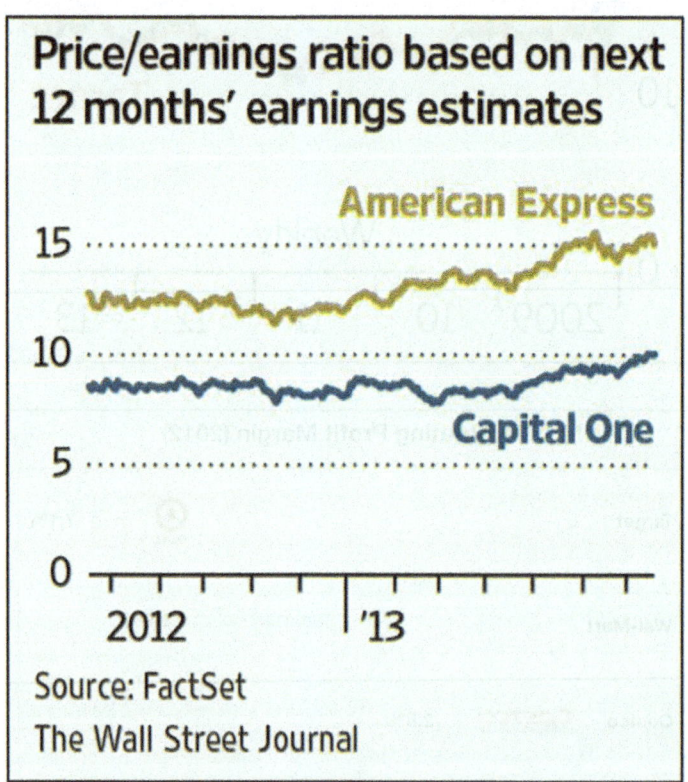

Figure 4-28. *American Express vs. Capital One (2013)*[97]

---

[95]Andrew Bary, "Everybody's Store," *Barron's*, February 7, 2007; Spencer Jakab, "Growth is Helping Costco at the Margins," *The Wall Street Journal*, March 12, 2013; Sarah Nassauer and Maria Armental, "Costco Increases Membership Fees as Profit Growth Slows Down," *The Wall Street Journal*, March 8, 2017.

[96]Matthias Rieker, "Capital One Likes Idea of Charging Ahead," *The Wall Street Journal*, July 17, 2013.

[97]Matthias Rieker, "Capital One Likes Idea of Charging Ahead," *The Wall Street Journal*, July 17, 2013. Reproduced by permission from *The Wall Street Journal*.

Assessing quality of revenue and quality of earnings is at the heart of understanding strategic success and failure. A P/E premium in comparisons of same-sector firms is a strong diagnostic of superior competitive fitness and business quality.

4.2.6.2 The Conglomerate Discount

It is well known that highly diversified multi-business firms (conglomerates) tend to trade at a discount to single-business "pure play" companies.[98] *Citigroup* produced a study in 2011 which documented the size of the conglomerate discount at about 10% in North America and Europe.[99] (See Figure 4-29.)

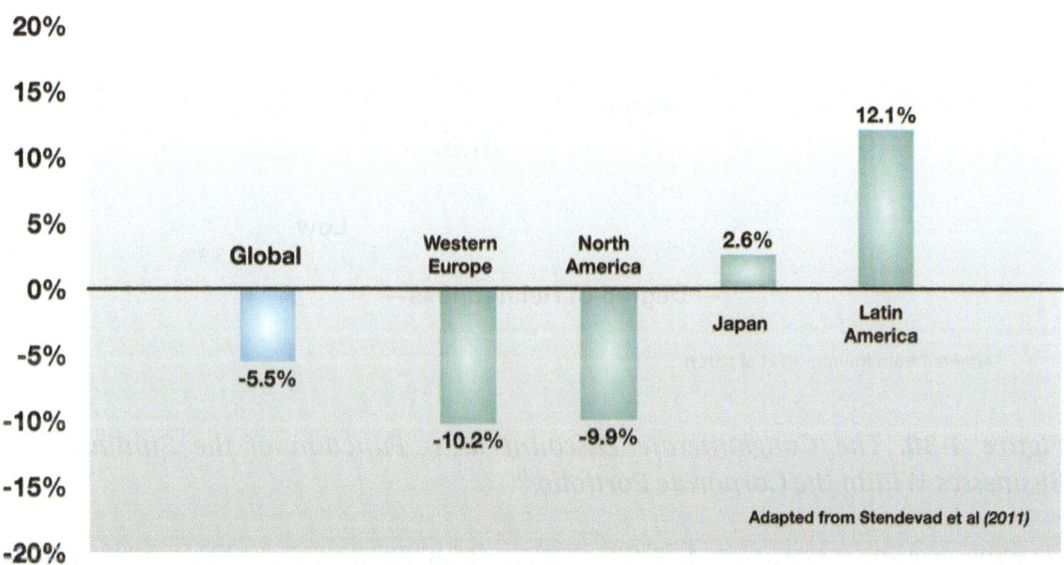

Figure 4-29. The Conglomerate Discount[100]

---

[98]There are various reasons for this, a full discussion of which is beyond the scope of this book.

[99]Carsten Stendevad et al., "Spin-offs: Tackling the Conglomerate Discount," *Citi Global Markets Inc.*, April 2011.

[100]Adapted from Carsten Stendevad et al., "Spin-offs: Tackling the Conglomerate Discount," *Citi Global Markets Inc.*, April 2011.

CHAPTER 4   INTERPRETATIONS: P/E AS A DEPENDENT VARIABLE

A depressed P/E is sometimes a function of the degree of diversification in the company's business model. The more diversified a company, the higher the discount, as shown here ("degree of relatedness" refers to the similarity among the businesses in the firm's portfolio). (See Figure 4-30.)

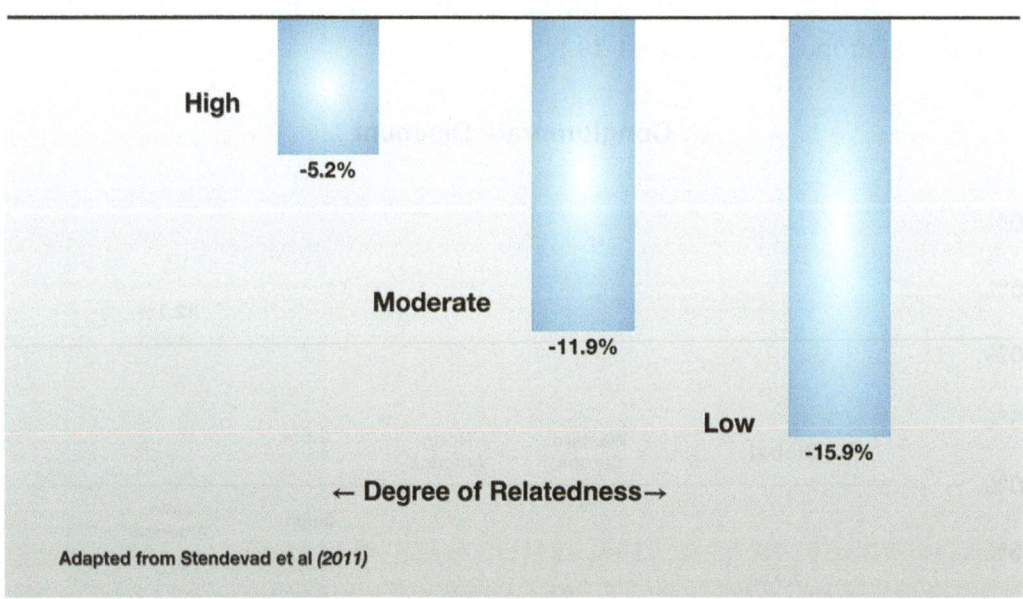

Figure 4-30. The Conglomerate Discount as a Function of the Similarity of Businesses Within the Corporate Portfolio[101]

Citi's study found that a strategic move to un-diversify the company by spinning off or selling business units leads to an increase in the P/E. (See Figure 4-31.)

---

[101]Adapted from Carsten Stendevad et al., "Spin-offs: Tackling the Conglomerate Discount," Citi Global Markets Inc., April 2011.

CHAPTER 4   INTERPRETATIONS: P/E AS A DEPENDENT VARIABLE

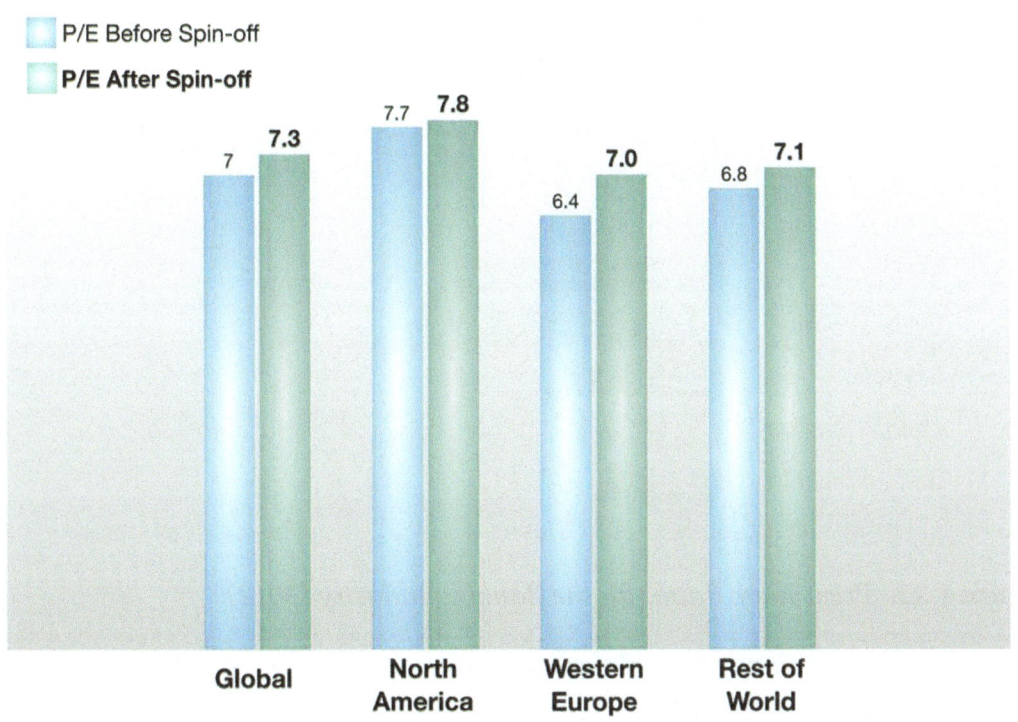

Figure 4-31. Effect of Divestiture on the P/E Ratio[102]

The banking sector offers an example of the conglomerate discount. Larger banks have more diversified business models, including retail banking, investment banking, extensive trading businesses, asset management, and international operations. Regional banks focus on domestic lending and retail banking – and receive significantly higher price-to-book ratios.[103] Here are the figures from 2012. (See Figure 4-32.)

---

[102]Adapted from Carsten Stendevad et al., "Spin-offs: Tackling the Conglomerate Discount," *Citi Global Markets Inc.,* April 2011.

[103]David Reilly, "Bank Investors Bail on Too Big to Fail," *The Wall Street Journal*, May 16, 2012. P/B is the preferred Multiple in the banking sector.

CHAPTER 4   INTERPRETATIONS: P/E AS A DEPENDENT VARIABLE

Figure 4-32. *Price/Book Ratios for the Banking Industry (2012)*[104]

The *Wall Street Journal* offers this explanation:

> Smaller banks don't suffer a conglomerate discount. They don't have big investment banking or trading arms.... [They] are more U.S. focused.

4.2.6.3 Is there a Conglomerate Premium?

The value effect of diversification apparently reverses from a discount to a premium in times of economic distress.[105] (See Figure 4-33.)

---

[104]David Reilly, "Bank Investors Bail on Too Big to Fail," *The Wall Street Journal*, May 16, 2012. Reproduced by permission from *The Wall Street Journal*.

[105]Liam Denning, "Companies Must Flex Spending Muscles," *The Wall Street Journal*, December 8, 2009.

178

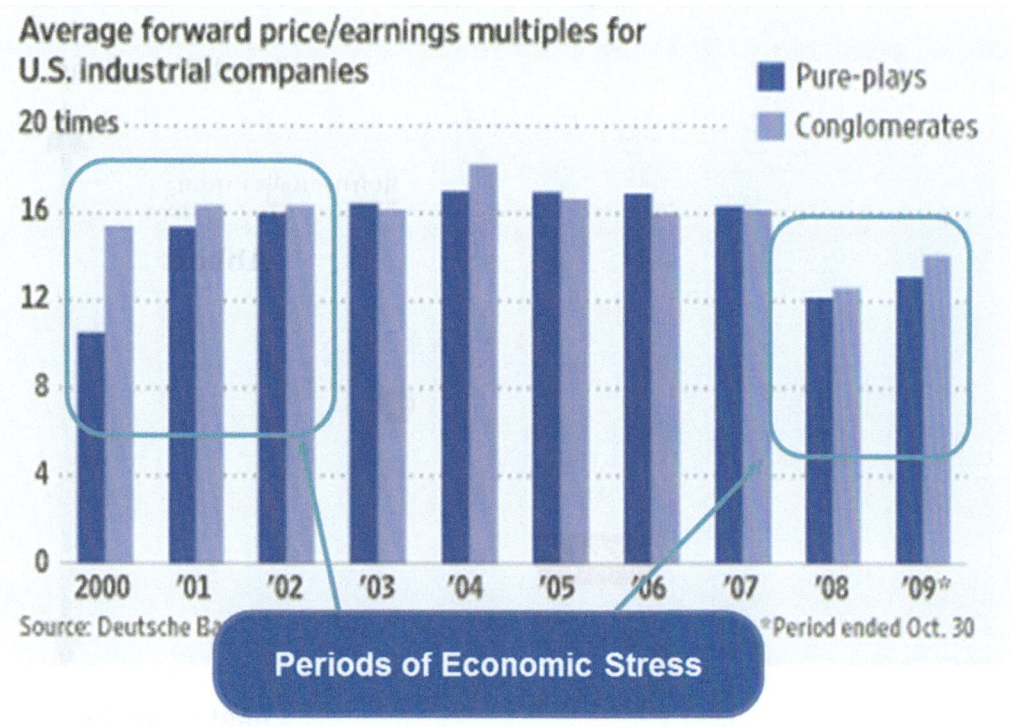

Figure 4-33. *Pure Plays vs. Conglomerates: P/E Comparison*[106]

Diversification is intended to help stabilize the business platform during periods of economic turbulence. The premium P/E reflects the value of that stability in those environments.[107]

Big Pharma presents a more complex case. A strategic problem for companies in this sector can be an overdependence on patent-protected blockbuster drugs. As the patents expire, these companies suffer significant shifts in their revenue streams. "Pure play" companies in this sector – those with high dependence on a limited number of patented drugs – carry lower P/E multiples than more diversified firms (such as *Johnson & Johnson*, with its consumer products business to cushion these shifts).[108] (See Figure 4-34.)

---

[106]Liam Denning, "Companies Must Flex Spending Muscles," *The Wall Street Journal*, December 8, 2009. Reproduced by permission from *The Wall Street Journal*.

[107]Venkat Kuppuswamy and Belén Villalonga, "Does Diversification Create Value in the Presence of External Financing Constraints? Evidence from the 2007–2009 Financial Crisis," *Harvard Business School Working Paper*, 2010.

[108]"Jagged Little Pills," *Financial Times*, October 23, 2010.

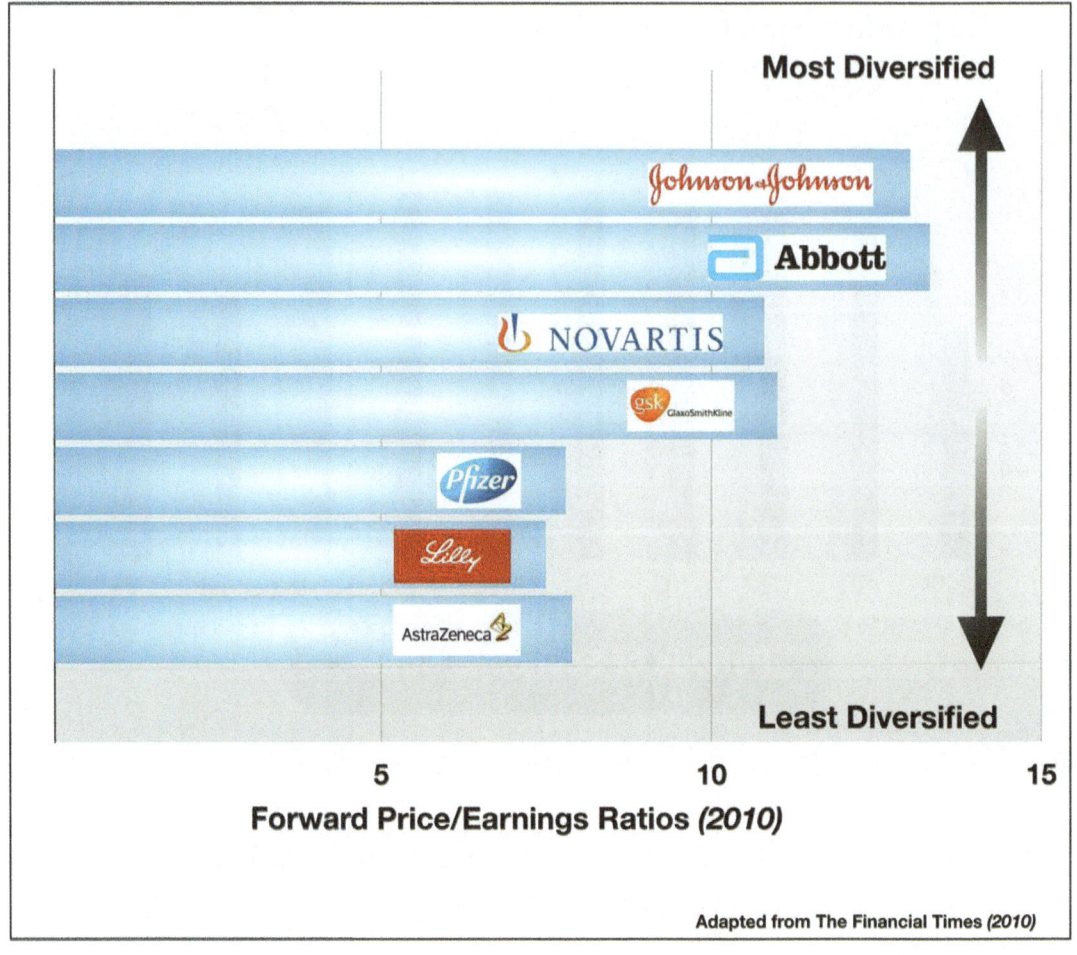

Figure 4-34. *Diversification and Valuation in the Pharmaceutical Sector*[109]

So, discount or premium for conglomerates? It seems that both are possible, depending on the context.[110]

The P/E multiple – it bears repeating – is not a univalent signal. It shifts perspective and provides different information, depending on the context. Despite this ambiguity, the Multiple often highlights the key strategic questions that underlie a firm's competitive market position, especially for comparisons with rivals within the same sector.

---

[109]Adapted from "Jagged Little Pills," *Financial Times*, October 23, 2010.

[110]Note also that conglomerates carry a premium in Japan and Latin America. In this case, the "country factor" outweighs the conglomerate discount. See Section 4.3.7.

4.2.6.4 Capex Intensity

Lower investment tends to mean better share price performance.[111]

The long-term shift in the developed world economies toward asset-light business models is reflected in the trends in market metrics. It appears that valuation ratios measure (and penalize) capital intensity. Within a sector, firms that use a "lighter" model may be rewarded with higher valuations. Here is a typical illustration based on the EV/EBITDA ratio for European retailers.[112] (See Figure 4-35.)

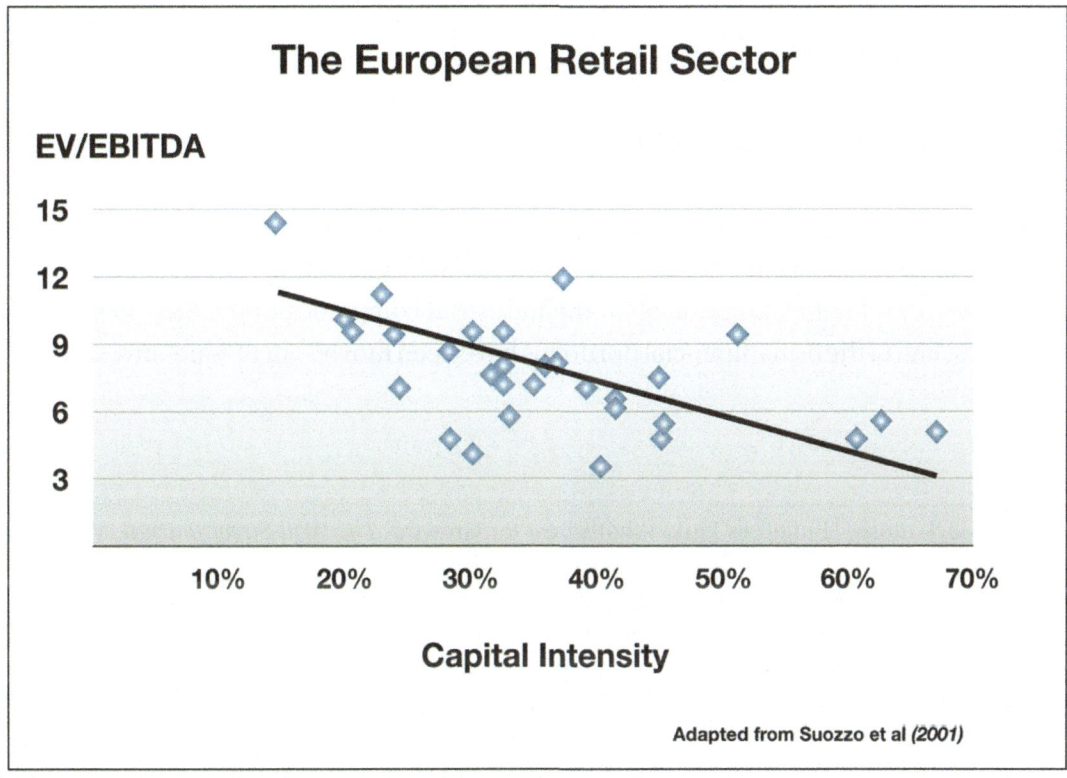

Figure 4-35. *EV/EBITDA and Capex*[113]

---

[111] James Mackintosh, "Buffett vs. Fink: What's Best for Growth," *The Wall Street Journal*, March 2, 2017.

[112] Peter Suozzo et al., "Valuation Multiples: A Primer," *UBS Global Equity Research,* November 2001.

[113] Adapted from Peter Suozzo et al., "Valuation Multiples: A Primer," *UBS Global Equity Research*, November 2001.

CHAPTER 4   INTERPRETATIONS: P/E AS A DEPENDENT VARIABLE

The effect also shows up at a larger scale, as a partial explanation for differences in valuations in different national markets.[114] (See Figure 4-22.) A dollar earned with lower Capex is more highly valued than a dollar that requires heavy fixed investment to generate.

4.2.6.5 Excess Cash Accumulation

Too much cash on the balance sheet can depress a company's P/E.[115] The effect is pronounced in the tech sector, but the trend is general. Cash as a percentage of total assets has nearly doubled in the last 25 years.[116] Estimates now set cash holdings by nonfinancial American companies at approximately $2 trillion (as of 2018), or around 10% of GDP – an unprecedented figure.[117]

Managing this cash creates a drag on valuation. On the one hand, "safe" investments[118] carry a very low return – typically no more than 2–3% over the past decade.[119] On the other hand, if CFOs feel pressure to "put the cash to work" by investing it in high-yielding and riskier securities, it moves them away from the primary mission of the company; they become portfolio managers, "hedge funds" in effect.[120] A recent academic study, using data drawn from financial reports of all the industrial companies in the S&P 500, found that almost half of the firms' financial portfolios have been moved out of "safe" investments

---

[114] James Mackintosh, "Buffett vs Fink: What's Best for Growth," *The Wall Street Journal*, March 2, 2017.

[115] The excessive accumulation of cash has been commented on in the previous chapter (see the discussion of CAPE$_2$, the Cash-Adjusted P/E, Section 3.11).

[116] Ben Casselman, "Cautious Companies Stockpile Cash," *The Wall Street Journal*, December 7, 2012.

[117] "Corporate Saving in Asia: A $2.5 Trillion Problem," *The Economist*, September 27, 2014; as noted in this article, Japanese corporations hold cash worth about 44% of Japan's GDP, and Korean companies hold cash worth about 34% of the country's GDP. These levels can only be viewed as serious distortions of the financial and economic framework.

[118] Defined as "highly liquid, risk-free near-cash securities."

[119] Martin Peers, "Cash Returns: Where Apple Lags Rivals," *The Wall Street Journal*, May 23, 2011.

[120] *Apple*, for example, has created a wholly owned subsidiary, *Braeburn Capital*, which manages a portfolio of $244 billion, sourced from *Apple's* undistributed earnings and supplemented by $115 Bn of debt (Thomas Gilbert and Christopher Hrdlicka, "Apple is a Hedge Fund that Makes Phones," *The Wall Street Journal*, August 23, 2018). As for *Google* – as early as 2010 – it was *"looking for bond traders and portfolio analysts"* in order to launch its own "trading floor" to manage its cash hoard ($26 Bn at the time) (Douglas MacMillan, "Google's Latest Launch: Its Own Trading Floor," *Bloomberg BusinessWeek,* May 27, 2010).

and into risky assets, often characterized by poor liquidity as well. The authors calculated a discount of 13–22% compared to safe assets.[121]

As value is thus impacted, the P/E should also be impacted – either through the value-reducing effects of low-yielding "safe" cash or the discounting of risky, yield-seeking, often illiquid investments, and perhaps both. In 2010, one analyst calculated that "the overabundance of low-yielding cash has shaved 1.4 points off the [entire] equity market's earnings multiple."[122]

4.2.6.6 Exposure to the Business Cycle

Firms differ in the extent to which their measures of performance – earnings, share prices, valuations – are impacted by the ups and downs of the broad economic cycles of expansion, slowdown, recession, and recovery.

> **Cyclical** stocks tend to exhibit a strong, positive correlation to the business cycle, generally outperforming **Defensives** when economic growth is accelerating and underperforming during periods when the economy is slowing or contracting. Additionally, the cyclical sectors all have a beta to the S&P 500 greater than one over the past 10 years, as well as a positive correlation to changes in interest rates.[123]

Cyclical sectors typically include consumer discretionary, financials, technology, and industrials. Defensives include healthcare, consumer staples, telecommunications services, and utilities.

The P/E ratios of Cyclicals and Defensives have varied considerably, relative to each other. However, since 1980, except for brief periods at the beginning of recoveries from recessions, Defensives have carried a premium in their forward P/E, which averages about 10% over that period. (See Figure 4-36.)

---

[121] Ran Duchin, Thomas Gilbert, Jarrad Harford, and Christopher Hrdlicka, "Precautionary Savings with Risky Assets: When Cash Is Not Cash," *The Journal of Finance*, December 2016.

[122] Roben Farad, "When Cash Takes a Vacation," *Bloomberg BusinessWeek*, July 12, 2010.

[123] David Leibovitz et al., "Cyclicals vs. Defensives: The Valuation Imbalance," *Market Bulletin*, JP Morgan Asset Management, July 29, 2016.

CHAPTER 4   INTERPRETATIONS: P/E AS A DEPENDENT VARIABLE

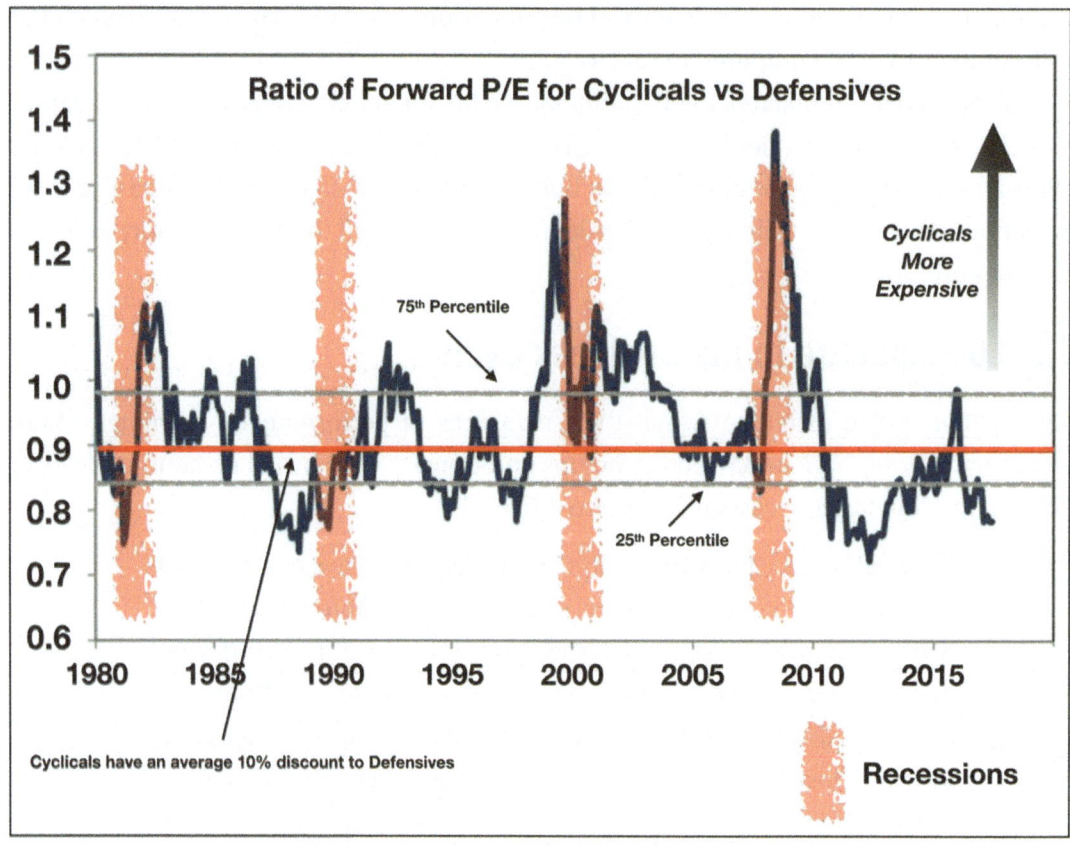

Figure 4-36. *Cyclicals vs. Defensives*[124]

The accepted interpretation is that investors are generally willing to pay a premium for Defensives' earnings stability – which accords with the evidence in the next section. Cyclicals outperform only at the start of the recovery phase, when strong future growth is expected. Cyclicals are also more exposed to foreign sales.[125] (See Figure 4-37.) As we saw in the case of the conglomerate discount in the banking industry, revenues (and earnings) generated by US companies in markets outside the United States appear to be subject to a discount.

---

[124]Adapted from Peter Suozzo et al., "Valuation Multiples: A Primer," *UBS Global Equity Research*, November 2001.

[125]David Leibovitz, Abigail Dwyer, and John C. Manley, "Cyclicals vs. defensives: The valuation imbalance," *Market Bulletin, JPMorgan Asset Management*, July 29, 2016.

CHAPTER 4   INTERPRETATIONS: P/E AS A DEPENDENT VARIABLE

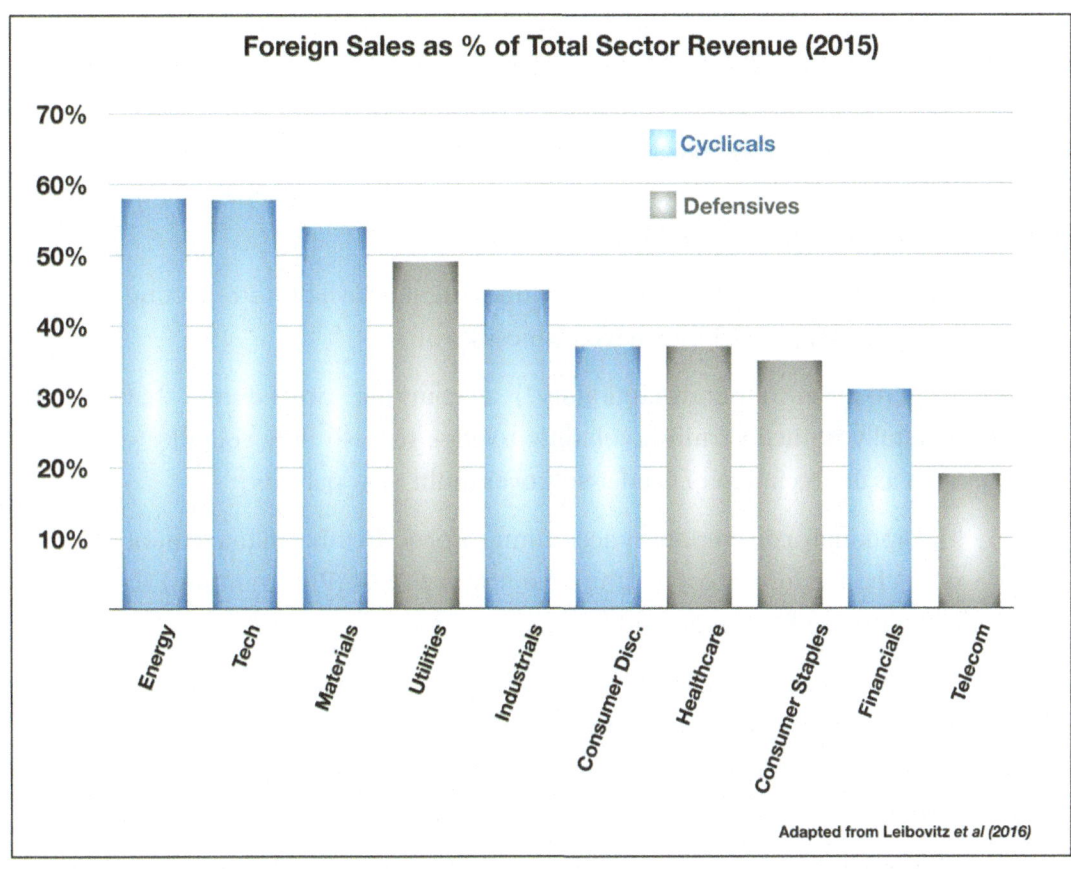

Figure 4-37. Cyclicals vs. Defensives: The Effects of Exposure to the Business Cycle[126]

4.2.7 Earnings Volatility

> In the consumer goods space...valuations, as measured by price-to-earnings ratios, continue to expand... Historically, high multiples in consumer goods were the price you paid for reliability.[127]

---

[126] Adapted from David Leibovitz, Abigail Dwyer, and John C. Manley, "Cyclicals vs. defensives: The valuation imbalance," Market Bulletin, *JPMorgan Asset Management*, July 29, 2016.

[127] Jonathan Eley, "Short View," *Financial Times*, October 20, 2017.

CHAPTER 4   INTERPRETATIONS: P/E AS A DEPENDENT VARIABLE

Earnings volatility seems an obvious candidate as a valuation driver. A company with steady predictable earnings should be a more attractive investment and command a higher multiple. Surprisingly, it has not been much studied.

Some of the published results of research on this topic include the following:

1. In a well-conceived working paper,[128] Jacobs and Zhang pull apart the question of earnings volatility into three plausible components:

- The raw volatility of the company's fundamental cash flows, reflecting the underlying variability of its business fortunes

- The required ("nondiscretionary") accounting procedures that generally reduce earnings volatility relative to cash flow volatility – such as depreciation of fixed assets over multi-year periods

- The optional or discretionary accounting procedures that management may choose to employ (within the scope of GAAP accounting) to further smooth earnings and reduce cash flow

The latter two categories are often classified together as "accruals" – that is, non-cash adjustments to Earnings. Jacobs and Zhang documented a modest correlation of the P/E (Forward P/E and two variants of Trailing P/E) with cash flow volatility (23–30%) and a weaker correlation with (smoothed) earnings volatility (10–21%). They conclude, brightly

> All three P/E measures are strongly positively correlated with the earnings volatility measure and the cash flow volatility, consistent with higher P/E ratios for smoother earnings....suggesting that managerial smoothing is associated with higher P/E ratios.
>
> Firms with less volatile reported earnings are valued more highly per dollar of earnings.

---

[128]Jacob K. Thomas and Huai Zhang, "Another look at P/E ratios," *Working Paper*, Yale School of Management (2006).

The modest correlations observed are suggestive, but a more granular analysis is probably required to get beneath the averaging.[129] It is likely that some firms, some sectors, may be more susceptible to earnings volatility effects (and investor concerns) and the relationship to P/E and other multiples[130] may be more pronounced.

2. In a paper from 1999, we learn that "firms with patterns of increasing earnings have higher price-earnings multiples than other firms."[131] This suggests that the market may reward consistency in earnings *growth*. Smoother earnings are a part of that process.

3. A concrete example of a premium for more predictable earnings comes from the steel industry. A 2010 article reported that *Nucor* carried a large premium P/E multiple (up to 60%) over its major competitors (although the P/B ratios and year-over-year earnings growth rates were similar).

> Nucor's earnings tend to be less volatile than those of other steel outfits... because of its consistent earnings... Nucor usually commands a price/earnings ratio above the industry's average.[132]

Insurance giant AIG (pre-crash) was also generally accorded a premium P/E for the same reason. By focusing on relatively less volatile components of the earnings stream (underwriting profits vs. investing results), the company achieved more predictable results and garnered a premium multiple in its sector.[133] *The Wall Street Journal* offered a similar explanation for the premium accorded to certain retailers:

---

[129] After all, averaging also cancels out much of the volatility in the data.

[130] Given that the underlying volatility here is cash flow volatility, it would be interesting to see the effect on cash flow multiples like EV/EBITDA.

[131] Mary Barth, John Elliot, and Mark Finn, "Market Rewards Associated with Patterns of Increasing Earnings," *Journal of Accounting Research*, Vol. 37, No. 2 (Autumn, 1999), pp. 387–413. I found this paper frustratingly obscure, such that I could not determine the magnitude of the effect they claim to have found, and can only quote their exquisitely brief summary here.

[132] Jacqueline Doherty, "Red Hot Opportunity," *Barron's*, June 17, 2010.

[133] Devin Leonard, Peter Elkind, and Doris Burke, "All I Want in Life is an Unfair Advantage," *Fortune*, August 8, 2005.

CHAPTER 4   INTERPRETATIONS: P/E AS A DEPENDENT VARIABLE

> In the volatile world of retail stocks, many are increasingly willing to pay up for consistency... [Investors are] not looking at the multiple like [they] used to.[134]

4.2.8 Share Price Volatility (Beta)

> It is well known that less volatile stocks get a higher PE ratio.[135]

> Lower PE's indeed had a lower average subsequent beta compared with higher PE's.[136]

Beta is a measure of the volatility of a company's share prices, relative to the volatility of the market as a whole. A beta of 1 means that if the market rises or falls by 10%, the company's share price will rise or fall also by 10%. A low beta – say, 0.5 – would mean the stock would rise or fall by only half as much, and a beta of 2.0 would describe a stock that was twice as volatile as the market average.

The relationship between beta and P/E is inconsistent. (See Figure 4-38.)

---

[134] Miriam Gottfried, "New retail Fashion: Consistency," *The Wall Street Journal*, April 3, 2017.
[135] Jeremy Blum, "A Perfect Storm Is Causing High PE Ratios: But For How Long?" *Seeking Alpha*, March 21, 2018.
[136] "Low P/E ≠ Low Volatility (At Least, Not All The Time)," *Seeking Alpha*, September 11. 2017.

CHAPTER 4   INTERPRETATIONS: P/E AS A DEPENDENT VARIABLE

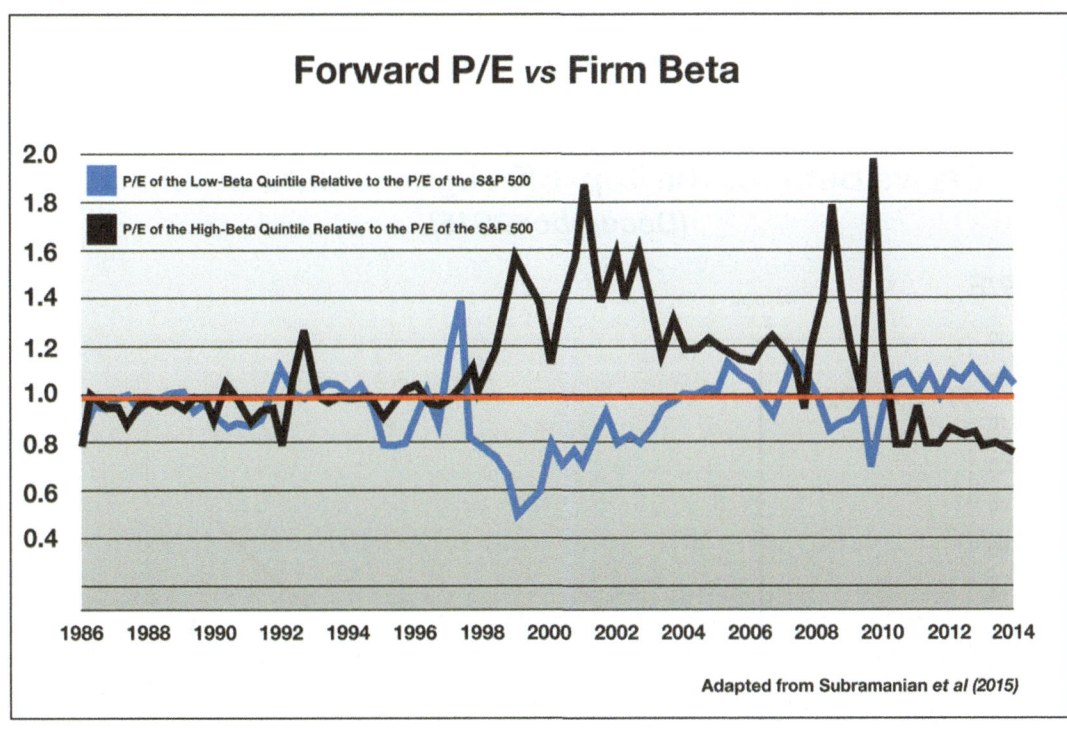

Figure 4-38. *Beta and P/E[137]*

From 1986 until the late 1990s, beta – high or low – had little effect on the P/E. From 1998 to 2010, high beta drove higher P/E multiples – that is, more volatile stocks in the market were commanding much higher relative valuations (up to 60–100% higher for brief periods). After 2010, the pattern reversed. For the next five years, low-beta, less volatile stocks carried a 7% premium P/E to the market P/E, while high-beta stocks traded at a 20% discount.[138]

---

[137]Adapted from Savita Subramanian et al., "What Do Oil and High Beta Stocks Have in Common?" *Equity & Quantitative Strategy, Bank of America, Merrill Lynch*, April 15, 2015.

[138]Savita Subramanian et al., "What Do Oil and High Beta Stocks Have in Common?" *Equity & Quantitative Strategy, Bank of America, Merrill Lynch*, April 15, 2015.

CHAPTER 4   INTERPRETATIONS: P/E AS A DEPENDENT VARIABLE

However, as of December 2018, the relationship between beta and P/E for the top 100 highest-beta stocks in the S&P 500 had become very weakly positive again.[139] (See Figure 4-39.)

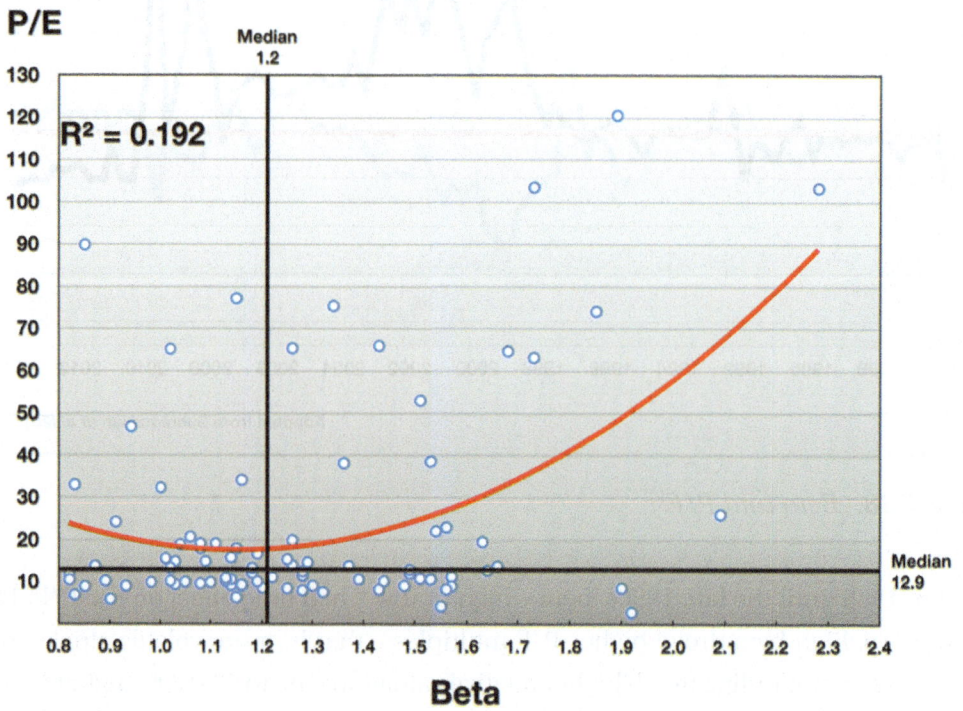

Figure 4-39. Beta and P/E (2018)

This effect may be related to the monetary policy regime. Quantitative Easing (large-scale purchases of bonds by the Federal Reserve) is said to have driven many would-be bond investors, with their low-risk/low-volatility investing preferences, out of the artificially yield-depressed fixed-income market and into bond-like equities ("safe stocks" which tend to be less volatile). This would account for the elevated P/E for low-beta stocks during the period of most active QE.

---

[139]Data source: Josh Arnold, "The 100 Highest Beta Stocks in the S&P 500," *Sure Dividend*, December 14, 2018. Available at www.suredividend.com/high-beta-stocks/#high-vs-low – I have excluded a handful of stocks with negative P/E ratios. It should also be noted that eliminating a few extreme values from the set reduces the R^2 to nearly zero (but not to negative values).

An earlier study (1996) found a strong but noisy *negative* long-term relationship between overall market-level *monthly* volatility and the Trailing P/E[140]:

> The market multiple is highly sensitive to volatility. Our empirical results suggest that a 1 percent increase in market volatility (e.g., from 12 percent standard deviation to 13 percent) can, over time, reduce the market multiple by 1.8.

The straightforward functional interpretation is that "market P/E multiples ought to be lower when the uncertainty surrounding those forecasts [of future growth] is higher." (See Figure 4-40.)

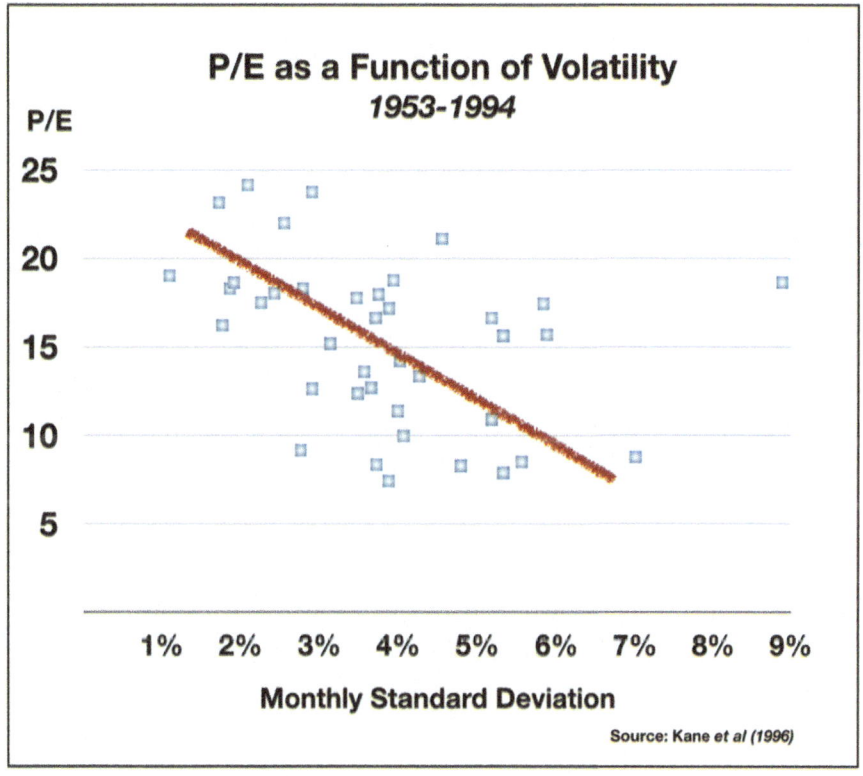

Figure 4-40. *P/E and Volatility*[141]

---

[140]Alex Kane, Alan J. Marcus, and Jaesun Noh, "The P/E Multiple and Market Volatility," *Financial Analysts Journal* (July/August 1996), pp. 16–23.

[141]Adapted from Alex Kane, Alan J. Marcus, and Jaesun Noh, "The P/E Multiple and Market Volatility," *Financial Analysts Journal* (July/Aug 1996), pp. 16–23.

CHAPTER 4   INTERPRETATIONS: P/E AS A DEPENDENT VARIABLE

In a study of the relationship of P/E to bond yields, Asness (2003) found that over the long term (1926–2001), the correlation was very low ($R^2=3\%$). *But* when he added in the volatility factor – actually the *difference* between the volatility of stocks and the volatility of bonds – the R^2 jumped to 62%.[142] Volatility is a strange variable.

"Volatility storms" in the equities market are becoming more common. They shear off value more dramatically from high P/E stocks. In October 2018, a spike in volatility was accompanied by a 1300-point decline in the market over two days. The carnage was focused on the tech sector, where high-P/E stocks declined much more than low-P/E stocks.[143] (See Figure 4-41.)

---

[142] Clifford Asness, "Fight the Fed Model," *Journal of Portfolio Management*, Vol. 30, No. 1 (Fall 2003), pp. 11–24. *"P/E is strongly related to the difference between stock and bond volatility… Investors have experienced more volatility in stocks versus bonds over the last generation…. [therefore] they also require a lower P/E versus Bond Yield."*

[143] Michael Wursthorn and Christopher Whittall, "Volatility Ripples Across the World," *The Wall Street Journal*, October 12, 2018.

CHAPTER 4   INTERPRETATIONS: P/E AS A DEPENDENT VARIABLE

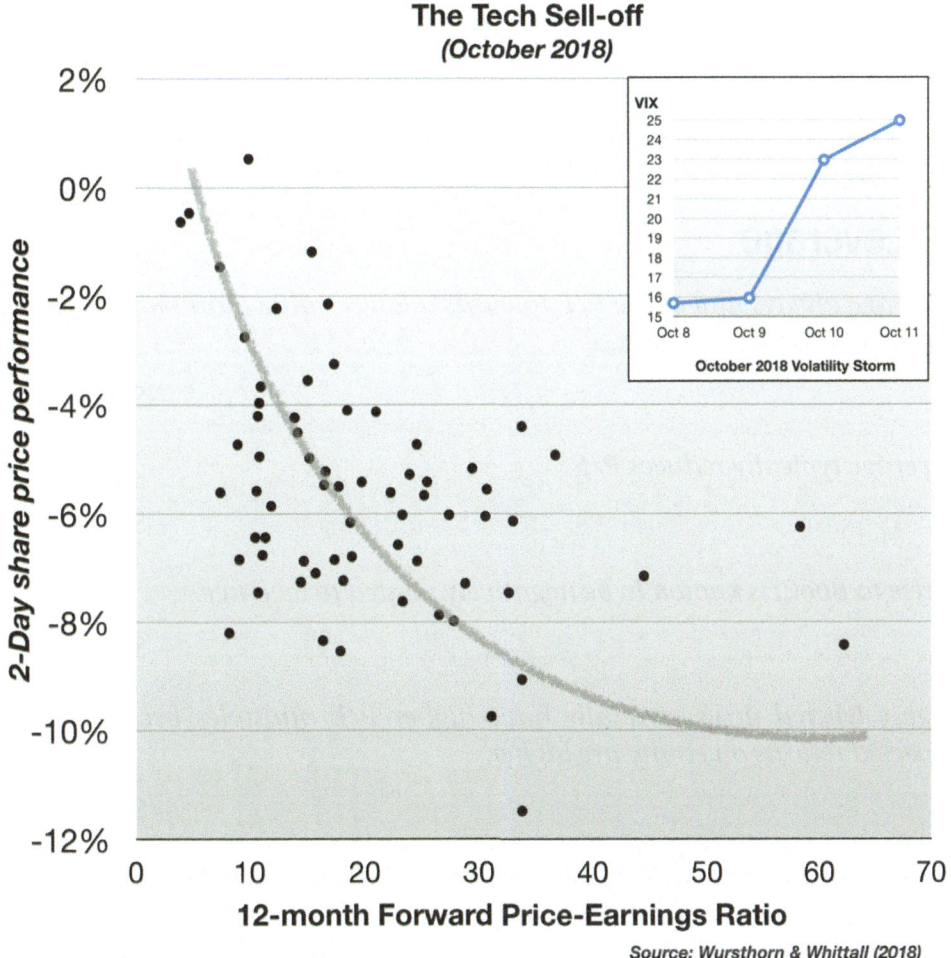

Figure 4-41. *P/E and Volatility*[144]

The relationship between volatility and valuation is complex. In the short term (daily, as in the volatility storm event shown here, or monthly), volatility drives lower valuations (as a rule). In the longer term, higher volatility (or "risk" in the finance-theoretic sense) is associated in many cases with higher P/E multiples (as cited in Section 4.2.3 with reference to the small cap anomaly). But "volatility" is really a compound variable – it blends the effect of earnings volatility ("fundamental" volatility), market

---

[144]Michael Wursthorn and Christopher Whittall, "Volatility Ripples Across the World," *The Wall Street Journal*, October 12, 2018. Reproduced by permission from *The Wall Street Journal*.

CHAPTER 4 INTERPRETATIONS: P/E AS A DEPENDENT VARIABLE

volatility (short-term market weather), market regime (long-term volatility-valuation relationships), and company beta – all these factors operating over different and varying timescales. The P/E multiple is caught in the swirl of these diverse forces and may lose coherence as a valuation signal.

4.2.9 Leverage

Leverage always moves the P/E towards a lower value than that obtained from the standard formula.

—Source 1[145]

Leverage typically reduces P/E.

—Source 2[146]

[Price to Book] is known to be negatively related to leverage.

—Source 3[147]

Highly levered firms generally have higher P/E multiples because their expected returns on equity are higher.

—Source 4[148]

A company with a relatively high all-equity P/E can artificially increase its P/E ratio by swapping debt for equity.

—Source 5[149]

---

[145] Stephen Penman, *Accounting for Value*, Columbia Press (2011), p. 94.

[146] Martin Leibowitz, "The Levered P/E Ratio," *Financial Analysts Journal,* November/December 2002, pp, 68–77.

[147] Malcom Baker, Mathias Hoyer, and Jeffery Wurgler, "Leverage and the Beta Anomaly," January 14, 2019. Available at https://papers.ssrn.com/sol3/papers.cfm?abstract_id=2832704

[148] A financial modeling web site: http://macabacus.com/learn

[149] Marc Goedhart, Timothy Koller, and David Wessels, "The Right Role for Multiples in Valuation," *McKinsey & Company,* March 2005.

CHAPTER 4   INTERPRETATIONS: P/E AS A DEPENDENT VARIABLE

The effect of leverage – that is, the use of debt capital rather than equity to finance the business – on valuation is the subject of long-standing controversy. The debate is rooted in the classical fictions of Miller and Modigliani, who postulated that leverage should in principle have *zero* effect on enterprise value. A vast literature has evolved in response to this misleading assertion, which it is beyond the scope of this book to address.[150]

The P/E ratio – where it has been studied in connection with leverage – seemingly pierces the complexity of the debate, presenting the case for a persistent discount associated with high debt levels.[151] In a study by Subramanian, the most highly leveraged firms in the S&P 500 incurred a *penalty* of approximately 30% P/E discount to the least leveraged firms over the past 30 years.[152] (See Figure 4-42.) However, different market regimes play a role. From the dot-com bubble until the financial crisis, for example, leverage seems to have depressed valuations significantly. But with the initiation of Quantitative Easing after 2008, which suppressed bond yields and interest rates, the sign

---

[150] Here is one of the friendlier assessments of MM: *"Thirty seven years and hundreds of papers after Modigliani and Miller's seminal work, what do we really know about corporate capital structure choice? Theory has clearly made some progress on the subject. We now understand the most important departures from the Modigliani and Miller assumptions that make capital structure relevant to a firm's value. However, very little is known about the empirical relevance of the different theories. Empirical work has unearthed some stylized facts on capital structure choice, but this evidence is largely based on firms in the United States, and it is not at all clear how these facts relate to different theoretical models. Without testing the robustness of these findings outside the environment in which they were uncovered, it is hard to determine whether these empirical regularities are merely spurious correlations, let alone whether they support one theory or another."* (Raghuram Rajan and Luigi Zingales, "What Do We Know about Capital Structure? Some Evidence from International Data," *The Journal of Finance*, Vol. 50, No, 5 (December 1995), pp. 1421–1460).

[151] Other market valuation metrics have been examined with generally similar results. A study of the firms listed on the New Zealand stock exchange found that Tobin's Q was significantly negatively correlated with leverage (Gurmeet Singh Bhabra, "Insider ownership and firm value in New Zealand," *Journal of Multinational Financial Management*, Vol, 17 (2007) pp, 142–154).

[152] Savita Subramanian, "2017 – The Year Ahead: Euphoria or Fiscal Fizzle," *Equity and Quant Strategy, Bank of America/Merrill Lynch*, November 22, 2016.

CHAPTER 4 INTERPRETATIONS: P/E AS A DEPENDENT VARIABLE

changed. US companies more than doubled their debt levels relative to cash flows, and the relative P/E's of leveraged companies also doubled, creating a "bull market for highly leveraged companies." (See Figure 4-43.)

> Investors 'rewarded' companies that borrowed during the period of near-zero interest rates from 2009-2016 which helped push the median ratio of net debt to EBITDA to historic highs for the S&P 500.[153]

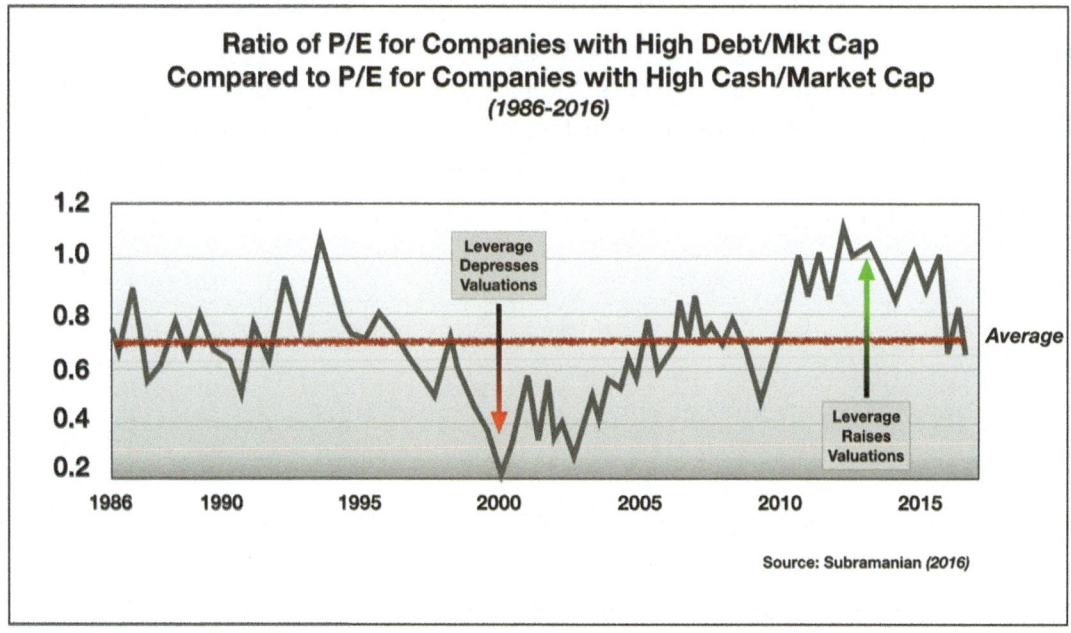

Figure 4-42. *P/E and Leverage*[154]

---

[153] Alexandra Scaggs, "Bull Market in Highly Leveraged US Groups Starts to Shift," *Financial Times,* June 18, 2018.
[154] Adapted from Savita Subramanian, "2017 – The Year Ahead: Euphoria or Fiscal Fizzle," *Equity and Quant Strategy, Bank of America/Merrill Lynch,* November 22, 2016.

CHAPTER 4   INTERPRETATIONS: P/E AS A DEPENDENT VARIABLE

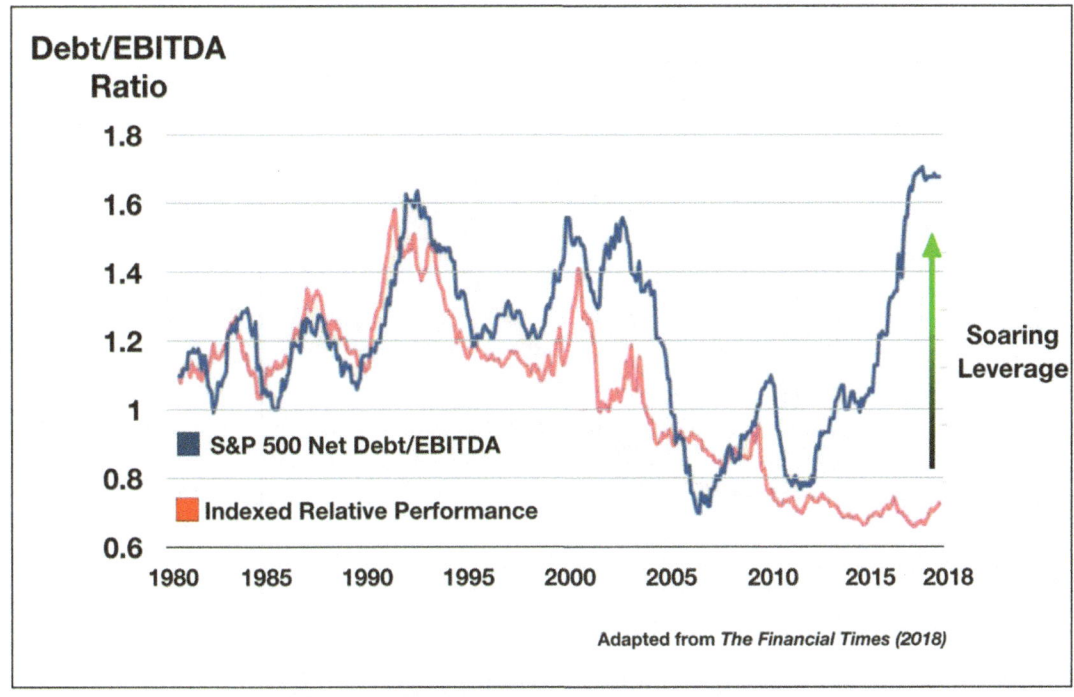

Figure 4-43. *Leverage and Performance*[155]

On the other hand…

Leverage has been increasing across the corporate spectrum. Since 1995, corporate debt has grown much faster than GDP.[156] Leverage as a financial strategy has been embraced by corporate America. Triple-A fortress balance sheets have virtually disappeared.[157] There are only two AAA-rated companies left in the United States (2019).[158] (See Figure 4-44.)

---

[155]Adapted from Alexandra Scaggs, "Bull Market in Highly Leveraged US Groups Starts to Shift," *Financial Times*, June 18, 2018.

[156]John D. McKinnon, "Potential Tax Change is Red Flag for Some Firms," *The Wall Street Journal*, April 4, 2011.

[157]Eric Platt, "US Corporate Downgrades Soar Past $1 Tn as Defaults Gain Pace," *Financial Times*, December 5, 2015.

[158]The last two were *Microsoft* and *Johnson & Johnson* [2018]. In 1992, there had been 99 AAA-rated companies in the United States. "Undaunted by Downgrades," *The Economist*, February 18, 2017.

CHAPTER 4   INTERPRETATIONS: P/E AS A DEPENDENT VARIABLE

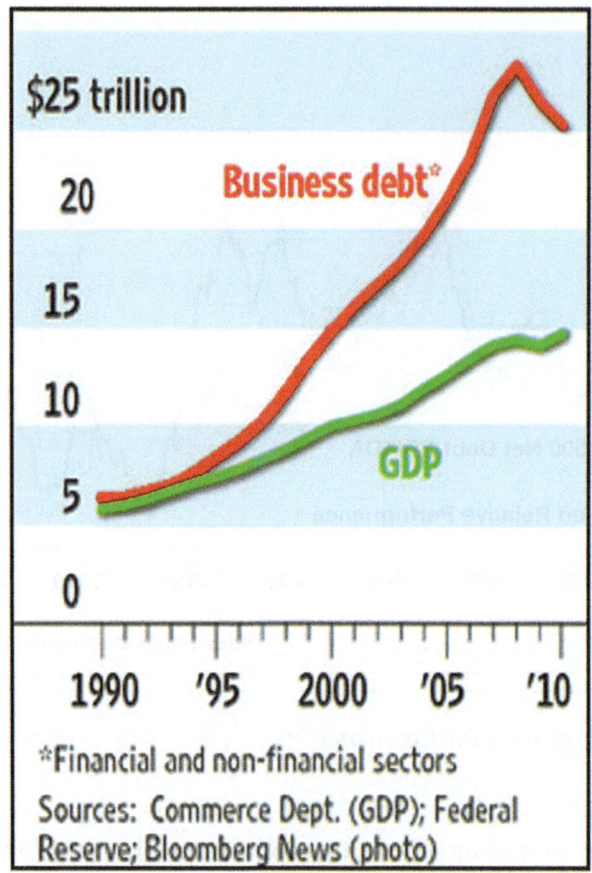

Figure 4-44. *Leverage Trends*[159]

Corporate management teams have reached a strategic conclusion that *leverage increases (shareholder) value*. Leverage today is added not only for operational purposes but to boost equity returns.[160] Presumably, given the highly competitive nature of capitalism, these trends would not be what they are if leverage resulted in value destruction. The market would not favor a systematically losing strategy over the long run.

---

[159]John D. McKinnon, "Potential Tax Change is Red Flag for Some Firms," *The Wall Street Journal*, April 4, 2011. Reproduced by permission from *The Wall Street Journal*.

[160]Ivo Welch, "Capital Structure and Stock Returns," *Journal of Political Economy*, Vol. 112, No. 1, pt. 1 (2004), pp. 106-131: *"Stock returns are a first-order determinant of debt ratios, that they are perhaps the only well-understood influence of debt ratio dynamics."*

CHAPTER 4   INTERPRETATIONS: P/E AS A DEPENDENT VARIABLE

Of course leverage also increases *economic* risk. It amplifies losses as well as gains and reduces flexibility in times of stress. Whether leverage increases *financial-theoretic* "risk" – meaning the *volatility* of returns – is unclear. How the market processes this increased economic risk, and any changes in volatility, and how it may offset these against the potential for amplified returns is unclear.

There is also a causality question: firms with lower P/B ratios often have more traditional, fixed asset-based business models. These assets are more available as collateral for adding debt and may be associated with more stable business outcomes. Hence, low-P/B firms may be able to carry more leverage. Companies with higher P/B often have large amounts of intangible assets (brands, technology) that are harder to borrow against. A 1995 study of P/B and leverage by sectors suggests such a conclusion.[161] (See Figure 4-45.)

---

[161] Michael J. Barclay, Clifford Smith, and Ross Watts, "The Determinants of Corporate Leverage and Dividend Policies," *Journal of Applied Corporate Finance* (January 1995), pp. 214–229. In another study of international markets and leverage *vs.* P/B, the negative relationship was confirmed – but the details of the relationship also suggest an alternative view of casualty: *"There may be other potential reasons for why the market-to-book ratio is negatively correlated with leverage. For instance, the shares of firms in financial distress (high leverage) may be discounted at a higher rate because distress risk is priced.... If this is the dominant explanation, the negative correlation should be driven largely by firms with low market-to-book ratios. In fact, the negative correlation appears to be driven by firms with high market-to-book ratios rather than by firms with low market-to-book ratios. It is unlikely that financial distress is responsible for the observed correlation."* In other words, the driving factor may be that firms with asset-light business models, lots of intangible assets, and these higher P/B ratios use relatively less leverage (Raghuram Rajan and Luigi Zingales, "What Do We Know about Capital Structure? Some Evidence from International Data," *The Journal of Finance*, Vol. 50, No. 5 (December 1995), pp. 1421–1460).

CHAPTER 4   INTERPRETATIONS: P/E AS A DEPENDENT VARIABLE

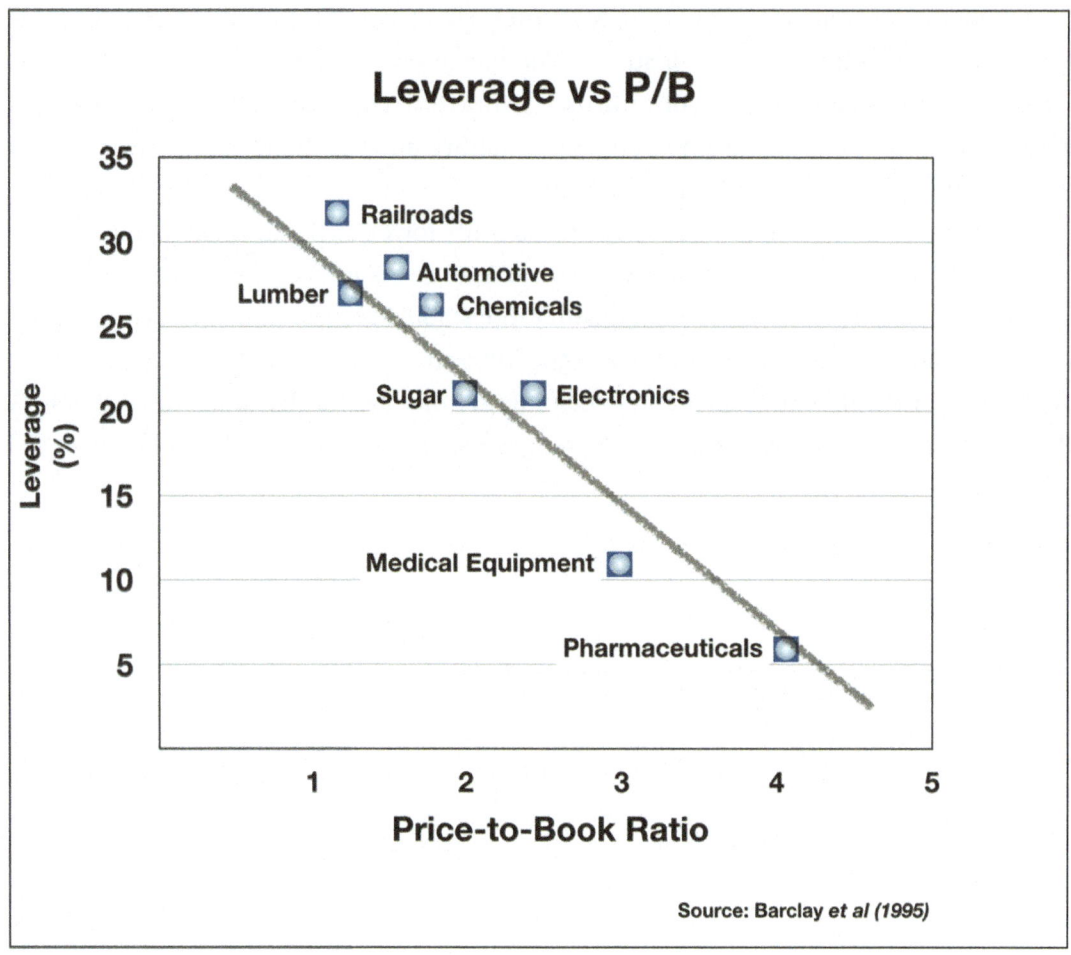

Figure 4-45. *Leverage and Price-to-Book*[162]

In summary, the effect of leverage on valuation is a surprisingly under-researched problem. This is especially so, given the tremendous expansion of the use of leverage in corporate capital structures in the United States in recent decades.[163] The Darwinian perspective of the market argues that it must be creating value and presumably raising the leveraged firm's P/E – or it wouldn't have survived as a strategy. But the mechanism and the scope of this effect are not well understood.

---

[162] Michael J. Barclay, Clifford Smith, and Ross Watts, "The Determinants of Corporate Leverage and Dividend Policies," *Journal of Applied Corporate Finance* (January 1995), pp. 214–229.

[163] Mike Cherney, "Renewed Embrace of Bonds Sparks Boom," *The Wall Street Journal*, March 8, 2014.

4.2.10 Accounting Issues

"Earnings" is an accounting construct, and even within the constraints of *Generally Accepted Accounting Principles (GAAP)*, firms have discretion as to how they calculate revenue, expenses, and profits. Some alternatives may be characterized as conservative, meaning that they take pains to avoid underreporting expenses (where those expenses are partially based on management assumptions). At first glance, conservative accounting ought to reduce final Net Earnings. If E is lower, the P/E will be higher, as a matter of arithmetic. Is the effect merely mechanical, or does it reflect a real increase in firm value associated with more prudent management?

It is a puzzle, and the issue has been studied less than it warrants, considering the power of accounting choices to determine the Earnings numbers that are central to all methods of valuation. One early study (1973) found that firms using accelerated depreciation had higher P/E ratios than firms using straight-line methods.[164] Another study (1983) found a "crude" association between conservative accounting generally and higher P/E's. Conservative accounting choices had an R^2 value of 33% in "explaining" P/E values.[165] This is of the same magnitude as the effect of *Earnings Growth* as previously described. As noted, however, this should be an arithmetic truism: if permitted discretionary accounting choices (e.g., the use of accelerated depreciation) reduce Earnings, the P/E will rise automatically. It is not clear from this data that conservatism as a management style drives a higher valuation.

Later studies have not clarified things. A 1990 study found that "differences in accounting methods explain no more than 15% of the variation in P/E ratios."[166] A 2002 study found that the stock market does not "penetrate" – that is, value correctly – the quality of earnings associated with conservative accounting.[167] There is more work to be done.

---

[164] W. Beaver and D. Morse. 1978. "What Determines Price-earnings ratios?" *Financial Analysts Journal* (July–August), 65–78.; W. Beaver and R. E. Dukes, "Delta-Depreciation Methods: Some Empirical Results," *Accounting Review* (July 1973).

[165] Darryl Craig, Glenn Johnson, and Maurice Joy, "Accounting Methods and P/E Ratios," *Financial Analysts Journal* (March/April 1987), pp. 41–45.

[166] Paul Zarowin, "What Determines Earnings-Price Ratios: Revisited," *Journal of Accounting, Auditing, and Finance,* Vol. 5, No. 3 (1990), pp. 439–57.

[167] Stephen Penman and Xiao-Jun Zhang, "Accounting Conservatism, the Quality of Earnings, and Stock Returns," *The Accounting Review*, Vol. 77, No. 2 (April 2002), pp. 237–264.

4.2.11 Governance

"Governance" – in the narrow financial-market sense used here – refers to the extent to which a company is managed "in the interests of the shareholders." It is rooted conceptually in the so-called principal-agent problem, widely discussed in the economic literature, which is said to arise where there is a separation between the owners (shareholders) of a business enterprise and the managers hired to run it. Good corporate governance is achieved when structural and policy measures are in place to safeguard the common shareholders.[168]

Thus, "governance," like "quality," *ought* by its very definition to drive valuation premia (for "good governance") and discounts (for "weak governance").

At the extremes, this is clearly evident. For example, Korean companies carry a large discount:

> The Kospi [the Korean Stock Market Index] has for years traded at least one-fifth below the valuation of comparable markets on a price-to-earnings basis, despite the rise of a clutch of dominant companies such as *LG, Hyundai,* and *Samsung Electronics.*

Some analysts estimate the penalty at perhaps as much as 30–50%.[169]

This severe discount is commonly attributed, in part, to "subpar governance," including complicated ownership structures, with circular shareholdings among different corporate units that help founding families keep control though they may hold, nominally, only small stakes. Analysts also cite "murky business ethics." Often, the governance concerns converge upon a critique of the traditional Korean "chaebol" model (which also reflects a "conglomerate discount" – as noted in Section 4.2.6).

Findings from studies of the mainstream US equity universe are less clear. As noted, the starting point for analyses of governance is the agency problem, which is typically presented as a given fact: "Separation of ownership from control has long been recognized to potentially have an adverse effect on firm value." The literature on corporate governance

---

[168] Of course, "good governance" may be construed more broadly, with reference to the interests of other stakeholders, including employees, customers, and society at large. The narrow construct here is perhaps distinctly American-flavored.

[169] Edward White, "Korean Valuations Groan Under Burden of Shoddy Governance," *Financial Times,* May 17, 2019.

CHAPTER 4 INTERPRETATIONS: P/E AS A DEPENDENT VARIABLE

is full of similar pronouncements. Yet the evidence is equivocal and hard to interpret. Let us consider some of the governance factors that have been studied by academics.

Insider Ownership: One dimension of governance relates to the firm's ownership structure – questions such as the concentration of ownership among the Board of Directors. Higher rate of insider ownership has sometimes been considered to be positive for corporate governance, as it implies greater alignment of the Board's interests with those of other shareholders. One of the earliest studies (1988) found an inverted U-shape for the relationship between Tobin's Q and the concentration of the Board ownership.[170] Subsequent studies have tended to confirm this pattern (sort of). Valuation metrics do increase as insider interests rise from zero – that is, as insiders' influence over the Board increases – up to a certain point. Then they decline. One large study looked at two time slices – one in the mid-1970s (a bear market) and one in the mid-1980s (a bull market). (See Figure 4-46.) The researchers found that

> For 1976, at low levels of insider ownership, the relation between [Tobin's] Q and inside ownership is approximately one-for-one – a 10% increase in inside ownership increases Q by approximately 10%. For 1986, at low levels of inside ownership, the relation is approximately three-for-one – a 10% increase in inside ownership increases Q by approximately 30%.[171]

---

[170]Randall Morck, Andrei Shleifer, and Robert Vishny, "Management ownership and market valuation," *Journal of Financial Economics,* 20 (January): 293–315.

[171]John McConnell and Henri Servaes, "Additional evidence on equity ownership and corporate value," *Journal of Financial Economics,* Vol. 27 (1990), pp. 595–612.

CHAPTER 4   INTERPRETATIONS: P/E AS A DEPENDENT VARIABLE

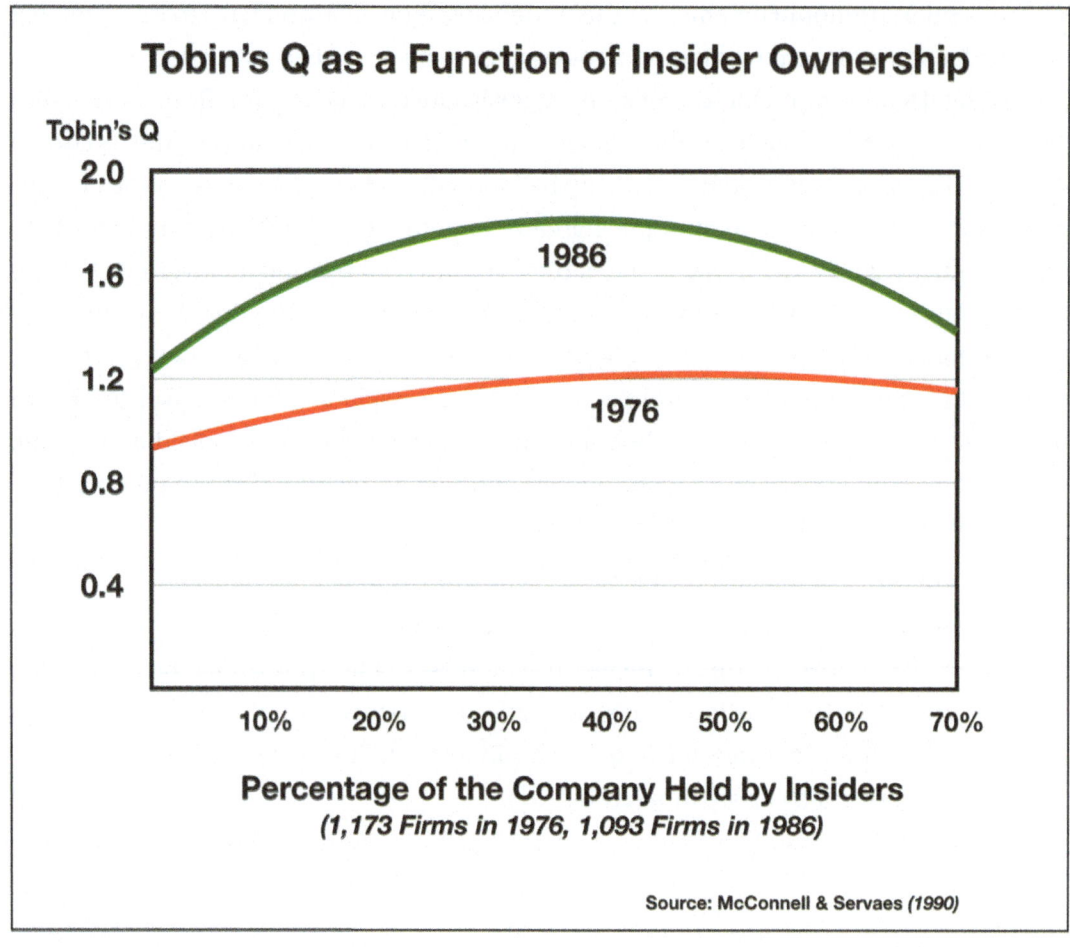

Figure 4-46. *Leverage and Price-to-Book*[172]

Other studies have found a "double-humped" relationship between ownership concentration and market multiples – with Tobin's Q peaking twice, at about 10% and again at about 40–50% insider ownership.[173] Other studies have found three "humps."[174]

---

[172] Adapted from John McConnell and Henri Servaes, "Additional evidence on equity ownership and corporate value," *Journal of Financial Economics*, Vol. 27 (1990), pp. 595–612.

[173] J. R. Davies, David Hillier, and Patrick McColgan, "Ownership structure, managerial behavior and corporate value," *Journal of Corporate Finance*, Vol. 11 (2005), pp. 645–660.

[174] A study of the firms listed on the New Zealand stock exchange found a "nonlinear cubic relationship" [essentially triple-humped] between Tobin's Q and ownership concentration (Gurmeet Singh Bhabra, "Insider ownership and firm value in New Zealand," *Journal of Multinational Financial Management*, Vol. 17 (2007), pp. 142–154).

A 2015 study found that "in the presence of high insider ownership, low P/E firms earn lower returns and high P/E firms earn higher returns" – a reversal of the typical "value anomaly" pattern.[175] It is not clear how to interpret this.

Staggered Boards of Directors: A "staggered" Board is one where only a subset of the Board members are up for election at any one time. This is considered to be a defense against takeover attempts, which is interpreted as a negative governance factor (since it may deprive shareholders of the opportunity to benefit from the takeover premium that is typically offered). It is also a defense against proxy challenges to current management, again seen typically as depriving shareholders of the opportunity to benefit from potentially improved performance and resulting higher share prices that "new management" or improved strategies might bring.

A 2005 study found that staggered boards reduced the Market Multiple (Tobin's Q, in this case) by 3–4%.[176] A more recent study of staggered boards from 1978 to 2015 found a "statistically and economically significant" negative correlation between staggered boards and the Price/Book multiple, "suggesting that firms with a staggered board have a firm value that is 2.1% lower than firms without a staggered board."[177]

These discounts are not large and may be unstable. Whether they are truly economically significant is open to doubt. Still, they indicate that market valuation multiples are at least somewhat sensitive to board structure.

Composite Governance Metrics: Multidimensional approaches to assessing governance risk are typically based on constructing specialized metrics from a large number of factors presumed to signal the quality of the firm's governance. For example, Gompers *et al.* employed a metric they called the GIM Index, a recipe of 24 separate governance risk factors, ranging from executive compensation policies to the use of multiple classes of stock.

---

[175] Robert Houmes and Inga Chira, "The effect of ownership structure on the price earnings ratio – returns anomaly," *International Review of Financial Analysis,* Vol. 37 (2015), pp. 140–147.

[176] Lucian A. Bebchuk and Alma Cohen, "The costs of entrenched boards," *Journal of Financial Economics,* Vol. 78 (2005), pp. 409–433.

[177] K.J. Martijn Cremers, Lubomir P. Litov, and Simone M. Sepe, "Staggered boards and long-term firm value, revisited," *Journal of Financial Economics,* Vol. 126 (2017), pp. 422–444. This article is incoherent in a number of respects. For one thing, the authors identify the market multiple they study as Tobin's Q, but the definition is that of Price/Book (i.e., the denominator is Book Value, not Replacement Cost). They also state in the abstract that they *"find no evidence that staggered board changes are negatively related to firm value"* – with the emphasis on "changes" presumably – despite the actual negative correlations cited here. They even suggest that *"staggered boards promote value creation for some firms"* – which is hard to square with the data.

CHAPTER 4   INTERPRETATIONS: P/E AS A DEPENDENT VARIABLE

Each factor was assigned an equal weight and a value of either 1 or 0 (present or absent). The authors examined some 1500 firms across the decade of the 1990s. Weaker governance was associated with lower valuation multiples (Tobin's Q, again).

> The Governance Index is highly correlated with firm value. In 1990, a one-point [i.e., one risk factor] increase in the index is associated with a 2.4 percentage-point lower value for Tobin's Q. By 1999, this difference had increased significantly, with a one-point increased in the index associated with an 8.9 percentage-point lower value for Tobin's Q.[178]

The governance effect on valuation is ambiguous – because governance itself is an ambiguous concept. For one thing, regulations change over time and often in the direction of mandating improved governance measures (e.g., Sarbanes-Oxley). For another, many governance issues seem to be not so much zero-or-one propositions (good or bad), but questions of calibration. For example, some degree of share ownership by Board members is likely a good thing ("skin in the game"), but when Board ownership dominates it becomes difficult to make changes ("entrenchment"). To some extent, the market multiples reveal this "Goldilocks" phenomenon (in those humped valuation graphs), but finding the sweet spot in the data is not always easy. Good governance is multidimensional, which implies the existence of complex trade-offs, and perhaps instability, as economic conditions evolve and strategic fashions come and go (e.g., the trends in shareholder activism). There was a time when staggered boards, for example, were seen as proper defensive measures against predatory "raiders" – and shareholders voted for them. Today, perhaps, the raiders are seen in a different light, and so staggered boards are being reevaluated. Good governance in one era may be seen as less good in another era.

---

[178]P. A. Gompers, J. L. Ishii, and A. Metrick, "Corporate governance and equity prices," *Quarterly Journal of Economics,* Vol. 118 (2003), pp. 107-155. See also Kenneth Lehn, Sukesh Patro, and Mengxin Zhao, "Governance indexes and valuation: Which causes which?" *Journal of Corporate Finance,* Vol. 13 (2007), pp. 907-928.

4.3 Sector-Level and Market-Level Drivers
4.3.1 Sentiment ("Animal Spirits")

> Market average P/E's vary through time, as investor confidence waxes and wanes.[179]

> The P/E ratio actually is a reflection of the market's optimism...[180]

> While a number of studies have explored the fundamental determinants of the price-earnings ratio, its sensitivity to investor sentiment has remained largely unexplored.[181]

Sometimes, when investors are confounded by an unexpected market move, or when a researcher has struggled with a complex statistical project that refuses to confirm the model... when they finally throw up their hands and invoke "sentiment" as the fallback explanation...[182] it can be quite refreshing.[183] The market processes all sorts of information – rumors, opinions (well founded or unfounded), fears, hopes, misinformation, and lazy conformity, right along with the "rational expectations" that economists presume. Recognizing this can be the starting point for a serious understanding of the role of non-rational factors that influence market outcomes. Under the heading of *Sentiment,* this vast and confused set of information vectors becomes an important subject in its own right.

---

[179] Keith Anderson and Chris Brooks, "Decomposing the Price-earnings Ratio," *Journal of Asset Management,* Vol. 6, No. 6 (March 2006), pp. 456–469.

[180] Zvi Bodie, Alex Kane, and Alan Marcus, *Investments* (McGraw-Hill, 2002), p. 572.

[181] Md Lutfur Rahman and Abul Shamsuddin, "Investor sentiment and the price-earnings ratio in the G7 stock markets," *Pacific-Basin Finance Journal,* Vol. 55 (2019), pp. 46-62.

[182] Here is how it might be couched in academic speak: *"Thus the limits to arbitrage, accompanied by* **irrational** *exuberance, may inflate the P/E ratio."* [Emphasis in the original] (Md Lutfur Rahman and Abul Shamsuddin, "Investor sentiment and the price-earnings ratio in the G7 stock markets," *Pacific-Basin Finance Journal,* Vol. 55 (2019), pp. 46-62).

[183] For example: *"Although P/E ratios form the essence of fundamental analysis, investor sentiment may also contribute to the movements in P/E ratios. For example, if the markets factor in sentiment, the stock prices may suddenly jump but the company earnings may not be up to the mark. Hence, a sentiment-driven firm but poor fundamentals still has a high P/E ratio. In this regard, we consider investor sentiment as one of the key determinants of P/E ratio."* (Boonlert Jitmaneeroj, "The impact of dividend policy on price-earnings ratios: The role of conditional and nonlinear relationship," *Review of Accounting and Finance,* Vol. 16, No. 1 (2017), pp. 125-140).

The idea that the P/E would reflect these influences would be a healthy extension of our conceptual framework. Unfortunately, it has not been deeply studied yet, and it lies beyond the scope of this book to enumerate the sources, forms, and components of Sentiment. But we can make a few very general observations.

First, Sentiment comes "in layers." There is *company-specific sentiment* that affects an individual firm and is rooted in investors' opinions that pertain specifically to that firm. And there is *market sentiment* that affects the value of the firm but originates from the macroeconomic context and manifests its effects across the entire market. In between, there may be a layer of *sector-specific sentiment,* which will affect the valuations of all the companies within a particular industry (e.g., when the banking sector fell out of favor in the aftermath of the 2008 financial crisis). Picking apart the effects of each component on the valuation for a particular company is challenging.

Second, Sentiment is of two sorts: un-informed, or less informed, and typically "unstructured" sentiment, on the one hand, and informed, structured sentiment, on the other. Roughly speaking, we might call the first sort *Retail Sentiment* and the second *Professional Opinion*. A full exploration of the topic of Sentiment would cover at least four types (Table 4-1).

Table 4-1. *Types of Sentiment*

	Firm Level	**Market Level**
Un-Informed Sentiment	1 Company Reputation among Investors	2 "Animal Spirits" "Consumer Sentiment" "Consumer Confidence"
Informed Sentiment	3 Analysts' Reports	4 Economists' Expectations, Forecasts

The category of most interest here is represented on box 2 of this matrix. The effect of general consumer sentiment on stock prices and values has become a focus of interest, especially in the context of quantitative easing and stimulative monetary policy generally. The relationship between consumer sentiment and asset values is the subject of much discussion among economists, especially with respect to the direction of causality – does consumer sentiment set the tone and drive stock values (and presumably P/E ratios), or is it the other way around?[184]

What is clear is that in Bear markets P/E multiples are depressed. In Bull markets, the P/E expands (though in a complex way – see Chapter 5, Section 5.6). And in "bubbles" the Multiples are superelevated. Bear, Bull, and Bubble are market regimes that can be characterized in terms of investor sentiment.

How important are these sentiment regimes in setting the P/E for a given company? In a study entitled "Decomposing the Price-earnings Ratio," Anderson and Brooks found that simply regressing the "Year" variable against returns provided the strongest of the several factors they considered in explaining P/E levels.[185] "Year" is seen in this study as a proxy for the large-scale market regime. For example, "Year" values in the 1970s would mostly represent Bear Markets, while "Year" values in the 1990s would mostly represent Bull Markets. The effect of "Year" on P/E was much stronger than the effect of "Size" (market capitalization), for example.

4.3.1.1 The Market P/E and "Animal Spirits"

So, does broad Consumer Sentiment itself have an effect on market valuations?

The economist John Maynard Keynes – and experienced and successful trader – argued that the market is truly driven by emotion, "animal spirits," rather than cold calculation of self-interest. His famous dictum is a splendid encapsulation of the argument for the importance of Sentiment, and Keynes is always worth quoting afresh:

> A large proportion of our positive activities depend on spontaneous optimism rather than mathematical expectations... Most of our decisions... can only be taken as the result of animal spirits – a spontaneous urge to action rather than inaction, and not as the outcome of a weighted average of quantitative benefits multiplied by quantitative probabilities.[186]

---

[184] The more common view today is that rising asset prices and values (a booming stock market) are the cause of improved consumer sentiment, which leads to increased spending. The Federal Reserve appeared to have committed itself to exploiting this "wealth effect" as a means to transmit a stimulus from the financial markets to the real economy. There is much debate as to whether the wealth effect exists and how significant it may be.

[185] Keith Anderson and Chris Brooks, "Decomposing the Price-earnings Ratio," *Journal of Asset Management*, Vol. 6, No. 6 (March 2006), pp. 456–469.

[186] Keynes, John M. (1936). *The General Theory of Employment, Interest and Money*. London. Macmillan, pp. 161–162.

CHAPTER 4   INTERPRETATIONS: P/E AS A DEPENDENT VARIABLE

However, a number of studies have failed to find a relationship between recognized consumer sentiment metrics, such as the University of Michigan's Consumer Sentiment Index.[187] (See Figure 4-47.)

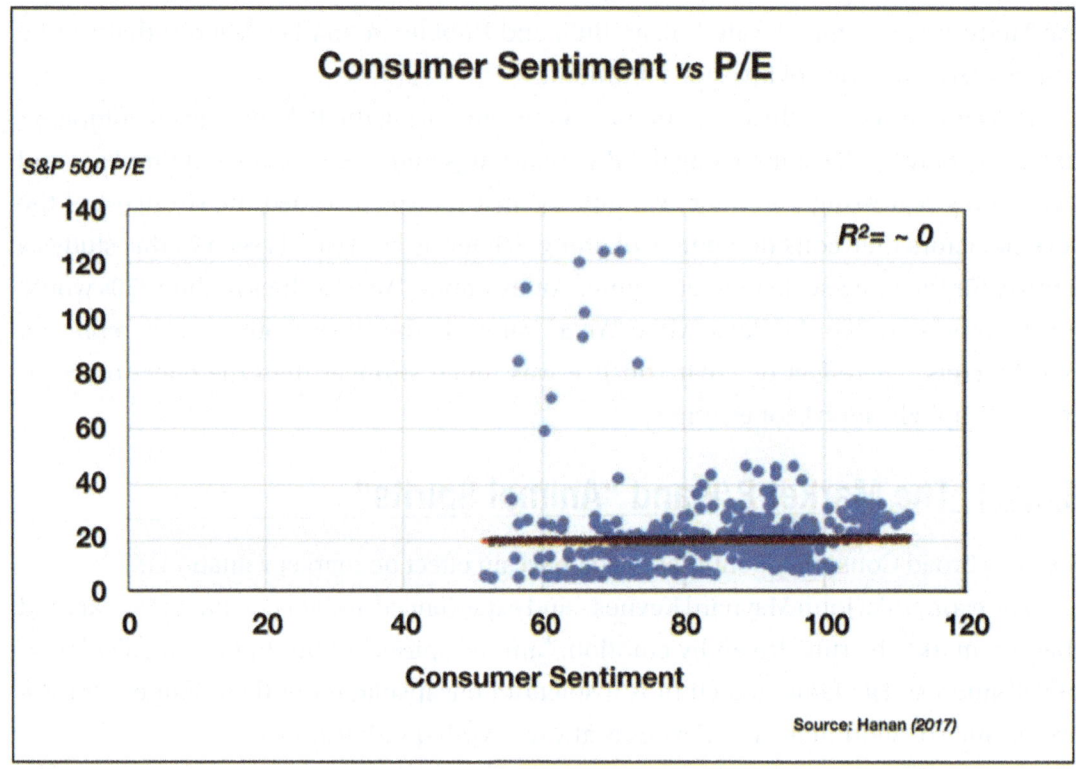

Figure 4-47. *Consumer Sentiment and P/E*[188]

---

[187]For example, Kevin Christ and Dale Bremmer, "The Relationship Between Consumer Sentiment and Stock Prices," July 15, 2003. Also see Ahmed Salhin, Mohamed Sherif, and Edward Jones, "Managerial sentiment, consumer confidence and sector returns," *International Review of Financial Analysis*, Vol. 47 (2016), pp. 24-38.

[188]Adapted from Martin Hanan, "The S&P 500 P/E Ratio: A Historical Perspective," *Valuescope White Paper* (2017), available at www.valuescopeinc.com/resources/white-papers/the-sp-500-pe-ratio-a-historical-perspective/

We see very little relationship between Consumer Sentiment Index and the P/E ratio. There is not adequate evidence to suggest that a change in Consumer Sentiment causes the P/E ratio to increase or decrease. None of the variability in the S&P 500 P/E ratios can be explained by regression with Consumer Sentiment.[189]

A very recent study of all the G7 markets (Canada, France, Germany, Italy, Japan, the United Kingdom, and the United States) makes the summary claim that "the P/E ratio *generally* increases with an improvement in investor sentiment in the G7 countries" [Emphasis added].[190] However, a closer examination of the data in the G7 study disappoints an attempt to find a clear relationship between the sentiment metrics and the P/E. The relationship is neither linear for any particular country nor consistent in shape across countries. The authors admit to "mixed results" and conclude that (for example) "business confidence does not exert any statistically significant influence in any P/E quantiles in the USA." In fact, the overall correlation of the P/E ratio with the Consumer Confidence index for the United States is essentially zero.[191] Another recent study found the same result for stock market returns: "consumer confidence is not a predictor of sector or aggregate returns."[192] Perhaps "animal spirits" are not being measured accurately. The study also calls attention to the accumulation of "evidence against the reliability of the consumer confidence indicator."

In any case, as the results stand today, Sentiment does not appear to show a significant relationship to the P/E.

---

[189] Martin Hanan, "The S&P 500 P/E Ratio: A Historical Perspective," *Valuescope White Paper* (2017), available at www.valuescopeinc.com/resources/white-papers/the-sp-500-pe-ratio-a-historical-perspective/. This study used the Michigan Consumer Sentiment Index.

[190] Md Lutfur Rahman and Abul Shamsuddin, "Investor sentiment and the price-earnings ratio in the G7 stock markets," *Pacific-Basin Finance Journal,* Vol. 55 (2019), pp. 46–62. This study used a different metric from the Hanan paper cited previously. The authors here used a combination of *consumer confidence* indices and *business confidence* indices in each country.

[191] The correlations for Consumer Confidence with the P/E did not exceed 0.2 for any country.

[192] Ahmed Salhin, Mohamed Sherif, and Edward Jones, "Managerial sentiment, consumer confidence and sector returns," *International Review of Financial Analysis*, Vol. 47 (2016), pp. 24–38.

CHAPTER 4   INTERPRETATIONS: P/E AS A DEPENDENT VARIABLE

4.3.2 Sector Discounts and Premiums

Industry sectors are defined on the basis of broad operational similarities, common product/service characteristics, similar cost structures, or a common customer set and consumption patterns.[193] The differences between sectors are often reflected in persistent differences in the P/E multiple.[194] (See Figure 4-48.) They can sometimes highlight important questions of economic substance connected with structural aspects of firm value. For example, the 30% premium accorded to the *consumer discretionary* sector (65 companies in the S&P 500 sector index) over *consumer nondiscretionary* sector (32 companies) is likely rooted in the lifestyle and psychological variables underlying consumer spending patterns, which affect the quality of earnings and, through that mechanism, the companies' valuations. Also, not surprisingly, there are often significant valuation spreads *within* sectors – which can identify "value" (low P/E) and "growth" (high P/E) companies in the same industry.[195]

---

[193]Companies in the "same" sector may have quite different business models, however. For example, in the semiconductor sector, some firms are Capex-intensive heavy manufacturers (*e.g., Intel*), while others are "asset-light," focusing on chip design and/or intellectual property licensing (*e.g., Nvidia, Qualcomm*), and do not open or operate their own fabrication facilities.

[194]Source for this data: www.gurufocus.com/sector_shiller_pe.php

[195]David Dreman and Eric Lufkin, "Do Contrarian Strategies Work Within Industries," *Journal of Investing*, Vol. 6 (1997), pp. 7–29.

CHAPTER 4 INTERPRETATIONS: P/E AS A DEPENDENT VARIABLE

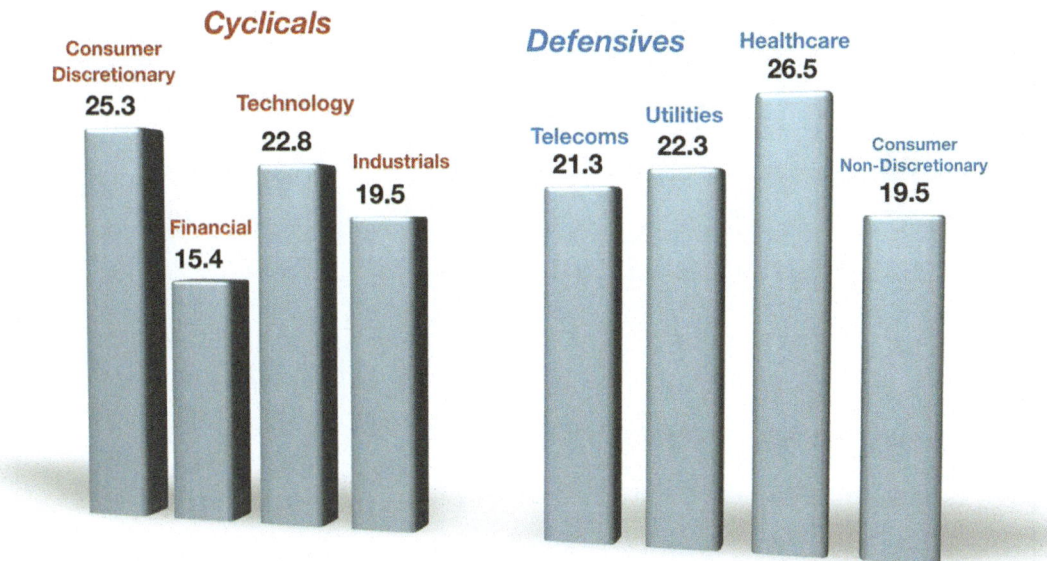

Figure 4-48. *Average Trailing P/E by Sector (2013–2018)*

Viewed over time, sector P/E multiples can signal important *changes* in the structural characteristics of the business model. For example, the energy sector saw a sharp spike in P/E multiples in 2016/2017.[196] This pronounced divergence from "normal" levels reflected a quasi-collapse in sector earnings when crude oil prices fell briefly below $30/barrel – while the market generally maintained the industry's prior valuations (share prices) on the correct view that the dip would prove temporary. (See Figures 4-49 and 4-50.)

---

[196]Edward Yardeni, Joe Abbott, and Mali Quintana, "Stock market Briefing: S&P 500 Sectors and Industries Forward P/Es," *Yardeni Research,* October 24, 2018.

CHAPTER 4   INTERPRETATIONS: P/E AS A DEPENDENT VARIABLE

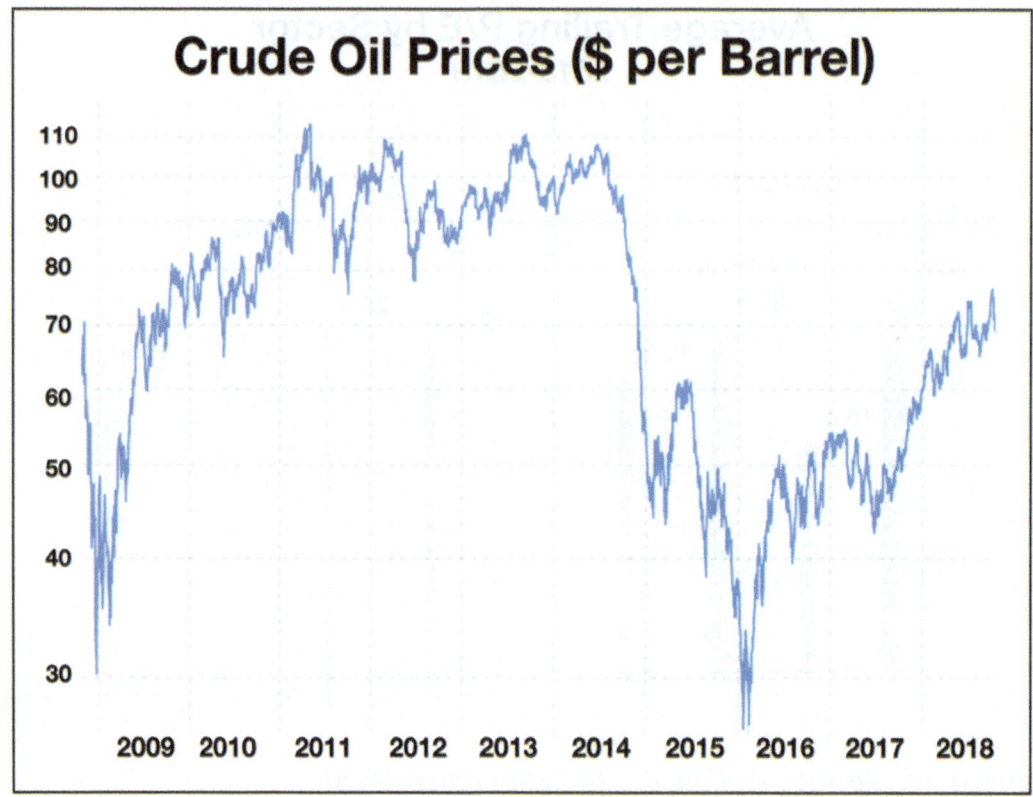

Figure 4-49. Crude Oil Prices – the Energy Sector Valuation Driver

CHAPTER 4　INTERPRETATIONS: P/E AS A DEPENDENT VARIABLE

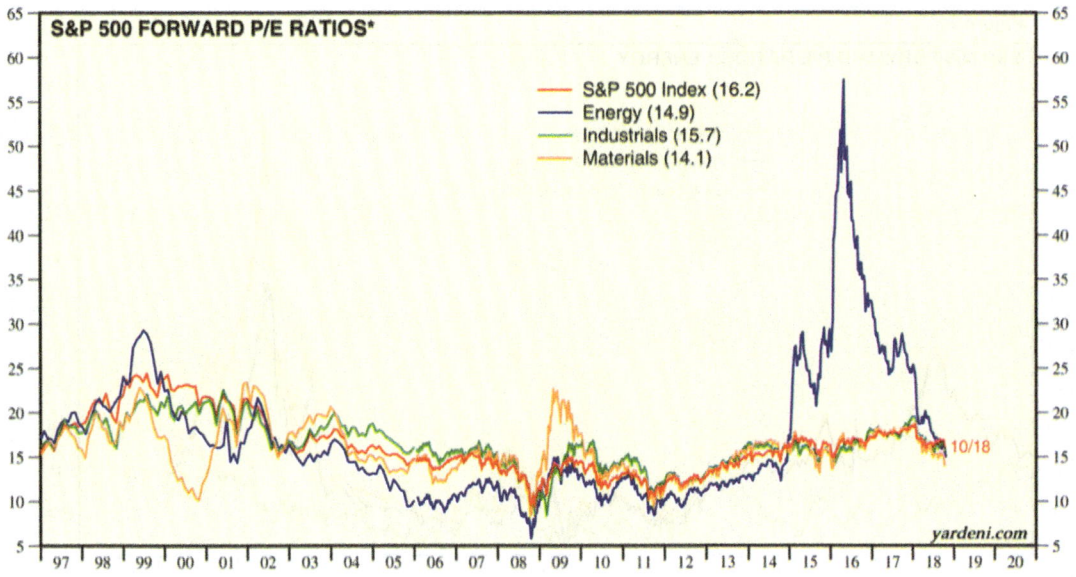

Figure 4-50. *Energy Sector P/E vs. S&P 500 P/E*[197]

Even more information can be gleaned from stepping down one level in the analysis, from the sector to the components of the sector. A closer look at the energy sector is revealing. (See Figure 4-51.)

---

[197]Edward Yardeni, Joe Abbott, and Mali Quintana, "Stock market Briefing: S&P 500 Sectors and Industries Forward P/Es," *Yardeni Research,* October 24, 2018. Reproduced by permission of *Yardeni Research.*

CHAPTER 4   INTERPRETATIONS: P/E AS A DEPENDENT VARIABLE

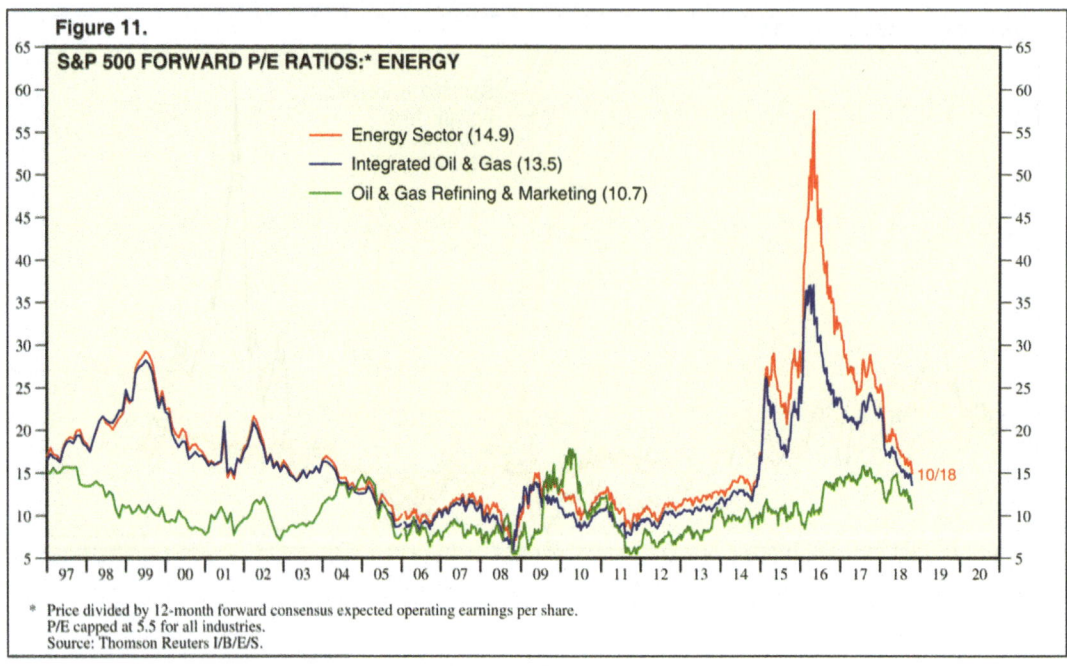

Figure 4-51. *Energy Sub-sector P/E's*[198]

As discussed in the previous chapter (Section 3.6), the Multiples for the energy sector illuminate interesting differences between upstream (exploration and extraction) energy companies and downstream (refining and marketing) companies. Here we see that the P/E spike did not affect companies in the downstream category, which largely benefit from cheaper crude (their main cost component).

Interestingly, this spike in the energy sector was so pronounced, and the companies involved carry so much weight (market capitalization), that it skewed the P/E for the entire S&P 500. It pulled up the market P/E by almost 10%, making equities as an asset class appear more expensive.[199]

---

[198] Edward Yardeni, Joe Abbott, and Mali Quintana, "Stock market Briefing: S&P 500 Sectors and Industries Forward P/Es," *Yardeni Research,* October 24, 2018. Reproduced by permission of *Yardeni Research.*

[199] James Mackintosh, "A New Way to Look at Crazy Valuations," *The Wall Street Journal,* February 28, 2017

Sometimes a sector is revalued upward by investors. This effect appears in the telecoms sector after the financial crisis. (See Figure 4-52.) Along with other Defensive sectors, telecoms rose to a nearly 60% premium over the S&P 500, reflecting a significant shift in investor psychology.[200] Telecoms companies are defensive not only in terms of the underlying stability in the pattern of consumer demand (e.g., which they share with Consumer Staples) but also because they enjoy a high Quality of Revenue, deriving from their subscription-based business model. In periods of market stress, they may present one of the most defensive of the Defensive sectors and draw unusual investor support, reflected in a premium P/E multiple.

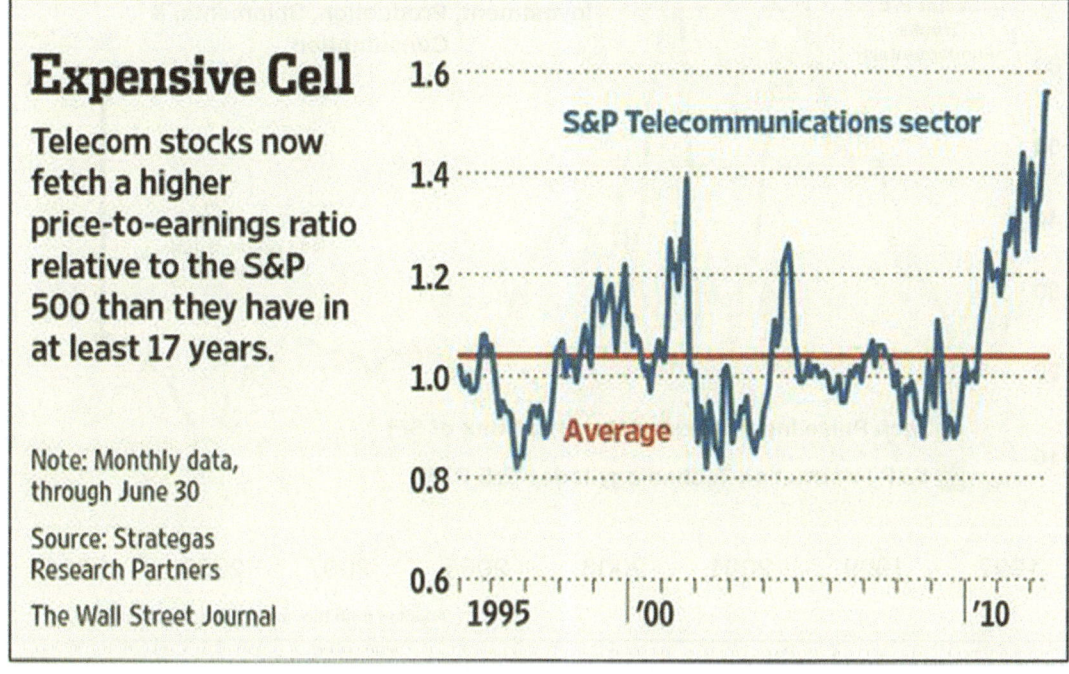

Figure 4-52. Telecom Sector P/E[201]

---

[200]Jonathan Cheng, "Investors Testing Limits of Defense," *The Wall Street Journal*, July 23, 2012.
[201]Jonathan Cheng, "Investors Testing Limits of Defense," *The Wall Street Journal*, July 23, 2012. Reproduced by permission from *The Wall Street Journal*.

CHAPTER 4   INTERPRETATIONS: P/E AS A DEPENDENT VARIABLE

A sector may also fall out of favor despite generating strong fundamentals, analogous to the "maturity reset" that can affect individual companies (as described in Section 4.2.1 earlier). After the dot-com crash, investors soured on technology companies generally, and sector valuations dropped and stayed low for the next decade, despite a robust recovery in the companies' fundamental performance, as reflected in the Federal Reserve's Tech Pulse Index.[202] (See Figure 4-53.)

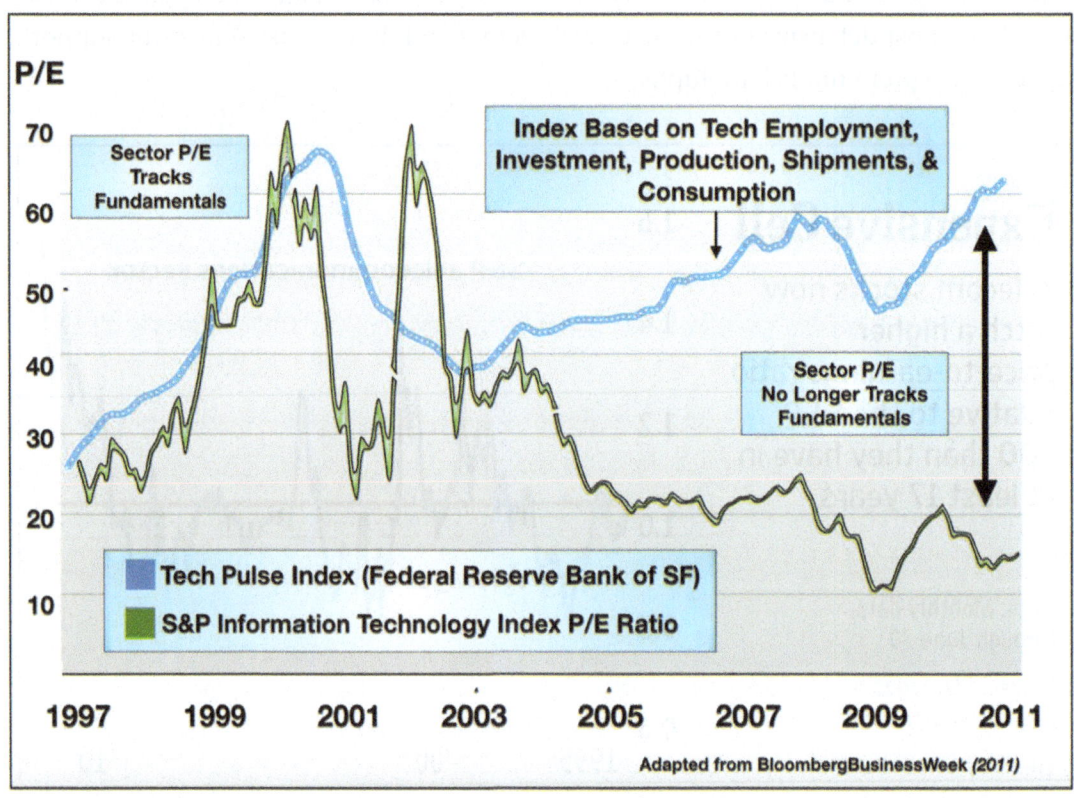

Figure 4-53. *Tech Sector P/E Diverges from Fundamental Performance*[203]

Sector membership is an important determinant of a company's valuation multiples. Looking across sectors, we often see companies with similar earnings streams which nevertheless carry very different valuations in the capital markets. A Discounted Cash Flow model might not capture this. We would like to understand better the relative

---

[202] *Bloomberg/BusinessWeek*, February 28, 2011.

[203] Adapted from *Bloomberg/BusinessWeek*, February 28, 2011.

218

contributions of sector membership, *vs.* overall market sentiment, to a company's P/E valuation. The subject has been little studied. One of the few relevant papers, from 2006, focused on UK companies, found that Sector membership had "a decidedly moderate predictive power,"[204] quite a bit less than Size.[205] This finding would seem to be at odds with the strong and persistent sector differences shown earlier, which are of the same rough magnitude as Size effects (Large Cap vs. Small Cap). Further research could help clarify this relationship.

4.3.3 Regulation

Government regulations impose external constraints on how a business may operate or add requirements that increase costs or reduce risks, in the interest of some larger social objective or in return for protection from competition. Regulation often has a negative effect on valuation multiples.

Unfortunately the subject has not been systematically studied. What we can observe are "anecdotal" examples which invite an interpretation based on the effect of regulation on P/E values. In 2007 and 2008, the healthcare sector – which had been trading at a premium to the overall market – saw a decline of nearly 40% in "equivalent EPS dollars" to trade at a significant discount to the market.[206] (See Figure 4-54.)

---

[204]British understatement for "not much."
[205]Keith Anderson and Chris Brooks, "Decomposing the Price-earnings Ratio," *Journal of Asset Management*, Vol. 6, No. 6 (March 2006), pp. 456–469.
[206]Mina Kimes, "Returning to Health," *Fortune*, February 8, 2010.

CHAPTER 4   INTERPRETATIONS: P/E AS A DEPENDENT VARIABLE

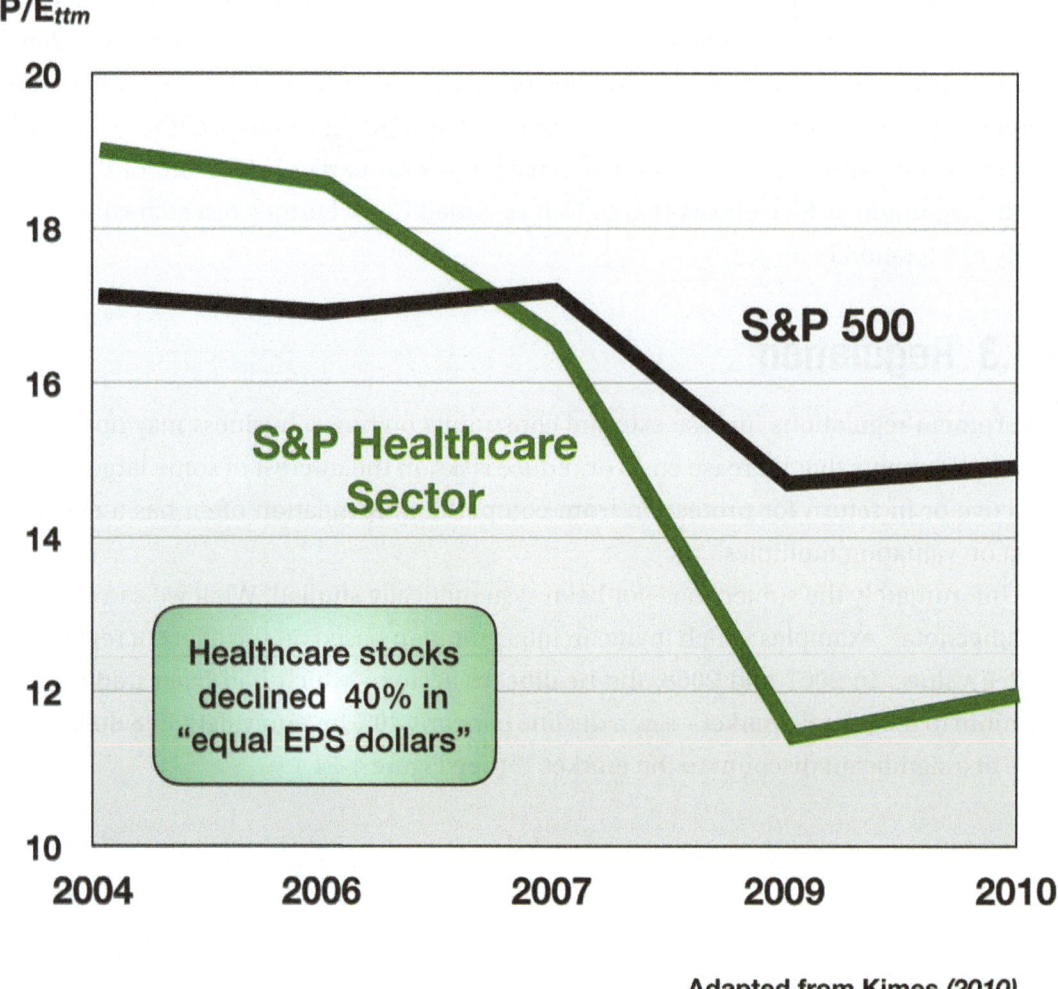

Figure 4-54. *P/E Shift in the Healthcare Sector*[207]

The likely explanation was the looming impact of comprehensive new healthcare regulation (the Affordable Care Act of 2010), which altered the cost structures and business models of many segments of the industry.

In the aftermath of the 2008 financial crisis, the financial sector – especially the largest, "systemically important" banks – became subject to much more stringent regulation, imposing significant new costs on the banking business model, including higher capital

---

[207] Adapted from Mina Kimes, "Returning to Health," *Fortune*, February 8, 2010.

CHAPTER 4   INTERPRETATIONS: P/E AS A DEPENDENT VARIABLE

requirements which (probably permanently) reduced their profitability. This heavier regulatory regime may have contributed to a dramatic reduction in the industry's Price-to-Book ratios.[208] (See Figure 4-55.)

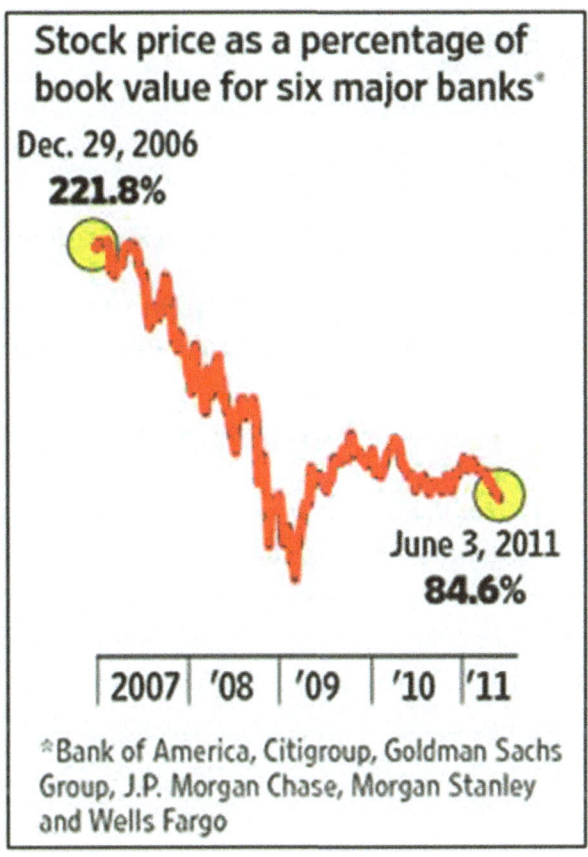

Figure 4-55. *P/B Shift in the Banking Sector*[209]

---

[208]David Reilly, "Banks Caught in a Squeeze Play," *The Wall Street Journal*, June 3, 2011; Jonathan Cheng and Randall Smith, "Bulls and Bears in Tug of War on Bank Stocks," *The Wall Street Journal*, June 6, 2011.

[209]Jonathan Cheng and Randall Smith, "Bulls and Bears in Tug of War on Bank Stocks," *The Wall Street Journal*, June 6, 2011. Reproduced by permission from *The Wall Street Journal*.

CHAPTER 4   INTERPRETATIONS: P/E AS A DEPENDENT VARIABLE

Such examples suggest in a general way that regulation may be a significant driver of market valuations. It would be useful to be able to tie these valuation shifts more closely, and more quantitatively, to specific economic consequences of regulatory changes.[210]

4.3.4 Monetary Policy

Stock returns and monetary policy: Are there any ties? The interdependence between asset prices and monetary policy is a central issue in financial economics.[211]

—A typical academic study (2013)

Since 1994 about 80% of realized excess stock returns in the U.S. have been earned in the 24 hours before scheduled monetary policy announcements.[212]

—The New York Federal Reserve (2013)

Asked and answered? The link between monetary policy – that is, central banks' statements and actions regarding interest rates, asset purchase programs (such as "Quantitative Easing"), and other policy tools employed to either stimulate or restrain the real economy – and the prices of financial assets such as stocks or bonds is an enormous subject, of central importance to macroeconomic theory and practice. It lies outside the scope of this book to review or even to summarize the work done on this topic, beyond a few general remarks.

---

[210]The quantitative changes in the capital requirements for banks following the 2008 crisis could be analyzed for their measurable impact on P/E or P/B ratios, for example. The impact of the Volcker Rule limitations on proprietary trading by banks could also be studied in terms of its effects on bank profit margins (lower?) and securities inventories (much lower). Regulation (e.g., Dodd-Frank) is often quite multidimensional, and it would be useful to understand what specific measures drive valuation shifts. This would require complicated and carefully designed research programs. I am not aware of detailed academic research in this vein, however.

[211]Hafedh Bouakez, Badye Essid, and Michel Normandin, "Stock returns and monetary policy: Are there any ties?" *Journal of Macroeconomics*, Vol. 36 (2013), pp. 33–50.

[212]David O. Lucca and Emanuel Moench, "The Pre-FOMC Announcement Drift," *The Federal Reserve Bank of New York, Staff Report No. 512*, revised August 2013.

First, from a "theory" perspective, actions by the central bank may transmit their effects to the financial market through other variables that have been studied more narrowly in terms of their effect on P/E and market valuations. These include

- Interest rates – see Section 4.3.7.
- Inflation – see Section 4.3.6.
- Effects on the use of leverage by firms – see Section 4.2.9.

Second, and perhaps more to the point, the actual effect of the Fed's moves on the market is very large. One study compared the market returns *with* and *without* the days of the Federal Open Market Committee (FOMC) meetings – typically about ten days per year – and found that from 1985 to 2016 more than 25% of the total returns of the stock market came on just those few days.[213] (See Figure 4-56.) From 2008, and the advent of "unconventional" monetary policy (characterized by asset purchases by the Fed on a trillion-dollar scale), FOMC days accounted for fully 60% of market returns. The average gain on FOMC days was 50 times higher than the average gain on other days.[214]

---

[213] James Montier and Philip Pilkington, "The Stock Market as Monetary Policy Junkie: Quantifying the Fed's Impact on the S&P 500," *GMO*, March 23, 2016, available at www.advisorperspectives.com/commentaries/2016/03/23/the-stock-market-as-monetary-policy-junkie-quantifying-the-fed-s-impact-on-the-s-p-500

[214] Richer Sharma, "Trump Tees Up a Necessary Debate on the Fed," *The Wall Street Journal*, September 29, 2016.

CHAPTER 4   INTERPRETATIONS: P/E AS A DEPENDENT VARIABLE

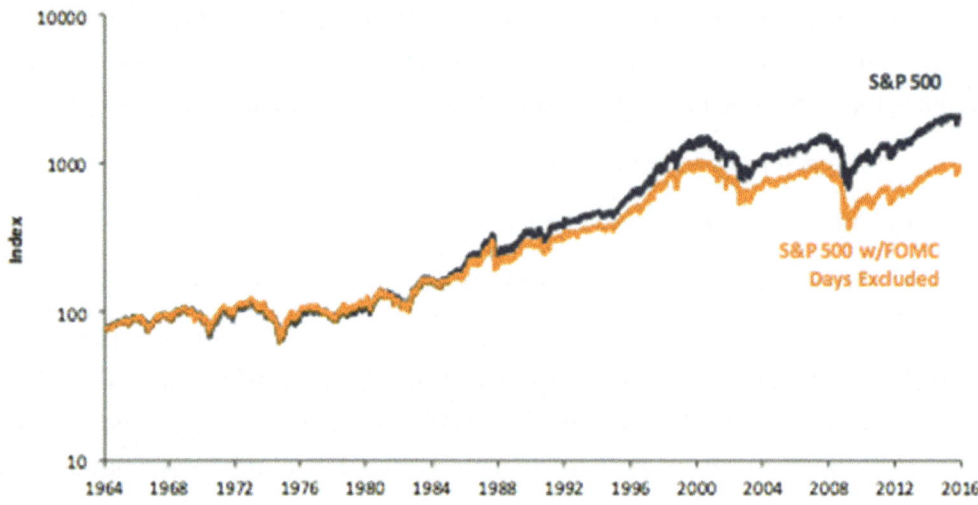

As of 1/4/16
Source: GMO

Figure 4-56. Impact of the Federal Reserve on Market Returns[215]

Most striking is a 2013 study by the Fed's own economic staff.

> Since 1994, the S&P500 index has on average increased 49 basis points in the 24 hours before scheduled FOMC announcements. These returns do not revert in subsequent trading days and are orders of magnitude larger than those outside the 24-hour pre-FOMC window. As a result, about 80% of annual realized excess stock returns since 1994 are accounted for by the pre-FOMC announcement drift. The statistical significance of the pre-FOMC return is very high.[216]

---

[215]James Montier and Philip Pilkington, "The Stock Market as Monetary Policy Junkie: Quantifying the Fed's Impact on the S&P 500," *GMO*, March 23, 2016, available at www.advisorperspectives.com/commentaries/2016/03/23/the-stock-market-as-monetary-policy-junkie-quantifying-the-fed-s-impact-on-the-s-p-500. Reproduced by permission of GMO.

[216]David O. Lucca and Emanuel Moench, "The Pre-FOMC Announcement Drift," *The Federal Reserve Bank of New York, Staff Report No. 512*, revised August 2013.

CHAPTER 4   INTERPRETATIONS: P/E AS A DEPENDENT VARIABLE

The authors blandly present several "trading strategies" of their own design.

The impact of this factor on P/E multiples has not been studied, to my knowledge, with one exception. A version of the Cyclically Adjusted P/E has been constructed which extracts the effects of the FOMC meetings, which they call the Monetary Policy–Adjusted CAPE, or MAPE.[217] It reduces the numerator by the amount of the gains due to the FOMC effect and thus lowers the P/E. This renders a view of the market as less overvalued, compared to the CAPE. (Note that by 2015, the MAPE was about half the value of the CAPE.) (See Figure 4-57.)

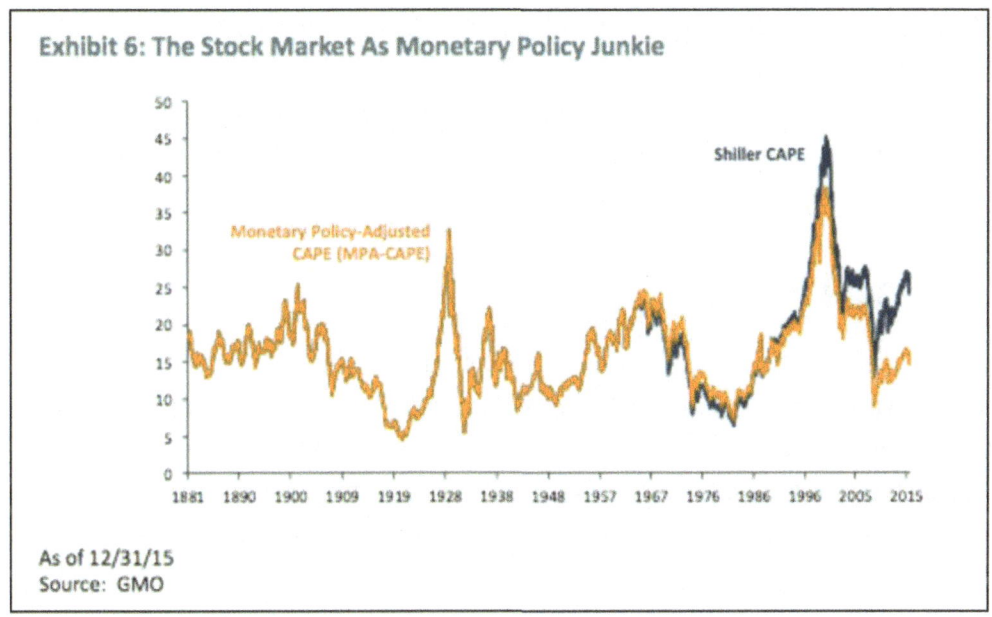

Figure 4-57. *P/E Adjusted for Effects of Fed Meeting Announcements*[218]

---

[217] James Montier and Philip Pilkington, "The Stock Market as Monetary Policy Junkie: Quantifying the Fed's Impact on the S&P 500," *GMO*, March 23, 2016, available at www.advisorperspectives.com/commentaries/2016/03/23/the-stock-market-as-monetary-policy-junkie-quantifying-the-fed-s-impact-on-the-s-p-500

[218] James Montier and Philip Pilkington, "The Stock Market as Monetary Policy Junkie: Quantifying the Fed's Impact on the S&P 500," *GMO*, March 23, 2016, available at www.advisorperspectives.com/commentaries/2016/03/23/the-stock-market-as-monetary-policy-junkie-quantifying-the-fed-s-impact-on-the-s-p-500. Reproduced by permission of GMO.

CHAPTER 4 INTERPRETATIONS: P/E AS A DEPENDENT VARIABLE

Finally, we must take account of the fact that the Fed and its leaders have become more explicit in recent years about the goal of raising asset prices (equities) by driving down bond yields and "forcing" investors to move to riskier asset classes. Why? One of the benefits of "quantitative easing" is said to be the stimulus it provides to investor psychology, called the wealth effect. A rising stock market generates consumer confidence, which leads to increased willingness to spend, which drives economic growth, and so on. The United States is perhaps now (2018) just emerging from a decade of "unconventional" monetary policy. Europe and Japan are still pursuing their versions of quantitative easing, which have in some respects surpassed in scope the US experiment.[219] It is widely assumed that market valuations have been inflated to some degree – perhaps to a very significant degree – by these policies.

In short, it seems clear that monetary policy is a major factor in setting, and perhaps distorting, valuations and in determining the level of market multiples. But little work has been done so far to quantify the effect.

4.3.5 Fiscal Policy

Fiscal policy refers to the effect of the economic stimulus created by government spending (or withdrawn through austerity measures). Tax cuts, infrastructure spending, boosting of entitlements, and direct subsidies to certain industries – all can drive higher valuation ratios, which may focus on specific sectors or firms. A *Bank of America* study looked at the P/E increases for 35 companies in the S&P 500 considered to be most "exposed" to benefit from fiscal stimulus effects.[220] (See Figure 4-58.)

---

[219]In Europe, unlike in the United States, the Central Bank has bought corporate bonds as well as sovereign debt. In Japan, the Bank of Japan has bought equities (ETFs) on a very large scale.

[220]Savita Subramanian, "2017 – The Year Ahead: Euphoria or Fiscal Fizzle," *Equity and Quant Strategy, Bank of America/Merrill Lynch,* November 22, 2016. See also Michael Hartnett et al., "150 stocks with exposure to the Fiscal Stimulus theme," *Investment Strategy: Global, Bank of America/Merrill Lynch,* August 21, 2016.

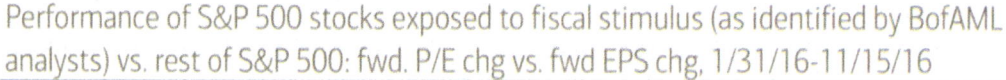

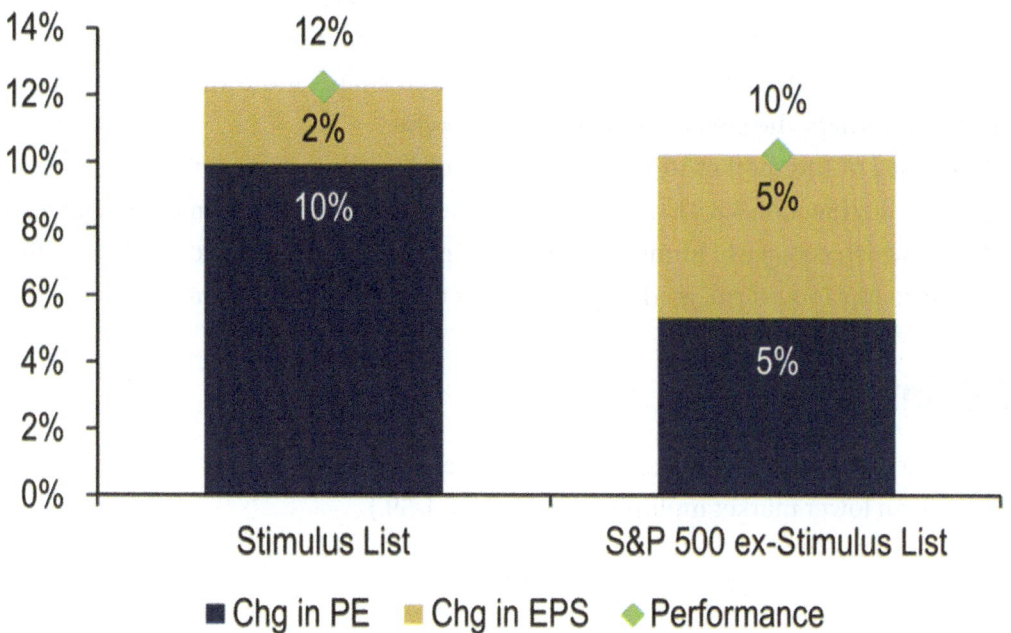

Note: Stimulus list based on S&P 500 stocks in US list as published in 150 stocks with exposure to the Fiscal Stimulus theme 21 August 2016
Source: FactSet, BofA Merrill Lynch US Equity & US Quant Strategy

Figure 4-58. *P/E and Fiscal Policy*[221]

The chart indicates that the companies considered to be the beneficiaries of government spending and tax cuts gained 12% over the period, 200 basis points better than the rest of the market. The more important point is that this was *not* because their earnings were growing; in fact, the EPS of that group grew *less than half as much as the earnings growth of the rest of the S&P 500*. This was offset by the expanding Multiple.

---

[221] Savita Subramanian, "2017 – The Year Ahead: Euphoria or Fiscal Fizzle," *Equity and Quant Strategy, Bank of America/Merrill Lynch*, November 22, 2016. Reprinted by permission. Copyright © 2019 Bank of America Corporation ("BAC"). The use of the preceding reference in no way implies that BAC or any of its affiliates endorses the views or interpretation or the use of such information or acts as any endorsement of author's use of such information. The information is provided "as is," and none of BAC or any of its affiliates warrants the accuracy or completeness of the information.

CHAPTER 4   INTERPRETATIONS: P/E AS A DEPENDENT VARIABLE

Evaluating the effects of fiscal policy can be difficult. The 2017/2018 US Reform lowered the corporate tax rate from 35% to 21%. *Goldman Sachs* estimated that it would boost S&P 500 Profits by 5%. If so, all things equal, the P/E should rise – by 5%? Or would it fall by 5%?[222] An increase in Earnings alone would reduce the Multiple. But a structural increase in corporate profitability might make businesses and shares more valuable, raising the Multiple. Or perhaps the effects would offset each other.

Responses of the market to fiscal policy have been less studied than responses to monetary policy (Section 4.3.4). Central Bank pronouncements have come to be perceived as "events" which can cause immediate changes in bond and stock prices, whereas fiscal policy is seen as a long-term, gradual influence of more uncertain character.

4.3.6 Inflation

There is a negative correlation between inflation and valuation ratios.[223] Higher inflation tends to mean lower market multiples. (See Figure 4-59.)

---

[222]Justin Lahart, "Can the Tax Cut Boost Stocks?" *The Wall Street Journal*, December 15, 2017.

[223]Tom Lauricella, "Skeptics See Stocks Mired in the Muck," *The Wall Street Journal*, June 16, 2008. Also Steven A. Sharpe, "Reexamining Stock Valuation and Inflation: The Implications of Analysts' Earnings Forecasts," *The Review of Economics and Statistics,* Vol. 84, No. 4 (November 2002), pp. 632–648.

CHAPTER 4   INTERPRETATIONS: P/E AS A DEPENDENT VARIABLE

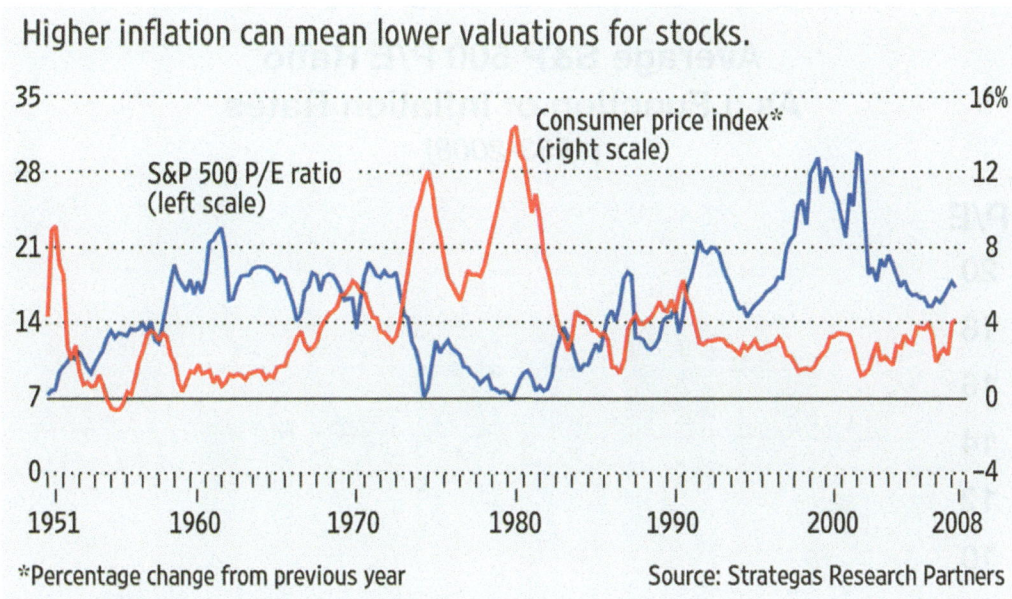

Figure 4-59. *P/E Levels vs. Inflation*[224]

A close study of several measures of actual and expected inflation for the period 1979–1998 found overall negative correlations of 80–90% with the P/E:

> The coefficient on inflation expectations...implies that a 1 percentage point increase in the expected inflation rate is associated with a 26 percent decline in the price-earnings ratio.
>
> Clearly inflation's 'effect' on stock valuation is not only tight, as suggested by simple correlations, but also quite large.[225]

The relationship is not linear, however. Regimes of very low inflation (deflation) and very high inflation both depress market valuations. (See Figure 4-60.)

---

[224] Tom Lauricella, "Skeptics See Stocks Mired in the Muck," *The Wall Street Journal*, June 16, 2008. Reproduced by permission from *The Wall Street Journal*.

[225] Steven A. Sharpe, "Reexamining Stock Valuation and Inflation: The Implications of Analysts' Earnings Forecasts," *Division of Research and Statistics, Federal Reserve Board*, July 2000. A revised version was published in *The Review of Economics and Statistics*, Vol. 84, No. 4 (November 2002), pp. 632–648.

CHAPTER 4   INTERPRETATIONS: P/E AS A DEPENDENT VARIABLE

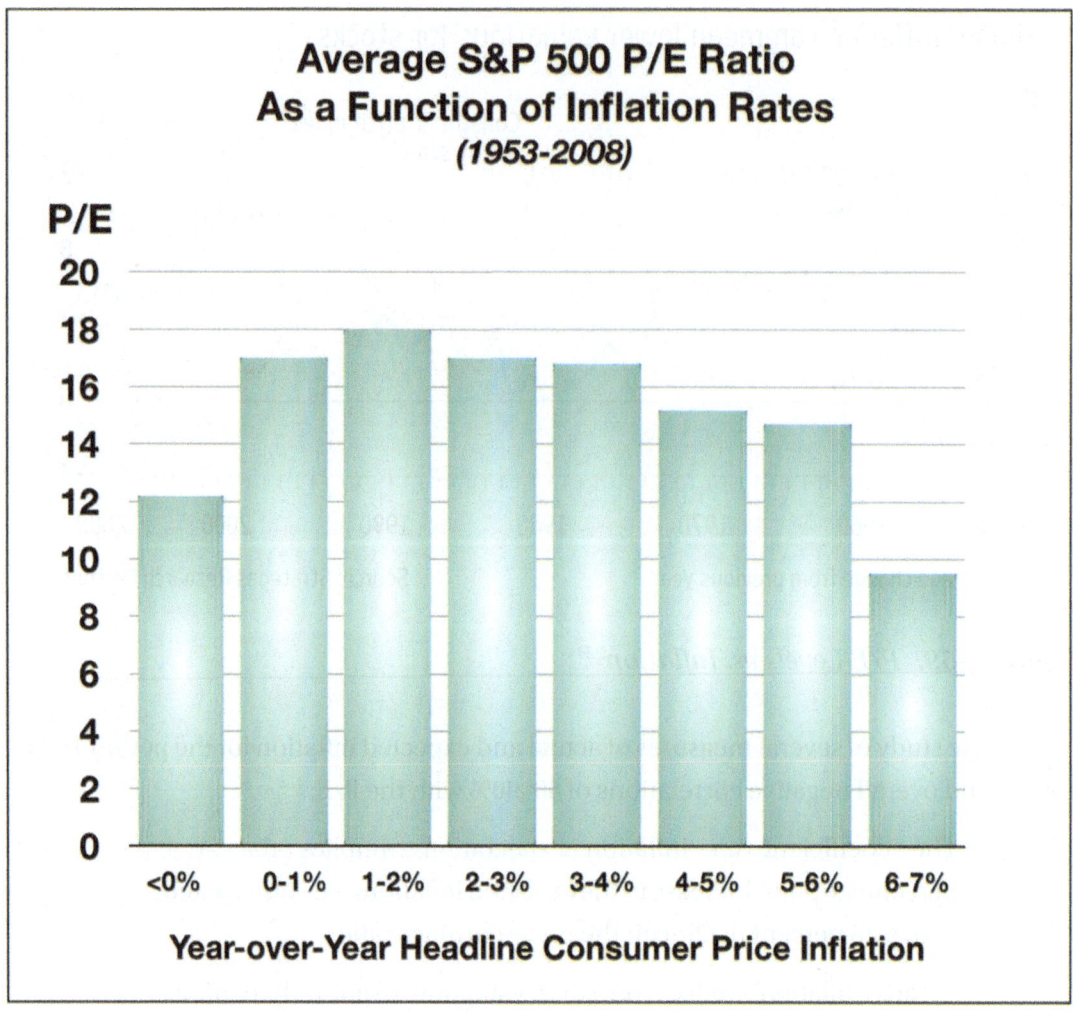

Figure 4-60. Inflation Regimes and P/E Levels

The effect is significant. A 2% inflation regime drives a level of market valuation twice as high as a 6-7% inflation regime. A long "Goldilocks" period of "just right" inflation – largely in the 1-2% range over the last three decades[226] – has been associated with structurally elevated average levels of the market valuation multiples.

---

[226]David Harrison, "Central Bankers Rethink Strict 2% Inflation Target," *The Wall Street Journal*, April 3, 2017

CHAPTER 4　INTERPRETATIONS: P/E AS A DEPENDENT VARIABLE

Ilmanen charts inflation against both P/E *and* market volatility (in the following). The market generates higher P/E values and exhibits less volatility, in the zone around 1–3% inflation.[227] This seems to endorse the Inflation Target of 2% set by the Federal Reserve (and the European Central Bank, informally). (See Figure 4-61.)

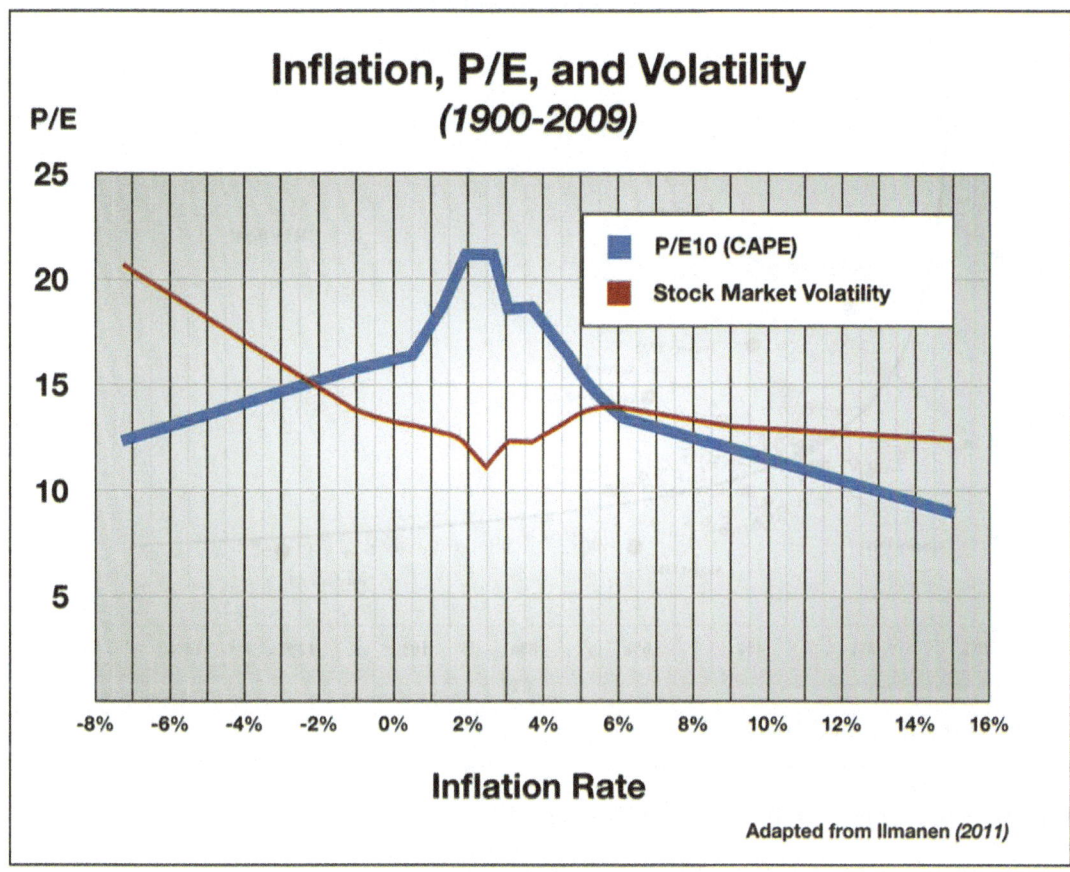

Figure 4-61. *Inflation, P/E, and Volatility*[228]

---

[227] Antti Ilmanen, *Expected Returns: An Investor's Guide to Harvesting Market Rewards,* Wiley (2011), p. 135. It would be interesting to update this chart with respect to inflation and market volatility; volatility has increased in the last decade despite near-optimal inflation levels.

[228] Adapted from Antti Ilmanen, *Expected Returns: An Investor's Guide to Harvesting Market Rewards*, Wiley (2011), p. 135.

CHAPTER 4 INTERPRETATIONS: P/E AS A DEPENDENT VARIABLE

Overall, Inflation "explains" about half the variation in the market P/E since 1965, according to Subramanian.[229] (See Figure 4-62.)

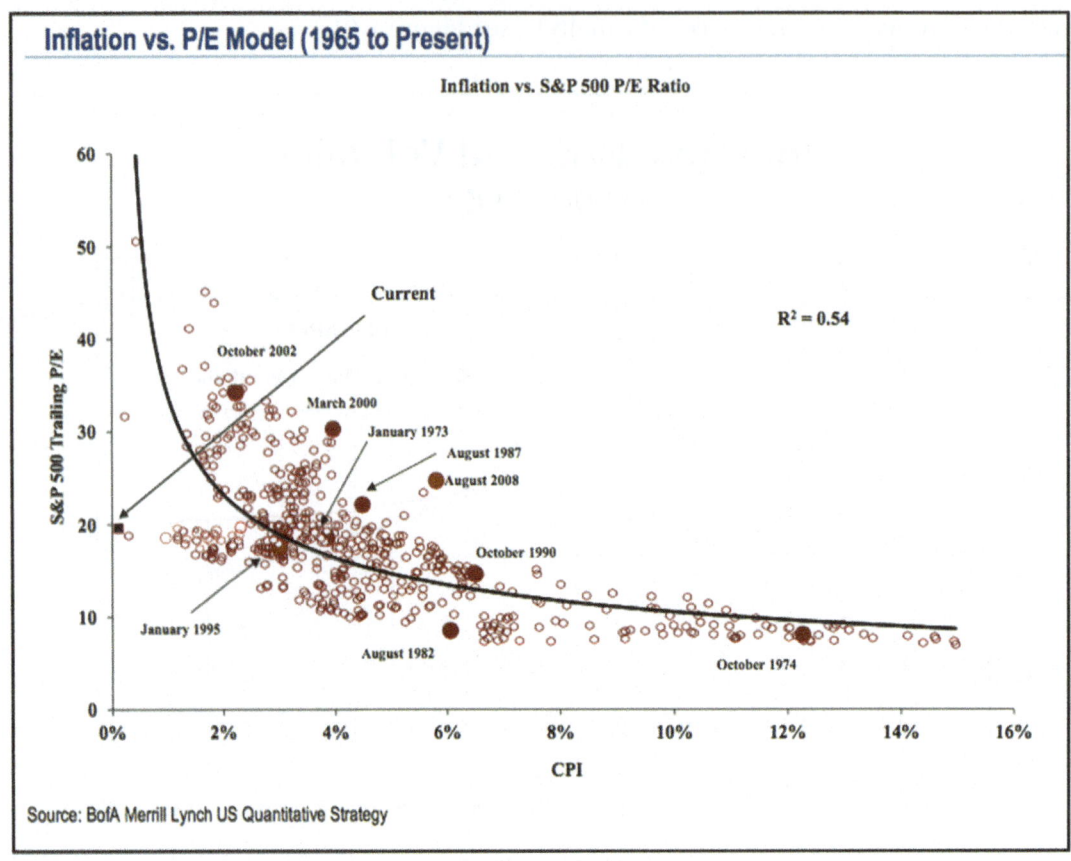

Figure 4-62. Inflation vs. P/E (1965-2015)[230]

---

[229]Savita Subramanian, "Episode 1: High Valuations," *Equity and Quant Strategies, Bank of America/Merrill Lynch*, May 26, 2015.

[230]Savita Subramanian, "Episode 1: High Valuations," *Equity and Quant Strategies, Bank of America/Merrill Lynch*, May 26, 2015. Reprinted by permission. Copyright © 2019 Bank of America Corporation ("BAC"). The use of the preceding reference in no way implies that BAC or any of its affiliates endorses the views or interpretation or the use of such information or acts as any endorsement of author's use of such information. The information is provided "as is," and none of BAC or any of its affiliates warrants the accuracy or completeness of the information.

Interpreting the impact of inflation on asset prices (market valuation) is becoming more difficult, as the economy shifts from asset-heavy to asset-light business models and becomes more technology-intensive. The long-range effect of technological innovation is generally understood to be deflationary – although that term may carry inappropriate connotations. Technology improvements generally lead to cost reductions for a wide range of products and services, and some have questioned whether this process should be considered in the same overall framework as traditional commodity-driven inflation analyses. It is likely that inflation plays a different role in determining stock values today than it did in, say, the early 1980s.

For this reason, the effect of "inflation" on P/E multiples is uncertain today. We need a better understanding of the role of prices in the real economy, before we can factor that into an improved understanding of the impact on prices in the equities market.

4.3.7 Interest Rates and Bond Yields

Market-level P/E ratios are strongly correlated with market interest rates, as reflected in the 10-year Treasury Yield, at least during certain periods. From 1965 to 2001, the correlation was an impressive 81%.[231] A 2006 study found that at the level of the *market as a whole*, there was "a strong negative link between forward P/E ratios and prevailing long-term interest rates."[232] On the other hand, the same study found that at the level of the *individual firm,* the correlation between the P/E and the 10-year Treasury bond yield was essentially *zero.*[233]

---

[231]Clifford Asness, "Fight the Fed Model," *Journal of Portfolio Management*, Vol. 30, No. 1 (Fall 2003), pp. 11–24.

[232]Jacob Thomas and Huai Zhang, "Another Look at P/E Ratios," *Working Paper*, Yale School of Management, 2006.

[233]The study covers 41,348 firm-quarters between 1992 and 2002. Regarding the puzzling discrepancies in their findings, the authors comment: *"[Theory] predicts that all three E/P measures should be positively related to the risk-free rate... The results suggest that the risk-free rate is only weakly positively related to forward E/P and is negatively related to the two trailing E/P measures. We conjecture that the apparent inconsistency between these results is due partially to our sample being limited to the years after 1992. (The co-movement between the Risk-Free Rate and E/P ratios appears weaker for years after 1992.)"* (Jacob Thomas and Huai Zhang, "Another Look at P/E Ratios," *Working Paper*, Yale School of Management, 2006). If I have understood their results correctly, I would say that *none* of the P/E measures show a significant relationship at the firm level: Correlations between the 10-year Treasury Yield and the Forward Firm-Level P/E are 0.03 and 0.00 for the Trailing Firm-Level P/E. See Table 1 in the report.

CHAPTER 4   INTERPRETATIONS: P/E AS A DEPENDENT VARIABLE

The "theoretical" problem is that it is hard to articulate the connection between the "risk-free rate" – a general factor that presumably impacts the performance of thousands of diverse private sector players – and the outcomes for any specific firm. Treasury rates act as a broad and blunt force on the economy and the markets, yet there is a huge range of persistent P/E value differences across the economy. The cost of funding should affect leveraged companies much more than cash-rich ones, for example, and we have seen evidence earlier that it does. The values in some sectors (utilities, real estate) are usually impaired by rising rates. Financials and consumer goods companies are said to benefit. Much information is lost in these averages.

4.3.7.1 The "Fed Model"

Nevertheless, the concept of a causal connection between interest rates (with Treasury Yields as the proxy) and equity market value has received considerable attention as a result of its "endorsement" by Alan Greenspan back in 1997:

> The ratio of prices in the S&P 500 to consensus estimates of earnings over the coming twelve months has risen...*Changes in this ratio have often been inversely related to changes in long-term Treasury yields.*[234] [Emphasis added]

The Fed moves markets, as we have seen, and Greenspan's authority at that time was near its peak. Market participants seized on this bit of Fedspeak, as an astute speculative answer to the challenging question of what drives stock market valuation. The linkage between bond yield, and the Multiple quickly became known as the Fed Model and has given rise to an extensive literature, much of it critical. But because of the importance of monetary policy and interest rate changes to the overall market (described in Section 4.3.4), the model remains popular.

---

[234] Alan Greenspan, "Monetary Policy Report to the Congress, Pursuant to the Full Employment and Balanced Growth Act of 1978," *The Federal Reserve*, July 22, 1997.

Many analysts, portfolio managers, and financial commentators often (explicitly or implicitly) assume a negative relationship between the stock market's P/E ratio and the level of interest rates. In this view, high P/E ratios may not necessarily suggest an expensive stock market if prevailing interest rates are low. The Fed model is the best-known and most widely used "formalization" of this argument.[235]

The implicit – and perhaps plausible – assumption here is that stocks and bonds are viewed by investors as fungible alternatives, which means that the equilibrium mechanism in the market should drive both toward a similar volatility-adjusted return.[236] If one or the other is yielding higher than it should, it argues for mispricing. It also can be taken to mean that the Treasury Yields effectively set the "normal" valuation level for the stock market – the "equilibrium P/E." Or it can be taken the other way – as the Fed is sometimes presumed to take it – that the Market P/E points to the correct interest rate target. In recent years, "equilibrium" has swung back and forth.

One question is whether the correlation underlying the Fed Model is an artifact of a particular time period. If so, times may have changed.

> The "Fed model" was developed based on market data from the 1960s to the 1990s. Before the 1960s and after the 1990s, the model fails. Data from before the 1960s was readily available when the "Fed model" was in its heyday, but was conveniently ignored. It has subsequently failed miserably post-2000, yet the model retains many adherents.[237]

---

[235] Javier Estrada, "The fed model: The bad, the worse, and the ugly," *The Quarterly Review of Economics and Finance*, Vol. 49 (2009), pp. 219–238.

[236] *"The Fed model is based on the idea that investors view stocks and bonds as competing assets in their portfolio and therefore switch from one to the other whenever one yields more (or costs less) than the other. Note that, in order for this argument to be plausible, it must be the case that stocks and bonds are 'comparable' assets. Although this may sound implausible, it is however what must be assumed if the Fed model is to be considered a special case of a standard equity valuation framework."* (Estrada, *op. cit.*).

[237] Robert Arnott, Denis B. Chaves, and Tzee-man Chow, "King of the Mountain: Shiller P/E and Macroeconomic Conditions," *Journal of Portfolio Management* (Fall 2017), pp. 55–68.

CHAPTER 4   INTERPRETATIONS: P/E AS A DEPENDENT VARIABLE

Asness, in an often-cited polemic ("Fight the Fed Model"), advances the rather strange argument that the Fed Model "works" *not* because it should work – it is theoretically flawed, in his view – but only because it describes accurately the pattern of false reasoning that somehow investors collectively fall into.

> The Fed model documents a consistent investor error (or a strange pattern in investors' taste for risk)... If investors mistakenly set the market's P/E as a function of inflation or nominal interest rates, then [the high correlation of the two variables] is just documenting this error, not justifying it.
>
> There is strong evidence that investors contemporaneously set stock market P/E's as a function of nominal interest rates. All else equal, higher [interest rates] imply lower P/E.... While it may have all been because of the error of money illusion, investors have indeed been following the Fed model.[238]

Another study applied the logic underlying the Fed Model in 20 countries found that the model did not work well and showed many shifts in its behavior over time.

> Most investors do seem to be willing to pay higher (lower) P/E's when interest rates and inflation are low (high), though not necessarily the P/E's suggested by the Fed model.[239]

4.3.7.2 The Interest Rate Level and the P/E: Is There a Sweet Spot?

Another approach to the question is to look at the relationship between the *level* of interest rates and prevailing P/E levels. Tracking interest rates since 1950, the zone of maximum P/E seems to occur when the yield on the 10-year Treasurys is between 4% and 6%.[240] (See Figure 4-63.)

---

[238]Clifford Asness, "Fight the Fed Model," *Journal of Portfolio Management,* Vol. 30, No. 1 (Fall 2003), pp 11–24.

[239]Javier Estrada, "The fed model: The bad, the worse, and the ugly," *The Quarterly Review of Economics and Finance*, Vol. 49 (2009), pp. 219–238.

[240]Joe Light, "Rethinking Rising Rates," *The Wall Street Journal*, April 13, 2013.

CHAPTER 4 INTERPRETATIONS: P/E AS A DEPENDENT VARIABLE

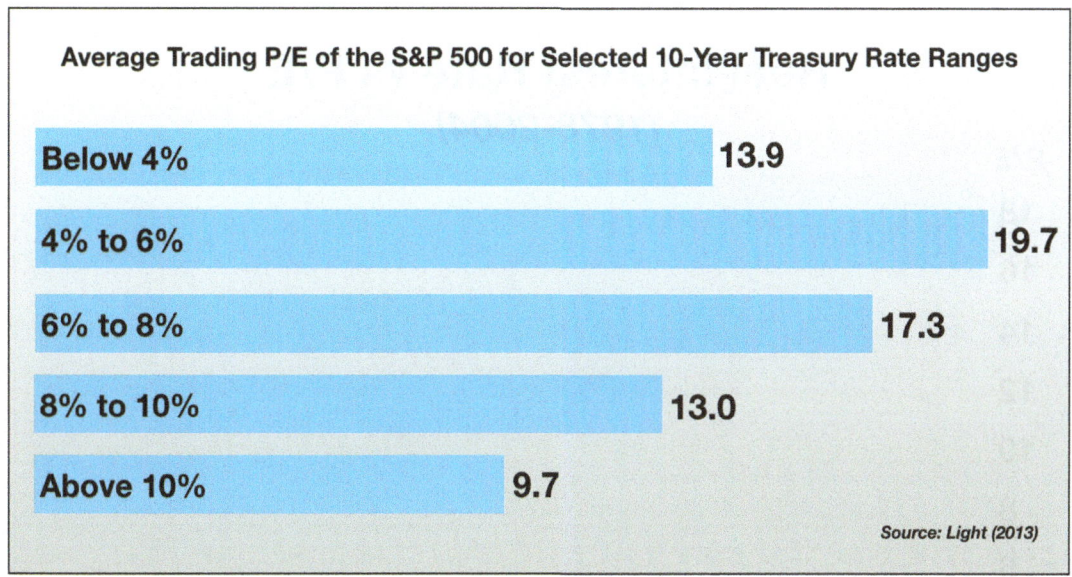

Figure 4-63. *P/E and Interest Rate Regimes*[241]

Using *real* interest rates (i.e., adjusting for inflation), what emerges even more clearly is what has been called a "tent" pattern – reminiscent of the inflation "sweet spot" described in the preceding section, showing a P/E peak (and presumably maximum market "happiness") during periods when *real* 10-year Treasury Yields are 2–3%.[242] (See Figure 4-64.)

---

[241] Joe Light, "Rethinking Rising Rates," *The Wall Street Journal*, April 13, 2013. Reproduced by permission from *The Wall Street Journal*.

[242] Martin L. Leibowitz and Anthony Bova, "P/Es and Pension Funding Ratios," *Financial Analysts Journal*, Vol. 63, No. 1 (2007), pp. 84–96.

CHAPTER 4   INTERPRETATIONS: P/E AS A DEPENDENT VARIABLE

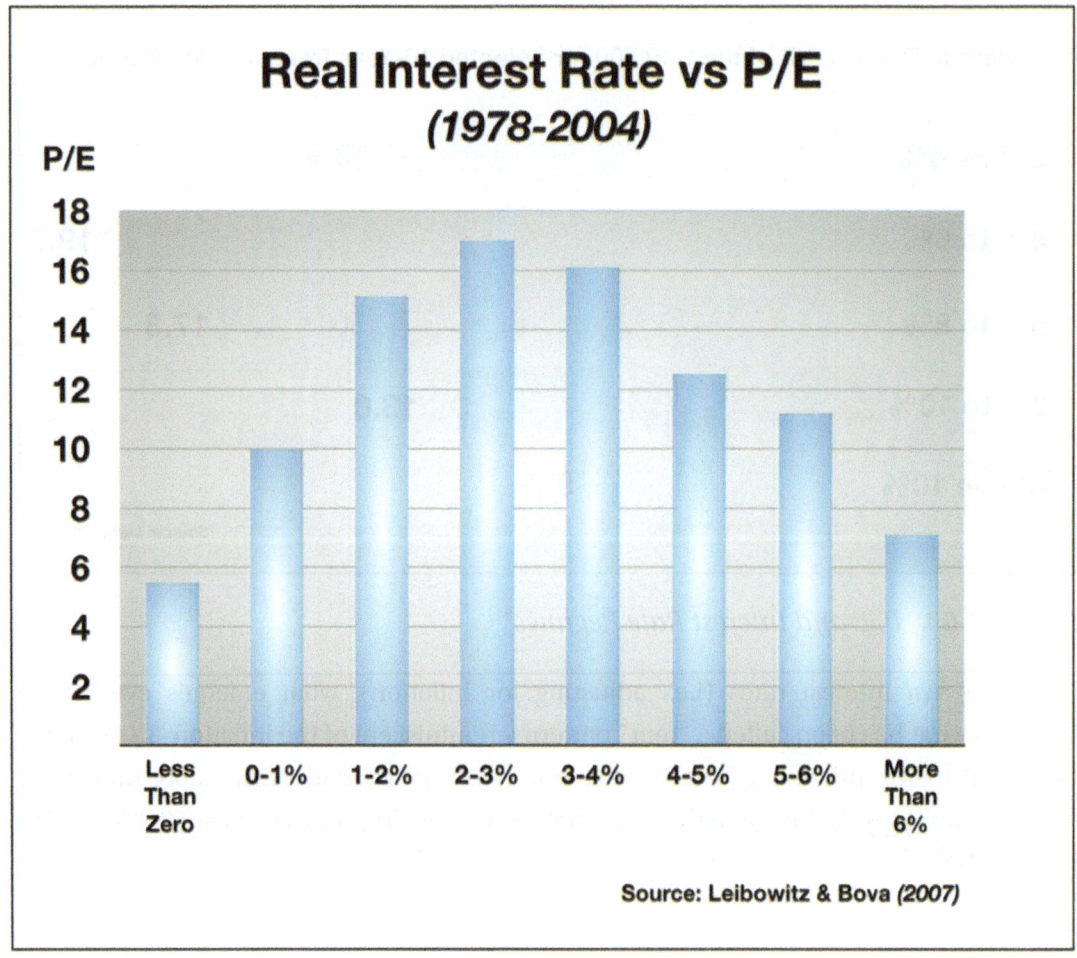

Figure 4-64. *P/E and Real Interest Rates*[243]

The authors of this study develop an interesting interpretation of this pattern. Drawing on the "Base + Growth" concept of the P/E Multiple discussed in Section 4.2.1, they divide the valuation model into two components: a steady-state "tangible value" component "associated with a firm's current book of business" and a component they call the "franchise value...derived from the growth of productive investment opportunities" – and with complicated reasoning about discount rates and equity risk premiums, they use this to construct a map of valuation potential that tracks the interest rate sweet spot, as shown here. (See Figure 4-65.)

---

[243]Adapted from Martin L. Leibowitz and Anthony Bova, "P/Es and Pension Funding Ratios," *Financial Analysts Journal*, Vol. 63, No. 1 (2007), pp. 84–96.

CHAPTER 4   INTERPRETATIONS: P/E AS A DEPENDENT VARIABLE

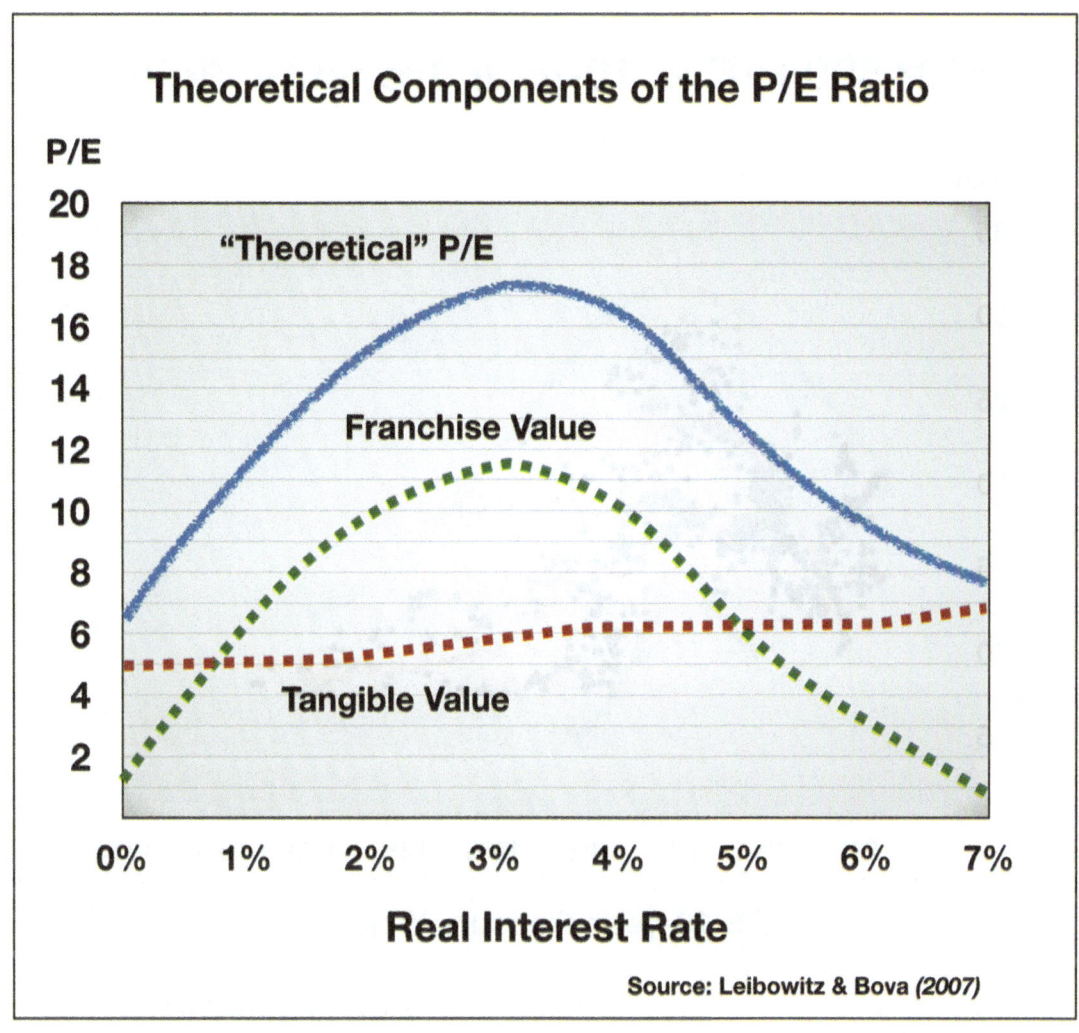

Figure 4-65. *Theoretical Components of the P/E Ratio vs. Real Interest Rates*[244]

Like all formulas that require a discount factor, this one seems to be difficult to wield accurately. However, a plot of the monthly (nominal) 10-year Treasury Yields from 1954 to 2017, although noisy, does seem to display the same "tented" pattern and "explains" about 30% of the valuation of the P/E.[245] (See Figure 4-66.)

---

[244] Adapted from Martin L. Leibowitz and Anthony Bova, "P/Es and Pension Funding Ratios," *Financial Analysts Journal*, Vol. 63, No. 1 (2007), pp. 84–96.

[245] Russ Koesterich, "Yes, rates and stocks can rise together.... for now," *BlackRock Blog*, February 21, 2018. Available at www.blackrockblog.com/2018/02/21/rates-stocks-rise-together/

CHAPTER 4   INTERPRETATIONS: P/E AS A DEPENDENT VARIABLE

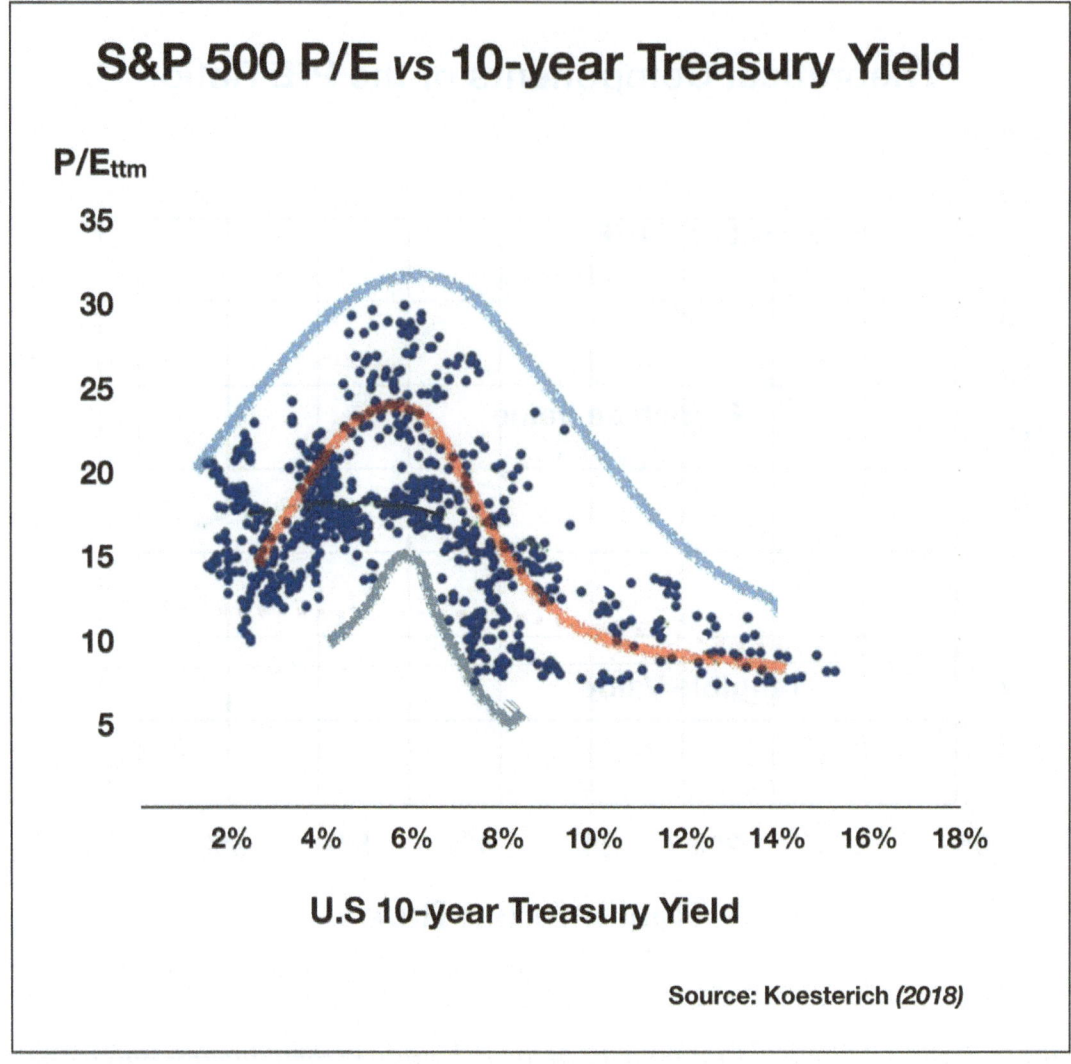

Figure 4-66. *S&P 500 P/E vs. 10-Year Treasury Yield*[246]

4.3.8 International Differences

Finally, valuation multiples differ considerably depending on which country the firm is headquartered in and on which market its shares trade. The variation in country-specific multiples is nearly 5 to 1.

---

[246]Adapted from Russ Koesterich, "Yes, rates and stocks can rise together.... for now," *BlackRock Blog,* February 21, 2018. Available at www.blackrockblog.com/2018/02/21/rates-stocks-rise-together/

CHAPTER 4   INTERPRETATIONS: P/E AS A DEPENDENT VARIABLE

Over the last 20 years, European shares have generally traded at an average discount of 15–30% compared to the multiples in the US markets.[247] (See Figure 4-67.)

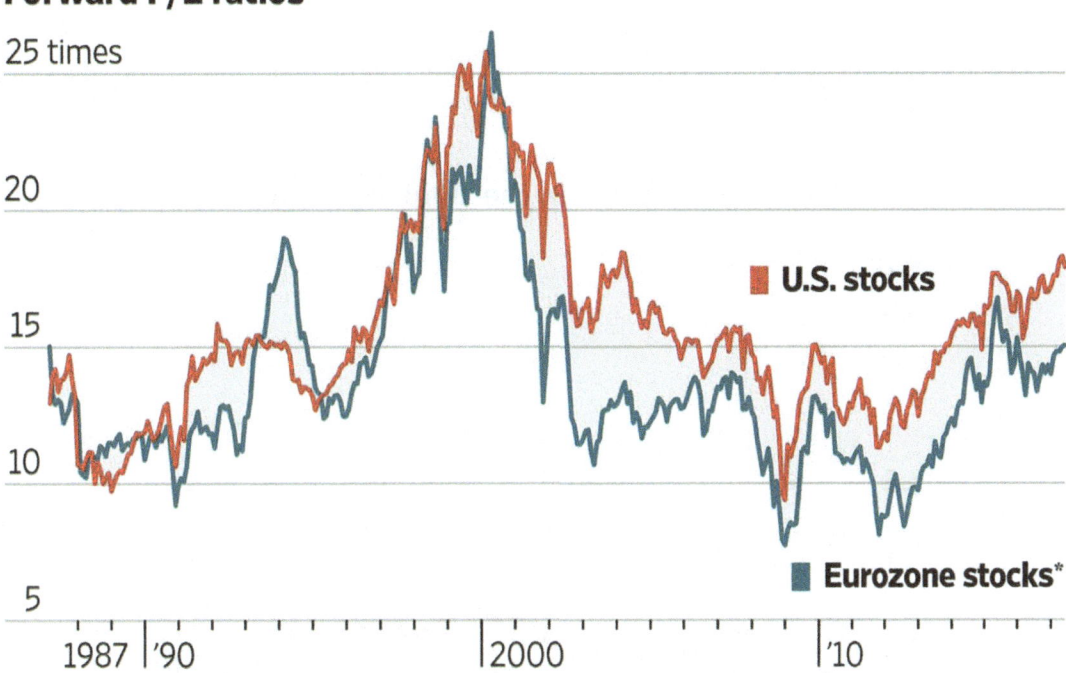

Figure 4-67. *US vs. European P/E Ratios*[248]

Korean companies carry an even larger penalty.[249] Emerging Market equities have generally traded at a steep discount.[250]

---

[247]James Mackintosh, "European Shares Aren't as Cheap as They Look," *The Wall Street Journal*, April 25, 2017.

[248]James Mackintosh, "European Shares Aren't as Cheap as They Look," *The Wall Street Journal*, April 25, 2017. Reproduced by permission from *The Wall Street Journal*.

[249]Edward White, "Korean Valuations Groan Under Burden of Shoddy Governance," *Financial Times,* May 17, 2019.

[250]Emerging Markets did experience a transitory surge in their relative valuations (measured as Price-to-Book) during the financial crisis, which affected the developed economies more severely. "Hedge Funds: Law of Averages," *The Economist*, August 27, 2016.

CHAPTER 4   INTERPRETATIONS: P/E AS A DEPENDENT VARIABLE

Sectors that should trade at similar valuations can diverge significantly, and structurally, based on their home markets. Banking is a good example. The basic business model of banking is very similar across the developed world, and yet during the Eurozone crisis of 2012, banks in that region traded at a third less than the P/B multiple of their US counterparts and less than half of the multiples of Japanese banks. This reflects not only local economic conditions but also differences in culture, regulations, and investor psychology.[251] (See Figure 4-68.)

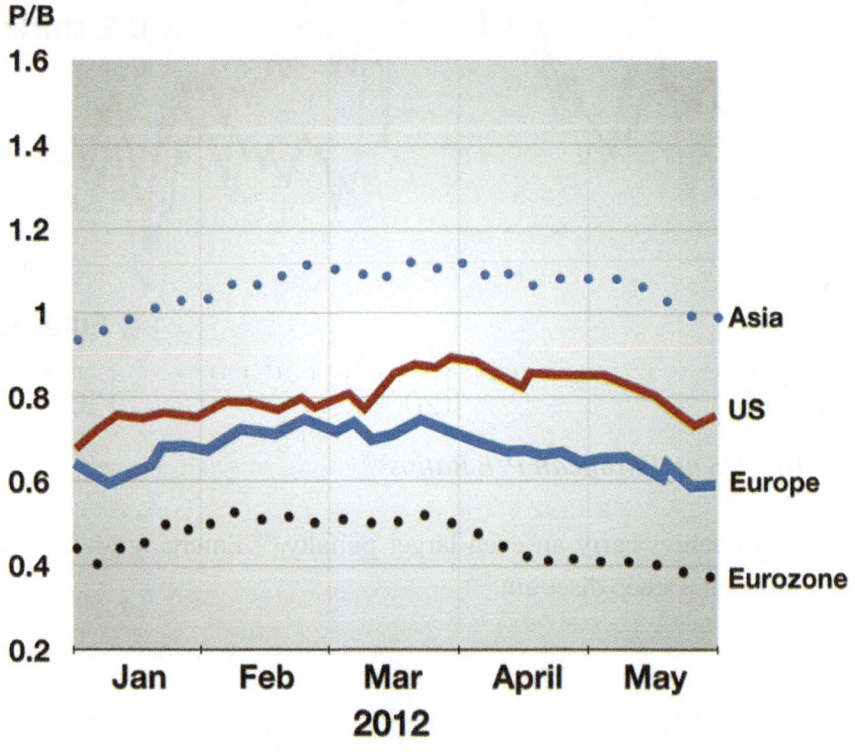

Figure 4-68. Banking Sector P/E's by Region During the 2012 Euro Crisis[252]

---

[251]"Risk Waiting," *Financial Times*, May 25, 2012.
[252]Adapted from "Risk Waiting," *Financial Times*, May 25, 2012.

CHAPTER 4   INTERPRETATIONS: P/E AS A DEPENDENT VARIABLE

The country-specific effect is quite significant, even for countries that would be considered as quite similar in terms of their economic and regulatory frameworks. For example, the United States and Canada have significantly different market multiples – and the country "factor" discount for Canada is much larger than the variation of the Canadian multiple over time.[253] In other words, the fact that a company is "Canadian" (listed on the Canadian exchange) matters a great deal in terms of its P/E market valuation. The Country effect is much larger than the typical "Size" effect (Small Cap vs. Large Cap), for example.[254] Figure 4-69 shows the comparison based on the CAPE version of the multiple.

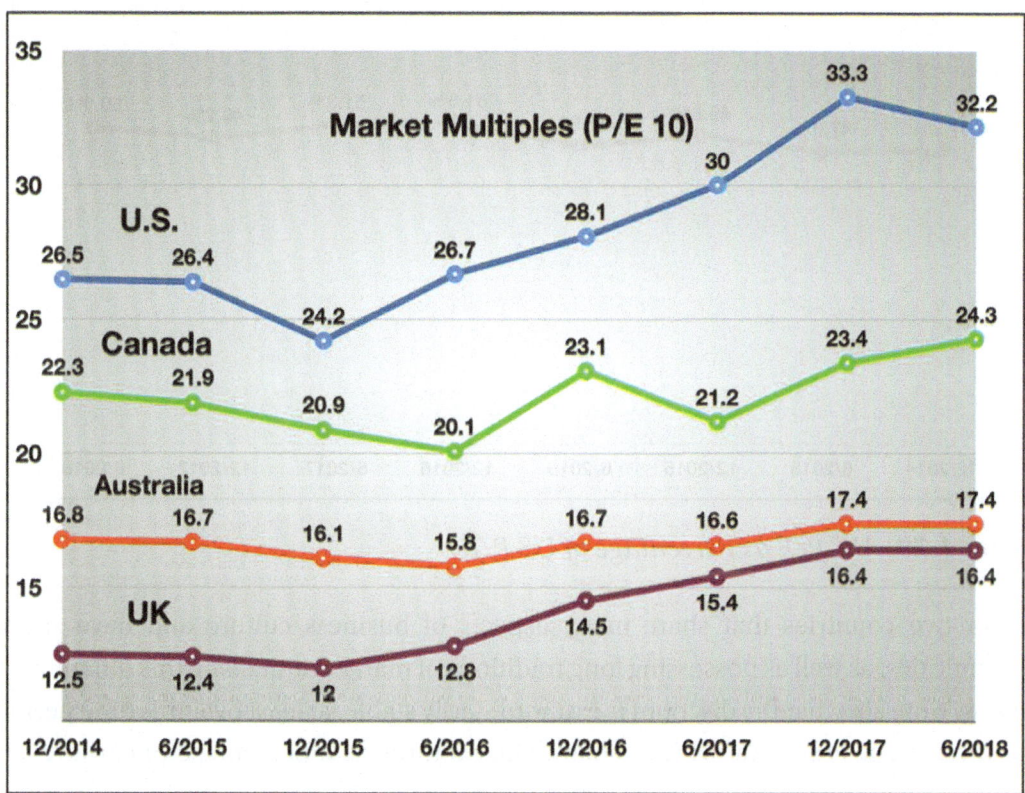

Figure 4-69. P/E Comparison: US, Canada, UK, Australia

---

[253]Data from *Siblis Research*, 2018: http://siblisresearch.com/data/cape-ratios-by-country/

[254]A *KPMG* study of companies in Germany, Austria, and Switzerland from 2017, for example, finds that the "Country Risk Premium" for calculating the cost of capital is about six to seven times larger than the "Small-Size Company Risk Premium." While not directly related to the P/E value, this shows the relative impact of these factors on a company's returns. Marc Castedello and Stefan Schöniger, *Cost of Capital Study 2017, KPMG.*

CHAPTER 4   INTERPRETATIONS: P/E AS A DEPENDENT VARIABLE

The UK comparison is even more striking. UK companies command, on average, only half the market value per dollar (or pound sterling) earned as compared to their US counterparts, based on CAPE. (See Figure 4-70.)

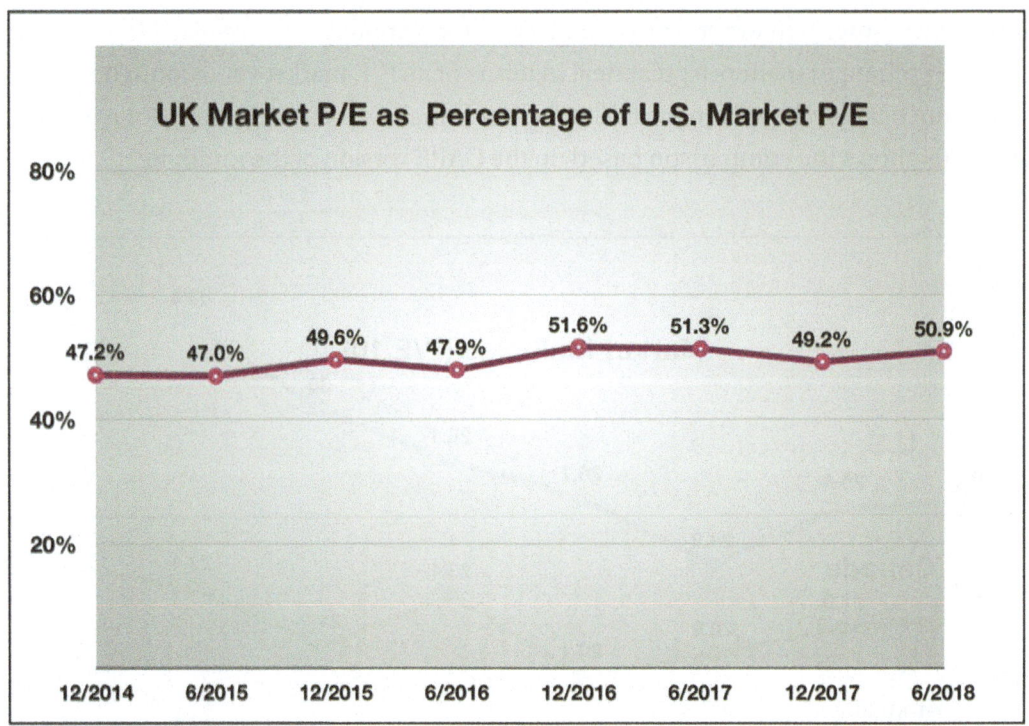

Figure 4-70. *UK P/E as Percentage of US P/E*

For two countries that share many aspects of business culture and have strong economic ties, as well as possessing long traditions of market capitalism, this difference is striking. Note also that the discount is extraordinarily stable, at least over this time period. The Investment/Payout ratios (i.e., shareholder returns as a percentage of earnings) in both countries are nearly identical.[255] And the size of the UK "Country" discount dwarfs the intrinsic variability in UK market multiples.[256] (See Figure 4-71.)

---

[255] Robert Buckland et al, "Market Wants Cash Cows," *Citi Research*, March 19, 2015.

[256] The CAPE ratio runs high, as noted elsewhere in this book. Using CAPE may exaggerate the difference between the United States and other countries somewhat. The discrepancy between the PE1 (forward) for the United States and the United Kingdom is smaller – but still large; as of September 2019, the UK market traded at a 30% discount to the US market (James Mackintosh, "U.S. Stocks Cost a Premium, for Good Reason," *The Wall Street Journal*, September 25, 2019).

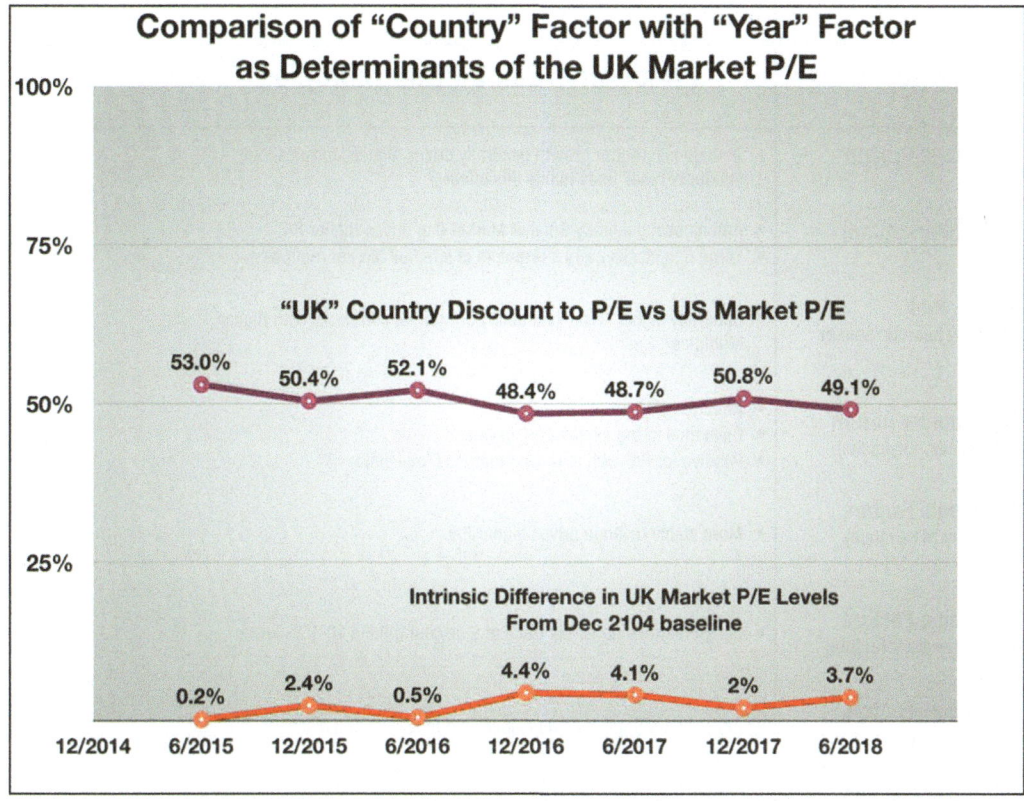

Figure 4-71. UK P/E: Country Factor vs. Year Factor

All in all, the "Country" factor may be the single most important determinant of the P/E for many firms.

4.4 Summary

Tables 4-2 and 4-3 summarize the various "factors" that help determine a company's P/E multiple. As indicated throughout this chapter, the general effect of many of these factors can be somewhat ambiguous, and the *sign* of the effect may change over time (i.e., from determining a premium to determining a discount on the Multiple).

CHAPTER 4 INTERPRETATIONS: P/E AS A DEPENDENT VARIABLE

Table 4-2. *Firm-Specific Factors*

Factor	Effect on P/E and Other Multiples
Earnings Growth	• Ambiguous: Higher growth generally drives higher Multiples, but "maturity reset" may nullify this effect
Size (MarketCap)	• Ambiguous; generally Smaller Market Cap drives Higher P/E • Large Cap stocks carry a premium in late Bull Market regimes
Risk (Finance-Theoretic Sense)	• Generally higher "risk" (variability of returns) correlates with Higher Multiples
Shareholder Return (Dividends, Buybacks)	• Ambiguous • Dividends losing explanatory power • Positive for P/E with improved metrics (Total Yield)
Strategic Factors (Quality of Revenue)	• More stable revenue drives higher P/E
Strategic Factors (Conglomerate Structure)	• Conglomerates generally trade at a discount, P/E's 10-15% lower
Strategic Factors (Capex)	• Asset-heavy (high capex) business models trade at a discount
Strategic Factors (Cash Accumulation)	• Firms carrying a lot of cash trade at a discount
Strategic Factors (Cyclicality)	• Ambiguous • Cyclical Companies trade at a premium in Bull market regimes • Defensives may command a premium during and after recessions
Earnings Volatility	• Companies with more stable earnings command a premium multiple
Share Price Volatility	• Less volatile companies seem to trade at higher multiples
Leverage	• Ambiguous
Accounting Issues	• High P/E companies often have more accruals • Firms using accelerated depreciation have higher P/E's • In general, higher multiples are associated with more aggressive accounting choices. • The direction of causality not clear
Governance	• Weak corporate governance drives lower P/E

CHAPTER 4   INTERPRETATIONS: P/E AS A DEPENDENT VARIABLE

Table 4-3. *Market-Wide or Sector-Wide Factors*

Factor	Effect on P/E and Other Multiples
Sentiment	• Complex and ambiguous • Market "weather" or regime type has an obvious effect on P/E's • Soft "consumer sentiment" metrics have little effect • "Rational" growth expectations drive a premium multiple
Sector	• Significant sector differences; not well studied
Regulation	• Higher regulation drives lower P/E's
Monetary Policy	• Complex and ambiguous • Fed moves have a very large effect on asset values
Fiscal Policy	• Companies exposed to stimulus effects show expansion of the P/E
Inflation	• Complex and ambiguous • A sweet spot for inflation of 2-3% seems to exist • P/E's reduced above or below that range
Interest Rates	• Complex and ambiguous • A sweet spot for treasury rates of 3-6% seems to exist • P/E's reduced above or below that range
Country Factor	• Very large effects on P/E

CHAPTER 5

Applications: P/E As an Independent Variable

In the previous chapter, the P/E and other multiples are considered as signals generated by underlying explanatory factors (such as earnings growth). In this chapter, the P/E itself is viewed as the factor that explains or predicts future outcomes and can therefore be used to support, or trigger, significant decisions.

The chief applications of market multiples include

- Guiding investment strategies
- Valuing corporate transactions – acquisitions, divestitures, mergers, joint ventures, and private equity investments
- Illuminating macro-trends in the market and potentially providing warnings of shifts in the market regime

The first of these – providing investment guidance – is the most important in practical terms. The P/E and other multiples are employed extensively by investors to analyze prospective investments, develop strategies, construct indexes, and design financial instruments, to improve returns. The most prominent example of this, and in many ways the conceptual starting point, is the so-called "Value" Anomaly: stocks with low P/E ratios, low P/B ratios, or high Dividend Yields (low Price/Dividend ratios) have all shown a tendency to outperform the market over the long term.

CHAPTER 5   APPLICATIONS: P/E AS AN INDEPENDENT VARIABLE

Other "anomalies" have since been uncovered, some of which also rely on Market Multiples for definition and detection. These include "Growth" and "Quality."[1]

The systematic exploitation of market anomalies has become a growing industry, with a vast set of product offerings and service providers. Multiples are used at all stages of "productization" (see Figure 5-1).

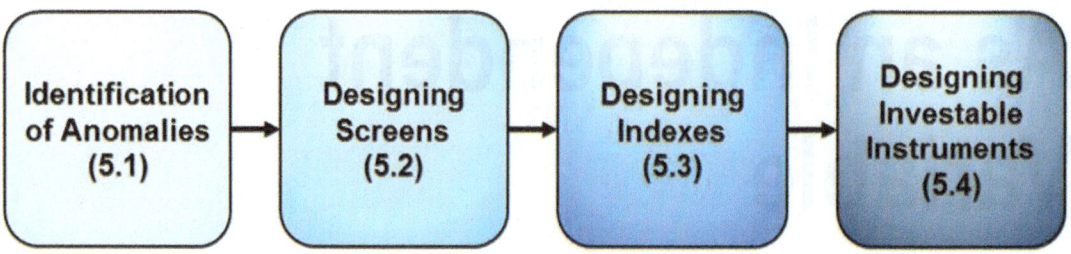

Figure 5-1. The "Productization" of Market Multiples

5.1 Using Multiples to Forecast Stock Prices

5.1.1 The General Case: P/E As a Contrarian Indicator

> A large number of papers provide evidence that low P/E stocks tend to outperform high P/E stocks.[2]

The most common application of the P/E and other multiples is to predict future stock market returns. There are three general points to make about this practice.

First, **the P/E is a powerful predictor of long-term share prices**. At the 10-year horizon, the Forward P/E explains up to 80% of the market return pattern.[3]

Second, **it is a relatively poor predictor of short-term prices** (see Figure 5-2).

---

[1] The concept has been extended to other factors (as they are often called today) that do not rely on market multiples per se, such as "Size" and "Momentum." But the concept of a persistent, exploitable mispricing – which is arguably derived from the original understanding of the "Value" anomaly – underlies all of them. In a sense, market valuation metrics have opened the door.

[2] Donna Dudney et al., "Do residual earnings price ratios explain cross-sectional variations in stock returns?" *Managerial Finance*, Vol. 41, No. 7 (2015), pp. 692–713.

[3] Savita Subramanian, "2017 – The Year Ahead: Euphoria or Fiscal Fizzle," *Equity and Quant Strategy*, Bank of America/Merrill Lynch, November 22, 2016.

Over the 1926-2001 period, the power of simple P/E to forecast 20-year stock returns is truly impressive [R^2=65%].... At shorter horizons R^2 values fall dramatically [R^2 for 1-year forecasts varies between 1% and 10% depending on the period].[4]

The correlations between ten-year forward annualized returns and P/E [was] -0.52... On the other hand, for one-year returns...the ability of multiples to forecast...largely vanishes.... The correlations between one-year forward returns and P/E [was] -0.10.[5]

---

[4] Clifford Asness, "Fight the Fed Model," *Journal of Portfolio Management*, Vol. 30, No.1 (Fall 2003), pp 11-24. Note: The discrepancy between this study reporting a 65% R^2 for a forecast of returns and the Subramanian study reporting an 80% R^2 is likely due the different time periods (1926-2001 vs. 1971-2015) and different time windows (20 years vs. 10 years forward).

[5] Javier Estrada, "Multiples, Forecasting, and Asset Allocation," *Journal of Applied Corporate Finance*, Vol 27, No. 3 (Summer 2015), pp. 144-151. Note that these correlations are negative - which means that the variations in these metrics are correlated but move in the opposite direction - e.g., **low** P/E is associated with **high returns**.

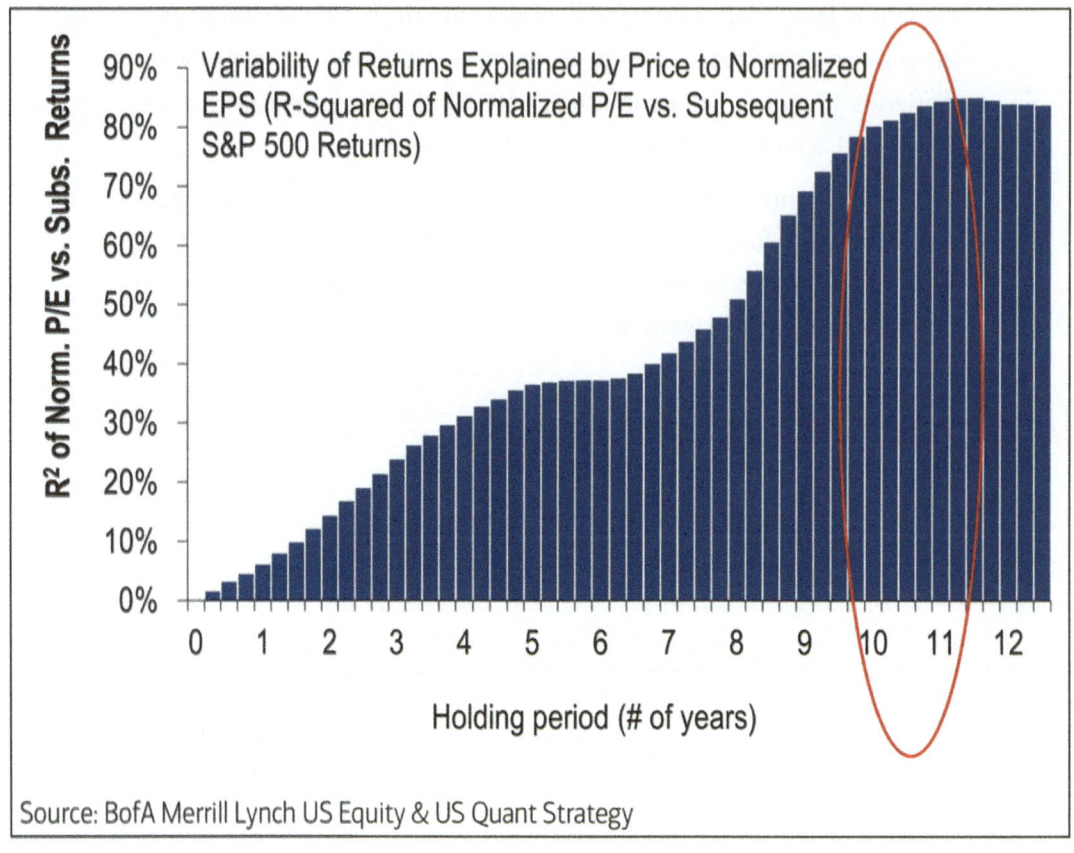

Figure 5-2. *Predictive Power Improves with Longer Holding Periods*[6]

Third, **the signal is *contrarian***. Lower P/E values predict higher returns (especially over the long term) (see Figure 5-3). The lowest P/E category yields the highest performance going forward (see Figure 5-4 and Figure 5-5).

---

[6]Savita Subramanian, "2017 – The Year Ahead: Euphoria or Fiscal Fizzle," *Equity and Quant Strategy, Bank of America/Merrill Lynch*, November 22, 2016. Reprinted by permission. Copyright © 2019 Bank of America Corporation ("BAC"). The use of the preceding reference in no way implies that BAC or any of its affiliates endorses the views or interpretation or the use of such information or acts as any endorsement of author's use of such information. The information is provided "as is," and none of BAC or any of its affiliates warrants the accuracy or completeness of the information.

CHAPTER 5   APPLICATIONS: P/E AS AN INDEPENDENT VARIABLE

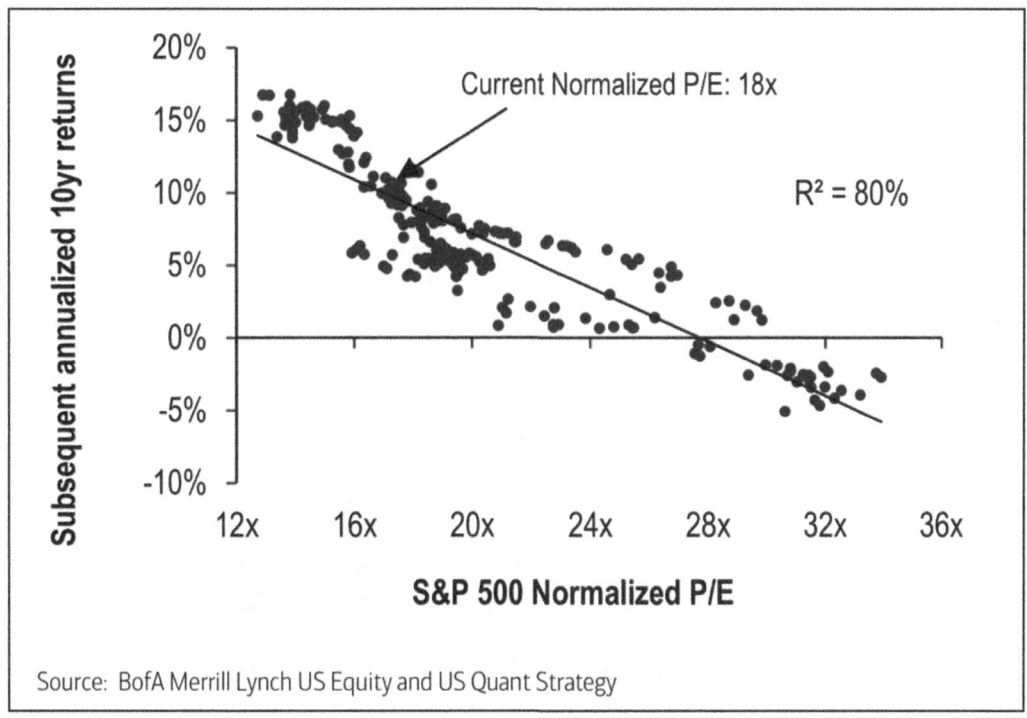

Figure 5-3. *P/E Is a Contrarian Signal for Future Returns*[7]

---

[7]Savita Subramanian, "2017 – The Year Ahead: Euphoria or Fiscal Fizzle," *Equity and Quant Strategy, Bank of America/Merrill Lynch,* November 22, 2016. Reprinted by permission. Copyright © 2019 Bank of America Corporation ("BAC"). The use of the preceding reference in no way implies that BAC or any of its affiliates endorses the views or interpretation or the use of such information or acts as any endorsement of author's use of such information. The information is provided "as is," and none of BAC or any of its affiliates warrants the accuracy or completeness of the information.

CHAPTER 5   APPLICATIONS: P/E AS AN INDEPENDENT VARIABLE

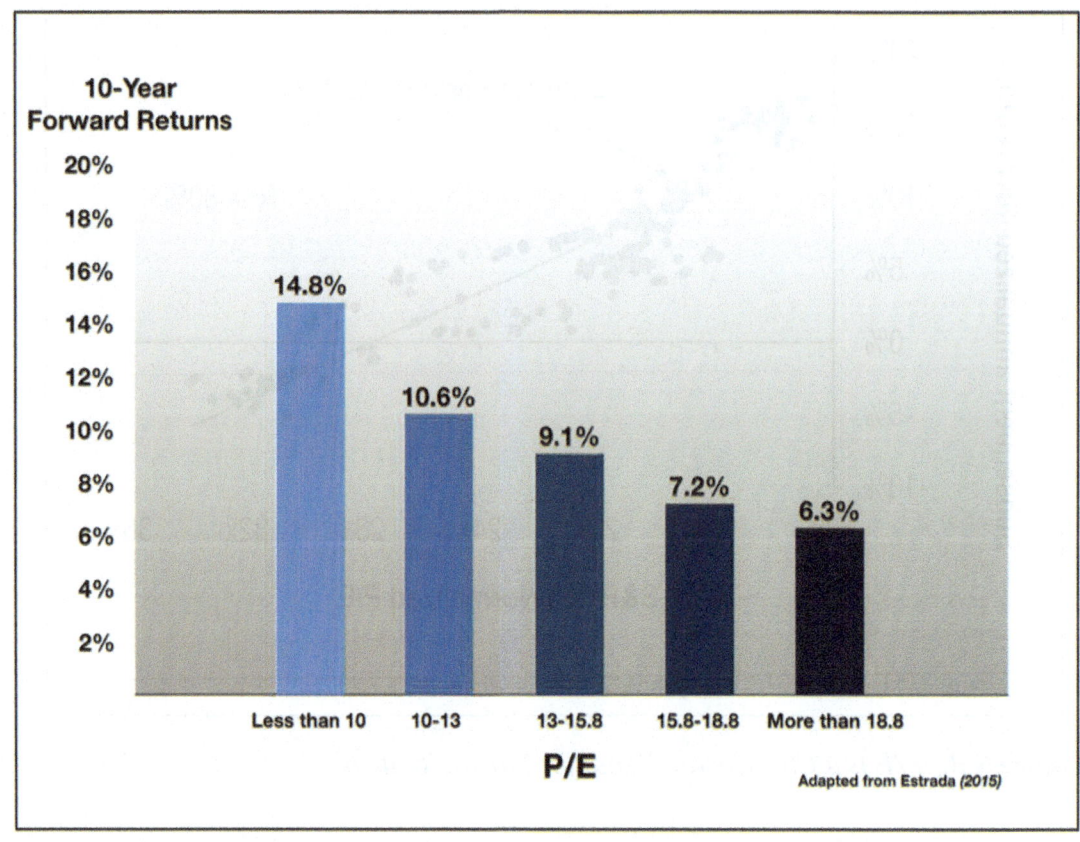

Figure 5-4. *P/E vs. 10-Year Returns*[8]

This result is unexpected, "contrarian." A high P/E is normally a sign of corporate health and competitive success. It shows that the company has been able to create significant shareholder value. It indicates positive market sentiment: investors are willing to bid up the price of the earnings dollar, in the hope of more to come. However, the shares of such successful firms, carrying high P/E's, will – on average – *underperform* going forward. On the other hand, a low P/E usually signals the existence of problems or structural challenges facing the company and negative investor sentiment, directed either at the firm or the sector. Yet, an investment in the shares of such troubled companies will – on average – *outperform* an investment in their more "successful" peers. Thus, a classic way to succeed as an investor is to search for the "poor performers." A low P/E multiple

---

[8]Adapted from Javier Estrada, "Multiples, Forecasting, and Asset Allocation," *Journal of Applied Corporate Finance*, Vol 27, No. 3 (Summer 2015), pp. 144–151.

CHAPTER 5   APPLICATIONS: P/E AS AN INDEPENDENT VARIABLE

can help identify them. This has historically been one of the most important practical applications of market multiples: to construct signals or screens to identify investment opportunities. See Figure 5-5.

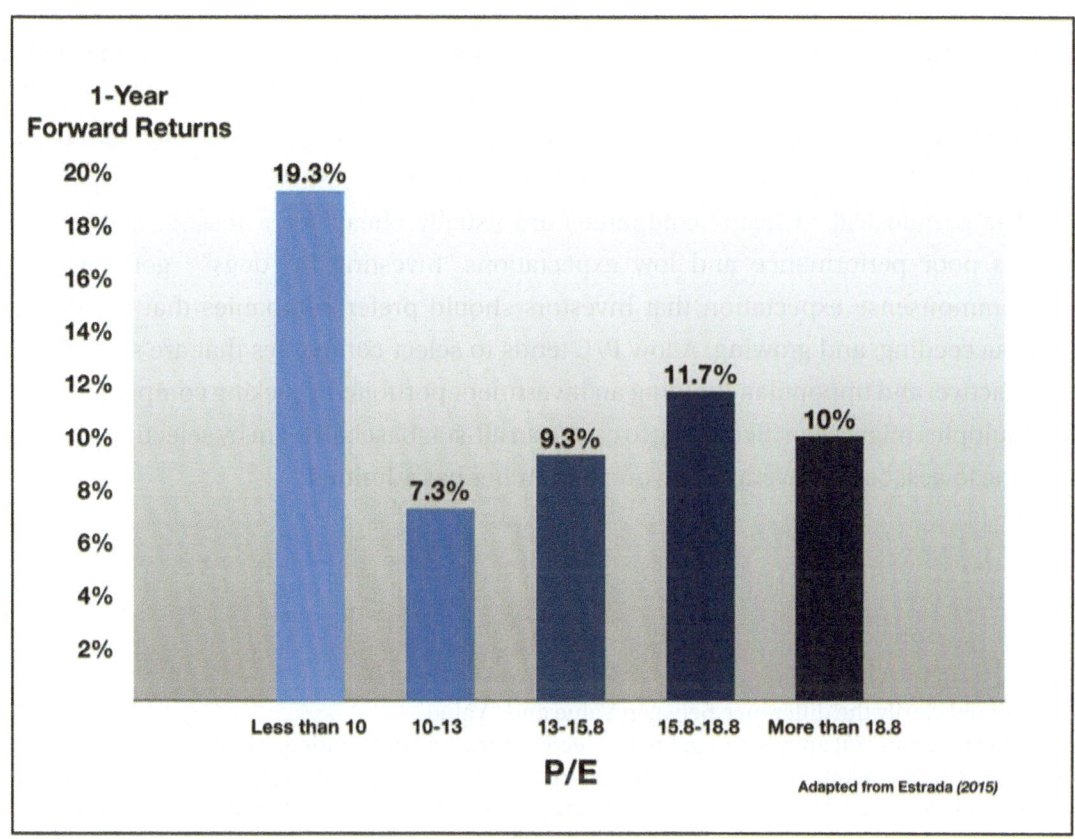

Figure 5-5. *P/E vs. 1-Year Returns*[9]

---

[9]Adapted from Javier Estrada, "Multiples, Forecasting, and Asset Allocation," *Journal of Applied Corporate Finance*, Vol 27, No. 3 (Summer 2015), pp. 144–151.

5.2 Screening for "Value"[10]

All market ratios tend to be contrarian. Low values usually predict higher returns. That is, companies with low values of P/E, P/B, Price/Dividend, and EV/EBITDA – stocks that are in some sense "cheap" – tend to outperform companies with higher values in the subsequent period. Screening for low P/E (etc.) has acquired a label – *"Value Investing"* – and is now recognized by academics and practitioners as a reliable way to exploit a fundamental quirk in the behavior of the stock market. This approach has worked well, over long periods of time, and is followed by some of the world's most successful investors.[11]

It is paradoxical. "Cheap" companies are usually cheap for a reason. A low P/E reflects poor performance and low expectations. Investing in "dogs"[12] goes against the commonsense expectation that investors should prefer companies that are doing well, succeeding, and growing. A low P/E tends to select companies that are struggling, unattractive, and unpopular. Building an investment portfolio by picking companies with low multiples might seem like trying to create an all-star baseball team by selecting players with the lowest batting averages. As one researcher has admitted

---

[10]We should clarify the difference between Value and "Value."

Value has many meanings, but in finance, economics, and accounting, it is always related more or less to the "exchange value" of an asset, good, or service – the price it will fetch in a free and fair transaction between a willing seller and a willing buyer. This notion of "fair value" has been codified by the accounting profession and adopted by the legal profession *(e.g., "The* amount *for which an asset or liability could be exchanged in an arm's length transaction between unrelated, willing parties who are reasonably well-informed").* In other words, in the world of finance and economics, Value is a quantitative notion. "Valuation" comprises the various methodologies designed to calculate this amount (see Chapter 2).

"Value" – here placed in quotes – refers to a very specific pricing anomaly, where a company is viewed as "undervalued" by the market – that is, where the market price is lower than the purported intrinsic value of the enterprise. Whether "Value" in this sense exists has been the subject of controversy. The negative answer is given by some academics, who claim that the "anomaly" is really an entirely rational pricing of a particular type of risk. We will touch on that question in the following. Other academics and most practitioners hold that "Value" does exist and can be exploited for profit by savvy investors.

The second usage will prevail throughout this chapter, although "Value" will not always be placed inside quotation marks.

[11]Of course, Warren Buffett is the preeminent example and advocate.

[12]The "Dogs of the Dow" is a classic Value Strategy, based on Dividend Yield.

Value stocks tend to be companies that lack growth, require balance sheet restructuring, feature incompetent management, need a new corporate strategy, are rated "Sell" by brokers, or have some other issue. Effectively Value investors provide a service to the market by holding undesirable stocks.[13]

Moreover, in an efficient market, "Value" should not exist, or at least it should not *persist*. If "everyone knows" that low-P/E stocks will do well in the future, someone will go out and buy them. Increased demand will drive the price up. The P/E will rise. The buying will continue until the price reaches the "correct" value. The mispricing should vanish.

But this does not happen. The persistence of low P/E, mispriced "Value" opportunities over decades, is referred to as an "anomaly" – the "Value" Anomaly.[14]

5.2.1 Evidence for the Value Anomaly

Value Investing embraces this anomaly and the counterintuitive mind-set it implies.

The existence of the "Value" Anomaly (also sometimes called the P/E Anomaly) has been known to practitioners for a long time. It was "discovered" by academics in the 1960s and 1970s, who ran simple regressions of stock market performance against the P/E multiple. Basu (1977) was one of the first to document this effect in the academic literature. In his study, the lowest quintile of stocks by P/E outperformed the highest P/E quintile, as well as the market portfolio as a whole, and with lower risk[15] (see Figure 5-6).

---

[13] Nicolas Rabener, "Improving the Odds of Value," *FactorResearch*, October 2018.

[14] *"An anomaly is a deviation from the presently accepted paradigms that is too widespread to be ignored, too systematic to be dismissed as random error, and too fundamental to be accommodated by relaxing the [theory]"* (A. Tversky and D. Kahneman, "Rational Choice and the Framing of the Decision," *The Journal of Business*, Vol. 59, No. 4 (1986), p. 252).

[15] S. Basu, "Investment Performance of Common Stocks in Relation to Their Price-Earnings Ratios: A Test of the Efficient Market Hypothesis," *The Journal of Finance*, Vol. 32, No. 3 (June 1977), pp. 663–682.

CHAPTER 5   APPLICATIONS: P/E AS AN INDEPENDENT VARIABLE

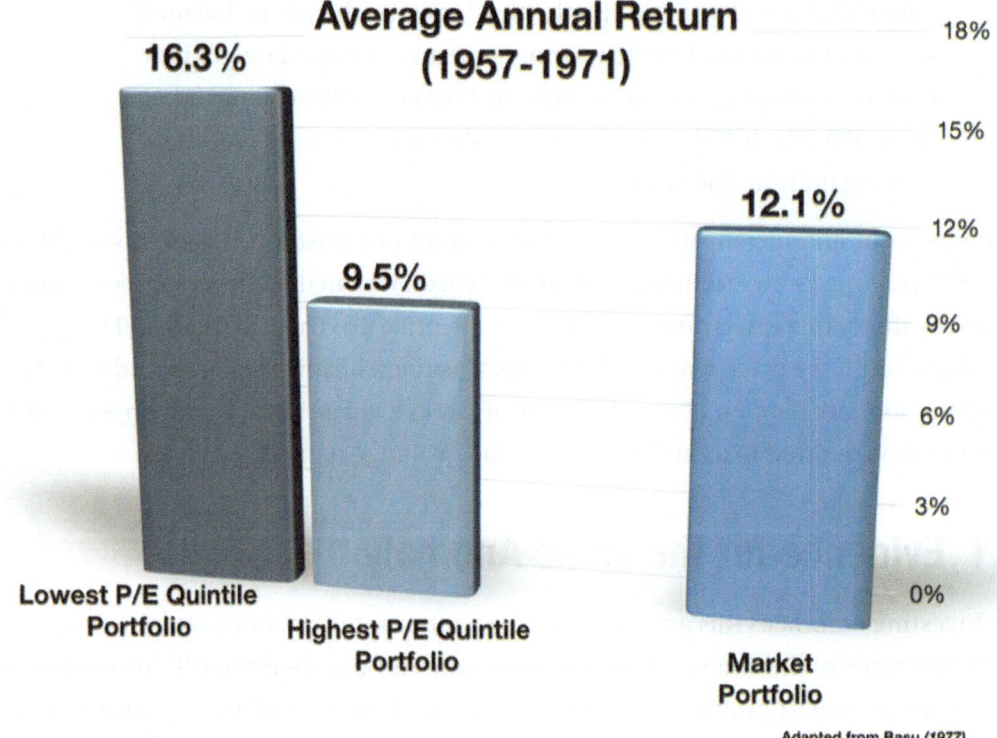

Figure 5-6. *P/E Signal, 1957–1971*[16]

Four decades later, a report by the Federal Reserve Bank of San Francisco plotted the monthly P/E of the entire market (the X-axis) against the share price growth over the subsequent ten years (the Y-axis). The pattern is more pronounced in the recent period[17] (see Figure 5-7).

---

[16] Adapted from S. Basu, "Investment Performance of Common Stocks in Relation to Their Price-Earnings Ratios: A Test of the Efficient Market Hypothesis," *The Journal of Finance*, Vol. 32, No. 3 (June 1977), pp. 663–682.

[17] Thomas Mertens, Patrick Shultz, and Michael Tubbs, "Valuation Ratios for Households and Businesses," *FRBSF Economic Letter*, Research from *Federal Reserve Bank of San Francisco*, January 8, 2018. Note that given the requirement for 10 years of follow-on returns to define each data point, the "later data" here must apparently end in 2007 – prior to the "stall out" of the "Value" anomaly discussed later in this chapter.

CHAPTER 5   APPLICATIONS: P/E AS AN INDEPENDENT VARIABLE

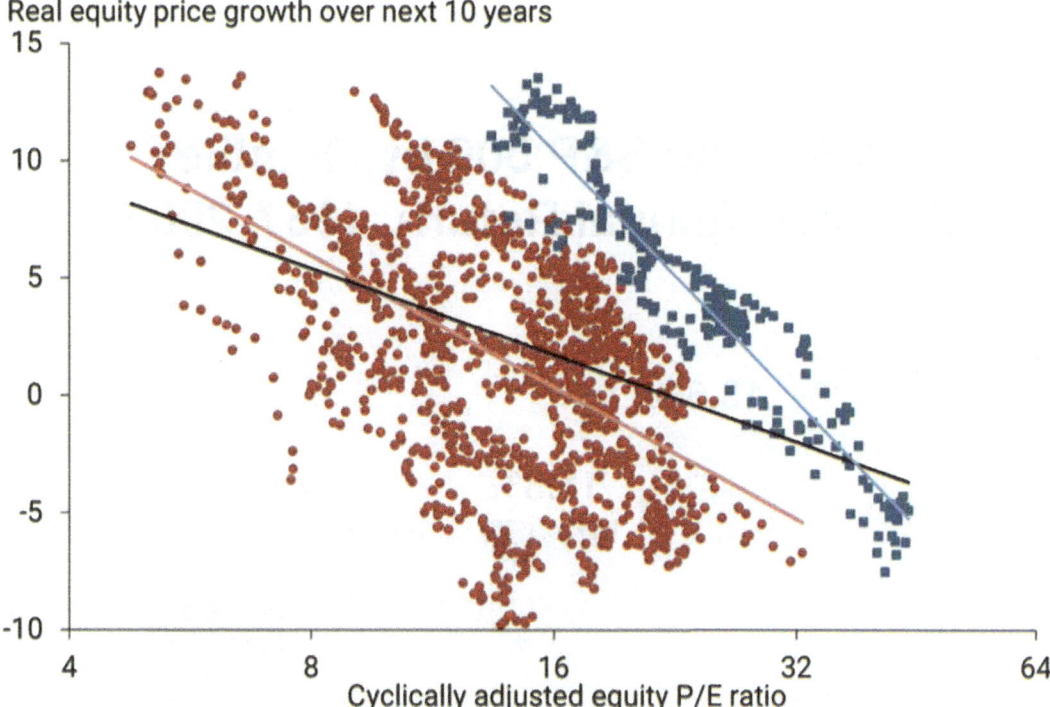

Figure 5-7. CAPE vs. 10-Year Returns[18]

This result has been confirmed in hundreds of studies ever since, for markets all around the world, and in all sorts of economic conditions. Like many factors in Finance, "Value" waxes and wanes. In certain market regimes, it can seem to vanish. But over the long term, the Value Anomaly has remained one of the strongest of the many market

---

[18]Reprinted from *the Federal Reserve Bank of San Francisco's "Valuation Ratios for Households and Businesses," FRBSF Economic Letter 2018-01,* January 8, 2018, www.frbsf.org/economic-research/publications/economic-letter/2018/january/valuation-ratios-for-households-and-businesses/. *The opinions expressed in this article do not necessarily reflect the views of the management of the Federal Reserve Bank of San Francisco or of the Board of Governors of the Federal Reserve System.*

CHAPTER 5 APPLICATIONS: P/E AS AN INDEPENDENT VARIABLE

anomalies that have been studied by academics. The following chart shows a 500–basis point annual advantage for low-P/E stocks over high-P/E stocks, which would amount to a 1000% premium over a 46-year period, across the entire S&P 500[19] (see Figure 5-8).

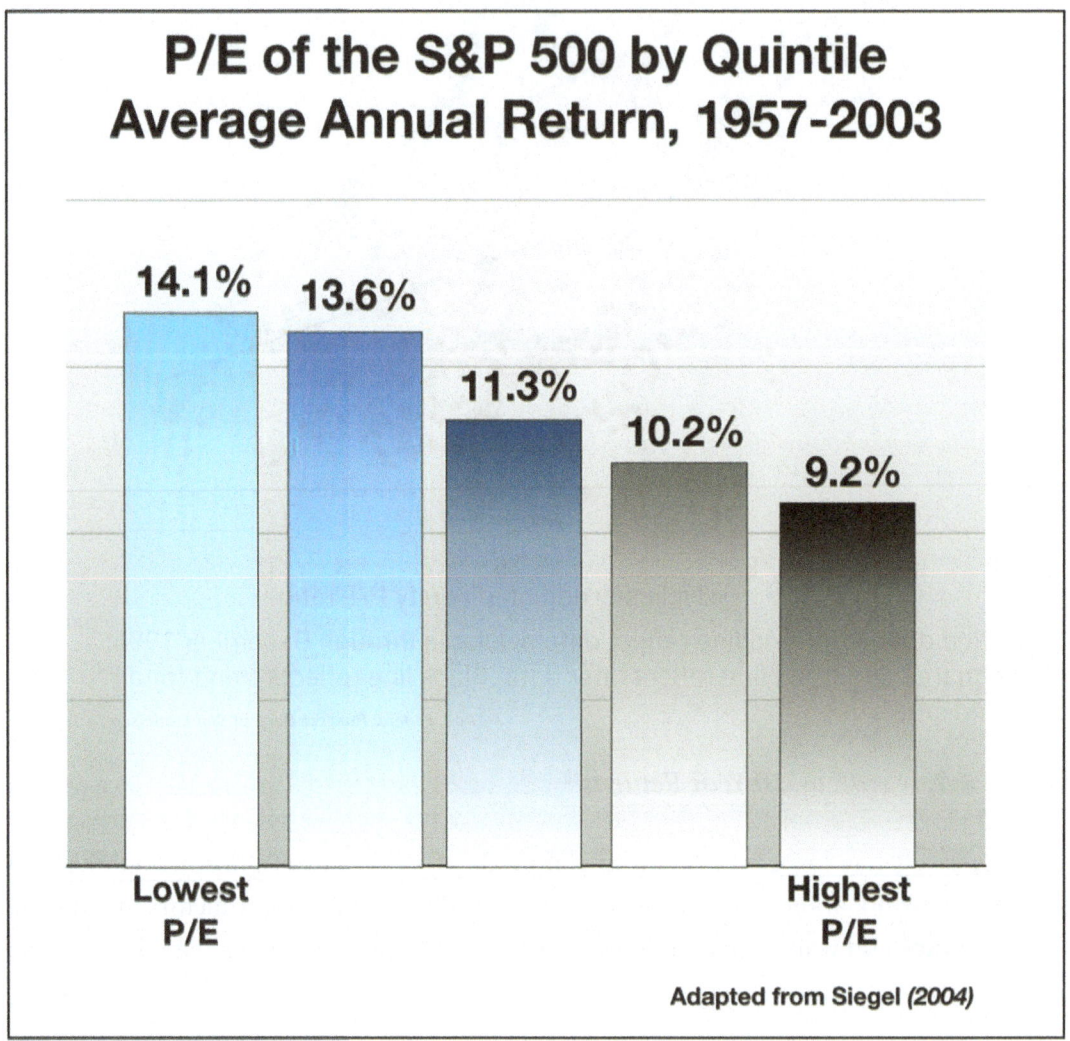

Figure 5-8. *The S&P 500 – Returns by P/E Quintile (1957–2003)*[20]

---

[19]Jeremy Siegel, "The Growth Trap," *Fortune*, December 27, 2004.
[20]Adapted from Jeremy Siegel, "The Growth Trap," *Fortune*, December 27, 2004.

5.2.2 Explanations of the Value Anomaly

Why does the "Value Anomaly" exist? Why does "Value Investing" work?

There are a number of explanations:

- **The Statistical Explanation**: "Value" as simple "mean reversion" (or "regression to the mean"[21])

- **The Traditional Finance-Theoretic Explanation**: "Value" as a form of "Risk"

- **A Modified Finance-Theoretic Explanation**: "Value" as a delayed response to new information

- **The Behavioral Finance Explanation**: "Value" as an outcome of biased decision-making

- **The Commonsense Explanation**: "Value" as the trajectory of the firm's learning process

5.2.2.1 Mean Reversion

A simplistic explanation of the Value Anomaly is based on the observation that many statistical processes (time series) are "mean-reverting" – a phenomenon which is also called "regression to the mean." The formal meaning of this concept is expressed as follows:

> If a variable is extreme on its first measurement, it will tend to be closer to the average on its second measurement.[22]

Applied to stock prices, it is argued that "high flyers" or so called "Growth" stocks for example, companies with much higher-than-average PE multiples – will tend to fall back to the average P/E level over time. "Value" companies with much lower-than-average multiples will tend to see their P/E's rise over time. This provides an explanation of sorts

---

[21]Some argue that "mean reversion" and "regression to the mean" are different phenomena. If so, the difference is quite subtle.

[22]See *Oxford Dictionary of Statistics*, Oxford University Press (2008), p. 335; for a much more nuanced discussion, see Stephen Stigler, "Regression to the Mean, Historically Considered," *Statistical Methods in Medical Research*, Vol. 6 (1997), pp. 103–114.

for the outperformance of undervalued companies: their earnings may grow in absolute terms, but more importantly, those earnings will be revalued upward in *relative* terms, providing a "tailwind" to the stock market returns (see Figure 5-9).

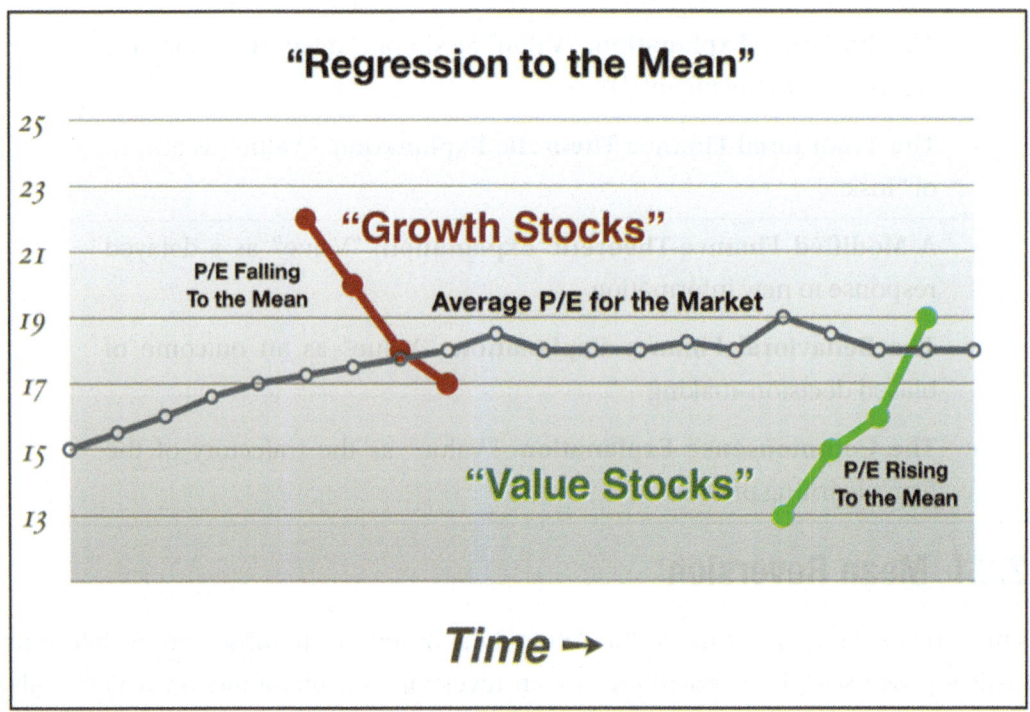

Figure 5-9. Regression to the Mean

"Mean reversion"[23] is not really an explanation; it is a relabeling of the phenomenon and a theory-free interpretation of the valuation process. It assumes that share prices will simply "return to normal" at some point, without any reference to causation.[24]

---

[23]John Campbell and Robert Shiller, "Valuation Ratios and The Long-Run Stock Market Outlook," *The Journal of Portfolio Management*, (Winter 1998).

[24]Shiller and Campbell put it this way: *"We should first understand what the stability of a valuation ratio itself implies about mean reversion. If we accept the premise for the moment that valuation ratios will continue to fluctuate within their historical ranges in the future, and neither move permanently outside nor get stuck at one extreme of their historical ranges, then when a valuation ratio is at an extreme level either the numerator or the denominator of the ratio must move in a direction that restores the ratio to a more normal level."* ["Valuation Ratios and The Long-Run Stock Market Outlook," *The Journal of Portfolio Management*, (Winter 1998)]. There is no causality or true "theory" here, merely the idea that "what goes up must come down," cast in statistical language.

Mean-reverting patterns can be found in most financial time series, at all scales, from very short-term, intraday, or high-frequency to multi-year time frames. Models to detect mean reversion are very popular with investors.

The practical challenge for Value Investing lies in predicting the time frame. How long do we have to wait for the mean reversion to occur? Different mean reversion processes, driven by different underlying causal mechanisms, operate on different timescales. The type of mean reversion that the P/E and other multiples signal is likely to be long. The revaluation of a company's earnings is a strategically significant process that operates on scale commensurate with the development of strategic initiatives, the execution of new policies and programs, and the gradual realization of improved business outcomes. It seems likely that this "turnaround" process occurs on a scale measured in multiple quarters or even years.[25] Without a causal model, predicting the reversion becomes simply a waiting game.

5.2.2.2 "Value" As a "Risk Factor"

Orthodox Finance Theory relates future returns to "risk"[26] – usually taken to mean simply the variability of past returns, measured in various ways. Returns are said to be positively correlated with such "risk" – higher returns imply the existence of higher variability of returns. Originally, the only type of "risk" that was considered was the overall variability of the market portfolio. This "market risk" acquired the label "beta."[27] In early versions

---

[25] Benjamin Graham wrote *"the interval required for a substantial undervaluation to correct itself averages approximately 1.5 to 2.5 years"* [*The Intelligent Investor* (1959)]. Werner F. M. De Bondt and Richard Thaler used a 3-year window in their well-known study of the P/E anomaly, and indeed most of the effect was delayed until the 15–24-month window. "Does the Stock Market Overreact?" *The Journal of Finance*, Vol. 40, No. 3 (July 1985), pp. 793–805. There are certainly cases where the P/E adjustment takes place much more rapidly. For example, in 2013, *Best Buy's* P/E jumped from 5.4 to 11.5 in less than four months, driving the stock up 120%: Justin Lahart, "You Needn't Be Best to Be a Buy," *The Wall Street Journal*, May 1, 2013.

[26] The use of the word "risk" is really a misnomer. In Finance Theory, "risk" refers only to the variability of outcomes (e.g., stock returns). It is in that sense a neutral statistical concept. It does not imply loss. For this reason, more careful authors will replace "risk" with measures of variability such as "standard deviation" of returns. I will generally place the word in quotation marks when referring to its use in the finance-theoretic sense.

[27] The original significance of the term *beta* is mathematical. But it has floated free of the equations and is now applied to a range of different concepts all related in some way to the idea of the broad trends and forces moving the market as a whole, as opposed to the specific trends and factors that move individual stocks, which in the same spirit is labeled *alpha*.

CHAPTER 5   APPLICATIONS: P/E AS AN INDEPENDENT VARIABLE

of Finance Theory, beta was considered to be the only factor determining returns, the only form of risk for which investors could expect a reward for taking on (since company-specific risks could be diversified away through proper portfolio construction).

Over time, it became clear that there was more to the story. The decisive consolidating step to admit other forms of "risk" came with the work of Fama and French in the 1990s, who identified additional "risk factors" – that is, sources of variability in stock prices, which were not explained by or subsumed in overall market "risk." Initially they identified just two additional factors: Value and Size.[28] (Later, many other factors were identified by researchers.)

The Value Factor was defined by Fama and French in terms of the Price/Book ratio (rather than P/E).[29] The "Value Anomaly" was explained as originating in the existence of a separate component of return variability ("risk") – an additional risk factor – that was related to low P/B. The market is said to offer investors an additional return premium to entice them to bear this new type of risk.

One test of this explanation is whether Value stocks, as selected by P/B or similar screens, do actually show higher "risk" – greater volatility or variability of outcomes than the market average. Research results are contradictory. Some academic studies have argued that Value stocks (low P/B) show higher volatility, at least under some circumstances.[30] But the actual measure of "risk" most often cited – standard deviation of stock returns – shows a different picture. Stocks screened for low P/B ("value stocks") were less volatile than stocks screened for high P/B ("growth stocks") over a long period (1963–2002)[31] (see Figure 5-10).

---

[28] It is worth mentioning that academic researchers usually refer to the inverse of the P/B ratio – the B/P or Book-to-Market. Of course it contains exactly the same information, but the "sign" is reversed, so to speak, such that it is a High B/P that signals a Value stock. Eugene Fama and Kenneth French, "The Cross-Section of Expected Stock Returns," *The Journal of Finance*, Vol. 47, No. 2 (June 1992), pp. 427–465.

[29] Academics have tended to continue using P/B as the screen for the Value Factor, while most practitioners prefer P/E (because of the structural deficiencies associated with the calculation of Book Value, as described in Chapter 3 and in Appendix 2).

[30] Angela J. Black and David G. McMillan, "Asymmetric risk premium in value and growth stocks," *International Review of Financial Analysis*, 15 (2006), pp. 237–246. See also Yakup Eser Arisoy, "Volatility risk and the value premium: Evidence from the French stock market," *Journal of Banking & Finance*, 34 (2010), pp. 975–983.

[31] William Bernstein, "Are Value Stocks Riskier Than Growth Stocks?" at www.efficientfrontier.com/ef/902/vgr.htm

CHAPTER 5   APPLICATIONS: P/E AS AN INDEPENDENT VARIABLE

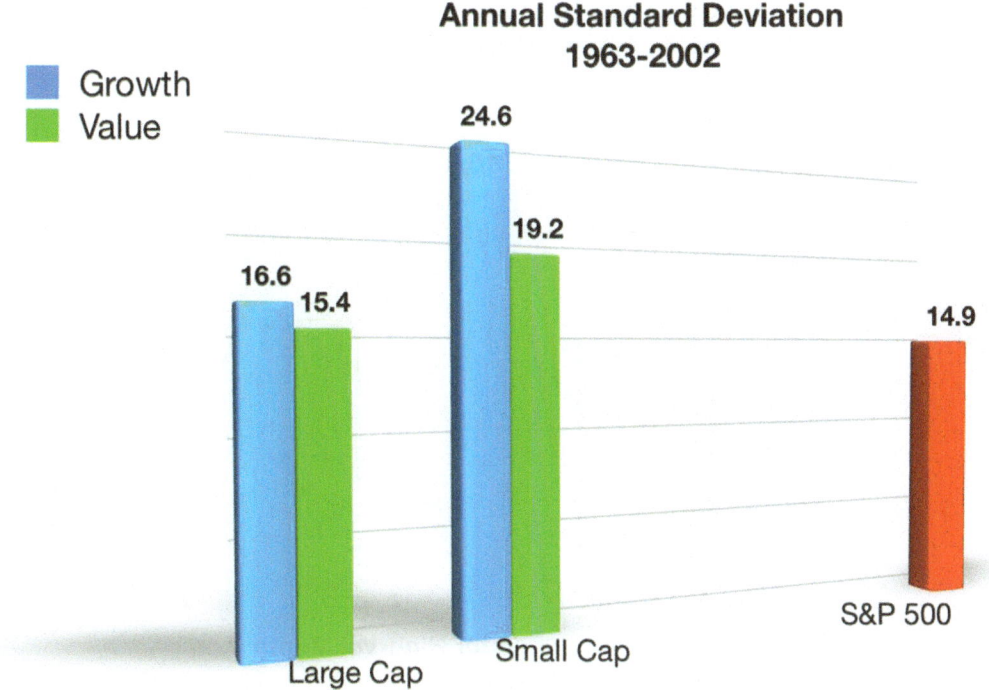

Figure 5-10. *Risk" for Small/Large Cap, Growth/Value vs. the Market*[32]

A later study (1980–2011) confirmed this pattern and found that the returns for Value stocks were less volatile for the year following both low-volatility months and high-volatility months, reflecting the persistence of a low-volatility/low-P/B relationship in different market environments (see Figure 5-11). (This study also found that the *5-year* returns for Value Stocks were also less volatile than the overall market.)[33]

---

[32]Adapted from William Bernstein, "Are Value Stocks Riskier Than Growth Stocks?" at www.efficientfrontier.com/ef/902/vgr.htm

[33]The Brandes Institute, "Volatility: Implications for Value and Glamour Stocks," available online at www.brandes.com/docs/default-source/brandes-institute/volatility-implications-for-value-and-glamour-stocks

CHAPTER 5   APPLICATIONS: P/E AS AN INDEPENDENT VARIABLE

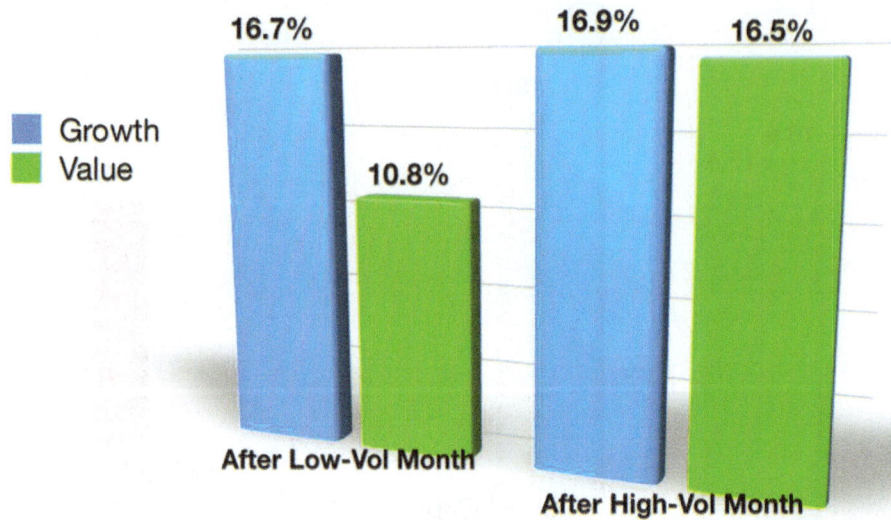

Figure 5-11. *"Risk" vs. Growth/Value*[34]

5.2.2.3 "Value" as a "Delayed Response"

Efficient Market theory, as originally formulated, required drastic simplifying assumptions about the market and investor behavior.[35] This exposed the theory to criticism that it does not provide a valid description of real markets. In recent years, it is claimed the Efficient Market theory has been "refined…to reflect the realism of the marketplace" and especially the recognition of "frictions" of various kinds.[36]

One such "friction" relates to the potential delays in processing new information. Perhaps the "Value" Anomaly exists because the market processes new information more slowly than the standard theory assumes. That is, perhaps the anomaly arises from a gap in

---

[34] Adapted from the Brandes Institute, "Volatility: Implications for Value and Glamour Stocks," available online at www.brandes.com/docs/default-source/brandes-institute/volatility-implications-for-value-and-glamour-stocks

[35] Such as the absence of transaction costs.

[36] Andrew Ang, William Goetzmann, and Stephen Schaefer, *"Evaluation of Active Management of the Norwegian Government Pension Fund – Global,"* December 14, 2009.

time between the arrival of new information and the full incorporation of that information into revised prices. The lag allows time for an agile investor to anticipate and exploit the temporary mispricing of Value stocks.

> Contrary to the growing belief that publicly available information is instantaneously impounded in security prices, there seem to be lags and frictions in the adjustment process. As a result, publicly available P/E ratios seem to possess "information content" and may warrant an investor's attention at the time of portfolio formation or revision.[37]

This is also sometimes described as "under-reaction":

> Over horizons of perhaps 1 to 12 months, security prices underreact to news. News is incorporated only slowly into prices, which tend to exhibit positive autocorrelations over these horizons. A related way to make this point is to say that current good news has power in predicting positive returns in the future.[38]

Other studies have found that the under-reaction-followed-by-correction (mean reversion) process can take as long as five years or more.[39] This offers plenty of opportunities for investors to profit ahead of the trend reversal.

5.2.2.4 Behavioral Finance Explanations

The preceding "under-reaction" paradigm is based on a relatively neutral terminology – it invokes little more than processing delay in terms of causality. But it suggests and shades into an alternative view of the Value Anomaly based on the idea that there are systematic biases in investors' decision-making processes. A richer psychological framework is invoked: "Individuals are slow to change their beliefs in the face of new evidence" – processing delay becomes *conservatism*. Referencing Bayesian Inference, a classical

---

[37] S. Basu, "Investment Performance of Common Stocks in Relation to Their Price-Earnings Ratios: A Test of the Efficient Market Hypothesis," *The Journal of Finance*, Vol. 32, No. 3 (June 1977), pp. 663–682.

[38] Nicholas Barberis, Andrei Shleifer, and Robert Vishny, "A model of investor sentiment," *Journal of Financial Economics*, 49 (1998), pp. 307–343.

[39] David N. Dreman and Michael A. Berry, "Overreaction, Underreaction, and the Low-P/E Effect," *Financial Analysts Journal*, July/August 1995, pp. 21–30.

CHAPTER 5   APPLICATIONS: P/E AS AN INDEPENDENT VARIABLE

statistical perspective on the way in which probabilities for a hypothesis are updated – that is, the way in which opinions change as new information becomes available – one research psychologist has observed

> Opinion change is very orderly, and usually proportional to numbers calculated from the Bayes Theorem – but it is insufficient in amount. A conventional first approximation to the data would say that it takes anywhere from two to five observations to do one observation's worth of work in inducing a subject to change his opinions.[40]

But is it "under-reaction" or "overreaction"? Conservatism and inertia, or fear and pessimism? Apparently, human beings are prone to both forms of bias.

> The return performance of low PE stocks with low earnings expectations is based on an anomaly known as the "overreaction to earnings effect."...
>
> Studies show that extremely good/bad years are temporary and that future earnings invariably return to more normal level. If investors view these temporary aberrations as permanent, an unfavorable earnings report results in the market setting overly pessimistic forecasts of future earnings, causing the stock price to fall below its equilibrium level. Once investors become aware that they have been overly pessimistic, stock prices adjust upward to their intrinsic value.[41]

This discussion merges with a range of other psychological observations and interpretations of investor decision-making, collected under the heading of Behavioral Finance – which has emerged as an important challenge to traditional rationalistic Finance Theory. The P/E Value Anomaly has played a key role in stimulating the development of this new field.[42]

---

[40]W. Edwards, "Conservatism in human information processing," in B. Kleinmutz (Ed.), *Formal Representation of Human Judgment*, John Wiley and Sons, New York (1968), pp. 17–52.

[41]April Klein and James Rosenfeld, "P/E Ratios, Earnings Expectations, and Abnormal Returns," *The Journal of Financial Research*, Vol. 14, No. 1 (Spring 1991), pp. 51–64.

[42]The under-reaction vs. overreaction debate is an example of the incoherence that sometimes attaches to these behavioral narratives. It is perhaps too easy to invent psychological explanations for the anomalies we observe. As with other tangential topics, a fuller treatment of Behavioral Finance will be deferred to another volume.

5.2.2.5 "Value" As a Reflection of a Learning Process

The previous explanations are all mechanistic and, in a sense, deterministic. The first three explanations portray the Value Anomaly as a fixed response of the market mechanism to either the nature or the timing of information about the companies that carry the "Value" label. The Behavioral Finance explanation is based on a *psychological* mechanism presumed to operate within the mind of the investor, which also processes new information in a quasi-deterministic manner. None of these first four approaches make any reference to the behavior of the companies in question or responses of management to the challenges of the business, including a depressed valuation.

But firms are of course socio-technical systems, managed by human agents who can observe the causes of low valuation and respond with policies designed to correct those problems and raise the company's value. There is a learning process. A company that finds itself in trouble is subject to intense competitive pressure to find successful corrective strategies. Management may be replaced with "better" management. The firm may engage outside advisors and consultants to diagnose its shortcomings and recommend improvements. Throughout the firm, at all levels, incentives are usually in place to promote effective problem-solving, learning, and innovation. Over time, we should expect that most companies in difficulty today will improve in the future and the valuation metrics should rise in response to this improvement.

This is a commonsense explanation. Companies with low P/E's usually deserve them, because they are in difficulty and have disappointed investors. However, those companies are managed by intelligent agents who are capable of identifying these problems, coming to grips with them, and making adjustments in the business strategy to improve performance. As this improvement manifests itself, the P/E will respond. Viewed as such, mean reversion is an accurate reflection of a learning or adjustment process brought about by management's constructive response, to solve problems and increase the value of the business. The delay inherent in the process reflects the natural course of diagnosing the problems, considering alternative solutions, introducing changes in business strategy, and allowing time for the improvements to take effect. Whether or not investors are tracking these matters imperfectly, the organic nature of economic change is in this view the real driver of the trajectory of returns and valuation. As the situation improves, valuation metrics will rise. This is why the Multiple can be employed as a screen for the "Quality" or "Profitability" factor.

> The long-short Profitability factor generated consistently positive returns in the US and Europe since 1990. Companies that are more profitable than others *should be trading at higher valuations*.[43] *[Emphasis added]*

Interesting to note: in this case the signal provided by the Multiple is not contrarian. As Rabener observes, "the Profitability factor could therefore be regarded as the opposite of the Value factor." It carries similar information, but screened for the opposite sign. The P/E Multiple is a barometer of competitive success, whether we screen for low or high values.

(On the other hand, "growth" companies that have done well in the prior period may tend to become complacent or gradually grow more inefficient and less profitable or miss some strategic change in their business situation because of a natural inertia and commitment to past policies. Their learning process has been "disrupted" by their success – a common observation.[44])

5.2.2.6 The "Cyclicals" Exception

It is sometimes argued that the significance of the P/E signal may be reversed for "Cyclical" companies – those with earnings that surge and fall dramatically with either the general business cycle (e.g., automotive companies) or the effects of a cycle related to the sector (e.g., oil prices or semiconductor inventory cycles). A low Multiple for such companies may reflect the effect of a very good earnings period at the "top" of the cycle, which is likely

---

[43]Nicolas Rabener, "The Odd Factors: Profitability & Investment," *FactorResearch,* available online at www.factorresearch.com/research-the-odd-factors-profitability-investment

[44]Clayton Christensen has developed a "theory" of strategy based on this tendency, which he calls the Innovator's Dilemma. Essentially, he indicts established and successful companies for failing to respond creatively to emergent challenges to their business models, precisely because it would involve deviating from long-running successful policies and, at least in the short term, going against the interests and desires of their existing customers. Clayton Christensen, *The Innovator's Dilemma: When New Technologies Cause Great Firms to Fail,* Harvard Business Review Press, 1997.

to decline in the coming (and "inevitable") down-cycle. The Price forecasts this decline and stays relatively low. So a low P/E, instead of representing a value play or a buying opportunity, can be a warning that the fleeting good times are about to change. The relatively low Price in the numerator is a forecast by the market, based on a recognition that the impressive earnings of the moment are not sustainable.

5.2.2.7 Is "Value" Disappearing?

A recent study (2014) has argued that "both the Shiller PE [i.e., $CAPE_1$] and the conventional PE ratios fail a critical statistical test: they are not mean-reverting – and as a consequence, both ratios can be expected to indicate either undervaluation or overvaluation for very long periods of time."[45] In other words, the Value Anomaly may have stopped working. Underpriced stocks may simply not recover, or they may take much longer to do so. Indeed, since 2008, the returns on Value Investing seem to have dried up. Rabener charts long/short strategies using P/E and P/B – that is, he buys the low-P/E or low-P/B stocks and shorts the high-multiple stocks. The P/E strategy was very powerful from 2000 to 2007, gaining 600%. But following the 2008 crisis, "Value" has disappeared as a driver of returns, with P/E screens showing a slight loss in the following decade (screens based on P/B multiples were worse)[46] (see Figure 5-12).

---

[45]Brian Kantor and Christopher Holdsworth. "2013 Nobel Prize Revisited: Do Shiller's Models Really Have Predictive Power?" *Journal of Applied Corporate Finance*, (Spring 2014), pp. 101–108. I have not been able to read more than the abstract of this paper, so I am not sure if what they mean is that the time required for mean reversion to occur has lengthened (which is what I suspect). I would hope the authors would make their work more available.

[46]Nicolas Rabener, "Value US: Sectoral Analysis," *FactorResearch,* May 2017.

CHAPTER 5   APPLICATIONS: P/E AS AN INDEPENDENT VARIABLE

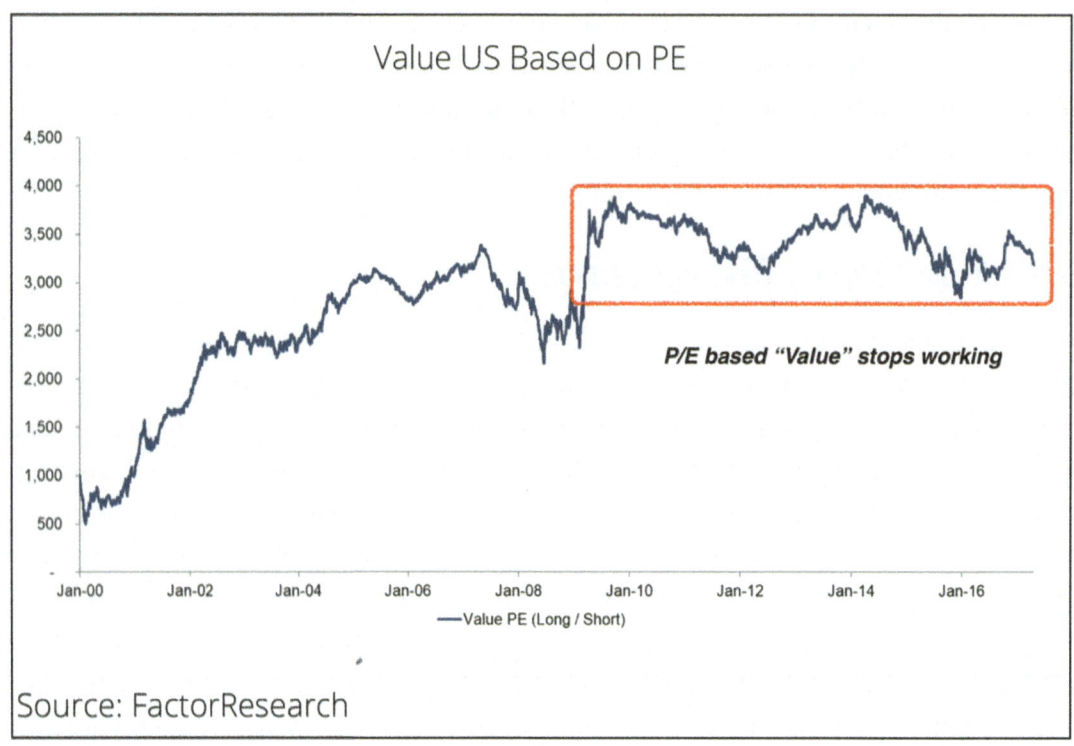

Figure 5-12. *P/E Signal for "Value" Disappears*[47]

What explains this? Aggressive monetary easing by the Federal Reserve may play a role. There is also speculation that Value Investing strategies are weakened by the rise of cap-weighted index-based investing. Index funds which are weighted by market capitalization will, in a rising market, create a positive feedback (pro-cyclical) process, channeling more money into larger cap and growth stocks, indeed into any overvalued stock, and away from undervalued stocks, which tends to reinforce the "growth factor" (high-P/E stocks) and attenuate the "value factor" (low P/E).

> Passive funds could conceivably contribute to price overshooting if their fund flows are sizeable. As indices are typically weighted according to market values, the share of overvalued stocks or bonds in them tends to increase in a rising market ... Large flows into and out of passive funds could exacerbate these investment trends.[48]

---

[47]Nicolas Rabener, "Value US: Sectoral Analysis," *FactorResearch*, May 2017. Reprinted by permission of the author.

[48]V. Sushko and Grant Turner, "The Implications of Passive Investing for Securities Markets," *BIS Quarterly Review* (March 2018), pp. 113–131.

CHAPTER 5   APPLICATIONS: P/E AS AN INDEPENDENT VARIABLE

In any case, "Value" (low-P/E stocks) has underperformed relative to "Growth" (high-P/E stocks) over the past few years[49] (see Figure 5-13).

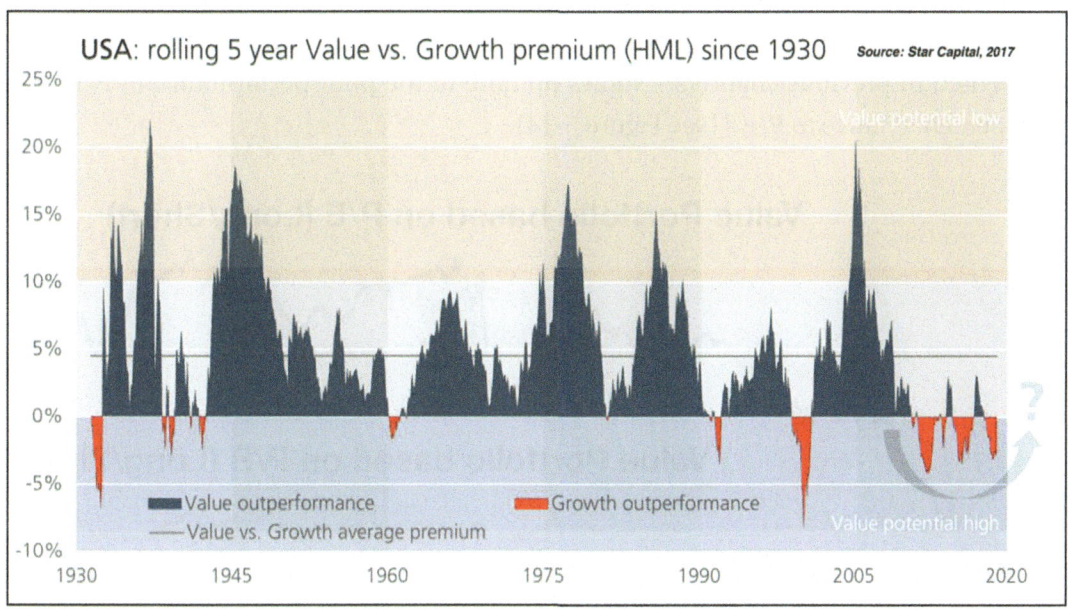

Figure 5-13. *"Value" Premium Weakens Under Quantitative Easing*[50]

5.2.3 Comparing Multiples As Value Screens

Which metric does the best at predicting future returns when used as a Value Screen?

This is subsidiary to a more general question: How well can market metrics (and other indicators) predict future stock market returns? As with many such questions in Finance, there is as yet no clear answer to either the larger or the smaller question. There are some intriguing indications.

---

[49]Norbert Keimling and Nora Imkeller, *Star Capital Research* (2017), available at www.starcapital.de/en/research/research-in-charts/

[50]Norbert Keimling and Nora Imkeller, *Star Capital Research* (2017), available at www.starcapital.de/en/research/research-in-charts/. Reprinted by permission of the author.

CHAPTER 5   APPLICATIONS: P/E AS AN INDEPENDENT VARIABLE

5.2.3.1 Price/Book Is Ineffective

P/B is the metric preferred by many academics, going back to the original three-factor model of Fama and French.[51] However, P/B is no longer as effective as it once was. The failure of Book Value accounting to keep up with the transformation of the economy – commented in previous chapters – shows up here in the poor performance of P/B as a Value Screen, relative to P/E[52] (see Figure 5-14).

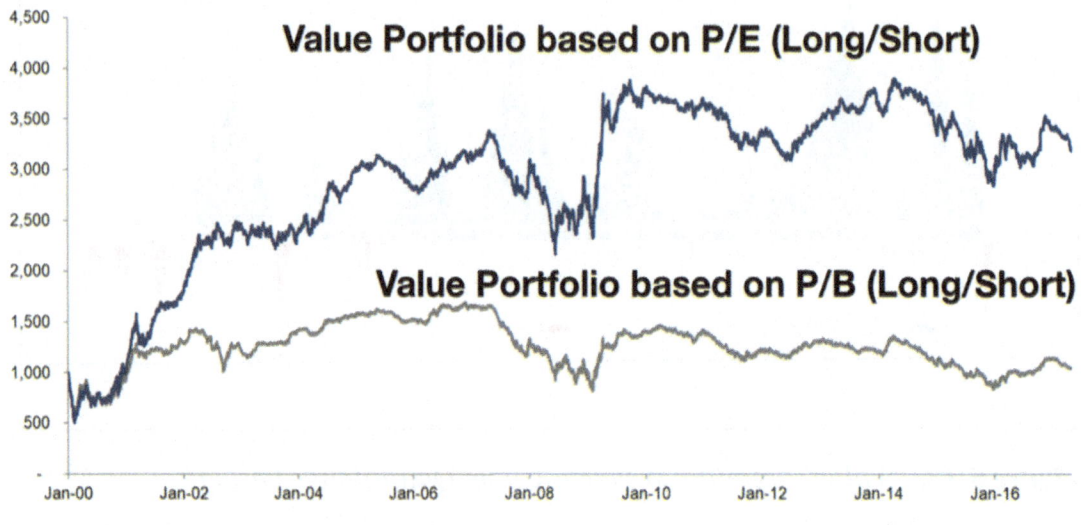

Source: Rabener, Factor Research, 2018

Figure 5-14. *P/E vs. P/B as "Value" Signals*[53]

---

[51]Eugene F. Fama and Kenneth R. French, "The Cross-Section of Expected Stock Returns," *The Journal of Finance*, Vol. 47, No. 2 (June 1992), pp. 427–465.

[52]"*Systematic value investors face a lot of options when deciding which value metric they should utilize when constructing their portfolios. Historically, investors have focused on the price-to-book ratio… But there's a problem with price/book: today's economy. Price/book, perhaps the most conventional measure of value, evaluates stock prices based on a company's book value – the worth of all tangible assets but no intangible ones…Today's service economy is filled with companies whose biggest assets are their brands, intellectual property, or customer loyalty, which don't show up on the balance sheet*" (Nicolas Rabener, "Value Factor: Comparing Valuation Metrics," *FactorResearch*, May 2018. Available online at www.factorresearch.com/research-value-factor-comparing-valuation-metrics).

[53]Nicolas Rabener, "Value Factor: Comparing Valuation Metrics," *FactorResearch*, May 2018. Available online at www.factorresearch.com/research-value-factor-comparing-valuation-metrics. Reprinted by permission of the author.

In a study of Brazilian equities, the P/E metric was found to be much more effective than the P/B to identify "value" stocks, offering "significantly better risk-adjusted performance for investors."[54] (The authors noted that the high inflation rate in Brazil "makes the book values of companies less meaningful, especially for firms with older assets" – in short, another reason that the P/B multiple is to be avoided.)

5.2.3.2 Cash Flow Multiples: Mixed Results

Rabener also charts two Cash Flow multiples: Price/Free-Cash-Flow and EV/EBITDA. P/FCF is modestly superior to Price/Book, while the EV/EBITDA is much better and only slightly underperforms P/E (see Figure 5-15).

---

[54]Rafael Falcão Noda, Roy Martelanc, and Eduardo Kazuo Kayo, "The Earnings/Price Risk Factor in Capital Asset pricing Models," Paper presented at the *BALAS Annual Conference 2014*, Port of Spain, Trinidad and Tobago, 2014. The authors emphasize an important general point: we do not understand fully the effect of inflation on the accuracy of the multiples and other valuation metrics. *"Another possible extension is checking whether E/P ratios constitute better explanatory factors for returns in other countries with historically high inflation rates and whether B/M ratios are more suited for countries with historically low inflation rates."* This comment illuminates the general academic inattentiveness to the need for a more systematic analysis of the problem of valuation.

CHAPTER 5   APPLICATIONS: P/E AS AN INDEPENDENT VARIABLE

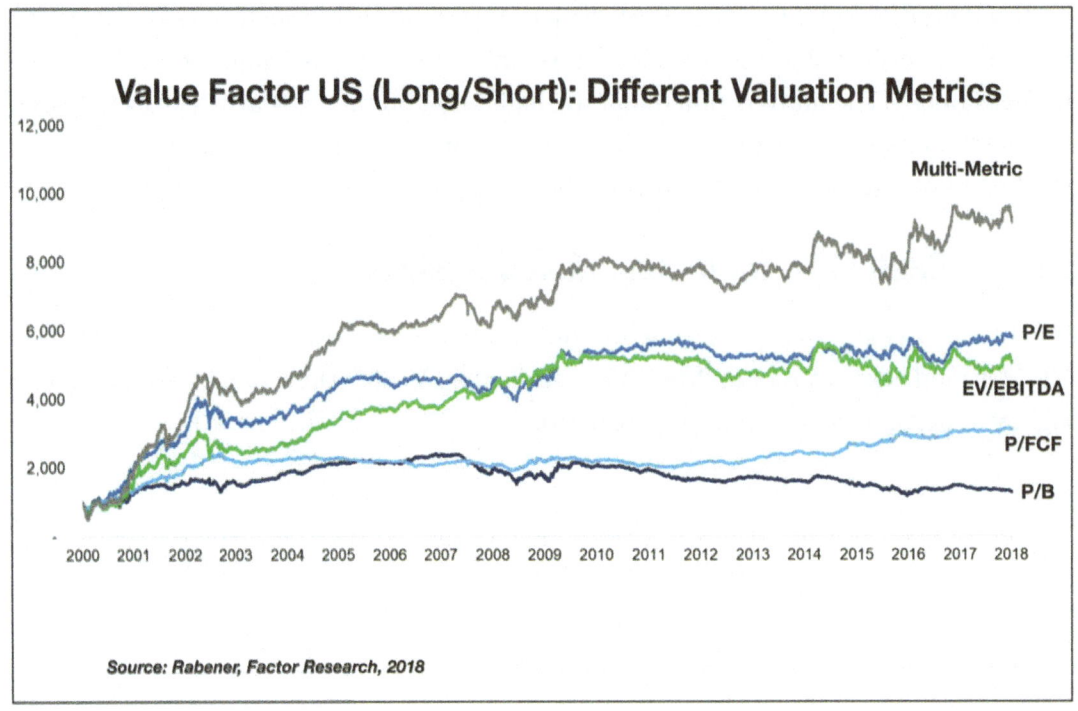

Figure 5-15. "Value" Signals Derived from Several Metrics[55]

A different study found that cash flow metrics were superior to metrics based on GAAP earnings.

> A strategy of buying the 50 cheapest S&P Stocks based on the enterprise-value-to-free-cash-flow ratio has outperformed a similar strategy using forward P/E's by at least 2% since 1986, with less volatility.[56]

Another perspective is provided by MSCI, a leading index provider. They use three Multiples to build their flagship Value Index: Forward P/E, P/B, and EV/OCF (Enterprise Value/Operating Cash Flow).[57] Interestingly, the Cash Flow multiple seems to generate

---

[55] Nicolas Rabener, "Value Factor: Comparing Valuation Metrics," *FactorResearch*, May 2018. Available online at www.factorresearch.com/research-value-factor-comparing-valuation-metrics. Reprinted by permission of the author.

[56] Ben Levisohn, "Is It Time to Scrap the Fusty Old P/E Ratio?" *The Wall Street Journal*, September 4, 2010.

[57] *MSCI Factor Investing, Focus: Value* (2018).

the most coherent "Value" signal, when plotted in deciles. The cash flow multiple is the only metric that shows a monotonic relationship with future returns, and it has the largest spread between highest and lowest deciles. The patterns for P/E_{fwd} and P/B are less regular and non-monotonic, with smaller spreads between highest and lowest deciles (see Figure 5-16).

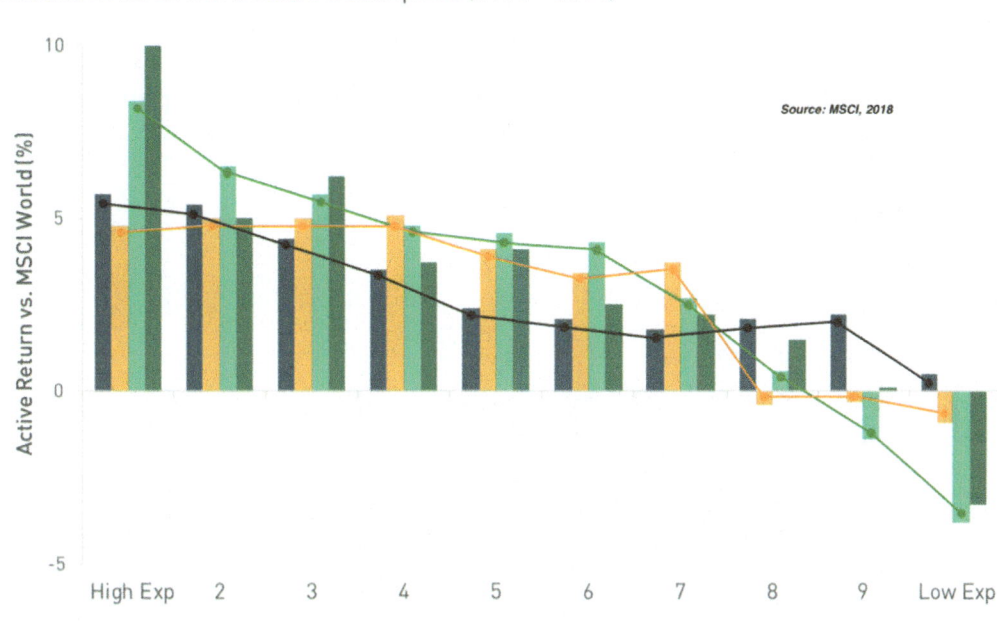

Figure 5-16. *Returns for Several "Value" Metrics*[58]

The diverse findings in the literature regarding the effectiveness of cash flow as a predictor of returns are due in part to the fact that there are so many definitions of cash flow, both in terms of the research protocols of particular studies and in terms of the "raw" data from corporate financial statements and other sources. It is a difficult topic to control.

---

[58]Adapted from *MSCI Factor Investing, Focus:Value* (2018).

5.2.3.3 Dividend Yield vs. P/E

Dividend Yield is another market metric that is frequently used to create Value screens.[59] It presents the same contrarian pattern as the P/E Multiple[60] (see Figure 5-17). High Dividend Yield correlates well with Low P/E multiples.[61]

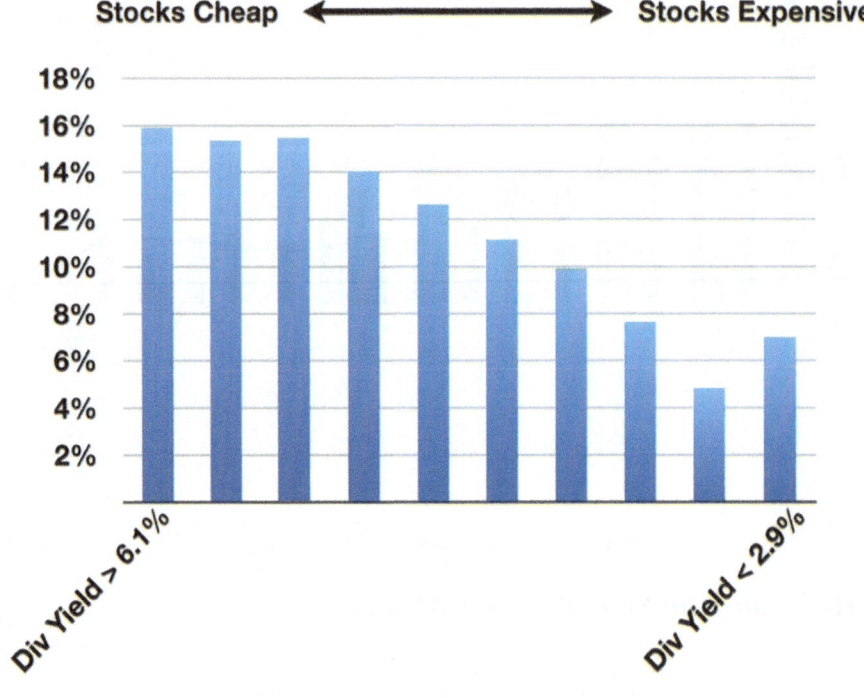

Figure 5-17. Returns for Several "Value" Metrics[62]

---

[59] A classic example is the "Dogs of the Dow" technique, in many variations: https://en.wikipedia.org/wiki/Dogs_of_the_Dow

[60] Burton G. Malkiel, "The Efficient Market Hypothesis and its Critics," *Journal of Economic Perspectives*, Vol. 17, No. 1, Winter 2003, pp. 59–82.

[61] See Chapter 4, Section 4.2.4.

[62] Adapted from Burton G. Malkiel, "The Efficient Market Hypothesis and its Critics," *Journal of Economic Perspectives*, Vol. 17, No. 1, Winter 2003, pp. 59–82.

CHAPTER 5 APPLICATIONS: P/E AS AN INDEPENDENT VARIABLE

The trend to substitute buybacks for dividends in recent years has diluted the power of this multiple. In the last decade, the Dividend Yield screen appears to have weakened considerably.[63] Returns from a Long/Short strategy based on this factor have stagnated. This mirrors the decline of Value strategies based on the P/E multiple shown earlier (see Figure 5-18).

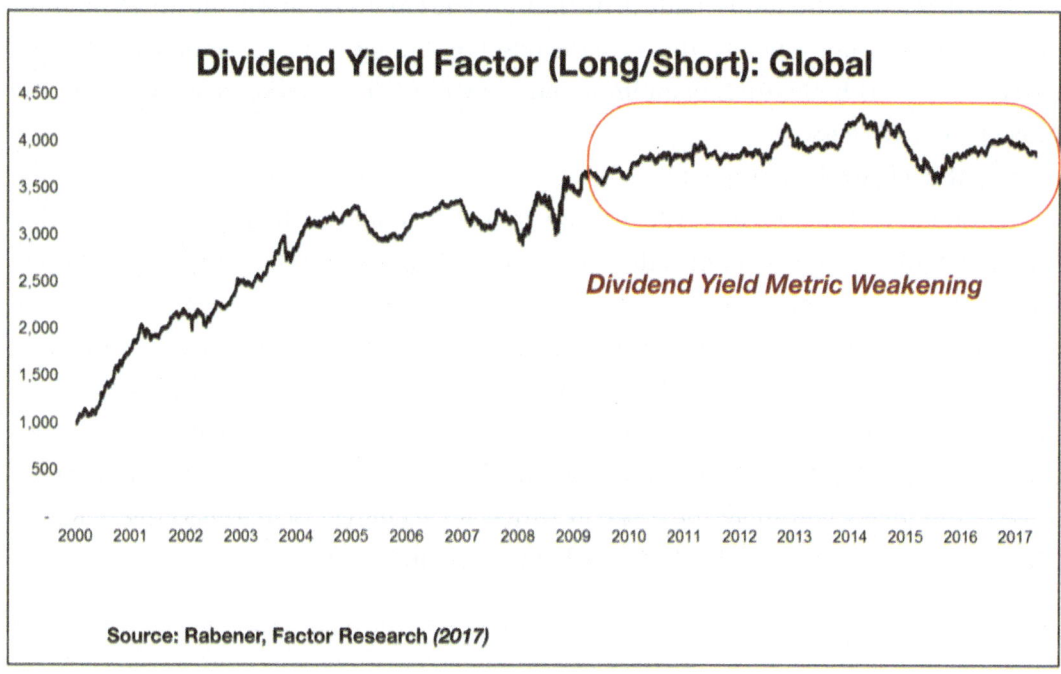

Figure 5-18. *Dividend Yield Signal Weakening*[64]

5.2.3.4 Does CAPE Improve Performance?

Yale economist Robert Shiller in a recent piece in the *New York Times* [in 2017] noted his CAPE ratio (cyclically adjusted price-earnings ratio), a valuation measure applied to the S&P 500, is at levels only surpassed historically in 1929 and around 2000.

---

[63]Nicholas Rabener, "Resist the Siren Call of High Dividend Yields," *FactorResearch*, October 2017.
[64]Adapted from Nicholas Rabener, "Resist the Siren Call of High Dividend Yields," *FactorResearch*, October 2017.

CHAPTER 5   APPLICATIONS: P/E AS AN INDEPENDENT VARIABLE

"The current level of CAPE suggests a dim outlook for the American stock market over the next 10 years or so, but it does not tell us for sure nor does it say when to expect a decline," he wrote. "Investors should not let themselves be tempted to bet aggressively on the Trump bull market."[65]

This pronouncement was made in April 2017. The Dow rose 30% in the next 8 months. In 1996, in testimony before the Federal Reserve, Shiller made a similar prediction, based on his CAPE measure, of an imminent downturn. The market rose by 50% in the subsequent five years.

Is CAPE a flawed instrument?

As noted in Chapter 3, CAPE has an inherent tendency to run high – flashing "overvaluation" – especially since the 2008 crisis. Whenever the economy and corporate profits are growing, an average of the past ten years earnings will always tend to be lower than the current year's earnings, and CAPE will be higher than the current P/E. In the case of individual stocks, CAPE can be quite skewed. For a stock growing its EPS a steady rate of 5% per year, the CAPE will be about 23% higher than the current P/E. For companies growing faster or those recovering from a setback, the effect can be much more pronounced. For *Apple*, the CAPE in 2018 was 84% higher than *Apple's* then-current P/E. For *Bank of America*, it was 275% higher (see Figure 5-19).

---

[65]Emily Stewart, "Here's How to Spot a Market Bubble," The street.com, April 17, 2017.

CHAPTER 5   APPLICATIONS: P/E AS AN INDEPENDENT VARIABLE

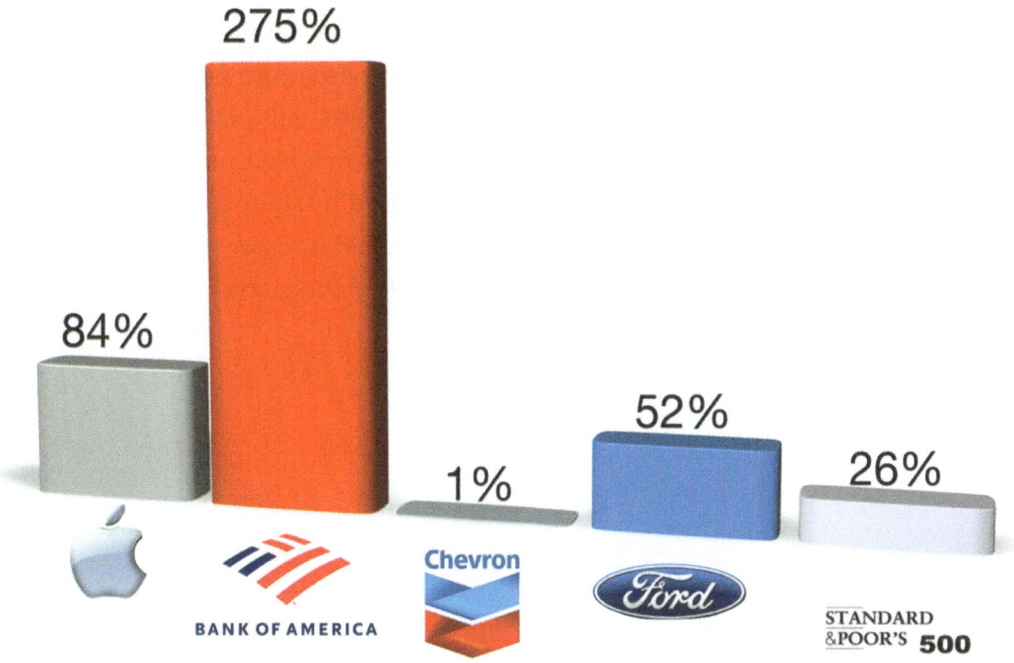

Figure 5-19. *The CAPE "Premium"*

At the very least, some calibration is needed. To interpret CAPE in the same way as the current-year P/E would seem to predispose the analyst to pessimism, even in the face of contrary evidence.[66]

---

[66]Shiller's "non-apology" for the failure of the CAPE call in 1996 is telling in this regard: *"On December 3, 1996, we testified before the Federal Reserve Board that, despite all the evidence that stock returns are hard to forecast in the short run, this simple theory of mean reversion is basically right and does indeed imply a poor long-run stock market outlook. We amplified our testimony and published it in 1998, continuing to assert our pessimistic long-run scenario. The stock market did not immediately move to encourage faith in our theory. Since our testimony, the stock market, as measured by the real (inflation-corrected) Standard & Poor Composite index, has increased by 80% above its value when we testified, and 30% above its value when we published. Despite these developments, we believe that our original testimony and article are even more relevant today."* [John Campbell and Robert Shiller, "Valuation Ratios and the Long-Run Stock Market Outlook," *NBER Working Paper No. 8221* (April 2001)].

5.2.3.5 Market Regimes: Bull Markets Favor Growth over Value (As a Rule)

The "value signal" that the P/E and other multiples normally provide can disappear for periods of time, especially in bull markets. During the market surge of 2018, the typical pattern was disrupted. High-P/E stocks significantly outperformed low-P/E stocks. Unprofitable companies also outperformed (see Figure 5-20). This pattern – paying more for earnings growth and even for potential future earnings that have not yet materialized, rather than betting on low-priced value stocks – is viewed by some as a "warning sign," even an "unnatural distortion," an indication of overexcited investor sentiment, perhaps associated with a developing bubble in certain segments of the market.[67]

---

[67]Corrie Driebusch, "Unprofitable Growth Stocks Are Soaring," *The Wall Street Journal,* September 20, 2018.

CHAPTER 5   APPLICATIONS: P/E AS AN INDEPENDENT VARIABLE

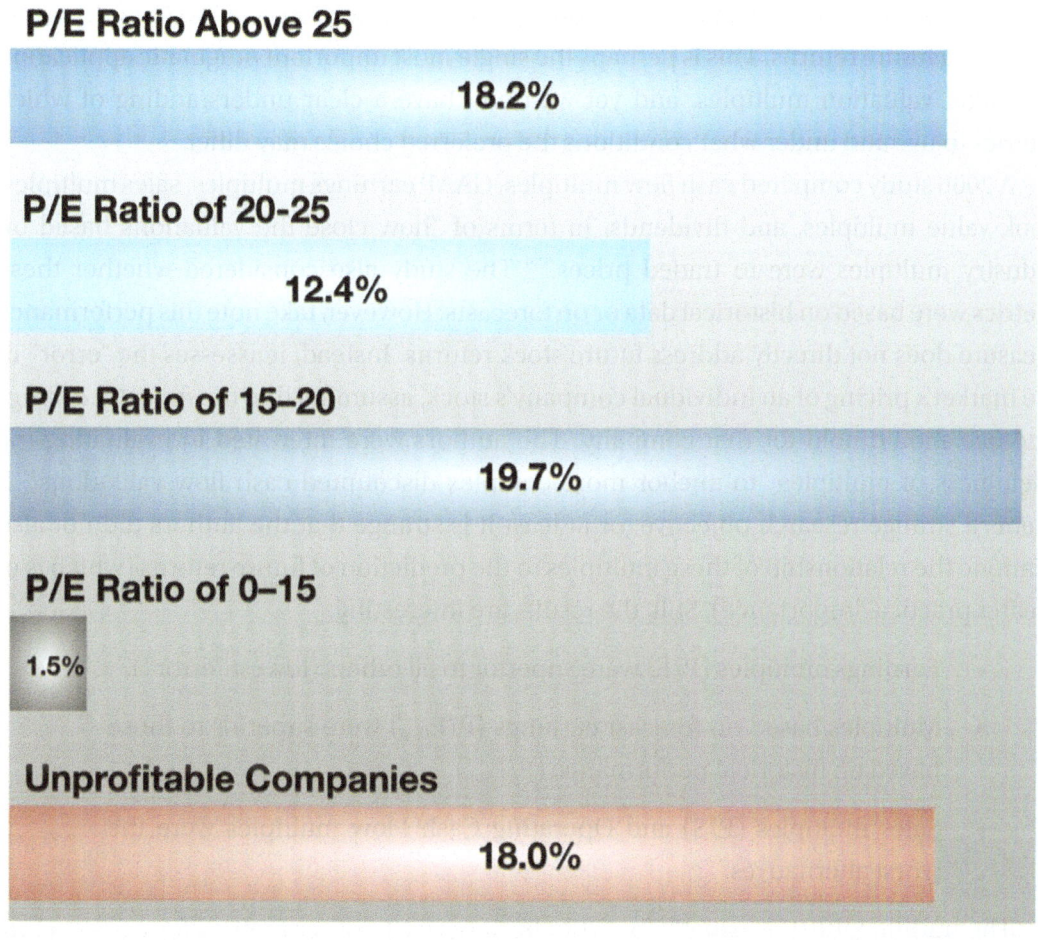

Figure 5-20. *The P/E Signal Sometimes Fails*[68]

---

[68]Adapted from Corrie Driebusch, "Unprofitable Growth Stocks Are Soaring," *The Wall Street Journal,* September 20, 2018.

5.2.3.6 Multiples and Expected Returns: Summing Up

Where does this leave us? Which metric works best? Oddly, there are few systematic comparisons of the effectiveness of alternative market metrics applied to the purpose of predicting future returns. This is perhaps the single most important pragmatic application of market valuation multiples, and yet we don't have a clear understanding of which metrics to use and under what conditions the preferred choice may differ.

A 2006 study compared cash flow multiples, GAAP earnings multiples, sales multiples, book value multiples, and dividends, in terms of "how close the valuations based on industry multiples were to traded prices."[69] The study also considered whether these metrics were based on historical data or on forecasts. However, take note this performance measure does not directly address future stock returns. Instead, it assesses the "error" in the market's pricing of an individual company's stock, assuming that the *industry average multiple* should hold for that company. The authors were interested in evaluating the usefulness of multiples "to anchor more complex discounted cash flow valuations." It seems a strange research objective, or at least it is strange that the authors did not also examine the relationship of these multiples to the prediction of future returns (which is of greater practical importance). Still, the results are interesting:

- Earnings multiples (P/E) were superior to all others (lowest "error").
- Multiples based on forecast earnings (P/E$_{Fwd}$) were superior to those based on historical performance (P/E$_{ttm}$).
- Sales multiples (P/S) and Operating Cash Flow multiples were the worst alternatives.

The traditional P/E is usually found to be superior to other metrics for constructing value screens to select "cheap" or undervalued stocks that will outperform in the future. The Forward P/E is generally better than the trailing P/E, and both are better than P/B (compromised by problems with accounting standards) and apparently better than valuation metrics based on cash flow such as EV/EBITDA, although some versions of cash flow–based multiples seem promising. The Dividend Yield signal has lost much of its predictive power lately.

---

[69] Jing Liu, Doron Nissim and Jacob Thomas, "Is Cash Flow King in Valuations?" *Financial Analysts Journal*, Vol. 63 No. 2 (2007), pp. 56-68.

As for CAPE, the debate continues. Two recent studies, examining essentially the same data, have turned up very different statistical answers. In one, the relationship between CAPE (from 1881 to 2015) and average real returns over the subsequent 10–15 years was quite strong – CAPE "explained" almost 50% of the variation in returns.[70] But in the other, CAPE managed to account for only 13–16% of the variations in 10-year returns. Worse, the CAPE prediction 1 year ahead had virtually *zero* reliability (see Figure 5-21). The author refers to this as a failure to provide support for "market timing." But the real significance here is that the signal does not provide useful guidance with respect to reasonably near-term prospects. It is not actionable for most "ordinary" investment decisions, which may not envision a 10-year horizon. In particular, it is less than 5% accurate in predictions based on "high-Multiple" scenarios (when CAPE measures above 32), the "danger signal" episodes, where the accuracy of the metric is most critical.[71] It appears that CAPE may fail when it is most needed.

---

[70] Norbert Keimling, "Predicting Stock Market Returns Using the Shiller CAPE," *StarCapital Research,* January 2016.

[71] Wim Antoons, "The CAPE Ratio and Future Returns: A Note on Market Timing," *The Brandes Institute,* November 2018.

CHAPTER 5 APPLICATIONS: P/E AS AN INDEPENDENT VARIABLE

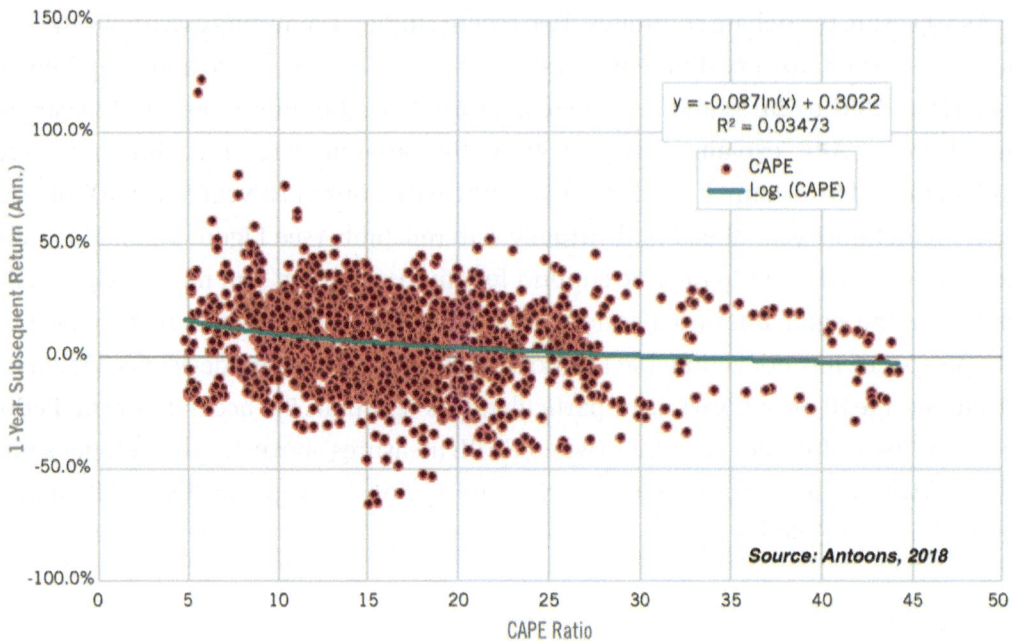

Source: Robert Shiller data (http://www.econ.yale.edu/~shiller/data.htm), as of 6/30/18. U.S. equity represented by the S&P Composite Price Index. Past performance is not a guarantee of future results. Log = Logarithmic regression.

Figure 5-21. *CAPE Fails as a Short-Term Signal*[72]

5.3 Index Construction

The use of market ratios to construct specialized indexes to capture the Value Anomaly and other factors is a mainstay of the indexing business. Value indexes like the Russell 1000 Value Index, the S&P Value Index, various "Quality" indexes, and many others use P/E and P/B screens to select their component companies. Here is the Value Indexing methodology used by index provider CRSP[73] (see Figure 5-22). Three different multiples are used. Note that the P/E_{fwd} is weighted twice as heavily as the P/E_{ttm} and the combined P/E factor is weighted twice as heavily as P/B.

---

[72]Wim Antoons, "The CAPE Ratio and Future Returns: A Note on Market Timing," The Brandes Institute, November 2018.

[73]*CRSP Indexes: Methodology Guide, January 2019* – published by the University of Chicago's **Center for Research in Security Prices**.

CHAPTER 5 APPLICATIONS: P/E AS AN INDEPENDENT VARIABLE

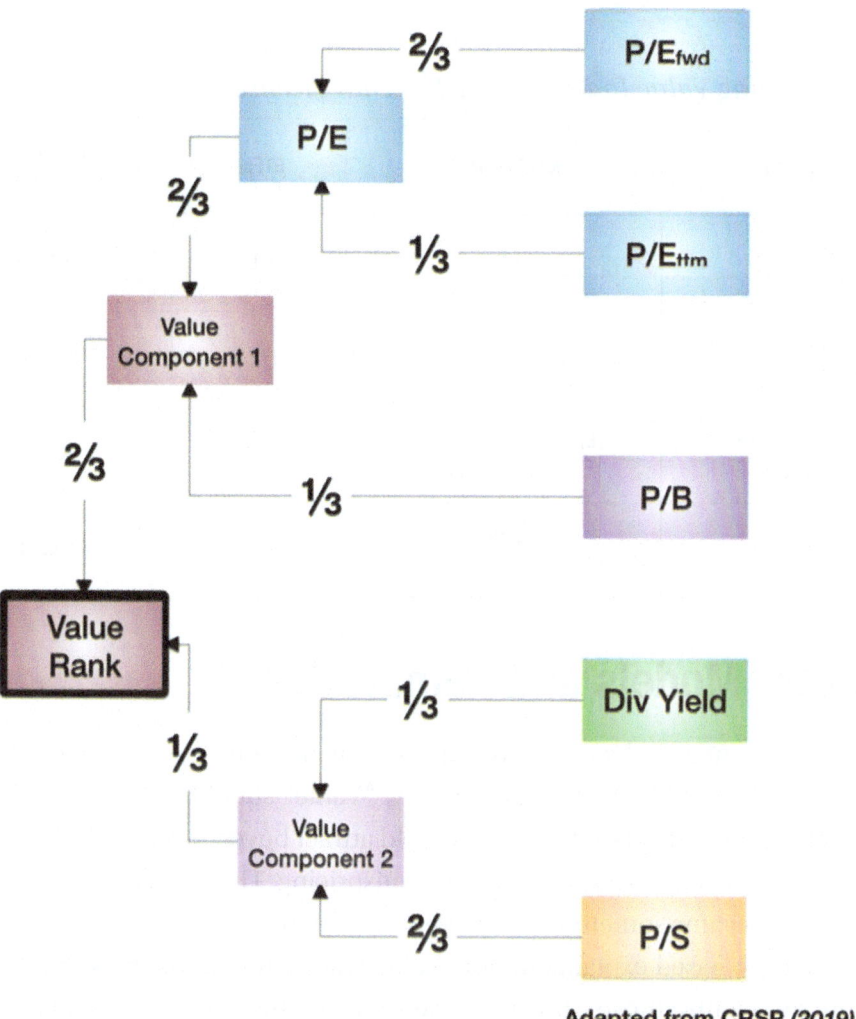

Figure 5-22. Example of Value Index Construction Methodology[74]

Growth indexes are sometimes constructed in the same way, but with a reverse "sign" (e.g., high P/E instead of low P/E). "Quality" Indexes often employ P/B.

---

[74]Adapted from *CRSP Indexes: Methodology Guide,* January 2019 – published by the University of Chicago's **Center for Research in Security Prices**

The indexes are then licensed to providers of Exchange Traded Funds (ETFs). Several of the leading value indexes and some of the ETFs that license them are shown in Table 5-1.

Table 5-1. Leading Value Indexes and ETFs That License Them

Index Name	Key Metrics	ETFs	Assets Under Mgmt. (2019)
Russell 1000 Value Index	P/B	IWD	$39 Bn
S&P 500 Value Index	P/E, P/B, P/S	IVE	$15 Bn
CRSP US Large Cap Value Index	P/E_{fwd}, P/E_{ttm}, P/B, P/S, Dividend Yield	VTV	$80 Bn
MSCI Value Index	P/B, P/E_{fwd}, Price/Operating Cashflow	VLUE	$3.2 Bn

5.4 Factor Models and "Smart Beta"

The "Value" phenomenon has been recognized for decades.[75] As we have said, from the perspective of strict Efficient Market theory, "Value" should not exist. Undervalued stocks – that is, incorrectly priced stocks – should attract buyers who will bid the price up to the "correct" level and quickly eliminate the mispricing. This does not happen.

"Value" thus became something of an embarrassment for some academics. Attempts to provide a theory-based explanation for "Value" (and other anomalies) tend to divide the field into two camps: those who would view the anomaly as a rational phenomenon, a correct pricing for a specific new source of "risk" – different from the broad market risk ("beta") – and those who view the anomaly as stemming from non-rational biases or errors inherent in human decision-making. To explain "Value," the first camp argues

---

[75] The understanding of the Value principle predates the development of academic Finance Theory; it has been observed and exploited at least since the time of Graham and Dodd (1934).

that stocks with a low P/E reflect a specific risk or set of risks associated with companies in distress of various kinds, such as "earnings depression."[76] The second camp – Behavioral Finance – explains "Value" as a manifestation of a tendency of investors to overreact to bad news (and perhaps other biases) – leading to a misperception of the company's "true value," which may persist and depress the price of the stock for a considerable period of time.

An expedient solution has been to relabel the anomalies as *Factors*.[77] This seems to have facilitated the marketing of financial products based on "Value" while sidestepping the academic controversies.[78]

---

[76] Eugene Fama and Kenneth French, "Common risk factors in the returns on stocks and bonds," *Journal of Financial Economics*, Vol. 33 (1993), pp. 3-56. Members of the "rationalist" camp often offer rather casual interpretations of the "risks" associated with supposedly undervalued companies. However, a recent study of "Value" in relation to a range of distress indicators, including credit ratings, credit spreads, leverage, and other measures, has concluded that value stocks (defined by price-to-book ratios) do **not** reflect distress risk. *"We find no evidence supporting the pricing of distress risk, and no evidence of a positive relation between distress risk and the value premium."* (Wilma de Groot and Joop Huij, "Are the Fama-French factors really compensation for distress risk?" *Journal of International Money and Finance*, Vol. 86 (2018), pp. 50-69).

[77] The term "factor" implicitly acknowledges a leaning toward the "rationalist" perspective, which now generally speaks of anomalies as "risk factors." The source of the idea is often identified as the Arbitrage Pricing Theory (APT), developed by Ross and others in the 1970s. In so many words, the theory holds simply that the expected return of a stock can be modeled by a series of "factors" – which may be seen as different types of "risk" that each carry a separate "risk premium." This structure lent itself to the (pseudo-)resolution of the problem of the anomalies by reconceptualizing them as "risk factors" that somehow contribute to the total expected return. So "Value" is related to a kind of "risk" – and the apparent mispricing of "Value" stocks is actually a correct valuation, based on including this new risk, and the accompanying risk premium, into the calculation. Market efficiency is supposedly preserved (Stephen Ross, "The arbitrage theory of capital asset pricing," *Journal of Economic Theory*, Vol 13, No. 3 (1976), pp. 341-360; and Richard Roll and Stephen Ross, "An empirical investigation of the arbitrage pricing theory," *Journal of Finance*, Vol. 35, No. 5 (1980), pp. 1073-1103).

[78] Conceptual problems remain. "Factors" are as opaque as the "anomalies" they once were. For example, two prominent "factors" today are *Low Volatility* and *Quality*. Stocks with lower-than-average volatility tend to outperform the market. Fine. But it is specious to describe low volatility as a "risk" – in fact *volatility is risk* in classical Finance Theory. Lately, a *Profitability* Factor has been identified. To no one's surprise (we assume), more profitable companies do better than less profitable companies. See R. Novy-Marx, "The Other Side of Value: The Gross Profitability Premium," *Journal of Financial Economics*, Vol. 108, No. 1 (2013), pp. 1-28; also Vikas Klara and Christan Celas, "Introducing the Profitability Factor," *MSCI*, June 2016. Available at www.msci.com/documents/10199/2ef5bba7-8448-44da-bdb3-0a102374c8d3. Even Fama and French have embraced the Profitability factor. Eugene F. Fama and Kenneth R. French, "A five-factor asset pricing model," *Journal of Financial Economics*, Vol. 116 (2015), pp. 1-22. Clearly, there is no serious argument to be made that Profitability constitutes a "risk factor."

5.4.1 The Proliferation of Factors

"Value" and "Size"[79] were the first Factors to be accepted – along with the "Market Beta" Factor – hence the "three-factor model" proposed by Fama and French.[80] In time, the official list expanded to four factors,[81] then five,[82] then six,[83] and then (less officially) hundreds...[84]

The productization of these Factors has created a new investment strategy called Factor Investing and a new category of investment vehicles, also often now known as "Smart Beta" funds,[85] which track indexes based on Factor screens. These vehicles are presented as "beta-capture" instruments because they track the indexes mechanically, without any attempt to analyze or select individual stocks.[86]

"Smart beta" reconfigures our view of the source of market risk and return. The "Risk Premium" is now seen as comprising several distinct components, each driving a putatively independent portion of the potential return[87] (see Figure 5-23). The investment premise is that by applying factors like Value or Size (but in a "passive" manner), an investor can hope to outperform the overall market. Some even claim that active stock picking ("alpha") only succeeds, where it rarely does, by providing exposure to "factor beta":

---

[79]"Size" captures the small cap anomaly, in which smaller companies have a higher return than larger companies.

[80]Eugene F. Fama and Kenneth R. French, "Common risk factors in the returns on stocks and bonds," *Journal of Financial Economics*, Vol. 33 (1993), pp. 3-56.

[81]Mark Carhart, "On Persistence in Mutual Fund Performance," *The Journal of Finance*, Vol. 52, No. 1 (March 1997), pp. 57-82.

[82]Eugene F. Fama and Kenneth R. French, "A five-factor asset pricing model," *Journal of Financial Economics*, Vol. 116 (2015), pp. 1-22.

[83]Eugene F. Fama and Kenneth R. French, "Choosing Factors," *Journal of Financial Economics*, Vol. 128 (2018), pp. 234-252.

[84]As the standard theory came apart. Campbell Harvey, Yan Liu, and Heqing Zhu, "...and the Cross-Section of Expected Returns," *The Review of Financial Studies*, Vol. 29 (2016), pp. 5-68. This study declares that a great many of these "factors" are likely spurious.

[85]Another nice marketing phrase. Many "smart beta" funds add proprietary adjustments to the basic Factors.

[86]"Beta-capture" is contrasted with "alpha-capture" – which is based on active investing and fundamental research to identify winners and losers out of the broad universe of stocks.

[87]Actually there is considerable discussion, and disagreement, concerning the degree of independence among the different factors.

CHAPTER 5　APPLICATIONS: P/E AS AN INDEPENDENT VARIABLE

> The real value of ... active management does not reflect true skill (alpha), but can in fact be explained by implicit exposures to systematic factors (betas).[88]

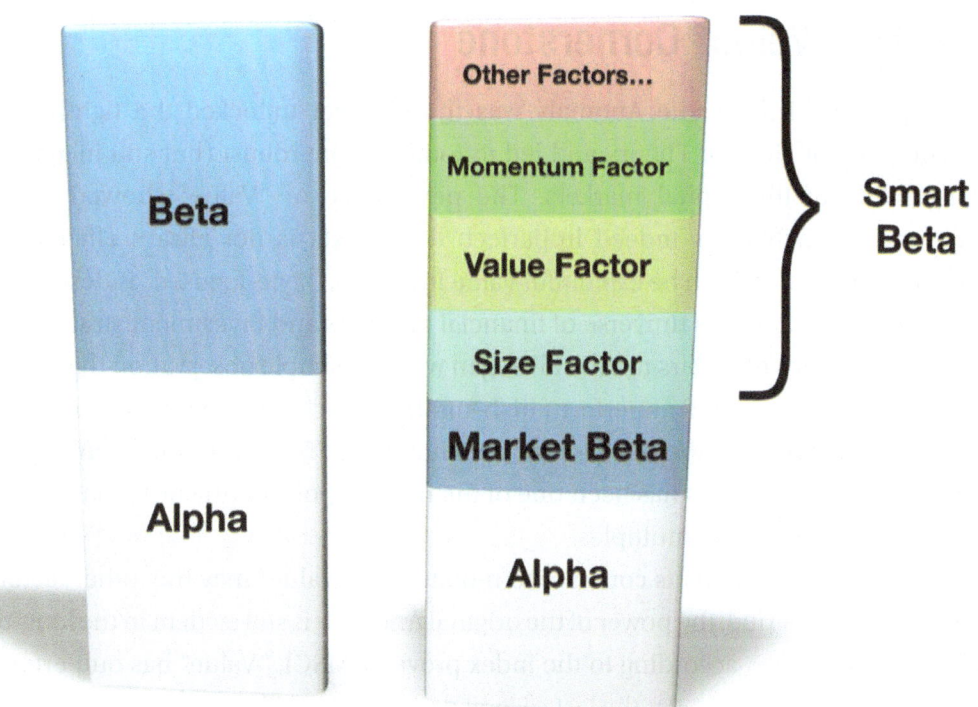

Figure 5-23. Composition of Returns – "Smart Beta"

In any case, Market multiples are among the metrics used to screen for "factors" and "smart beta," especially for the Value anomaly.

> Smart beta funds take an ordinary index and tweak it based on so-called factors, such as comparing prices of the underlying stocks with earnings.[89]

---

[88]Joop Huij et al., Robeco, *Factor Investing: Case Studies,* 2019. Available at: https://fi.intms.nl/fi_43a1c02c/files/downloads/factor-investing-case-studies.pdf

[89]Attracta Mooney, "Smart Beta Growth Engine Sputters," *Financial Times,* November 5, 2018.

CHAPTER 5   APPLICATIONS: P/E AS AN INDEPENDENT VARIABLE

Other factors – such as "Quality" – have been based on the Price/Book ratio,[90] on Return-on-Assets, or some similar ratio such as Cash Flow to Total Assets.[91]

The extension of smart beta and factor investing into the mainstream has led to the creation of many Exchange Traded Funds (ETFs) based on these principles. By 2018, "smart beta" funds were said to exceed $1 Tn in assets.[92]

5.4.2 The "Value" Cornerstone

The recognition of the Value Anomaly was the key that unlocked the tightly closed model of classical Finance Theory and led to today's more robust (but still incomplete) understanding of the capital markets. The persistence of "Value" showed that the equilibrium mechanism is indeed imperfect, the market is not always efficient, and mispricings do exist and can be exploited. Value Investing, "style-focused" indexes, Factor models, and Smart Beta – a universe of financial products and investment strategies that accounts for trillions of dollars today – all began with the simple observation that low-P/E (or P/B) stocks consistently outperform high-multiple stocks and the market as a whole. Once "Value" had pointed the way for new thinking; other "factors" began to emerge from the statistical shadows. This has been one of the most important practical consequences to date of the use of market multiples.

Even today, as the markets continue to mutate, and "Value" may trail other factors in performance for a period, the power of the original Anomaly is still evident in the long-term results. As shown here, according to the index provider MSCI, "Value" has outperformed all other important Factors over the last several decades[93] (see Figure 5-24).

---

[90]Clifford S. Asness, Andrea Frazzini, and Lasse H. Pedersen, "Quality Minus Junk," *Review of Accounting Studies*, (November 2018), pp. 1–7 (published online at: https://ezproxy.stevens.edu:2122/content/pdf/10.1007%2Fs11142-018-9470-2.pdf).

[91]Jean-Philippe Bouchaud, Stefano Ciliberti, Augustin Landier, Guillaume Simon, and David Thesmar, "The Excess Returns of Quality Stocks: A Behavioral Anomaly," *HEC Paris Research Paper No. FIN-2016-1134* (2016).

[92]Inevitably, with the growth in popularity of "smart beta," there has been a reaction; some critics now argue it has been overdone and may be a passing fad. The underlying principle of exploiting market anomalies (factors) to achieve market-beating returns is well established, however.

[93]MSCI Factor Investing, *Focus: Value* (2018).

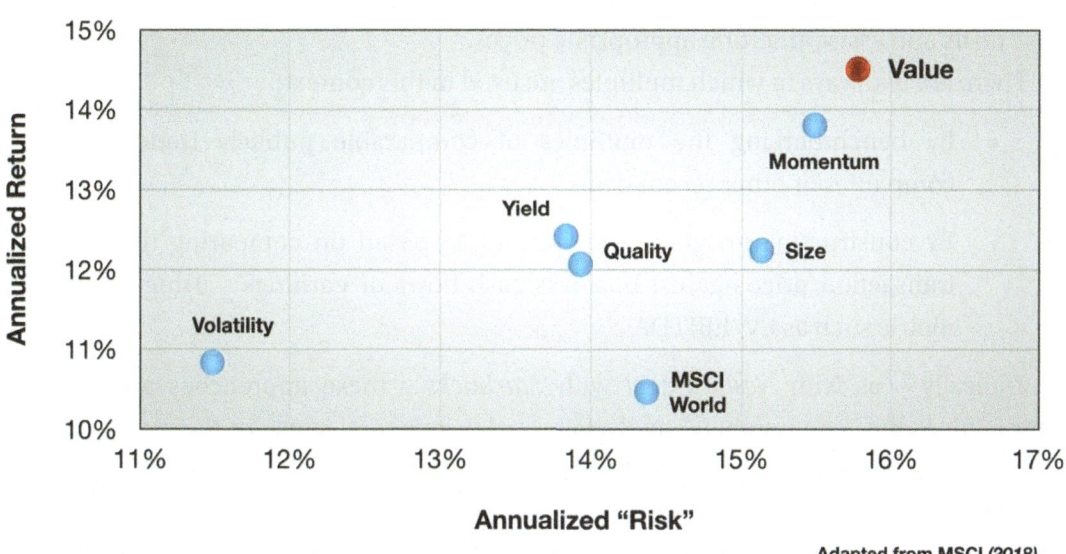

Figure 5-24. *Factor Performance Over the Long Term*[94]

5.5 Valuing Corporate Transactions

5.5.1 Deal Pricing

A lead article in the *Financial Times* begins

> *Nestlé* has agreed to a $7.15bn deal with *Starbucks* to sell its coffee products outside the U.S. brand's café chain as the Swiss group ramps up its US and global expansion plans... The $7.15bn upfront cash payment was equivalent to *15 times earnings before interest, tax, depreciation and amortization* – in line with other deals in the sector, analysts said.[95] *[Emphasis added]*

---

[94]Adapted from *MSCI Factor Investing, Focus:Value* (2018).
[95]Ralph Atkins, "Nestlé Adds Starbucks to US Blend," *Financial Times*, May 8, 2018.

CHAPTER 5 APPLICATIONS: P/E AS AN INDEPENDENT VARIABLE

Large transactions involving complex businesses can be difficult to value. They often lack an immediate reference point of a public market price. Multiples can shed light on these deals and assist in setting appropriate prices.

There are two ways in which multiples are used in this context:

- By benchmarking the multiples of comparable publicly traded companies or other recent deals[96]
- By constructing an endogenous multiple based on comparing the transaction price against business cash flows or earnings – using a metric such as EV/EBITDA

Typically – as with *Nestlé's* deal with *Starbucks* – these approaches are used in combination: the "comparables" analysis provides a general sense of the market value, and the endogenous analysis of cash flows provides a window on the fundamental value of the business at the proposed transaction price.

Private equity investors rely heavily on multiples – especially EV/EBITDA[97] – to understand the "market value" of their transactions, to compare potential entry and exit prices.[98] Even where external benchmarks are unavailable, an alternative form of the ratio can be calculated: it is simply the proposed purchase price (including the assumption of the firm's debt – assumed to be equal to EV), set against the current or projected cash flows, to yield a serviceable version of the EV/EBITDA ratio. This can be benchmarked to suitable public or private comparables.

---

[96] **The American Institute of Certified Public Accountants** has a draft Valuation Guide for valuing venture capital and private equity investments. The use of Multiples from comparables is described as follows: *"Once the guideline public companies have been identified, financial information is gathered on each and comparative metrics that can be applied to the subject portfolio company are calculated... These metrics, commonly called multiples, are typically ratios of enterprise value or market value of equity to an underlying financial data point such as revenue, EBITDA, net income, or book value."* (AICPA Task Force, *Valuation of Portfolio Company Investments of Venture Capital and Private Equity Funds and Other Investment Companies*, Draft (May 15, 2018), paragraph 5.19).

[97] *"The EBITDA multiple is the most important valuation ratio in the PE industry."* (Ann-Kristin Achleitner, Reiner Braun, and Nico Engel, "Value creation and pricing in buyouts: Empirical evidence from Europe and North America," *Review of Financial Economics*, Vol. 20 (2011), pp. 146–161).

[98] The AICPA Valuation Guide offers extensive advice on the selection, weighting, and adjustment of multiples for private equity transactions: AICPA Task Force, *Valuation of Portfolio Company Investments of Venture Capital and Private Equity Funds and Other Investment Companies*, Draft (May 15, 2018), paragraphs 5.19–5.45.

CHAPTER 5   APPLICATIONS: P/E AS AN INDEPENDENT VARIABLE

A large study examined over 3300 private equity transactions (leveraged buyouts) over a 25-year period and found that "besides leverage and operational improvements, EBITDA multiple expansion is a fundamental factor in explaining equity returns."[99] Indeed, to measure the value creation of a particular investment, EV/EBITDA is the essential metric, as stylized in Figure 5-25.

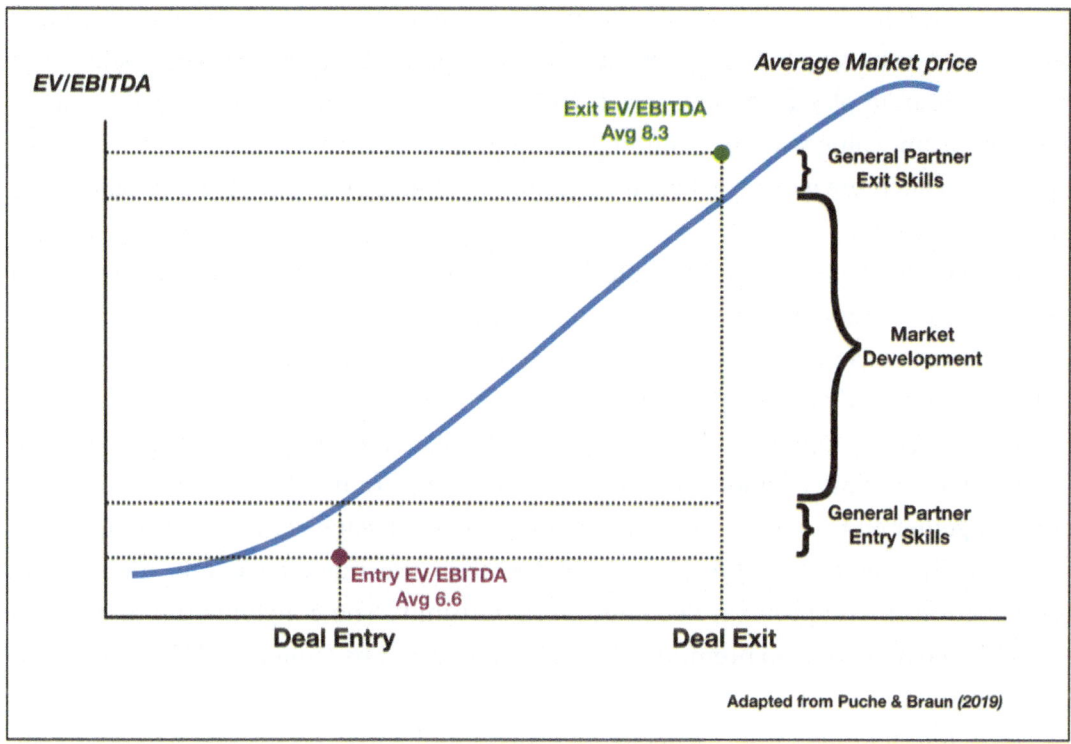

Figure 5-25. *A Private Equity Model*[100]

The authors found that the median entry point for the deals in their sample carried an EV/EBITDA of 6.6. The median exit price had an EV/EBITDA of 8.3. (The average holding time of the investment was a little over 4 years.) Multiple expansion accounted for a third of the value created.

---

[99]Benjamin Puche and Reiner Braun, "International Evidence on Value Creation in Private Equity Transactions," *Journal of Applied Corporate Finance*, Vol. 27, No. 4 (Fall 2015), pp. 105–122.

[100]Adapted from Benjamin Puche and Reiner Braun, "Deal pricing and returns in private equity," *The Journal of Alternative Investments*, Vol. 21, No. 3 (Winter 2019), pp. 70–85.

5.5.2 Sum-of-the-Parts Analyses (the Conglomerate Discount)

Multiples are useful in the analysis of the phenomenon known as the "conglomerate discount" – as described in the previous chapter (Section 4.2.6). There we saw how the P/E multiple can signal the existence, and severity, of the penalty for an over-diversified business portfolio. Multiples can also be used to calculate the increase in value that could result from breaking up the company into its components. Restructuring a diversified firm into a set of pure play companies, each focused on a single business, is often a way to gain significant value without assuming earnings growth. The use of multiples to make the case for such breakups has become a common strategy for activist shareholders and managements.[101]

The technique is called Sum-of-the-Parts Analysis. Essentially, each business unit in the diversified company is analyzed separately and valued as though it were a standalone entity. Its earnings or cash flows are calculated separately. An appropriate comparable public company – a "pure play" in the same line of business – is identified.[102] The pure play's market multiple is applied to the earnings of the isolated business unit, and a valuation is arrived at. Similar valuations for all the business units of the diversified company are added together and compared against the current market value of the entire company.

Typically, the sum of the parts is higher than the market capitalization of the diversified firm. The problem becomes an opportunity. The conglomerate discount is reenvisioned as a breakup premium, the value that would be "unlocked" if the company were broken up.

Tyco International was a highly diversified industrial conglomerate. Following a scandal in the 2000s, the company languished. In January 2007, a *Barron's* article made the case for a breakup.[103] Analyzing the three main business units (in healthcare,

---

[101] Note that we do not comment here on the rationale for the existence of the conglomerate discount or why "over-diversification" is strategically disadvantageous. There are a variety of arguments to explain the phenomenon, which it is beyond the scope of this book to review. The existence of the discount is now well established, regardless of its exact causes.

[102] **The American Institute of Certified Public Accountants** offers extensive guidance on the selection of appropriate comparable companies for such valuations. AICPA Task Force, *Valuation of Portfolio Company Investments of Venture Capital and Private Equity Funds and Other Investment Companies*, Draft (May 15, 2018), paragraphs 5.10–5.17 especially.

[103] Jonathan Laing, "Cleaning Up on Tyco's Breakup," *Barron's*, January 7, 2007. The idea of a breakup had already been floated by Tyco's management, but not yet executed.

CHAPTER 5   APPLICATIONS: P/E AS AN INDEPENDENT VARIABLE

electronics, and security systems) as hypothetically separate companies that would achieve higher multiples of earnings (based on comparisons with pure play companies in the respective sectors), *Barron's* estimated that "shares of the three spin-offs together could be worth 30% more than *Tyco's* current stock, thanks to higher price-earning ratios"[104] (see Figure 5-26).

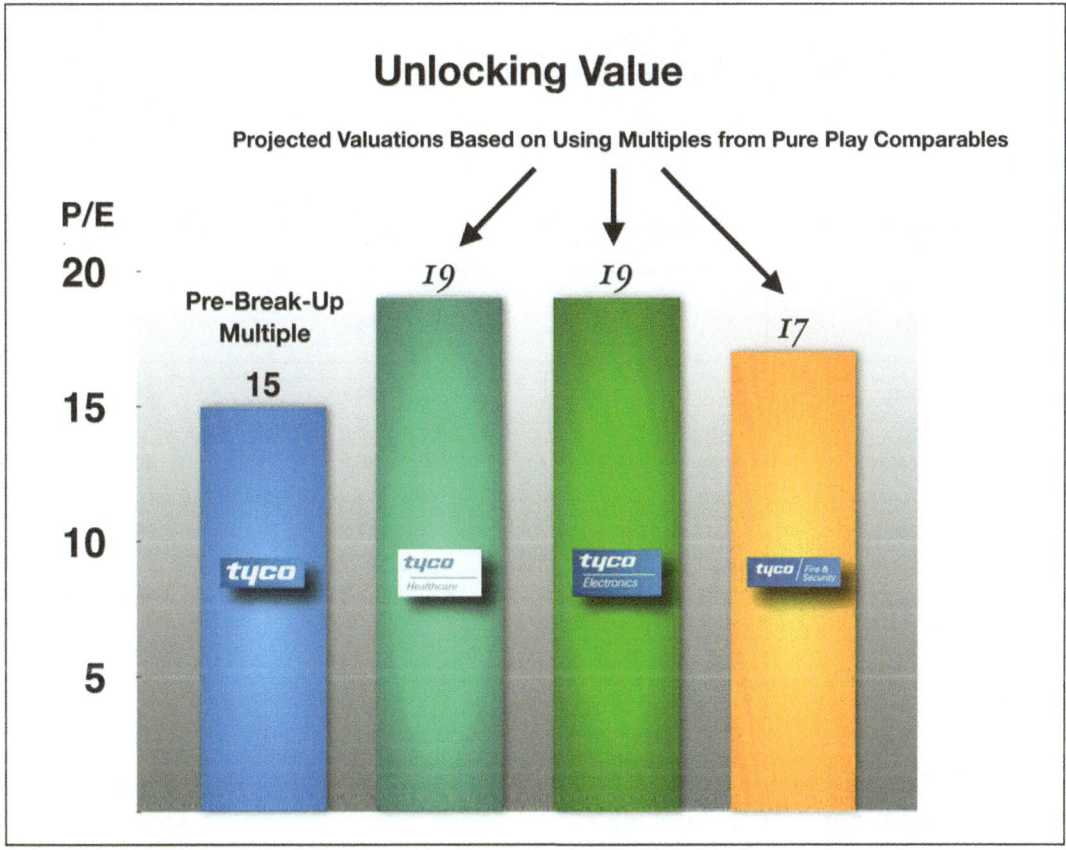

Figure 5-26. Sum-of-the-Parts

---

[104]In the event, the breakup did occur later in 2007 and was followed by a further breakup in 2012. The value creation was more modest than *Barron's* hoped, but still beat the market average in the following several years.

297

CHAPTER 5   APPLICATIONS: P/E AS AN INDEPENDENT VARIABLE

Even companies with more similar businesses may offer a potential for value creation through a breakup. In 2015, *Barron's* reported on a sum-of-the-parts analysis of the Fortune 50 consumer products giant *Proctor & Gamble*, which argued for a breakup premium of 21%[105] (see Table 5-2).

Table 5-2. Sum-of-the-Parts Analysis of Proctor & Gamble

Proctor & Gamble (2015)			P&G
Segment	2016E EBITDA ($Bn)	EV/EBITDA (from pure play comparables)	2016E EV ($Bn)
Beauty	3.2	15.2	49.2
Grooming	2.6	11.7	31.0
Healthcare	1.9	16.2	30.8
Fabric & Home	4.5	17.2	78.0
Baby, Feminine & Family	4.8	12.1	58.2
Total Company			247.2
Value per Share			~ $91/share
Then-Current Stock Price			$75/share
Breakup Premium			~ 21%

---

[105] Leslie P. Norton, "It's Time for P&G To Split Up," *Barron's*, November 23, 2015.

At the time, *P&G* resisted the call for a radical restructuring, but did move to spin off several business units and consolidate others. The analysis of the pure play multiples has pointed the way, in part.

Is sum-of-the-parts an accurate value-forecasting technique? The actual recovery of "locked up" value can be difficult to assess. In some cases, the improvement is obvious and dramatic. In 2016, *Alcoa* broke up into two companies focusing on different parts of the aluminum industry supply chain (roughly extraction and refining aluminum as a commodity *vs.* engineering and manufacturing high-value aluminum products). In the four months before *Alcoa* announced its plan, its share price had languished, rising just 1.8% (vs. 3.3% for the S&P 500 index). In the four months following the breakup, the combined value of the two new entities surged 60% (against a 12% rise in the S&P 500).

Sum-of-the-parts analysis is a cornerstone of much M&A analysis today and an important application of market ratios such as the P/E and EV/EBITDA.

5.6 Diagnosing Market Regimes

Passive investing strategies now account for nearly 50% of the investment universe. This has refocused many investors away from following company-specific events and more on understanding broad market trends. "Regime changes" in the financial markets – volatility spikes, market price corrections, the reverberations of central bank policy shifts – have become more important in determining market returns over the past two decades. There is an obvious interest in being able to predict these shifts.

Multiples are sometimes seen as providing useful signals of coming changes in broad market trends. For example, regular attention is drawn to the market P/E as it reaches high levels, based on the view that bear markets are pre-signaled by unusually high market multiples. Dividend yield (D/P) levels in the stock market are often compared to bond yields to discern market turning points:

> If dividend yields exceed bond yields, that tends to signal that equities have reached a trough. In the past 20 years, the dividend yield on the S&P 500 exceeded the two-year bond yield for only about a year. That was from 2002 to 2003, closely matching what turned out to be a bottom in the market.[106]

---

[106]John Authers, "The Short View," *Financial Times,* February 5, 2008.

CHAPTER 5   APPLICATIONS: P/E AS AN INDEPENDENT VARIABLE

Unfortunately, this was written in February 2008 as the dividend yield again surpassed the bond yield. But of course that time it was not a trough, but a top; just months later we saw the near collapse of the US stock market. The signals are not always accurate. Still, the use of multiples to predict changes in the "weather" in the stock market is very popular.

Two examples of market shifts where equity investors have a strong interest in receiving an early and accurate warning are (1) the effects of monetary policy changes on equity values and (2) the development of "bubbles."

5.6.1 Monetary Policy Impact

The long-term relationship between stocks and bonds (especially Treasurys) is a vexed topic in investing theory and practice. It highlights the linkage between monetary policy and stock market values. This relationship has gone through very different phases. The chart here shows the relevant multiples – P/E (reversed as E/P) *vs.* Treasury bond yield – for the equities market and the bond market. The relationship was essentially negative (or disconnected) from the 1920s until the 1970s, at which point the growing influence of monetarist economic thinking on Fed policy contributed to the emergence of a strong positive correlation[107] (see Figure 5-27).

---

[107]Clifford Asness, "Fight the Fed Model," *Journal of Portfolio Management,* Vol. 30, No.1 (Fall 2003), pp 11–24.

CHAPTER 5   APPLICATIONS: P/E AS AN INDEPENDENT VARIABLE

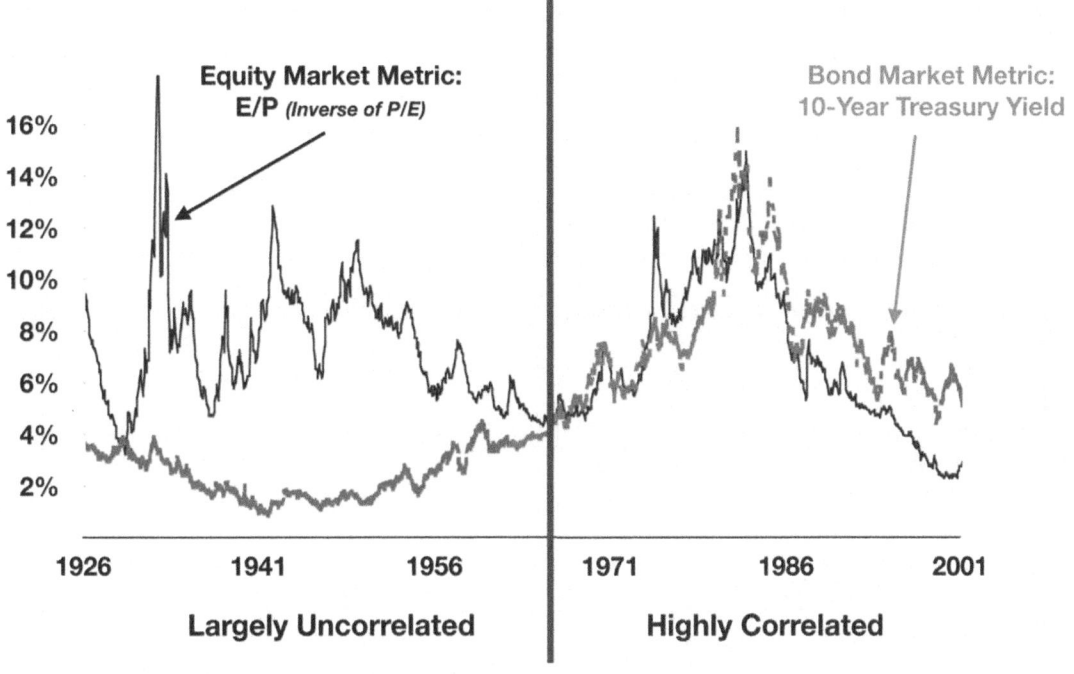

Figure 5-27. Equity vs. Bond Market Valuations[108]

The correlation became so strong that investors began to lean on the so-called "Fed Model" (see Chapter 4, Section 4.3.7), looking to Fed interest rate policy to drive market valuations, using the multiples as a guide.

Following the 2008 financial crisis, the relationship has mutated. Massive central bank bond-buying – "Quantitative Easing" – drove up bond prices and drove down bond yields[109] (see Figure 5-28). The equities multiple (E/P, or "Earnings Yield" here) has surged ahead of bond yields, both causing and reflecting a massive transfer of investor demand away

---

[108]Adapted from Clifford Asness, "Fight the Fed Model," *Journal of Portfolio Management,* Vol. 30, No. 1 (Fall 2003), pp. 11–24.

[109]Ed Yardeni, Joe Abbott, and Mali Quintana, "Stock Market Briefings: S&P 500 Earnings Yield," *Yardeni Research,* June 1, 2019.

CHAPTER 5   APPLICATIONS: P/E AS AN INDEPENDENT VARIABLE

from low-yielding bonds and toward equities, driving the long Bull market that followed the crisis. By many measures, the market regime of the last decade (2009–2019) has been unusual, with many traditional indicators and strategies undergoing significant shifts in behavior. (We have noted the languishing of "Value" strategies in Section 5.2.) Yardeni inverts these metrics to portray the relative valuations of earnings derived from these two asset classes; the regime shift is dramatic (see Figure 5-29).

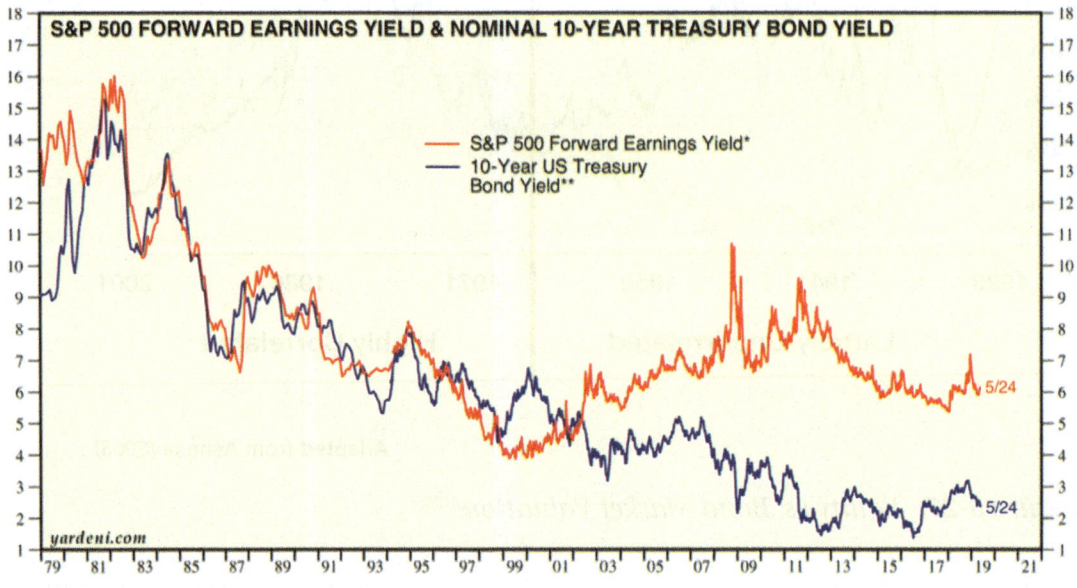

Figure 5-28. *Equity vs. Bond Market Valuations – Post-Crisis*[110]

---

[110]Ed Yardeni, Joe Abbott, and Mali Quintana, "Stock Market Briefings: S&P 500 Earnings Yield," *Yardeni Research*, June 1, 2019. Reproduced by permission of Yardeni Research.

CHAPTER 5   APPLICATIONS: P/E AS AN INDEPENDENT VARIABLE

Of course much attention is given to the *direct* signals from the Fed: policy statements, ratings increases, minutes of Fed meetings, and public comments by the Fed members (see Chapter 4, Section 4.3.4). But the transmission of these signals to the stock market is not always straightforward, and the effects are not always the same.[111] Quantitative Easing policies have generally stimulated equity valuations (raising P/E levels). Quantitative Tightening might be expected to reverse this process. But the relationship is not mechanical; valuations, and market movements, seem also to depend upon the macroeconomic context within which the Central Bank is acting. Market multiples are therefore closely watched for signals of just *how* the market will interpret the Fed's moves and what the effects on equity values may be.

---

[111] In June 2013, Ben Bernanke proposed a modest slowdown in bond purchases by the Fed – and the financial markets erupted in turmoil, the so-called "Taper Tantrum." The equity markets fell 5% in the next week, and effects on bond prices were even more exaggerated. Five years later, the Fed chairman (Powell) recalled *"The taper tantrum left scars on anybody who was working at the Fed at that time"* (Binyamin Appelbaum, "Effects of the 2013 'Taper Tantrum' Linger Over Fed Policy," *The New York Times*, January 11, 2019).

Five years later the Federal Reserve began actually reducing its holdings of Treasures – "Quantitative Tightening" – and the stock markets seem to have taken it in stride, or even as a bullish signal, rising strongly in the months following. Matt Phillips, "'Quantitative Tightening': The Hot Topic in Markets Right Now," *The New York Times,* January 30, 2019. The equity markets rose nearly 10% in the month following the initiation of QT.

CHAPTER 5 APPLICATIONS: P/E AS AN INDEPENDENT VARIABLE

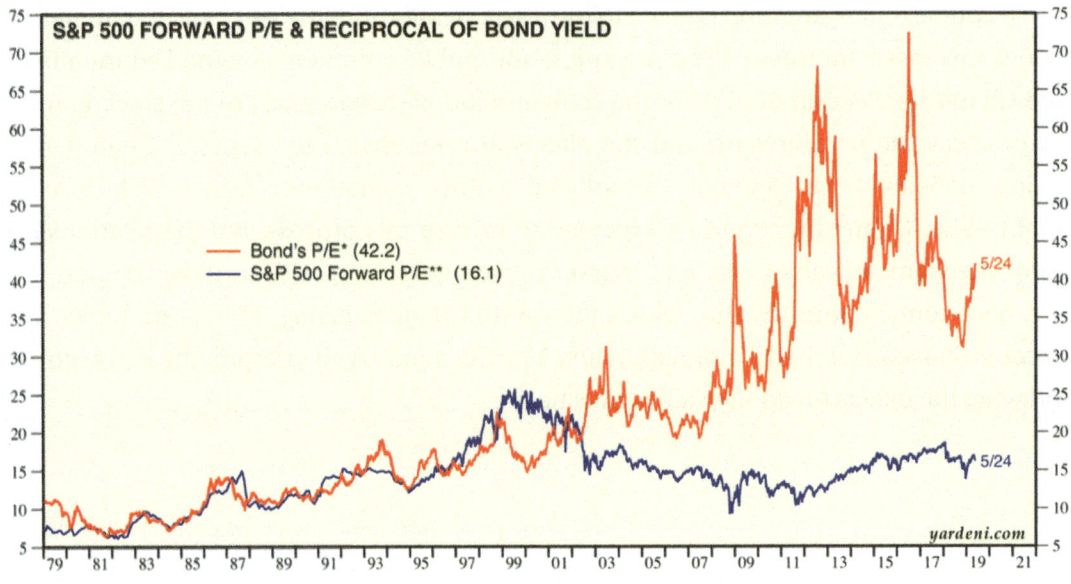

* Reciprocal of 10-year US Treasury bond yield.
** 52-week forward consensus expected S&P 500 operating earnings per share. Monthly through March 1994, weekly thereafter.
Source: Standard & Poor's and I/B/E/S data by Refinitiv.

Figure 5-29. Equity P/E vs. Bond P/E[112]

5.6.2 Bubble Detection

When bubbles are forming...another warning sign is when prices [surge past] an asset's underlying value. With stocks, one popular way to measure value is to divide the markets price by 10-year average earnings after adjusting for inflation *[i/.e., use the CAPE$_1$]*.[113]

Journalists commonly cite the P/E to forecast, or to retrospectively diagnose, the development of a "bubble" – a state of severe overvaluation affecting a sector or an entire market. For example, the dot-com bubble of 1998–2001 is clearly visible in the P/E trend. The Market P/E briefly reached double its prior "normal" level[114] (see Figure 5-30).

---

[112]Ed Yardeni, Joe Abbott, and Mali Quintana, "Stock Market Briefings: S&P 500 Earnings Yield," *Yardeni Research,* June 1, 2019. Reproduced by permission of *Yardeni Research.*

[113]Joe Light, "How to Spot a Market Bubble," *The Wall Street Journal,* April 18, 2014.

[114]Savita Subramanian, "2017 – The Year Ahead: Euphoria or Fiscal Fizzle," *Equity and Quant Strategy, Bank of America/Merrill Lynch,* November 22, 2016.

CHAPTER 5   APPLICATIONS: P/E AS AN INDEPENDENT VARIABLE

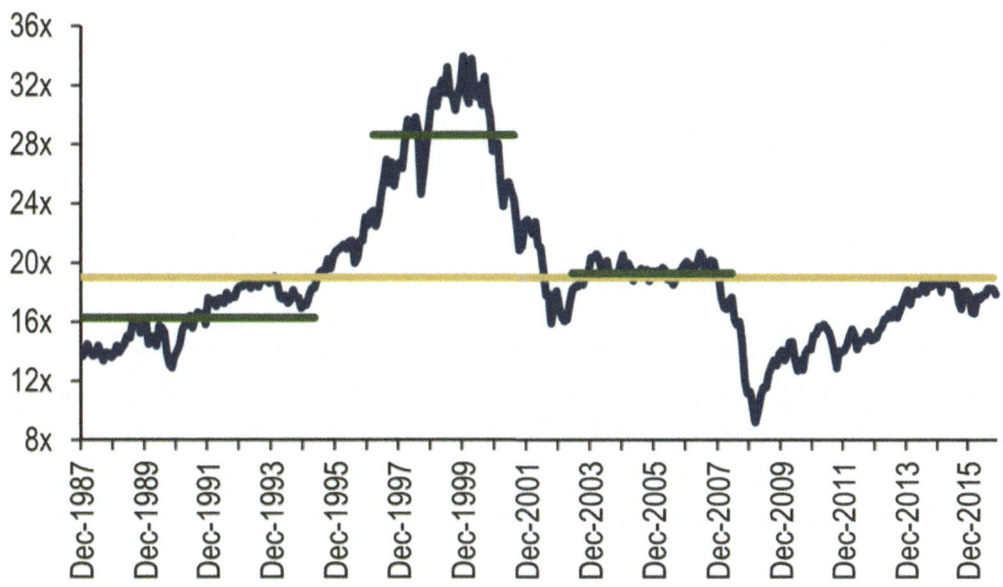

Source: BofA Merrill Lynch US Equity & US Quant Strategy

Figure 5-30. *Bubble Detection with the P/E: The Dot-Com Case*[115]

Detecting and understanding bubbles has been an important concern for investors, and central bankers, for centuries.[116] Market multiples ought to provide clear warning signs. The difficulty is that P/E ratios vary a great deal even within the "normal" range. From 1982 to 1998 (a bull market), the S&P price-earnings ratio more than tripled – a larger percentage increase than the "bubble" that followed. When did the market cross the line into overvaluation? How can we distinguish between a healthy bull market and an unhealthy and dangerous bubble?

---

[115]Savita Subramanian, "2017 – The Year Ahead: Euphoria or Fiscal Fizzle," Equity and Quant Strategy, *Bank of America/Merrill Lynch,* November 22, 2016. Reprinted by permission. Copyright © 2019 Bank of America Corporation ("BAC"). The use of the preceding reference in no way implies that BAC or any of its affiliates endorses the views or interpretation or the use of such information or acts as any endorsement of author's use of such information. The information is provided "as is," and none of BAC or any of its affiliates warrants the accuracy or completeness of the information.

[116]The coinage of the term "bubble" to refer to overexcited, overvalued financial markets dates back to the 1700s.

CHAPTER 5 APPLICATIONS: P/E AS AN INDEPENDENT VARIABLE

Once again, the "Fed Model" is thought to be useful:

> The Federal Reserve Model...captures the tendency of P/E multiples to rise and fall (inversely) with interest rates. Such a model has never been officially sanctioned by the Federal Reserve but is widely followed in the financial community. [It] posits an empirical relationship between the P/E (or earnings/price (E/P)) ratios and the 10-year Treasury rate of interest.[117]

The relationship between these two valuation metrics – one for the stock market and the other for the bond market – can be interpreted as a "mispricing metric," by calculating the hypothetical value of the "P/E-in-equilibrium" (i.e., assuming the past correlation) and comparing it to the actual P/E, to identify periods of significant overvaluation (bubbles). This relationship "explains" about two-thirds of the variation in the P/E between 1970 and 2004 (statistically, a rather strong result) (see Figure 5-31).

---

[117]Burton Malkiel, "Models of Stock Market Predictability," *The Journal of Financial Research*, Vol. 27, No. 4 (Winter 2004), pp. 449–459.

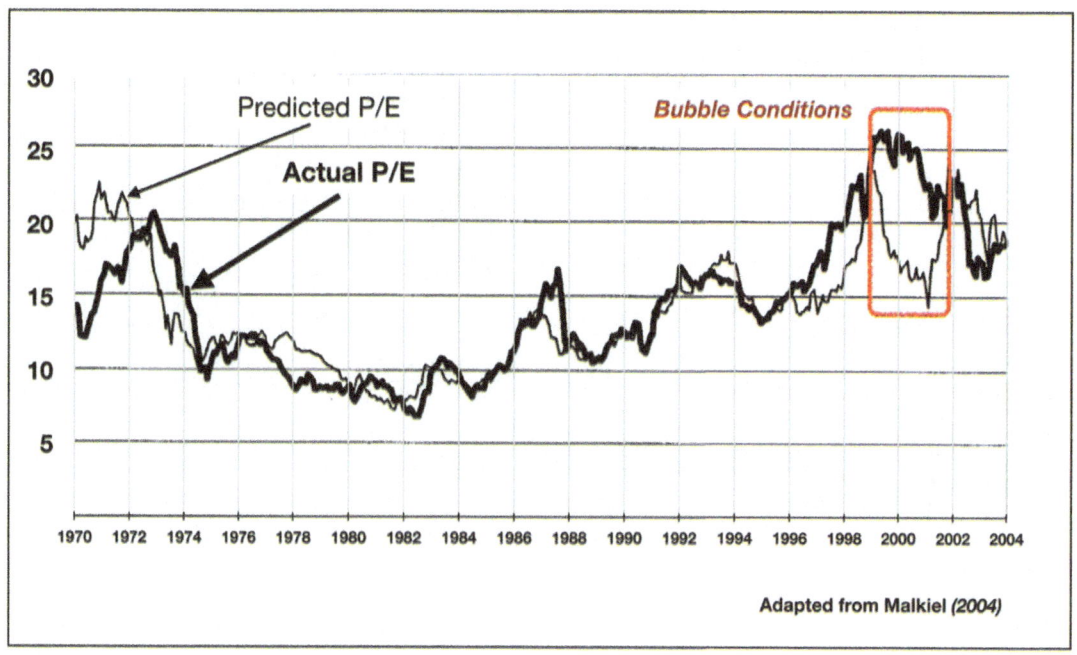

Figure 5-31. *Actual P/E vs. "Predicted P/E"*[118]

Of course, the same measure can potentially signal mispricings in the bond market. By this metric, the market never "returned to normal" after the dot-com bubble. This is in line with the comment cited earlier regarding the missing mean reversions in the equities market and the disappearance of "Value" over the last several years.[119] Especially after the 2008 financial crisis, the Fed Model metric began to signal a very different relationship, with Bonds much more expensive relative to Stocks than had been the case before 2003[120] (see Figure 5-32).

---

[118]Adapted from Burton Malkiel, "Models of Stock Market Predictability," *The Journal of Financial Research*, Vol. 27, No. 4 (Winter 2004), pp. 449–459.

[119]Brian Kantor and Christopher Holdsworth, "2013 Nobel Prize Revisited: Do Shiller's Models Really Have Predictive Power?" *Journal of Applied Corporate Finance*, (Spring 2014), pp. 101–108.

[120]James Mackintosh, "Uber Poisoned an Already Sick IPO Market," *The Wall Street Journal*, May 15, 2019.

CHAPTER 5   APPLICATIONS: P/E AS AN INDEPENDENT VARIABLE

Figure 5-32.   *Relative Prices for Equities vs. Bonds*[121]

5.6.3 Illuminating the "Fine Structure" of Market Regimes

Bull markets are associated with high and rising P/E ratios and bear markets with low and falling ratios. But market multiples can also reveal the internal structure and dynamics of these trends, as well as illuminating some of the more opaque market regimes.

---

[121]James Mackintosh, "Uber Poisoned an Already Sick IPO Market," *The Wall Street Journal*, May 15, 2019. Reproduced by permission from *The Wall Street Journal*.

CHAPTER 5   APPLICATIONS: P/E AS AN INDEPENDENT VARIABLE

For example, the phenomenon described as a "Maturity Reset" in Chapter 4 (Section 4.2.1) is created by a decline in a firm's P/E multiple – even while revenues and earnings are rising steadily. Highly successful companies – such as Walmart, Microsoft, Cisco, Intel, Coca-Cola – went through the decade of the 2000s without gaining significant value – despite impressive growth in their businesses[122] (see Table 5-3).

Table 5-3. Maturity Reset

Company	Sales Growth 2000-2010	Earnings Growth 2000-2010	Market Cap Growth 2000-2010	P/E 2000	P/E 2010
WMT	2.5x	2.8x	0.81x *(19% decline)*	45	14
MSFT	2.7x	2.0x	0.88x *(12% decline)*	64	11
CSCO	2.1x	2.9x	0.43x *(57% decline)*	100	15
INTC	1.3x	1.1x	0.51x *(49% decline)*	24	11
KO	1.8x	5.4x	0.97x *(3% decline)*	67	12

A fundamental investor looking just at the company's performance metrics (sales and earnings) would likely find this pattern confounding. Robust earnings growth is classically supposed to be the main driver of the P/E ratio itself (this is almost a point of orthodoxy in Finance theory). Yet there are times when it doesn't hold or where the significance of the P/E and other multiples changes.

In fact this phenomenon was not limited to these few companies; the same pattern prevailed for the market as a whole during these ten years, as shown in Table 5-4.

---

[122] Figures here are based on year end for 2000 and year end for 2010.

CHAPTER 5   APPLICATIONS: P/E AS AN INDEPENDENT VARIABLE

Table 5-4. Market Maturity Reset

	Sales per Share Growth 2000-2010	Earnings per Share Growth 2000-2010	Market Cap Growth 2000-2010	P/E 2000	P/E 2010
S&P 500	1.3x	2.3x	0.97x (3%decline)	26.4	16.2

It has been called a "range-bound market." The strong fundamental performance of these companies, and indeed of the entire private sector – doubling earnings per share over the decade – is offset by a decline in the multiple. As expressed by a prominent practitioner

> Over the last 100 years, every time we had a secular bull market it lasted 16-17 years. But the markets that followed were not bear markets; they were range-bound markets…. In a range bound market, you have high starting valuations, which are a byproduct of the secular bull market….
>
> There are two forces working against each other: growing earnings and contracting P/E multiples… Range-bound markets are not caused by horrible earnings growth; in fact, earnings growth during range-bound markets is not much different from bull markets. As P/E's compress they go from being your friend to your enemy.[123]

A range-bound market is a true macro-regime – similar to bull and bear markets. It is a long-term process of structural adjustment which should signal to investors a need for adapting different strategies – and, in particular, paying more attention to the behavior of the market multiples than to the traditional fundamentals alone.

---

[123]The concept of a range-bound market has been developed in detail by Vitaliy Katsenelson. His books include *Active Value Investing: Making Money in Range-Bound Markets,* Wiley (2007), and *The Little Book of Sideways Markets: How to Make Money in Markets That Go Nowhere*, Wiley (2010). The quotes here are drawn from an interview with Katsenelson that appeared in *Barron's*: Lawrence C. Strauss, "Home on the Range," *Barron's*, September 21, 2009. Note that the term "range-bound market" is also used in a more tactical sense to describe a stock that is stuck in a trading range, which may have nothing to do with the complex dynamics of fundamentals vs. P/E multiple described here.

Another example: *Goldman Sachs* has analyzed the pattern of recent recoveries after a bear market, to reveal an interesting pattern in the evolution of P/E multiples as the market rallies from a major setback. In a report entitled "The Multiple Mystery: At What P/E Should the Market Trade?" *Goldman* analyzed the 2008/2009 market crisis and mapped the recovery pattern onto the average of other recoveries from 1980 to 2002.[124] They found that a recovery (leading often to the beginnings of a new bull market) goes through two distinct phases. In the first phase, share prices are driven by an expansion of the Multiple, rather than Earnings. In the second phase, Multiple expansion slows, stops, and may even reverse slightly. But share prices continue to climb as Earnings improve. The first phase anticipates the recovery of corporate Earnings by about three quarters. The second phase comprises the realization of the Earnings rebound as the economy actually emerges from the recession (which officially ended in June 2009). Writing in October, the authors summarized their argument:

> Historically, the market multiple has expanded by an average of 34% during the first 10 months following the bear market troughs in 1982, 1987, 1990, and 2002 (10 months post-trough in the current episode would be year-end 2009). After the initial expansion period, P/E multiples typically remained flat or contracted slightly over the subsequent 12 months.
>
> Multiple compression does not necessarily mean the S&P 500 must trade lower. In fact, history suggests that the market index level continues to rise even as the multiple stays flat or even declines. Multiple expansion typically drives market returns during the initial 10-month period after a bear market trough. Subsequent equity market returns are primarily earnings-driven as rising forward EPS estimates drive share prices higher.

Two charts portray this phenomenon. The first chart aligns the market price patterns for the S&P 500 for the five bear markets in this period. The price troughs are set at *zero* on the X-axis. Although the 2008 crisis involved a decline from a much higher initial level than the past average, the recovery in market prices tracked the pattern of the average of the previous recoveries (see Figure 5-33).

---

[124]David Kostin et al., "The Multiple Mystery: At What P/E Should the Market Trade?" *US Equity Views – Goldman Sachs Global Economics*, October 1, 2009.

CHAPTER 5   APPLICATIONS: P/E AS AN INDEPENDENT VARIABLE

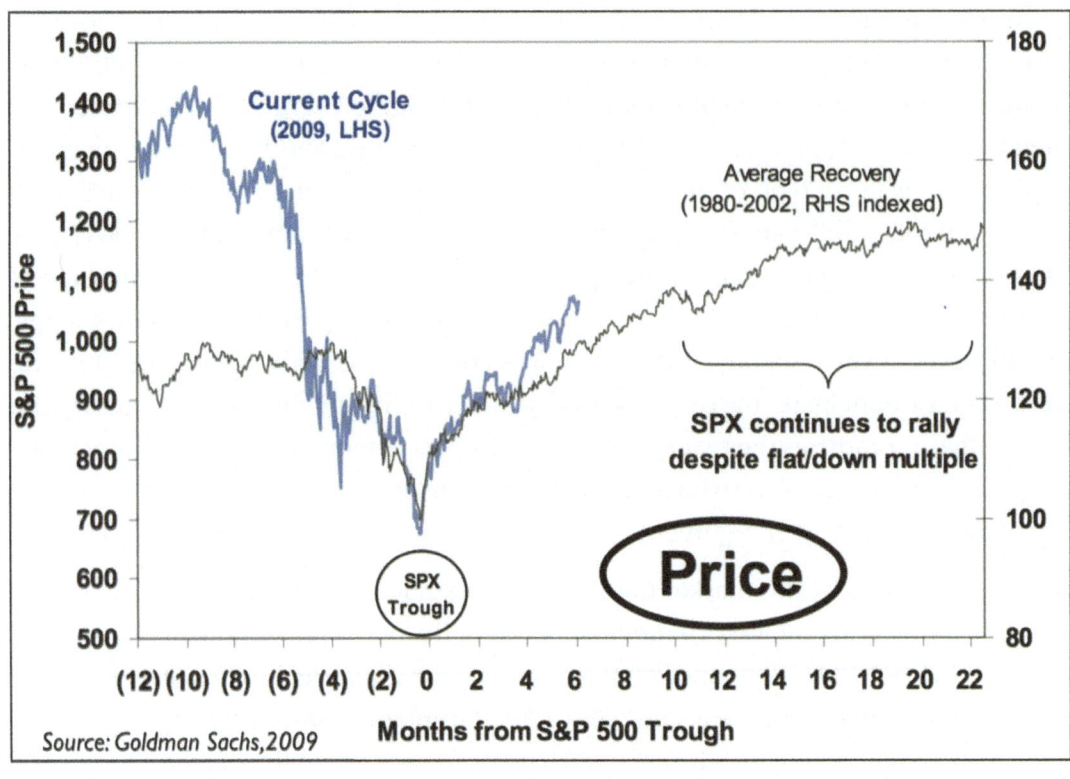

Figure 5-33. The Shape of Price Trends in Bear Markets and Recoveries[125]

The second chart shows the pattern in the P/E multiples. Note that in the case of the 2008 crash, *the P/E multiple began to turn four months before the average turning point of the previous recoveries.* The expansion of the multiple was dramatic – nearly 60% from the absolute bottom of the P/E trough (month -4) and 30% from the price trough (month 0). Also note that in the average of the previous recoveries, the multiple expansion stalled after month 10 (second chart), but prices continued to rise because earnings growth was beginning again (first chart) (see Figure 5-34).

---

[125]David Kostin et al., "The Multiple Mystery: At What P/E Should the Market Trade?" *US Equity Views – Goldman Sachs Global Economics,* October 1, 2009. Reproduced by permission.

CHAPTER 5   APPLICATIONS: P/E AS AN INDEPENDENT VARIABLE

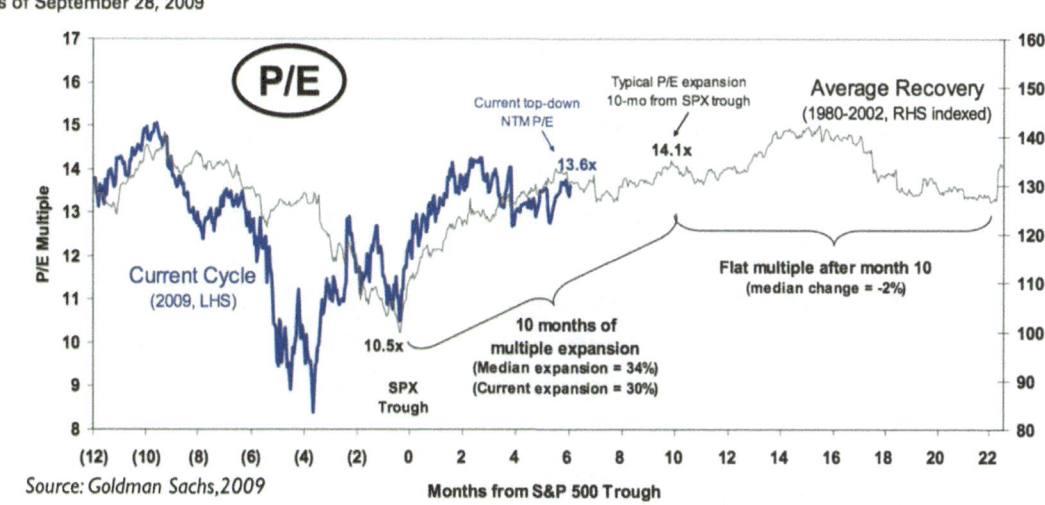

Figure 5-34. *P/E Trends in Bear Markets and Recoveries*[126]

Based on this analysis, the *Goldman* study predicted a decline in the multiple in the following quarters, and this was observed. But by then, the fundamentals were driving share prices once again.

Market multiples have found their primary application as a tool for creating simple investing strategies through the construction of "Value" screens. They have also been looked to for signals of the potential onset of changes in the market regime (although they prove less accurate in this application).

Where do we go from here?

The *Goldman* study displays a creative use of the P/E multiple to forecast market movements. It is suggestive of the rich information that the multiples contain – beyond the simple "overvalued or undervalued?" question that is usually posed. The study shows how more nuanced guidance can be derived from a careful and more granular analysis of the behavior of market multiples.

The broader challenge is to bring the study of market multiples into a more coherent and rigorous framework, to determine with greater precision how levels and changes in the Multiples can be used to assist investment analysis. We need to become less simplistic: it is

---

[126]David Kostin et al., "The Multiple Mystery: At What P/E Should the Market Trade?" *US Equity Views – Goldman Sachs Global Economics,* October 1, 2009. Reproduced by permission.

313

clear that the significance of the various multiples is not constant. Meanings change based on the macroeconomic context and other aspects of the "market weather." But that does not mean that these metrics are capricious or unreliable. Just as an elevated heart rate in a human being may signal health or illness, long-term conditions, or a momentary episode, so the market metrics likely have patterns to their complexity.

Beyond offering guidance to investors, the use of multiples in the valuation of business transactions is another well-developed application. Private equity investors, investment bankers involved in mergers and acquisitions analysis, and legal professionals making the case for (or against) particular transactions or involved in the settlement of disputes all rely on market multiples as their first choice for valuations and as a check on model-based valuations. Corporate management teams increasingly look to the signals derived from market multiples to inform strategic decisions, such as the structure of the business portfolio. Even the accounting profession has recognized "officially" that market multiples offer the surest path to understanding "fair value" – the cornerstone of their business.[127]

5.7 Summary

Table 5-5 summarizes the important applications of market multiples discussed in this chapter.

---

[127]AICPA Task Force, *Valuation of Portfolio Company Investments of Venture Capital and Private Equity Funds and Other Investment Companies*, Draft (May 15, 2018), paragraphs 5.19–5.45.

CHAPTER 5   APPLICATIONS: P/E AS AN INDEPENDENT VARIABLE

Table 5-5. Summary of Important Applications of Market Multiples

Application	Comments	Multiples Used
Investment Screens	• Used to identify attractive investment prospects • Mainly used for the Value Anomaly	P/E, Dividend Yield, P/B, EV/EBITDA
Index Construction	• Used to construct equity indexes that reflect an investment style • Always used for Value indexes • Also used for some Indexes designed to track Growth and Quality	P/E, Dividend Yield, P/B, P/S, P/OCF
Factor Models, "Smart Beta"	• Used to define certain "factors"– especially Value, Growth, Quality • Used to screen companies or portfolios for "factor exposure"	P/E, P/B, ROA, Cashflow/Total Assets
Valuing Corporate Transactions	• Used to evaluate and price potential acquisitions and divestitures • Used to support and calibrate Discounted Cash Flow valuations for private equity transactions	EV/EBITDA
Evaluating the Conglomerate Discount	• Used in Sum-of-the-Parts analyses to assess the discount attached to over-diversified firms	EV/EBITDA, P/E

Analyzing Market Regimes	• Used to compare Equity and Bond markets relative valuations
	• Used to diagnose Market regimes, such as
	  • Bubble detection
	  • Range-bound markets
	• Used to understand changes in Market Regimes, such as
	  • phases of post-recession recoveries
		P/E, Dividend Yield

CHAPTER 6

Assessments and Qualifications

6.1 The Best Metric Today (2019): The P/E

The best and most consistent results for most valuation applications are (still) obtained from the traditional Price-to-Earnings Multiple.[1] It benefits from the immediacy, completeness, and actionable realism of the market component ("Price"), paired with the least problematic constituents of the company's financial statements (income statement components like "Earnings" or "Cash Flow"). The P/E, in its several versions, triangulates the intrinsic value of the enterprise with greater effectiveness than Book, Model, or Market alone and is superior to the other triangulating perspectives (Price-to-Book and Return-on-Assets).

---

[1] *"Forward earnings perform the best"* (Jing Liu, Doron Nissim and Jacob Thomas, "Equity Valuation Using Multiples," *Journal of Accounting Research*, Vol. 40, No. 1 (March 2002), pp. 135–172).

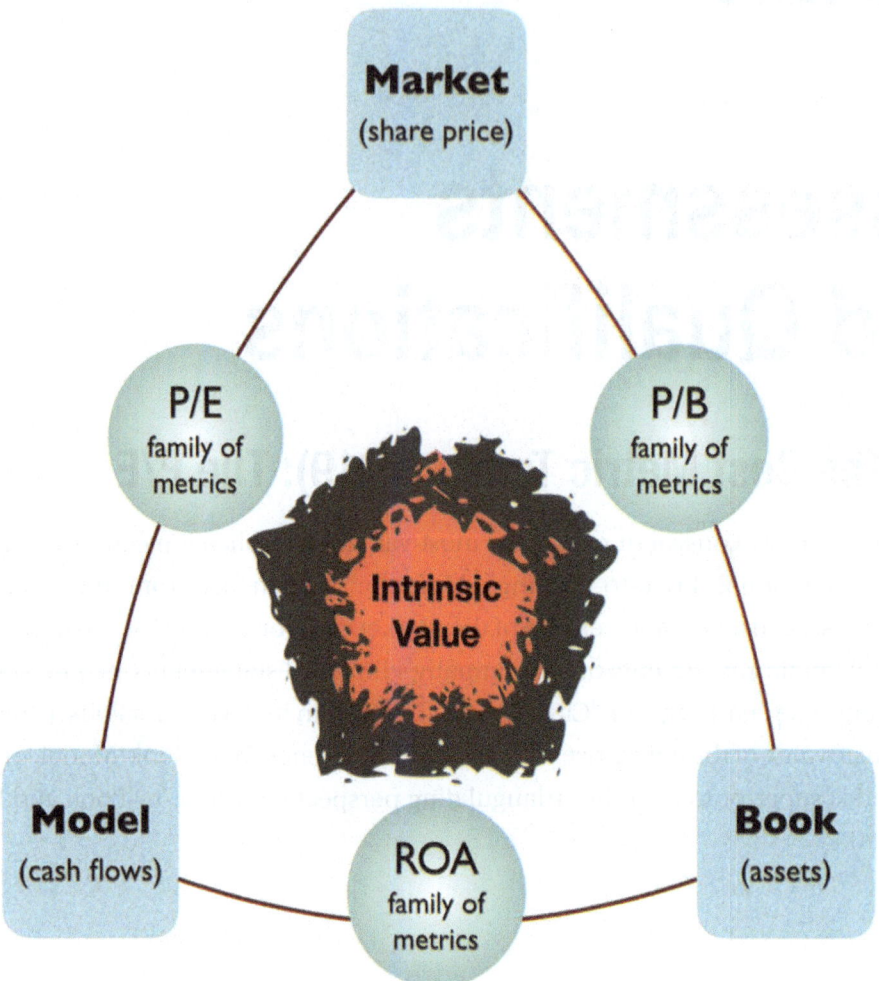

But what does "best" mean? Is the best metric the one that is most accurate? For what purpose? Predicting future stock market returns? Or explaining past returns? Is it the one that is easiest to use (perhaps conceding on accuracy a bit)? Is it the one that is most widely accepted and facilitates the construction of useful time-series data sets or best enables cross-company comparisons? How much does "best" depend upon the application?

A common answer is **the best metric is the one that most accurately predicts/ explains share prices**. It is assumed (probably correctly) that success in this regard will correlate with success in other applications, such as M&A analysis or private equity valuations.

What can we say about the performance of the various market multiples with respect to this criterion?

CHAPTER 6   ASSESSMENTS AND QUALIFICATIONS

6.1.1 P/E Tends to Prevail (but Not Always), and It Only Explains So Much

A typical study by *Vanguard* in 2012 examined some of popular metrics. Over the very long run (1926–2011), the P/E$_{ttm}$ and CAPE predicted market returns the best[2] (see Figure 6-1).

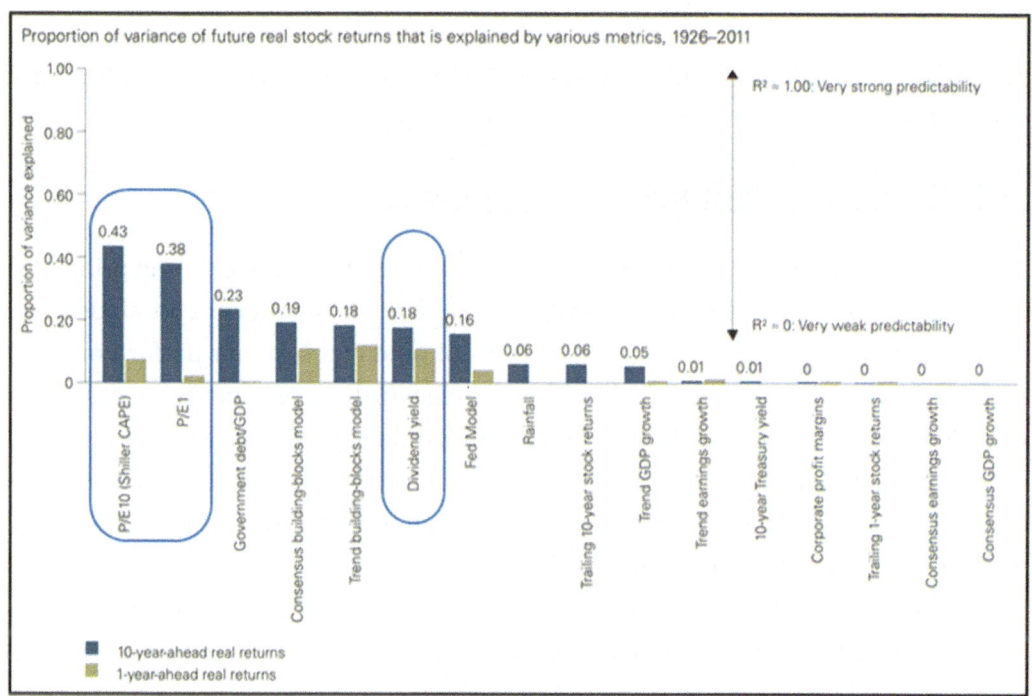

Figure 6-1. *A Comparison of Several Predictive Metrics*[3]

Nevertheless, as the authors point out, "even the P/E ratios leave approximately 60% of historical variation in long-term real returns unexplained."[4]

---

[2]Joseph Davis, Roger Aliaga-Díaz, and Charles Thomas, "Forecasting Stock Returns: What Signals Matter, and What Do They Say Now?" *Vanguard Research*, October 2012.

[3]Joseph Davis, Roger Aliaga-Díaz, and Charles Thomas, "Forecasting Stock Returns: What Signals Matter, and What Do They Say Now?" *Vanguard Research*, October 2012. Reproduced by permission of *Vanguard*.

[4]Jeremy Siegel calls the CAPE version of P/E *"one of the best forecasting models for long-term stock returns"* based on an R² of 35% ("The Shiller CAPE Ratio: A New Look," *Financial Analysts Journal*, Vol. 72., No. 3 (May/June 2016), pp. 41–50. "Best," I suppose, is best when it's all you've got.

6.1.2 Substituting Earnings Measures Other Than GAAP-Compliant Net Earnings Does Not Reliably Improve Performance (Yet)

Plausible arguments have been advanced in favor of various alternative measures of Earnings – including Operating Earnings, "normalized earnings," gross profits, "Core Earnings," and others. So far, none of these alternatives has shown a *consistent* performance advantage over the traditional GAAP-based P/E, although there are promising indications that free cash flow (non-GAAP) metrics may be improving.

6.1.2.1 Cash Flow Multiples are Promising

The use of cash flows in the construction of valuation metrics, while appealing in principle, has not always worked well. There are many inconsistencies in the way cash flow is defined from one company to the next. But there are hints of potential superior performance in the some of published results, which should encourage further concentrated research in this direction. A recent study by Morgan Stanley analyzed the performance of 81 different metrics as predictors of stock performance, applied to 4000 global stocks from 1997 to 2019. Free Cash Flow (defined consistently as operating cash flow minus net capital expenditures) provided a strong value signal.

Free Cash Flow based factors have generated the highest and most consistent returns historically relative to other valuation metrics (e.g. P/E, P/B).[5]

6.1.3 The Performance of All Multiples Is Highly Dependent on the Market Regime

Joseph Mezrich of *Nomura* analyzed the performance of 22 "representative factors" – including six market multiples (PE_{ttm}, P/E_{fwd}, P/B, Dividend Yield, EV/EBITDA, and PEG) – over four time periods, corresponding to four different market regimes, between 1985 and 2011. Here are the rankings among just the six Multiples (see Table 6-1).

---

[5]Morgan Stanley Quantitative Equity Research, Global Factor Guide (November 5, 2019)

CHAPTER 6   ASSESSMENTS AND QUALIFICATIONS

Table 6-1. *Ranking the Six Multiples*

	1985-1999 (Bull Market)	2000-2005 (Range Bound Market)	2006-2010 (Recession, Crisis, Recovery)	2011 (Moderate Expansion)	Average Position
P/E$_{ttm}$	5	1	1	2	2.25
P/E$_{fwd}$	3	2	2	4	2.75
EV/EBITDA	2	3	4	3	3
Dividend Yield	4	4	5	1	3.5
P/B	1	5	6	6	4.5
PEG	6	6	3	5	5

6.1.4 The Performance of Some Multiples Has Diminished Significantly over Time

As shown in Mezrich's rankings, the Price-Book ratio has gone from first to last over this period. As noted in earlier chapters, the growing divergence between Book Value and Market Value, caused by the shifts in the nature of corporate business models toward "intangible" or "invisible" assets, casts doubt on the accuracy of metrics that depend upon Book Value. Dividend Yield is another metric that may have been compromised in recent years by the surge of share buybacks as an alternative for returning cash to shareholders.

6.1.5 Sensitivity Varies, but Favors P/E

A value metric may also be judged superior if it tracks changes in the underlying intrinsic value more closely – that is, if it eliminates mis-valuations (reverts to the mean) more quickly. A study cited earlier found that P/E is indeed much more sensitive to market mispricings than any other metric:

> The sustainability of valuation difference between value and glamour portfolios [i.e., an anomalous mispricing] varies a lot among classification criteria; the difference remains significant for 5 years on the basis of P/B and P/S criterion, while decreases to insignificant much faster on the basis of earnings multiples...

> The valuation difference based on P/E ratios fades away remarkably faster than the corresponding differences that are based on [cash flow multiples]. The finding might be explained by the popularity of P/E as a measure of relative valuation of stocks; as investors are more aware of P/E ratios than they are of other valuation ratios the relative undervaluation (overvaluation) of low (high) P/E stocks smoothens out more rapidly due to smaller information asymmetry among investors.[6]

6.1.6 A Future Orientation Tends to Improve Short-Term Performance, but Only So Much

With respect to Earnings-Based Multiples – as noted in Chapter 3, Section 3.2 – the Forward P/E based on analysts' forecasts is generally found to be superior to the Trailing P/E based on historical earnings as reported. But as to the forecast horizon, the results are diverse. Bradshaw *et al.* found that the advantage of analysts' forecasts compared to a simple trend line forecast only held for the first year.[7] Liu et al. found a 2–3-year horizon for analysts' advantage:

> We examine the valuation performance of a comprehensive list of drivers and find that multiples derived from forward earnings explain stock prices remarkably well... and performance improves if the forecast horizon lengthens (1-year to 2-year to 3-year out EPS forecasts).[8]

---

[6]Eero Patari and Timo Leivo, "Persistence in Relative Valuation Difference between Value and Glamour Stocks: The Finnish Experience," *Banking and Finance Letters*, Vol. 2, No. 3, pp. 319–324.

[7]Mark T. Bradshaw, Michael S. Drake, James N. Myers, and Linda A. Myers, "A re-examination of analysts' superiority over time-series forecasts of annual earnings," *Review of Accounting Studies*, Vol. 17 (2012), pp. 944–968.

[8]Jing Liu, Doron Nissim, and Jacob Thomas, "Equity Valuation Using Multiples," *Journal of Accounting Research*, Vol. 40, No. 1 (March 2002), pp. 135–172.

A comprehensive study of the German stock market confirmed the 2-year horizon:

> forward-looking multiples, in particular the two-year forward-looking P/E multiple, outperformed trailing multiples....
>
> [the data] reveal a clear dominance of the two-year forward-looking P/E multiple across industries.[9]

6.1.7 Prediction Tends to Improve Significantly as the Holding Period Increases

Forecast accuracy for the P/E (usually forward) for predicting *short-term* results is limited, as noted earlier. Strangely, perhaps, the predictive power improves as the holding time increases. Different studies have calculated R^2 values ranging from 38% to 80% over a longer term[10] (see Table 6-2).

Table 6-2. Predictive Power of Holding Time

Source	% of Variation in Returns Explained: 1-Year Horizon	% of Variation in Returns Explained: 10-Year Horizon
Estrada, 2015	10%	52%
Vanguard, 2012	"close to zero"	38-40%
Asness, 2003	1-10%	65% (20 years)
Subramanian, 2017	~ 6%	~ 80%

---

[9]Andreas Schreiner, "Equity Valuation Using Multiples: An Empirical Investigation," *Doctoral Dissertation,* the University of St. Gallen Graduate School of Business Administration, 2007.

[10]Javier Estrada, "Multiples, Forecasting, and Asset Allocation," *Journal of Applied Corporate Finance,* Vol 27, No. 3 (Summer 2015), pp. 144–151.Joseph Davis, Roger Aliaga-Díaz, and Charles Thomas, "Forecasting Stock Returns: What Signals Matter, and What Do They Say Now?" *Vanguard Research,* October 2012.Clifford Asness, "Fight the Fed Model," *Journal of Portfolio Management,* Vol. 30, No. 1 (Fall 2003), pp. 11–24.Savita Subramanian, "2017 – The Year Ahead: Euphoria or Fiscal Fizzle," *Equity and Quant Strategy, Bank of America/Merrill Lynch,* November 22, 2016.

6.1.8 Cash Flow Multiples Are Less Reliable

The use of cash flows in the construction of valuation metrics, while appealing in principle, seems oddly not to work very well. There are too many inconsistencies in the way cash flow is defined from one company to the next. But there are hints of potential superior performance in some of the published results, which should encourage further concentrated research in this direction.

6.1.9 Averaging (Trend-Smoothing) Multiples: An Under-explored Concept

The recent popularity of $CAPE_l$ has raised important questions of how to handle short-term variability vs. long-term trends and how to apply averages in valuation exercises. CAPE, as it stands, is still essentially a rule of thumb, with a plausible but so far rather superficial rationale for its key assumptions (such as the 10-year averaging window) and a mixed predictive track record.

6.1.10 P/E Wins the Industry Popularity Contest

Finally, there is the market for ideas. In a fiercely competitive environment, the popularity of a particular technique – persisting over long periods – often conveys important information. Alternatives that work well tend to win out, numerically, over those that do not – nonnatural selection at work.

Price/Earnings is by far the most popular. Two decades ago, it was far and away the dominant choice among professionals[11] (see Figure 6-2).

---

[11] Mark Bradshaw, "The Use of Target Prices to Justify Sell-Side Analysts' Stock Recommendations," *Accounting Horizons,* Vol. 16, No. 1 (March 2002), pp. 27–41.

CHAPTER 6 ASSESSMENTS AND QUALIFICATIONS

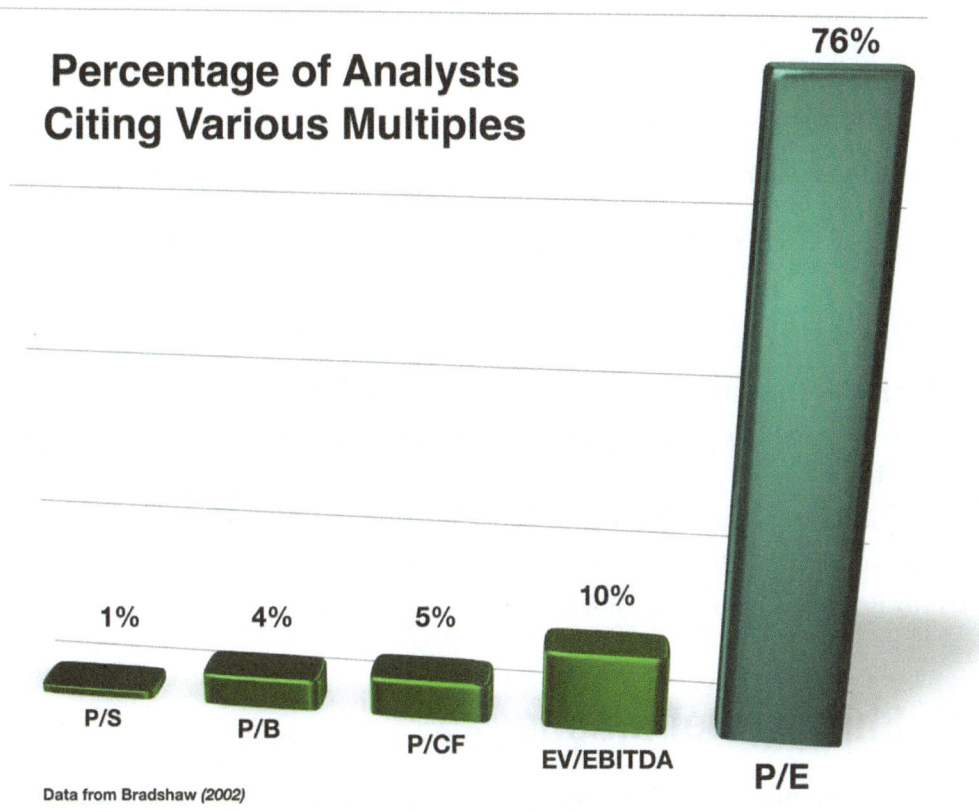

Figure 6-2. *Percentage of Analysts Citing Various Multiples (2002)*[12]

In recent years, other multiples – especially EV/EBITDA and versions of Price-to-Free-Cash-Flow – have gained "mindshare" among analysts studying individual companies and are more frequently used in conjunction with the traditional P/E. CAPE has won favor with many commentators looking at broad market trends. But the traditional P/E (especially Forward P/E) is still the preferred alternative for enterprise valuation at the individual firm level.

It is perhaps surprising that a formula so basic, so long in use, has not been superseded. Some of the other ratios discussed here have been viewed as improvements upon the vanilla P/E. These concepts have their merits: "Book" is conservative; "Sales" is less volatile; "Cash" is cash; "Averaging" seems plausible. But they have not dislodged the Earnings Multiple from its place of primacy, at least among practitioners.

---

[12]Data taken from Mark Bradshaw, "The Use of Target Prices to Justify Sell-Side Analysts' Stock Recommendations," *Accounting Horizons*, Vol. 16, No. 1 (March 2002), pp. 27–41.

So, to summarize the more helpful findings

- The traditional P/E – based on GAAP net earnings – is still the preferred choice and, by most measures, the best performing of the multiples.
- The Forward P/E is generally found to be superior to the trailing P/E.
- The P/E predicts better for the long term than the short term.
- Ratios that use cash flow in the denominator are becoming more important.

We should remember, however, that a metric like the P/E is in some sense only as sound as its components. In the remainder of this chapter, we will review a series of methodological questions concerning the reliability of the basic constituents of the market ratios – questions pertaining to the stability and interpretability of "Earnings" and "Price." We will also summarize briefly the case for the other two "sides" of the Value Triangle – Price-to-Book and Return-on-Assets (and related ratios).

6.2 Shifting Definitions

Many people approach the financial world with the assumption that all the key terms are well defined and that the definitions are stable. This is a misconception. Simple-seeming accounting categories like "Sales" or "Earnings" are in truth quite complex and subject to subtle biases. They incorporate many judgment factors, some of which are transparent and standardized (although the standards can change!) and some of which may be hidden deep in the fabric of the corporate accounts. These figures can be massaged or tweaked or "managed" (which is legal, up to a point); they can also be manipulated or rendered so obscure that their meaning is lost.

Definitional uncertainty in finance is a large subject. The sections that follow are a brief catalog of some of the definitional issues that can affect the meaning and usefulness of the market multiples, with a focus on the P/E in particular and its components – "Price" and "Earnings."

6.2.1 GAAP,[13] Non-GAAP, Core, and So On: The Validity Problem for "Earnings"

In early 2018, *Barron's* magazine reported the following:

> In the fourth quarter [2017], 28 of the 30 companies in the Dow, or 93%, reported non-GAAP EPS in addition to GAAP EPS...
>
> Some Dow component fourth-quarter results illustrate the unusual nature of the quarter. For example, *McDonald's* (ticker: MCD) fourth quarter GAAP EPS showed a 40% decline, but non-GAAP EPS a 19% increase. Similarly, *Intel* (INTC)'s GAAP EPS was down 121% but non-GAAP up 37%.

A breakdown in Western civilization? Perhaps not. *Barron's* advice:

> Investors should probably pay closer attention to non-GAAP numbers... The numbers generated from non-GAAP EPS for Dow companies were less volatile and more likely *a better reflection of profit growth from day-to-day operations than GAAP*.[14] *[Emphasis added]*

Indeed. Here's more, from the academic literature:

> The decrease in conditional conservatism from *adjusting GAAP earnings to Street earnings*[15] *leads to improvements in persistence, smoothing, and informativeness and reduces analysts' forecast errors and dispersion*.[16] *[Emphasis added]*

Accounting is an evolving field, often playing catchup to changes in the economy and in the nature of corporate operations. What may start out as an alternative, non-GAAP accounting treatment – motivated by genuine concerns that GAAP may not be presenting

---

[13]That is, Generally Accepted Accounting Principles – short-hand for accounting that is conducted according to the recognized rules of the profession, and regulated by the **Financial Accounting Standards Board**.

[14]Vito Racanelli, "Should Investors Still Mind the GAAP when it Comes to Earnings," *Barron's*, February 26, 2018

[15]On "Street Earnings" – a version of non-GAAP earnings – see the next section.

[16]Frank Heflin, Charles Hsu, and Qinglu Jin, "Accounting conservatism and Street earnings," *Review of Accounting Studies*, Vol. 20 (2015) pp. 674-709

an accurate picture as business models change – may eventually be accepted into the GAAP framework. For example, until 2009, *Apple* (like many other tech companies) was required to account for a sale of a product like the iPhone – which combines hardware and software in a single device – by spreading a portion of the revenue over the presumed lifetime of the product (2 years was judged the correct figure), instead of when the payment was received (up front). This "bundled revenue" problem had the effect of reducing reported Apple's GAAP earnings by more than one-third in 2009. Apple issued its own non-GAAP numbers to bring this distortion (as they saw it) to the attention of the investing public. It was estimated at the time that over 10% of the companies in the S&P 500 index were similarly affected. Eventually, the Financial Accounting Standards Board was moved to revise the rule "to align the accounting better with what the economics of the transaction were... [in which case] the big gap between GAAP and non-GAAP earnings per share will mostly close."[17]

In short, what is non-GAAP today can become GAAP tomorrow.

All well and good, but this also means that in 2009 the definition of E in the P/E ratio changed, quite significantly, for quite a large number of public companies. If we would accept the revised rule as more accurate and more in line with true economic value, then in Apple's case, prior to the change, the P/E was 30–35% higher than it should have been.

"Earnings" must be understood as a dynamic, flexible, and evolving concept (which sounds better than saying it is "inconsistent" or "incoherent"). But that means that the P/E is potentially unstable. It raises questions about the validity of long-term smoothing of the Multiple through techniques such as CAPE (Cyclically Adjusted P/E). It also should call into question the validity of long-term studies of valuation ratios that would compare today's P/E multiple with the P/E from 20, 30, or 50 years ago. Conclusions drawn from close comparisons of the value of these and other metrics from, say, the 1960s vs. those of today are likely less valid than they may appear.

6.2.2 Street Earnings

Public companies are required to use GAAP standards for the preparation of their financial statements. But they have more latitude in how they present their results in earnings announcements and earnings calls. It is assumed that the availability of GAAP-compliant

---

[17]Martin Peers, "Investors Should Focus on Apple's Core," *The Wall Street Journal*, September 24, 2009. Also Michael Rapoport, Yukare Iwatani Kane, and Ben Worthen, "U.S. Accounting to Aid Tech Firms," *The Wall Street Journal,* September 24, 2009.

figures in the financial statements is cover for offering alternative interpretations of the company's performance. These may be referred to as "pro forma" earnings, insofar as they originate from the company directly. But these figures may also be picked up and republished by outside analysts, who prefer and accept the validity of the company's alternative interpretation. These are the so-called "street numbers."[18]

> Earnings performance has been traditionally measured using the net income and earnings per share (EPS) figures produced according to 'generally accepted accounting principles' (GAAP). However, recent years have witnessed an increasing focus on 'Street' earnings numbers, which are the numbers announced by corporations in their press releases and tracked by analyst estimate clearinghouse services, such as *I/B/E/S*, *Zacks*, and *First Call*.[19]

Through this republication by analyst clearinghouses and others, "Street Earnings" may become – in their own way – "generally accepted."

It goes further. Analysts working for companies that aggregate and supply financial market data, such as *Thomson Reuters* (now *Refinitiv*), *FactSet Research*, *S&P Capital IQ*, and *Bloomberg*, study companies and make their own assessments as to what to include or exclude from "Earnings." These differences can be quite significant, as shown here in a chart from *The Wall Street Journal*[20] (see Figure 6-3).

---

[18] Jo Craven McGinty, "Results May Vary: Why Companies' Earnings Reports Differ," *The Wall Street Journal*, April 25, 2015.

[19] Mark Bradshaw and Richard Sloan, "GAAP versus The Street: An Empirical Assessment of Two Alternative Definitions of Earnings," *Journal of Accounting Research*, Vol. 40, No. 1 (March 2002), pp. 41–66.

[20] Jo Craven McGinty, "Results May Vary: Why Companies' Earnings Reports Differ," *The Wall Street Journal*, April 25, 2015.

CHAPTER 6   ASSESSMENTS AND QUALIFICATIONS

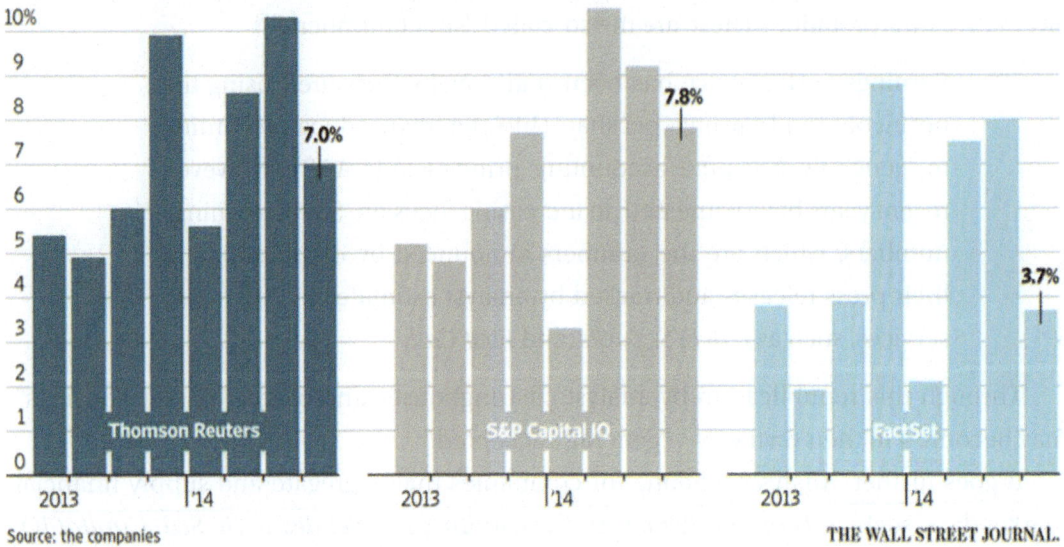

Figure 6-3. *Street Earnings*[21]

There is a large literature on the topic, focusing on questions such as whether Street Earnings are more "value-relevant" than GAAP earnings for various purposes (they are), whether investors understand Street Earnings or are misled by them (generally they are not), and whether firms that release pro forma figures, which become Street Earnings, carry higher multiples than other firms (they do not).[22] Research has also looked at what kinds of expenses are typically excluded from Street Earnings and whether the practice is related to the desire to meet or beat analysts' earnings forecasts. A critical review of the literature published in 2005 concluded that

> The key question of whether pro forma earnings are used to mislead or to inform has not been resolved.[23]

---

[21] Jo Craven McGinty, "Results May Vary: Why Companies' Earnings Reports Differ," *The Wall Street Journal*, April 25, 2015. Reproduced by permission from *The Wall Street Journal*.

[22] Chih-Ying Chen, "Do analysts and investors fully understand the persistence of the items excluded from Street earnings?" *Review of Accounting Studies*, Vol. 15 (2010), pp 32–69.

[23] Philip Berger, "Discussion of 'Are Investors Misled by "Pro Form" Earnings,'" *Contemporary Accounting Research*, Vol. 22, No. 4 (Winter 2005), pp. 965–976.

In short, we don't know if this non-GAAP medicine kills or cures.

The relevant point here is that quite often the most readily accessible form of "Earnings" may be Street Earnings, which, whatever its merits, constitutes a different denominator for the P/E and other multiples. As *The Wall Street Journal* summarizes

> There are multiple definitions of earnings that include, or omit, different kinds of information. Street earnings, the most coveted figures produced by Wall Street analysts and data providers, are regarded by investors as the best indicators...
>
> They are also unregulated numbers that often paint a substantially different picture than earnings prepared according to generally accepted accounting principles.[24]

6.2.3 IFRS vs. GAAP

The "World War" in accounting, between the advocates of GAAP – the American standard – and IFRS (International Financial Reporting Standards) which is used almost everywhere else, is a war the Americans probably will lose. But for the time being, US corporations construct "Earnings" differently from firms based elsewhere. An often-cited difference between the two systems is that GAAP requires companies to expense all development costs associated with R&D activities that often lead to significant new intangible technology and intellectual property assets. IFRS allows for much of the development cost to be viewed instead as an investment and capitalized – carried on the balance sheet as an asset. IFRS "Earnings" will be higher than GAAP "Earnings" – and IFRS Book Value will also be higher. Clearly, these differences will affect the Multiples. The IFRS version of the P/E will be lower – which may help to explain the typical discount borne by European and Canadian companies, relative to their US counterparts.

---

[24] Jo Craven McGinty, "Results May Vary: Why Companies' Earnings Reports Differ," *The Wall Street Journal*, April 25, 2015.

CHAPTER 6   ASSESSMENTS AND QUALIFICATIONS

Several countries that have recently switched from GAAP to IFRS provide interesting natural experiments to study the effect on business valuations. In the United Kingdom, for example, it was found that there were significant differences in profitability and capital structure – that is, "Earnings" and Book Value – before and after the switch, which would certainly affect the market valuation ratios.[25]

6.2.4 Changing Accounting Standards

GAAP accounting rules are subject to change. Some changes impact fundamental components of the financial statements, reverberating through the valuation framework. A recent example (2018) involving revenue recognition highlights the potential for disruption and uncertainty:

> More than half of the S&P 500 companies disclosed some impact on their accounting for revenue... Finance teams spent months rewriting accounting processes and procedures and preparing new financial statements. Roughly one in five public companies surveyed...said they spent...$1 million or more on the effort.
>
> Some companies expect the new rules to accelerate revenue, while others say the timing of [revenue recognition] will be delayed, even though the underlying business remains unchanged.[26]

Since a change in revenue will drive changes in earnings, the denominators of market multiples will be affected. "Before" and "After" may no longer be commensurate.

Beyond the issue of consistency from one period to the next, some accounting changes may introduce outright "distortions." Warren Buffett has criticized recent accounting changes that in his view have misrepresented *Berkshire Hathaway's* earnings:

> A large portion of our gain did not come from anything we accomplished at Berkshire...

---

[25]Yhlas Sovbetov, "How IFRS Affects Value Relevance and Key Financial Indicators? Evidence from the UK," *International Review of Accounting, Banking and Finance,* Vol. 7, No. 1 (Spring 2015), pp. 73–96.

[26]Tatyana Shumsky, "Updated Accounting Rules Reverberate," *The Wall Street Journal,* June 13, 2018.

> I must tell you about a new accounting rule – a generally accepted accounting principle (GAAP) – that in future quarterly and annual reports will severely distort *Berkshire's* net income figures and very often mislead commentators and investors.
>
> The new rule says that the net change in unrealized investment gains and losses in stocks we hold must be included in all net income figures we report to you. That requirement will produce some truly wild and capricious swings in our GAAP bottom-line. *Berkshire* owns $170 billion of marketable stocks (not including our shares of *Kraft Heinz*), and the value of these holdings can easily swing by $10 billion or more within a quarterly reporting period. Including gyrations of that magnitude in reported net income will swamp the truly important numbers that describe our operating performance. For analytical purposes, *Berkshire's* "bottom-line" will be useless.[27]

If the bottom line is truly "useless for analytical purposes," then what is the Price-Earnings ratio good for?

There are many examples of such changes, some of which have been discussed in earlier chapters. Recent changes cited as particularly important for their effects on valuation multiples include the following:

- Changes in the accounting for employee stock options – treating them as expenses[28]

- Changes requiring "Mark-to-Market" or "fair value" assessment of many assets, in place of traditional balance sheet items "carried at cost"[29]

- The change to require testing for impairment of goodwill and other intangibles[30]

---

[27]Warren Buffett, *2017 Annual Letter to Berkshire Hathaway Shareholders.* See also Donald E. Graham, "I Can't See Berkshire's Bottom Line," *The Wall Street Journal*, November 8, 2018.
[28]SFAS 123 (1995).
[29]FAS 157 (2007).
[30]FAS 142 (2001).

All of these changes will generally have the effect of reducing current earnings, lowering the denominator of the P/E ratio, and thus forcing the multiple upward. The trend toward higher P/E readings in recent years (discussed in earlier chapters) is a consequence in part of these more conservative accounting treatments. Each such change creates a break in the financial time series:

> Starting in 2001, goodwill and other long-lived assets must instead be tested annually for impairment – that is, if the asset is found to have lost value, it must be written down. But if a goodwill asset has gained in value, it cannot be written up!
>
> This new practice reduces post-2001 earnings relative to pre-2001 earnings.[31]

The effect is especially troublesome for averaged multiples such as $CAPE_l$, which straddle the "Before" and "After" periods created by such changes.

6.2.5 Earnings Management 1: Gaming the Numbers

Microsoft at one time was famous for managing its quarterly earnings to achieve regular, consistent, slightly-better-than-expected results:[32]

> In January [1997], for the 41st time in the 42 quarters since it went public, *Microsoft* reported earnings that met or beat Wall Street estimates. The 36 brokerage analysts who make the estimates were, as a group, quite happy about this – the 57 cents per share announced by the software giant was above their consensus of 51 cents, but not so far above as to make them look stupid.
>
> The pressure to report smooth, ever higher earnings has never been fiercer... "Managing earnings" has a pejorative, slightly sleazy ring to it, but even at the most respected of companies, accounting and business decisions are regularly made with smoothing or temporarily boosting earnings in mind. [33]

---

[31] Laurence Siegel, "CAPMing the CAPE: Shiller-Siegel Shootout at then Q Group Corral, Part 2," available online at https://larrysiegeldotorg.files.wordpress.com/2016/09/siegel_capming-the-cape_2016_09_08.pdf

[32] John Markoff, "Microsoft's Accounting Under Scrutiny," July 1, 1999.

[33] Justin Fox, "Learn to Play the Earnings Game," *Fortune*, March 31, 1997.

"Earnings Management" refers to the still-widespread practice of making small, legal (or at least defensible) adjustments to various accounting categories, to raise or lower reported GAAP earnings, often by shifting revenue or expense recognition slightly (or not so slightly) from one time period to another. *Fortune* cited one example from the *Microsoft* case, which will suffice to make the point:

> Starting in August 1995, *Microsoft* has followed a uniquely conservative method of accounting for the software it ships – deferring recognition of large chunks of revenue from a product until long after the product is sold. The reasoning is that when somebody buys software in 1996, they're also buying the right to upgrades and customer support in 1997 and 1998. If it hadn't been for the new accounting technique, the company would have had to report a sharp rise in profits in the latter half of 1995 [when Windows 95 was launched], then a sharp drop in the first half of 1996 – a turn of events that might have sent its stock price reeling – instead of the smoothly rising earnings that it did post. By the end of 1996, *Microsoft* had taken in $1.1 billion in "unearned revenue" that it had yet to recognize on its income statements.[34]

"Earnings management" takes many forms, and some of them shade into improper or illegal accounting practices. *Microsoft* was eventually sanctioned by the *Securities and Exchange Commission* and (without admitting wrongdoing) agreed to mend its ways.[35] But the general practice is still in play at many companies, in a perhaps less egregious fashion.

---

[34] Justin Fox, "Learn to Play the Earnings Game," *Fortune*, March 31, 1997.

[35] Rebecca Buckman, "Microsoft, SEC Settle Probe Into Earnings Misstatements," *The Wall Street Journal*, June 4, 2002. A few more details: *"Microsoft Corp. agreed to settle Securities and Exchange Commission civil allegations the software company misstated its earnings during certain periods during the 1990s by illegally maintaining different 'reserve' accounts for such expenses as marketing and obsolete inventory, the SEC said.... The case is regarded as somewhat unusual, because it involved a cash-rich company setting aside reserves that in some cases understated quarterly income, rather than inflating it. Such techniques can have the effect of smoothing out quarterly results and providing better predictability to Wall Street.... The SEC...said 'senior Microsoft financial personnel' frequently added to the estimates for reserve accounts – in effect increasing expenses – without adequate analysis."*

The subject is vast and has been studied extensively. It is not the place to explore this issue in detail, but once again, it is obvious that "managed earnings" will have an effect on the denominator of market multiples, creating another source of instability affecting the interpretation of these metrics.

6.2.6 Earnings Management 2: Buybacks and EPS Enhancement

Following changes in SEC rules in 1982 to permit companies to purchase their own shares in the open market, such "buybacks" have become a dominant force in the financial markets. (See Chapter 4, Figure 4-21.)

In the first quarter of 2018, buybacks by firms in the S&P 500 reached $189 Bn, up 41% from the previous year. The buyback payout ratio rose to 48% of earnings.[36] The full-year rate is now (2019) nearly $1 trillion, far surpassing dividends.[37] The demand for shares coming from buybacks was more than twice the demand coming from the growth of Exchange Traded Funds (ETFs).[38]

There are at least three important effects of buybacks:

1. **Dividends have lost importance**. As noted, buybacks have displaced dividends as the preferred means of "returning cash to shareholders." This has apparently reduced the information quality (or "value relevance" as the academic literature often describes it) of dividend payments as a value signal. Dividend Yields have dropped by half since the 1980s. The Dividend Yield metric appears to have lost much of its predictive power.

2. **Buybacks increase earnings per share**. A company can increase its EPS in two ways: (i) by increasing actual earnings from operations in the numerator or (ii) by reducing the number of shares in the denominator. Buybacks produce the second effect.

---

[36]"Six Muddles About Buybacks," *The Economist*, June 2, 2018.
[37]Lawrence Strauss, "Stock Dividends Aren't What They Used to Be," *Barron's*, April 29, 2019.
[38]Matt Phillips, "Buybacks Dip Could factor Into Sell-Off," *The New York Times*, October 12, 2018.

CHAPTER 6   ASSESSMENTS AND QUALIFICATIONS

Companies have discovered how to use buybacks to drive up EPS. In Q2 2018, *Southwest Airlines* saw its earnings from its business operations decline by 2.1%. But the company bought back 28 million shares and drove the *reported* EPS up 2.4%.[39] In the first three quarters of 2015, *Microsoft* bought back 3% of its outstanding shares – and turned a 1.3% drop in earnings from its operations into a 3.1% gain.[40]

Microsoft has been at this game for a long time. From 2004 to 2013, the company repurchased $110 billion of its own shares, reducing its share count by 22% (see Figure 6-4).

Thanks to such buybacks, the company's average annual earnings growth rate was 46% higher than it would have been holding the share count constant.[41]

Microsoft has discovered a much more powerful way to manage its earnings than through the accounting tricks it was sanctioned for previously, along with dozens of other companies. *The Wall Street Journal* reported in 2015 that over the previous 12 months, "more than 20% of all companies in the S&P 500 reduced share count by at least 4%."[42]

---

[39] Michael Rapoport and Theo Francis, "Buybacks Dress Up Profits," *The Wall Street Journal*, September 24, 2018.

[40] E. S. Browning, "Surge in Buybacks Stirs Up Worries," *The Wall Street Journal*, November 23, 2015.

[41] Rolfe Winkler, "Microsoft Buys Back Earnings Growth," *The Wall Street Journal*, September 18, 2013.

[42] E. S. Browning, "Surge in Buybacks Stirs Up Worries," *The Wall Street Journal*, November 23, 2015.

CHAPTER 6   ASSESSMENTS AND QUALIFICATIONS

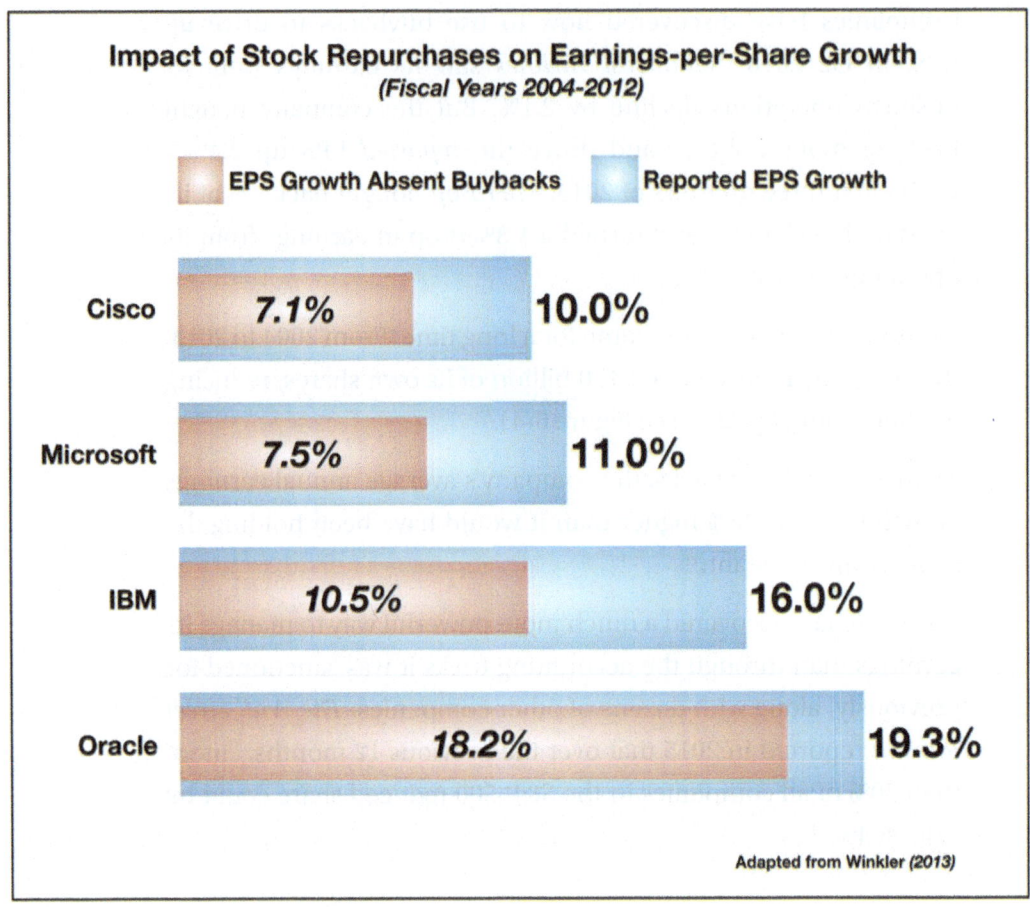

Figure 6-4. *Effect of Buybacks on EPS*[43]

What is the effect of this practice on "true value"? Does the market distinguish between EPS that grows by increasing the numerator and EPS that grows by shrinking the denominator? Does the P/E respond to both kinds of EPS growth in the same way? It is not clear.[44]

---

[43]Adapted from Rolfe Winkler, "Microsoft Buys Back Earnings Growth," *The Wall Street Journal*, September 18, 2013

[44]To me, this is one of the most intriguing unanswered questions related to valuation in general and the significance of market multiples in particular. I am not aware of any studies that have really focused on this issue.

3. **Buybacks drive up "Price" even apart from the increase in EPS.** Buybacks increase demand for the company's shares. This puts upward pressure on the Price, quite apart from the EPS effect. *Goldman Sachs* has estimated that buybacks add 1 point to the Forward P/E of the S&P 500.[45] That would imply a valuation enhancement of 5% or so – attributable solely to the extra buy-side volume. Other analysts have calculated a much larger effect: a report cited by *The Wall Street Journal* estimates that the S&P would have been 19% lower in Q1 2019 if companies had not bought back any stock.[46] (This figure may blend both the EPS increase and the effect of the additional buying pressure.)

Some confirmation of this effect may be seen during "blackout periods" around earnings announcements, which force a temporary halt to buybacks.[47] The stock market appears in some cases to sag in line with these blackout periods, although the effect has not been studied much.[48] The volatility of the market also seems to increase.[49]

In short, buybacks have become a powerful force in the financial markets, introducing large changes in reported "Earnings" and, separately, somewhat more modest changes in "Price." Neither effect has been carefully studied, in relation to the impact on valuation metrics.

---

[45]Allison Nathan and David Groman, "Buyback Realities," *Goldman Sachs Global Macro Research*, Issue 77, April 11, 2019.

[46]Jessica Menton, "Volatility Unlikely to Derail Buybacks," *The Wall Street Journal*, May 17, 2019; the report referenced in this article is by Ed Clissold, *Ned Davis Research*, May 2019.

[47]Corrie Driebusch, "Volatility Sets Up a Boom in Buybacks," *The Wall Street Journal*, October 24, 2018; Matt Phillips, "Buybacks Dip Could factor Into Sell-Off," *The New York Times*, October 12, 2018.

[48]Matt Phillips, "Buybacks Dip Could factor Into Sell-Off," *The New York Times*, October 12, 2018; Corrie Driebusch, "Volatility Sets Up a Boom in Buybacks," *The Wall Street Journal*, October 24, 2018.

[49]Allison Nathan and David Groman, "Buyback Realities," *Goldman Sachs Global Macro Research*, Issue 77, April 11, 2019.

6.2.7 Cash Dilution ("Nonoperating Financial Assets")

The question of how to adjust the valuation metrics to account for the effects of large cash accumulations – recognizing that cash is an asset that generates very low returns – has been addressed in Chapter 3, Section 3.11, with the Cash-Adjusted P/E concept ($CAPE_2$). But the problem may go beyond just stripping out the cash value from the market value, as $CAPE_2$ attempts to do. Excessive cash balances may actually damage valuations, impacting the P/E and other valuation multiples even more than $CAPE_2$ allows for.

The type specimen for this problem is *Apple*.

> When you buy a share of *Apple* stock, you do not simply buy into a $1 trillion technology company. You also buy a share of one of the world's largest investment companies: *Braeburn Capital*, a wholly owned subsidiary of *Apple*. Braeburn manages a $244 billion financial portfolio – 70% of Apple's book assets. Apple acts like a hedge fund by supporting this portfolio with $115 billion of debt.[50]

Seventy-six percent of this cash was held in risky securities (i.e., other than Treasurys and equivalent instruments), including corporate equities and bonds and mortgage-backed securities.[51] The authors calculate that these risky assets are discounted by 12–22%, which would imply that *Apple's* Book Value is reduced by 7–12% – and that the Price/Book ratio is increased (overvalued?) by about the same amount.[52] This is on top of the adjustment that $CAPE_2$ would propose. The subtitle of the study is *"When Cash Is Not Cash"* – which seems appropriate.

---

[50]Thomas Gilbert and Christopher Hrdlicka, "The Hedge Fund That Makes iPhones," *The Wall Street Journal*, August 27, 2018.

[51]In their research, Gilbert, Hrdlicka, et al. applied several tests for liquidity, relying on reporting under FASB 157 (Fair Value Measurements). They classified 74% of non-Treasury government debt, 90% of corporate debt, and 97% of asset- and mortgage-backed securities as illiquid (Ran Duchin, Thomas Gilbert, Jarrad Harford, and Christopher Hrdlicka, "Precautionary Savings with Risk Assets: When Cash is Not Cash," *The Journal of Finance,* Vol. 72, No. 2 (April 2017), pp. 793–852).

[52]In an earlier version of the paper, the estimate of the discount was higher: *"The value of risky reserves is 23.2-29.7% lower than the value of safe reserves."* (Ran Duchin, Thomas Gilbert, Jarrad Harford, and Christopher Hrdlicka, "Precautionary Savings with Risky Assets: When Cash Is Not Cash," July 2014).

Large holdings of risky assets are associated with the destruction of value. The market values a risky dollar of financial assets at substantially less than a dollar.[53]

Regarding the size of the discount, we noted in Chapter 3 that the credit rating firm *Moody's* has reportedly applied a 30% discount to the cash reserves of certain firms.[54] The phenomenon is widespread.

Shadow hedge funds abound within S&P 500 industrial companies... In 2012 these corporations managed a combined portfolio of *$1.6 trillion of nonoperating financial asset*s.[55] *[Emphasis Added]*

The putative status of cash as an asset, *prima facie*, of unimpeachable value ("cash is king" and so on) may blind us to the negative consequences of excessive cash holdings, which in turn confuses the interpretation of P/E Multiples. Too much cash, or excessive Free Cash Flow, may signal underinvestment or lack of growth opportunities or management entrenchment or a tax problem – all of which undercut a straightforward reading of the valuation metrics.

6.2.8 Taxes

For many companies, for many reporting periods, taxes are the largest single expense. Tax obligations are often driven by factors unrelated to the operational performance of the business in a given period (which is why they are excluded from Operating Income). Changes in the tax laws can therefore have significant effects on the market ratios that use "Net Earnings" in the denominator.

---

[53] Thomas Gilbert and Christopher Hrdlicka, "The Hedge Fund That Makes iPhones," *The Wall Street Journal*, August 27, 2018.

[54] John Jannarone and Sara Silver, "Cash (Kept at Home) is King," *The Wall Street Journal*, January 14, 2009.

[55] Thomas Gilbert and Christopher Hrdlicka, "The Hedge Fund That Makes iPhones," *The Wall Street Journal*, August 27, 2018. See

CHAPTER 6   ASSESSMENTS AND QUALIFICATIONS

The tax law change in 2018 had a large impact. Twenty-eight of the 30 companies included in the Dow Jones Industrial Average reported non-GAAP earnings figures (in addition to the required GAAP numbers of course). The non-GAAP numbers were different from the GAAP figures, on average, by 110% – eight to ten times the "normal" level (see Figure 6-5).

The cause of the discrepancy was the tax law.

> 19 DJIA companies reported a net charge [i.e., a loss] because of the tax law, while nine reported a net gain and these were typically the largest single item accounting for the unusually large differences between GAAP EPS and non-GAAP EPS for these companies for the quarter.[56]

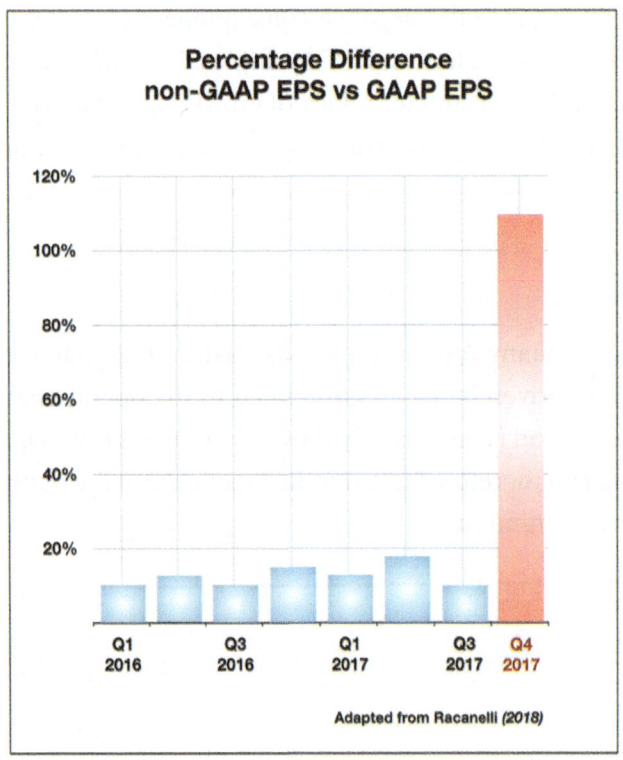

Figure 6-5. *Tax Impact on EPS*[57]

---

[56]Vito Racanelli, "Should Investors Still Mind the GAAP when it Comes to Earnings," *Barron's*, February 26, 2018.

[57]Adapted from Vito Racanelli, "Should Investors Still Mind the GAAP when it Comes to Earnings," *Barron's*, February 26, 2018.

Taxes also seem to play a role in stimulating the accumulation of excess cash reserves, mentioned in the previous section.[58] Tax advantages associated with maintaining cash "overseas" – and avoiding US corporate income taxes – may encourage cash accumulation, which finds its way into "risky assets."

> Firms with more foreign income hold more risky assets as a fraction of their total book assets.
>
> Foreign income is positively correlated with both liquid and illiquid reserves as a fraction of total book assets.[59]

If these risky assets are discounted, raising the P/B and potentially distorting other ratios, this would be another channel for tax effects to impair the reliability of market metrics.

6.2.9 The Effect of Asset-Light Business Models

Corporate operating profit margins have been rising in recent decades, from an average of about 5-6% in the mid-1990s to 11-12% in 2018[60] (see Figure 6-6).

---

[58]C. Fritz Foley, Jay C. Hartzell, Sheridan Titman, and Garry Twite, "Why do firms hold so much cash? A tax-based explanation," *Journal of Financial Economics,* Vol. 86 (2007), pp. 579-607.

[59]Ran Duchin, Thomas Gilbert, Jarrad Harford, and Christopher Hrdlicka, "Precautionary Savings with Risky Assets: When Cash Is Not Cash," *The Journal of Finance,* Vol. 72, No. 2 (April 2017) pp. 793-852.

[60]Edward Yardeni and Joe Abbott, *Stock Market Briefing: S&P 500 Sectors & Industries*, May 22, 2018.

CHAPTER 6   ASSESSMENTS AND QUALIFICATIONS

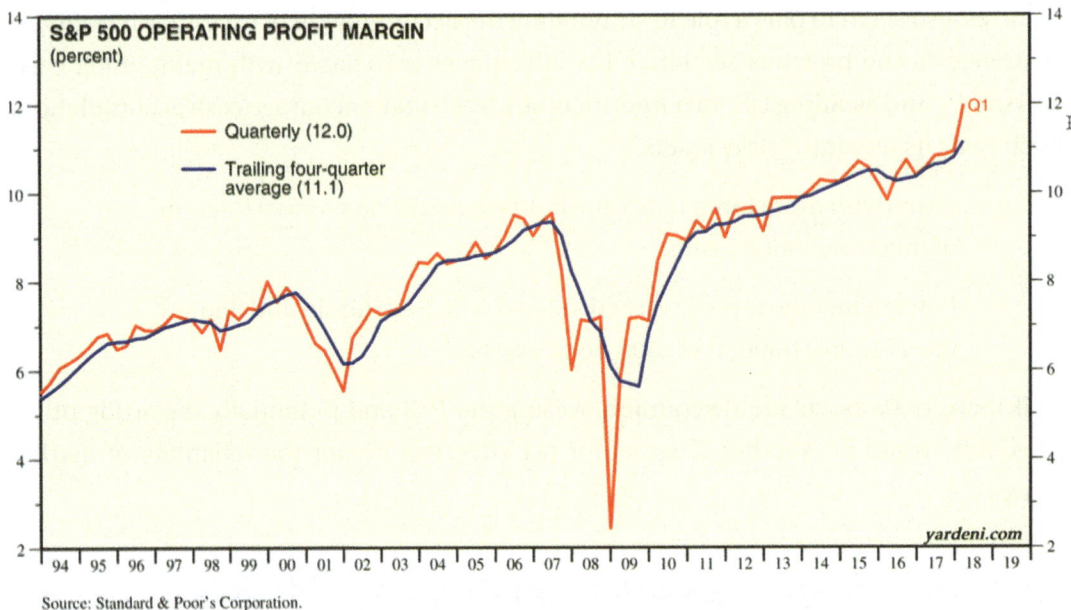

Source: Standard & Poor's Corporation.

Figure 6-6. *The Rising Profitability Trend*[61]

According to the *St. Louis Federal Reserve*, corporate *net* profits as a percentage of the US Gross Domestic Income rose from about 1.5% in the 1970s to over 4% by 2016.[62] As a share of the entire US GDP, over the past 25 years, corporate profits are up from 3% to 9%[63] (see Figure 6-7).

---

[61]Edward Yardeni and Joe Abbott, *Stock Market Briefing: S&P 500 Sectors & Industries*, May 22, 2018. Reproduced by permission of *Yardeni Research*.

[62]FRED, Federal Reserve Economic Data, *Federal Reserve Bank of St. Louis*, https://fred.stlouisfed.org/series/A449RE1A156NBEA

[63]FRED, Federal Reserve Economic Data, *Federal Reserve Bank of St. Louis*, https://fred.stlouisfed.org/graph/?g=cSh

CHAPTER 6   ASSESSMENTS AND QUALIFICATIONS

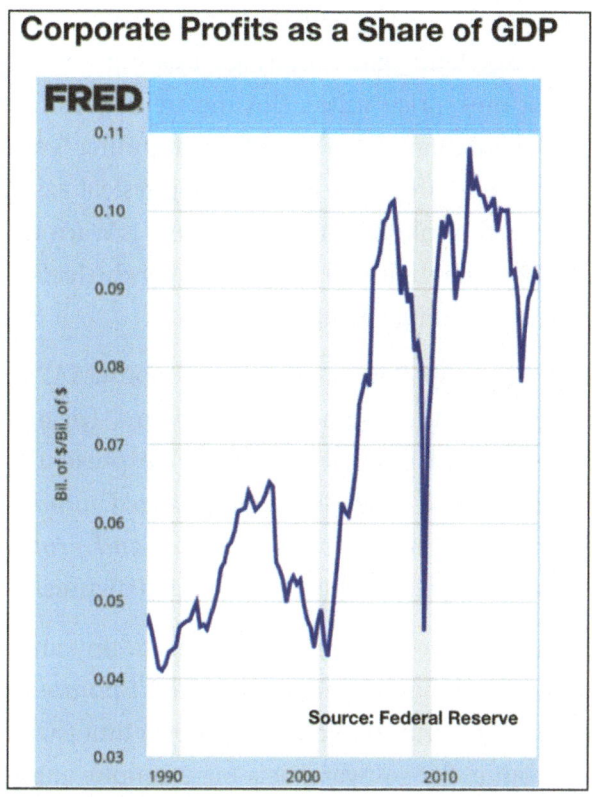

Figure 6-7. *The Rising Profitability Trend (2)*[64]

Researchers are beginning to focus on the growth of intangible assets at many firms and the role this may play in this expansion of profitability. Intangible assets, like brand equity, do not require investment that fits the traditional "capital expenditure" category. One recent study concludes

> Increased use of intangible assets enables firms to have high profitability without a corresponding increase in investment.[65]

What effect does this have on the integrity of valuation metrics like the P/E? As "intangible assets" become the core of the business franchise for many (perhaps a majority of) American companies, traditional "industrial era" accounting treatments

---

[64]Data from FRED, Federal Reserve Economic Data, *Federal Reserve Bank of St. Louis.*

[65]Ozgur Orhangazi, "The role of intangible assets in explaining the investment–profit puzzle," *Cambridge Journal of Economics* (Nov 2018), available online at https://doi.org/10.1093/cje/bey046

are increasingly inadequate. This is certainly felt on the balance sheet, where invisible assets like brand, technology, and data simply go missing and Book Value is deeply impaired as a measure of enterprise value. But the trend toward asset-light business models also impacts the calculation of expenses for computing "earnings." Concepts like depreciation – which may be appropriate for valuing physical assets like machinery or inventory – are inappropriate for valuing intangibles. Here is Warren Buffet (from his 2015 letter to *Berkshire Hathaway* shareholders), explaining why he feels compelled to deviate from Generally Accepted Accounting Principles:

> The operating expense figures above are non-GAAP because they exclude some purchase-accounting items (primarily the amortization of certain intangible assets). We present the data in this manner because we believe *the adjusted numbers more accurately reflect the true economic expenses and profits* of the businesses aggregated in the table than do GAAP figures.
>
> I won't explain all of the adjustments, some are tiny and arcane, but serious investors should understand the *disparate nature of intangible assets*. Some truly deplete in value over time, while others in no way lose value. For software, as a big example, amortization charges are very real expenses. Conversely, the concept of recording charges against other intangibles, such as customer relationships, arises from purchase-accounting rules and clearly does not reflect economic reality. GAAP accounting draws no distinction between the two types of charges. Both, that is, are recorded as expenses when earnings are calculated, even though, from an investor's viewpoint, they could not differ more. *[Emphasis added]*[66]

The Economist points out that fundamental valuation anomalies – such as "Value" – can be seen as linked to the distinction between tangible and intangible assets.

> The profits of firms with tangible assets suffer in economic downturns, when costly plant and buildings cannot be redeployed. The value premiums thus a reward for bearing business-cycle risk.[67]

---

[66] Luke Kawa, "Warren Buffett's [2015] Shareholder Letter, Annotated," *Bloomberg Online*, February 27, 2016.

[67] "Striking Out: The Agony of the Value Investor," *The Economist*, October 27, 2018.

CHAPTER 6   ASSESSMENTS AND QUALIFICATIONS

It is not just *reported* Earnings that are affected. *Forecast* earnings – the denominator for the Forward P/E – are also subject to greater uncertainty as a result of new business models. A 2005 study looked at the relationship between intangibles and the accuracy of analysts' earnings forecasts:

> The rise of intangible assets in size and contribution to corporate growth over the last two decades poses an interesting dilemma for analysts. Most intangible assets are not recognized in financial statements... The increasing importance of intangible assets and the absence of explicit information about the contribution of intangibles to earnings imply strong market incentives for analysts to provide value-added information (e.g., accurate earnings forecasts) for high-intangibles firms.[68]

And indeed

> We find a significantly positive association between analysts' forecast error and the amount of the firm's intangible assets – technology-based intangibles, brand names, and recognized intangibles.

It seems clear that changes in corporate business models in the direction of greater reliance on intangible assets may alter the value significance of historical *and* forecast earnings figures.

6.2.10 The Effect of Alternate Growth Strategies: Acquisition vs. Internal Development

Another factor that can skew earnings and distort the P/E signal is the growth strategy the company follows. Consider two outwardly similar companies, pursuing different growth strategies. One company chooses to grow principally through acquisition of other companies. Such a company will recognize the full purchase price on its balance sheet, as a combination of hard assets acquired with the target company and "goodwill" – which is defined as the difference between the price paid to acquire the company and the target's

---

[68]Feng Gu and Weimin Wang, "Intangible Assets, Information Complexity, and Analysts' Earnings Forecasts," *Journal of Business Finance & Accounting,* Vol. 32, Nos. 9 and 10, (November/December 2005), pp. 1675–1702.

original book value. Goodwill accounting is complex and problematic – the relevance here is that over time the acquired hard assets will be depreciated and the goodwill "assets" will potentially suffer "impairment." Both processes result in non-cash charges against earnings in future periods. The second company grows through internal investment and development. Such a company will expense most of the costs of those investments along the way, as R&D expenses, for example. In a reporting period where the first company makes a strategic acquisition (booked as a balance sheet asset) while the second company simply spends internally to achieve a similar result (expensed on the income statement), the latter will likely show lower GAAP earnings and carry a higher P/E. In future periods, the relationship may be reversed as the first company's acquired assets are gradually written down while the second company has no such charges. The effects would extend to many other important ratios and metrics:

> Take two identical firms, with the same operations, cash flow, strategy, and value. The firm built through past acquisitions would have a bloated asset base. As a result, its ratio of debt to assets would look healthier. Its shares would look artificially cheap compared with their book value. And it would have a lower return on equity.[69]

Thus, the P/E signals may differ, perhaps significantly, from one company to another very similar company, and relative valuations may shift from one period to another – when they really shouldn't. (Assume for this argument that absolute debt levels are also the same for both companies – that is, that the first company's acquisition was funded from cash on hand and not through debt issuance. In other words, any difference is not an effect of leverage.) This complicates all comparisons, across sectors, and over time. I am not aware of any studies that would shed light on the scale of these differences between acquisition-driven companies and those that rely on internal development, but the enormous amount of "goodwill" carried by so-called "deal-junkies" like *AT&T* ($143 Bn), *Anheuser-Busch InBev* ($137 Bn), and *General Electric* ($82 Bn) suggests that the effect may be consequential.[70]

This section has skimmed lightly over some of the important concerns related to the definitions of key components of the valuation metrics, especially "Earnings." These concerns do not invalidate the application of these metrics for the purposes described in

---

[69]Schumpeter, "As Good As It Gets," *The Economist*, September 1, 2018.
[70]Schumpeter, "As Good As It Gets," *The Economist*, September 1, 2018.

Chapter 5, but they should remind us that these instruments are not simple, mechanical gauges, like a thermometer or a bathroom scale. The readings they give us always require a degree of judgment in forming the proper interpretation and especially an alertness to possible sources of bias – in short, a critical mind-set.

6.3 Problems with Price-to-Book

Speaking of which, an additional comment is necessary. As Barron's magazine puts it:

> There's a problem with price/book: today's economy.
>
> Price/book, perhaps the most conventional measure of value, evaluates stock prices based on a company's book value – the worth of all tangible assets but no intangible ones. Price/book and similar accounting-based metrics worked better in an industrial-based economy, when companies owned valuable tangible assets, like manufacturing plants and equipment. Today's service economy is filled with companies whose biggest assets are their brands, intellectual property, or customer loyalty, which don't show up on the balance sheet.[71]

The "conservative academic wing" of Financial Economics has generally accepted that Book Values are accurate measures of enterprise value – that the denominator of the P/B ratio is reliable. The P/B metric[72] is the preferred filter used by academics to identify the "Value factor" – which is one of the three factors (or four or five or six) that have been identified as anomalies within the framework of the Efficient Market Hypothesis. Kenneth French, a representative of the orthodox view, has argued recently that P/B is perfectly sound:

---

[71] Reshma Kapadia, "Are Value Stocks About to Grow?" *Barron's*, April 30, 2018.
[72] Or, as the academic literature somewhat stubbornly insists, the Book-to-Market ratio, or BE/ME – "Book Equity to Market Equity" – and similar inverted forms.

CHAPTER 6   ASSESSMENTS AND QUALIFICATIONS

> [Prof.] French... whose work with [Eugene] Fama helped make price/book a classic gauge for value maintains that price/book is still the best measure of value. 'We have tested the hypothesis several times and haven't been able to convince ourselves that another measure – including a combination of measures – is better.'[73]

However, there are indeed fundamental problems with Book Value.

First, many asset values on the balance sheet are **out of date**. Accounting standards require in most cases that *assets* be carried on the books **at cost** – that is, for the price that was paid to acquire them originally. This is considered "conservative" – but it means that there is an inherent structural bias built into balance sheet values. These values may then be further reduced by depreciation (for tangible assets) or by an assessment of impairment (for recognized intangible assets). But in general, assets are never "marked up" in value. So, for certain kinds of assets that over longer periods of time clearly experience some appreciation in value, such as acquired technology, brands, data sets, or even real estate, the reported balance sheet figures will be inaccurate.

Second, **the "Assets" half of the balance sheet is incomplete**. Key intangible assets that actually drive revenue growth and profitability are not recognized or accounted for. In many cases, these assets were developed by years of internal investment rather than being acquired from an external source – so there is no clear cost basis for accountants to work with. This is true for so-called "brand equity" that has been homegrown by companies like *Coca-Cola* over long periods of time and clearly constitutes a very significant portion of the company's true value.[74]

The P/B ratio of the entire S&P 500 is over 3 today[75] – which implies that most of the enterprise value of the American economy is invisible to the Accounting profession (see Figure 6-8). This discrepancy varies considerably over time,[76] with market conditions, and

---

[73]Quoted in Reshma Kapadia, "Are Value Stocks About to Grow?" *Barron's*, April 30, 2018.

[74]This failure to account for brand equity within the standard accounting framework has given rise to the emergence of a number of firms specializing in the valuation of brands, which have developed elaborate quantitative methodologies for this purpose. *Interbrand* (http://interbrand.com); BrandZ, of *Millward Brown* (www.millwardbrown.com/brandz/brandz); and *Brand Finance* (http://brandfinance.com) are three leading providers of brand equity valuation services.

[75]May 2018.

[76]Source: *Standard & Poor's* (www.multpl.com/s-p-500-price-to-book).

CHAPTER 6   ASSESSMENTS AND QUALIFICATIONS

from one sector to another. The P/B for energy companies is typically under two, while the P/B for soft drink companies is almost 10 (see Figure 6-9).[77] It is very hard to know what to make of a ratio that is as unstable and inconsistent across the economic spectrum.

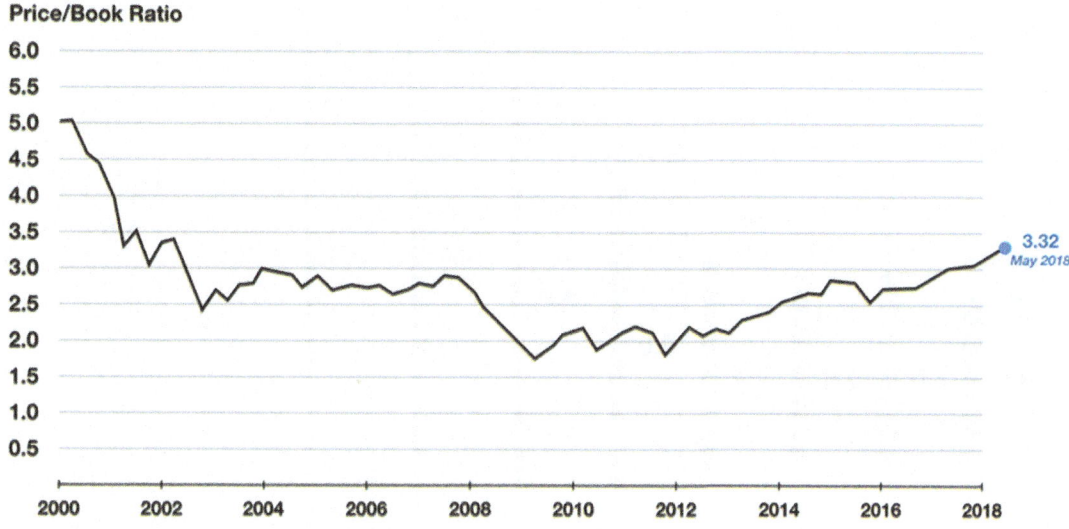

Figure 6-8. *Price/Book Ratio (2000–2018)*[78]

Finally, as we have seen in previous chapters, many of the "assets" that accountants do recognize and record on the balance sheet are really best seen as liabilities, in the sense that they **reduce or even destroy enterprise value** rather than adding to it. We have considered the Cash-Adjusted version of the P/E multiple – which essentially recognizes the value-destructive (or at least dilutive) character of carrying excessive cash on the balance sheet and removes the cash from the calculation of the P/E ratio. It is well understood that large inventories ("assets" in the accountants' eyes) are almost always a sign of corporate distress. Similar analyses can be applied to show the value-impairment potential in many situations of excessive investments in Accounts Receivable and Property, Plant, and Equipment (Capex).

---

[77]Data from *NYU Stern* (http://pages.stern.nyu.edu/~adamodar/New_Home_Page/datafile/pbvdata.html).
[78]Data from *Standard & Poor's* (www.multpl.com/s-p-500-price-to-book).

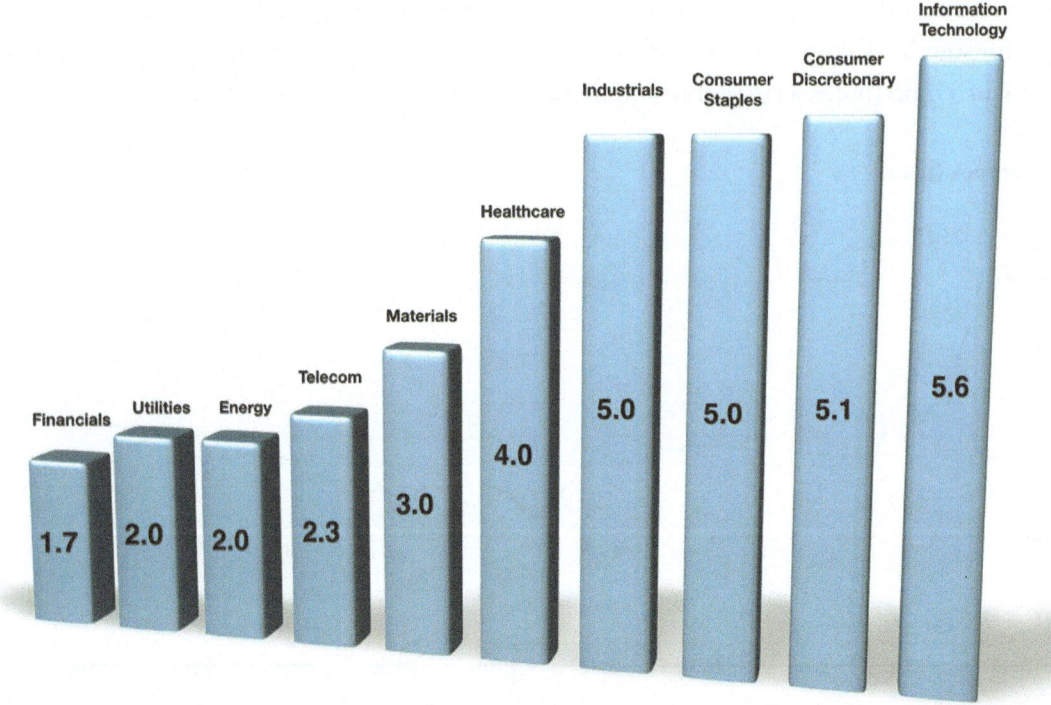

Figure 6-9. *Price/Book by Sector*

In short, the "Book Value" denominator of the P/B ratio is incomplete, stale, and tainted with value-destroying components. These disparities are not consistent across the market, so it is not a matter of applying a simple "correction factor." Price-to-Book is no longer appropriate as a measure of enterprise value and should be retired from most uses.

6.4 ROA: An Incomplete Picture

Return-on-Assets is also problematic as a valuation metric, for several reasons.

In principle, it should be a very powerful indicator of value. Companies that use their assets efficiently should be more valuable. ROA is highly correlated with Operating and Net Profit margins (as it should be). But all of these measures may be skewed in the same way and away from accurate reflections of enterprise value. Lacking a corrective

CHAPTER 6   ASSESSMENTS AND QUALIFICATIONS

reference point to the financial market valuations, ROA is doubly exposed to uncertainties in the accounting calculations described in Section 6.2 – in both the numerator and the denominator. It is essentially uncorrelated with P/E (or P/B) – that is, it does not predict market value.[79]

ROA should give us a reading on profitability, above all. Yet a recent study by *Deloitte* argues that ROA is somehow undergoing a long-term *deterioration* (see Figure 6-10).

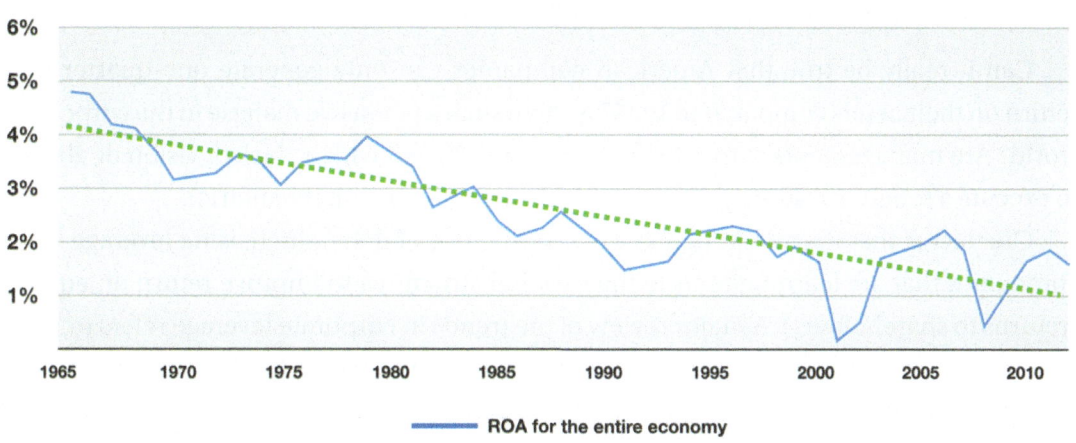

Adapted from Deloitte *(2013)*

Figure 6-10. *Trend in ROA*[80]

The authors comment

> [There has been] an economy-wide, secular decline in return on assets (ROA) over the last 47 years. The decline signals companies' decreasing ability to find and capture attractive opportunities relative to the assets they have. Companies lack a clear vision or the ability and commitment to execute a long-term strategy. [81]

---

[79] I have run a number of simple regressions on different sets of companies; some sets are chosen for diversity and others for sector similarities. The correlation between P/E and ROA is always low and often essentially zero.

[80] Adapted from John Hagel, John Seely Brown, Tamara Samoylova, and Michael Lui, "Success or struggle: ROA as a true measure of business performance," *Deloitte Insights*, October 30, 2013.

[81] John Hagel, John Seely Brown, Tamara Samoylova, Michael Lui, "Success or struggle: ROA as a true measure of business performance," *Deloitte Insights*, October 30, 2013.

CHAPTER 6   ASSESSMENTS AND QUALIFICATIONS

But this assertion is clearly at odds with trends for most other indicators of business fitness and performance, such as the strong rise in corporate profit margins cited previously in this chapter – as the Deloitte authors actually admit:

> Corporations report record profit levels. The economy has recovered at a steady pace of 1.8–2.4 percent over the last three years. Stock market rallies restored major indices to prior levels and beyond. Housing prices have stabilized and have begun to increase nationally. Manufacturing activity is showing signs of expansion. All aggregate signs point to positive outcomes.

Can it really be true that American companies can only generate one-quarter the return on their assets compared to 1965? Is there such a pervasive malaise in the corporate world? Are managements across the board really afflicted with a "lack of vision or ability to execute a long-term strategy"? Or could it be a problem with the metric?

One factor that may be in play is the growing use of debt – increasing leverage – by companies that are learning to tune their capital structures to improve return on equity (returns to shareholders). A major review of the trends in corporate leverage refers to "the significant transition of the corporate sector from equity-based funding to debt-based funding over the last century" – the amount of debt, as a percentage of business capital, carried by major US corporations has approximately tripled since the 1960s. The ratio of liabilities to assets on corporate balance sheets has at least doubled.[82]

Presumably, this trend might have raised the ROA by reducing the value of the denominator (especially if the borrowed cash was used to fund investments in intangibles). But that does not seem to be happening.

What can we conclude about this metric? Its behavior is puzzling. Still, if the sun is shining, but your watch tells you it is midnight (and you're not in Alaska)… maybe you need a new watch. There is something wrong with the way the ROA metric is being calculated. It is not a reliable metric for valuation purposes.

---

[82]John R. Graham, Mark T. Leary, and Michael Roberts, "A Century of Capital Structure: The Leveraging of Corporate America," *Journal of Financial Economics*, Vol. 118 (2015), pp. 658–663.

6.5 Concluding Comments: The Uncertainty Principle(s) in Finance

Stepping back from the more particular difficulties reviewed earlier, there are four general comments to make about the nature of Finance as a discipline, which bear on the challenges of enterprise valuation and the use of market metrics like the P/E ratio.

6.5.1 The Academic Confusion Factor

A standard textbook on investment analysis assures us that

> "Analysis of P/E ratios is such a simple procedure."[83]

The most prestigious academic journal in Finance confirms that the P/E and the other market multiples will solve all our problems:

> It is now widely accepted that excess returns are predictable by variables such as dividend-price ratios, earnings-price ratios, dividend-earnings ratios, and an assortment of other financial indicators.[84]

The matter is often presented as "settled science." It is not. As we have seen throughout this book, almost every hypothesis finds both supporting and contradictory evidence. All our conclusions seem tentative. The latest studies often overturn the consensus reached just a few years ago. Metrics that "worked" at one time suddenly stop working. Taken as a whole, the literature is riddled with methodological inconsistencies. Received opinions – dignified as "stylized facts"[85] – retain currency long after they have actually been discredited.[86]

---

[83]Zvi Bodie, Alex Kane, and Alan Marcus, *Investments* (McGraw-Hill, various editions).

[84]Martin Lettau and Sydney Ludvigson, "Consumption, Aggregate Wealth, and Expected Stock Returns," *The Journal of Finance*, Vol. 56, No. 3 (June 2001), pp. 815-84.

[85]For those unfamiliar with the term, a stylized fact is not an actual fact, but "a broad generalization that summarizes data, which although essentially true may have inaccuracies in the detail" *(Wikipedia definition)*. In other words, these are statements that economists feel free to regard as facts without worrying about whether they are true or not.

[86]The Efficient Market Hypothesis is a good example.

CHAPTER 6   ASSESSMENTS AND QUALIFICATIONS

The preceding views, expressed with a casual confidence, are examples of stylized facts that are not actually true. These market valuation metrics, apples-and-oranges ratios, are protean in nature, versatile, mutable, rich in significance, and unstable. They are difficult to interpret and apply.

Honest analysts will acknowledge the intellectual confusion this creates. A candid review article from 2008, entitled "A Comprehensive Look at the Empirical Performance of Equity Premium Prediction," ranges across a dispiriting landscape:

> The literature is difficult to absorb. Different articles use different techniques, variables, and time periods. Results from articles that were written years ago may change when more recent data is used. Some articles contradict the findings of others. Still, most readers are left with the impression that "prediction works" – though it is unclear exactly what works...

> Most models are unstable or even spurious. Most are no longer significant even in-sample, and the few models that still are usually fail simple regression diagnostics. Most models have performed poorly for over 30 years...

> [they exhibit] poor out-of-sample performance...and they predict poorly in the sample...

> ...although it is possible to occasionally stumble upon, and then to defend some seemingly significant models...skepticism is appropriate...most models have lost statistical significance...

> Our evidence suggests that the models would not have helped an investor.[87]

---

[87]Ivo Welch and Amit Goyal, "A Comprehensive Look at the Empirical Performance of Equity Premium Prediction," *The Review of Financial Studies,* Vol. 21, No. 4 (July 2008), pp. 1455–1508. This is a very thorough treatment, recommended for anyone who may need the statistical details. "*Out-of-sample, most models not only fail to beat the unconditional benchmark (the prevailing mean) in a statistically or economically significant manner, but underperform it outright. If we focus on the most recent decades, that is, the period after 1975, we find that no model had superior performance Out-of-sample and few had acceptable performance In-sample. With 30 years of poor performance, believing in a model today would require strong priors that the model is well specified and that the underlying model has not changed.*"

Unfortunately, this is still it seems the minority opinion, as the authors concede:

> The belief that the variables that we have explored in our article can predict stock returns and/or equity premia is not only widely held, but the basis for two entire literatures: one literature on how these variables predict the equity premium *[i.e., more or less our Chapter 4]* and one literature on how smart investors should use these variables in better portfolio allocations *[more or less our Chapter 5]*.

6.5.2 Reflexivity and the "Human Uncertainty Principle"

The problem is that the market is not analogous to a physical system with invariant patterns of behavior that can be discovered and set up as causal "laws." It is a complex socio-technical system, a learning system – that is, the thinking/reasoning/emoting agents (investors, traders, the managers of companies, the regulators) whose behavior sum up to create the market price – these living agents react to and learn from experience and change their strategies and behaviors, in response to business outcomes, and indeed in response to the market signals themselves. The market mutates. It interacts with itself, with its own price signals – a phenomenon some have called "reflexivity":

> Reflexivity is inconsistent with equilibrium theory, which stipulates that markets move towards equilibrium and that non-equilibrium fluctuations are merely random noise that will soon be corrected. In equilibrium theory, prices in the long run at equilibrium reflect the underlying fundamentals, which are unaffected by prices. Reflexivity asserts that prices do in fact influence the fundamentals and that these newly influenced set of fundamentals then proceed to change expectations, thus influencing prices; the process continues in a self-reinforcing pattern. Because the pattern is self-reinforcing, markets tend towards disequilibrium.[88]

---

[88]This is a pretty standard *Wikipedia* definition.

CHAPTER 6   ASSESSMENTS AND QUALIFICATIONS

The idea of Reflexivity in financial markets has been championed by the "legendary hedge fund investor", George Soros and has begun to attract interest from a broader audience. In 2009, Soros gave a series of lectures developing the concept in general terms, and specifically as applied to the financial markets, which were republished by the *Financial Times*.[89]

The theory goes beyond what we can entertain here.[90] But the essence of it, applied to financial market behavior, is that "market prices always distort the underlying fundamentals."[91] A simple way to construe this is that since market prices look forward, they will always run ahead of reality, of actual performance, alternatively overshooting and undershooting the putative equilibrium point. This implies that the P/E cycles between overvaluation and undervaluation, which conforms to what we have seen in the evidence presented throughout this book (see Figure 6-11).

---

[89] *Financial Times*, October 26, 27, and 29, 2009. Highly recommended. In 2013, the *Journal of Economic Methodology* devoted a special issue to the topic of reflexivity. Soros' introduction for that issue is also useful: "Fallibility, Reflexivity, and the Human Uncertainty Principle," Vol. 20, No. 4 (2013), pp. 309–329.

[90] Soros and others connect these ideas to larger issues in philosophy and the philosophy of science and a critique of economic thinking about markets in and out of equilibrium.

[91] George Soros, "Financial Markets," *Financial Times*, October 27, 2009.

CHAPTER 6   ASSESSMENTS AND QUALIFICATIONS

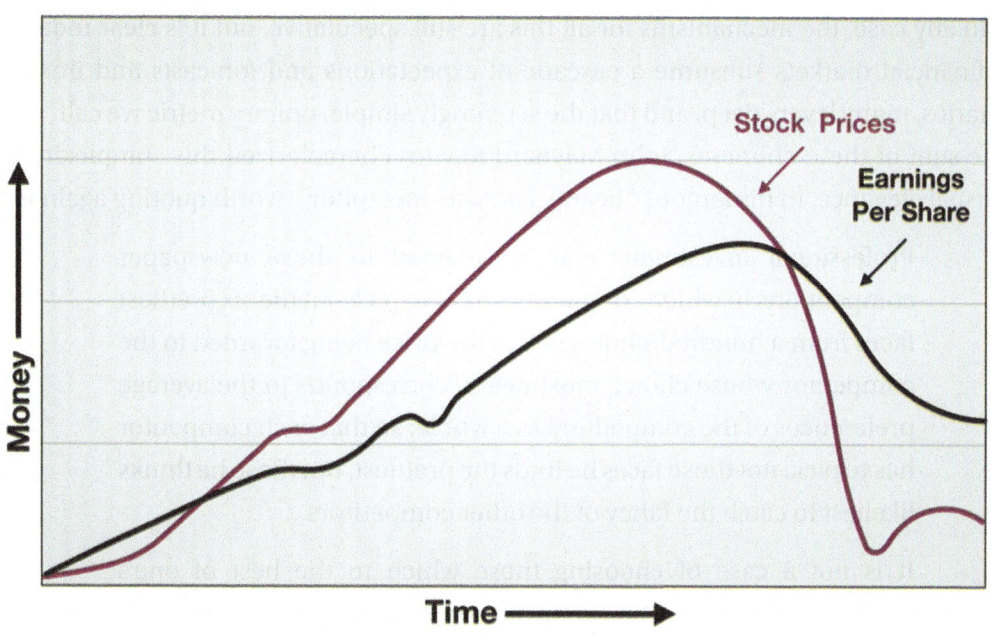

Adapted from Soros (2009, 2013)

Figure 6-11. *Reflexivity*[92]

In this view, the P/E is almost never accurate, as a measure of value. But, paradoxically, therein lies its usefulness. We can often reach a reasonable conclusion that the P/E is too high, or too low, even if we cannot say exactly how large the deviation from "true value" may be. These mis-valuations signal investment opportunities (if we interpret them properly). Paradoxically, *it is the "error" in the P/E which endows it with predictive power.*

To this we may add another factor which Soros does not explicitly address: technological change. The financial industry today is going through a period of accelerated and disruptive technological change. Evolving technologies frequently open new opportunities and close down old ones and often amplify the "pro-cyclical" or positive feedback processes that create the overshoot/undershoot patterns.

---

[92]Adapted from George Soros, "Financial Markets," *Financial Times*, October 27, 2009.

CHAPTER 6   ASSESSMENTS AND QUALIFICATIONS

In any case, the mechanisms for all this are still speculative, but it is clear today that the financial markets subsume a cascade of expectations and forecasts and imagined scenarios, many layers deep, and that the seemingly simple, unitary metric we call "price" is the sum of these chimeras. John Maynard Keynes characterized this complexity with his usual elegance, in his famous "beauty contest" metaphor – worth quoting again here:

> Professional investment may be likened to those newspaper competitions in which competitors have to pick out the six prettiest faces from a hundred photographs, the prize being awarded to the competitor whose choice most nearly corresponds to the average preferences of the competitors as a whole; so that each competitor has to pick, not those faces he finds the prettiest, but those he thinks likeliest to catch the fancy of the other competitors...
>
> It is not a case of choosing those which to the best of one's judgment, are really the prettiest, nor even those which average opinion genuinely thinks the prettiest. We have reached the third degree where we devote our intelligences to anticipating what average opinion expects average opinion to be. And there are some, I believe, who practice the fourth, fifth, and higher degrees.[93]

6.5.3 Fischer Black's Proposition

Returning to the mystery we started with in Chapter 1...

Have we really answered the question of the value of the Ford Dollar? Shouldn't one dollar of corporate earnings be worth... one dollar? Regardless of whether it comes from *Ford Motor Company* (P/E 5.5) or *Amazon* (P/E 120)?[94]

---

[93]John Maynard Keynes, *The General Theory of Employment, Interest, and Money*, (1936) p. 156. Keynes and Soros both bring significant experience as successful investors to their theorizing.

[94]P/E figures from Q4 2018.

One answer – and probably the one that most of us subscribe to – calls for an expansion of our understanding of what "Price" means. We view the share price not just as the value of a claim on an ongoing earnings stream, but as also including the expected value of an *option* to sell that claim (the share of stock) at some point in the future. In other words,

Price = Value (Claim on $1.00 on Earnings, t_0 to t_F) + **Expected Value** (Option to Sell, at t_F)

which translates to the familiar Dividend Discount Model or the Discounted Cash Flow formula:

Price = Discounted Cash Flows from Earnings or Dividends (t_0 to t_F) + Terminal Value (at t_F)

or something along those lines. If so, since the value of the $1.00 claim (or dividend) should be the same regardless of the source ("a dollar is a dollar…"), the difference between *Ford's* P/E and *Amazon's* P/E would be due entirely to the difference in the expected value of the option to sell the shares in the future, that is, the expected future share price. Since *Amazon's* share price has climbed 24-fold in the last ten years, while *Ford's* price has not changed (the comparison is close to the ratio of *Amazon's* current P/E to *Ford's* P/E), this interpretation makes some sense.[95]

But what if it is the "Earnings" figure that is unstable, and variable in its meaning, from one company to the next? What if the accounting rules that create "Earnings" are inconsistent or incomplete?

The late Fischer Black – one of the most original thinkers in the history of Finance – once proposed exactly this.[96] He argued that "the ideal set of accounting rules is one that makes the price-earnings ratio as constant as possible."[97]

> The objective of a set of rules for estimating earnings or normalized earnings is to give a figure that can be multiplied by a constant (say, 10) to give an estimate of the value of a firm's stock. When price-earnings ratios differ from this constant, the usual reason is that the earnings figure is distorted.

---

[95] Although of course the price looks forward – so the past trend is only indicative.
[96] For a good intellectual biography, see Perry Mehrling, *Fischer Black and the Revolutionary Idea of Finance*, Wiley (2011).
[97] Fischer Black, "The Magic in Earnings: Economic Earnings versus Accounting Earnings," *Financial Analysts Journal*, November/December 1980, pp. 19–24.

CHAPTER 6   ASSESSMENTS AND QUALIFICATIONS

His reasoning was rooted in his faith in the fully efficient market:

> It's very rare for an unusual price-earnings ratio to mean an underpriced or overpriced stock, because that would imply an obvious profit opportunity that investors are overlooking. When the price-earnings ratio is out of line, *one should normally assume that the price is correct and the earnings figure is incorrect* (as a guide to value). *[Emphasis added]*

Black wrote these words in 1980. We have come a long way since then in understanding how the financial markets can in fact be inefficient, and persistently so. "Anomalies" have been identified that do create "obvious profit opportunities" – over reasonably long time horizons. The market does indeed set different values on different dollars, depending upon the characteristics of the firm and the market that created them.

Still, Black was correct in this sense: the market offers a better measure of value than the official accounting numbers. By this line of reasoning, the "Earnings" reported by *Amazon* are significantly understated. This is plausible, since *Amazon* has been investing very heavily in its growth and infrastructure, and perhaps even more important, by aggressive pricing it has actually been trading current profitability to acquire reliable customers (another "intangible" and invisible asset). If the customer acquisition costs are taken out of the income statement and capitalized as assets, *Amazon's* "Earnings" would rise significantly, and its P/E would come down.[98] By the same reasoning, *Google's* offer of free search to its customers could be interpreted as an investment equal to the value of a hypothetical user fee (not charged), to acquire loyal customers who support its advertising business. *Google's* loyal user base is a critical un-accounted asset which it leverages to generate ad revenue. If the foregone user fees were recognized and "added back" to revenues, *Google's* "earnings" would rise and its P/E would also come down.

---

[98]The idea of capitalizing "customers" as assets is not far-fetched. In some industries, where the subscription mode of revenue is the rule – such as telecommunications – the idea of calculating a Customer Lifetime Value (CLV) has taken hold, as a useful way of understanding the enterprise value overall. CLV is calculated much like any stream of discounted cash flow: the subscription revenues are projected out as far as the average "churn" point – where on average customers discontinue their subscriptions, the customer acquisition costs and other expenses are subtracted, and the net cash flows are discounted back to a present value. A *McKinsey* study from 2003 calculated the CLV for several wireless carriers and arrived at values between $900 and $1800 per customer added. Adam Braff, William J. Passmore, and Michael Simpson, "Going the Distance with Telecom Customers," *The McKinsey Quarterly*, 2003, No. 4.

Making these adjustments is an exercise that lies outside of the framework of GAAP accounting and is full of uncertainty. The goal of stabilizing P/E by changing the accounting rules is perhaps more of an intellectual proposition than a practical one, a kind of thought experiment. But in light of the several ways in which accounting for "Earnings" has proven to be problematic (Section 6.2), the nature of the denominator may be just as indeterminate as that of the numerator.

6.5.4 Price-Insensitive Markets

Passive index-based investing has become a major force in the financial markets. Passive funds now account for something approaching half of the total funds invested. This includes broad-based index funds, exchange-traded funds, smart beta, and so-called "closet indexers" (active funds that apparently follow strategies designed to closely track their benchmarks).[99]

Passive investing is indifferent to the price, or the fundamental performance, of the individual components of the index. An investor who buys a share of an index fund or an ETF based on the S&P 500 index spreads that investment over all 500 companies included in the index at that moment. If we assume an equal-weighted index, it means that 0.2% of the funds are converted into demand for each company's shares. It cannot be the case that all 500 companies are performing equally well or carry the same valuation ratios. Some are undoubtedly underpriced and others overpriced, relative to their "true values." But the passive investor does not care about price or value in the traditional sense. He or she is simply trying to "match the market" and keep costs down (the mantra of the indexing evangelists).

There are other forms of market activity which generate transactions that are also arguably price-insensitive. These include high-frequency traders and market makers and corporate buybacks, as well as perhaps the general attenuation of price/value relationships created by extraordinarily loose monetary policies over the last decade. How

---

[99]True indexers are generally easy to identify; they openly advertise their index-tracking strategies. Closet indexers are harder to identify, and the category is not as definitive. One study in 2009 estimated that *"the fraction of closet indexers increased even more significantly* [than true indexers]: Funds *with low Active Share (20-60%) had about 30% of all assets in 2003, compared with almost zero in the 1980s."* (K. J. Martijn Cremers and Antti Petajisto, "How Active Is Your Fund Manager? A New Measure That Predicts Performance," *The Review of Financial Studies*, Vol. 22, No. 9 (September 2009), pp. 3329–3365; also Antti Petajisto, "Active Share and Mutual Fund Performance," *Financial Analysts Journal*, Vol. 69, No. 4 (July/August 2013), pp. 73–93.

far this phenomenon has pervaded the equities market is hard to say, but it is certainly significant. In 2017, one analyst estimated that

> discretionary, research-based stock selection now accounts for only 10% of average trading volume. The offsetting deviations in company performance that were once the hallmark of a boldly diversified stock portfolio have been overwhelmed by marketwide buy or sell orders.[100]

If large swaths of the buying and selling volume in the market are no longer focused on price or on fundamentals (earnings) or on the relationship between the two... then we have entered a new kind of market environment. Clearly the P/E and other ratios that served as useful guideposts in the traditional market must be impacted by this trend. There are signs of this sort of shift underway. Dividend yield no longer possesses the predictive power it once did. Price/Book is no longer meaningful for most American companies. CAPE has been stuck on "Danger!" – signaling severe overvaluation – all the while that the market has risen fourfold in the last ten years (2009-2019). Even the classic "Value" signal, based on screening for low P/E, seems to have stopped working in recent years. Perhaps in ten years' time we will look back upon these metrics as relics of the 20th century, no longer suitable for valuation purposes.

More likely, and hopefully, we will finally get serious about developing more rigorous procedures for interpretation. The central problem, I believe, is the assumption that simple metrics must carry simple, fixed messages. The literature reviewed only very sketchily in this book supports the opposite idea – that the P/E and other market ratios reflect a wide range of influences and the mix of "drivers" is constantly shifting. The information content is rich, dense, and somewhat opaque. We may recur to the biological metaphor – a "simple" metric like pulse rate or body temperature has many different "causes" and many different meanings, for individuals of different backgrounds, prior conditions, ages, and temperaments. We should not deny complexity, when it is obvious. The financial market is clearly a challenging subject to master; why should it be simple to understand or predict? We need greater intellectual discipline, greater subtlety in dealing with the data, greater honesty with respect to the results, and more attention to the quality of the underlying intuitions that motivate and guide our research programs in the first place – and probably somewhat less reliance on mere statistical technique.

---

[100] Jason Thomas, "Where Have All the Public Companies Gone?" *The Wall Street Journal*, November 17, 2017.

APPENDIX A

A Critical Examination of Discounted Cash Flow Valuation Methods

This book makes the case, not uncritically, for the usefulness of market metrics, as a rich, reality-based source of information relevant to the valuation of a business enterprise, and for the superiority of these metrics over other methods. In Chapter 2, we have considered briefly and dismissed GAAP Book Value and Discounted Cash Flow modeling as inferior techniques for valuation purposes. In this appendix, we will expand on this position.

The End of Book Value

The case against Book Value is clearer, perhaps. Accounting methods were developed in an era when most business models were built on tangible assets, with solid valuations based on historical cost. In most cases, these assets had finite lives of short-to-medium duration,[1] and the replacement cycle meant that the historical costs carried on the balance sheet were usually reasonably in line with current replacement costs (i.e., market prices).

This changed with the emergence of new types of value-creating assets – such as brands, design, technological innovation, subscription-based customers, and monetizable data – which are usually deemed "intangible" assets and which differ from traditional tangible assets in two important ways. First, they are long-lived and often grow in value through cumulative investment – although the "investment" in question is usually treated as a period expense by GAAP accounting and written off. Second, they do not appear on the

---

[1] Other than real estate (land), and certain types of structures, most tangible assets depreciate and are replaced within a few months or years.

company's balance sheet in most cases and so are not counted as contributing to the book value, although it has become clear to investors that they drive true enterprise value very significantly, and share prices have come to reflect that.

It has been a central conceit of accounting traditionalists that accounting data provide a complete picture of "true value" or even "market value" of the firm – for example:

> A firm's current earnings, book value, and (net) dividends suffice to infer market value.[2]

But this is no longer even remotely the case, at least with respect to book value. As detailed in Chapters 2 and 6, the Price-to-Book ratio for the US economy as a whole today is something like 3 or 4 to 1, and for many companies it is much higher. This means the accounting perspective captures only a small fraction of the value-creating substance of the modern business enterprise. Moreover, as to the accuracy of "current earnings" – when *95% of the companies in the S&P 500 feel compelled to provide alternative, non-GAAP measures of their earnings to investors* – even the Book Value stalwarts will reach the conclusion that GAAP is not doing its job.[3] For many years, Warren Buffett was a staunch advocate of Book Value, but he has recently revised his view:

> For nearly three decades, the initial paragraph [of the annual shareholder's letter] featured the percentage change in *Berkshire's* per-share book value. It's now time to abandon that practice.
>
> The fact is that ... book value is a metric that has lost the relevance it once had... Accounting rules require our collection of operating companies to be included in book value at an amount far below their current value, a mismark that has grown in recent years...

---

[2]James A. Ohlson and Xiao-Jun Zhang, "Accrual Accounting and Equity Valuation," *Journal of Accounting Research*, Vol. 36, Studies on Enhancing the Financial Reporting Model (1998), pp. 85–111.

[3]Tatyana Shumsky and Theo Francis, "Accounting Blurs Profit Picture," *The Wall Street Journal*, June 28, 2016. In a recent conference held in New York (September 2019), the chief economist of the Securities and Exchange Commission, S. P. Kothari – a renowned professor of accounting from MIT – acknowledged this point explicitly and (I thought, given the audience) a bit surprisingly. See S. P. Kothari, Karthik Ramanna, and Douglas J. Skinner, "Implications for GAAP from an analysis of positive research in accounting," *Journal of Accounting and Economics*, Vol. 50 (2010), pp. 246–286.

The book-value scorecard to become increasingly out of touch with economic reality. In future tabulations of our financial results, we expect to focus on Berkshire's market price.[4]

Historically, accounting methods were not developed to value companies or even to value assets. True, they create dollar-denominated entries, itemized on the balance sheet, that can be labeled "values" – but the "value" the accountant places on an asset is usually nothing more than a record of the price paid to acquire it, decremented by a simple depreciation rule. Balance sheet values are not intended, or methodologically designed, to reflect *current* asset values, meaning the prices that the assets might fetch if they were sold today, or the cost of replacing them.

Eighty years ago, Benjamin Graham could observe that "book value ... is in most cases... artificial."[5] Despite this, Book Value has often been assumed to stand for the actual value of the business, and for many years this assumption seemed to hold up. But as the disconnect between GAAP values and market values grew ever wider, it became untenable.[6]

The Accounting profession itself has begun to recognize this. The American Institute of Certified Public Accountants (AICPA) is engineering a shift away from historical cost and toward an embrace of market metrics – precisely the same metrics discussed

---

[4] Warren Buffett, "Berkshire Hathaway Shareholders Letter," 2018.

[5] Benjamin Graham, *The Interpretation of Financial Statements*, Chapter XX (1937).

[6] The Accounting profession has made piecemeal concessions, such as introducing the idea of impairment. Impairment is triggered when an asset carried on the books at (depreciated) cost is clearly no longer worth that amount, by reference to similar assets trading in the market (N.B. the role of the market price). If, say, the asset in question is a bond, pledged as collateral for some liability, and the true (market) value of the bond has dropped, demonstrably and significantly, then accounting principles may require the recognition of an impairment to the stated balance sheet value. But impairment is far from being a true valuation procedure. It is an episodic adjustment, forced by the reality of a large divergence from market prices for similar assets or by major changes in the structure of the business, and it is always driven by an "excess of caution" and it is always late.

APPENDIX A   A CRITICAL EXAMINATION OF DISCOUNTED CASH FLOW VALUATION METHODS

in this book, such as P/E and EV/EBITDA – as a new anchor for enterprise valuations. In recent proposed rules for enterprise valuation, they explicitly endorse the use of "fair market value"[7] and note that "a historical reporting basis, such as cost, does not provide meaningful comparability across investments."[8] Indeed, "of the three approaches to valuing an enterprise...[book value] is considered to be the weakest from a conceptual standpoint."[9] Instead, the AICPA offers extensive guidance on the selection and use of market multiples.[10]

The end of Book Value, or at least of its role as a measure of enterprise value, is not the end of accounting, of course. Accounting has always been said to perform two functions: a valuation function (which is now called into question) and a so-called stewardship function, based on providing audited financial statements for the benefit of shareholders, management, and others. With a certain appropriate humility, perhaps, accountants can refocus on that primal role and leave the hard work of enterprise valuation to the market.

> The high-wire game of calculating the market value of entire companies is what the stockmarket does. The goal of accounts is more modest: to measure past performance and provide useful information that helps investors.
>
> —*The Economist* magazine (2018)[11]

---

[7]Defined as follows: *"Fair value is a market-based measurement... the price at which an orderly transaction to sell the asset or to transfer the liability would take place between market participants under current market conditions."* (American Institute of Certified Public Accountants, *Valuation of Portfolio Company Investments of Venture Capital and Private Equity Funds and Other Investment Companies, Draft (*2018), paragraph 2.09). The final version of this document was released on August 19, 2019.

[8]*Ibid.*, paragraph 2.07.

[9]*Ibid.*, paragraph 5.95.

[10]*Ibid.*, throughout, but paragraphs 5.19–5.55 especially.

[11]Schumpeter, "As Good as it Gets," *The Economist*, September 1, 2018.

APPENDIX A   A CRITICAL EXAMINATION OF DISCOUNTED CASH FLOW VALUATION METHODS

Discounted Cash Flow Modeling: A Critical Assessment

Asset prices should equal expected discounted cashflows.

—John Cochrane, University of Chicago (The opening sentence of the 2010 Presidential Address to the American Finance Association)[12]

Price is assumed to be equal to the present value of the expected future dividends.

—Stephen Penman, Professor and Director of the Center for Excellence in Accounting, Columbia University[13]

Once you have estimated and discounted cash flow, you have completed the valuation.

—McKinsey & Co.[14]

You just want to estimate a company's cash flows over time, discount them back and buy for less.

—Warren Buffett[15]

As you learn in finance 101, the value of an asset is based on its future cash flows. To get a present value, you must discount this cash flow.

—A Random Investment Advisory Blog[16]

---

[12]John Cochrane, "Discount Rates," *The Journal of Finance*, Vol. 66, No. 4 (August 2011), pp. 1047–1108.
[13]Stephen Penman, "The Articulation of Price-Earnings Ratios and Market-to-Book Ratios and the Evaluation of Growth," *The Journal of Accounting Research* Vol. 34, No. 2 (Autumn 1996), pp. 235–259.
[14]Tim Koller, Marc Goedhart, and David Wessels, *Valuation, 4th Edition,* Wiley (2005), p. 56 - *"over 350,000 copies sold!"*
[15]Quoted in Peter J. Wallison, "Give Us Disclosure, Not Audits," *The Wall Street Journal*, June 2, 2003.
[16]www.private-investment.at/posts/view/692

APPENDIX A   A CRITICAL EXAMINATION OF DISCOUNTED CASH FLOW VALUATION METHODS

"Truisms" like these – repeatedly so frequently, and so prominently, and expressed with such a bland definitiveness, as though there were truly no need for further discussion – are usually not quite true. They go together with the so-called "stylized facts" – which are not quite facts – as part of the rhetorical repertoire of a field that is prone to oversimplification, and often seems to be trying (perhaps unconsciously) to sidestep some awkward realities.

But unlike the case with GAAP Book Value, the proponents of Discounted Cash Flow valuation are still quite ready to defend their approach. Indeed, DCF is a huge intellectual franchise. There are dozens of textbooks that promote the topic and thousands of university-level courses to drill hundreds of thousands of students every year in DCF methods. You can't get an MBA without mastering DCF. In the financial industry, DCF is an obligatory element of the "business case" prepared in support of major investments or acquisitions.

Is this enthusiasm warranted?

The DCF Best Case

Here is a summary of the "best case" for the use of DCF in enterprise valuation – from a report by *Credit Suisse*:

> Take as an example two companies, Apple, Inc. (AAPL) and Edison International (EIX), which had the same price-earnings multiple, 12.8, based on year-end 2013 prices and 2014 consensus earnings estimates. Setting aside any perceived mispricing, it stands to reason that the prevailing price-earnings multiple implies radically different outlooks for these two companies. They are in separate sectors (information technology and utilities), with vastly disparate economic returns on capital (AAPL's CFROI® is 25 percent versus EIX's 5 percent), substantial variance in the outlook for earnings growth (the expected 5-year earnings per share growth is nearly 50 percent for AAPL and 7 percent for EIX), and very different capital structures (AAPL has net cash while EIX has a healthy amount of debt).
>
> How can two companies so unalike have the same price-earnings multiple? Contemplating how these two stocks arrive at the same multiple from very different directions provides a mental warm-up for the process of carefully considering what comprises

a price-earnings multiple. Without a proper appreciation for the factors that determine a multiple, there is no way to apply it intelligently in exercises of relative or absolute valuation.

The value of a financial asset is the present value of future cash flows. Few serious market practitioners would disagree. But many investors shun models that project and discount future cash flows because they deem them too complicated or sensitive to assumptions. Yet these same individuals seem blithely content to rely on multiples.

Here's the challenge. With discounted cash flow models, the value is sensitive to the inputs. But the assumptions underlying the inputs are explicit. You can compare them to base rates, discuss them, and debate them. With multiples, those assumptions are buried. The assigned multiple becomes a point of persuasion rather than a thoughtful case based on the economic drivers of value.[17]

This has the appearance of a strong argument: yes, the future is uncertain, but better to spell out all the assumptions and uncertainties explicitly, than to bury them in a single atomic data point (the share price), which, moreover, is so jittery we cannot be sure where we will find it in an hour or a day – certainly the share price is a much more "high-frequency" phenomenon than any underlying view of true value of the enterprise could be construed.

But the question is not whether DCF is useful for teasing out hidden assumptions or raising interesting questions. The question is whether it can be used as an accurate method for *measuring enterprise value.*

What Is DCF, Really?

DCF originated as a bond-pricing method. The fair price of a bond is the present value of the stream of cash flows it is expected to generate. Bonds offer a highly predictable stream of cash flows (they are "fixed income" instruments after all), as well as a straightforward procedure to discount them back to a present value (based on current interest rates). Is it plausible to value a share of *Ford's* stock, or the entire operating business of the company,

---

[17]Michael J. Mauboussin and Dan Callahan, "What Does a Price-Earnings Multiple Mean? An Analytical Bridge between P/Es and Solid Economics," *Global Financial Strategies, Credit Suisse,* January 29, 2014.

the same way we value its bonds? Is there a difference between stocks and bonds, between equity and debt? Does the same method we would use for valuing a Treasury bill apply to valuing, say, the entire business of *The Walt Disney Company*?

But more to the point, we should realize that the DCF method doesn't actually *measure* anything. DCF is *not* a measurement tool; *it is a forecasting procedure.* Forecasting is not measuring. The forecast for next Tuesday's weather doesn't actually measure Tuesday's weather. Measuring the temperature today is easy and highly accurate. A thermometer reading is high-quality information. Forecasting the temperature two weeks from today is so difficult that it may require a supercomputer and yet still end up being quite off the mark. A forecast of that sort contains much lower quality information.

Besides this, DCF suffers from a number of problems, which were summarized in Chapter 2. Among other things, to construct a DCF model with sufficient care is very time-consuming, which limits its applicability to a small subset of the potentially interesting questions we might raise. It is also not anchored to an *actionable* transaction price. A DCF model may give you an "answer," but the price at which the deal (the purchase of shares or the acquisition of a company) can be done may be very different.

But the more serious problems have to do with the lack of methodological rigor and hence the lack of control over the results. That is to say, the DCF methodology is loose enough that different users can all-too-easily generate very different answers, wittingly or unwittingly. It is easy to misuse, misconstrue, or misrepresent.

Uncertainties, Compounded

The DCF method combines, or compounds, two estimation processes. The Forward Process (as we may call it) involves forecasting future cash flows to some cutoff point, 5, 10, 15 years out – plus a terminal value ("TV") to represent the sum of all future periods beyond the cutoff point, "to infinity." The Backward Process involves converting these future cash flow estimates, plus the TV, into today's dollars by a process of discounting the future sums. The discount rate is the key variable: it may be constructed in different ways, but the most common formula is based on an estimate of the company's "cost of capital":

> The cost of capital, in a financial market equilibrium, will be the same as the market rate of return on the financial asset mixture the firm uses to finance capital investment.

This is often called the Weighted Average Cost of Capital ("WACC"), reflecting both debt and equity components of the firm's capital structure. The cost of equity is one of these components, and it also can be calculated in different ways, but is almost always inferred in some fashion from the market values. A standard answer is to base the WACC on the Capital Asset Pricing Model ("CAPM"),[18] which is of course a market-based metric.

> CAPM shows that the cost of equity capital is determined only by beta [market risk]. Despite it failing numerous empirical tests, and the existence of more modern approaches… the CAPM still remains popular due to its simplicity and utility in a variety of situations.

Other methods are now recommended by some:

> The implied cost of equity capital is an increasingly popular alternative to the factor models such as the CAPM. There are several closely related alternative methods. In these models, the cost of equity is *backed out from the current stock price… [Emphasis added]*[19]

(Note that these definitions reference market values. We will come back to that point in the following.)

Both the Forward and the Backward estimation procedures introduce uncertainty, of several kinds. There is substantive uncertainty – that is, whether or not the forecast of cash flows for, say, five years from now is accurate. There is also structural uncertainty, especially in the choice of assumptions used to calculate the TV and the WACC for the discount rate.

Finance theory and financial models deal with uncertainties and errors in many contexts. It is often plausible (though not necessarily correct) to assume that uncertainties or errors are distributed in such a way that they tend to cancel each other out. This is the view that some take of the minor "frictions" and fluctuations in share prices, namely, that errors are more or less normally distributed around a mean which is the "correct" price.[20] But in the DCF procedure, because any errors in the Forward Process of estimating future

---

[18] Steven N. Kaplan and Richard S. Ruback, "The Valuation of Cash Flow Forecasts: An Empirical Analysis," *The Journal of Finance*, Vol. 50, No. 4 (September 1995), pp. 1059–1093.

[19] Murray Z. Frank and Tao Shen, "Investment and the Weighted Average Cost of Capital," *Journal of Financial Economics*, Vol. 119, No. 2 (February 2016), pp. 300–315.

[20] The literature often speaks of this as "noise."

cash flows will be fed back into the Backward discounting process, we speak of these uncertainties as compounding, rather than self-canceling.

How serious are these uncertainties?

Regarding the errors introduced by the Forward Process, it is immediately obvious that they are considerable. All we have to do is look at the earnings forecasts prepared for the shortest term (one quarter), by the most experienced professional forecasters (Wall Street equity analysts), to see that accuracy is not the hallmark of this procedure. In comparing results reported for the third quarter of 2019, analysts correctly forecast earnings for just 6% of the 342 companies belonging to the S&P 500 which had reported by November 1. In 75% of the cases, the analysts erred on the low side, and in 18% they erred high.[21] Other examples of earnings forecast uncertainties have been cited throughout this book. The scale of the error is not trivial, amounting to hundreds of basis points per year. One study has found the average bias of analysts to be about 30%, typically on the upside (i.e., overly optimistic).[22]

But the more serious problem with the Forward Process has to do with the terminal value. The TV typically accounts for over half of the future total cash flow forecast. It is generated (in most cases) by applying a simple fixed annual growth rate to the last pre-cutoff cash flow number – the so-called "perpetual growth rate." The most common approach is to use the annual growth rate in the GDP – which is of course itself a forecast and known to vary considerably.

Steiger's study of the sensitivities of the DCF approach (cited in Chapter 2) finds that cash flow forecasts are inherently "very complex." But the choice of the perpetual growth rate has an inordinately large impact.

> Due to the fact that the TV often accounts for more than half of the total company value, special attention has to be paid to its calculation and input coefficients. Even very small changes that might not even be significant from an economist's perspective will result in substantial changes in the company value. Therefore it is very easy to move the TV into the desired direction without having to drastically change any underlying business predictions.

---

[21]Gunjan Banerji, "Better Than Expected Earnings Ease Growth Fears – for Now," *The Wall Street Journal*, November 1, 2019.

[22]Marc Goedhart, Rishi Raj, and Abhishek Saxena, "Equity Analysts: Still Too Bullish," *The McKinsey Quarterly*, 2010, No. 3.

APPENDIX A   A CRITICAL EXAMINATION OF DISCOUNTED CASH FLOW VALUATION METHODS

Steiger concludes, on this point

> The TV, together with its underlying assumptions, is the most important and influential part of the whole discounted cash flow analysis.[23]

The AICPA Draft on Enterprise Valuation Procedures cited earlier also points to the concern caused by the fact that the TV is "the single largest component" of the DCF valuation.[24]

This overweighting of the TV is also of concern because the TV is probably the least relevant component of the model to most investors. Notwithstanding Warren Buffett's quip that his "favorite stock holding period is forever," few investors adopt a 10-15-year perspective, let alone one that stretches to "forever" – which is what the TV figure represents. It is likely that most of us operate with investment horizons of 5 years or less, which means that the DCF model is giving greatest weight to the portion of the company's future that figures least in most investors' calculations.

Regarding the Backward estimates and the Discounting procedure, Steiger finds that the choice of the WACC – which is an unobservable variable – has also a very large impact. As cited in Chapter 2, his case study showed that a 50-basis point change in the WACC assumption led to as much as a 1000-basis point change in the valuation.

Once again, the problem is exacerbated by the wide range of values that have been applied.

> A survey of 150 corporate finance and valuation textbooks found that they recommended a range of equity risk premiums from 3 to 10 percent, and one-third of the books used different premiums within their own pages. Bradford Cornell, a professor of finance, looked at the equity risk premium over time and concluded that it "is probably nonstationary." He adds, tellingly, "Recognition that the risk premium may be nonstationary provides a warning signal regarding the projection of past averages into the future."[25]

---

[23]Florian Steiger, "The Validity of Company Valuation Using Discounted Cash Flow Methods," *European Business School*, 2008.

[24]American Institute of Certified Public Accountants, *Valuation of Portfolio Company Investments of Venture Capital and Private Equity Funds and Other Investment Companies*, Draft (2018), paragraph 5.85.

[25]Michael J. Mauboussin and Dan Callahan, "What Does a Price-Earnings Multiple Mean?" *Global Financial Strategies, Credit Suisse*, January 29, 2014.

APPENDIX A   A CRITICAL EXAMINATION OF DISCOUNTED CASH FLOW VALUATION METHODS

DCF Manipulation

> Discount cash flows – a notoriously flexible measure…[26]

> The lack of constraints [on assumptions] can render any deal 'fair.'[27]

The extreme sensitivity of the DCF calculations to very small, economically insignificant changes in input values – all of which are assumptions, based on unobservable variables – heightens the risk that the models are far too easy to manipulate.

> Valuation models, expressed as mathematical formulas, look precise, but can be abused to convey fake precision.

> Due diligence teams in IPOs, acquisitions, and other corporate transactions, as well as expert witnesses in valuation cases, all understand how a formula can be used to justify any desired value through the choice of a growth rate.[28]

Steiger concludes

> It is very easy to manipulate the DCF analysis to result in the value that you want it to result in by adjusting the inputs. This is even possible without making changes that would be significant from an economist's point of perspective, e.g. a change in the perpetual growth rate or in the WACC by just a few base points. Analysts or business professionals have no tools to estimate the input factors with that kind of exactness.

This comment gives operational meaning to the statement that these models are overly sensitive. If we accept that there are limits on the acuity with which analysts can estimate the input variables, then if changes small enough to fall below that threshold are nevertheless capable of causing very large and economically significant differences in the outcomes – that is, the valuations – the procedure must be deemed methodologically unstable.

---

[26] Jon Sindreu, "Defense Deal's Valuation Puzzle," *The Wall Street Journal*, June 21, 2019.

[27] Matthew Shaffer, "Truth and Bias in M&A Target Fairness Valuations: Appraising the Appraisals," *Harvard Business School*, October 2018. Available online at https://matthewshaffer.online/job-market-paper/

[28] Stephen Penman, "Handling Valuation Models," *Journal of Applied Corporate Finance*, Vol. 18, No. 2 (Winter 2006), p. 48.

Because of this concern, Steiger urges "special precaution" in verifying the "validity of the underlying assumptions."[29] The AICPA urges that "the assumptions embedded in the calculation should be subject to heightened scrutiny."[30] The *Financial Accounting Standards Board*, in its landmark pronouncement on Fair Value Measurement, urges heightened disclosure requirements related to the use of unobservable variables for valuation purposes. They note that

> IFRSs [the Rest-of-World Accounting standards] require a quantitative sensitivity analysis for financial instruments that are measured at fair value and categorized within Level 3 of the fair value hierarchy. The [FASB – i.e., U.S. Accounting standards] will analyze the feasibility of incorporating information about interrelationships between unobservable inputs into a quantitative measurement uncertainty analysis disclosure.[31]

We should read between the lines here: the DCF method is inherently fragile and unreliable. It should be handled with great care, and as with any dangerous instrument, its use should be fully disclosed. Small mistakes can lead to large inaccuracies. In general, users should be alert to the risks of manipulation. In many situations, a sole reliance on DCF modeling for business valuation constitutes an act of financial malpractice.

Is DCF Actually Used by Market Practitioners?

First of all, academics don't count. Nor do "valuation specialists" whose franchise is based on promoting the mysteries of DCF to laymen. The question here is whether DCF methods are actually used by market professionals – equity analysts and investors – to value public companies for purposes of investment.

---

[29] Florian Steiger, "The Validity of Company Valuation Using Discounted Cash Flow Methods," *European Business School*, 2008.

[30] **American Institute of Certified Public Accountants**, *Valuation of Portfolio Company Investments of Venture Capital and Private Equity Funds and Other Investment Companies, Draft* (2018), paragraph 5.85.

[31] **The Financial Accounting Standards Board**, *Fair Value Measurement (Topic 820) Amendments to Achieve Common Fair Value Measurement and Disclosure Requirements in U.S. GAAP and IFRSs No. 2011-04* (May 2011), pp. 7–8.

And the answer is no, or not much, or not really.

Based on survey data, the use of DCF models by analysts is limited. Several studies show a strong preference among professionals for ratio-based market metrics,[32] with DCF models playing a secondary role. But even so, these surveys probably overstate the prevalence of DCF. It is likely that a lot of analysts say they use DCF methods because they feel they are *supposed* to use them (after all, they spent several semesters in Business School grinding away at WACC and DCF and the rest – it acquired the patina of intellectual credibility). And it may be that sometimes a DCF exercise will be employed either as a parallel exercise, to strengthen confidence in a valuation result developed from the application of market metrics, or as a way to dress up a valuation report in formal clothing (especially when it is to be submitted to a paying customer).

But – speaking anecdotally, from experience and conversations over many years with industry professionals – investment decisions are not made based on forecasts of future cash flows.[33] They are made based on forecasts of future share price. In other words, the market metrics dominate.

DCF: Assessments

Early on – even before the rise of "modern finance theory – Benjamin Graham had identified the problem with valuation methods based on the assumptions about unrealized future outcomes:

> The concept of future prospects and particularly of continued growth in the future invites the application of formulas out of higher mathematics to establish the present value of the favored issue. But the combination of precise formulas with highly imprecise assumptions can be used to establish, or rather justify, practically any value one wishes.[34]

---

[32]Efthimios G. Demirakos, Norman C. Strong, and Martin Walker, "What Valuation Models Do Analysts Use?" *Accounting Horizons*, Vol. 18, No. 4 (December 2004), pp. 221–240.

[33]A recent profile of Jim Simons, founder of *Renaissance Technologies*, the most successful hedge fund of all time, revealed that for all his success Mr. Simons *"didn't have a clue how to estimate cash flows"* (Gregory Zuckerman, "The Making of the World's Greatest Investor," *The Wall Street Journal,* November 2, 2019).

[34]Benjamin Graham, *The Intelligent Investor* (1949).

APPENDIX A   A CRITICAL EXAMINATION OF DISCOUNTED CASH FLOW VALUATION METHODS

Seventy years on, the *Financial Times* published a series of lead editorials in the same vein, addressing the "Big Flaw" in public accounting – namely, its approach to valuation:

> [There has been] a dangerous decline in public trust [driven by] one overarching problem: the latitude given to the use of models, estimates, and projections.[35]
>
> It has made for volatile, at worst fictitious, valuations.
>
> Companies can value illiquid assets with no verifiable market price, using questionable estimates based on "models."
>
> Straightforward market valuations are one thing. But when models and estimates are used as proxies...[36]

From his Olympian perspective, the great John Maynard Keynes agreed:

> The outstanding fact is the extreme precariousness of the basis of knowledge on which our estimates prospective yield have to be made. Our knowledge of the factors which will govern the yield of an investment some years hence is usually very slight and often negligible. If we speak frankly, we have to admit that our basis of knowledge for estimating the yield ten years hence for a railway, a copper mine, a textile factory, the goodwill of a patent medicine, an Atlantic liner, a building in the City of London, amounts to little and sometimes to nothing; or even five years hence.[37]

McKinsey provides a gently worded summary:

> Not all valuation methods are created equal. In our experience, managers dedicated to maximizing shareholder value gravitate toward discounted-cash-flow (DCF) analyses as the most accurate and flexible method for valuing projects, divisions, and companies. Any analysis, however, is only as accurate as the forecasts it relies on. Errors in estimating the key ingredients of corporate value – ingredients such as a company's return on invested capital (ROIC),

---

[35]"A Shake-up of Audit's Oligopoly is Long Overdue," *The Financial Times,* September 3, 2018.
[36]"Reform Accounting Rulers to Restore Trust in Audit," *The Financial Times*, August 3, 2018.
[37]John Maynard Keynes, *The General Theory of Employment, Interest and Money* (Harcourt, Brace, 1935), pp. 149–150.

its growth rate, and its weighted average cost of capital – can lead to mistakes in valuation and, ultimately, to strategic errors.

We believe that a careful analysis *comparing a company's multiples with those of other companies can be useful in making such forecasts,* and the DCF valuations they inform, more accurate. Properly executed, such an analysis can help a company to stress-test its cash flow forecasts, to understand mismatches between its performance and that of its competitors, and to hold useful discussions about whether it is strategically positioned to create more value than other industry players are. As a company's executives seek *to understand why its multiples are higher or lower* than those of the competition, *a multiples analysis can also generate insights into the key factors creating value in an industry. [Emphasis added]*[38]

The American Institute of Certified Public Accountants identifies "unobservable inputs" as "inputs for which market data are not available."[39] This would of course include every single input used in a DCF exercise: future cash flows, terminal value, cost of equity, and so on, all "unobservable." The AICPA then defines its "fair value hierarchy" as follows:

The fair value hierarchy gives the highest priority to quoted prices (unadjusted) in active markets for identical assets or liabilities and the lowest priority to unobservable inputs. Valuation techniques [should] maximize the use of relevant observable inputs and minimize the use of unobservable inputs. As such, even in situations in which the market for a particular asset is deemed not to be active, relevant prices or inputs from this market would still need to be considered in the determination of fair value. *It would not be appropriate to default solely to a model's value based on unobservable inputs. [emphasis added]*[40]

---

[38] Marc Goedhart, Timothy Koller, and David Wessels, "The Right Role for Multiples in Valuation," *McKinsey & Co.*, March 2005.

[39] **American Institute of Certified Public Accountants**, *Valuation of Portfolio Company Investments of Venture Capital and Private Equity Funds and Other Investment Companies, Draft* (2018), paragraph 2.23.

[40] American Institute of Certified Public Accountants, *Valuation of Portfolio Company Investments of Venture Capital and Private Equity Funds and Other Investment Companies, Draft* (2018), paragraph 2.21.

AFTERWORD

Fair Price, True Value

Price and Value are incongruous concepts. They seem to belong to different dimensions of the human condition. Price is transactional, commercial, a part of day-to-day practical experience, and measured in cash passed from hand to hand. Price is observable, verifiable, but somehow superficial and transitory. It is a signal standing for something more important, and yet its concreteness commands our attention. Prices can easily change. They come to life in the marketplace, mediating between individuals with symmetrical, but opposite, interests.

Value is existential, although also ethereal. It is "intrinsic" (where price is "extrinsic"). It relates to the fundamental nature of the thing that it is attached to and not just to a particular transaction. It changes only slowly, organically. We tend to feel it cannot really be measured, and attempts to convert the value of a thing to dollars and cents are often resisted. We accept that "true value" is fundamentally unobservable – yet still "real." The idea of Value extends into the moral sphere. We speak of the value of a human being or the value of friendship or of trust.

The process of valuation fuses these incongruities together, not always successfully. We turn whichever methodological crank we have selected, and then we find ourselves staring at a number, unsure whether we are seeing Price rather than Value or the other way around. This uncertainty has confounded finance theorists, accountants, and practical investors, since the beginning.

The community of interested parties tends to divide itself into two camps. There are those who perforce assume that Price=Value, at least more or less. There are others who have concluded that Price≠Value, or at least hardly ever.

AFTERWORD FAIR PRICE, TRUE VALUE

The P=V folks have developed the Efficient Market Hypothesis (EMH) to explain their position. They invoke the idea that markets process new information accurately and find the equilibrium, quickly, between supply and demand, and there, at that price point there lies... true value. They embellish the vocabulary of the field with synonymous expressions: the law of one price, the "no-arbitrage" principle, the market's random walk, "you can't beat the market."

The P≠V camp demurs, based on the obvious and far-too-numerous exceptions to the EMH (which the P=V people have vainly tried to isolate as "anomalies" so as to preserve the main body of their theory). The P≠V-ers are a diverse crowd, ranging from simple practitioners who stubbornly persist in making money in the face of the EMH nihilism to psychologists and statisticians who study the systematic biases and flaws in human decision-making that underpin these anomalies to investment gurus who have rebranded the "anomalies" as "factors" and make a good living selling models and indices based on them. But the P≠V partisans all share the basic idea that the market is often out of equilibrium, for long periods of time, which means that there are mispricings and profit opportunities to be had by someone clever enough to discover them.

In this book, we have not had to choose a theoretical position: P=V or P≠V – that is *not* the question. We have surveyed a range of empirical findings connected with the use of market valuation metrics, largely without needing or attempting to explain them. That said, the spirit of the material generally runs to the P≠V side of the argument, for the simple reason that markets seem to run on mispricings, logically speaking. Otherwise, what would drive trading activity? As an astute scholar has observed

> Price has to move away for value in order to attract buyers and sellers.[1]

Indeed. Yet the relationship is unclear, even so. Even if we accept that P≠V, what is the dynamic view of that inequality? Is it that P tracks V imperfectly, slowly perhaps, deviating and then converging, and the ≠ symbol reflects nothing more than "friction" or "noise"? This could allow us to preserve some sort of equilibrium perspective, say P=V+N (noise). Or is P a signal that is inherently unstable, and ambiguous, with a complex and perhaps nonstationary relationship to V? The "reflexivity" perspective of George Soros and others cited in Chapter 6 would be an example of such a viewpoint. In that case, we leave equilibrium behind and embrace a *dis*equilibrium model of the market.

---

[1] Perry Mehrling, *Fischer Black and the Revolutionary Idea of Finance*, Wiley (2012), p. xxiii.

In the P=V+N approach, it is possible to develop straightforward interpretations of the meaning of the price signal. All we need to do is to "average out" the noise term. In the hard P≠V view, the challenge of interpreting the price signal is perhaps greater, but there is a reward: instead of meaningless "noise," there is real and useful information contained in the disequilibrium, which can serve as the basis of interesting trading or investing strategies.

But again, this assessment is not within the scope of this book. The facts of the market's behavior are the facts, regardless of one's theoretical perspective. The next volume in this series will turn to this question, the linkage of Fact and Theory, to understand whether and how, and why P≠V.

Index

A

Accounting valuations
    GAAP, 24
    intangible assets, 23
    Price-to-Book ratios, 21, 22
    public accounting, 21
American Express *vs.* Capital One, 174
Assessments and Qualifications
    best metric, The P/E
        averaging multiples, 324
        CAPE predicted market, 319
        cash flows, 324
        Earnings measures, 320
        industry popularity
            contest, 324, 325
        M&A analysis/private equity
            valuations, 318
        market regimes, 320
        performance, some multiples, 321
        predictive power, time, 323
        sensitivity varies, 321
        short term performance, 322, 323
    Finance, uncertainty principles
        Academic confusion
            factor, 355, 356
        Fischer Black's Proposition,
            360–362
        Price-insensitive markets, 363, 364
        reflexivity, 357–360
        shifting, definitions (*see* Shifting)

B

Bank of America Corporation
    ("BAC"), 227, 232, 252, 253, 305
Base *vs.* growth component, 137–140
Beta *vs.* P/E ratio, 189, 190
Borrowing valuation, 25
Bubble detection
    actual P/E *vs.* predicted P/E, 307
    dot-com case, 305
    equities *vs.* bonds, relative prices, 308
    federal reserve model, 306
    valuation metrics, 306
Business strategy
    accounting issues, 201
    capex intensity, 181
    Colgate *vs.* Proctor & Gamble, 168
    conglomerate discount, 178–180
    economic cycles, 183
    excess cash accumulation, 182, 183
    factors, 170
    GE Valuation, 170
    governance, 202
    quality of revenue, 171, 174

C

Capital Asset Pricing Model
    (CAPM), 112, 373
Cash-Adjusted P/E (CAPE2)
    Apple *vs.* Exxon, 114–116

INDEX

Cash-Adjusted P/E (CAPE2) (*cont.*)
    cash holdings, 113
    Corporate Cash, 119
    EV/EBITDA, 119
    Price-to-Earnings Ratio, 117
Cash Flow Growth *vs.* EV/EBITDA
    Ratio, 137
Cash Flow, metrics
    definition, 76
    EBITDA, 75
    EV/EBITDA, 76
    FCF (*see* Free Cash Flow (FCF))
Company-specific sentiment, 208
Composite P/E ratios
    aggregate set, 125
    emerging markets, 123
    financial time series, 125
    qualitative characteristics, 125
    S&P 500 index, 125, 126
Conglomerate discount, 175–177, 296
Consumer Sentiment Index, 210
Costco *vs.* Walmart, 173
Country Factor *vs.* Year Factor, 245
Cyclically Adjusted P/E (CAPE), 328
    accounting changes, 94, 95
    averaged metric, 108
    business cycle, 93, 107
    defined, 92
    Earnings metric, 110
    large losses, few firms, 95, 96
    P/E Multiple, 91, 112
    performance
        averaging mechanics, 104
        averaging window, 100, 101
        bias, 104
        errors, forecasting, 102, 103
        P/E Multiple, 99, 100
        ratio, 97
        regression analysis, 101
        rising trend, 106
        Sell Signal, 107
        valuation metrics, 97, 98
    time window, 109
    Total Yield, 111
    under-researched questions, 92, 93
    volatility, 91
Cyclicals *vs.* defensives, 183–185

D

Defensives, 183
Discounted Cash Flow
    modeling (DCF), 26, 27, 40
    assessments, 378, 379
    bond-pricing method, 371, 372
    enterprise valuation, 370, 371
    manipulation, 376
    market practitioners, 377
    uncertainties, compounds, 372–375
Dividend Discount
    Model (DDM), 25, 59, 64, 361
Dividend ratios
    Dividend Yield, 60–63
    P/D, 60
    valuation metric, 64
Dividends *vs.* buybacks, 166

E

Earnings Before Interest, Taxes,
    Depreciation, and Amortization
    (EBITDA), 75–76, 78–81, 196, 295
Earnings growth, 201
Earnings Management, 335
Earnings per share (EPS), 6, 8, 42, 44, 56,
    103, 142, 329

Earnings volatility, 186–187
Economic risk, 199
Efficient Market Hypothesis (EMH), 30, 34, 83, 91, 349
EPS Growth *vs.* P/E Ratio, 142, 143
Equity *vs.* Debt, 160, 161
EV/EBITDA ratio, 75–76, 181
Exchange Traded Funds (ETFs), 77, 153, 154, 288, 292, 336

F

Federal Open Market Committee (FOMC), 112, 223–225
Fed Meeting Announcements, 225
Fed Model, 234–236, 301, 306
Financial Models, shortcomings
    DCF, 26, 27, 29
    DDM, 26
    sensitivity analysis, 28
    WACC, 28
Firm-level drivers
    growth, 135
    profitability, 146
    risk/cost of capital, 159
    size, 156
Firm-specific factors, 246
Fiscal policy, 226–228
Ford Dollar
    vs. GM, 8
    Mysterious multiple, 16, 17
    P/E measure
        Decile, 9–11, 13, 14, 16
        expensive company, 4, 5
        future share price, 6
Ford Motor Company
    enterprise value, 20
    value triangle, 19

Forecast stock prices
    P/E, contrarian indicator
        future returns, 253
        vs. 1-year returns, 255
        predictive power improves with longer holding periods, 252
        vs. 10-year returns, 254
Forward P/E
    common form, 44
    Discounted Cash Flow approach, 44
    normalized P/E, 49
    P/E, improve, 50
    random-walk time-series models, 45, 46
    relative P/E, 49
    vs. Trailing P/E
        deflation effect, 48
        forecast earnings, 47
        Wall Street equity analysts, 47
Forward-to-Earnings Ratio *vs.* Return on Equity, 152
Free Cash Flow (FCF)
    accounting rules, 77
    concept, 76
    earnings-based multiple
        EBITDA, 80, 81
        enterprise value, 79
        traditional metrics, 80
    idle cash, 78

G, H

Generally accepted accounting principle (GAAP), 24, 201, 333
Governance
    multidimensional, 206
    ownership structure, 203
    staggered boards, 205

Government regulations
    banking sector, 221
    healthcare sector, 220
Gross Profit vs. Market Value, 148, 254
Growth, effect of Walmart vs. Amazon, 135

I, J, K

Index construction
    market ratios, usage, 286
    methodology, 287
    value indexes/ETFs, 288
Industry sectors
    crude oil prices, 214
    definition, 212
    P/E vs. S&P 500, 215
    sub-sector P/E, 216
    tech sector, 218
    telecom, 217
    trailing P/E, 213
International Financial Reporting Standards (IFRS), 331–332, 377
Investment/payout ratio, 167

L

Leverage, 194
    P/E, 196
    performance, 197
    price-to-book, 200, 204
    trends, 198

M, N

Market-Based valuation metrics
    Disney vs. Netflix, 31–32
    EMH, 30, 31
    Ford vs. Tesla, 33, 35
    irrational biases, 31
Market multiples, 249, 250
Market regimes
    bear markets and recoveries
        P/E trends, 313
        shape of price, 312
    bubble detection (see Bubble detection)
    business transactions, 314
    corporate earnings, 311
    dividend yield (D/P) levels, 299
    maturity reset, 309, 310
    monetary policy (see Monetary policy)
    range bound market, 310
    share prices, 311
Market returns, 223, 224
Market sentiment, 208
Market-to-Book ratio, 21
Market valuations, 223
Market volatility, 191, 193
Market-wide/sector-wide factors, 247
Mean reversion
    behavioral finance, 267, 268
    concept, 261
    cyclical exception, 270
    learning process, 269, 270
    patterns, 263
    risk factor, 263, 264
        growth/value, 266
        P/E signal, 272
        quantitative easing, 273
        small/large cap, growth/value vs. the market, 265
    stocks, 267
    "Value" Disappearing, 271–273
Monetary policy, 222, 226
    asset classes, 302

equity *vs.* bond market
    valuations, 301, 304
    fed model, 303
    quantitative easing, 301
Multi-period models, 26

O

Operating earnings
    core earnings, 57, 59
    definition, 51
    vs. GAAP Earnings, 53
    income, excludes, 51
    net earnings, 53
    one-time charges or write-offs, 52
    pro forma measure
        Facebook, 54
        GAAP earnings, 56
        non-GAAP, 55
        non-real charges, 55
Ownership concentration *vs.* market multiples, 204

P

Payout ratios *vs.* P/E multiples, 162–165
P/E compression, 144, 145
P/E ratio
    beta, 189, 190
    cyclicals and defensives, 183
    divestiture, effect of, 177
    ROE, 149
    stock market, 146
    value, 256
P/E Ratio *vs.* Real Interest Rates, 239
P/E (reversed as E/P) *vs.* Treasury bond yield, 300

Price-to-Book (P/B), 37, 38, 83–85, 172, 178
Price-to-Dividend (P/D), 60
Price-to-Earnings/Earnings-Growth (P/EG or PEG ratio)
    defined, 120
    earnings growth rate, 120, 121
Price-to-Earnings (P/E), 39, 256
Price-to-Sales (P/S)
    Amazon *vs.* Walmart, 70, 71
    defined, 65
    Energy Sector P/E Ratios, 72, 73
    EV/S, food retailers, 69
    financial reporting, 68
    market performance, 69, 70
    PER strategy, 74
    revenue, 66
    revenue recognition, 67
Productization, 250
Professional opinion, 208
Profitability, 147
Pure plays *vs.* conglomerates, 179

Q

Quality factor, 147
Quality metrics, 155
    factor research, 153
    MSCI, 153
    S&P 500 *vs.* Leading Exchange Traded Funds, 154

R

Range-bound market, 310
Reflexivity, 357
Retail sentiment, 208
Return-on-Assets (ROA), 38, 39, 88–90, 149, 352

INDEX

Return on Capital Employed (ROCE), 147
Return on Equity (ROE), 38, 147, 149, 154
    vs. Forward-to-Earnings Ratio, 152
        Price-to-Book, 151
        Quality Factor, 150
Return on Invested Capital (ROIC), 88, 147, 380
Return on Investment (ROI), 38, 88
Revenue growth vs. P/E, 136
Risk/Return framework, 157

S

S&P 500 P/E vs. 10-Year Treasury Yield, 240
Sector-level/market-level drivers
    Euro crisis, 242
    inflation vs. P/E, 228–230, 232
    interest rates, 233, 236–238
    regulations, 219
    sectors, 212, 213
    sentiment, 207
        animal spirits, 209, 211
        P/E levels, 209
        types, 208
    technological innovation, 233
    UK vs. US, P/E comparison, 244
    US/Canada/UK/Australia, P/E comparison, 243
Sector-specific sentiment, 208
Shareholder return
    business strategy (see Business strategy)
    buybacks, 166
    dividends, 162, 163
Shifting
    Acquisition vs. Internal development, 347, 348
    Asset-light business models, 343–347
    cash dilution, 340, 341
    Earnings Management
        buybacks and EPS enhancement, 336, 338, 339
        gaming the numbers, 335
    GAAP accounting rules, changes, 332–334
    GAAP, non-GAAP, core, 327, 328
    IFRS vs. GAAP, 331, 332
    Price-Book ratios, problems, 350–352
    ROA, 353, 354
    street earnings, 328, 330, 331
    taxes, 343
Small Cap companies, 157
Small cap stocks, 159
Smart beta, 288, 290
    composition of returns, 291
    ETFs, 292
    value cornerstone, 292, 293
Spreadsheet software, 25
Staggered boards, 205
Steady-state earnings, 141
Street earnings, 328, 330, 331

T

Taper Tantrum, 303
Tobin's Q
    Book Value, 86
    Mark-to-Market approach, 86
Trading strategies, 225
Trailing Price/Earnings ratio, 42, 44

U

Under-reaction paradigm, 267
US vs. European P/E Ratios, 241

V

Valuation ratios, 41, 129
"Value" anomaly, 256–258
    bull markets, 282, 284, 286
    CAPE, 279, 281
    cash flow multiples, 275
    dividend yield *vs.* P/E, 278, 279
    GAAP earnings, 276
    P/B, 274
    value investing, 261
Value corporate transactions
    sum-of-the-parts, 296
        analysis of Proctor & Gamble, 298
        Barron's article, 296
Value investing, 256
Value triangle, 19
    comparative approach, 36
    financial market, 36
    Market to Book Value, 37
    P/B, 37, 38
    P/E, 39
    ROA, 38, 39
Valuing corporate transactions, 293–295
Volatility of stocks *vs.* volatility of bonds, 192
Volatility storms, 192

W, X, Y, Z

Weighted average cost of capital (WACC), 28, 29, 373, 375, 376, 380

The manufacturer's authorised representative in the EU is Springer Nature Customer Service Centre GmbH, Europaplatz 3, 69115 Heidelberg, Germany. If you have any concerns regarding our products, please contact ProductSafety@springernature.com

Printed and bound by CPI Group (UK) Ltd, Croydon, CR0 4YY
24/03/2026
02077557-0001